The Last Dance

SECOND EDITION

Encountering Death and Dying

LYNNE ANN DeSPELDER
Cabrillo College

ALBERT LEE STRICKLAND

 Mayfield Publishing Company

Copyright © 1987 by Lynne Ann DeSpelder and Albert Lee Strickland
Second edition

Library of Congress Catalog Card Number: 86-062996
International Standard Book Number: 0-87484-745-1

Manufactured in the United States of America

Mayfield Publishing Company
1240 Villa Street
Mountain View, California 94041

Sponsoring editor: Franklin C. Graham
Manuscript editor: Victoria Nelson
Production editor: Jan deProsse
Art director: Cynthia Bassett
Cover and text designer: Albert Burkhardt
Production manager: Cathy Willkie
Compositor: Skillful Means Press
Printer and binder: R. R. Donnelley & Sons Co.

Contents

Preface xv

Prologue, by David Gordon 1

C H A P T E R I

Attitudes Toward Death: A Climate of Change 5

 Patterns of Death and Dying: Then and Now 5

 Factors Lessening Familiarity with Dying and Death 7

  Life Expectancy and Mortality Rates 9
  Geographical Mobility 9
  Changing Causes of Death 11
  Reduced Contact Among Generations 13
  The Displacement of Death from the Home 13
  Life-Extending Technologies 14

 Expressions of Attitudes Toward Death 16

  Language 17
  Humor 18
  Mass Media 20
  Literature 26
  Visual Arts 28
  Music 30

The Present Milieu   *33*

    Precursors of Current Interest in Death and Dying   33
    The Rise of Death Education   35
    Examining Assumptions   37

Further Readings   *39*

CHAPTER 2

Perspectives on Death: Cross-Cultural and Historical   *41*

Death in Early and Preliterate Cultures   *41*

    The Power of the Dead   42
    The Names of the Dead   44
    The Origin of Death   45

Cultural Case Studies   *48*

    Indians of North America   48
    The LoDagaa of Africa   52
    Mexican Culture   55

Death and Dying in Western Civilization   *57*

    Anticipated Death   62
    The Deathbed Scene   62
    Burial Customs   64
    Invisible Death   70

Further Readings   *71*

CHAPTER 3

Socialization: How We Learn About Death as Children   *73*

Components of a Mature Concept of Death   *75*

Developmental Studies of the Child's Understanding of Death   *76*

    Early Encounters with Death   77
    The Psychoanalytic Model: Death Anxiety in Children   83
    Erik Erikson: Stages of Psychosocial Development   84
    Jean Piaget: Cognitive Transformations   87
    Cognitive Development and Children's Concepts of Death   90
    A Mature Concept of Death   92

Sources of Attitudes Toward Death   *94*

    Early Parental Messages   94
    Cultural Influences   95
    Life Experiences   100

Talking with Children About Death   *101*
Further Readings   *107*

C H A P T E R   *4*

Health Care Systems: Patients, Staff, and Institutions   *109*

The Modern Hospital   *109*

    Health Care for the Dying: An Overview   111
    Emergency Care Confrontations with Death   116

The Patient-Caregiver Relationship   *117*
Dealing with the Dying: Stress in the Helping Professions   *119*
Public Health Response to AIDS   *123*
Terminal Care: Alternatives   *125*

    Modern Hospice Care   126
    Hospice Programs in the Hospital   129
    Hospice Organizations   130
    Support Groups for the Terminally Ill   132

The Social Role of the Dying Patient   *133*
Further Readings   *136*

C H A P T E R   *5*

Facing Death: Living with Life-Threatening Illness   *139*

The Taboo of Terminal Illness   *139*
Personal and Social Costs of Life-Threatening Illness   *141*
The Experience of Life-Threatening Illness   *144*
Patterns of Coping with Life-Threatening Illness   *146*
Treatment Options   *150*

    Surgery   154
    Radiation Therapy   156
    Chemotherapy   157
    Other Therapies*   158
    Infection and the Cancer Patient   161

Coping Mentally and Emotionally with Life-Threatening Illness   *162*

Helping a Loved One Who Is Dying   *166*

Further Readings   *167*

CHAPTER 6

Last Rites: Funerals and Body Disposition   *169*

Social Aspects of Last Rites   *171*

Notification of Death   172
Mutual Support of the Bereaved   174
Bereavement as Social Change   175
Funerals as a Coping Mechanism   175

The American Funeral: History and Criticisms   *177*

Selecting Funeral Services: Awareness and Alternatives   *184*

Funeral Service Charges   185
Comparing the Costs   188

Body Disposition   *193*

Burial and Entombment Costs   197
Memorials and Endowment Costs   197
Cremation Costs   198

Making Meaningful Choices   *202*

Further Readings   *203*

CHAPTER 7

Survivors: Understanding the Experience of Loss   *205*

Perspectives on Grief   *206*

Bereavement, Grief, and Mourning   *206*

The Experience of Grief   *208*

Duration of Grief   208
Symptoms of Grief   210
Phases of Grief   212
The Mortality of Bereavement   217

Variables Influencing Grief   *219*

The Survivor's Model of the World   221
Mode of Death   222

Relationship of Survivor to Deceased   223
Unfinished Business   225
Intellectual Versus Emotional Responses   226

Coping Mechanisms for Survivors   228

Funerals and Rituals   229
Survivor Support Groups   230
Practical Management of Life's Affairs   231

Bereavement as an Opportunity for Growth   231
Further Readings   233

CHAPTER 8

Death in Children's Lives   235

Major Causes of Death in Childhood and Adolescence   236
Children with Life-Threatening Illness   237

The Child's Perception of Illness   237
The Child's Coping Mechanisms   240

Children as Survivors of a Close Death   241

The Bereaved Child's Experience of Grief   241
The Death of a Pet   242
The Death of a Parent   245
The Death of a Sibling   247

Helping Children Cope with Change and Loss   250

Guidelines for Sharing Information   251
Using Books as Tools for Coping   253
When a Family Member has a Life-Threatening Illness   254
Support Groups for Children   258

Further Readings   259

CHAPTER 9

Death in the Lives of Adults   261

Psychosocial Stages of Adulthood: A Developmental Perspective   261
Loss Experiences in Adulthood   262

Individual Differences in Meaning of Death and Coping Styles   262
Aging and the Incidence of Loss   265

Parental Bereavement　266

    Pregnancy Loss and Perinatal Death　267
    Loss of the "Perfect" Child　270
    Sudden Infant Death Syndrome　271
    The Critically Ill or Dying Child　271
    The Death of an Adult Child　277
    Peer Support Groups for Specific Parental Bereavements　278

Spousal Bereavement　279

    Factors Influencing Spousal Bereavement　279
    Social Support for Widows and Widowers　285

The Death of a Parent　286
Illness and Aging　287

    Chronic and Debilitating Illnesses　289
    Caring for the Chronically Ill and Aged Adult　291

Further Readings　296

CHAPTER 10

Medical Ethics: Dying in a Technological Age　*299*

Truth Telling and the Terminal Patient　*301*
Informed Consent to Treatment　*303*
Choosing Death: The Decision Not to Prolong Dying　*308*
Allowing to Die: The Special Care Nursery　*312*
Organ Transplantation　*317*
The Need for a New Definition of Death　*319*

    The Traditional Signs of Death and the New Technology　319
    Conceptual and Empirical Criteria　322
    Four Approaches to the Definition and Determination of Death　323
    Legislation Defining Death　327

Further Readings　*331*

CHAPTER 11

The Law and Death　*333*

Living Wills　*333*
Organ Donation　*336*

The Death Certificate   *338*

The Coroner and the Medical Examiner   *338*

Autopsies   *341*

Laws Regulating Body Disposition   *341*

Wills   *343*

    Definitions and Elements of Wills   344
    The Formally Executed Will   346
    Codicils   347
    Revoking a Will   349

Probate   *350*

    The Duties of the Executor or Administrator   350
    Avoiding Probate   353

Laws of Intestate Succession   *354*

Estate and Inheritance Taxes   *355*

    Estate Taxes   356
    Inheritance Taxes   358
    Trusts   358

Life Insurance and Death Benefits   *359*

    Policies and Considerations   359
    Other Death Benefits   362

Further Readings   *363*

CHAPTER *12*

Environmental Encounters with Death   *365*

Risk Taking   *366*

Accidents   *369*

Disasters   *371*

Violence   *376*

    Capital Punishment   382
    Courting Death   383
    Dysfunctional Strategies   383

War   *384*

The Nuclear Threat   *390*

Stress   *395*

Further Readings   *401*

CHAPTER *13*

Suicide   *403*

    Comprehending Suicide   *406*

    Two Models of Suicide   *407*

        The Social Context of Suicide   *408*

        The Mental and Emotional Dynamics of Suicide   *410*

    Types of Suicide   *412*

        Surcease Suicide   *413*

        Psychotic Suicide   *414*

        Cultural Suicide   *414*

        Referred Suicide   *415*

        Other Dynamics of Suicide   *417*

        Subintentional Suicide   *418*

    Childhood and Adolescent Suicide   *418*

        Factors Influencing Youthful Suicide   *420*

        Categories of Youthful Suicide   *422*

    Contemplating Suicide   *423*

        Choice of Method   *424*

        Order of Lethality   *427*

        Suicide Attempts   *428*

        Suicide Notes   *429*

    Suicide Prevention, Intervention, and Postvention   *430*

    Helping the Suicidal Person   *431*

    Further Readings   *437*

CHAPTER *14*

Beyond Death/After Life   *439*

    Concepts of Death and Immortality   *440*

        Age-old Beliefs About Afterlife   *440*

        Death and Resurrection in the Hebrew Tradition   *441*

        Hellenistic Concepts of Immortality   *444*

        Christianity: Death, Resurrection, and Eternal Life   *446*

        The Place of Death and Immortality in Eastern Thought   *450*

Near-Death Experiences: At the Threshold of Death   457

    NDEs: A Composite Picture   458
    Dimensions of Near-Death Experiences   458
    Interpreting Near-Death Experiences   460

Death in the Psychedelic Experience   466
Beliefs About Death: A Wall or a Door?   468
Further Readings   470

C H A P T E R 15

The Path Ahead: Personal and Social Choices   473

    The Value of Exploring Death and Dying: New Choices   474
    Societal Applications of Death Education   479
    New Directions in Death Education   482
    Death in the Future   483
    Living with Death and Dying   487

        Humanizing Death and Dying   488
        Defining the Good Death   489

    Postscript and Farewell   493
    Further Readings   494

    Epilogue, by David Gordon   495

    Notes   497
    Name Index   545
    Subject Index   551
    Credits and Sources   559

Preface

*T*he person who sets out to increase his or her knowledge of death and dying is embarking on an exploration that must be in part a journey of personal and experiential discovery. The study of death is concerned with questions that are rooted at the center of human experience, the most important of which are not fully answerable in terms of a standard textbook definition. In writing *The Last Dance: Encountering Death and Dying,* our aim has been to compose a comprehensive and readable introduction to the study of death and dying by providing a text that conveys the salient points of the major issues and questions. We highlight the dominant points of view and the most interesting problems in the field, and we are also sensitive to the reader's need for a well-organized, rhythmic text. Thus, intensity is balanced with relief.

This book is a comprehensive survey of a field of study that is still very much in the process of formation. It is not an indoctrination to any one point of view, but an introduction to diverse points of view. The reader is invited to join in the process of discovering the assumptions, orientations, and predispositions that have for much of this century inhibited discussion of death and dying in this country. Readers may well form their own opinions, but we hope that, when they do, they will choose them only after considering other possibilities in a spirit of tolerance and open-mindedness. A major theme of this book is that such an unbiased investigation makes choices available that might otherwise be neglected because of prejudice or ignorance.

This text evolved out of the practical experience of teaching college and university courses in death and dying. It provides the reader with a solid theoretical grounding as well as methods for applying what is learned about death and dying to real-life situations. Each chapter conveys the depth of research and range of applications pertinent to its particular topic area. For those wishing to pursue further study, each chapter includes a list of recommended readings, and the chapter notes also provide suggested source materials for consultation. In this way, the reader is introduced to a wide range of topics in thanatological studies and is also guided toward more detailed presentations on topics of particular interest. Concepts and principles are made more meaningful by the use of examples, anecdotes, and other illustrative materials. Contributions from anthropology, art, ethics, health science, history, literature, philosophy, psychology, public policy, religion, and sociology can all be found here in their relevant contexts. Although topics are organized in a way that we believe serves the needs of most readers, some may wish to exercise their own preferences, perhaps by rearranging the sequence in which chapters are read. Accordingly, the book has been written to allow for such flexibility.

In short, *The Last Dance: Encountering Death and Dying* embodies an approach to the study of death and dying that combines the intellectual and the emotional, the social and the individual, the experiential and the scholarly. The book emphasizes the positive and necessary values of compassion, listening, and tolerance for the views of others, and it encourages the reader to engage in a constructive process of self-discovery about death and dying.

With the publication of the second edition of *The Last Dance: Encountering Death and Dying,* we again express our appreciation to the many individuals who contributed to the success of the first edition; their contributions are evident in this subsequent edition as well. Additionally, we thank the many teachers who offered suggestions for improving the text as it made its way into a second edition. The following instructors who reviewed various incarnations of this manuscript: Thomas Attig, Bowling Green State University; Linda C. Kinrade, California State University, Hayward; Anthony Lenzer, University of Hawaii at Manoa; Wendy Martyna, University of California, Santa Cruz; Marsha McGee, Northeast Louisiana University; Walter L. Moore, Florida State University — Tallahassee; Judith M. Stillion, Western Carolina University; Jeffrey S. Turner, Mitchell College; and Joseph M. Yonder, Villa Maria College of Buffalo. Assistance in gathering both text and art materials was provided by staff members at a number of museums, libraries, and governmental institutions. Other individuals helped with a variety of research, clerical, and production tasks. We especially wish to mention Carol Foote, whose photographic images once again enliven the book's presentation, and Barbara Jade Sironen, whose efforts on behalf of the book ranged the gamut and are most evident in her collaboration on the *Instructor's Guide* accompanying this text. To all who helped us in producing this book, our sincere thanks.

L. A. D.
A. L. S.

---

*I don't know how much time I have left. I've spent my life dispensing salves and
purgatives, potions and incantations — miracles of nature (though I admit that
some were pure medicine-show snake oil). Actually, half the time all I offered was
just plain common sense. Over the years, every kind of suffering person has made
his or her way here. Some had broken limbs or broken bodies . . . or hearts. Often
their sorrow was an ailing son or daughter. It was always so hard when they'd lose
a child. I never did get used to that. And then there were the young lovers. Obtaining
their heart's desire was so important to them. I had to smile. I always made them
sweat and beg for their handful of bark, and for those willful tortures I'll probably
go to hell . . . if there is one. My God, how long has it been since I had those feelings
myself? The fever, the lump in the throat, the yearning. I can't remember. A long
time . . . maybe never. Well, there have been other passions for me. There's my dusty
legion of jars. Each one holds its little secret. Barks, roots, soils, leaves, flowers,
mushrooms, bugs — magic dust, every bit of it. There's my book — my "rudder," a
ship's pilot would call it. That's a good name for it. Every salve, every purgative . . .
they're all in there. (Everything, that is, except my stained beard, scraggly hair, and
flowing robes — they'll have to figure those out on their own.) And then there's my
walking stick (always faithful) . . . and the ballerina. And ten thousand mornings,
ten thousand afternoons, ten thousand nights. And the stars. Oh, I have had my
loves.*

*It hurts to move. My shelf and jars seem so far away, though I know that if
I tried I could reach them. But no. It's enough and it's time . . . almost. I hope he
makes it back in time. He burst through my door only two days ago. A young man,
well spoken. Tears were streaming down his face. He looked so bent and beaten that
I could not refuse him. He told me that his wife had died over a month ago and that
he had been inconsolable since.*

"*Please help me,*" *he pleaded,* "*or kill me.*" *He covered his face with his hands.* "*Perhaps they're the same thing. I don't know anymore.*"

I let him cry awhile so I could watch him, gauge him. When at last he looked up, with my good hand I motioned him to take a seat. Then, between coughing fits, I went to work. "*Do you see that toy there?*" *I said.* "*The little ballerina . . . Yes, that's it. Pick it up.*"

"*Pick it up?*"

"*It won't bite. Pick it up.*" *(He probably thought it was a trick—that's what they expect.) He grasped it carefully, with one hand, then wiped his eyes with the other.* "*That's better,*" *I continued.* "*That's just a toy to you. You don't know what meaning to put to it, yet. So I want you to look at that ballerina.*"

He was hesitant, but I waited, stubbornly, until he looked down and fixed his attention on the little toy dancer. I went on: "*I knew a young man once who was very handsome—always had been. He not only turned every head, he was strong and smart, and his family was wealthy. His main concern each day was which girl he should court that evening. He had planned that after several seasons of playing at love he would marry a beautiful girl, have beautiful children, and settle down to spend the money his father had promised him. And he had plans for that money. He had already purchased the land he wanted to live on and was having built there the biggest house in the area. He was going to raise and race horses, I think. One morning he got on his favorite horse and went for a ride. He whipped that horse into a gallop; it stepped in a hole and threw him. The young man broke his neck, and died.*" *I stared at my guest and waited.*

"*That's a tragedy,*" *he finally croaked.*

"*For whom? For those he left behind, perhaps. But was it for him? When he opened his eyes that morning, he didn't know he would die that day. He had no intention of dying for another sixty years—if then. None of us does.*" *The young man looked confused.* "*His mistake was that he forgot that he could die that day.*"

"*That's a morbid thought,*" *he replied, and he looked as though he had just smelled something putrid.*

"*Is it? A moment ago you asked me to end your grieving by ending your own life. Suppose I oblige?*" *I stared at him for a few moments with my most practiced penetrating glare.* "*Suppose I did agree to kill you. How would you spend your last few minutes?*"

He was still a little wary of me, but relieved that I seemed to be suggesting a hypothetical situation, rather than a serious course of action. He considered the possibilities for a while, then straightened in his chair. "*Well, I guess I would step outside and take a last, best look at the sky, the clouds, the trees.*"

"*Suppose you lived that way all the time?*" *He stared at me, then looked down at his hands, searching them.* "*That young man I told you about . . . perhaps the tragedy for him was not that he died, but that he failed to use the eventual certainty of his death to make him* live! *Did he woo each of those ladies as though it might be his last romance? Did he build that house as though it might be his last creation? Did he ride that horse as though it would be his last ride? I don't know; I hope so.*" *My young guest nodded, but he was still sad. I pointed to the toy ballerina he was holding.* "That was given to me by a young lady who understood these things."

He looked at the figure closely. "Is she a dancer?"

"Yes, she is, and she is dead." The young man looked up, once again off balance. "She has been dead for, oh, a very long time." After all these years, a tear fell onto my cheek. I let it go. "She was many things. A child, a woman, a cook and a gardener, a friend, lover, daughter . . . But what she really was—who she was—was a dancer. When she was dying, she gave that doll to me, smiled, and whispered, 'At the moment of my death, I will take all of my dancing and put it in there, so my dancing can live on.' "

Tears welled in my guest's eyes.

"I can help you," I said, "but first there is something that you must do." He became very attentive. "Go to town and knock on the door of the first house you come to. Ask the people inside if their family has ever been touched by death. If so, go to the next house. When you find a family that has not *been touched by death, bring them to me. Do you understand?" He nodded, and I sighed. "I'm tired now."*

He got up, set the ballerina back on the table, and started for the door. I stopped him. "Young man!" He faced me from the doorway. "Come back as soon as you can."

David Gordon

In a Spanish village, neighbors and relatives peer through the doorway upon the deathbed scene of a villager.

Attitudes Toward Death: A Climate of Change

Of all human experiences, none is more overwhelming in its implications than death. Yet, for most of us, death remains a shadowy figure whose presence is only vaguely acknowledged. Although American attitudes toward death have changed greatly in the last decade, our predominant outlook and social customs regarding death are marked by a queasy uncertainty that some observers characterize as a denial of death. Anxiety about death is not new, of course. Death has always represented the central question of human experience, but one that, for the greater part of the present century, most Americans have tried in various ways to avoid.

Life styles influence death styles. Attitudes develop out of the interplay between individuals and their environment. It should be noted that an attitude includes components of belief, emotion, and behavior. To understand our own attitudes toward death, it is useful to glance backward a bit in time. Examining the past can provide some clues about how and why present attitudes evolved. Let us consider the shape of American attitudes toward death in the late nineteenth century — the way that people believed, behaved, and felt about death.

Patterns of Death and Dying: Then and Now

In contrast to the death-related experiences of most Americans today, consider those that were commonplace to someone living before the turn of the century. Death usually

5

© Albert Lee Strickland

The churchyard cemetery is a reminder of human mortality as well as a focal point for memories of deceased members of the community. Here, the tombstones face the doorway of the church, so that the names of the memorialized dead can be seen as parishioners exit this Canadian church.

took place in the home, with all family members present, down to the youngest child. After death, the family washed and prepared the body for burial. The local carpenter, or perhaps the family members themselves, built a coffin that was then set up in the parlor of the home.

Friends and acquaintances from the community and other relatives came to the family's home to view the body of the deceased in an open coffin and to share in the ritual of mourning. Children kept the vigil along with adults, sometimes sleeping in the same room as the corpse. Later, the body was carried to the gravesite, perhaps in a family plot on the property or in a nearby cemetery, and a local parson would read a few appropriate verses from the Bible as the coffin was lowered and the grave filled in by relatives. Each person learned about death firsthand. From caring for the dying family member through disposition of the corpse, death was within the realm of the family.

If you were a person of the nineteenth century suddenly transported through time to the present, you would find a rich source of information about current attitudes toward death by observing modern funeral practices. Walking into the "slumber room" of a typical mortuary, you'd probably experience culture shock. The familiar coffin has been replaced by a more elaborate "casket," and the corpse shows the mortician's skill in cosmetic "restoration." In every way, the stark appearance of death is diminished.

At the funeral, you would observe the ritual as family and friends eulogize the deceased. Ah, that's familiar, you say — but where is the dear departed? Off to the side a bit, the casket remains closed, death tastefully concealed.

When the service at the gravesite concludes, you look on with amazement as the mourners prepare to leave although the casket lies yet unburied. The cemetery crew will complete the actual burial. As a nineteenth-century onlooker at a twentieth-century funeral, you are perhaps most struck by a sense that the family and friends of the deceased are observers rather than participants: The tasks of preparing the dead for burial are handled by others who are paid to perform these services. Compared to a time when skills for dealing with a dead body were an ordinary part of common domestic life, our participation in the rituals surrounding the dead is minimal.

Factors Lessening Familiarity with Dying and Death

The changes in how Americans have dealt with death and dying over the past hundred years result from a combination of social and technological factors. The size, shape, and distribution of the American population — that is, its demographics — have undergone major changes since the turn of the century. Increases in average life expectancy, coupled with lower mortality rates, have

Death brought the community into play for the last time: the food discreetly left in the kitchen; the condolence calls; the preparation of the corpse in the bed in which [the person] had died—and perhaps slept in for many years—without benefit of the mortician's cosmetics; the laying out in the parlor; a stream of people filing softly by throughout the day paying respects to the family; the old friends who sat up with the body through the long lonely night; and then the funeral the next day, with family, friends, numerous townspeople, members of the husband's lodge, ladies of the burial society who had decorated the grave site. Funerals were long and doleful; the minister droned on interminably about the virtues of the deceased and hymns were sung; then the black hearse with white-gloved pallbearers in attendance and a black-plumed horse drawing it made its slow progress to the cemetery. It was not unusual for town businesses to close down completely for a funeral, and nearly everyone joined the procession to the burying-place, where at graveside a few last words were said, before the finality of the earth raining down on the coffin. Back at home neighbors had cleaned and dusted, leaving a neat—and empty—home for the grieving family to return to. There they sank down wearily and talked in numbed voices and at last went to bed, to try to get some rest in preparation for the new day.

Richard R. Lingeman,
Small Town America

had a tremendous influence on our attitudes and implicit expectations about life and death. The extended family has been replaced by a smaller family unit, the nuclear family — a significant demographic change, the effects of which have been accentuated by increased geographical mobility. Advances in medical science and in applied health care technologies have not only contributed to demographic change, they have altered the usual causes of death as well as the setting where dying most often occurs.

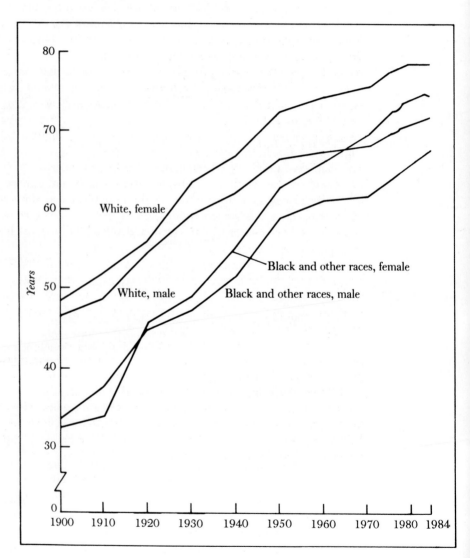

Figure 1-1   *Life Expectancy at Birth, by Race and Sex, 1900 – 1984*
Source: U.S. Department of Commerce, Bureau of the Census, *Social Indicators III,* p. 71; *Statistical Abstract of the United States 1986,* p. 68.

Life Expectancy and Mortality Rates

Since the turn of the century, average life expectancy at birth in the United States has increased from forty-seven to about seventy-five years.[1] Figure 1-1 gives changes in life expectancy by sex and race over a period of more than eighty years. In 1900, over half (53 percent) of reported deaths involved persons fourteen years of age and younger. Today, less than 5 percent of total reported deaths occur among this age group.[2]

Imagine a time when death at an early age was not uncommon. Today we might characterize such persons as "struck down in their prime." Most Americans take for granted the expectation that a newborn child will live on into his or her seventh decade, perhaps beyond.

Of course, the expectation that a baby will survive and mature into old age is not shared equally by all Americans, and it is certainly not shared by people who live in areas of the world where poverty and poor living conditions contribute to a high death rate. The death rates among people living in conditions of bare subsistence have been altered only minimally by the advances in modern medicine and health care. For most Americans, however, the expectation of a long life seems almost a birthright.

How unlike times past, when it was possible that one or both parents would die before their children had grown to adolescence. Mothers died during childbirth; babies were stillborn. Most people experienced the deaths of brothers and sisters during the early years of childhood from such diseases as whooping cough, diphtheria, and polio.

At the turn of the century, the death rate in America was about 17 per 1000. Today, at about 8.6 per 1000, the death rate has declined to its lowest point ever (see Figure 1-2).[3] A high mortality rate, which included a considerable percentage of infant deaths, made it nearly impossible for a person living in earlier times to deny the fact of death.

Young and old experienced death as a natural and inevitable part of the human condition. A typical household of the nineteenth century could be made up of an extended family: aged parents, uncles, aunts, and grandparents, as well as children of varying ages. In this extended family, the likelihood of experiencing death firsthand was considerably greater than is the case with today's typical nuclear family, consisting only of a mom, a dad, and the kids. Today, as Robert Fulton reports, the typical American family "may expect statistically to live twenty years without the passing of one of its members."[4]

Geographical Mobility

Besides changes in the composition of the typical American family, geographical mobility has also contributed to the lessened incidence of firsthand experiences of death. Every year, about 20 percent of us pull up stakes, say goodbye to our relatives, friends, and neighbors, and move elsewhere.[5]

Whereas in previous times relationships were closely tied to place and to kinship, today's relationships are characterized more by present function than by a lifetime of shared experiences. How many college friendships continue

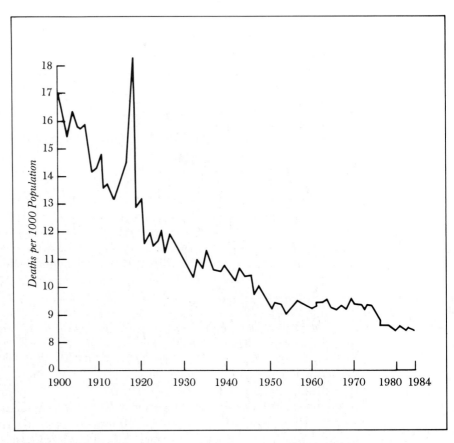

Figure I-2   *Death Rates, 1900–1984*
Source: National Center for Health Statistics, *Vital Statistics of the United States; Statistical Abstract of the United States 1986.*

through marriage and the childrearing years on into retirement? Children, once grown, rarely live in the same house with their parents — or, even less likely, with brothers and sisters in an extended family.[6]

Family and friends become separated from one another by large distances as changes in life style and changes of employment necessitate moving onward. In such circumstances, death is unlikely to occur among family and friends. This highly mobile pattern of living is, of course, experienced in varying degrees. Among those ethnic or socioeconomic groups that place an exceptionally high value on family ties, several generations may exhibit a notable degree of intimacy and closeness. But, for most Americans, a highly mobile life style contributes to making the impact of death less immediate.

*Five generations of the Machado family form an extended family network rarely
seen today. Firsthand experiences of death in such a family come through the
closeness of multigenerational living.*

Gordon Parks, FSA Collection, Library of Congress

Changing Causes of Death

Changing causes of death represent another major reason why experience
of death today is so different from what it was at the turn of the century. Then
the typical death was rapid and sudden, often caused by acute infectious diseases
such as tuberculosis, typhoid fever, syphilis, diphtheria, streptococcal septi-

TABLE I-I   *Leading Causes of Death, 1982*

Cause of Death[a]	Estimated Death Rate per 100,000	% of Total
All causes	852.0	100.0
Diseases of heart	326.0	38.3
Malignancies (cancer)	187.2	22.0
Cerebrovascular diseases	68.0	8.0
Accidents	40.6	4.8
Chronic pulmonary diseases	25.8	3.0
Pneumonia and influenza	21.1	2.5
Diabetes mellitus	14.9	1.8
Suicide	12.2	1.4
Chronic liver disease	11.9	1.4
Atherosclerosis	11.6	1.4
Homicide	9.6	1.1
Perinatal (early infancy) diseases	9.0	1.1

Source: U.S. National Center for Health Statistics, *Vital Statistics of the United States; Statistical Abstract of the United States 1986*, p. 73.
[a] The top four causes of death currently account for nearly 75 percent of all deaths in the U.S. population.

cemia, and pneumonia. In 1900, these microbial diseases accounted for about 40 percent of all deaths in the United States; today they account for only about 4 percent. People still contract these infectious diseases, but the outcome has been dramatically altered by improvements in health care.[7] Now the typical death is a slow, progressive process resulting from diseases such as heart disease and cancer (see Table 1-1). As a result of these changing causes of death, many people now have the notion of death as something that happens in old age.[8]

Although most demographers consider the maximum possible lifespan of human beings to have remained fairly constant at about eighty-five years, in earlier times few individuals actually survived to such a ripe old age. In modern societies, however, a diminishing mortality rate among younger members of the population has resulted in a larger, and steadily increasing, proportion of aged persons.

In 1900, persons sixty-five or older made up 4 percent of the American population, whereas today they make up 12 percent, or about 28 million persons. In 1900, this segment of the population accounted for 17 percent of all deaths; today, of the slightly more than 2 million deaths each year in the United States, more than two-thirds occur among persons sixty-five and older.[9] These persons tend to be somewhat disengaged from the social situations that would make their deaths more visible to the rest of society.

Reduced Contact Among Generations

Geographical mobility, an increasing proportion of elderly people in the population, a declining percentage of deaths among the young, and the rise of the nuclear family combine to create a situation wherein few people are present when close family members die. Typically, grandparents and grandchildren do not reside in the same home and thus have intermittent rather than the daily contact of times past. Indeed, the goal of independent living, a home of one's own, has become the norm for both old and young in American society.

Although there are many reasons for the age segregation prevalent in American society — the desire for independence, fear, lack of community, differing life styles, unsuitable housing — the result is that many elderly people are isolated to a significant extent from even close friends and family members. Retirement homes or retirement subdivisions and trailer parks, for example, tend to discourage close intermingling of the generations.

Consider, for instance, the unfortunate experience of two small children on a Halloween trek, going door to door in their neighborhood. After knocking on several well-lighted doors in a large mobile home park, their cries of "Trick or treat!" were finally answered by a woman who said, "You'll not get any Halloween treats in this place. Only old people live here, and they leave their lights on for security and safety, not to welcome children on Halloween!"

In addition, some elderly persons are confined to hospitals or reside in nursing or convalescent facilities because of illness or poor health. Such circumstances are not conducive to death occurring amid familiar surroundings with family and friends present. Even when an older person is able to continue living more or less independently in his or her own home, the onset of the final illness usually brings admittance to a hospital followed by death in an institutional setting. Thus, reduced contact between the generations is yet another reason why few of us are likely to experience directly an actual death.

The Displacement of Death from the Home

Not only is death less prevalent than it once was, it is less visible, as is dying. Institutionalized and given over to professional caretakers, death is kept apart from the rest of us. Most urban deaths, as many as 90 percent, now occur in institutional settings. In 1900, two-thirds of the Americans who died were less than fifty years old. Most died in their own beds, at home. This was true even in the cities, where perhaps 75 to 80 percent of deaths occurred in the home.

The present pattern of death in our society is such that, regardless of age, about 80 percent of all persons die in an institutional setting — hospital, nursing or convalescent facility, or retirement home providing care for the aged — perhaps surrounded by an astonishing array of machinery that is dedicated to sustaining life until the last electrical impulse fades from the monitor. A long-distance phone call announcing the passing of grandpa or grandma often takes the place of the intimate, firsthand experience of a loved one's death in an earlier time.

Grandmother,
When Your Child Died

Grandmother, when your child died
hot beside you
in your narrow bed,
his labored breathing kept
you restless
and woke you when
it sighed,
and stopped.

You held him through the bitter dawn
and in the morning
dressed him, combed his hair,
your tears welled, but you didn't weep
until at last he lay
among the wild iris in the sod,
his soul gone inexplicably to God. Amen.

But grandmother, when my child died
sweet Jesus, he died hard.
A motor beside
his sterile cot
groaned, and hissed, and whirred
while he sang his pain—
low notes and high notes
in slow measures
slipping through the drug-cloud.
My tears, redundant,
dropped slow
like glucose or blood
from a bottle.
And when he died
my eyes were dry
and gods wearing white coats
turned away.

Joan Neet George

Life-Extending Technologies

Changes in how Americans relate to death have also resulted from striking advances in modern medical practice. With its invention in 1954, the kidney machine became the first in a steadily lengthening line of sophisticated technologies designed to aid in prolonging life. These new biomedical technologies offer us a multitude of choices in health care that people of an earlier time would find unfathomable, and they have altered our attitudes about death and dying.

Biological malfunctions that once were lethal are now repaired by highly skilled surgical techniques. The replacement or repair of dysfunctional organs is an accepted, and even expected, part of current medical practice. These surgical procedures take advantage of companion technologies that extend the surgeon's skills. Sophisticated machinery monitors various biological functions, including brainwave activity, heart rate, body temperature, respiration, blood pressure, pulse, blood chemistry, and a host of others. Signaling changes in body function by light, sound, and computer printout, such apparatus often becomes the crucial difference in situations of life or death.

Current developments in biomedical science reflect the contributions of many scientific and technological disciplines, including electronics, materials science, engineering, nuclear physics, molecular biology, cell biology, immunology, and biochemistry. Recombinant DNA technologies are beginning to provide clues that can aid in treating some of our major diseases.

The computer is also becoming an important tool in medicine, both in the laboratory and in clinical applications. Computers aid in physiological monitoring as well as in diagnostic and therapeutic procedures. Used with infusion pumps, computers ensure constant-rate administration of intravenous fluids. In the technology of prosthetics, the replacement of body parts, computers are performing both physiological and sensory functions for persons whose natural mechanisms are impaired.

The familiar X-ray machine has been joined by innovative imaging systems

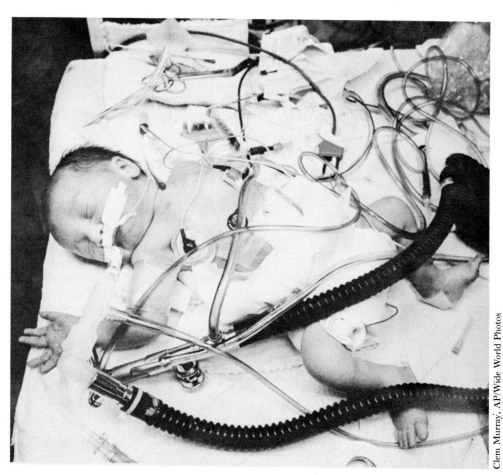

Clem Murray, AP/Wide World Photos

Lifelines — tubes and wires monitoring heartbeat, breathing, and blood pressure — increase this premature baby's chances of survival in the intensive care unit of Philadelphia's Children's Hospital. The special-care nursery often becomes an arena for many of the most difficult ethical decisions in medicine.

such as the CAT scanner, which by its "computerized axial tomographic" scanning provides images of plane sections through the patient's body. Ultra-sound systems, positron emission tomography, nuclear magnetic resonance (NMR) zeugmatography, and the germanium camera are yet other new imaging systems whose development promises to have far-reaching applications in modern medicine.

Yet this marriage of medicine and technology also brings confusing consequences. The same technological device that seems to one person a godsend that extends life, may to another person seem to prolong dying. These modern medical miracles raise new questions concerning their use. To what degree should we rely on life-saving technologies for sustaining biological functions? What degree of normal activity is possible for a person whose life has been saved but whose function is otherwise impaired? What are the personal and financial costs? Who should make decisions about the use of such technologies? The highly publicized case of Karen Ann Quinlan, whose death in 1985 came nearly a decade after being removed from a respirator as a result of a New Jersey Supreme Court decision, is a familiar example of the complexities that are frequently associated with such life-sustaining machines and the decision about the extent of their use.[10]

Even the definition of death has become hazy: "cessation of life, the total and permanent cessation of all vital functions" is now superseded by a complex medicolegal definition. Defining death has moved a considerable distance from the child's simple statement, "When you're dead, you're dead."

With far-reaching consequences, life-extending technologies have changed the way we understand death and dying. Our attitudes seem to reflect the view that, given the appropriate medical expertise and the right tools, death is an event that can be indefinitely postponed. Indeed, many of our attitudes toward death are closely connected with our notions about what medical technologies can and cannot accomplish. Coupled with the ethical maxim that whatever *can* be done *should* be done to keep an individual alive, these technological factors have reduced the intimate contact with death experienced by our forebears. Thus, for the variety of reasons given on the preceding pages, experiences of death and dying are segregated from the rest of life.

As a society, we have given over the care of our dying to specialists. Likewise, as we have seen, caring for the dead is no longer part of our common experience. Instead, there are death professionals — ranging from the coroner to the cremator — to whom we turn when confronted by death. In stark contrast to a time when family and friends cared for the body of the deceased and prepared it for burial, the prevalent attitude now is, "You sure couldn't get me to touch a dead body, not for love or money!"

Expressions of Attitudes Toward Death

The prevailing cultural attitude toward death can be seen in the language used to describe the fact of death, as well as in the portrayal of death by the media and in literature. Although direct contact with death is far less common than it once was, death nevertheless occupies a significant place in the larger cultural environment. The manner in which death is presented in news reports, dramatic features, and even in various forms of humor is an expression of current attitudes toward death and dying within American culture.

Language

It seems that many people have difficulty talking about death at all. The language used to discuss the process of dying and subsequent death is rarely direct. More often, we take refuge in euphemisms, substituting mild, indirect, or vague expressions for ones considered harsh or blunt (see Table 1-2). The words a person uses to talk about the fact of death often reveal attitudes toward

TABLE 1-2 *Euphemisms*

Passed on	Made the change
Croaked	Got mertelized
Kicked the bucket	On the other side
Gone to heaven	God took him/her
Gone home	Asleep in Christ
Expired	Departed
Breathed his/her last	Transcended
Succumbed	Bought the farm
Left us	With the angels
Went to his/her eternal reward	Feeling no pain
Lost	Lost the race
Met his/her Maker	His/her time was up
Wasted	Cashed in
Checked out	Crossed over Jordan
Eternal rest	Perished
Laid to rest	Lost it
Pushing up daisies	Was done in
Called home	Translated into glory
Was a goner	Returned to dust
Came to an end	Withered away
Bit the dust	In the arms of the Father
Annihilated	Gave it up
Liquidated	It was curtains
Terminated	A long sleep
Gave up the ghost	On the heavenly shores
Left this world	Out of his/her misery
Rubbed out	Ended it all
Snuffed	Angels carried him/her away
Six feet under	Resting in peace
Consumed	Changed his/her form
Found everlasting peace	Dropped the body
Went to a new life	Rode into the sunset
In the great beyond	That was all she wrote
No longer with us	

death or the circumstances surrounding a death. We rarely speak of someone dying; instead they "passed away" or "were called home." The dead person is then "laid to rest," and burial becomes "interment"; the undertaker is replaced by the "funeral director." These terms all suggest a well-choreographed production for disposing of the dead in a tasteful manner.

In our etiquette for acknowledging a person's bereavement, death is seldom mentioned without the adornment of euphemistic language. In more than 200 sympathy cards studied, death was mentioned directly in less than 3 percent. Most cards allowed the sender to express condolences without violating the cultural taboo against explicitly mentioning the event of death. In another study of 110 sympathy cards, none mentioned the word "death" or "died."[11] Nor was there any reference to the end of life. The person who had died was referred to only indirectly, usually within the context of memories or the healing process of time.

Death is a metaphor in such sentiments as "What is death but a long sleep?" and is denied in verses like James Whitcomb Riley's "He is not dead, he is just away." It seems that the greeting card companies, perceiving American attitudes toward death, have chosen to agree with Amy Vanderbilt's advice that words like "death," "died," or "killed" should be avoided when writing letters of condolence.[12] Such advice reflects the view that euphemisms can be a way of talking about death without offending another person's sensibilities, a way of avoiding any disrespect of the bereaved's feelings of loss. However, euphemisms may also be used to distance oneself from the experience by masking the reality of death.

Language may also be devised to devalue death. The military has added to our lexicon of substitutions for plain talk about death by citing "body counts" and by describing a person as "being wasted" by an adversary. Elaborate charts depict the capability of new weapons systems to inflict "mega-death" on the enemy. Substitutes are found for words that would more directly describe the harsh and horrible reality of death in battle. Death is depersonalized. Thus, language can be used in ways that allow us to distance ourselves from death, to deny its reality, to make it somehow more acceptable, more manageable.

Humor

People sometimes use humor to counteract their anxiety. Serious and somber matters may be made easier to deal with when there is some comedic relief. Clowns poke holes in our pretensions, thereby shedding a glimmering light on ourselves and the situations that we deem so crucial to our secure self-identity. Laughter can release some of the anxiety that accompanies the human predicament. Casting a humorous light on death is not new, of course. But now that death has come out of the closet enough to receive the attention bestowed by the media, we sometimes discover a bravado in the face of death that many find startling.

At least one university campus has organized a "cadaver party" that includes among its aims the restoration of voting rights for the dead. "Rent-a-caskets" have been used at birthday parties and mock wakes, and as cocktail bars. One hostess expressed a desire to be placed in the casket and rolled into her yule party so that, at the appropriate moment, she could leap up dressed as Santa Claus—thus laying to rest, no doubt, the rumors of Santa's untimely demise. And in California, passing motorists are taken aback by a white hearse with the cryptic license plates, "Not Yett." Efforts to deflate some of the seriousness or to defuse some of the anxiety about death may be entirely frivolous or they may have a practical side, depending upon one's point of view.

It is possible, for instance, to obtain a build-it-yourself coffin that doubles (before it's needed for its ultimate purpose) as a stereo cabinet, wine rack, or coffee table. One firm offers the option of having a coffin built in the shape of an elephant, an airplane, a fish, or a car. A recent news story described a woman who chose to be buried in a luxury convertible (with the top down?) while she was adorned in furs and jewelry, apparently in an effort to prove that it *is* possible to take it with you.

Poking fun at death or casting it in an unconventional light may or may not be genuinely confronting death. Such acts may be intended frivolously, or they may reflect what the participant sees as quite practical considerations. Finding humorous aspects to death, or considering it in a less than somber fashion, may make it possible to reduce the anxiety that comes with an awareness of one's own mortality.

Mary Hall observes that "what is humorous to each of us depends on our particular cultural set, our own experience, and our personal inclination."[13] She notes that humor can function in several ways relative to death. First, it can

---

 The Undertakers

Old Pops had been stone cold dead for two days. He was rigid, gruesome and had turned slightly green and now he lay on a slab at the undertakers, about to be embalmed by two lovable old morticians.

"At least he lived to a ripe age," said one.

"Yep," said the other. "Well, let's get to 'er."

Suddenly, Old Pops bolted upright and without opening his eyes, began to utter this story:

"In 1743, Captain Rice set sail from England with an unreliable and mutinous crew. After three days at sea, the mast of the mainsail splintered, and then broke completely in half. The ship tossed about at sea for two days; the men mutinied, and the ship tossed about for another two days. At the end of the third day, a ship appeared on the horizon and rescued them and good Captain Rice failed to mention to the admiral the incident of mutiny, and his crew became faithful and hard-working and devoted themselves to their captain."

Old Pops laid back down on the marble.

"Well," said one mortician, "there goes the old saying, 'dead men tell no tales'!"

Steve Martin, *Cruel Shoes*

raise our consciousness about a taboo subject, allowing us to talk about the indescribable. Humor can also give us an opportunity to rise above the immediate sadness of death, thus giving us momentary release from "the awfuls" and helping us feel more in control of the situation, even though it cannot be changed. Third, humor is a great leveler in that it treats us all alike and confronts us with the fact that there are no exemptions from humanness. Thus, humor binds us together and promotes the closeness we need when we fear the unknown. Finally, after a death has occurred, humor is a comfort to the survivors as they recall the funny as well as the painful events of a loved one's life.

Humor comes in many different forms, from humorous epitaphs to so-called *black* or *gallows* humor, which often reflects a thumbing of one's nose at death, as if attempting to minimize the power of death and regain some sense of mastery over it. Since the advent of the atomic bomb, the threat of horrendous death has given rise to humor that seeks to put such an incomprehensible possibility into a more manageable perspective.

Death is a topic frequently addressed by cartoonists. "In cartoon humor," Hall points out, "we find represented modern technology and its effect on the dying patient, as well as the characteristics of people who are attempting to carry on their normal activities, even in the dying trajectory." Cartoons demonstrate both that "we are all mortal, that there are no bargains with death," and that "we still all attempt to escape and be the exception."[14]

Humor also provides relief and release for caregivers whose jobs bring them into frequent contact with dying or death. A firm that distributes instructional materials for emergency medical technicians recognizes this need for relief by including in its catalog a musical recording entitled "You Respond to Everyone But Me." At a teaching hospital, a resident discussed how doctors avoided using the word "death" when a patient died, concerned that the other patients might be alarmed. One day, as a medical team was examining a patient, an intern came to the door to inform the team of another patient's death. Knowing that the word was taboo and finding no ready substitute, she stood in the doorway and announced, "Guess who's not going to shop at Woolworth's any more?" Soon, this phrase became the standard way of sharing information among the staff that a patient had died.

Death may be humorously treated as a way to put life's foibles into perspective, as in the offhanded remark, "Halitosis is better than no breath at all." For individuals with a life-threatening illness, humor can be an important means of coping with the debilitating effect of a shattering diagnosis as well as with the illness's attendant pain and anxiety. Joking about death can help us confront our fears and thereby gain a sense of mastery over the unknown.

Mass Media

Because most of us no longer experience death firsthand, the way we think about death is shaped largely through vicarious experiences provided by the

"The Far Side," drawing by Gary Larson, Chronicle Features

"Wouldn't you know it! Now the Hendersons have the bomb."

media. Newspapers, magazines, books, movies, and television have become the secondhand sources from which we learn about death and dying.

In the News

As you read your daily newspaper, what kinds of encounters with death vie for your attention? Perhaps, scanning the day's news, you find an assortment of accidents, murders, suicides, and disasters involving violent deaths. A jetliner crashes, and the newspaper announces the fact with banner headlines. Here you see a story about a family perishing when trapped inside their burning home; in another, a family's vacation comes to an untimely end when they become the victims of a spectacular fatal automobile collision on the interstate.

And there are the deaths of the famous. Whereas most deaths are reported in death notices — brief, standardized statements, usually printed in small type and listed alphabetically in a column of vital statistics "as uniform as a row of tiny grave plots"[15] — the deaths of the famous are announced by means of more-extensive "obituaries." Obituaries vary in length as well as in content and style. Prefaced by individual headlines and set in the same size of type used in other newspaper stories, obituaries indicate the newsworthiness that editors attribute to the deaths of famous persons.[16]

The death of a neighbor or of the person working alongside you on the job is not likely to be reported with such emphasis.[17] Ordinary deaths — the kind most of us can expect to experience — tend to be neglected or else mentioned only in the most routine fashion. The spectacular obscures the ordinary.

Whether routine or extraordinary, these encounters with death in the news influence the way we think about and respond to death. The nature of news has changed from providing information to sharing experience.[18] Celebrations as well as disasters are often experienced simultaneously by the news correspondent and the viewing or listening audience. When the space shuttle *Challenger* exploded shortly after lift-off, killing the seven crew members aboard, it evoked grief that was shared as people read newspapers and watched television. Reaction to the tragedy was intense, due partly to heightened public interest in a mission involving the first private citizen slated for space flight, Christa McAuliffe, a schoolteacher.

In describing the role of television during this crisis, some likened it to a "national hearth" around which Americans were symbolically gathered as they witnessed the disaster and contemplated its meaning, while others said television fulfilled its function no better and no worse than one would expect of any household appliance. Some questioned whether repeated broadcasts of the shuttle exploding exhibited a macabre fascination by the media for the "pornography of grief."

Whether they perceive television as a national hearth or simply as an appliance, most people have come to expect the media not only to provide information about events, but also to convey some sense of their meaning. When the news involves death, a question arises about the propriety of focusing upon those most closely affected. For example, during the memorial service for the *Challenger* crew, which was viewed on television by millions of Americans in their homes and offices, the astronauts' grieving families were shown. Was such coverage of the bereaved an intrusion on their private sorrow, or was it news that helped to focus the entire nation's shared experience of loss? The distinction between *public* event and *private* loss is not always easily drawn.

The media both reflect and help shape the attitudes held by the reading and viewing public. At times, however, the attitudes of the media and its audience do not coincide. When a newspaper in Ontario, Canada, ran a picture of a distraught mother at the scene of an accident as she learned of her daughter's fatal injuries, many readers were outraged, calling the picture "a blatant example of morbid ludicrousness" and "the highest order of poor taste and insensitivity."[19]

Interestingly, the girl's mother did not resent the newspaper for publishing the photograph. On the contrary, she said that seeing the photo had helped her to realize what had happened. Given the sudden and unexpected circumstances of the death, this mother's response was not unusual. Many survivors of sudden, unexpected deaths want to reconstruct, in as much detail as possible, the events surrounding the death as a means of coping with the reality of their loss.

In this context, then, the pertinent question concerns the attitudes expressed by the members of the community who were outraged at what they considered to be the paper's insensitivity. One writer suggested that, because most people are unfamiliar with death and the emotions it elicits, they are likely to "ascribe emotions to the grief-stricken that are not really present."[20] Were the outraged readers defending what they imagined to be the prerogatives of the grief-stricken mother as a victim of a too-intrusive press? Or did the photograph simply trigger volatile emotions related to their own uncomfortable feelings about death?

Such questions are not amenable to simple answers. The media's insistence on the dramatic does at times raise issues regarding its ethical integrity.[21] The newspaper editor's decision to print a photograph showing a grieving mother reflects a set of assumptions and attitudes about the role of the press and the tastes of its public. Another set of assumptions and attitudes was reflected by those readers who expressed outrage at the picture's appearance in the paper. Thus, the issues raised by this incident really pertain to attitudes about what is acceptable where death is concerned.

Like newspapers, television news programs are highly selective in determining what constitutes a newsworthy death; again the criteria are violence, disaster, or fame.[22] Our neighbor's death is not likely to be reported on network news. Indeed, deaths reported on television are likely to be even more remote from our experience. Recall from your experience both the types of death reported on television and the commentator's manner of presenting this information. The "detached and captionlike quality" of network news coverage, observes Michael Arlen, results in "snippets of information" about the deaths that are reported.[23] News of the bus crash or the mine disaster is interposed between reports about closing stock market prices and factory layoffs in Detroit.

Arlen contrasts these media messages about death with the experience of death in our own lives, where death evokes "myriad expressions of grief, incomprehension, and deep human response." Only rarely — as with the deaths of Martin Luther King, Jr., John F. Kennedy, Robert Kennedy, and, more recently, John Lennon — does television suspend its detachment somewhat to present the communal dimensions of death, the public as well as private loss that accompanies bereavement. With the deaths of these public figures, and the intense grief of the American public, the media played a key role in what was essentially a "national rite of passage."

Entertaining Death

The pervasive influence of television on the American consciousness is well known. Ninety-eight percent of American homes have at least one television set, and television programs are viewed an average of seven hours per day per household.[24] Far from being ignored, death is a central theme of much television programming. In a typical week of program listings in *TV Guide,* about one-third describe programs in which death or dying is a featured theme.[25] Out of a possible total of 168 hours of weekly viewing time, an avid television viewer could spend more than 70 percent of those hours watching programs that feature death in some way.

These figures are even more striking in that they take into account only such programs as talk shows, crime and adventure series, and movies. Not included are newscasts (which typically feature several stories about death in each broadcast); religious programming (which includes theological and anecdotal discussions of death); nature programs (which often depict death in the animal kingdom); children's cartoons (which often present caricatures of death); soap operas (which seem always to have some character dying or recently deceased); or sports programs (which give us descriptions such as "the ball is dead" and "the other team is killing them today").[26]

Despite this massive volume of programming in which death is prominent, the televised image of death is seldom designed to add to our knowledge of its reality. Few programs deal with such real-life topics as how most people cope with a loved one's death or dying.

Instead, television presents a depersonalized image of death, an image that is often characterized by violence. Consider, for example, the western or detective story, which glazes over the reality of death by describing the bad guy as "kicking the bucket" or as having "croaked" — relegated, no doubt, to Boot Hill at the edge of town, where the deceased now "pushes up daisies." Think about the last death you saw portrayed in a television entertainment or movie. Perhaps the camera panned from the dying person's face and torso to a closeup of hands twitching — then all movement ceases as the person's breathing fades away in perfect harmony with the musical score. Or, more likely, the death was violent: the cowboy gunfight at the OK Corral; high noon. The gent with the slower draw is hit, reels, falls, his body convulsing into cold silence.

Recall the Saturday morning cartoon depiction of death. Daffy Duck is pressed to a thin sheet by a steamroller, only to pop up again a moment later. Elmer Fudd aims his shotgun at Bugs Bunny, pulls the trigger, bang! Bugs, unmarked by the rifle blast, clutches his throat, spins around several times, and mutters, "It's all getting dark now, Elmer. . . . I'm going. . . ." Bugs falls to the ground, both feet still in the air. As his eyes close, his feet finally hit the dirt. But wait! Now Bugs pops up, good as new. Reversible death!

Facing the possibility of death heroically, lawman Will Kane (played by Gary Cooper) strides courageously toward a showdown with his adversary at "High Noon." Attitudes toward death portrayed in the movies help shape how we relate to risk and to death in our own lives.

Realistic portrayals of death are not the media's standard bill of fare. The television drama or cartoon picture of death would probably seem quite out of place to a child of an earlier time with firsthand experience of death in the home. When told of his grandfather's death, one modern seven-year-old asked, "Who did it to him?" The understanding of death offered by the media is that it comes from outside, often violently. Such notions of death reinforce the belief that dying is something that *happens* to us, rather than something we *do*. Death becomes an accidental rather than a natural process.

Persons who have been present at someone's death describe a very different picture. Many recall the gurgling, gasping sounds as the last breath rattles through the lungs; the changes in body color as flesh tones tinge blue; the feeling of a once warm and flexible body growing cold and flaccid. They often say, "Death is not at all what I thought it would be like; it doesn't look or sound or feel like anything I see on television or in movies!"

Although death is a major theme in movies, only rarely does a film deal realistically with dying and death. Even when there is some attempt at an accurate portrayal of individuals facing death, reality is often replaced by fantasy to enhance the story line. Many films exhibit what critic Roger Ebert calls "Ali McGraw Disease," in which characters with terminal illness are depicted as becoming more and more beautiful until ultimately "they're so great that they die."[27] Ebert's comment may pertain not only to the efforts of filmmakers to portray death as beautiful but to the common desire to see only a positive image of dying.

At the same time, perhaps because many of us do not have a close familiarity with dying, fascination with death can sometimes turn bizarre. This is evident, for instance, in documentary videos depicting graphic scenes of animal and human death, including suicide and autopsies, which have become popular at videocassette outlets.[28]

In the world of prime-time television death is rarely a quiet or natural event. The few exceptions to the usual portrayal demonstrate that it is possible for the media to provide a more thoughtful forum for considering death-related issues. For example, in the past several years, television documentaries have shown some of the ways that different individuals and families cope with the experience of terminal illness. The Public Broadcasting System has been particularly noteworthy in encouraging a greater discussion of the issues that relate to death and dying.

Similarly, a number of American newspapers have published a "Course-by-Newspaper" series on death and dying, thus providing readers an opportunity to educate themselves concerning some of the important topics covered in a survey course on death and dying. Such examples show that the media — print and television — can perform an educational service by presenting death and dying as other than sensational. Unfortunately, these positive contributions are nearly buried under an avalanche of messages about death that often bear little resemblance to its reality.

Literature

Death is one of the enduring themes in literature. From Sophocles' *Oedipus the King,* to Shakespeare's *King Lear,* to Leo Tolstoy's "The Death of Ivan Illych," death has been treated by writers as significant and meaningful to human experience. Recall for a moment a work of literature you have read recently. Was death an element of the plot? How did the author portray dying or death in the story? In works of poetry, prose, and drama, the meaning of death is explored as it relates to society as well as the individual. Thus, literature gives us a rich source of information about attitudes toward death. By expressing the human dimension and portraying the range and subtlety of death-related experiences, literature can balance a strict diet of facts and technical information.

Recently, literature has been applied in just this way as a teaching tool within the medical profession. At Johns Hopkins, the Mayo Clinic, and other such institutions, plays like Marsha Norman's *'night, Mother,* which dramatizes the factors behind suicide, and Laurence Housman's *Victoria Regina,* focusing

Buffalo Bill's
defunct
        who used to
        ride a watersmooth-silver
                                stallion
and break onetwothreefourfive pigeonsjustlikethat
                                        Jesus
he was a handsome man
                        and what i want to know is
how do you like your blueeyed boy
Mister Death

        e.e. cummings

on issues of aging, have been presented to audiences made up of physicians and other medical personnel. The aim of these programs is to foster insight into the human behaviors and problems common to medical practice that may be given little discussion during formal training.

Literary accounts by veterans of the Vietnam War have created a genre depicting the trauma of combat as well as the quest to restore meaning to a shattering experience of loss. The best of these accounts are more than mere war stories. The authors' personal experiences form a basis for dealing with the overwhelming magnitude of the losses resulting from the war, individually and as a society.[29]

Another literary category of special interest to the student of death and dying is that which seeks to express and understand the Holocaust. The experiences of Nazi incarceration and extermination, as well as life and death in Soviet labor camps, have been reported and analyzed through a rich literature. Written in all the major European languages as well as in Hebrew and Yiddish, Holocaust literature has found expression through victims' diaries as well as persecutors' memoirs, in novels as well as psychological studies. Examples include Anne Frank's *Diary of a Young Girl,* Chaim Kaplan's *Warsaw Diary,* Charlotte Delbo's *None of Us Will Return,* and Elie Wiesel's *Night.* Yet this literature is not merely topical. Rather, it forces the reader to contemplate fundamental aspects of human nature. As one writer says, "The human imagination after Auschwitz is simply not the same as it was before."[30] Some of these writings explore the syndrome of the observer-victim whose familiar self, by means of radical detachment bordering on schizophrenia, deteriorates to the point that it finally allows "business as usual" amid unspeakable horror. The victim becomes indistinguishable from the violence, a situation the cartoon character Pogo once described in the phrase, "We have met the enemy and he is us."

Increasingly, literature has focused on what Frederick Hoffman calls the "landscape of violence" that pervades life in the twentieth century.[31] Reflecting human experience in a century that has seen the mass deaths of two world wars and innumerable smaller conflicts, the modern fictional hero tries to come to terms with sudden and violent death in situations that allow no time for survivors to express their grief fully or to mourn the dead ceremonially.[32] It seems that whatever meaning death may have is no longer clear.

Modern warfare as well as the common street violence that receives so much attention in the daily newspaper has the effect of reducing individuals to the status of *things*. This can be seen, too, in the popular detective novel, which has been described as "vigilante literature."[33] The hero in these stories sets out to avenge evil but is corrupted by a self-justifying morality that perpetuates violence.

Frederick Hoffman points out that modern literature includes many attempts to delineate and explore the meaning of death in situations that are apparently absurd and ultimately incomprehensible. The modern writer, says Hoffman, tries to deal with death in a variety of ways: by creating a mythology or metaphor significant enough to account for the evil; by portraying the violence within an ideological melodrama or showing it as a farce, alternating between the trivial and the grotesque; or by simply presenting experiences in a manner that is as impersonal as the events themselves seem to be, to let the bare violence speak for itself. "The history of violence," Hoffman says, "is dominated by examples of ambiguous dying."[34]

As you review the messages conveyed by the literature with which you are familiar, you may find that much of it reflects the belief that death in the twentieth century is so horrendous in its violence and impersonality that it is impossible to truly comprehend. For modern writers, death often elicits less a contemplation of judgment or concern for immortality than a deep anxiety about annihilation and loss of identity.

Visual Arts

As with literature, the visual arts present a range of attitudes toward death. Death themes in art are revealed through the symbols, signs, images, and concepts used by the artists.[35] In Western art, one often finds themes and images related to classical mythology or to the Bible and other writings associated with the Judaeo-Christian tradition. Comparable sources inspire artists of other cultures with respect to death themes in art. Themes that draw upon the processes observed in nature with respect to life, growth, decay, and death transcend cultural boundaries.

Tomb art is a rich source of information about the predominant beliefs of a culture. Scenes inscribed in relief on the limestone sarcophagi of ancient Egypt, for example, often depicting the life of the deceased, attest to that culture's beliefs about what follows upon death. These beliefs can also be seen in the illustrations accompanying Egyptian religious texts. Graphically portrayed is the common expectation that, after death, a person will be judged according to his or her deeds during earthly life.

By contrast, the sarcophagi constructed by Greek and Roman artisans express the somewhat different views common to these later societies. A first-century Roman urn, whose text is addressed to the "Manes" or spirits of the dead, shows the deceased reclining on a couch before a table lavishly set with dishes while three slaves offer him food and drink. Birds, commonly used in art as a representation of the soul, are perched on laurel trees, and the urn's cover depicts a bird's nest with four young being fed by their parents. The use of such symbols as the banquet scene and the family of birds communicates visually the deceased's hopes for a peaceful afterlife.

The tomb figures of ancient China, hundreds of which were sometimes buried in a single tomb, represent persons of varied status and occupation. These works of art indicate the presence of a belief in the desirability of preserving and perhaps even recreating after death the social interrelationships of the time.

The artistic history of Western civilization is full of images of death. When we view a work like the thirteenth century French sepulchral effigy of Jean d'Alluye, which shows the recumbent knight in chain mail, sword girded and shield at his side, feet resting on the image of a lion, it expresses something of the intellectual and social milieu of medieval Christendom and the age of chivalry, the tension between faith and heroism that influenced the way people of that time related to death.

Several centuries later, there arose in Western Europe one of the most arresting expressions of death ever to emerge in the graphic arts: fifteenth- and sixteenth-century woodcuts of the Dance of Death. Growing out of widespread fears related to the spread of bubonic plague, known as the Black Death, the Dance of Death reflects a preoccupation with mortality and sudden, unexpected death regardless of one's station in life. As an artistic theme, the Dance of Death continues to fascinate contemporary artists. Fritz Eichenberg's woodcuts reveal the frightening possibilities inherent in our own time's Dance of Death: humankind facing the prospect of universal annihilation resulting from total war.[36]

The encounter with dying and death is also expressed through art depicting scenes of the deathbed and persons *in extremis*. One such painting is Francisco José de Goya's *Self-Portrait with Dr. Arieta*. This work, which Goya painted for the doctor who aided his recovery from life-threatening illness, shows the doctor holding medicine to Goya's lips and includes the figure of Death alongside persons who may be Goya's priest and his housekeeper.

Suicide, too, has been given artistic expression. In *The Death of Lucretia*, painted in 1666, Rembrandt portrays Lucretia with a tear in her eye, moments after she has stabbed herself with a dagger. Painted shortly after the death of his wife and one of his sons, this work expresses the artist's saddened mental state.

Early American attitudes toward death can be seen in Charles Wilson Peale's painting, *Rachel Weeping* (1772 and 1776), which shows a mother mourning her dead child. Lying on her deathbed, the child has her jaw wrapped with a fabric strap to keep it closed and her arms bound with a cord to keep them straight at her sides. Various medicines, all of which have proven ineffective, sit on a bedside table. The child's mother gazes heavenward and holds a handkerchief as tears roll down her face, a contrast to the dead child's peaceful countenance.

In the early nineteenth century, Americans combined both classical and Christian symbols of death to memorialize public figures and family members. Influenced by earlier practices in England and continental Europe, the images associated with American mourning reflected the Romantic views of the time toward death. Found on jewelry and pottery as well as textiles and prints, common motifs included the urn, trees and gardens, and the mourner — symbols that expressed qualities associated with the deceased as well as religious and secular meanings associated with death. Young women embroidered and painted mourning memorials on silk that were "shared with family and friends by being hung in the most important room of the house, the parlor."[37] The making of a memorial quilt, for example, provided not only a focus for physically working through grief, but also a means of perpetuating the memory of the loved one.

Death themes in art can be traced to our own time in the works of artists like Edvard Munch, Ernst Barlach, Käthe Kollwitz, and American sculptor Richard Shaw. Shaw's 1980 work *Walking Skeleton* expresses a whimsical attitude toward death: The skeleton is composed of twigs, bottles, playing cards, and similar found objects.

In the opinion of some commentators, few images of death appear in modern art in comparison, for example, with the artists of medieval Europe. It has been suggested that whereas people of medieval times sought relief by materializing their horrors, modern people prefer to deal with oppressive thoughts by burying them. When modern artists depict death, they often focus on the moment "after," thus portraying death as an accomplished fact.[38]

Music

Themes of death and loss can be heard in serious as well as popular music. The Requiem Mass, or Mass for the Dead, for example, has attracted numerous composers, including Mozart, Berlioz, and Verdi, to name a few.[39] One section of the Requiem Mass, the *Dies irae* ("Day of Wrath"), which dates from the early thirteenth century, has become a kind of musical symbol for death. In Berlioz's *Symphonie Fantastique* (1830), this theme is heard, first following the ominous tolling of bells and then, as the music reaches its climax, in counterpoint to the frenzied dancing of witches at a *sabbat*. The *Symphonie* tells the story of a young musician who, spurned by his beloved, attempts suicide with an overdose of opium. In a narcotic coma, he experiences five fantastic dreams, including a nightmarish "march to the gallows."[40] The *Dies irae* is also heard in Saint-Saëns' *Danse Macabre* (1874) and Liszt's *Totentanz* (1849), two of the

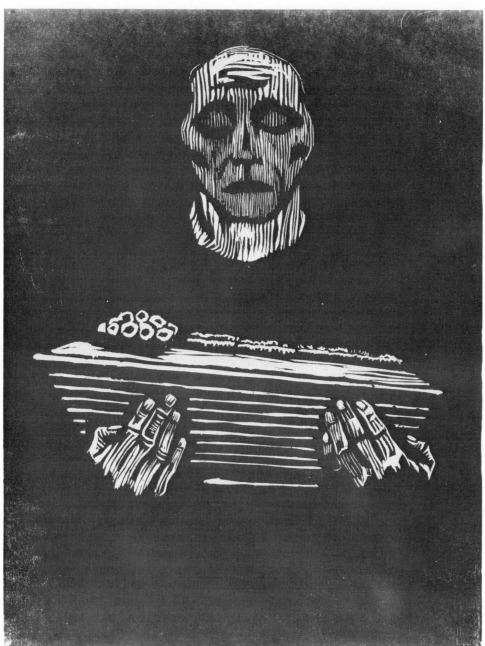

Of the modern artists who have expressed death themes in art, few have done so more frequently or more powerfully than German artist Käthe Kollwitz — as in this 1925 woodcut, Proletariat — Child's Coffin.

best known musical renditions of the Dance of Death, discussed in Chapter 2.

A century later, death themes became standard fare in rock music. Some believe that rock music may have played a role in breaking the taboo against public mention of death. Whether rock helped break the taboo or the lessening of the taboo encouraged writers and musicians to treat death themes, rock music has expressed these themes in songs ranging from the humorous to the poetic and deeply moving.[41] Examples of death themes in rock music include Elton John's "Candle in the Wind" (the death of Marilyn Monroe); Jackson Browne's "For a Dancer"; "Abraham, Martin, and John," by Dion (assassination); "Fire and Rain," by James Taylor (suicide); and "Richard Cory," by Simon and Garfunkel (suicide). Folk and country music has produced songs like "Where Have All the Flowers Gone" (war) and "Long Black Veil" (mourning). The next time you listen to music, note the references to death and ask yourself what attitudes are being expressed.

In the world of jazz and blues, the so-called "jazz funeral" is perhaps the best example of a popular version of the *dirge,* a musical form associated with the time of the funeral procession and burial. Related to the dirge are *elegies* and *laments,* musical settings for poems marking the loss of a person. Beethoven, Schubert, Schumann, Strauss, Brahms, Mahler, and Stravinsky are among those composers who have given us elegies in the Western musical tradition.

As a means of ritual leavetaking, the lament is a musical form found in many societies — as in the music for bagpipes played at Scottish clan funerals, for example. Typically, laments are characterized by a vocal expression of mourning called "keening," which conveys feelings of longing that are also heard in chants composed to mark the event of death.

In pre-Christian Hawaii, for instance, the *chant* was the basic form of musical expression and served to commemorate both happy and sad occasions.[42] One type of chant, known as *mele kanikau,* was the traditional Hawaiian lament to commemorate someone who has died.[43] *Kanikau* might be chanted at the funeral or sent to the surviving relatives. In more recent times, *kanikau* were published in newspapers as a tribute. The lament would be chanted only once at the appropriate occasion, and then it remained in the family as part of its chant repertoire. The *kanikau* could be either carefully composed ahead of time or used as a spontaneous chant during the funeral procession. Imagery related to the natural world is used to portray the writer's experience of loss.[44] Subtlety and levels of meaning are important. *Kanikau* might compare the deceased person to the wind, to the rain. Things that were experienced together are mentioned: "My companion in the chill of Manoa" or "My companion in the forest of Makiki." The things that bind you together are recalled. Not "I am bereft without you," but "These are the things I cherish about you."

Church music is another rich source of death-related themes. Passion music, for example, which centers on the suffering and death of Christ, is one such form of religious music. These themes can also be heard in psalms and psalmody, as well as in hymns and other popular church music.

The Present Milieu

We have been forced to contemplate our mortality. The experience of world war, the atomic bomb, and the aftermath of Hiroshima and Nagasaki have been followed in the more recent past by assassinations of political leaders, war in Vietnam, international terrorism, and nuclear brinkmanship, not to mention the prospect of global pollution. Robert Lifton and others have described children of the present era as *hibakusha,* a Japanese word meaning "explosion-affected" that was initially applied to the survivors of Hiroshima. Anxiety about the constant threat of nuclear annihilation is surely sufficient reason for searching out the meaning of life and death.

Most of us, however, want to learn about death and dying for the more obvious reason that we have been so ignorant of the experience. It's been kept hidden from our view. Our image of death has been blurred by euphemistic language, by the isolation of the dying and separation between generations, and by new technologies and the institutions that take on the tasks of dealing with the dying and the dead, as well as by our vicarious acquaintance with death through media presentations.

Our ambivalent attitudes toward death are reflected also when one educator applauds the study of death as the "last of the old taboos to fall" while another educator says, "It is not a fit subject for the curriculum." What price do we pay for the lack of firsthand experience with death?[45]

David Stannard tells us that in societies in which each individual is unique, important, and irreplaceable, death is not ignored but is marked by a "community-wide outpouring of grief for what is a genuine social loss." But in societies in which one individual is not considered to be very different from any other, "little damage is done to the social fabric by the loss of an individual," and outside one's immediate circle there is little or no acknowledgment of the death.[46]

The first step in learning of new choices among behaviors and attitudes regarding death is to become aware of how a climate of denial prevents us from experiencing death, thus estranging us from an integral aspect of human life. In the final analysis, sufficient motive for studying death and dying and for opening ourselves to the experience is framed by Octavio Paz: "A civilization that denies death ends by denying life."[47]

Precursors of Current Interest in Death and Dying

A few books serve as signal examples of the modern impulse to systematically study our experience of death and dying. A convenient watershed from which to date the beginnings of this effort is Herman Feifel's book, *The Meaning of Death.* Published in 1959, Feifel's compilation brought together a number of authorities from various disciplines whose essays encompassed theoretical approaches, developmental and attitudinal studies, cultural and religious concepts, and clinical aspects of death. Death was shown to be an acceptable and important topic for public consideration.

Ten years later, Elisabeth Kübler-Ross's *On Death and Dying* added to the growing demand for a more realistic assessment of how dying and death was being dealt with in this country. The book's major contribution was its penetrating focus on the needs and feelings of the dying patient. At that time, the notion that dying patients could provide important lessons for health care professionals and for their own families was regarded as a radical innovation by many people.

In the meantime, two books published in 1965 contributed to the development of studies dealing with death and dying. *Awareness of Dying,* by Barney G. Glaser and Anselm L. Strauss, used sociological fieldwork in six hospitals to study how a dying patient's awareness of his or her impending death affected hospital staff and family members. Glaser and Strauss found that medical professionals and the general public were reluctant to discuss the process of dying itself and tried to avoid telling a patient that he or she is dying. The second book, Robert Fulton's *Death and Identity,* brought together a rich collection of material from various fields bearing on death and dying from both theoretical and practical points of view. Other writers focused attention not on the processes of dying or the meaning of death, but rather on the social practices and customs for dealing with death.

Geoffrey Gorer's essay, "The Pornography of Death," published in 1955, was an early instance of this kind of sociological inquiry. It marks the beginning of what has become an energetic and often highly critical appraisal of how we deal with death. Jessica Mitford's *The American Way of Death* and Ruth Harmer's *The High Cost of Dying,* both published in 1963, criticized American funeral practices. Evelyn Waugh had earlier employed satire in *The Loved One,* published in 1948, to cast light on the hypocritical and death-denying attitudes so prevalent in American society. Books like these received considerable publicity. Popular attention was directed to practices relating to death and body disposal in this country. Indeed, publications of this kind stimulated subsequent efforts by the Federal Trade Commission and other consumer advocates to determine whether actions should be taken to regulate American funeral practices.

These death and dying studies are significant antecedents to the current public and professional interest in death and dying. During the past two decades, much has happened to increase our awareness about the ways people try to ignore the inevitability of death or construct elaborate deceptions to avoid its reality. Such writers as those mentioned help us see more clearly that the attempt to disguise death generally serves only to distance us from the actual experience.

Like a mysterious stranger at a costume ball, whose mask conceals the face beneath, death waits. Perhaps the disguise is more terrifying than the reality, yet how can we know unless we risk the experience of uncovering the face that lies hidden behind the mask? Learning about death and dying can help us identify the attitudes and behaviors that keep us from lifting the mask so that we may each confront our mortality in a way that is meaningful for our own lives.

The obituary pages tell us of the news that we are dying away, while the birth announcements in finer print, off at the side of the page, inform us of our replacements, but we get no grasp from this of the enormity of scale. There are 3 billion of us on the earth, and all 3 billion must be dead, on a schedule, within this lifetime. The vast mortality, involving something over 50 million of us each year, takes place in relative secrecy. We can only really know of the deaths in our households, or among our friends. These, detached in our minds from all the rest, we take to be unnatural events, anomalies, outrages. We speak of our own dead in low voices; struck down, we say, as though visible death can only occur for cause, by disease or violence, avoidably. We send off for flowers, grieve, make ceremonies, scatter bones, unaware of the rest of the 3 billion on the same schedule. All of that immense mass of flesh and bone and consciousness will disappear by absorption into the earth, without recognition by the transient survivors.

Less than a half century from now, our replacements will have more than doubled the numbers. It is hard to see how we can continue to keep the secret, with such multitudes doing the dying. We will have to give up the notion that death is catastrophe, or detestable, or avoidable, or even strange. We will need to learn more about the cycling of life in the rest of the system, and about our connection to the process. Everything that comes alive seems to be in trade for something that dies, call for call. There might be some comfort in the recognition of synchrony, in the information that we all go down together, in the best of company.

Lewis Thomas, *The Lives of a Cell: Notes of a Biology Watcher*

The Rise of Death Education

Considered broadly, death education includes both formal instruction dealing with dying, death, and grief, as well as informal exploration of these topics. Informal death education typically occurs in the context of "teachable moments" arising out of death-related events occurring in daily life. The event precipitating this instruction may be the death or bereavement of a child in a given classroom, or it may be more widely experienced, as in the case of the shuttle disaster which killed the *Challenger* astronauts. This event, watched as it happened by millions of school children in their classrooms, stimulated immediate discussion of issues related to death in schools throughout the country. Teachers were faced with the need to deal with students' concerns, questions, and anxieties.

Public discussion of death and dying is a fairly recent phenomenon in American society. Among the factors cited as responsible for the recent emergence of death studies and the death awareness movement are: (1) the increasing number of aged persons in American society; (2) the prolongation of the dying process; (3) the destruction of Hiroshima by the atomic bomb, ushering in the nuclear age and attendant anxieties; (4) the "psychology of entitlement," which became prominent in the 1960s and which asserted the rights of the dying as well as entitlements for other groups heretofore ignored in varying degrees by society; (5) a reaction against what has been characterized as a dehumanizing technology and advocacy of humane and natural approaches to such biological phenomena as birth and death; and (6) a sociocultural need to confront death meaningfully in a secularized society.[48]

Clearly, we are witnessing a period of transition. In 1964, a bibliography of death-related publications comprised about 400 references; by 1975, it had increased tenfold. Robert Fulton, who compiled a bibliography of nearly 4000 items that year, estimated that more books and articles about death and dying had been published in the previous decade than had been written during the whole of the previous hundred and fifty years.[49] This trend has continued. Of the 1100 books now in print relating to death, dying, and bereavement, more than half were published since 1975 and, during this period, the National Library of Medicine cataloged more than five thousand new journal articles in these subject areas.[50] Not long ago, a person seeking information about death would find precious little on the subject, and even that only after considerable effort. Today, books on death and dying often occupy a special niche in bookstores, with several feet of shelf space devoted to recent publications, many of them in the self-help category, offering advice to the bereaved and to the dying.

The number of courses dealing with death and dying has also grown dramatically. Whereas in 1970 there were only about twenty death education courses above the high school level, that number increased fiftyfold within just four years.[51] Today, it is estimated that between two and three thousand such courses are offered on college campuses. Death education is also found in high schools, professional curricula, and adult and continuing education, as well as, to a lesser extent, at the elementary and preschool level. In 1982, Brooklyn College began offering a master's degree in thanatology within its graduate program in community health, and similar programs are available at other graduate schools.

An organization for those working professionally in the field, the Association for Death Education and Counseling, is a catalyst for multidisciplinary communication about death and dying. Organizations of similar purpose, such as the Minnesota Coalition for Terminal Care, can be found at the regional and local level in many areas. These groups are yet another example of the growing acceptance of the idea that death is a topic that can be discussed openly and responsibly.

 Where death is concerned, the adage, "What you don't know won't hurt you," is a fallacy. Avoiding the thought of death doesn't remove us from its power. Such ostrichlike behavior only limits our choices for coping effectively with the experience of death. When we bring death out of the closet, we give ourselves the opportunity to clear away the accumulated rubbish and preserve what we find valuable. As Robert Kavanaugh said, "The unexamined death is not worth dying."

Examining Assumptions

Many people are rethinking their assumptions about death. In a society as pluralistic as ours, however, the quest for a more personally meaningful attitude toward death leads to diverse and even conflicting outcomes. For example, the consumer debate about funerals has caused many people to take another look at their own preferences for last rites. The trend away from traditional funeral rituals and the increasing popularity of memorial societies, with their emphasis on swift and inexpensive disposition of the body, is considered by many death researchers to be a significant indicator of changing attitudes toward death.

Although some criticize the conventional funeral as perpetuating death-denying behaviors, and call for reforms, others would as soon eliminate the funeral altogether. One-third of the responses to a *Psychology Today* question-naire reflected this attitude.[52] Whereas only 6 percent of the respondents expressed a wish to lie in state at their own funerals, a considerable majority (70 percent) stated definitely that they would not want their bodies displayed in an open casket.[53] Thus, it would seem that the services offered by memorial societies coincide very nicely with the wishes of many Americans. Many of the elements of the conventional funeral (such as embalming, cosmetic restoration, and the viewing of the body at the mortuary) are seen as irrelevant and even morbid by some who favor the less elaborate options provided by memorial societies.

Others find the trend away from traditional funeral practices disturbing, arguing that it is the approach taken by memorial societies that reflects a denial of the reality of death. Traditionally, ceremonies marking a person's death have provided a framework for meeting the social and psychological needs of survivors, and for acknowledging the place and meaning of death in human life. Something quite important is lost, they believe, when survivors are not given the opportunity to participate in a social ritual designed to commemorate the death of a significant other and to facilitate the mourning of his or her passing from the community (see Figure 1-3).

Underlying these contrasting attitudes, a common intention can be discerned; namely, the desire to find a personally meaningful response to the fact of death. That various options exist is itself a positive sign. As people examine their own attitudes and investigate the choices that are available to them, new ways of dealing with death and dying become evident.

The hospice movement, which focuses on giving emotional support for the dying person and for his or her family, is an example of how some people are attempting to acknowledge the reality of death by restoring some of the attitudes and practices that were prevalent in the past in ways that are appropriate for the present. Among the Amish, for example, death is considered part of the natural rhythm of life. Death becomes a time for reinforcement and support, for the bereaved family as well as the larger society. Researcher Kathleen Bryer summarizes the social patterns that the Amish find helpful in coping with death as including: the continued presence of the family, open

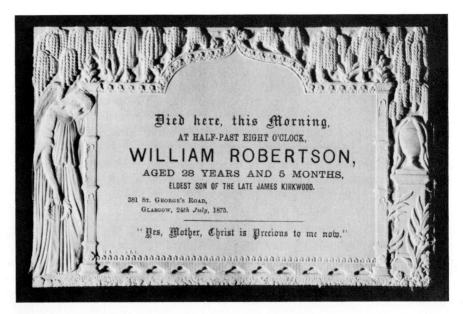

Figure 1-3   *Embossed Linen Death Notification Card, 1875*
This card exemplifies the formality of nineteenth-century mourning customs.
The etiquette books of the period often devoted considerable space to the
procedural details associated with the wearing of mourning clothes, the issuance
of funeral invitations, and other behaviors appropriate to the survivors of a
death.

communication about the process of dying and its impact upon the family,
maintaining a normal life style as much as possible during the course of illness,
commitment to the independence of the dying person, opportunities to plan for
one's own death, and continued support of the bereaved.[54] Hospice organizations provide an example of how such traditional attitudes toward dying and
death can be successfully adapted in a modern social setting.

When death or life-threatening illness touches our own lives, the experience transcends the merely academic or theoretical. Our inquiry must therefore
be practical. Death is universal, intrinsic to human experience. Yet many of us
try to cram it into a dark closet and shut the door. There death stays until,
bursting its hinges, the door flies open and death is once again forced upon our
awareness. We have to deal with it.

As you read this book, you will notice that each chapter contains material
based upon theory, research, and practice in a particular area of death and
dying, from the patterns of socialization through the dynamics of grief and
bereavement. You can teach yourself not only about the attitudes and practices
of others, but about your own as well.

Further Readings

D. J. Enright, editor. *The Oxford Book of Death.* New York: Oxford University Press, 1983.

James J. Farrell. *Inventing the American Way of Death, 1830–1920.* Philadelphia: Temple University Press, 1980.

John Langone. *Vital Signs: The Way We Die in America.* Boston: Little, Brown, 1974.

Robert J. Lifton and Eric Olson. *Living and Dying.* New York: Bantam, 1975.

Mary Jane Moffat, editor. *In the Midst of Winter: Selections from the Literature of Mourning.* New York: Random House, 1982.

Dan Nimmo and James E. Combs. *Nightly Horrors: Crisis Coverage by Television Network News.* Knoxville: University of Tennessee Press, 1985.

Martha V. Pike and Janice Gray Armstrong. *A Time to Mourn: Expressions of Grief in Nineteenth Century America.* Stony Brook, N.Y.: The Museums at Stony Brook, 1980.

Vanderlyn R. Pine. "The Age of Maturity for Death Education: A Socio-Historical Portrait of the Era 1976–1985," *Death Studies* 10:3 (1986): 209–231.

Stanley Joel Reiser and Michael Anbar, editors. *The Machine at the Bedside: Strategies for Using Technology in Patient Care.* New York: Cambridge University Press, 1984.

Robert F. Weir, editor. *Death in Literature.* New York: Columbia University Press, 1980.

In January 1879 frontier photographer L.A. Huffman recorded this scene
showing the burial platform of a Sioux warrior who had died and been
placed on the scaffold only a few days before. Surrounding the gravesite
is a vast plain, crisscrossed with the trails of wild herds of buffalo.

CHAPTER 2

Perspectives on Death: Cross-Cultural and Historical

*D*eath is a universal human experience, yet the response it elicits is shaped by the attitudes toward it and beliefs about it that are prevalent in a particular culture. This shared consciousness among its members makes a culture distinct; it gives a particular cast to experiences and the meanings ascribed to them, and death is such an experience. In the previous chapter, we saw how social and cultural changes in the United States from the nineteenth century to the present affected the characteristic American mode of dealing with death and dying. To gain a broader perspective on the present, we will expand our study by surveying attitudes and behaviors relative to death in cultures that in many respects are quite different from our own. In doing so, we may find that customs that at first seem unfamiliar or even exotic in fact share a common ground with many of our own practices.

Death in Early and Preliterate Cultures

As archeological evidence demonstrates, human concern for the dead predates the advent of written history. In the Neanderthal burials of more than 50,000 years ago, food, ornamental shells, and stone implements were buried with the dead, implying a belief that the deceased would find these items useful during the passage from the land of the living to the land of the dead. In many of these ancient burials, the corpse was stained with red ochre and positioned in a fetal posture, suggesting beliefs about the revitalization of the body after death

41

Figure 2-1   *Neanderthal Burial*

and subsequent rebirth (see Figure 2-1.)[1] This evidence from the earliest known burials demonstrates a characteristically human concern with beliefs about the meaning of death and with rituals that serve to formalize the relationship between the living and the dead.

Among prehistoric societies, death seems to have been viewed not as an end or as extinction but as a radical change of status: a transition from the land of the living to the world of the dead. With the death of the body, the soul passes on to another realm. Thus, the living took precautions to aid the deceased on the journey to the spirit world and — among some societies — to offset fears about the potential malevolence of the dead toward the living.

The Power of the Dead

It is clear from evidence such as the Neanderthal burials that speculations about death and what happens afterward date from the earliest human societies. Although the cultural environment of a primitive people, lacking a written language or an advanced technology, appears rudimentary by modern standards, it is a mistake to think that the terms *preliterate* or *primitive* imply ignorance or dullness. The primitive, whose learning simply takes place in a different schoolhouse, is capable of intelligent consideration of the fundamental areas of human experience. It may be that the essential lessons for living well — and for dying well — have a common basis in the experience of primitive and modern alike.

The study of contemporary preliterate cultures has shed light on the beliefs about death and the afterlife held by primeval peoples. In one such society, grief may be expressed with loud wails, in another with silent tears; but almost always there is deep respect for the still-powerful soul of the deceased. Often there is a concern that the soul or spirit of the deceased, if not treated properly, could inflict harm upon the living. Thus, elaborate funeral rituals are conducted to ensure not only the successful journey of the soul into the realm of the dead, but also the well-being of the living community.

In many preliterate societies, the dead are considered to be at least potentially harmful during this time of transition. Only by specific ritual practices can the living safeguard themselves from the unworldly presence of the dead. One must take care not to arouse the ghosts of the departed. Special concern is due malevolent spirits — often of those who suffered catastrophic deaths or deaths in childbirth — which wander about aimlessly, seeking to harm or disrupt the living.

To understand how these beliefs about the dead could have a very real effect on the living, think about the eerie feelings that people associate with "haunted houses," or the strange sense of foreboding experienced when passing through a cemetery at night. Often experiences that include an element of mystery provoke awe and uncertainty. In preliterate societies, the context may be different, but the impulse is strikingly similar: One simply has no wish to disturb the dead.

Yet this is not to say that people in preliterate societies shun their dead. Often the contrary is true. In many tribal societies, ceremonies are held periodically to celebrate and honor the dead, who are thought to be still present in some way as members of the community. The community is composed in its totality of both the living and the dead; in the rhythm and flow of communal life, the individual — in death as in life — is a part of the whole. As unseen members of a continuing social order, the dead may be valuable allies and may even perform services for the living — as interpreters, intermediaries, and ambassadors in the realm beyond the reach of sensory perceptions.

For the ancient Hawaiians living within the intimate relationships of the *'ohana*, or family clan, a close bond existed between the living members of a family and their ancestors.[2] Besides serving as role models upholding standards of conduct, ancestors provided a crucial spiritual link between human beings and powerful, but distant and impersonal, gods. Keeping alive the memory of one's ancestors and calling upon them to intercede with the gods sustained family loyalties beyond the boundaries of death. Furthermore, memo-

Death-Song

If they ask for me
Say: He had some
Business
In another world.

Sokan

rizing the names and characteristics of one's ancestor-gods was felt to enhance an individual's sense of identity and self-worth.

Individuals are born, procreate, and die. Yet, just as those who are now deceased gave life to the community while they were living, the community sustains the dead's participation by celebrating their shared identity in the whole. This communal consciousness embraces both living and dead who, together, comprise the clan, the tribe, the people. The proximity and deep relationship between the two worlds of living and dead may sometimes result in fear of what the dead may do to affect the living. Yet, this intimate relationship is also celebrated as a sign that the community endures — even beyond the limits imposed by death.

Thus, in societies that retain a strong sense of community between the living and the dead, it seems as if "the land echoes with the voices of the ancestors."[3] In Japan, where a deeply rooted reverence for ancestors continues to influence present practices, many Japanese consider the tomb to be the dwelling place of the deceased's spirit.[4]

We can see a semblance of this communal sense when someone mentions the "founding fathers" of a nation or of a college. Often, these deceased figures are spoken of metaphorically as "being with us in spirit" on those occasions when the members of the living group — be it nation or college convocation — meet to celebrate their common aims with those who preceded them in the life of the community.[5]

The Names of the Dead

In many preliterate societies, the living members fear that the spirits of the dead, once aroused, can do them harm. If calling a person's name is a good way of summoning the person, then refraining from using a name will presumably leave its bearer undisturbed. Hence, in preliterate societies one of the most prevalent of all quasimagical practices related to the dead is name avoidance: The deceased is never again mentioned, or else is referred to only obliquely, never by name. The nineteenth-century anthropologist Sir James Frazer reports instances of name avoidance among the Samoyed of Siberia and the Todas of southern India, the Mongols of Tartary and the Tuaregs of the Sahara, the Ainos of Japan and the Wa-Kamba and Nandi of central Africa, and among many others as well.[6]

Among some of the aboriginal tribes of Australia a dead person is never again mentioned by name after burial, but is referred to instead only as "that one." Elsewhere an allusion may be made to particular traits or to some special fame that the person was known for during his or her lifetime; the deceased may also be referred to by his or her relationship to the speaker, but again, never by name. Thus, "Uncle Joe," who gained great renown as an expert fisherman, might be referred to after his death as "that relative who caught many fish." Or a woman who had demonstrated extraordinary bravery might be called "that one who showed courage." In some societies, there is a demand that living members bearing the same name as the deceased must adopt new names, or even that words describing ordinary objects be erased from the society's vocabulary when they are the same as the name of the deceased.[7]

In some preliterate societies, the name of the deceased, rather than being avoided, may receive special emphasis, such as being conferred on a newborn in the deceased's family. In some societies this practice reflects simply the desire to honor the memory of a loved one; in other societies it is considered a means of ensuring that the soul of the dead person becomes reincarnated. When a Lapp woman is near the time of giving birth, a deceased ancestor appears to her in a dream and informs her which of her ancestors is to be reborn in her infant. This is the name her new baby receives.[8] Among the Hawaiians, children sometimes were named for ancestors or were named by the gods. Names bestowed by the gods, which came in a family member's dream, were most important, followed by names linking a child with his or her forebears, given for the sake of identification as well as commemoration. Sometimes the name of a child who died would be given to a child born later. It was felt that "to name a child for a deceased relative was to make the name live again."[9]

The desire to spare oneself or others grief may at least partly account for the effort to avoid mentioning the name of someone recently dead; this desire motivates the behavior of many in our own society. The deceased person may be referred to in terms of family relationship or by other substitutions. If a primitive avoids a name from fear of evoking the deceased's ghost, is this "ghost" much different from the mental images conjured up by mention of the deceased's name to a bereaved relative in a more developed society? While one society manages grief by postulating the existence of ghosts, another does so by relying on custom and etiquette. Likewise, when we name a child after a beloved parent or another person that we respect, aren't we hoping that some of the qualities we value in the namesake will be "reborn" in the child?[10]

The Origin of Death

Why do humans die? One might respond that death occurs because human beings are biologically programmed to die. In the scientific view, death is an intrinsic part of life: a natural event. In many primitive societies, however, there are no "natural" causes of death. Instead, death is always viewed as an unnatural event, an accident. Death may result from a wound sustained in battle, or from a mishap that strikes a person unexpectedly in the course of daily life. In such cases, the proximate cause of death is clear. When the cause of death is not obvious, it can be attributed to some unseen, malign influence, possibly induced by magical means. Although a magical explanation does not lend itself to either proof or disproof, it can provide a comfort by making sense of what otherwise seems inexplicable.

Something of this attitude can be seen occasionally even among modern people. Sometimes diseases that are not well understood become the objects of magical thinking, attempts to provide a rationale that satisfies despite the lack of clear and logical information. When the courses of such diseases as tuberculosis in the nineteenth century and cancer today are not scientifically clear, some people fall prey to magical explanations that seem to provide the missing link. Among the Senufo of Africa's Ivory Coast, for example, the unexpected death of a child or young person is considered abnormal and brings an obligation to discover the supernatural cause of such misfortune. Likewise, when death occurs suddenly, perhaps resulting from an accident or from violence outside the village, it threatens the welfare of the entire village and sets into motion "an elaborate series of precautions, sacrifices, and medicines that will purify the land and protect the villagers from further calamity."[11]

Magical explanations may be less convincing to people living in modern urban-industrial societies than they are to people whose environment has remained essentially unchanged for millenia. Nevertheless, there is a common human desire to find suitable explanations when death occurs. These explanations may satisfy those who seek the cause of an individual's death, but a larger question remains: How did death become part of human experience in the first place?

Preliterate cultures provide responses to this fundamental enigma in the form of myths. Although easily as useful and as pertinent to their believers as any provided by the modern, scientific frame of reference, the insights couched in myth can be coaxed out only by patient study and reflection. The outlines given here can only suggest the riches to be found in much primitive myth.[12]

Some myths portray death as originating because the ancestral parents or an archetypal figure transgressed against divine or natural law, through poor judgment or disobedience. Sometimes a person or a group is put to a test. When the test is failed, death becomes a reality. Among the Luba of Africa, one such myth describes how god created a paradise for the first human beings and endowed it with everything needed for their sustenance. However, they were forbidden to eat of the bananas in the middle of the field. When the humans ate the bananas, it was decreed that humankind would die and be buried in the earth after a lifetime of toil. This motif is akin to the Biblical story of Adam and Eve's transgression and subsequent expulsion from the Garden of Eden, an account of the origin of death that continues to have relevance in three major religious traditions: Judaism, Christianity, and Islam.

In other myths a crucial act that would have ensured immortality was not properly carried out; an *omission* rather than an *action* introduces death to humankind. Another mythic theme is that of a messenger whose task it was to

When Hare heard of Death, he started for his lodge & arrived there crying, shrieking, *My uncles & my aunts must not die!* And then the thought assailed him: *To all things death will come!* He cast his thoughts upon the precipices & they began to fall & crumble. Upon the rocks he cast his thoughts & they became shattered. Under the earth he cast his thoughts & all the things living there stopped moving & their limbs stiffened in death. Up above, toward the skies, he cast his thoughts & the birds flying there suddenly fell to the earth & were dead.

After he entered his lodge he took his blanket and, wrapping it around him, lay down crying. *Not the whole earth will suffice for all those who will die. Oh, there will not be enough earth for them in many places!* There he lay in his corner wrapped up in his blanket, silent.

Figure 2-2   *Winnebago myth: When Hare Heard of Death*

deliver the message of eternal life, but who "either garbled the message out of forgetfulness or malice, or did not arrive on time" to save the day. The Winnebago Indian myth involving the trickster figure, Hare, is an example of this motif (see Figure 2-2). Momentarily forgetting his purpose, Hare failed to deliver the life-saving message. A variant of this motif is seen in myths that tell how two messengers were sent — one bringing immortality, the other bringing death — and the messenger bringing death arrived first.

In the "death in a bundle" motif, death is introduced into human experience when a bundle containing the fate of mortality for all humankind is opened, either inadvertently or because of poor choice. Another motif, involving sleep and death, describes how a message of immortality was addressed to human beings, but people were not awake to receive it. Other myths describe death as resulting from a sexual transgression.

Although most myths portray death as something unwelcome, a few portray it as welcomed, even actively pursued. In some such myths, death is welcomed out of weariness with life or disgust with its misery; in other myths, death is sought in order to prevent overpopulation. Many such myths describe human beings bartering for or buying death from the gods so that life would not continue interminably.

Despite their variety, all these myths echo a theme that is surprisingly familiar: Death comes from outside; it impinges on and cuts short what would otherwise be an immortal existence. The notion that death does not originate within ourselves, but comes from outside, continues to influence our attitudes toward death. Death seems somehow foreign, not really part of how we experience ourselves. Even when we understand the biological processes of disease or deterioration, there is often a sense that, if only this defect could be repaired or the deterioration reversed, we would live forever. Although eons separate us from the preliterate myth makers, death still seems an anomaly. Yet when a friend or relative dies, it is difficult to avoid the recognition of our own mortality. An early work of literature on the theme of death, the epic of Gilgamesh, describes the awakening to one's own mortality.[13] Grieving at the death of his beloved friend Enkidu, Gilgamesh ultimately realizes that he too will die.

Cultural Case Studies

Up to now a broad outline has been sketched, showing some of the notable features of death-related cultural beliefs and customs that are more or less universal in human societies. To fill in this picture, we now focus on particulars, in cultures both historical and modern: We take up in turn the attitudes toward death in Native American culture; the death ceremonies of an African tribe, the LoDagaa; and finally the Mexican "Cult of Death" and "Day of the Dead."

Of the many different cultures that could be selected, the three chosen are sufficiently diverse and yet are similar to our own in ways that help to elucidate our present situation. The similarities may, however, be masked by unfamiliar emphases; among the LoDagaa, for example, expressions of grief are formalized in mourning rituals, and thus at first seem quite unlike our own prevalent style of mourning. Yet on closer examination we find significant correspondences that may give us new insights into the behaviors and attitudes most familiar to us.

Indians of North America

Traditional Native American culture has many features in common with cultures of other societies whose members live with an intimate knowledge of the cycles of the natural environment. Death is part of a cyclical process that can be observed wherever one chooses to look. Generally speaking, the attitude toward death of the tribes of North America can be summarized as follows: Death is not something to be ignored, but neither should it become an obsession, something to be feared. Death demands attention only when it impinges on the present, on one's situation, here and now. At such times, it is good to make room for death.

 Two Death Songs

In the great night my heart will go out
Toward me the darkness comes rattling
In the great night my heart will go out

Papago song by Juana Manwell
(Owl Woman)

The odor of death,
I smell the odor of death
In front of my body.

A song of the Dakota tribe

This characteristic way of relating to death in these traditional cultures is perhaps best typified, among the Plains Indians, in the Sioux battle cry: "It's a good day to die!" There are many accounts of individuals who faced death stoically, even indifferently. In some tribes, individuals composed "death songs" as expressions of their confrontation with death. Sometimes a death song would be "composed spontaneously at the very moment of death" and "chanted with the last breath of the dying person."[14]

These death songs express a resolve to meet death fully, to accept it with one's whole being, not in defeat and desperation, but with equanimity and composure. As part of the natural cycle, dying is not something to be feared or struggled against; a place can be made for death when the time comes. As an expression of this attitude, the death song represents a summary of a person's life and an acknowledgment of death as the completion of being, the final act in the drama of earthly existence.

For most traditional Native American societies, dying was less feared than were the ghosts of the dead. Among many tribes, the soul or spirit of the deceased was thought to linger for several days near the site of death before passing on to the after world. Typically, this was seen as a time that required great care, both to ensure the progress of the deceased toward the supernatural realm and to safeguard the living. To help accomplish these aims, some tribes destroyed the dead person's belongings, burning or burying them along with the corpse.

The Ohlones of the California coast, for example, adorned the corpse with feathers, flowers, and beads, and then wrapped it in blankets and skins. Dance regalia, weapons, medicine bundle, and other items owned by the deceased were gathered together and, along with the corpse, were placed on the funeral pyre. The mourners sometimes threw some of their own valued possessions onto the pyre as gifts for the deceased. The destruction of the deceased's

---

Burial Oration

You are dead.
You will go above there to the trail.
That is the spirit trail.
Go there to the beautiful trail.
May it please you not to walk about where I am.
You are dead.
Go there to the beautiful trail above.
That is your way.
Look at the place where you used to wander.
The north trail, the mountains where you used to wander, you
   are leaving.
Listen to me: go there!

Wintu tribe

possessions was intended to facilitate the soul's journey to the "Island of the Dead" and also to remove any reminders of the deceased that might cause his ghost to remain near the living. A Yokut funeral chant says: "You are going where you are going; don't look back for your family."

For the Ohlones, the dangerous period lasted from six months to a year; afterward, a ceremony was held to acknowledge that the widow was free of taboos and that her life could return to normal. However, it was still considered disrespectful to utter the deceased's name. In *The Ohlone Way*, Malcolm Margolin writes: "While the mere thought of a dead person brought sorrow, the mention of a dead person's name brought absolute dread."[15] By destroying the deceased's belongings and avoiding his or her name, the Ohlones confirmed the separation of the dead from the living.

Other tribes, however, showed less fear of the dead. Indeed, in some tribes, the dead were thought of as guardian spirits or as special envoys of the shamans or medicine men. The memory of deceased members of a tribe was sometimes sustained through rituals exhibiting reverence or even worship of the ancestors, whose burial places were considered sacred. This attitude toward the dead was stated eloquently by Chief Seattle: "To us the ashes of our ancestors are sacred and their resting place is hallowed ground. . . . Be just and deal kindly with my people, for the dead are not powerless. Dead, did I say? There is no death, only a change of worlds."[16]

Burial customs also reflect a society's attitude toward its dead. For many of the Plains tribes, it was customary to expose the corpse on a platform above ground or to place the corpse in the limbs of a tree. This not only hastened the decomposition of the body, but also was thought to speed the soul's journey to the spirit world. Later, the sun-bleached skeleton would be retrieved for burial in sacred grounds. As Old Chief Joseph of the Nez Perce lay dying, he told his son, "Never forget my dying words. This country holds your father's body. Never sell the bones of your father and mother."[17] These words would be remembered later by the Younger Chief Joseph as he led his warriors into battle to preserve the sanctity of the tribal lands that held the bones of the ancestral dead.

The attitude toward death and toward the dead in a society arises out of the general cultural life of the group and its members. Death rituals symbolize the separation of the dead from the living, the transition of the deceased to some afterlife state, and the reincorporation of the community after its loss of the deceased. However, tribal societies vary greatly in their ritual observances surrounding the dead and the elaborateness of such observances. But even when the dead are greatly feared and the corpse is disposed of quickly, the deceased nevertheless becomes the object of ritual attention. This is illustrated by David Mandelbaum's instructive comparison of death customs among the Hopi and the Cocopa.[18]

Traditionally, when a Cocopa dies, surviving family members wail and scream in an "ecstasy of violent grief behavior" that generally lasts twenty-four hours or more, continuing until the body is cremated. Clothes, food, and other articles are burned with the body. It is thought that the deceased will make use of these items in the afterlife, but the Cocopa also intend that they will help persuade the spirit of the deceased to pass on from the earth.

Later, the bereaved family gives a ceremony to mourn and commemorate the deceased. Speeches and lamentations are heard on this occasion. Although the names of the dead cannot be spoken at other times, at this special time relatives who have passed into the spirit world are publicly summoned, and their presence may be impersonated by living members of the tribe. Occasionally, a ceremonial house constructed especially for the spirits is burned as a gift.

The mourning ceremony is conducted both to honor the dead and to try to persuade lurking spirits to come out in the open and to depart from the earthly realm. Whereas the cremation ritual focuses on the grief and emotional needs of the bereaved family, the subsequent mourning ceremony is designed to affirm the integrity of the family and the community.

The Hopi, on the other hand, prefer to keep death at a distance. Death is unwelcome; a person's death causes fear. Death threatens the "middle way" of order, control, and measured deliberation that the Hopi cherish. As we would expect, this attitude toward death is reflected in Hopi funeral rituals, which are attended by very few and are held privately. The death is mourned, but without public ceremony. Mourners tend to be reticent in expressing their grief. The Hopi desire that the whole matter be "quickly over and best forgotten."

Among the Hopi, burial follows soon after death. Unlike the Cocopa, the Hopi have no wish to invite departed ancestors to a communal gathering. Once a person's spirit leaves the body, it becomes a different class of being, no longer Hopi. The Hopi want to make sure that the "dichotomy of quick and dead is sharp and clear."

Mandelbaum's discription of the death customs of these two Native American societies shows how, even within a similar cultural setting, different social groups may develop quite distinctive responses to death. The Hopi and the Cocopa both fear the dead, but the Hopi avoid the dead, whereas the Cocopa choose to invite the ghosts of deceased ancestors to come out in the open.

Probably each of us feels drawn more strongly to either the Hopi or the Cocopa style of mourning. Reflecting on the different emphases within each of these societies can help us evaluate our own attitudes and determine our own values relative to death. In thus pondering cross-cultural examples, we can ask, What is valuable about each of these ways of coming to terms with death? The common elements of the rites of passage surrounding death—the themes of separation, transition, and reincorporation—are present whether the ritual is elaborate or simple. But the manner in which these essential elements are realized through ceremony and other ritual practices is a reflection of a society's attitudes toward death and its particular way of finding resolution when death takes a member of the group.

The LoDagaa of Africa

The term *ancestor worship* has frequently been used to label customs in Africa that could be more accurately described as reverence for and continuing communication with the deceased members of a community who are still remembered by name. As time passes, generations come and go, and memory fades, these ancestral members of the community are replaced by the more recently deceased.[19] The ongoing community of the living dead consists, then, of deceased ancestors who are still recalled in the minds of the living.[20]

The relationship between the living and the dead is indicated quite clearly by the system of age grouping practiced by the Nandi in Kenya. Once past childhood, a male member of the tribe moves through the junior and senior warrior levels and eventually enters the age group of senior elders; he next becomes an old man and ultimately, at death, an ancestor, one of the living dead, whose personality is remembered by survivors. After a while, when he is no longer remembered by persons now alive, he merges with the anonymous dead. By this time, however, the Nandi believe that the dead man's "soul stuff" may have already reappeared in a newborn child of the tribe, thus continuing the recurrent pattern of a person's passage through the levels of the age-group system.[21]

The study of the LoDagaa of Northern Ghana by Jack Goody provides an excellent description of the death customs practiced within a traditional African tribal society.[22] Among the LoDagaa, funeral ceremonies span at least a six-month period, and sometimes continue over several years. They occur in four distinct, successive phases, each focusing on specific aspects of death and bereavement. Altogether, the LoDagaa funeral ceremonies last about twelve to fifteen days.

The first stage begins at the moment of death and lasts for six or seven days. During the first half of this initial stage, the body is prepared for burial; the deceased is mourned by bereaved relatives and other members of the community; rites are performed to acknowledge the separation of the deceased from the living; the solidarity of kinship ties are affirmed; and some minor social and family roles that had been occupied by the deceased are redistributed. These public ceremonies, which last about three days, end with the burial of the corpse. In the remaining three or four days of this first stage, in private ceremonies, preparations are made for redistributing the dead man's rights over his widow, children, and property.

About three weeks later, in a second funeral ceremony, the cause of death is established. Whereas modern people would typically consider, say, a snake-bite to be the cause of death, the LoDagaa would view it as an intermediate agent but not the final cause of death. Among the LoDagaa, the real cause of death "is seen as a function of the network of spiritual and human relationships." So inquiries are made to uncover any tension that may have existed between the deceased and others. The LoDagaa also frequently rely on divination as a mode of inquiry into the causes of a person's death.

At the beginning of the rainy season a third stage of the funeral ceremonies

Delmar Lipp, Eliot Elisofon Archives, National Museum of African Art

A woman and child in mourning are depicted in this Yombe memorial figure from Zaire. Installed in a shed constructed on the grave, such adornments are thought to provide the deceased with companionship or protection in the afterlife.

is held. Many of its rites, although resembling those of the first stage, mark a transitional stage in the deceased's "passage from the role of living father to that of ancestral father." A provisional ancestral shrine is placed in the dead man's grave.

The final stage follows the harvest, provided that sufficent time has elapsed since the death. The final ancestral shrine is constructed and placed in the grave, and the close relatives of the deceased are formally released from mourning. The care of offspring is also formally transferred to the deceased's tribal "brothers," and final rites are conducted to conclude the redistribution of the deceased's property.

Virtually no one in our society is likely to experience such prolonged or extensive funeral rites as those of the LoDagaa. What is the function of the LoDagaa death ceremonies? Two purposes hold sway throughout the long period of mourning. First, some rituals *separate* the dead person from the bereaved family and from the larger community of the living; by these rites certain social roles formerly occupied by the deceased are gradually assigned to living persons. Second, some rites gather together, or *aggregate;* the dead person is joined with the ancestors, and the bereaved are reincorporated into the community of the living in a way that reflects their changed status.

This rhythm of separation and gathering together is, of course, common to all funeral ceremonies, even when only minimally acknowledged. The rites of the LoDagaa are noteworthy because of the formality with which these basic functions of funeral ritual are accomplished. They provide a model of explicitness in mourning against which our own customs for coping with death and bereavement can be compared and constrasted.

The explicitness of LoDagaa mourning is evident in the use of "mourning restraints," made of leather, fabric, and string. These restraints, which are generally tied around a person's wrist, indicate the relationship of the bereaved to the dead person. For example, at a man's funeral, his father, mother, and widow would wear restraints made of hide; his brothers and sisters would wear fiber restraints; and his children would wear restraints made of string, tied around the ankle. Thus, the strongest restraints are provided to the mourners who had the closest relationship with the deceased — usually through kinship and marriage, but sometimes through extraordinarily strong friendship bonds. Weaker mourning restraints are given to persons who had been correspondingly less intimate with the deceased. One end of the mourning restraint is attached to the bereaved person while the other end is held by a "mourning companion" who assumes responsibility for the bereaved's behavior during the period of intense grief.

Mourning restraints thus serve two related purposes: Being something that can be seen and felt, they validate that the bereaved's expression of grief at the loss of someone close is commensurate with the intensity of relationship with the deceased. Second, they discourage expressions of grief that would exceed the norms of LoDagaa society.

Immediately following the death, LoDagaa expressions of grief are likely to be fervent. Gradually, during the three-day period of the initial funeral ceremonies, expression of grief becomes more routine and systematized as the mourners begin adjusting to and accepting their loss.

The LoDagaa way of mourning invites considerable public participation by members of the community, but the grave is dug and made ready for the

> If we knew the home of Death, we would set it on fire.
>
> Acholi funeral song

burial by men specially designated and trained for this function. In their training they learn not only how to prepare a grave properly but also how to protect themselves against the mystical dangers that surround care of the dead. The LoDagaa pay for these funeral services by giving offerings of food and other goods to the gravediggers at the conclusion of the ceremonies.

Even though gravedigging is performed by specialists, the LoDagaa occasionally make therapeutic use of this task to counteract excessive fear of the dead. For example, if a LoDagaa boy displays debilitating fear at the sight of a dead person or during a funeral, he may be forced by his father to join in the work of digging the grave. The LoDagaa believe that a repulsive act performed under controlled circumstances can have curative as well as preventive effects. This kind of direct confrontation with the reality of death is considered to be a way of working through fears about death.

In LoDagaa society, people come to terms with death by confronting it directly. The prolonged and elaborate funeral ceremonies, the use of mourning restraints to show degrees of relationship to the deceased, and the therapeutic use of digging the grave as a means of confronting fears about death all demonstrate the LoDagaa choice to deal with death explicitly.

Mexican Culture

From very ancient times, Mexican culture has echoed the interrelated themes of life, death, and resurrection. Life and death are seen not as opposites, but as different phases of an underlying process of regeneration. The Aztecs of pre-Conquest Mexico believed that the very creation of the world was made possible by sacrificial rites enacted by the gods. The warrior killed in battle and the sacrificial victim in Aztec religious rites were confident that they were participating in a destiny that had been determined in the origins of the world.

The Spanish conquerors brought to Mexico a cult of death that in many respects resembled indigenous beliefs. The willingness to die for ideals espoused by the larger society is exemplified in Spanish history by the mass suicide at Sagunto in 219 B.C., when the city's leading citizens demonstrated that death was preferable to capture by the Carthaginians.[23] Such an acceptance of fate was familiar to the Aztecs.

For the Mexican, death is intimately related to identity. Octavio Paz says, "Death defines life. . . .Each of us dies the death he is looking for, the death he has made for himself. . . . Death, like life, is not transferable."[24] Common folk sayings reiterate this deep connection between death and identity, as in "Tell me how you die and I will tell you who you are." In the Mexican consciousness, death mirrors a person's life.

Symbols of death are visible everywhere. In churches, the suffering Savior is portrayed with a bloody vividness. Glass-topped coffins display the remains of martyrs, saints, and notables of the Church. Death is manifested in graffiti and in the ornaments that decorate cars and buses.[25] Newspapers seem to revel in accounts of violent deaths, and obituaries are conspicuously framed with black borders calling the readers' attention to the fact of death. Art and literature are replete with images of death, and in Mexican poetry one finds similes comparing life's fragility to a dream, a flower, a river, or a passing breeze.[26]

Whereas Anglo artists and writers seem in awe or even fearful of death, their Mexican counterparts seem to confront death with an attitude of humorous sarcasm. But it is not really death that is parodied, but life. In Mexican art and literature, death is portrayed not so much as an end, but as an equalizer that not even the wealthiest can escape; the emotional response it generates is often one of seeming impatience, disdain, or irony. Although the engravings of Antonio Guadalupe Posada, for example, may superficially resemble the woodcuts of the medieval *danse macabre,* in which people of all walks of life danced with their own skeletons, Posada's skeletons do not have the "anxious premonition of death" one associates with similar works by artists in other cultures.[27] Surrounded by references to death, Paz says, the Mexican "jokes about it, caresses it, sleeps with it, celebrates it," and makes it "one of his favorite toys and his steadfast love."[28]

Once a year, death is celebrated in a national fiesta, *El día de los Muertos,* the Day of the Dead. Occurring annually in November, the Day of the Dead generally lasts one or two days, though in some parts of Mexico it may continue for several weeks. Blending both indigenous and Roman Catholic elements into a unique commemoration of All Souls' Day, the fiesta is an occasion for communion between the living and the dead. Bread in the shape of human bones is eaten. Sugar-candy skulls and tissue-paper skeletons poke fun at death and flaunt it. The fiesta reveling is a time for excess and revolting against ordinary modes of thought and action. It is, says Paz, "an experiment in disorder, reuniting contradictory elements and principles in order to bring about a renascence of life.[29]

During the Day of the Dead, celebrants seek to break through the ordinary bonds that separate the dead from the living. Women dress the graves of deceased family members, placing food offerings and lighted candles before the souls of the ancestors. The dead are said to partake of the spirit of the foods and gifts brought to them.[30] The entire night is often devoted to meditative communion with dead loved ones, as the ancestors are urged to come forth this one special night of the year to aid and comfort the living. But fiesta night, as Paz observes, is also a night of mourning.[31] The failure to pay respect to the dead can bring scorn to the family that neglects its responsibilities.[32]

Familiarity with death, however, may breed contempt, not understanding. Paz argues that both the American and the Mexican deny the reality of death, albeit in different ways. In the one culture death is brought to the forefront of

An ironic attitude toward death characterizes the Day of the Dead fiesta in Mexico. Death is satirized while memories of deceased loved ones are cherished by the living. Family members often place the names of deceased relatives on ornaments such as this candy skull and these candy coffins. This practice assures the spirits of the dead that they have not been forgotten by the living and provides solace to the living in the form of tangible symbols of the presence of deceased loved ones.

consciousness, in the other it is pushed aside. It is possible to deny or avoid death even though surrounded by images that constantly suggest it. When death is devalued — is made to seem less than the radical event it truly is — then we are not looking squarely at death, and life loses meaning.

Death and Dying in Western Civilization

It could be expected that cultures like those just discussed reveal attitudes and behaviors different from our own. It might be surprising, however, to discover contrasts in the more familiar setting of Western civilization if we go back in time. To better understand our modern response to death, let us trace some earlier responses that were characteristic of Western culture during the last 1500 years or so.

For well over a thousand years (if we count from A.D. 500, roughly when the Middle Ages began), those living in the Western world accepted death as an integral part of human existence. Despite gradual changes, as Figure 2-3 shows, the attitude toward death remained generally consistent with a view of the universe as bound together by natural and divine law. Death was part of this natural design, and the teachings of the Church were a source of hope for the afterlife. This outlook, which would prevail from about the sixth to the nineteenth centuries, has been characterized by Philippe Ariès as one of "tamed death." [33]

Using Ariès' analysis, we can discern relatively distinct periods during this epoch of Western cultural history as regards death and dying. In the first period, during the early middle ages, a sense of collective destiny was prevalent. Death was understood in this context as the common fate of all people: "All people die." In the religious mentality of the time, the dead were "asleep in Christ," and their bodies entrusted to the Church until the Last Day when they would be resurrected at the time of Christ's Apocalyptic return. Salvation was achieved less through individual merit or freedom from sin than through the good graces of the Church.

By the twelfth century this mentality had gradually been transformed into a more particular awareness of one's own death as having a personal meaning: "Everyone dies," has become "I will die my own death." This transformation came about as a result of a general enrichment in medieval culture and greater complexity of social structure. Innovations had been made in commerce, agriculture, education, and political life. The works of the ancient writers having been preserved by Byzantine and Moslem scholars, Greek thought and Roman law became influential, opening the way for new intellectual pursuits. Above all, people in the West gained a new sense of individual identity and self-awareness. As a result, the act of dying became an event of supreme importance for the individual.

This increased emphasis on individual identity brought dramatic changes in the religious sphere as well. Whereas in times past, residing in the bosom of the Church was enough to assure resurrection on the Last Day and acceptance into heaven, now there were personal anxieties regarding the Judgment that would separate the just from the damned. The *liber vitae,* or Book of Life, which previously had been conceived of as a sort of vast cosmic census, now became the biography of an individual life, a balance sheet by which each person's soul would be weighed.

The third great transformation of the meaning of death occurred toward the end of the seventeenth century, when the death of the other, "thy death," began to receive emphasis. Death was romanticized, and the loss felt by the bereaved gave rise to impassioned expressions of grief and to desires to memorialize the dead. The romantic ideal of the beautiful death was part of a more general fascination with the imaginative and emotional appeal of the heroic, the mysterious. The sad beauty of death elicited feelings of melancholy,

Death Knells

During many centuries one item of expense for survivors was the fee that must be paid for the ringing of the soul bell. Every cathedral and church of medieval Christendom had such a bell, almost always the largest one in the bell tower.

By the time John Donne wrote the immortal line "for whom the bell tolls," ringing of the soul bell—in a distinctive pattern, or knell—was popularly taken to be merely a public notice that a death had occurred. This use of the soul bell came into importance relatively late, however.

Not simply in Christian Europe but also among primitive tribes and highly developed non-Christian cultures of the Orient, bells have been linked with death. Notes from bells (rung in special fashion) served to help convince a spirit that there was no need to remain close to a useless dead body. At the same time, noise made by bells was considered to be especially effective in driving away the evil spirits who prowled about hoping to seize a newly released soul or to put obstacles in its path.

Ringing of the soul (or passing) bell was long considered so vital that bell ringers demanded, and got, big fees for using it. Still in general use by the British as late as the era of King Charles II in the seventeenth century, bell ringers then regulated the number of strokes of the passing bell so that the general public could determine the age, sex, and social status of the deceased.

Webb Garrison,
Strange Facts About Death

tinged with optimism that there would be an eventual reunion of the family in a Heavenly home.

Survivors began more and more to visit the gravesites of beloved relatives and friends. Expressions of mourning became highly visible. The arts were pressed into service to memorialize the dead: Memorial brooches contained pictures of the deceased, and watercolors depicted such scenes as ladies weeping at receiving the news of a death. By the nineteenth century, the deaths of others tended to overshadow one's own sense of mortality.

Then, with great rapidity, all this changed. By the early decades of the twentieth century, the deathbed had been displaced from the home to the hospital. What had been a response to the death of another became a desire to spare the dying person the pain of knowing about the imminence of his or her death. Funerals became shorter, more discreet. Grief was suppressed. The customary signs of mourning disappeared. These changes were particularly dramatic in the United States. Attitudes and behaviors that had been common since the early Middle Ages, and that had remained essentially unchanged through most of the nineteenth century, were quickly superseded as death became taboo. No longer familiar, death was ugly and forbidden.

What was the significance of this break in the continuity of Western

Ritual of dying: the recumbent figure of the dying person, presiding amidst protocol and custom, over an essentially public ceremony. Everything done with simplicity, no great show of emotion. Custom and social observances dictate the style of dying and the deathbed scene. Death is familiar; there is an awareness of dying: "I see and I know that my death is near."

As the initiative passes from the dying person to the family and then to the medical arena, there arises a desire to spare the dying person, often by means of pretence, from the "ugliness" of death. Death becomes taboo.

Place of burial is the charnel house, the outer part or courtyard of the church. With the rise of the cult of martyrs there is a desire to be buried near the great saints of the church; burials take place near or in churches, instead of outside cities as during pagan times.

Gradually, a greater sense of individuality is reflected in death customs. A new self-awareness becomes evident first in the use of inscriptions and plaques to mark a person's biography and death; later, effigies and death masks herald the individuality of the dead. Eventually, the tombs of the notable dead are embellished with sculptures portraying both the appearance of the body when alive and its ultimate putrefaction after death, a stark reminder of mortality and individual responsibility.

The "cult of memory" demonstrated by ornate memorials to the dead was often accompanied by hysterical mourning on the part of the bereaved survivors. More recently, however, these once-customary signs of mourning have been largely replaced by the avoidance of emotional display and by discreet and brief funeral ceremonies. Uncertainty and anxiety become the characteristic emotions elicited by "forbidden death" in the twentieth century.

500 600 700 800 900 1000 1100 1200 1300 1400 1500 1600 1700 1800 1900 2000

500	600	700	800	900	1000	1100	1200	1300	1400	1500	1600	1700	1800	1900	2000

(Early Middle Ages)   (Late Middle Ages)   (Renaissance)

——— "All people die" ———   "One's own death"   ——— "Thy death" ———   "Forbidden death"

——— "Tamed death" ———

Universe bound together by natural and divine law. Death a familiar and accepted part of this order. Individuals experienced themselves as participants in a collective destiny of humankind, presided over by the Church.

General enrichment throughout culture; intellectual advances, influenced by Greek thought and Roman law.

Age of exploration and conquest; old geographic and intellectual boundaries giving way.

Increasing secularization of social and intellectual life.

Belief in the Apocalypse (Christ's return at the end of time). Resurrection of the dead on the Last Day. The dead "asleep in Christ," to awake in Paradise. Salvation based on participation in the communal Body of Christ, not on individual moral actions.

Concept of the Resurrection incorporates belief in the Last Judgment, when the soul will be judged on its record in the "Book of Life," an individual account that is closed on the Last Day.

Emphasis on Judgment predominates; the "Second Coming" fades into background. The time of Judgment shifts to the deathbed scene, which becomes the final test in the cosmic struggle. Between death and "the Last Day" there is an extension of being into purgatory.

Challenges to religious belief lead to a reexamination and reinterpretation of scripture and sacred traditions. The interplay between reason and faith creates a diverse and pluralistic religious and social environment.

Figure 2-3   *Death and Dying from the Middle Ages to the Present*

humanity's relationship with death? To answer this question, we must examine how patterns of dying and of death evolved from the Middle Ages to the present.

Anticipated Death

Dying was a grim business in the Middle Ages. In the absence of surgery or adequate means of alleviating pain, the pangs of death were real indeed. On pious deathbeds, the dying person offered up his or her suffering to God, expecting nothing more than to meet death in the customary manner.

Sudden death was rare. Even wounds received in battle or injuries resulting from accidents seldom brought instantaneous death. "I see and know that my death is near": Thus did the dying person acknowledge his or her impending demise. (The possibility of sudden, unexpected death was greatly feared because it caught the victim unaware and unable to properly close earthly accounts and turn toward the divine.)

Those who stood near the deathbed, too, could say with confidence that the dying person "feels her time has come" or "knows that he will soon be dead." Only rarely did death come without warning. Usually it was anticipated either by natural signs or by a conscious inner certainty. Death seemed manageable.

The Deathbed Scene

A person realizing that death was near began to prepare for it. The dying person customarily enacted certain ritual gestures to make sure that dying was done properly. Philippe Ariès describes the main features of a dignified death during the early Middle Ages: Lying down, with the head facing east toward Jerusalem, perhaps with arms crossed over the chest, the dying person first expressed sadness at his or her impending end, "a sad but very discreet recollection of beloved beings and things." Then, the many companions — family and friends — surrounding the deathbed received the dying person's pardon for any wrongs that they might have done, and all were commended to God.

Next, the dying person turned his or her attention away from the earthly and toward the divine. A confession of sins to a priest was followed by a short prayer requesting divine grace. The priest then granted absolution. With the customary rites completed, nothing more was said. The dying person was ready for death. If death came more slowly than expected, the dying person simply waited in silence.

The recumbent figure in the deathbed, surrounded by parents, friends, family, children, and even mere passersby, remained the predominant death scene until modern times. Dying was considered a more or less public ceremony, with the person who was dying clearly in charge. Emotion was neither suppressed nor given especially vivid expression. Everything was directed toward simplicity and ceremony.

As a new individualism evolved during the twelfth century, however, the scene around the deathbed began to change imperceptibly. Over the entourage

This deathbed vigil in a Spanish village is characteristic of the way in which human beings have responded to death for thousands of years. Only recently have such scenes been superseded in modern societies by the specter of dying alone, perhaps unconscious, amid the impersonal technological gadgetry of an unfamiliar institutional environment.

of public participants now hovered a great and invisible army of celestial figures, angels and demons, battling for possession of the dying person's soul. As the awareness of selfhood grew in the succeeding centuries, death became the *speculum mortis,* the mirror in which each person could discover his or her nature and destiny as an individual. Because free will implied moral responsibility for one's acts, each person facing death tallied the moral balance sheet of his or her life. As a unique occasion for reviewing one's actions and making a final decision for good or ill, the moment of death became the supreme challenge and the ultimate test of an entire lifetime.

From the seventeenth century on, the religious understandings of death began to gradually give way to secular understandings that emphasized reason and the natural order rather than the divine. Although still an important force in Western culture, religion now shared the stage with the more materialistic orientation of scientific rationalism. Thus, the world view of the Middle Ages, embodied in the iconography of the Church, with its attendant comforts and

A good teacher both of the body and the soul is perfect remembrance of death, when a man, looking beyond everything that is between (that is, between the present moment and the hour of death), is always seeing forward to that bed upon which we shall one day lie, breathing out our life; and at that which comes after.

Hesychius of Jerusalem, circa A.D. 400

fears, gave way to a mentality that viewed nature as chaotic and sometimes frightening, but also fascinating in its beauty.

The scene around the deathbed remained little changed outwardly; family and friends still gathered as participants in the public ritual of a person's dying. But, the religious images and understandings that had characterized the earlier world view no longer served to channel the spontaneous grief of the survivors. The idea of death as untamed yet beautiful, like nature, gave survivors a means to express their emotions. The old notions of Heaven and Hell that had so motivated people in an earlier time were replaced by a hoped-for immortality of the soul and an eventual reunion of loved ones in the afterlife. Whereas the Puritan child in seventeenth-century New England was counseled to contemplate the terrors of death and the torment of a fiery Hell as prods to good behavior, the Romantic child of the eighteenth and early nineteenth centuries was instructed to think of death as beautiful, graceful, and serene. Dying was likened to the emergence of a butterfly from its cocoon.

Along with this changed outlook, the initiative in the ceremonies surrounding death was transferred from the dying person to the grief-stricken survivors. But not until the twentieth century, with the displacement of the scene of death from the home to the hospital, would a major change in the manner of dying occur.

Burial Customs

Until the sixth or seventh century, burial customs remained much the same as they had been during Roman times. These customs reflected the pagan belief that the dead might come back to haunt the living. To prevent such unhappy events gravesites were usually located away from towns and cities. Despite the differences in their beliefs about the state of the dead, Christians followed the customary practices. Early Christians were buried in the pagan cemeteries; later, Christians were buried in their own cemeteries, but still outside of populated areas.

With the development of monasticism, however, a cult of martyrs arose that gradually introduced a new element into Christian burial practices. It came to be believed that the martyrs' saintliness remained powerful even in death, and could help others avoid the pitfalls of sin and the horrors of hell. The early martyrs had been buried alongside the pagan dead, as was the custom. But, over time, many Christians wanted to be buried near the graves of the martyrs in hopes of gaining merit by such proximity. (A rough, modern analogy might be that of a person wishing to be buried near a famous personage at Forest Lawn or a verteran requesting burial near a Medal of Honor winner, although those living in the early Middle Ages were concered with eternal welfare rather than earthly prestige.)

Pilgrims also journeyed to venerate the martyrs, creating a need to establish a focal point for their worship, and altars, chapels, and eventually churches were built on or near the graves. At first these developments took place in the old pagan burial grounds because burials were still prohibited within the cities. However, as the cemeteries adjoining rural churches became increasingly used for Christian burials, the great urban cathedrals also began allowing burials to take place within their precincts, although initially this practice was limited to the notables and saints of the Church. But, by the ninth century or so, the burials of the faithful were taking place in the churchyards and surrounds of the urban cathedrals as well as the rural churches. Thus, the state of the dead had become intimately linked with the Church.

The Charnel House

The custom of burial within the churchyards of the urban cathedrals eventually led to the development of *charnel houses,* arcades and galleries that ran the length of the churchyard, where the bones of the dead were entrusted to the Church. Limbs and skulls were arranged artistically along various parts of the churchyard, as well as within and near the church. Many of these bones came from the great common graves of the poor, which were periodically reopened to remove the bones and give them over to the church for safekeeping until the Resurrection. The final destination of the bones was unimportant, so long as they were associated with the church or with some saint or holy relic. "As yet unborn," Ariès says, "was the modern idea that the dead person should be installed in a sort of house unto himself, a house of which he was the perpetual owner or at least the long-term tenant, a house in which he would be at home and from which he could not be evicted."

Most burials were anonymous; except for those of a few notables of the Church, gravesites had nothing to identify who was buried in them. With the coming of the new individualism in the twelfth and thirteenth centuries, however, there was a growing tendency to preserve the identity of the person buried in a particular place. Simple grave markers, usually of the "Here lies John Doe" variety, began to appear on the graves of even common folk, although not until the seventeenth century or so would this practice become prevalent.

Throughout the Middle Ages, burial practices remained little changed; the characteristic resting place of the dead was an unmarked grave in the charnel house, a place where the dead awaited eventual resurrection in the care of the Church. The charnel house itself was a public place, which reflected the medieval familiarity with death. Much as the Romans had congregated in the Forum, their medieval counterparts met in the charnel houses. There

Library of Congress

This ossuary located at a European monastery is a survival of the medieval charnel house, a gallery of skeletons and skulls and bones.

they would find shops and merchants, conduct business, dance, gamble, or simply enjoy being together.

The Dance of Death

As funeral inscriptions and tombs — at least of the notable — became more personalized, macabre themes also developed. Effigies of the dead appeared, and as time passed became increasingly realistic. By the early seventeenth century,

Hans Holbein the Younger, British Museum

Antonio Guadalupe Posada, Swann Collection
Library of Congress

MIGUEL Y LA CRIADA.

The somber mood of Hans Holbein's depiction of Die Totentanz, *or Dance of Death, contrasts with the treatment of the same theme by Mexican artist Antonio Guadalupe Posada. In Holbein's medieval woodblock print,* The Preacher, *we see the congregation assembled below the pulpit as the skeletal figure of Death ominously taps on the shoulder of the minister; in Posada's print, there is a sense of gaiety and festivity. Although expressed differently, the two works convey a common message: Death comes to people in all walks of life; no one is exempt.*

the striving for realism had become so great that sometimes the deceased was portrayed twice; first as he or she looked while alive, and a second time as a severely decomposed corpse. In death as in life, the focus was on the individual. Although these effigies portrayed only the most notable personages, they nevertheless represent an important development in how the dead were perceived by the living. Survivors had found a means for continuing their relationship with the dead in the custom of perpetuating the *memory* of the deceased.

To understand some of the influences leading to this change, we can trace the evolution of the Dance of Death, or *Danse Macabre,* which found expression in a variety of art forms including drama, poetry, music, and the visual arts. The Dance of Death is thought to have its origin in ecstatic mass dances that date from the eleventh and twelfth centuries. But it is not until the late thirteenth and early fourteenth centuries that the Dance of Death begins to become formalized, combining ideas of the inevitability of death and its impartiality.

The Dance of Death was sometimes performed as a masque, a short dramatic entertainment in which actors costumed as skeletons danced with other figures representing persons of all levels of society. The rich as well as the poor were invited to join in the Dance of Death, which conveyed the notion that death comes to *all* people, and to *each* person. A series of paintings, dating from the early fifteenth century, depicted the living being escorted to their destination by skeletons and corpses, a grim reminder of the imminence of death and a call to repentance.[34]

A major influence on the Dance of Death was the mass deaths caused by the plague, called the Black Death, of the mid-fourteenth century. The devastation of the Hundred Years' War (1337–1453) between France and England also contributed to the sense that death was omnipresent.

In the oldest versions of the Dance of Death, death seems scarcely to touch the living to warn and designate the person. Even as death took on a more personal meaning with the rise of individualism, it was still an accepted part of the natural order of things. But, about the end of the fifteenth century and the beginning of the sixteenth, a great shift in attitudes is reflected in the Dance of Death: The person was now portrayed as being forcibly taken by death. Death was seen as a rupture, a radical and complete break between the living and the dead.

With this change, the Dance of Death took on certain erotic connotations. Death was seen as a radical break with ordinary modes of consciousness, and thus was likened to the "small death" that occurs during the sexual act when, for a moment, there is a break with ordinary consciousness.[35] These blatantly erotic ideas about death were sublimated by the larger society, so that death was transformed into the obsession with beauty that became the hallmark of the Romantic ideal of death. The relationship between love and death that previously was seen in martyrdom now extended to include romantic love as well. Romances like those of Tristan and Isolde or Romeo and Juliet demonstrated the notion that where there is love, death can be beautiful—and even desirable.

By the Romantic period of the late eighteenth and nineteenth centuries, these concepts, which bear a historical relationship to the code of chivalry and the notion of courtly love, would find currency in the popular imagination. Thus, we have followed the progression from the communal mentality that "we all die," to the personal awareness that "I will die," to finally arrive at the death of the other, "thy death." Exalted and dramatized, death became important because it affected the loved one, the other person, whose memory was perpetuated in the ornate cemeteries of the eighteenth and nineteenth centuries.

Memorializing the Dead

We have already noted how as individualism took hold, practices evolved to preserve the identity of the deceased. These practices came into broad use in the seventeenth century or so, when all the various social and cultural changes combined to produce a fascination with the death of loved ones and a desire to perpetuate their memory. In the eighteenth and early nineteenth centuries this

Death is a subject to me which you can see and think of but cannot talk of. Indeed however ill he be I could never think of the death of one I love. It may be reconed [*sic*] as a want of faith! I know it is not. I do not mean by that, that I shall not be prepared to die when the time comes.

> From the *Diary* (1858) of Annie de Rothschild,
> age thirteen

memorialization of the dead was evidenced by elaborate mourning rituals, ornate tombstones, and a variety of mourning paraphernalia. The acceptance of death as universal and inevitable, an attitude that reflected religious and social concepts of order that had endured for more than a thousand years in Western culture, began to give way to a desire to mute the harsh reality of death, to blunt its finality. The finality of death was made less severe by perpetuating the memory of the deceased and by imagining his or her continued existence in heaven, where survivors hoped to be eventually reunited with loved ones (see Figure 2-4).

The untended graveyards of the seventeenth-century Puritans, who disdained the body whether living or dead, were replaced by lush, well-kept cemeteries like Mount Auburn in Cambridge, Massachusetts, and Woodlawn in New York City. By the 1830s, the rural cemetery movement had begun in

DIED,

On the 23d instant, Mrs. HARRIET R. DAILEY, aged 44 years
The friends of the family are respectfully invited to attend her funeral, to-morrow, at 3 o'clock. from the residence of her husband, corner Seventh and F sts, south.

On the morning of the 24th instant, WILLIAM, aged 4 years and 10 days, youngest child of M. H. and Susan B. Stevens
His funeral will take place from No. 49 Missouri avenue, to-morrow (Friday.) at 2 o'clock. The relatives and friends of the family are respectfully invited to attend, without further notice.

On the morning of the 24th instant, at 4½ o'clock. after a brief but painful illness of pneumonia, which she patiently bore as only an humble believer in Him of Calvary can bear, and in the peaceful hope of an eternal life to come, surrounded by the family circle, ELIZABETH LARCOMBE. wife of John Larcombe, Sr., aged 61 years and 7 months.
The relatives and friends of the deceased are cordially invited to attend her funeral, from her late residence, on Virginia avenue, below 6th st, to-morrow (Friday) afternoon, at 3 o'clock, without further notice.

On the 23d instant, at 5 o'clock, of chronic croup, JOSEPH WM ARTHUR, aged 2 years and 5 months, eldest child of Richard and Rachel Gormley.
The friends of the family are invited to attend the funeral, from the residence of the parents, on Third st. east. between D and E sts. south, at 2 o'clock to-morrow evening.

Figure 2-4 *Newspaper Death Notice from the 1860s*

America, and resplendent monuments were erected to honor the dead in perpetuity. In these parklike settings, the bereaved could come to commune in memory with the deceased.[36]

Invisible Death

Beginning about the turn of the twentieth century, the Romantic attitude toward death waned. Care of the dying and of the dead would be delegated to professionals, and death would become no longer a familiar element of life. Care of the dying would come to be dominated by efforts to delay death by all means available. In recent times the quality of a person's final days or the meaning of death is hardly considered at all. Especially in technological societies, death is generally thought to be synonymous with extinction. The answers that were provided by the creeds of the Church for nearly two millennia no longer suffice for many people. Some despair about the meaning and value of life itself.[37]

It might be argued that Ariès' portrait of a time when people died more serenely than people do today is drawn too much in black-and-white. Were there not as many reasons to fear death in the past, especially during epidemics of plague, as we have today with the threats of environmental pollution and nuclear weapons? Was religion necessarily a comfort for the dying, given that the terrors of hell as well as the joys of heaven were likely to be among the images envisioned by a dying person? And what about the physical agony of dying? Today we have access to modern medical techniques for alleviating pain.

Whether or not the portrait drawn by Ariès is oversimplified, it is generally agreed that dying persons previously had access to a source of comfort that may be lacking in modern health care institutions: the presence of other people. Fulfillment, as Norbert Elias says, is closely tied to "the meaning one has attained in the course of one's life for other people."[38]

Even when a person has reached his or her goals in life and feels a sense of completion, the act of dying may be painful and difficult if it is felt to be meaningless. Caregivers may try to alleviate pain and attend to physical comfort, but this effort may seem mechanical and impersonal. Family members, in an unaccustomed situation and unfamiliar setting, may be at a loss for what to say or do. Thus, during the evolution of attitudes toward death in Western culture, the most significant change may be the dying person's sense of his or her meaning for others. Feeling that he or she has scarcely any significance for other people, the dying person today may feel truly alone.

Although we don't doubt the inevitability of death, it is questionable whether any of us truly believes in his or her own death. In every age, death has been confronted with the aid of various cultural and institutional support systems.[39] In our own time, the understanding of death is communicated through the processes of socialization by which children learn the concepts and conventions that have currency in modern society. We explore these processes in the next chapter.

Further Readings

Philippe Ariès. *Images of Man and Death*. Cambridge, Mass.: Harvard University Press, 1985.

Elizabeth P. Benson, editor. *Death and the Afterlife in Pre-Columbian America*. Washington, D.C.: Dumbarton Oaks, 1975.

Maurice Bloch and Jonathan Perry, editors. *Death and the Regeneration of Life*. New York: Cambridge University Press, 1982.

Peter Brown. *The Cult of the Saints: Its Rise and Function in Latin Christianity*. Chicago: University of Chicago Press, 1981.

James Stevens Curl. *A Celebration of Death*. New York: Charles Scribner's Sons, 1980.

Loring M. Danforth. *The Death Rituals of Rural Greece*. Princeton, N.J.: Princeton University Press, 1982.

Elisabeth Darby and Nicola Smith. *The Cult of the Prince Consort*. New Haven, Conn.: Yale University Press, 1983.

Richard A. Etlin. *The Architecture of Death: The Transformation of the Cemetery in Eighteenth-Century Paris*. Cambridge, Mass.: MIT Press, 1984.

Robert S. Gottfried. *The Black Death: Natural and Human Disaster in Medieval Europe*. New York: The Free Press, 1983.

Åke Hultkrantz. *The Religions of the American Indians*. Berkeley: University of California Press, 1979.

Richard Huntington and Peter Metcalf. *Celebrations of Death: The Anthropology of Mortuary Ritual*. New York: Cambridge University Press, 1979.

Jacques LeGoff. *The Birth of Purgatory*. Chicago: University of Chicago Press, 1984.

John S. Mbiti. *African Religions and Philosophy*. Garden City, N.Y.: Anchor Press/Doubleday, 1970.

Phyllis Palgi and Henry Abramovitch. "Death: A Cross-Cultural Perspective," *Annual Review of Anthropology* 13 (1984): 385–417.

Paul Radin. *The Road of Life and Death: A Ritual Drama of the American Indians*. Princeton, N.J.: Princeton University Press, 1973.

The "Endings" exhibit at the Boston Children's Museum, with its range of activities for learning about various aspects of death, offers an innovative means of sharing attitudes about death in our culture.

Socialization: How We Learn About Death as Children

*I*magine yourself as a child. Someone says, "Everybody's going to zittze one of these days. It happens to all of us. You, too, will zittze." Or, one day as you're playing, you are told, "Don't touch that, it's zittzed!" Being an observant child, you might notice that when a person zittzes, other people cry and appear to be very sad. After a time, as you put together all your experiences of "zittzing," you would begin to develop some personal feelings and thoughts about what it means to zittze.

A child's understanding of death evolves in much this way. As the child grows older, incorporating a variety of experiences related to death, his or her concepts and emotional responses to death begin to more closely resemble those prevalent among adults in the child's culture. This adult understanding of death does not emerge fully realized, but, like other aspects of children's development, gradually evolves during the years of childhood. Just as a child's understanding of "money" changes over time — at first it is a matter of little or no concern; later it seems to come into the child's experience almost magically; and finally, it engages the child's attention and participation in many differrent ways — so, too, does the child develop new understandings about what death means.

In all these stages of understanding, the child's responses change over time through the interplay between experiences and the level of maturity that he or she brings to understanding them. In other words, the child's understanding of death usually fits with his or

Death has a different emotional meaning to young children. In the game of Cowboys and Indians death is not final; the game must continue. The common threat when angered may be, "I'll kill you." One can readily see that the concept of killing is not viewed as final and that there is no association of pain with killing. Perhaps the following example will best prove the point. Upon arriving home from a business trip, a young child's father brought her a gun and holster set. After buckling on her new present she took out the gun, pointed it at her father and said, "Bang, bang, you're dead! I killed you." Her father replied, "Don't hurt me." His daughter's innocent answer was, "Oh, Daddy, I won't hurt you, I just killed you." To many children death is seen only as something in the distant future; "only old people die."

Dan Leviton and Eileen C. Forman,
"Death Education for Children and Youth"

her model of the world at each stage of development. Thus, an adult could give a young child a lengthy, detailed explanation of the concept of death as adults understand it, yet the child will grasp its components only when developmentally ready to understand. However, a child's cognitive and emotional readiness to understand is not simply a matter of age: Experience plays an important role; a child who has had firsthand encounters with death may arrive at an understanding of death beyond that which is characteristic of children in the same age group.

Our understandings about death take shape during childhood through continuous adjustments and refinements as new experiences cause us to reexamine our values and responses. During childhood, this process of reexamination is quite rapid; a child's understanding of death can change dramatically in a very brief time. This progression of a child's understanding about death can be placed in a framework that gives the adult observer an orderly picture of the relevant processes. By observing and questioning to gather information, and then analyzing the data, researchers begin to discern certain characteristic patterns of childhood development. (You have probably done this yourself, by observing the changes that occur in children with whom you have frequent contact. For example, the kinds of play activities that engross a child change over time; the toy that elicited great excitement at one age becomes uninteresting at a later time.) By such observations of children's behaviors developmental psychologists and theorists devise models to describe the characteristic concerns and interests of children at various ages. These models are like maps that describe the large patterns and characteristics of the territory of childhood; they describe how children relate to the world at different stages of their development. These models can be very useful for describing the characteristics of a typical child at, say, age two or age seven. They give a general picture of each particular stage of development. As instruments of observation become refined, so, too, does the picture of the territory. But the map should not be mistaken for the territory.

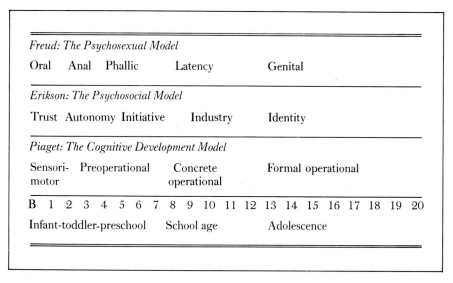

Freud: The Psychosexual Model

Oral   Anal   Phallic   Latency   Genital

Erikson: The Psychosocial Model

Trust Autonomy Initiative   Industry   Identity

Piaget: The Cognitive Development Model

Sensori-   Preoperational   Concrete   Formal operational
motor   operational

B 1   2   3   4   5   6   7   8   9   10   11   12   13   14   15   16   17   18   19   20

Infant-toddler-preschool   School age   Adolescence

Figure 3-1 *Comparison of Major Developmental Models, or Theories, Concerning Childhood Phases of Development*

Like maps, models of childhood development are abstractions, representations, interpretations of the actual territory (see Figure 3-1). Such maps can be useful for guiding one's way, for locating certain landmarks, and for sharing knowledge about a particular area with others. But the particular features of the landscape will always possess a uniqueness that cannot be fully described by a map.

Indeed, many researchers, on the basis of evidence, now believe that children vary widely in individual rates of development — not only physically but also emotionally and cognitively, or intellectually. Thus, with respect to any human trait, developmental levels do not correspond directly and neatly to chronological age.

Components of a Mature Concept of Death

Whatever our beliefs about death or what it is like to die or what happens afterward, the known facts can be easily summarized: Death is inevitable, and happens to one and all. Death is final; physical death spells the end of our known existence. A formal statement of these empirical, or observable, facts includes three components. These are the understanding that:

1. Death is irreversible and permanent.
2. Death involves the cessation of physiological functioning.
3. Death is universal and inevitable.

Recognition of these facts constitutes possession of a mature concept of death, although other, nonempirical ideas about death may be associated with an understanding of these observable facts.

Such nonempirical issues, for adults as well as children, are: What happens after someone dies? Where do the dead go? Does the self or soul continue to exist after the death of the body? What is the meaning of death? Such questions impinge on our understanding of death, and children also deal with them in various ways as they develop their own concepts and feelings about death.

In addition, what a person "knows" about death may differ from time to time, according to circumstances. Even as adults, we may discover that we harbor conflicting notions about death, especially our own. Under certain conditions a hard-nosed acceptance of the facts may give way to a more childlike attitude that presumes an ability to bargain where death is concerned. For example, a patient told by a doctor that he or she has only six months to live may imagine that by some kind of "magical" act, some bargain with the universe, the death sentence can be staved off. A child's understanding of death may also fluctuate among different ways of "knowing" as he or she develops a personal framework in which to place it.

Developmental Studies of the Child's Understanding of Death

Children first conceive of death as partial, reversible, and avoidable. As they broaden their understanding, they eventually arrive at a concept of death as final and inevitable. When and how this understanding is acquired are being investigated by a growing number of researchers.[1] Until recently, although important studies had been done on the general parameters of child development, few focused on how children learn about death.

As some of the blanks are being filled in by current research, the picture provided by earlier researchers is being refined.[2] From early studies, undertaken in the 1930s and 1940s, it was generally concluded that children had little or no awareness of death before the age of three or four. Early theoretical models proposed a series of stages with fixed corresponding ages within which particular kinds of behaviors and conceptual developments occurred. Current research, however, demonstrates that *sequence* is more reliable than correlating stages of understanding to ages in describing how children learn about death. In addition, until recently it was generally thought that the cognitive resources to conceive of death as final and inevitable were acquired at around the age of nine.

I was astonished to hear a highly intelligent boy of ten remark after the sudden death of his father: 'I know father's dead, but what I can't understand is why he doesn't come home to supper.'

Sigmund Freud, *The Interpretation of Dreams*

Despite deemphasizing a correlation between age and stage, current research nevertheless places this occurrence between the ages of five and seven for most healthy children.[3]

Early Encounters with Death

When does a child first become aware of death? By the time children are four or five, death-related thoughts and experiences are usually evident in their songs, their play, and their questions. Early researchers typically interpreted such evidence as indicating the younger child's lack of concern about death. More recent observations, however, tend to confirm the theory that death discoveries frequently occur even among children under the age of two. The younger child's awareness of death is manifested in ways different from those of the child of four or five, of course, but recent research has reversed the tendency to ignore such manifestations altogether.

Adah Maurer suggests that such experiences begin quite early.[4] In the infant's experience of the difference between sleep and wakefulness, for example, Maurer believes there is a perception of the distinction between being and nonbeing, and that children begin to experiment with this difference at a very early age. In their play, for instance, the "peekaboo" game may represent the polarities of being and nonbeing. The infant's experience of having a cloth thrown over her face, shutting out sensory awareness of the environment, is analogous to death. The "boo," when the cloth is removed, is like being alive

---

 Summaries of Early Studies of Children's Concepts of Death

Paul Schilder and David Wechsler (1934): Schilder and Wechsler listed general statements about children's attitudes toward death:

1. Children deal with death in an utterly matter-of-fact and realistic way.
2. Children exhibit skepticism concerning the unobservables.
3. Children often accept conventional definitions.
4. Children often remain insensitive to contradictions between convention and observation.
5. Children exhibit naivete in solving problems.
6. Children regard death as deprivation.
7. Children believe the devil punishes orally by withdrawing food or by devouring the dead.
8. Children do not believe in their own death.
9. To very young children, death seems reversible.
10. Children believe death may result from disease.
11. Children have a tendency toward undue generalization of limited knowledge.
12. Children believe in death from overeating, violence, and acts of God.
13. Fear of death is rare.
14. Children often fail to understand the meaning of death, but base their attitudes on the actions of adults.

continued

continued from previous page

15. Children may exhibit suicidal ideas.
16. Children are always ready to believe in the deaths of others.
17. Children are ready to kill.
18. The tendency to kill may come only in play.
19. The degree of preoccupation of children with violence and death can be seen by the way in which they react to ghost pictures.
20. God appears as a stage magician, controlling ghosts and death, etc.
21. Appearance and reality are not sharply differentiated.
22. Children exhibit the urge to pass moral judgments on every person and picture.
23. Children's professed morality is utilitarian, since children fear punishment.
24. Religious morality enters relatively rarely into children's attitudes toward death.

Sylvia Anthony (1940): Before the age of two years, the child has no understanding of death. After age two, most children think often of death. The idea of death seems to take much of its emotional component from its links with birth anxiety and aggressive impulses. Magical thinking pervades much of the child's thoughts about death (i.e., belief that events happen in a certain way because he or she thinks about them happening in a certain way; for example, angry thoughts directed toward someone who subsequently dies makes the child feel himself or herself to be a murderer). As a result, guilt is one of the child's reactions to death.

Maria H. Nagy (1948): Nagy identified three major developmental stages among children three to ten years of age.

Stage 1 (3–5 years): Death is understood as separation, a state of being less alive, a departure or disappearance (i.e., the dead go away and continue to "live" on under changed circumstances). The child does not yet recognize that death involves complete cessation of life; nor is the finality (irreversibility) of death comprehended.

Stage 2 (5–9 years): Death now understood as final. However, still present is the notion that one might be able to elude death; the inevitability (all die) and personal reference (I die) components are not yet established. Belief that one might be able to outwit or outluck the "Death Man."

Stage 3 (9 or 10 years and older): Death recognized as final and inevitable.

Irving E. Alexander and Arthur M. Adlerstein (1958): Death has a greater emotional significance for children with less stable ego self-concepts than for children with adequate self-concepts. The ages five to eight and the period of adolescence are times of great emotional upheaval and changing demands of growth, which are likely to put existing self-images to a severe test. As a result, the concept of nonbeing (death) may be more threatening during these periods of development.

Sources: Paul Schilder and David Wechsler, "The Attitudes of Children Toward Death," *Journal of Genetic Psychology* 45 (1934): 406–451; Sylvia Anthony, *The Discovery of Death in Childhood and After* (New York: Basic Books); Maria H. Nagy, "The Child's View of Death," *Journal of Genetic Psychology* 73 (1948): 3–27; Irving E. Alexander and Arthur M. Alderstein, "Affective Responses to the Concept of Death in a Population of Children and Early Adolescents," *Journal of Genetic Psychology* 93 (1958): 167–177.

again. Thus, death may be experienced in games of this kind as separation, disappearance, and return.

Some theorists believe that much of the behavior shown by infants and very young children is protothanatic — that is, preparation for concepts about life and death that will eventually emerge in the child's later interactions with the environment. To what degree such early experiences influence the child's later concepts about death is not altogether clear at present. However, that children do exhibit some awareness of death quite early is becoming more certain.

The child's earliest encounter with death usually comes with the ability to distinguish between the animate and the inanimate. In other words, the child perceives whether or not something has life. The following story illustrates how this may occur in quite ordinary circumstances. An eighteen-month-old boy was out for a walk with his father when the father inadvertently stepped on a caterpillar. The child kneeled down, looked at the dead caterpillar lying on the sidewalk, and said, "No more!"[5] That is the typical genesis of a child's awareness of death: *No more.*

It should be recognized that similar experiences may produce quite different responses in different children. Encountering a dead caterpillar or dead bird may set off a reaction in one child that lasts for several days, during which the child is eager to find some answers. Another child may seem to pay such an encounter little heed, apparently without a moment's reflection about an event that the first child found provocative and mysterious.

Death-Experienced Children, Ages One to Three

Many early researchers assumed that children between the ages of one and three are simply too young to know anything about death. Because of this

I saw death. At the age of five: it was watching me; in the evenings, it prowled on the balcony: it pressed its nose to the window; I used to see it but I did not dare to say anything. Once, on the Quai Voltaire, we met it: it was a tall, mad old woman, dressed in black, who mumbled as she went by: 'I shall put that child in my pocket.' Another time, it took the form of a hole: this was at Arcachon; [we] were visiting Madame Dupont and her son Gabriel, the composer. I was playing in the garden of the villa, scared because I had been told that Gabriel was ill and was going to die. I was playing at horses, half-heartedly, and galloping round the house. Suddenly, I noticed a gloomy hole: the cellar, which had been opened; an indescribable impression of loneliness and horror blinded me: I turned round and, singing at the top of my voice, I fled. At that time, I had an assignation with it every night in my bed. It was a ritual: I had to sleep on my left side, my face to the wall; I would wait, trembling all over, and it would appear, a very conventional skeleton, with a scythe; I then had permission to turn on my right side, it would go away and I could sleep in peace.

Jean-Paul Sartre, *Words*

assumption, and because research on very young children requires greater effort to obtain data, most research has been conducted on children older than four years. However, a study conducted by Mark Speece to investigate the impact of death experiences on children ages one to three suggests that very young children do indeed try to come to terms with death-related experiences.[6] Speece says, "It seems safe to conclude that death experiences occur in the lives of a sizable proportion of children of this age and that those children who do have such experiences attempt to deal with and integrate their specific death experiences into their understanding of the world in general."

In the course of his investigation, Speece found that slightly over half of his sample study population had some experience with death: in some cases, a human death (for example, a grandmother, a cousin, a neighbor); in others, a nonhuman death such as that of a pet (most often birds, dogs, and fish). Speece found that these young children responded to death in observable ways. For example, some actively looked for the deceased pet or person. Questions about the immobility of the deceased and what happens after death, and expression of concerns for the welfare of the living indicated that these children were trying to come to terms with their experience of death. Some children also display emotions in response to death, including anger. One child became angry because a pet bird that had died would not come back to life. Thus, the notion that very young children do not experience a meaningful response to the deaths that occur in their environment is rapidly falling away as new evidence, such as the results of Speece's study, reveals this notion to be a fallacy.

The Very Young Child and Death: An Example

So, how does one answer the question, "When does the understanding of death begin, and what governs its development?" The dialogue between a twenty-seven-month-old child and his psychologist father provides an illuminating and suggestive case study.[7] (Note how the father's professional skills in listening and his sensitivity to his child's behavior helped him engage in this kind of conversation.)

For two months the child had been waking several times each night and screaming hysterically for a bottle of sugar water. The father describes getting up one night, for the second or third time, and deciding with his wife to use firmness in refusing to meet the child's demand. He went into his son's room and told him that he was too old to have a bottle and would have to go back to sleep without it. The father, his mind made up that enough was enough, started to leave the room.

But then he heard a frightened cry, one of desperation that sounded like the fear of death. Wondering what could be causing the child such alarm, the father turned back into the room, took his son out of the crib, and asked, "What will happen if you don't get your bottle?" The child, no longer hysterical, but very tearful and sniffling, said, "I can't make contact!" The father asked, "What does that mean, 'you can't make contact'?" His son replied, "If I run out of gas, I can't make contact — my engine won't go. You know!"

Edward C. Clark, UPI/Bettman Newsphotos

Children who experience the death of someone close may look to adults for models of appropriate behavior. Amidst the regalia of high military and political office that characterized the funeral of President John F. Kennedy, young John F. Kennedy, Jr., salutes the flag-draped coffin containing his father's body as it is transported from St. Matthew's Cathedral to Arlington National Cemetery. The day also marked John-John's third birthday.

The father then remembered several family excursions during the previous summer, when vehicles had run out of gas. "What are you afraid will happen if you run out of gas?" Still crying, the child replied, "My motor won't run and then I'll die." At that point, the father recalled another incident his son had witnessed. Some time earlier, when they were selling an old car, the prospective buyer had tried to start the engine, but the battery was dead and the engine wouldn't turn over. The child had heard remarks like, "It's probably *not making contact*," "the *motor died*," and "I guess *the battery's dead.*"

With this incident in mind, the father asked, "Are you afraid that your bottle is like gasoline and, just like when the car runs out of gas, the car dies; so, if you run out of food, you'll die?" The child nodded his head, "Yes." The father explained, "Well, that's not the same thing at all. You see, when you eat food, your body stores up energy so that you have enough to last you all night. You eat three times a day; we only fill up the car with gas once a week. When the car runs out of gas, it doesn't have any saved up for an emergency. But with people it isn't anything like that at all. You can go maybe two or three days without eating. And, even if you got hungry, you still wouldn't die. People aren't anything like cars."

This explanation seemed to do little toward alleviating the child's anxiety, so the father tried a different tack. "You're worried that you have a motor, just like a car, right?" The child nodded, "Yes." "So," continued the father, "you're worried that if you run out of gas or run out of food you'll die, just like the motor of a car, right?" Again, the child nodded yes. "Ah, but the car has a key right? We can turn it on and off anytime we want, right?"

Now the child's body began to relax. "But where is your key?" The father poked around the boy's belly button: "Is this your key?" The child laughed. "Can I turn your motor off and on? See, you're really nothing like a car at all. Nobody can turn you on and off. Once your motor is on, you don't have to worry about it dying. You can sleep through the whole night and your motor will keep running without you ever having to fill it up with gas. Do you know what I mean?" The child said, "Yes."

"Okay. Now you can sleep without worrying. When you wake in the morning, your motor will still be running. Okay?" Never again did the child wake up in the middle of the night asking for a bottle of warm sugar water.

Think of the impressive reasoning that goes on in a child's mind — the way of stringing together concepts. In this case, the father speculates that two experiences contributed to his child's understanding: First, the child had decided that sugar water would give him gas because he had overheard his parents saying that a younger sibling had "gas" from drinking sugar water; second, when the child's parakeet died, his question "What happened to it?" was answered by his father: "Every animal has a motor inside that keeps it going. When a thing dies, it is like when a motor stops running. Its motor just won't run anymore."

A child's understanding of death is composed of a series of concepts, strung together like beads in a strand that is worked with until it eventually becomes a necklace, a coherent understanding of death. Thus, although there is still some uncertainty about when infants begin to develop concepts about death, the description of this twenty-seven-month-old's complex associations of language and death demonstrates that children do formulate some kind of understanding about death very early in life.[8]

The Psychoanalytic Model: Death Anxiety in Children

Psychoanalytic theory suggests that an infant's experiences of separation and loss mark the beginning of death-related anxieties that continue throughout life.[9] According to this view, the infant's lack of physical and psychological resources of self-care leads to anxiety, which is mitigated by the parent's nurture and care. The infant's cries result in some action on the parent's part to relieve the child's discomfort. Diapers are changed; the child is fed.

A central feature of an infant's existence is helplessness. During the earliest period of life, the infant's needs are met by the mother or her surrogate. From the infant's perspective, care takes place because of his or her own control over the environment. As James McCarthy says, "It is as if the breast has only to be imagined or thought about for it to appear."[10] The symbiotic union with the parent is so complete that there seems to be no separation between the child's subjective and objective realities.

However, inevitably, there will be times when the infant's attempt to satisfy needs meets with frustration. Over time, the infant gradually perceives that the parent is a separate entity; the child is alone, a separate self. This perception is the beginning of a kind of love-hate relationship with the parent — who both satisfies and frustrates the striving to have needs met. If mother arrives at the crib for feeding because she has been wished there, then angry thoughts may lead to her disappearance as well. This kind of magical thinking — which operates on the premise that wishing something can make it a reality — equates separation or disappearance with nonbeing or "death."

McCarthy relates anxiety about death to the emergence of the self as separate from others. This process of individuation, of arriving at a separate self-identity, occurs most notably within the context of the intimate bonding between an infant and parent, and anxiety is likely to be especially acute at the major turning points in a child's development — such as weaning, toilet training, beginning school, or the birth of siblings. According to the psychoanalytic model, even when death anxiety does not present obvious difficulties, it can still have an important bearing on the child's development.[11]

The fears associated with the separation-individuation process during infancy and early childhood may appear in an altered context during adolescence. Just as the infant comes to perceive separation from parents, so too the adolescent strives to come to terms with that separateness on a much broader scale. Since the adolescent's developmental tasks with regard to forging an individual identity are conceptually quite different from the younger child's,

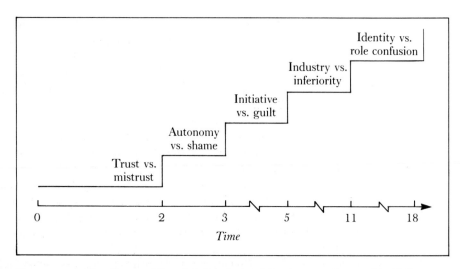

Figure 3-2   *Five Stages of Preadult Psychosocial Development Proposed by Erikson*
Source: Based on Erik H. Erikson, *Childhood and Society* (New York: Norton, 1964),
pp. 247–274.

the anxieties aroused by death also differ. But, McCarthy says, death may be no
less frightening to the ten-year-old than to the younger child; "it is just comprehended and symbolized differently."[12]

Erik Erikson: Stages of Psychosocial Development

The model of human development devised by the psychologist Erik
Erikson focuses on the psychosocial milestones that occur successively throughout a person's life (see Figure 3-2).[13] Here only the stages of childhood will
be discussed. In Erikson's model, psychosocial development is linked to the
individual's relationships with others. Each stage of development involves a
turning point, or crisis, that requires a response from the individual.

During the first stage, infancy, the individual must develop an adequate
sense of trust concerning the environment. If the infant's needs are not
adequately met, the result may be distrust. Thus, other persons in the infant's
environment — typically, the parents at this stage — play an important part in his
or her psychosocial development.

During the second stage, toddlerhood, roughly between one to three years,
the child begins to grapple with the issues of autonomy versus shame and doubt.
As the toddler explores the environment, developing greater independence,
there is sometimes a clash between what the child wants to do and what others
want the child to do. Toilet training typically occurs during this time, and it
may become a focal point of some of the conflicts between greater autonomy and
self-doubts and a sense of shame. In both physical and psychosocial development, this is a period of "letting go" and "holding on."

Between the ages of three to five years, typically the years of preschool and kindergarten, the child's psychosocial development involves issues of initiative versus guilt. The child increasingly desires to find his or her own purpose and direction, yet is also concerned about how parents (or other adults) may perceive these tentative efforts to express initiative and individuality. Thus, the overwhelmingly egocentric orientation of the infant is giving way to the more socially integrated self of the older child, which assumes its place as one among many. Trying things out may lead to situations that induce feelings of guilt. For instance, a child who has fantasies of doing away with a parent — expressed perhaps by the frustrated scream, "I wish you were dead!" — may feel guilt about having such thoughts. Again, how others respond to this conflict plays an important part in determining whether the crisis is resolved positively for the child's development. This period marks the beginning of the child's moral sense, the ability to function effectively within socially sanctioned modes of behavior.

One of the fears that may surface during this psychosocial stage is that of bodily mutilation. Children during these years of development are racing around on tricycles or big wheels, learning to cut small pieces of paper very precisely, making their muscles work for them, gaining greater control over their bodies. The body becomes very important to the child's self-image.

This preoccupation with the body can be illustrated: A five-year-old witnessed the death of his younger brother, who was killed when the wheel of a truck rolled over his head. The parents, who were considering having a wake in their home, asked their surviving son how he might feel if his younger brother's body was brought into the house for a wake. This five-year-old's question was, "Does he look hurt?" This child's concern about bodily disfigurement, which in this instance was directed toward the appearance of another's body, is characteristic of this stage of psychosocial development (see Figure 3-3).

In Erikson's model the years from about six to eleven are the stage of industry versus inferiority. This is typically a time when the child is busy in school, interacting with peers in a variety of ways. As the child's efforts begin to gain recognition and bring satisfaction, there may be anxieties about those areas in which the child senses a failure to measure up. Overcoming these feelings of inadequacy or inferiority becomes the major task of this psychosocial stage. As in all of the psychosocial stages, encouragement from others is crucial to the child's well-being.

Finally, from about ages twelve to eighteen, the years of adolescence, the milestone of development involves establishing an individual identity. This period is considered to be a particularly important time of personality development. A bridge must be established between the past — the years of childhood and dependency — and the future — the years of adulthood and independence. Thus, this is a time of integration as well as separation.

Remember what it's like being a teenager? Becoming more your own person? Striving to express your own ideas and beliefs? Sorting out the

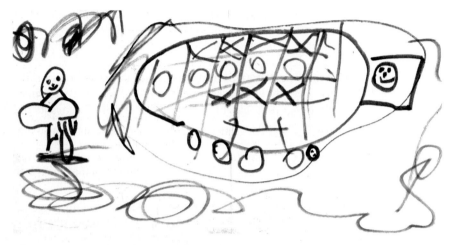

Figure 3-3   *Drawing of an Accident by a Five-Year-Old*
In this drawing by a five-year-old who witnessed his younger brother's accidental death, the surviving child is depicted as riding a "Big Wheel" on the left side of the truck that ran over his brother. The four wheels of the truck are shown, and the younger brother's head is drawn next to the wheel farthest to the right. This drawing is similar to one drawn by the child on the night of the fatal accident when he told his parents, "I can't sleep because I can't get the pictures out of my head." The act of externalizing these disturbing images by making a drawing had therapeutic value for this child in coming to terms with the traumatic experience of his sibling's death.

unbelievable tangle of all that's happening to you? Deciding what you want for your life?

These years can be confusing as well as challenging. With the desire for a greater sense of one's own identity — an answer to the question "Who am I?" — there may also come anxieties about how to arrive at an adequate answer to that central question. Adolescents are just on the edge of beginning to achieve what they want for themselves. The achievement of their goals and dreams seems nearly within their grasp. The possibility of death is a serious threat to that achievement.

In Erikson's model, psychosocial development at each stage depends significantly on the environment and the person's relationships with others. At each psychosocial stage certain aspects of death may be more important than others. For instance, to an infant, the sudden loss of a parent may be a major blow to the child's development of trust in the environment. The preschooler's fantasies of a parent's death may be accompanied by feelings of guilt. The adolescent's experience of a close friend's death may trigger anxieties concerning whether death could thwart the realization of one's own goals and dreams as

T A B L E 3-1   *Piaget's Model of Cognitive Development*

Age (approximate)	Developmental Period	Characteristics
Birth – 2 years	Sensorimotor	Focused on senses and motor abilities; learns object exists even when not observable (object permanence) and begins to remember and imagine ideas and experiences (mental representation).
2 – 7 years	Preoperational	Development of symbolic thinking and language to understand the world. (2–4 years) *Preconceptual subperiod:* sense of magical omnipotence; self as center of world; egocentric thought; all natural objects have feelings and intention (will). (4–6 years) *Prelogical subperiod:* beginning problem-solving; seeing is believing; trial and error; understanding of other points of view; more socialized speech; gradual decentering of self and discovery of correct relationships.
7 – 12 years	Concrete operational	Applies logical abilities to understanding concrete ideas; organizes and classifies information; manipulates ideas and experiences symbolically; able to think backwards and forwards; notion of reversibility; can think logically about things experienced.
12 + years	Formal operational	Reasons logically about abstract ideas and experiences; can think hypothetically about things never experienced; deductive and inductive reasoning; complexity of knowledge; many answers to questions; interest in ethics, politics, social sciences.

well. Thus, Erikson's model can help to supply some insight into what kinds of issues children may pay particular attention to at different times in their lives.

Jean Piaget: Cognitive Transformations

Jean Piaget is generally considered to have been the world's foremost child psychologist, a profound theorist as well as an astute observer of children's behavior. Many death researchers consider Piaget's model of cognitive development to be fundamental to an understanding of how children learn about death (see Table 3-1).[14]

According to Piaget's theory, an individual's mode of understanding the world changes significantly, in sequential stages, from infancy into adulthood. Piaget postulates four different periods of cognitive, or intellectual, development based on the characteristic ways in which children organize their experience of the world:

1. Sensorimotor
2. Preoperational
3. Concrete operational
4. Formal operational

Although each child exhibits a different rate of cognitive development, all move through these periods in the same order. Thus, Piaget's theory emphasizes *sequence*, not a direct age-stage correlation. Although particular cognitive abilities tend to fall within a specific age range, they develop earlier in some children and later in others. Therefore, the ages mentioned in discussing Piaget's model should be understood as approximations, not as norms.

In Piaget's model, the first two years of life are characterized as the *sensorimotor* period. The child begins to develop and strengthen sensory and motor abilities, becoming acquainted with the body and learning about the environment. This is not a period of conceptual development, because the child has not yet acquired the ability to name objects by use of language. A parent who leaves the room has simply vanished from the scene; there is no thought "My parent is in the other room." Piaget says, "As long as there is no subject, that is, as long as the child does not recognize itself as the origin of its own actions, it also does not recognize the permanency of objects other than itself."[15]

As the child experiences the changing flow of events in the environment, however, gradually certain patterns of continuities are perceived. These patterns become generalized into what Piaget terms schemes, which tie together the common features of actions carried out at different times. During this stage of development, Piaget says, "a Copernican revolution takes place," with the result that "at the end of this sensory-motor evolution, there are permanent objects, constituting a universe within which the child's own body exists also."

The next stage, between the ages of about two and seven, is what Piaget terms the *preoperational* period. The child's development centers on learning to use language and symbols to represent objects. Vocabulary develops at an astounding rate as the child becomes interested in naming everything in sight. Yet this period, as Piaget's term suggests, is prelogical — that is, characterized by an inability to visualize possible relationships or implications of events.

During the preoperational period, the child's primary developmental task is to explore and appraise his or her situation in the world. Frequently, this entails an intense questioning about nearly everything the child comes into contact with in the environment. Whereas during the sensorimotor period — from birth to about eighteen months — the child perceives the subjective and objective worlds as more or less fused into a single reality, during the preoperational period, the child seeks causes and explanations. The child tries to come to terms with the changes that result from the divorce between his or her subjective experience and the objective environment.

Between the ages of about seven to eleven or twelve, the third period, that of *concrete operations,* predominates. At this stage, the child begins to use logic to solve problems. The child can think logically about things without having to have their relationships demonstrated directly. The ability to do arithmetic, for instance, requires the recognition that the numbers are symbols for quantities. The child is able to manipulate such concepts in a logical fashion, although still unable to engage in abstract thinking. That is, the ability to think logically can be applied to objects, but not yet to hypotheses, which require the ability to

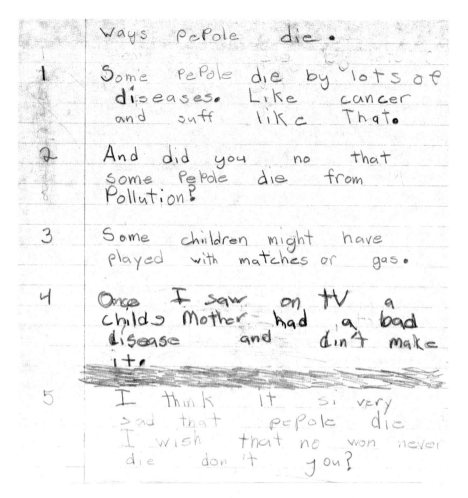

Figure 3-4 *Ways People Die: A Child's Explanation*

carry out operations on operations. Thus, the characteristic mode of thought in the preoperational period emphasizes simultaneously the concreteness and the logic of *things* (see Figure 3-4). During this period, children can think forward and backward in time, and they demonstrate an appreciation of time as "passing," although their comprehension of such measurements as time and space does not yet allow them to manipulate these concepts with the flexibility or abstraction that comes with the ability to engage in formal operations of thought.

The fourth and final period, that of *formal operations,* begins at about the age of eleven or twelve and extends into adulthood—although a person's fundamental way of seeing the world is thought to be fairly well established by about the age of fifteen. With the arrival of formal operational thinking, the child is able to "think about thinking," that is, to formulate or master concepts that are purely abstract or symbolic. As the endpoint of a complex process of cognitive development, this period is characterized by highly sophisticated operations of thought.

Relations of correspondence or implication between complex sets of statements can be perceived, analogies recognized, and assumptions or deductions made. Such operations make it possible to predict outcomes without having to try them out in the real world. In a chess game, for example, formal operations of thought allow the player to consider a number of complicated strategies, and to predict the likely result of each move, without having to touch a single piece on the board. Likewise, by mentally manipulating a wide range of related ideas and possibilities, the child can hypothesize the implications of an ethical or political issue. At the level of formal operations, the child is capable of using analysis and reflection to make sense of his or her experience and to formulate a coherent model of the world.

Cognitive Development and Children's Concepts of Death

How does Piaget's model of cognitive development apply to children's concepts of death? A partial answer is supplied by a study conducted by Gerald Koocher of children ranging in age from six to fifteen.[16] After the children were tested to determine which of Piaget's periods each fitted into, each child was asked four questions about death.[17] We take the first question asked through three periods, and then look briefly at responses to the other three questions. You might want to answer each of these questions for yourself.

Preoperational Understandings of Death

The first questions asked was, "What makes things die?" Children in the preoperational stage (which in Koocher's study included children from six to ten years of age) made use of fantasy reasoning, magical thinking, and realistic causes of death expressed in some cases in egocentric terms. Here are some sample responses:

Carol (age 7.3): "They eat poison and stuff, pills. You'd better wait until your Mom gives them to you." [*The researcher asks, "Anything else?"*] "Drinking poison water and stuff like going swimming alone."

Nancy (6.5): "When they eat bad things, like if you went with a stranger and they gave you a candy bar with poison on it. [*Anything else?*] Yes, you can die if you swallow a dirty bug."

David (7.8): "A bird might get real sick and die if you catch it. [*Anything else?*] They could eat the wrong foods like aluminum foil. That's all I can think of."

Koocher's findings were given general corroboration in a study done by Helen Swain, describing some general traits of the preoperational child.[18] In addition, Swain studied children two to four years of age—earlier in the preoperational stage than Koocher's subjects. When the concept of finality was investigated, most of the children in Swain's study expressed the notion that

My Gold Fish

My gold fish dies	And I feel very sad.
lots of times and	And I learned a
last week she died	rhyme and this is
And every time	how it goes
she dies I don't cry.	Too sad
But in my heart I cry	Too bad.

A six-year-old

death was reversible. They attributed the return of life to the good effects of ambulances, hospitals, or doctors whose participation is often summoned magically, as if a dead person could ring up the hospital and say, "Will you send me an ambulance over here? I'm dead and I need you to fix me up."

About two-thirds of Swain's study group said that death is unlikely or avoidable, or is brought on only by unusual events such as an accident or catastrophe. About one-third expressed disbelief that death could happen to them or to their families. Nearly half were uncertain whether they would ever die, or else thought they would die only in the remote future.

Concrete Operational Understandings of Death

During the concrete operational period of cognitive development, children tend to name intentional as well as unintentional means by which a person may die. The child has become familiar with, and can name, a wider range of causes of death. In Koocher's study, most of the children in this group were between ages nine and twelve.

Deborah (12.0): "Accidents, cars, guns, or a knife. Old age, sickness, taking dope, or drowning."

Kenny (9.5): "Cancer, heart attacks, poison, guns, bullets, or if someone drops a boulder on you."

Todd (7.5): "Knife, arrow, guns, and lots of stuff. You want me to tell you all of them? [*As many as you want.*] Hatchets and animals, and fires and explosions, too."

Formal Operational Understandings of Death

The final period of cognitive development in Piaget's model comprises children who use formal operations of thought. This period extends from about the age of eleven or twelve into adulthood. (Although in Koocher's study most of the children in this category were twelve or older, some as young as nine or ten used formal operations of thought.) By this point children typically demonstrate possession of a mature concept of death: They understand that death is irreversible and permanent, that it is universal and inevitable, and that it involves the cessation of physiological functioning. This understanding is reflected in their responses to the question "What makes things die?"

Ed (15.7): "You mean death in a physical sense? [*Yes.*] Destruction of a vital organ or life force within us."

George (13.5): "They get old and their body gets all worn out, and their organs don't work as well as they used to."

Dean (10.5): "When someone gets too old. You can also die of a sickness, or if you couldn't have enough to eat."

Paula (12.2): "When the heart stops, blood stops circulating. You stop breathing, and that's it. [*Anything else?*] Well, there's lots of ways it can get started, but that's what really happens."

A Mature Concept of Death

Thus, through three successive periods of cognitive development, children's responses to the question "What makes things die?" reflects progress toward the mature understanding of death. The answer to the other three questions asked by Koocher also elicited recognizable differences among the three stages.

Asked "How do you make dead things come back to life?" children who conceived of death as reversible gave answers like: "You can help them; give them hot food and keep them healthy so it won't happen again." Another child said, "No one ever taught me about that, but maybe you could give them some kind of medicine and take them to the hospital to get better." Children in the later stages, however, were able to recognize death as permanent: "If it was a tree, you could water it. If it's a person, you could rush them to the emergency room, but it would do no good if they were dead already." Another child said, "Maybe some day we'll be able to do it, but not now. Scientists are working on that problem."

Asked the third question, "When will you die?," children in the preoperational period provided answers ranging from "When I'm seven" (from a six-year-old) to "Three hundred years." At this age, children understood too little about time and death to be able to relate the two to make sense of them realistically. In contrast, the older children typically expected to live out a statistically correct lifespan, or a bit more; the usual age at which death was expected was about eighty.

In answer to the researchers' fourth question, "What will happen when you die?," one nine-and-a-half-year-old said, "They'll help me come back alive." The researcher asked, "Who?" "My father, my mother, and my grandfather," the child responded, "They'll keep me in bed and feed me and keep me away from rat poison and stuff."

According to some early developmental models of how children learn about death, a child of nine would understand that none of those measures would work. Thus, this example illustrates the point that age-and-stage correlations provide, at best, a rule of thumb concerning how children develop. As with any

Childhood activities such as "playing dead" can be a means of experimenting with various concepts, trying them on for size, and thus arriving at a more comprehensive and manageable sense of reality.

model of human behavior, the age-stage developmental framework is indicative, not rigorously descriptive.

In answer to the same question, an eight-and-a-half-year-old replied, "You go to heaven and all that will be left of you will be a skeleton. My friend has some fossils of people. A fossil is just a skeleton." Notice how the child makes use of comparison to help interpret what happens when death occurs. An eleven-year-old said, "I'll feel dizzy and tired and pass out, and then they'll bury me and I'll rot away. You just disintegrate and only your bones will be left."

A twelve-year-old said, "I'll have a nice funeral and be buried and leave all my money to my son." One ten-year-old said, "If I tell you, you'll laugh." The researcher assured the child, "No, I won't, I want to know what you really think." Thus encouraged, the child continued, "I think I'm going to be reincarnated as a plant or animal, whatever they need at that particular time." The ability to imagine what things might be like in the future is seen in these responses.

Play activities can help the child deal with his or her concerns about death. Play can be a means of exorcizing fears, trying out roles, making decisions, investigating consequences of actions, experimenting with value judgments, and finding a comfortable self-image.[19] Games like cowboys and Indians and cops and robbers reflect, in part, the child's attempt to reach some understanding about the place of death in his or her world.

Sources of Attitudes Toward Death

Just as the cognitive ability to grasp a mature concept of death develops gradually throughout childhood, so too do attitudes toward death. These attitudes derive from a complex array of interrelated sources, such as the cultural environment, personal experiences with death, and messages from parents and peers.

It is often difficult, if not impossible, to pinpoint the genesis of ideas about death that a child may acquire in the natural course of social interactions. Take, for example, the following incident: Two children, ages eight and ten, were asked to draw a picture of a funeral (see Figure 3-5). They got out their colored pencils and immersed themselves in the task. After a while, Heather (who is ten) said to Matt (eight), "Hey, you've got smiles on those faces! This is supposed to be a funeral. What are they doing with smiles on their faces?" In her model of appropriate death-related behavior, people don't smile at funerals; to her younger brother, smiles are perfectly acceptable. One can only surmise the influences that led to such a strong statement about what kind of behavior is appropriate at funerals; but in interactions such as this one between siblings, attitudes about death that are expressed by others become incorporated into a child's understanding of death.

Early Parental Messages

To consider parental messages about death, think back to your childhood. What messages did you receive about death that remain to this day in the back of your mind? Possibly some messages were conveyed directly: "This is what death is," or, "This is how we behave in relation to death." Or perhaps some messages were indirect: "Let's not talk about it. . . ." How would the rest of that sentence go? Let's not talk about it — because it's not something that people talk about? One woman, for example, was told, "You shouldn't look at it." When there was a dead animal on the highway, her mother admonished, "Put your head down, children shouldn't see that." That is a very clear message about what kind of behavior is appropriate toward death.

Other messages about death may be communicated unconsciously. Consider the notion of replaceability. A child's pet dies, and the parent says, "It's okay, dear, we'll get another one." When one woman was talking about the shock of her husband's recent death, her young child broke in and said, "Don't worry, Mommie, we'll get you another one."

Parental attitudes shape the behavior not only of the child but also of the adult that child will become and how that adult conveys attitudes toward death to his or her own children. A woman now in her thirties tells the following story: "I can remember a time when my mother ran over a cat. I wasn't with

The Shroud

A mother once had a little seven-year-old boy with such a sweet, beautiful face that no one could look at him without loving him, and she loved him more than anything in the world. Suddenly, the child fell sick, and God took him. The mother was inconsolable and wept day and night. Soon after he was buried, the child began to appear in places where he had sat playing in his lifetime. When his mother wept, he too wept, and when morning came he vanished. Then when the mother could not stop crying, he appeared one night wrapped in the little white shroud he had been buried in and wearing a wreath of flowers on his head. He sat down at her feet and said: "Oh, mother, if you don't stop crying I won't be able to sleep in my coffin, for my shroud is wet with all the tears that fall on it." When she heard that, the mother was horrified, and from then on she shed no tears. The next night the child came again. He held a candle in his hand and said: "You see, my shroud is almost dry. Now I can rest in my grave." After that, the mother gave her grief into God's keeping and bore it silently and patiently. The child never came again, but slept in his little bed under the ground.

Grimm's Tales for Young and Old

her in the car, but I recall my mother coming home and just totally falling apart. She ran into the bedroom and cried for hours. Since that time, I've never killed anything. I'm extremely conscientious about that — if there's an insect on me or in my house, I'll pick it up and carry it outside."

Cultural Influences

The cultural factors described in Chapter 1 as influencing attitudes toward death affect children as well as adults. Television programs, cartoons, movies, and jokes frequently make reference to death; even when not directed specifically toward children, these cultural influences are pervasive.

News reports of disasters or death, and the reactions of adults to such reports, convey to the child information about cultural attitudes toward dying and death. A child's response to such messages is related to his or her level of cognitive development, as Martha Wolfenstein and her colleagues found when they conducted a study of children's reactions to the death of President John F. Kennedy.[20] From the mass of details about the president's assassination, children tended to select those particular aspects related to their own developmental concerns: Children of elementary-school age tended to express concerns about the appearance of the president's body and the effect of the death on members of his immediate family; older children voiced concerns about the impact of the president's death on American politics and society.

Similar developmentally related concerns appear to be present in reports of children's reactions to the deaths of the *Challenger* astronauts. For example, when a group of first graders was asked to draw pictures of the shuttle accident, the astronauts were often depicted returning safely to earth where they could be saved by rescue teams.[21]

A

B

Figure 3-5 *Children's Drawings of a Funeral*
Instructed to draw a picture of a funeral, a sister (age ten) and brother (eight) did so. The ten-year-old's drawing (A) emphasizes the emotional responses of the survivors. We see the picture as if we are looking in (and down) upon their grief. The figures in the first two pews have tears streaming down their faces and one woman shouts "No!" At ten, this child reflects on the sorrowful and unwelcome nature of death. When questioned about the empty pews, she said they were for anyone who came late.

The eight-year-old's drawing (B) is viewed from a similar perspective (looking in and down at the scene). Here we see the survivors group around a flag-draped and flower-bedecked coffin. The figures are portrayed with smiles on their faces. The focus in this drawing is on the symbols of death (e.g., the casket) and on the ceremony rather than emotions. During the drawing session, the older sister commented that her brother's picture was "too happy" for a funeral scene.

In some of the drawings, the astronauts' bodies were shown as intact; in others, although the bodies were in pieces, the children said they could be made whole again by rescue crews or hospital workers. As we have seen, this interest in the condition of the astronauts' bodies and in the possibility of rescue is appropriate and usual for children of this age group.

Children's literature also communicates messages about life and death related to cultural attitudes. Of about two hundred nursery rhymes examined in one study, about half described the wonder and beauty of life and the other half dealt with "the many ways in which humans and animals die or are mistreated."[22] These rhymes included accounts of murder, choking to death, torment and cruelty, maiming, misery and sorrow, stories of lost or abandoned children, and themes depicting poverty and want. A significant proportion of classic children's stories also depict deaths, near-deaths, or the threat of death.

These classic stories, rhymes, and fairytales have been joined in the recent past by a genre of children's books designed especially to help children find answers to their questions about dying and death. (A selected listing of these books can be found in Chapter 8.) In many of these books, particularly those for very young children, death is presented as an event occurring within the natural cycle. Often these stories include the suggestion that, like the transition from one season to the next, after each ending in nature there is renewal. One writer has remarked that "it is consistent that a society which produced children's books explaining the mysteries of molecules and atoms, of evolution and birth, should also produce works of facts and fiction which attempt to define and explain death."[23]

Cultural attitudes toward dying and death also can be communicated through educational programs and presentations designed to provide opportunities for children to discuss these topics with parents and other adults. One of the most innovative examples of this phenomenon occurred when the Boston Children's Museum held a participatory show entitled "Endings: An Exhibit

---

 ### The Three Little Pigs

. . . This made the wolf so angry that he vowed he would eat the pig, and that nothing should stop him. So he climbed up on the roof and jumped down the chimney.

But the wise little pig was ready for him, for he had built a big fire and hung a great kettle of water over it, right under the chimney. When the pig heard the wolf coming he took the cover off the kettle, and down fell the wolf right into it. Before he could crawl out, the little pig popped the lid back on again, and in a trice he had the wolf boiling.

That night the little pig had boiled wolf for supper. So he lived in his brick and mortar house till he grew too big for it, and never was he troubled by a wolf again.

Journeys Through Bookland, Volume One

Little Red Riding-Hood

. . . "Dear me, Grandmamma, what great arms you have!"
   The wolf replied:
   "They are so much better to hug you with, my child."
   "Why, Grandmamma, what great legs you have got!"
   "That is to run the better, my child!"
   "But, Grandmamma, what great ears you've got!"
   "That is to hear the better, my child."
   "But, Grandmamma, what great eyes you've got!"
   "They are so much better to see you with, my child."
   Then the little girl, who was now very much frightened, said:
   "Oh, Grandmamma, what great teeth you have got!"
   "THEY ARE THE BETTER TO EAT YOU UP!"
   With these words the wicked wolf fell upon Little Red Riding-Hood and ate her
up in a moment.

Journeys Through Bookland, Volume One

About Death and Loss." Included were songs, stories, games, videotapes, and other exhibits designed to stimulate the sharing of thoughts and feelings about death between parents and children. Although many parents, educators, and other professionals praised the exhibit, it was criticized by some for impinging upon children's "innocence" and "sense of joy" by forcing them to think about dying and death.

Cultural influences on children's socialization are also found in distinctions that appear to be correlated with gender roles. For example, a study of junior high students found that attitudes toward death differed between males and females. These differences, said researchers, were normally "in the direction expected based on traditional sex roles."[24]

In comparison with males, for example, females were generally more in favor of abortion, valued funerals, and expressed greater concern about what might happen to their bodies after death. On the issue of capital punishment, boys were about equally divided, pro and con, whereas girls expressed uncertainty or disagreement. With respect to the students' beliefs about life after death, males were described by researchers as "more decisive" and females as "more variable" in their beliefs.

Developmental models and surveys of cultural factors are useful in gaining a perspective on ways in which children generally formulate understandings about death. For any given child, however, we must fill in this general framework with specific information: the child's personality, unique life experiences, and the kind of family and social resources available for learning about death. All these factors are influential.

Life Experiences

Self-concept seems to influence a child's ability to cope with death. Research indicates that a child with a good self-concept is generally less fearful about death. This correlation also applies to adults. People who feel good about themselves and are comfortable with themselves, who see themselves as active, vital, and interesting, and who have caring relationships with others tend to be less fearful about dying and death.

Consider adult responses to death that you may have observed. How did different persons demonstrate their particular understandings and attitudes about death? What kind of personal and social resources were mobilized to cope with death? Whereas one person might be curious about all the details surrounding a death, someone else might prefer to know as little as possible. The ten-year-old's phrase, "It's sickening, don't talk about it!" can sometimes survive into adulthood.

Significant experiences, such as the death of someone close, are likely to influence the child's attitude as well as understanding. The attitude of a child who is allowed to ask questions about such an experience is likely to be quite different from that of the child who is given to understand that death is not an appropriate topic for children's questions. The experience of a young child who observes the dramatic changes occurring among family members as a result of death, but who is not permitted to participate in any of the funeral rituals or to ask questions, may long afterward carry the notion that death is mysterious and unmentionable.

I recall with utter clarity the first great shock of my life. A scream came from the cottage next door. I rushed into the room, as familiar as my own home. The Larkin kids, Conor, Liam and Brigid, all hovered about the alcove in which a mattress of bog fir bedded old Kilty. They stood in gape-mouthed awe.

I stole up next to Conor. "Grandfar is dead," he said.

Their ma, Finola, who was eight months pregnant, knelt with her head pressed against the old man's heart. It was my very first sight of a dead person. He was a waxy, bony specimen lying there with his open mouth showing no teeth at all and his glazed eyes staring up at me and me staring back until I felt my own ready to pop out of their sockets.

Oh, it was a terrible moment of revelation for me. All of us kids thought old Kilty had the magic of the fairies and would live forever, a tale fortified by the fact that he was the oldest survivor of the great famine, to say nothing of being a hero of the Fenian Rising of '67 who had been jailed and fearfully tortured for his efforts.

I was eleven years old at that moment. Kilty had been daft as long as I could recall, always huddled near the fire mumbling incoherently. He was an ancient old dear, ancient beyond age, but nobody ever gave serious consideration to the fact he might die.

Leon Uris, *Trinity*

On the other hand, the child who experiences the death of a close family member or a friend may arrive at an understanding of death that generally would be associated with a later stage of development. A 1979 study showed that when children younger than six years had experienced a concrete encounter with death, they gained an understanding of it that was precocious for their stage of development.[25] One six-year-old who witnessed the accidental death of her sibling expressed what seemed to be a very clear understanding that death is final, that people die, and that she herself could die. She was concerned about how she could protect herself and her friends from the dangerous circumstances that led to her brother's death. This attitude toward death was reflected in her admonitions to schoolmates to be especially aware of preventing accidents. Along with her understanding of the reality of death, she possessed an attitude toward death that reflected the particulars of her experience.

Another kind of experience is reflected in drawings made by Cambodian children in refugee camps.[26] Death is the predominant theme in those drawings. These children had experienced starvation, and they represented that fact in their drawings. One child's picture depicted a woman in the midst of about six smaller bodies; the caption read, "Mother's Dead Children." In such catastrophic experiences of death, children seem to develop understandings of death earlier than they would in more ordinary circumstances. Children who experience the horror of widespread death during times of war or prolonged catastrophe are likely to develop a much more fatalistic attitude toward death than their counterparts whose experiences with death occur under more benign conditions.

The child as survivor of the death of someone close or as victim of a life-threatening illness involves issues beyond those discussed in connection with the general characteristics of children's socialization. Chapter 8 is devoted to the experience of bereavement and life-threatening illness in children's lives.

In the present context, the point is that life experiences, and particularly those that involve an intimate encounter with death, may shape an individual's unique beliefs about death. Perhaps only later in life, as an adult, does a person become aware of the real and lasting impact of a childhood experience.

Talking with Children About Death

However tempered they may be by the influence of peers and what is learned in the classroom and elsewhere outside the home, parental attitudes significantly influence the child's attitude toward death. Thus, parents have natural concerns regarding what to tell their children about death.[27] What can be told? What should be told? How can I talk about it? What will the child understand? We have already seen that children develop their own concepts about death, whether or not they receive parental instruction — or even if the topic is considered taboo by parents. Indeed, it seems that children want to learn about death, just as they want to learn about everything that touches their lives.

Cpl. Edward Belfer, U.S. Army Photo

Children's early encounters with death may come in ways that are extraordinary. The child seen here was one of many German citizens who, at the end of World War II, were ordered by the provisional military government of the U.S. Third Army to view the exhumed bodies of some 800 Russians, Poles, and Czechs who had been killed while imprisoned in the concentration camp at Flossenberg.

One child wrote, "Dear God, what's it like when you die? Nobody will tell me. I just want to know. I don't want to do it."

Parents explaining death to children should put honesty foremost. Be straightforward. How much to disclose to a child must be based on how willing the parent is to face the consequences of the issues that are raised in the child's mind. A parent who sets a ground rule that it's okay to be open and honest in talking about death ought to be aware that there will probably be times when the child wants to start a discussion and the parent is tired or would rather avoid the subject.

Second, don't put off introducing the topic of death to a child. When the experience of a close death precedes the discussion, the parent is faced with the need to provide an explanation in the midst of the crisis. This unfortunate circumstance arises when a parent puts it off "because it's not really going to

He lived a long way from here
Lew's mother explained.
You never asked
so I never told you
Grandpa died.

I want him to come back.
I miss him, Lewis said.
I have been waiting for him
and I miss him especially tonight.

I do too
said Lew's mother.
But you made him come back
for me tonight
by telling me what you remember.

Charlotte Zolotow, *My Grandson Lew*

happen," only to find that "I'm confronted with it happening right now in my family and the child has to be told something." When a family member is dying or someone has died suddenly and unexpectedly, the explanation to the child is charged with all the emotions that the parent is dealing with, making the aim of a clear explanation much more difficult to attain.

Third, set your level of explanation to the child's powers of understanding. This is determined partly by the child's cognitive stage and partly by his or her experience. By using the child's interest and ability to comprehend as a guide, the parent can provide an explanation that is appropriate to the child's particular circumstances. Such an explanation can assist the child in coping with his or her general concerns about death as well as the specific issues that may arise in conjunction with the experience of a close death.

A supportive listener goes a long way toward increasing the child's openness to dealing with death. Valuing a child's ideas and encouraging their candid expression is an excellent way to facilitate exploration and discussion of his or her understandings about death. As their children's mainstay, parents who are open to an interchange with their children on any subject will have a number of skills and resources that can be employed when the discussion turns to death.

When you talk to children about death, it is important to verify what it is they think you've told them. Have them tell you what they learned or what they heard you saying about death. Children tend to generalize from known concepts to make new experiences fit. This technique can result in a very literal-minded interpretation of new information, especially as practiced by young children, who tend to emphasize the concreteness of things. Recognizing this, try to keep your communication free of associations that might lead to confusion in the child's mind. Metaphorical explanations about death can help provide a child-sized picture that aids understanding, but unless fact is clearly separated from fancy, the child may grasp the literal details instead of the underlying message the analogy was intended to convey.

A story can illustrate how easily confusion can arise when death is explained to children. A girl of age five was told that her grandfather's cancer was like a seed that grew in his body; it grew and grew until he couldn't live in his body anymore and he died. Her parents didn't notice that ever afterward, all through childhood, she never ate another seed. Not one. Not a cucumber seed, watermelon seed, no seeds. Finally, at age twenty-one, she was asked, "Why are you avoiding the seeds? Isn't that a little bizarre? What's wrong with the seeds?" Her automatic response was, "You swallow them and you die." After all those years, she saw the fallacy of her compulsion to avoid eating seeds. It would have been useful if someone had asked her when she was five, "What will happen if you swallow that seed?"

We give children a great deal to get ahold of in their learnings about death. A child told that her goldfish "went to heaven" may make an elaborate picture of the pearly gates and different sections of heaven. Here is goldfish heaven, this is cat heaven, and over here is people heaven — a very organized concept that makes sense to a child. But we have to be careful that the concepts we convey to a child don't turn out to be dysfunctional.

One woman recalled that when she was three or four a favorite old black dog had to "go away for a long sleep." It wasn't until she was about seven years old that she realized that the dog wasn't away just napping someplace, at the puppy farm having a long sleep. If it was just "off somewhere to sleep," then a casual goodbye was fine. When she discovered that in fact her beloved dog was dead, she felt angry that she hadn't had the opportunity to give it the right kind of goodbye.

Another woman's first experience with death occurred when she was three-and-a-half and her mother died. It seemed that her mother had just disappeared; she didn't know what had happened to her. Several years later, she began to realize that her mother had died and she started asking questions. Some people told her that her mother had been buried, and her thought was, "Why don't they dig her up?" Others said that her mother had gone to heaven, so she kept looking at the sky, watching for her. With both of these concepts running through her young mind, she did her best to figure out, "How can my mother be buried in heaven?" That's a good example of the concreteness of a child's concepts about death.

A similar confusion is illustrated in the following story about a four-year-old whose brother (nine) told him that daddy had gone to heaven. The four-year-old promptly went and told his mother, "My daddy's on the roof!" She said, "What? Who told you that?" He said, "Andrew did." The older brother then explained, "We were looking out the window and I told him that daddy was in heaven up there." To the four-year-old, the highest "up there" was up on the roof.

One of the most helpful things we can do in relation to children and death is to gain an understanding of what is "normal." In other words, what is realistic for a child? If you tell a four-year-old that someone who has died is "up there" and you also say that Santa Claus lands on the roof on Christmas Eve, he

The Dead Mouse

We had been out of town and the neighbors had been caring for our various pets. When we returned, we found that our cat had, as cats will, caught and killed a mouse and had laid it out ceremoniously in front of his bowl in the garage. I discovered that that had happened when I heard loud screams from the garage. "Pudley's killed a mouse. There's a dead mouse in the garage!" Loud screams, for the whole neighborhood to hear. I went downstairs. It was the first time that I had a chance to observe how my children dealt with death. I said, "Oh, there is?" "Right here," they said, "Look!" They began to tell me how they had determined it was dead. It was not moving. They had poked at it several times and it didn't move. Matthew, who was five years old, added that it didn't look like it was ever going to move again. That was his judgment that the mouse was dead.

I said to him, "Well, what are we going to do?" I could feel myself being slightly repulsed; my fingers went to my nose. It was obvious to me that the mouse was dead—it had started to decay. Matt said very matter-of-factly, "Well, we'll have to bury it." Heather, seven, climbed on a chair and announced, "Not me. I'm not going to touch it. Don't bring it around here. Aughhh, dead mouse!" At that time, she was intent on being what she thought was feminine, and part of the stereotype involved not getting herself dirty.

So Matt volunteered for the job. "I'm going to need a shovel," he said. I stood back and watched, interested to see what would happen. I noticed that he didn't touch the mouse. From somewhere he already had gotten the idea that it wasn't appropriate to touch dead things. He carefully lifted it with the shovel and took it into the backyard to dig a hole. Heather peered around and watched at a safe distance.

After the mouse was buried, Matt came back and said, "I'm going to need some wood, a hammer, and a nail." I thought, "Oh great! He's going to perform some kind of little ceremony and place a symbol of some kind on the grave." Matt went to the woodpile and carefully selected a piece of wood maybe two inches long and another piece a bit wider, perhaps three inches wide and about four or five inches long. I thought, "Tombstone?" He got the nail and put the pieces of wood together in the shape of a cross.

I thought, "Oh. A cross, religious symbol, burial, funeral—all the things I knew about what happens with a dead body." Matt picked up a marking pen and wrote on the front of the cross: "DEAD MOUSE. KEEP OUT!" And he pounded it into the ground in front of where the mouse was buried. I thought, "What's going on in this kid's mind?"

I asked him, "Does that mean that when I die there should be a sign saying, "Dead Mommie. Keep out"? He put his hand on his hip and looked at me with that disgust that five-year-olds can muster for somebody who is *so* dumb, and said, "Of course not. You're going to be buried in one of those places where they have bodies. This is a backyard. Kids could ride their bikes over it. Who would know that there is a mouse buried back here?" I was flabbergasted.

A few weeks later there was a long discussion about what the mouse would look like at that time. My first thoughts were, "Don't do that! You can't dig it up. It's not

continued

---

continued from previous page

nice. It's not good. The mouse has to rest his spirit." Then I realized that all those things were coming from that place in me that didn't want to see what a month-old dead mouse looked like.

So I kept quiet. They dug and dug, and I could feel the sweat dripping off me. They dug a huge hole, but could find no remnants of the mouse. I was a bit relieved. But that brought up all kinds of questions about what happened to the mouse. I made this elaborate picture of a compost pile, really a lengthy explanation. Finally I realized that they didn't understand at all and that what I was saying was of no interest to them.

I said, "Well, it's like if you buried an orange." Something safe, I thought, something I can deal with that can be dug up day by day to see how it goes back into the earth.

They buried an orange and dug it up and dug it up and dug it up. And it wasn't an orange anymore.

I came away from that experience thinking, "Where did they learn all that? Matt's behavior, particularly. . . . Where did he get that from?"

---

may decide that Santa Claus and the person who has died are great buddies. He might make up stories about how they work together, making toys, feeding the reindeer, and so on.

Children are apt to point out any inconsistencies in what we tell them about death. When one three-year-old's young playmate was killed, his mother explained to him that Jesus had come and taken his friend to heaven. His concrete response was, "Well, that's an awful thing to do; I want to play with him. Jesus isn't very nice if he comes down here and takes my friend from me."

In discussing death with a child, it helps if you understand the child's belief system, the kind of thought processes he or she uses to understand the world; and then from your very first statement ask yourself, How can this path go in the child's mind? Where's the end of the road? If I explain death in this way, which I think is appropriate, how will it wind up in his or her understanding?

The most useful approach is to simply talk with the child about what he or she believes, to enter into the child's understanding of what death is all about. It is useful to ask the child the four questions mentioned earlier: How do people die? What will happen when you die? When will you die? How do you bring things back to life?

Many adults tend to worry a lot about children, especially about their encounters with death. Are they doing all right? Will they be okay? Is death going to be too hard for them to handle? Can they survive this particular loss? (Underlying this concern is worry about ourselves too.) In general, children do remarkably well. Erik Erikson said, "Healthy children will not fear life if their parents have integrity not to fear death."[28]

© Carol A. Foote

The most important contribution of an adult talking with a child about death is often to be simply a good listener.

Further Readings

Sylvia Anthony. *The Discovery of Death in Childhood and After*. New York: Basic Books, 1972.

Audrey K. Gordon and Dennis Klass. *They Need to Know: How to Teach Children About Death*. Englewood Cliffs, N.J.: Prentice-Hall, 1979.

Earl A. Grollman, editor. *Explaining Death to Children*. Boston: Beacon Press, 1967.

Stephen V. Gullo, Paul Patterson, and John E. Schowalter, editors. *Death and Children: A Guide for Educators, Parents, and Caregivers*. Dobbs Ferry, N.Y.: Tappan Press/Center for Thanatology, 1985.

Edgar N. Jackson. *Telling a Child About Death*. New York: Hawthorne Books, 1965.

Richard Lonetto. *Children's Conceptions of Death*. New York: Springer, 1980.

Roger Rosenblatt. *Children of War*. Garden City, N.Y.: Anchor Press/Doubleday, 1983.

Marguerita Rudolph. *Should the Children Know? Encounters with Death in the Lives of Children*. New York: Schocken Books, 1978.

Judith Stillion and Hannelore Wass. "Children and Death," in *Dying: Facing the Facts*, edited by Hannelore Wass, pp. 208–235. Washington, D.C.: Hemisphere, 1979. Also reprinted in *Death: Current Perspectives*, Third Edition, edited by Edwin S. Shneidman, pp. 225–249. Palo Alto, Calif.: Mayfield Publishing Co., 1980.

Hannelore Wass and Charles A. Corr, editors. *Childhood and Death*. Washington, D.C.: Hemisphere, 1984.

Robert Westall. *Children of the Blitz: Memories of Wartime Childhood*. New York: Viking, 1986.

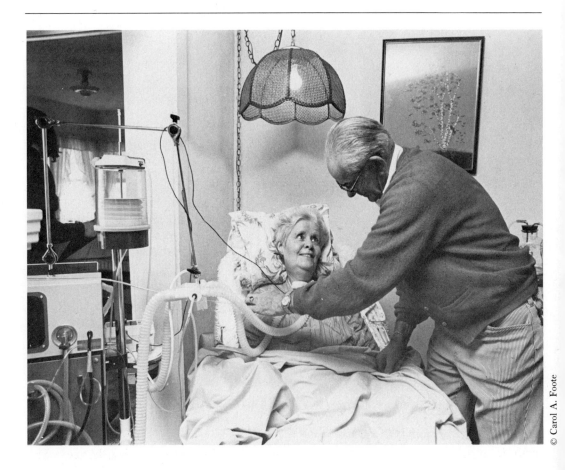

Home care may not come immediately to mind when one thinks of health care systems, yet this centuries-old tradition of care for the ill and the dying is once again emerging as an option for many. Innovations in sophisticated medical life-support equipment often make it possible for the seriously ill to be cared for at a high level of medical technology within the home.

CHAPTER 4

Health Care Systems: Patients, Staff, and Institutions

Most people fear death less than they fear the process of dying. Whereas the struggle to come to grips with the finitude of physical existence is a constant of human experience, the way we die is not, and has been significantly altered by technology and the rise of the modern hospital. Our medical institutions are designed to soothe and heal; yet it seems that their salve is not always comforting for the dying.

Think about the end of your own life. What do you fear about dying? Many people say that they fear dying in pain and loneliness, amid complicated machines that hum softly in an impersonal setting. Oriented toward the goal of preserving life, hospitals have sometimes been remiss about meeting the specific needs of patients and their families. Death is often treated as an anomaly.

The Modern Hospital

The first hospitals were established, centuries ago, to aid the homeless and the hopelessly ill. (The word *hospital* derives from the Latin *hospitum,* meaning a place that receives guests.) The distant relative of our modern hotels, hostels, and hospices, early hospitals aided sick travelers and victims of disaster. Physicians generally functioned independently of hospitals; members of religious communities provided the nursing care available within them.

In contrast to the hospital as a place primarily for the dying stands the modern hospital as a setting for acute intensive care. The association between physicians and hospitals is also a comparatively recent development. Highly specialized care is made available to patients who usually stay in the hospital only a brief time. The typical hospital patient expects to regain well-being and return to normal life.

The 7000 registered acute care hospitals in the United States provide care for more than 1 million Americans, on average, each day.[1] Hospital care accounts for the largest proportion of personal health care costs, and hospital costs have been increasing rapidly for nearly two decades. This increase is attributed to four main factors: price inflation, more hospital employees, wage increases, and changes in both the quantity and quality of the medical technologies used by hospitals. Annual health care expenditures in the United States totaled $387.4 billion in 1984, nearly 11 percent of the gross national product, with an average cost per person of $1580.[2] In less than a decade, per capita health care costs have more than tripled (see Figure 4-1).

The resident population of nursing homes has also grown rapidly. Nearly 26,000 nursing care facilities offer longer-term care to 1.5 million residents, with about one-fifth providing skilled nursing care.[3] In 1980, about 10 percent of persons age 75 and over lived in nursing homes, and nearly $21 billion was spent on nursing home care, with Medicaid providing about half of the financial support.[4] The rising cost of health care is among the reasons many people are

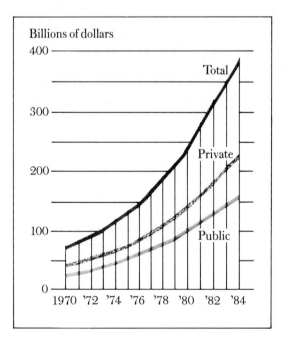

Figure 4-1   *National Health Expenditures: 1970 – 1984*
Source: Statistical Abstract of the United States 1986, 106th ed. (Washington: Government Printing Office, 1985), p. 94.

now questioning whether some chronically ill and dying persons, including those who are aged, could receive comparable care in less expensive alternative settings.

Health Care for the Dying: An Overview

A person entering a health care facility does so to receive medical and nursing care appropriate to a particular malady. The kind and quality of care provided depends largely on the nature of the relationships among three fundamental aspects of institutional health care: (1) the patient; (2) the institution's administrative and organizational patterns; (3) the medical and nursing staff and their attitudes and methods in carrying out the institution's goals. Each side of this triangle — the patient, the institution, and the staff — contributes to the overall shape of health care.

Consider first the patient's relationship to the structure of the institution and to its personnel. What conditions cause many people to fear the possibility of dying in an institutional setting? Why do institutions designed to provide care and comfort often seem impersonal and unfeeling?

The patient's experience is influenced by the hospital's rules, regulations, and conventions — written and unwritten. Because hospitals are generally organized to deal with many different patients, their capacity to meet the needs of each individual patient may be limited. When the elderly aunt did her dying at home, as was common during the last century, she could be spoon-fed her favorite homemade soup by a member of her family. Today, in the hospital or nursing home, she is more likely to receive a standardized diet, perhaps served rather impersonally by an overworked and harried aide.

Because providing health care for many people requires maximally efficient use of facilities and staff, hospital procedures tend to be standardized and routine. The trade-off for more sophisticated health care, in many instances, seems to be less personal comfort and care.

The patient's family, instead of taking an active role as caregivers, may be relegated to maintaining a deathwatch in the hospital corridor or the waiting room down the hall, with one family member at a time squeezing into the patient's room to keep the bedside vigil. Often there is little or no private space where relatives can gather to discuss their concerns with hospital staff. Hallway meetings between staff and family symbolize for many the impersonality of the hospital.[5]

The hospital's unwritten rules, no less faithfully executed by staff, may contribute to this alienation. For example, it is a common convention that only a physician can respond to a patient's or family's questions concerning treatment or prognosis; nurses are expected to reply to such queries, "Ask your doctor." This convention can result in needless fears and unfounded suspicions, adding to the anxiety of patients and their families.

Death often seems taboo in the hospital. A patient near death may be given medication so that the schedule is not disrupted or the staff or other patients upset. Family members, too, may be urged to accept a tranquilizer to subdue their emotional reaction to a loved one's death. Few hospitals are prepared to cope with such emotional responses. Rather than encouraging their expression, the emphasis is on subduing, controlling, and restricting any reaction that might jeopardize institutional decorum.[6]

When death occurs in the institutional setting, it is often treated so secretly that one would hardly be aware that sometimes patients die. Aside from the few staff members charged with the task of preparing the body and trundling it off to be picked up by the mortician, even those who work in hospitals are sheltered from direct confrontation with death. The false-bottom gurney, which transports the corpse to a nondescript exit, camouflages its odious human cargo. Death is compartmentalized, shut away from public view.

This faceless bureaucratization carries over to public announcements of death. Rarely do newspaper obituaries or death notices name the hospital or nursing home where death occurred, referring instead to a nameless "local hospital." Apparently this evasiveness is meant to confirm the message that hospitals are in business to effect cures and to save lives; acknowledging that patients sometimes die might be deleterious to a hospital's image in the community.

To educate the interns in a large hospital about the special needs of the dying, Dr. Elisabeth Kübler-Ross wanted to let the patients speak their own case. She was initially told by staff members that no one was dying on their ward—there were only some patients who were very critically ill.[7] Even when death is a fairly common reality in one's environment, the operative response may still be denial.

Kübler-Ross's pioneering work in educating hospital personnel about the dying became a springboard for the current movement toward increased awareness of the special needs of the dying patient. By constantly asking hospital staffers for their gut reactions to the experiences of dying patients, she helped them become more aware of their thoughts and feelings about death.

Dedicated to saving lives, those who work in hospitals may suppress the feelings of helplessness that arise when they are unable to prevent death. The physician who relates to a dying patient in a cold, detached manner may be compensating for underlying feelings that are painful to acknowledge. The nurse who recognizes that death will soon sever a relationship with a patient may respond in a way that is predicated on the fear of becoming too personally involved. Moreover, because medicine is primarily devoted to meeting patients' physical needs, the emotional and psychological side of patient care is sometimes neglected.

Increasingly, however, hospital personnel are becoming aware that meeting the emotional needs of patients and their families can be as important as caring for bodily needs (see Figure 4-2). Contact that spans the usual professional distance reduces the sense of alienation between patients and medical staff. A nurse who steps into the room, sits down by the patient's bed, and demonstrates a willingness to listen is more likely to be successful in providing comfort than one who merely breezes in, remains standing, and

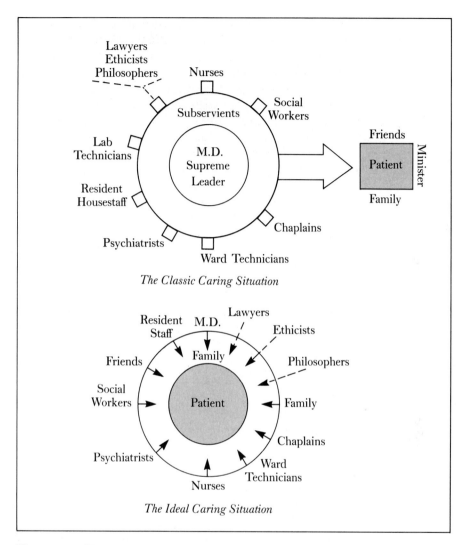

Figure 4-2 *Classic and Ideal Caring Situations*
Source: David Barton, ed., *Dying and Death: A Clinical Guide for Caregivers* (Baltimore: Williams & Wilkins, 1977), p. 181.

quips, "How're we today? Did we sleep well?" Skillful communication is a key to providing health care for the whole person.

A century ago, physicians did perhaps as much to console as to cure the patient. Indeed, consolation and palliative measures were sometimes all the medical practitioner could offer the patient. Today, our expectations are such that if a cure is not forthcoming, we feel somehow cheated. Medical malpractice has become a frequent allegation in the nation's courtrooms and a topic debated

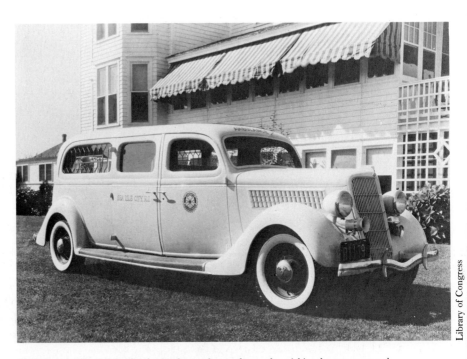

Library of Congress

Our expectations of medical care have changed greatly within the past several decades, from a time when ambulance service consisted mainly of transportation — as provided here by the Rotary Club in Sea Isle City, New Jersey — to the present, when sophisticated medical care is provided en route to the hospital by mobile paramedic units outfitted with life-sustaining devices and trained caregivers.

in state legislatures across the country. It is argued that, despite good medical practice, physicians may become scapegoats when a course of treatment does not result in the desired outcome.[8] We think medical science should provide us with an antidote for whatever ails us. Death seems less a natural event than a medical failure.[9] With the focus on cure so pervasive within the medical establishment, it comes as no surprise that funds and other resources are generally allocated most to acute care, less to chronic care, and least to care of the terminally ill and dying. In such a cultural context, biological death, the cessation of physical functions, may be preceded by social death.[10]

In a medical community where patients are supposed to get well, the dying patient may be treated as something of a deviant. The dying patient not only challenges the capabilities of medical science, but may confront medical practitioners with their own sense of mortality. Objectivity and detached concern may turn to avoidance when a patient clearly begins to die. Lawrence LeShan found that nurses characteristically took longer to answer the bedside calls of terminally ill patients than they took to answer calls of patients who were less severely ill.[11]

"I think in the next 10–20 years we'll have 'warehouses' with patients on life support systems, if the American public and physicians don't come to grips with and resolve the inherent conflicts involved in the present 'common' method for handling the terminally ill patient." *General practitioner*

"I do not think anybody should have the right to be God and decide death. In view of age and circumstances life may be prolonged to the benefit of patient and family." *Orthopedic surgeon*

"I am a doctor and I feel I should do all in my power to diagnose disease and sustain life." *Internist*

"We should not prolong misery when it's not indicated for other reasons. Everyone has a time to die and should be allowed to die with some dignity." *Urologist*

"The Physician Speaks,"
The Newsletter of Physician Attitudes

Avoidance of the dying is also demonstrated by the aversion of hospital personnel to discussing death when that topic is raised by the dying patient. Robert Kastenbaum has identified five strategies used by staff members in responding to a patient's desire to discuss death: (1) reassurance ("You're doing so well"); (2) denial ("Oh, you'll live to be a hundred"); (3) changing the subject ("Let's talk about something more cheerful"); (4) fatalism ("Well, we all have to die sometime"); (5) discussion ("What happened to make you feel that way?"). Few choose this last strategy, discussing death with the patient. The typical response tends to be evasion.[12]

We cannot expect institutional health care to be as personal as the care that the patient's family could give at home. However, because changes in family structure and health care practices make it likely that most of us will die in an institutional setting, the question remains whether the present model of health care for terminal patients is adequate. Can we do better? Just as many hospitals are instituting new concepts and practices in maternity care, is it possible to infuse more human values into care of the dying? How much professional detachment is necessary for objective and wise decisions to be made about medical care for a dying patient? What are the consequences when the patient and the patient's family are treated impersonally by physicians and nurses? Can dying be made a more meaningful part of human experience? We need to investigate the alternatives that might facilitate personal and compassionate care of the dying.

One such alternative has been proposed by William Buchholz, an oncologist and hospice consultant. Referring to the Greek word *eschaton,* meaning "last things," he suggests that we implement a "medical eschatology," in which the roles of caregiver and scientist are combined to increase our knowledge of a phenomenon that "begins not with death, but when the end first draws into sight."[13]

Buchholz says medical eschatology begins when the illusion of immortality is broken and we recognize that all our biographies have an end. This recognition paves the way for asking the questions that can lead to a better understanding of the human experience of dying and, as well, better care for the dying person. We need to ask: Which coping mechanisms are most effective, and under what circumstances? What is an appropriate response when a person is seemingly "stuck" in a particular stage, and what is the validity of expectations we may have regarding stages? What patterns can be seen related to life-threatening illness, and what is the relationship between the host and the disease? What role do psychosocial and transpersonal factors play with respect to life-threatening illness?

Prerequisite to answering such questions is the awareness that *caring* is not always synonymous with active *doing*. Despite the value we place on knowledge, it is also important to be open to *not* knowing. "Learning," as Buchholz reminds us, "can occur only when something is as yet not understood."

Although suffering commonly accompanies terminal disease, there may be no easy answer to the question of how best to approach the emotional and spiritual care of a person whose body is disintegrating. Some persons counsel disidentification with the body or emphasize the afterlife. But the issue, as Buchholz says, is really whether a caregiver can put aside his or her own beliefs and recognize what is appropriate for the person. Given the many belief systems, those who care for dying persons need to attend to the clues that can lead to discovery of what is appropriate for a particular person in a given situation. Dying, like birthing, is a natural event, often better witnessed than managed.

Emergency Care Confrontations with Death

The emergency room drama of immediate response to a life-or-death situation makes for a compelling image. Perhaps at no other place in the hospital is the pressure to perform more intense than in the emergency room or trauma unit. As an ER staffer at one hospital put it, "You can be sitting there almost lulled to sleep during a quiet period, then suddenly everything is happening at once because there's just been a five-car crackup." Medical intervention must be rapidly and efficiently mobilized if life is to be sustained. For some, this kind of pressure is overwhelming. They find the more routine rhythms of patient care in other wards more suitable, less stressful. Others gain satisfaction from being thrust into situations in which their skills must be quickly brought to bear in order to save lives.

Since emergency room care tends to be given in crisis, it may also seem impersonal. Trauma usually allows little or no opportunity to establish a relationship with the patient while administering treatment. Emergency room patients are frequently comatose or incoherent because of shock.[14] The ER staff must take action that can make the difference between life and death while

Generally, the doctor's announcement of the death was made within the first or first two sentences, usually in the course of one long sentence. An interesting feature of his presentation, more common in the DOA situation than in announcements of the deaths of hospital patients, was that in announcing the death he provided, in some way, that the death be presented as having followed a course of "dying." In nearly every scene I witnessed, the doctor's opening remarks contained an historical reference. . . . This was true in accident as well as "natural" deaths, and true whether or not the physician had any basis for assuming a likely cause of death. . . . Physicians seem to feel in such situations that historicizing their delivery of news, no matter how much their limited knowledge of the case may restrict the range of possibilities, helps not only reduce some of the shock value of "sudden deaths" but aids in the very grasp of the news. The correctness of the physician's supposed cause of death is of secondary significance relative to the sheer fact that he provides some sequential formulation of its generation, some means whereby the occurrence can be placed in a sequence of natural or accidental events. This is felt particularly to be necessary in the DOA circumstance, where many deaths occur with no apparent "reason," particularly the so-called "sudden unexpected deaths," not uncommon among young adults.

David Sudnow,
Passing On: The Social Organization of Dying

receiving little or no feedback from the patient. The patient who survives to be transferred to the intensive care unit may not be seen again by those who labored so energetically to sustain his or her life.

The impersonality of the patient-caregiver relationship may affect the way ER staffers respond to a patient's death, lessening its impact. Still, frequent exposure to death is itself stressful. The notion that everyone can be saved may represent a desirable objective, but it is not conducive to coping with the realities of the emergency room. Like other hospital personnel, the person working in the emergency room responds to a patient's death both personally and professionally. Analysis of the patient's condition and decisions about what care to provide are accompanied to a varying degree by an emotional response.

When the circumstances surrounding a death elicit the caregiver's own anxieties about death, or when the death seems an uncommon tragedy — the death of a child, for example, or the death of a family in an automobile accident on Christmas Eve — hospital personnel are likly to be affected more profoundly than by deaths that occur under more routine circumstances.

The Patient-Caregiver Relationship

What happens after the physician diagnoses the patient's illness as life threatening? This is a crucial time in the patient's care that can significantly determine the patient's response to treatment, attitude toward the illness, and ability to cope with it constructively. The patient should be given a truthful report of the diagnosis and the proposed course of treatment. The physician should give general information about the disease, with as much detail as the patient desires, so that the patient is informed about what to expect and any options that he or she can exercise as treatment proceeds. What is said in this meeting between physician and patient depends on a number of factors, including how the doctor prefers to break the news of a life-threatening illness to a patient, the patient's receptivity to the facts as presented, and the prognosis. Because this initial meeting between the patient and physician can have an important influence on their subsequent interaction and the type of relationships they maintain during the course of treatment, sufficient time should be made available to explore the patient's questions and concerns.

Dr. Ernest Rosenbaum provides a helpful model of sensitivity to the patient's needs at this crucial stage of treatment.[15] Once testing is complete and a malignancy indicated, Dr. Rosenbaum arranges for an interview with the patient, encouraging family members to attend as well. Advocating candor and stressing partnership between the patient and the physician, he describes the nature of the diagnosis, proceeding in a way that is mindful of the patient's willingness to learn the medical facts and their implications. The usual progress of the disease is described, as are appropriate forms of treatment, and, finally, the treatment that will be implemented initially.

These meetings, usually lasting about half an hour, are taped so the patient can listen again at home. Dr. Rosenbaum points out that in the office the patient is likely to be upset, anxious, and bewildered, too distracted to listen attentively or really hear much of what is said. Having the interview available on tape allows the patient to listen to it later when there is likely to be a better opportunity to reflect on what was discussed and to take appropriate actions.

Dr. Rosenbaum emphasizes the importance of establishing an atmosphere of openness and trust in order to mobilize the patient's will to live, a key element in any therapeutic effort. To further support this positive approach, Dr. Rosenbaum frequently recommends that patients participate in some type of group counseling program that deals with concerns of importance to patient's with life-threatening illness. "Sharing frustrations with others in similar circumstances," says Dr. Rosenbaum, "often relieves the sense of isolation that cancer patients experience."

I clearly made Dr. Mueh nervous. He was clearly up to his ears in patients and spread very thin.

He took 90 minutes to talk to me and my wife about my disease. He started out with terminal care and told me I'd get all the narcotics I would need to eliminate pain and that tubes could be used to provide nourishment.

I was amazed that he talked that way, as if I were dying.

Pierre Bowman, Honolulu *Star-Bulletin*

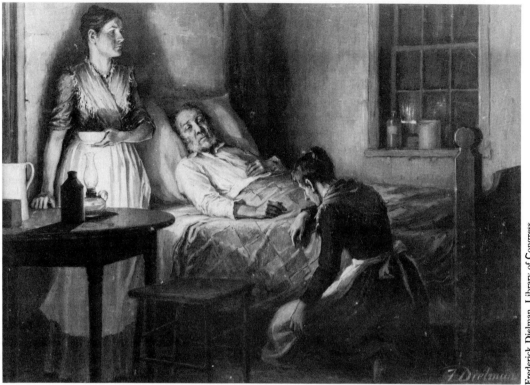

Frederick Dielman, Library of Congress

This 1895 illustration captures, in posture and expression, the weariness that accompanies round-the-clock care for the seriously ill and dying. Today's caregivers may feel this burden as much as ever while expecting themselves to put such feelings aside to conform to an image of professionalism.

Dealing with the Dying: Stress in the Helping Professions

Nurses and other health care professionals work in environments where death is experienced much more frequently than in most walks of life.[16] Although working with the dying may make death more familiar, it doesn't necessarily make the experience less stressful. Besides the ordinary human emotional response to the death of another person, the health professional may be exposed to other causes of stress related to the helping role. The inability to produce a cure may be perceived as inadequate care for the patient. The "what ifs" that anyone may experience at a loss may confound the helping professional as well. If not dealt with adequately, these doubts can produce harmful stress.

Health professionals sometimes question what constitutes the proper degree of involvement with a patient. How much should a nurse personally care about a dying patient? Aside from the professional commitment, what about personal and emotional involvement with the patient? Conflicts between emotions and professional responsibilities can contribute to guilt, confusion, and avoidance behavior — all factors that can increase stress.[17]

The professional relationships among members of the health care team may also contribute to stressful situations. Once a terminal diagnosis is made, nurses are likely to come into contact with the patient much more frequently than the patient's physician. Yet the physician's decision about the extent to which life should be sustained, or whether heroic measures should be avoided, influences the type of treatment the patient receives. It is not always possible to simply "follow doctor's orders." For instance, if a doctor has indicated that heroics are to be avoided, who will decide whether a particular procedure is "heroic" or "ordinary" in the circumstances? Should medical measures be taken to sustain life even when not ordered by the doctor? Resentment may arise at being thrust into what one nursing educator calls "the instrument of death by delegation."[18]

How can nurses and other helping professionals deal with these difficulties? The first step involves establishing a supportive environment in which death can be discussed openly among those involved in the patients' care. Policies can be implemented to meet the special care needs of the dying as well as to mitigate the stresses experienced by those who care for them. Procedures can be established that allow flexibility and confidence in responding to the circumstances surrounding a patient's death. Nurses and other members of the health care team should be given ample opportunity to discuss their feelings and the issues that arise in providing care for the dying.

A study of stress experienced by nurses at a cancer research center in Toronto found that nurses seemed to focus on the problems of caring for the dying patient almost as a displacement of more basic concerns. These concerns included feelings of inadequacy, a sense of isolation from colleagues, questions about the effectiveness of active treatment for dying patients, reluctance to express these concerns openly with colleagues because of fear of criticism and mistrust, and frustration stemming from the failure of physicians to resolve these problems omnipotently. When the nurses asked for and received a series of weekly sessions to facilitate communication and promote understanding of their problems, they reported that their major difficulty was in dealing with patients'

A person's in the room with me and they're very close to dying and afraid. I can feel the fear of death in myself. I'm working through my fear. I give them an opportunity, silent though it may be, to work through theirs. If I come into a room saying, "Oh, there's nothing to be afraid of. We go through death and then into another rebirth," that's not very useful. That's a way of not dealing with the power of the moment—the suffering in that room in the fellow on the bed, and the suffering in the mind of the fellow next to the bed.

Stephen Levine, *A Gradual Awakening*

feelings about illness, prognosis, and death. They felt "impotent because their training had led them to believe there should be answers where often there are none."[19]

Physicians who work in cancer settings may also experience stress particularly when the commitment to medical research and standards of patient care, including the patient's quality of life, come into conflict. One way to deal with this conflict is through rigorously applying all possible treatment regimens up until the moment of death, with the aim of advancing medical science for the sake of the greater good. Another is to search for a balance between research and quality of life for terminal patients.[20]

One of the most important avenues for reducing stress among medical and nursing staff involves developing an effective referral system. Such a referral system, along with seminars and regular meetings designed to educate as well as provide opportunities for communication and mutual support, can be potent means whereby the stress experienced by helping professionals can be alleviated.[21]

In one nursing home, for example, staff members' schedules are rotated so that as death nears, someone is with the patient almost constantly. The patient's family is notified and, if desired, a member of the clergy is called to the patient's bedside. If no relatives live nearby, the nursing home's staff assist in making arrangements for the funeral or disposition of the body. Staff members who had developed a close relationship with the patient are given time off to attend funeral services if they wish. Other patients who express an interest are informed of the death.

Staff members who cared for the patient in any way — the nursing staff, housekeeping personnel, dieticians, recreational and special service personnel — gather to discuss their responses to the patient's illness and death. Positive aspects of care are noted and encouraged while methods of improving patient care are discussed and plans made for implementation. Thus, staff members are given an opportunity to discuss their professional as well as personal relationship with the patient and their responses to the death.[22] This kind of health care approach, which recognizes the needs of patients, staff members, and surviving family members, is a model of what can be achieved when health care institutions devise methods that allow more personal and human care of the dying.

Those who care for the dying must have confidence in their methods of caregiving and must believe that the care they provide is appropriate and beneficial and in the best interest of the patient. An attitude of caring and support must be communicated to patients, to foster trust and feelings of self-worth and value in the patient as well as the caregiver.

Personal care is not limited to the patient's physical needs and well-being; the patient's personality must also be taken into account. According to Jeanne Quint Benoliel, personal care requires continuity of contact between at least one caregiver and the patient, opportunity for the patient to remain informed of his or her condition and treatment, participation by the patient in decisions that

Dr. Elisabeth Kübler-Ross, seen here with a patient who has been diagnosed with a life-threatening illness, is widely recognized for her pioneering efforts toward increased awareness on the part of the patient, family, and medical staff relative to the issues that arise in caring for the dying.

affect him or her, and behavior by staff members that elicits the patient's trust and confidence.[23] Someone who has established a supportive and trustful relationship with the patient offers a sense of the familiar amid what might be otherwise strange surroundings. Such a person may be able to act as counselor and advocate, a trusted friend to the patient in possibly difficult times.

Another source of continuity in patient care involves returning the patient to the same hospital or nursing home — or even the same unit — when institutional care is warranted. Seeing familiar faces in unfamiliar surroundings can help the patient feel less emotionally fragmented, and can give the comfort that comes from a sense of knowing what to expect. There is less doubt, less anxiety, about what might happen next.

Everyone who confronts the reality of dying — whether as a patient, family member, or health care professional — needs to experience a supportive environment nurtured by openness, compassion, and sensitive listening. If appropriate, the patient's family and friends can be encouraged to participate in the patient's care, thus providing a concrete way to alleviate their feelings of helplessness.[24]

Health care professionals are uniquely situated to offer sensitive and caring support for the dying and their families. In most instances, these resources represent an untapped potential that is likely to be realized only when society acts to improve the second-class citizenship of the dying.

Public Health Response to AIDS

What images and feelings do you become aware of as you think about AIDS? For many, AIDS is synonymous with death; a dread disease, contagious and epidemic, a twentieth-century plague. When we examine the psychosocial response to AIDS, we find a history marked by decisions concerning allocation of economic, medical, and social resources.[25]

The first cases of acquired immune deficiency syndrome (AIDS), a disease that destroys the body's natural defenses against infection, were reported in 1981. By early 1982, most researchers believed that AIDS was caused by an infectious agent, and identification of HTLV-III as the cause of AIDS was confirmed by Robert Gallo in January 1984.[26] By late 1985, a virus had been identified and linked to the disease, its genetic sequence determined, and a blood test devised to detect antibodies to AIDS.

The rapid pace of medical discoveries was more than matched, however, by the spread of AIDS. Many people criticized the lack of a well-financed and concerted effort by the U.S. Public Health Service. Some argued that early efforts were comparatively small and slow in coming because AIDS at first seemed to occur almost entirely among the population of homosexual and bisexual men. Indeed, through 1985, nearly three-quarters of the persons diagnosed with AIDS were members of this population. For single men aged twenty-five to forty-four years old in Manhattan and San Francisco, AIDS was cited as the leading cause of premature mortality, as measured by years of potential life lost.[27] Despite the high incidence of the disease among homosexual and bisexual men, they were not the only ones affected. Other high-risk groups included heterosexual drug users, persons infected from blood transfusions or blood products, and a third group, mostly women, who had apparently acquired the disease through heterosexual contact. The remaining AIDS victims did not fit into any of these high-risk categories.

By the end of 1986, approximately 35,000 cases of AIDS had been diagnosed, and it was estimated that perhaps as many as 2 million people in the United States had been infected with the AIDS virus. With the number of AIDS cases nearly doubling each year, the Public Health Service said it hoped to slow the spread of the disease by 1990 and to halt its transmission completely by 2000. Meeting these goals would require the investment of large amounts of money, energy, and talent in programs ranging from fundamental biological research to public education. Because of concern that the disease could indeed become epidemic, funding for work on AIDS has grown rapidly. The funds appropriated for AIDS research and education rose from $5.5 million in 1982 to about $109 million in 1985, a twentyfold increase. In 1986, Congress appropriated more than $240 million, with 10 percent of this amount earmarked for public education and risk reduction programs. Even this, however, was seen as merely one installment in what will be a long and expensive struggle to understand this disease.[28]

Federal funding is concentrated on public education, vaccine development, and drug testing, but the treatment costs remain largely the responsibility of the patient. The cost of treating AIDS is reported to be three times the average for other patients. Hospital and medical expenses for the first 10,000 cases of AIDS came to $1.5 billion. Although insurance covers much of the cost, the unpaid balance has been borne by hospitals and taxpayers. In New York City, for example, it was reported that about two-thirds of the cost of caring for AIDS patients had been paid by local taxpayers. Many hospital administrators and others involved in health care financing refer to AIDS as a catastrophe that is doubly damaging to communities.

The community response to AIDS has been mixed. Whereas some communities have responded with a variety of health and public service programs, others have reacted by narrowing and closing off any type of outreach. When Elisabeth Kübler-Ross proposed developing a hospice at her center in rural Virginia for infants with AIDS, for example, many local citizens acted swiftly to deny the necessary permits. Fear of contagion won out over the desire to help sick and dying infants.

Similar concerns about AIDS were initially voiced by some health care personnel. Patients with AIDS were sometimes placed in rooms distant from nurses' stations and told to stay in their rooms. As hysteria gave way to better information about the disease, however, care improved, as did communication between patients and caregivers. At San Francisco General Hospital, for example, procedures and options are explained to patients, allowing them to be in control of their own decisions, and hospital staff members are encouraged to "talk and touch and hug" AIDS patients just as they do with other dying patients.[29]

In reviewing the public and private responses to this disease, we are struck by the magnitude of the social, emotional, and financial consequences associated with AIDS, a modern dread disease that has provided many people an especially dramatic confrontation with mortality.

Terminal Care: Alternatives

Patients with life-threatening illness usually receive a combination of both acute and long-term care. As conditions change, a patient may sometimes need the skills and resources provided by a hospital, and at other times need the supportive services of a nursing home. Institutional care is often alternated with home care on those occasions when outpatient services are sufficient to meet the patient's needs.

Although 80 percent of terminal patient care in the United States is provided by hospitals and nursing homes, hospice care has become increasingly important. As a comprehensive term, hospice care is distinguished by its orientation specifically toward the needs of the dying patient. Such care may be provided in an institution devoted exclusively to caring for the terminally ill, or it may be one emphasis of a large medical center. Another form of hospice care

---

 ## *The Dying Person's Bill of Rights*

I have the right to be treated as a living human being until I die.

I have the right to maintain a sense of hopefulness however changing its focus may be.

I have the right to be cared for by those who can maintain a sense of hopefulness, however changing this might be.

I have the right to express my feelings and emotions about my approaching death in my own way.

I have the right to participate in decisions concerning my care.

I have the right to expect continuing medical and nursing attention even though "cure" goals must be changed to "comfort" goals.

I have the right not to die alone.

I have the right to be free from pain.

I have the right to have my questions answered honestly.

I have the right not to be deceived.

I have the right to have help from and for my family in accepting my death.

I have the right to die in peace and dignity.

I have the right to retain my individuality and not be judged for my decisions which may be contrary to beliefs of others.

I have the right to discuss and enlarge my religious or spiritual experiences, whatever these may mean to others.

I have the right to expect that the sanctity of the human body will be respected after death.

I have the right to be cared for by caring, sensitive, knowledgeable people who will attempt to understand my needs and will be able to gain some satisfaction in helping me face my death.

Marilee Ivars Donovan and Sandra Girton Pierce,
Cancer Care Nursing

is provided by organizations that offer various support services to terminally ill patients living at home or in one of the institutional settings mentioned. Each of the three major categories of institutional medical care—hospitals, nursing homes, and hospices—serves a specific purpose within the health care delivery system.

Hospitals primarily provide short-term, acute care. Aggressive techniques are employed to diagnose symptoms, provide treatment, and sustain life. The most recent data indicate that the average length of a hospital stay has been decreasing and is now about seven days. Among the factors contributing to this decline may be increased use of outpatient facilities and home care, as well as advances in treatment.[30] Most hospital patients are discharged back into the community after their well-being has been restored. The hospital's sophisticated equipment and diverse medical and surgical resources combine to emphasize its primary goal: rehabilitation.

Nursing homes and other nursing facilities provide less sophisticated care than do hospitals. Because they are chiefly intended to provide care for the chronically ill, the average length of their patients' stay is substantially longer than that for hospital patients. About three-quarters of nursing home patients eventually return to the community; the remaining one-quarter include both those who require ongoing nursing care and supervision and those who ultimately die while in a nursing home. Nursing homes categorized as skilled nursing facilities have a registered nurse on duty around the clock and a sophisticated paramedical staff. Homes categorized as intermediate care facilities offer less intensive care and have either a registered nurse or licensed vocational nurse on duty during day shifts.

The hospice, the third type of institutional care, is designed especially for the terminally ill. The goal of hospice care is to allow patients to be free of physical and psychological pain and to provide a comfortable, homelike environment in which dying can be experienced amid relatively familiar surroundings. Friends and family members often participate to a significant extent in the patient's care. Because the hospice is a relatively new alternative in America, there have been a variety of experimental approaches.

Although there are few residential care hospices in the United States, an increasing number of community-based organizations support home care for the dying or supplemental care provided by the more conventional health care institutions. Hospice care emphasizes keeping the patient as pain-free and comfortable as possible while refraining from dramatic medical interventions to resuscitate the patient when death approaches.[31]

Modern Hospice Care

The hospice movement came about in response to what many people—patients and medical practitioners alike—perceived to be inadequate care for the dying within the conventional hospital. The modern hospice concept originated in the late 1950s and 1960s; its most notable model is St. Christopher's Hospice in Sydenham, England, organized in 1967 by Dr. Cicely Saunders.[32] Located in a close-knit neighborhood in southeast London, St. Christopher's has become the model most often cited by those wishing to establish hospice care in this country. The patients who come to St. Christopher's are largely drawn from within a six-mile radius of the hospice, an area that contains approximately 1.5 million inhabitants. Of the seventy beds available, fifty-four are allocated to cancer patients, with the remainder occupied by elderly patients who can no longer function independently. On average, the length of stay for a cancer patient is about twelve days.

Filled with flowers, photographs, and personal belongings, the four-bed bays at St. Christopher's create an atmosphere that is cheerful and familiar. Patients are treated as mature, responsible individuals and are given opportunities to discuss their illness or not, depending on their mood and inclination. Patients who are accustomed to smoking or to having a cocktail before dinner are not prohibited from enjoying these familiar pleasures. Visiting hours extend from eight in the morning until eight at night, allowing considerable interaction between patients and their families. Children are encouraged to visit, and even family pets are allowed; a nursery for offspring of the hospice staff is operated on the grounds. The personal approach to patient care at St. Christopher's is accentuated by the parties that are held frequently for patients, staff, and families.

With patient care costing about 80 percent of comparable costs in a British general hospital, the largest percentage of operating costs at St. Christopher's is for staff salaries, reflecting what Dr. Saunders calls a "high person, low technology and hardware" system of health care.[33] Intravenous apparatuses, respirators, and related devices for prolonging life are absent. Instead, St. Christopher's encourages an atmosphere of tranquility and an acceptance of the process of dying. The highest priority is making the patient comfortable. Painful and distressing symptoms are controlled by skillful use of narcotics and other medications.

Death comes frequently at St. Christopher's. When a patient dies, the curtains are drawn around the bed while nurses and members of the patient's family gather to express their farewells. Relatives can sit with the body for a time if they wish. Afterwards, the body is taken to a private room where it is bathed and prepared for viewing in a small chapel at St. Christopher's. If the family wishes, a member of the clergy may be invited to come in and speak a few words of comfort regarding the deceased. The family is encouraged to participate to the extent that members desire. Allowing the family to spend time sitting with the body, for example, contrasts with the practice of quickly removing the body and handing it over to the mortician as efficiently and as secretly as possible. Death is treated more familiarly at St. Christopher's.

Another feature of the program at St. Christopher's that has been emulated by many hospice groups in this country is the home care program. Through this program, carried out jointly by the nurses at St. Christopher's and various community health practitioners in the vicinity, hospice care is provided to nonresidential patients. Some home care patients have not previously been patients at St. Christopher's; others are patients who have been released from the residential care program to return to their homes. About 10 percent of the patients in the residential program do return home periodically when symptoms are controlled or for a brief visit during holiday periods.

The home care program operates essentially as an outpatient program; medication schedules are planned by the hospice staff, and hospice nurses periodically visit patients at home to monitor their condition. In addition, a nurse is on call around the clock to provide help or answer questions from patients and family members. Knowing that such backup is available is an important source of confidence for the patients and families participating in St. Christopher's out-patient program.

When patients come in for examination or to review their treatment programs, the clinical schedule is so arranged that they need not wait to see the doctor. Discussion time is allowed so that questions from patients or their families can be satisfactorily answered. During these clinical visits, the patient's home care routine or drug maintenance schedule is altered if symptoms warrant. Maintaining the outpatient's comfort receives the same emphasis at St. Christopher's as maintaining the residential patient's.

Augmenting the residential program with a home care program greatly increases the number of persons who can be served by the staff at St. Christopher's. Residential patients can be returned home when their condition is such that home care is feasible and desirable. Patients from the home care program can be admitted as residents when the family is worn out, emotionally drained, or otherwise unable to provide the patient support necessary. The patterns of health care for the dying practiced at St. Christopher's are now being emulated in varying degrees in this country, both within the conventional medical system and by hospice organizations devoted to making support services available for the terminally ill.

The first American hospice, the Hospice of New Haven in Connecticut, began serving patients through a home care program in 1974.[34] Its development was stimulated partly by a visit in the early 1960s of Dr. Cicely Saunders to Yale University, where she reported on efforts to organize St. Christopher's in London. When the program in New Haven got underway, Dr. Sylvia Lack of St. Christopher's became its first medical director. Hospice care has grown rapidly since the establishment of the New Haven program. There are hundreds of hospice programs nationwide, and hospice care is now reimbursible under Medicare/Medicaid programs and through some private insurance companies.[35]

The philosophy of hospice care includes "pain control, symptom control (physical and psychological), continuous medical and nursing accessibility, medical direction, utilization of volunteers, home care, training of family members as care givers, and a bereavement program for the survivors."[36] Pain control and alleviation of symptoms are of primary importance in terminal care. When free of pain and suffering, the patient is better able to respond to family and friends.

A recent development has been the inauguration of hospice programs for dying children. Children's needs have not been addressed to the same extent as programs for terminally ill adults and geriatric patients. Of some eight hundred programs in the United States offering various forms of hospice care, fewer than twenty incorporate services for terminally ill children.[37] This imbalance is influenced by reluctance on the part of parents and others to accept that a child is dying. Other contributing factors may include the fact that children with life-threatening illnesses are often treated at major centers distant from their homes and the comparatively greater difficulty in communicating openly with a child about his or her fatal illness.

Hospice Programs in the Hospital

In recent years, a number of hospice care programs have been instituted within conventional hospitals. The willingness of hospital administrators and others in the medical community to find innovative ways to care for the dying represents an important step toward recognizing and responding to the special needs of the terminally ill and their families.

Broadly speaking, we can distinguish two types of hospice care programs within the hospitals. In the first a separate ward is designated for terminal care; in the second terminal care programs are integrated within the usual hospital organization. Each type has advantages and disadvantages.

Those who favor the creation of a separate ward to house terminal patients argue that this makes possible a general relaxation of hospital regulations and procedures, making the hospital environment more conducive to satisfying the needs and desires of the terminally ill and their families. For example, the age requirements for visitors are often relaxed so that children can be with a dying relative. The rules governing the length of visits and the visiting hours themselves may be made less stringent than elsewhere in the hospital. The supervisory and nursing personnel on the terminal care ward focus their energies on controlling pain and making the patient comfortable rather than on instituting life-sustaining (or death-postponing) interventions.

However, creating a separate ward for the terminally ill usually requires considerable reorganization of hospital facilities and resources, and this can be quite costly. Too, some argue that isolation from the general patient population places a stigma on the dying. Once a patient is admitted to the terminal ward, the message is clear that the prognosis is death — which may have dysfunctional effects on those who prefer not to face death so openly. Also, although terminal care is increasingly recognized as an important part of any total health care program, many practitioners want to work with patients whose odds for recovery are favorable; thus, some believe it would be difficult to recruit staff whose sole duties involved ministering to the terminally ill. In an environment where death is commonplace, even a highly motivated caregiver is exposed to possibly harmful stress.

Because of these potential difficulties, some health practitioners advocate providing the second type of hospice care program: integrated care for the terminally ill within special programs that supplement conventional hospital practices and procedures. Because this approach usually requires less reorganization of facilities and personnel, it is typically less expensive to administer. Integrated care of the dying can range from counseling support to specially trained hospital staff members who participate in a comprehensive treatment program for the dying. Hospice volunteers, members of the clergy, or other interested persons may provide supplemental support by visiting patients, discussing their concerns, counseling, and generally assisting in whatever way seems appropriate. Such help is usually made available to both patients and their families. The presence of someone familiar with the hospital routine and its organization — and who can therefore act as an informal liaison between staff and patients and family members — is frequently a source of great comfort to those experiencing the trauma of terminal illness.

Staff members who are sensitive to the needs of the dying and volunteers who are adequately trained to provide support for patients and their families can do much to enhance the care provided to the terminally ill. Integrated care of the terminally ill has typically been most successful through the persistence and vision of someone who becomes an advocate for the dying. That person may be a minister, a hospice volunteer, a nurse or physician, or anyone committed to easing the plight of the dying. Unless those who participate in a program designed to serve the terminally ill — whether the pattern followed tends toward separate ward care or integrated care — sustain their commitment and open-hearted concern for the dying, it is unlikely that terminal care needs will be adequately met.

It appears that more hospitals and more communities are investigating ways of incorporating a more personal and human approach to care for the dying. Some choose to establish a separate terminal ward with a specially trained staff and a less institutional environment; others provide integrated care, combining conventional medical and hospital care, counseling support, and volunteer help. Hospice and similar organizations are playing a major role in current efforts to ameliorate the conditions that foster denial of death and dying amid impersonal circumstances.

Hospice Organizations

The attractiveness of the hospice concept is reflected in the growth of community organizations designed to put it into practice. Most hospice programs start as relatively informal groups staffed largely by volunteers and later become more developed organizational structures. Although some groups providing hospice care are profit making, the majority are nonprofit. As conventional health care agencies and institutions assume a larger role in hospice care, it is likely that there will be an increase in the number of commercially operated hospice care facilities.

Designed specifically to meet the needs of dying patients and their families, hospice care is both more appropriate and more sensitive than the patient might receive in conventional health care facilities. A major attraction of hospice care is its emphasis on participation by the patient's family. In all, hospices try to

© Carol A. Foote

Institutional care becomes more personal when the environment reflects something of the patient's own life style and values. Here, surrounded by photographs of her relatives, a nursing home patient is able to reflect on her personal and family connections outside the institutional setting.

provide services that can help the dying patient experience a greater sense of self-worth and dignity than might otherwise be possible.

However, although the hospice concept has been received enthusiastically by many people in this country, and it promises to become a significant alternative to conventional programs, at present only a fraction of those who might wish to avail themselves of hospice care can obtain it. Most hospice organizations are small and limited in their resources, because they depend upon voluntary contributions of both time and money.

Although a few hospice groups in this country provide residential care for the dying — similar to that provided at St. Christopher's in London — most hospice organizations are composed of volunteers who provide support services to patients who are either at home or in an institutional health care setting. The hospice organization administers the program, provides training for volunteers, coordinates volunteer and patient interaction, and offers presentations to the local community about the hospice concept.

Support Groups for the Terminally Ill

Often, institutional health care programs for the terminally ill are supplemented by various groups that focus on specific interests and needs. Such groups range from national organizations like the American Cancer Society to small community-based groups meant to meet the needs of dying patients and their families in a particular locality.

Many of the community groups are composed of volunteers who desire to make some of the elements of hospice care available to local patients. A variety of pursuits may be followed in seeking to realize this goal, including patient visiting programs and educational programs for health care professionals as well as laypersons. Some of these community groups are working toward the establishment of a permanent residential care hospice program, while others concentrate on supplementing the programs in conventional health care facilities or in home care.

One of the first such programs to achieve prominence is the Shanti Project, organized in Northern California by Dr. Charles Garfield in 1974.[38] At the suggestion of Stewart Brand, editor of the *Whole Earth Catalog* and the *CoEvolution Quarterly,* a central telephone number was established that interested persons could call in order to be put in touch with volunteers willing to aid the dying. From the beginning of the Shanti Project, a policy of accepting only firsthand referrals was followed, allowing Shanti to focus its efforts on those who themselves request help or information. Shanti provides aid in the form of counseling and companionship for patients and families as well as conducting educational programs for the benefit of community and medical groups.

Once a referral is made, the Shanti volunteer becomes an advocate for the patient, a role that can include emptying ashtrays and cleaning the patient's room as well as consulting on the patient's behalf with medical personnel and health care agencies. Above all, the volunteer acts as the patient's companion and friend. Shanti encourages the use of peer counseling, whereby one cancer patient helps another cancer patient and someone who has experienced grief helps another undergoing a similar experience. Screened before entering the program and then given training seminars, Shanti volunteers must commit themselves to working with the project for at least one year, during which time they agree to spend eight to ten hours per week working with clients. The Shanti Project has achieved notable success in helping to ameliorate the social isolation and emotional alienation that often accompany terminal illness. Recently, the Shanti Project has concentrated its efforts on helping patients with AIDS.

Another community-based group providing volunteer emotional support services is Kara in Palo Alto, California. Taking its name from the Gothic root of the word *care* — meaning to reach out, to care, and to grieve with — Kara works closely with the hospice program of the local Veterans Administration Hospital, as well as with other hospitals and hospices in neighboring communities. In addition to direct volunteer counseling with dying and bereaved clients, Kara provides training and consulting services to professionals and laypersons, and, cooperatively with the VA Hospice, sponsors an annual conference. In the past ten years, 350 individuals were trained as volunteer counselors. These volunteers provided counseling services to more than two thousand clients, with an average case duration of five months. One-time counseling services were provided to an additional four thousand persons. A similar pattern of emotional support and educational programs can be found in many places across the country where community-based support groups exist.

At the national level, one of the best-known support services is "I Can Cope," a program originated in 1977 by two oncology nurses at the North Memorial Medical Center of Minneapolis and sponsored by the American Cancer Society. Designed for cancer patients and their families, "I Can Cope" is organized as a learning experience to help participants "develop a better understanding of cancer and various treatments, learn to manage side effects, deal with fears and feelings, and improve their sense of physical and emotional well-being."[39] Educational experiences are provided through a variety of lectures, reading materials, and audiovisual media, as well as through the sharing of problems and concerns currently being experienced by the participants. For many, the program results in decreased feelings of helplessness and passivity along with increased self-satisfaction, self-esteem, and confidence.

Another type of support organization is represented by the Elisabeth Kübler-Ross Center. Located in Virginia, the Center coordinates a variety of programs related to life-threatening illness, bereavement, and the "promotion of physical, intellectual, emotional, and spiritual health."[40] In addition to its educational program, which includes seminars and workshops presented by Dr. Kübler-Ross and others, the Center is active with projects involving the control of chronic pain, the institution of "screaming rooms" in hospitals, and care for babies with AIDS.

The Social Role of the Dying Patient

Why are hospitals seen as places not especially well suited to the needs of the dying patient? In most hospitals, the dying patient is something of an anomaly, the "uncooperative" exception to the rule that patients are supposed to get well and return to normal life. As sociologist Talcott Parsons discovered in the 1950s, a particular social role accompanies illness.[41] Like all social roles — parent, child, student, employee, spouse — the role of the "person who is sick" includes certain rights as well as responsibilities. For example, when we are ill, others usually exempt us from our usual tasks. We may stay home from work. Someone else may take on our share of housecleaning or child care. Commitments may be neglected. We are granted the right to be sick. We assume a particular social role that causes others to make allowances for our behavior that otherwise might result in social penalties. Whereas taking off from work just to enjoy a day in the sun is likely to be frowned upon, an absence due to illness elicits sympathy rather than reprimands.

The sick person not only enjoys exemptions from many of the usual social obligations, but also receives special consideration and care. Others put forth efforts to make sure the patient is comfortable and is receiving adequate treatment and so on. Personal and financial resources may be devoted to the patient's care and treatment. Such care is part of the social role of being sick, of being a patient.

But these rights are balanced by responsibilities. The sick person must want to get well. Malingerers, those who pretend to be sicker than they really are, receive little or no respect from those whose job it is to provide care or help carry the additional burden imposed by their supposed illness. It's okay to receive special treatment when you're really ill or when you've suffered an injury, but the role of the patient demands that you demonstrate that you'd really rather be well. You've got to take your medicine. You're expected to cooperate with those who are prescribing and administering treatment.

At one time or another most people have experienced the role of patient as well as the role of caregiver. The role of the dying patient is quite different. Although sharing some aspects of the curable patient's social role, the dying person's illness does not fit the pattern of a temporary condition allowing eventual return to wellness. Yet, in our society, a social role for the dying is not well defined. The same expectations may be placed upon the dying person as on patients whose prognosis is rehabilitation and return to normal modes of living. Even when circumstances are clearly contrary, the dying person may be urged to maintain a hope of recovery, to deny the reality of what he or she is experiencing. If the dying person does not exhibit this cheerful will to live, friends and family may feel angry or rejected.

The person who is dying also assumes a different role in relation to the medical community. When cure is no longer perceived as a medical possibility, supportive and palliative care takes the place of more active intervention and treatment. Typically, the patient's doctor begins to devote less and less time to mapping out hopeful strategies, and becomes more supervisory, expecting the patient to assume more responsibility for his or her own care.[42]

The lack of a clear consensus on care of the dying and the role of the dying

I know that, during my own illness in 1964, my fellow patients at the hospital would talk about matters they would never discuss with their doctors. The psychology of the seriously ill put barriers between us and those who had the skill and the grace to minister to us.

There was first of all the feeling of helplessness—a serious disease in itself.

There was the subconscious fear of never being able to function normally again—and it produced a wall of separation between us and the world of open movement, open sounds, open expectations.

There was the reluctance to be thought a complainer.

There was the desire not to add to the already great burden of apprehension felt by one's family; this added to the isolation.

There was the conflict between the terror of loneliness and the desire to be left alone.

There was the lack of self-esteem, the subconscious feeling perhaps that our illness was a manifestation of our inadequacy.

There was the fear that decisions were being made behind our backs, that not everything was made known that we wanted to know, yet dreaded knowing.

There was the morbid fear of intrusive technology, fear of being metabolized by a data base, never to regain our faces again. There was resentment of strangers who came at us with needles and vials—some of which put supposedly magic substances in our veins, and others which took more of our blood than we thought we could afford to lose. There was the distress of being wheeled through white corridors to laboratories for all sorts of strange encounters with compact machines and blinking lights and whirling discs.

And there was the utter void created by the longing—ineradicable, unremitting, pervasive—for warmth of human contact. A warm smile and an outstretched hand were valued even above the offerings of modern science, but the latter were far more accessible than the former.

Norman Cousins, *Anatomy of an Illness*

patient can lead to actions that seem quite incongruous. Consider, for example, the hopelessly ill patient in the final stage of a terminal condition who is rushed into the intensive care unit and subjected to heroic medical attempts to sustain life. Meanwhile, the patient's family may be waiting outside, experiencing a lingering uncertainty or false hopes for the patient's survival. In such circumstances, death may be far from peaceful or dignified. It may be difficult for the patient to deal with the prospect of death in a personally appropriate and comforting way.

Until about the middle of the twentieth century, a social role for the dying person was more or less fixed by custom and circumstance. The rapid and pervasive social and technological changes of recent times have largely eliminated the traditional role of the dying, while offering few guidelines in its stead.

What would a newly rediscovered and updated role for the dying look like? It would undoubtedly draw upon historical precedent while also reflecting the social and technological changes in our present modes of caring for dying patients.

Let us imagine some of the attributes of such a newly evolving role for the dying: No longer would the patient need to maintain an appearance of expecting to live forever, of getting well again, of sustaining false hope. At the same time, the patient assumes a more independent role, able to exercise more self-determination and entitled to a greater degree of cooperation from others involved in caregiving. The patient whose resources had been mobilized in the effort to effect a cure now turns his or her attention to preparing for death. Relatives and friends, understanding this change of perspective as natural, allow the patient to disengage from the activities and relationships that prevailed before the onset of illness.

 A "good" death — that is, one appropriate to the person who is dying — is as much anticipated as was the earlier hope of recovery. The dying person is recognized as the protagonist in an important and potentially valuable experience of life.

Further Readings

William Ray Arney and Bernard J. Bergen. *Medicine and the Management of Living: Taming the Last Great Beast.* Chicago: University of Chicago Press, 1984.

David Barton, editor. *Death and Dying: A Clinical Guide for Caregivers.* Baltimore: Williams & Wilkins, 1977.

Jeanne Quint Benoliel, editor. *Death Education for the Health Professional.* Washington, D.C.: Hemisphere, 1982.

Orville G. Brim, Jr., Howard E. Freeman, Sol Levine, and Norman A. Scotch, editors. *The Dying Patient.* New York: Russell Sage Foundation, 1970.

Deborah Chase. *Dying at Home with Hospice.* St. Louis: C. V. Mosby, 1986.

Charles A. Corr and Donna M. Corr, editors. *Hospice Care: Principles and Practices.* New York: Springer, 1983.

Norman Cousins. *The Physician in Literature.* Philadelphia: Saunders, 1982.

Diana Crane. *The Sanctity of Social Life: Physicians' Treatment of Critically Ill Patients.* New York: Russell Sage Foundation, 1975.

Thomas Andrew Gonda and John Edward Ruark. *Dying Dignified: The Health Professional's Guide to Care.* Menlo Park, Calif.: Addison-Wesley, 1984.

Ralph Hingson, Norman A. Scotch, James Sorenson, and Judith P. Swazey. *In Sickness and in Health: Social Dimensions of Medical Care.* St. Louis: C. V. Mosby, 1981.

Edmund D. Pellegrino and David C. Thomasma. *A Philosophical Basis of Medical Practice: Toward a Philosophy and Ethic of the Healing Professions.* New York: Oxford University Press, 1981.

Therese A. Rando. *Grief, Dying, and Death: Clinical Interventions for Caregivers.* Champaign, Ill.: Research Press, 1984.

Stanley Joel Reiser. *Medicine and the Reign of Technology.* New York: Cambridge University Press, 1978.

Paul Starr. *The Social Transformation of American Medicine.* New York: Basic Books, 1983.

Mary L. S. Vachon. *Occupational Stress in the Care of the Critically Ill, the Dying, and the Bereaved.* Washington, D. C.: Hemisphere, 1986.

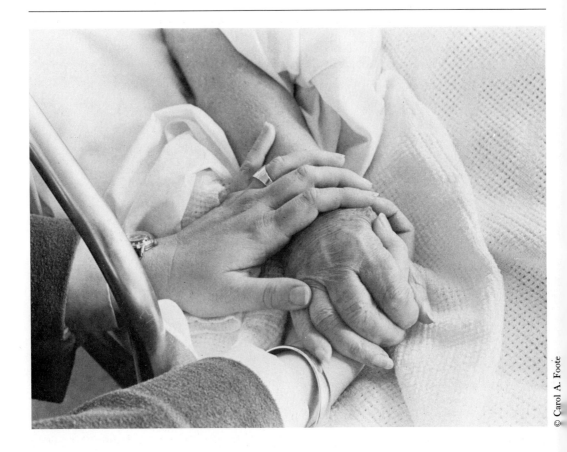

Total care for the patient with a life-threatening illness includes warm, intimate contact with caring persons who are able to listen and share the patient's concerns.

Facing Death: Living with Life-Threatening Illness

*C*ancer. Heart disease. For most of us these words send frightening repercussions echoing through the corridors of the mind. The famous as well as our friends and relatives die from these illnesses. Every day we read the death notices and the obituaries in the newspaper. To many people, cancer seems virtually synonymous with death and dying, though in fact the prognosis for a cancer patient is not always death.

In this chapter, we examine life-threatening illness and discuss various ways of responding to it, both medically and personally. Although cancer is preeminent in many people's minds as "the" long-term, life-threatening illness, the circumstances faced by individuals with other life-threatening illnesses are much the same. Patients diagnosed with heart disease, cerebrovascular disease, and other serious illnesses encounter similar kinds of medical and nursing care, methods of coping, and support systems. What we say here about cancer or heart disease, therefore, applies generally to other life-threatening illnesses as well.

The Taboo of Terminal Illness

A patient with acute leukemia compared her experience to that of someone with the Black Death during the fourteenth century in Europe.[1] The origin of the disease in one's body is somewhat mysterious, the result of factors not easily discernible. Nature seems somehow to have gotten out of control, and, though having no understanding of the chain of

When I first realized that I might have cancer, I felt immediately that I had entered a special place, a place I came to call "The Land of the Sick People." The most disconcerting thing, however, was not that I found that place terrifying and unfamiliar, but that I found it so ordinary, so banal. I didn't feel different, didn't feel that my life had radically changed at the moment the word *cancer* became attached to it. The same rules still held. What had changed, however, was other people's perceptions of me. Unconsciously, even with a certain amount of kindness, everyone—with the single rather extraordinary exception of my husband—regarded me as someone who had been altered irrevocably. I don't want to exaggerate my feeling of alienation or to give the impression that it was in any way dramatic. I have no horror stories of the kind I read a few years ago in the *New York Times*; people didn't move their desks away from me at the office or refuse to let their children play with my children at school because they thought that cancer was catching. My friends are all too sophisticated and too sensitive for that kind of behavior. Their distance from me was marked most of all by their inability to understand the ordinariness, the banality of what was happening to me. They marveled at how well I was "coping with cancer." I had become special, no longer like them.

> Alice Stewart Trillin,
> "Of Dragons and Garden Peas:
> A Cancer Patient Talks to Doctors"

events that led to such bleak fortunes, the patient feels a responsibility to put things right. "I must have done something wrong to get this disease. Now, what should I do to make it go away?"

Magical thinking—assuming oneself responsible though it's unclear just how—places a great burden on the patient with a life-threatening illness: "What did I do to bring this condition upon myself? If I had done this, or not done that, maybe I wouldn't be in this predicament." Throughout this self-questioning the patient usually feels a pervasive sense of helplessness, a sense of trying to combat unknown natural forces that have gone awry, forces that seem bent on destroying one's body.

Besides self-deprecation, the patient is likely to feel the effects of the social stigma associated with the disease. Many people tend to avoid the person who has a life-threatening illness, almost as if they feared it might be catching even when they know it not to be. More likely, we might catch a sense of the confrontation with death. This confrontation with death exposes our fear of loss and separation from all that we love, our fear of pain, and the imagined horror of dying. It shatters our image of ourselves and the plans we have made for the future.

Heart disease, the leading cause of death in the United States, is often thought of as a disease of superachievers, persons who are goal oriented and whose lives are active and filled with accomplishments. Cancer, on the other hand, is often portrayed as the uncontrollable madness of the body's cells gone

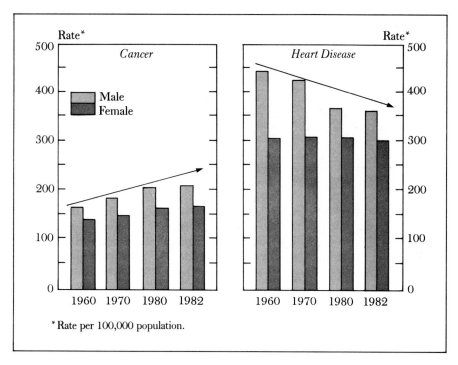

Figure 5-1   *Death Rates from Heart Disease and Cancer*
Source: Statistical Abstract of the United States 1986, p. 76.

wild, the body devouring itself from within. The cancer patient is seen as passive and powerless. Neither of these images is altogether true. What are the facts?

Heart disease, like cancer, affects all manner of people. Both illnesses are found at all strata of income and in all occupations, among people of widely divergent life styles. Among the primary causes of death in this country, cancer is second to diseases of the heart (see Figure 5-1).

Personal and Social Costs of Life-Threatening Illness

Although the mortality rate from heart disease has been declining, it remains the leading cause of death in the United States, accounting for nearly 40 percent of all deaths. Heart disease ranks first among all disease conditions relative to short-stay hospitalization, and it results in personal health care costs of about $14 billion annually in the United States.

Cancer, the second leading cause of death in the United States, caused about 450,000 deaths in 1984 — about 1230 persons a day, or one every 70 seconds. Whereas in 1900 about one of every twenty-seven deaths was attributable to cancer, it now accounts for roughly one in five. It is estimated that

I remember her as she lay in her hospital bed in July. Unable finally to deny the pain. And for the first time in our relationship of 21 years forced to allow someone else to take care of her. My father could not stand the sight and so he stayed outside, pacing up and down in the hallways. I could not help staring at her. Disbelief that this person with tubes running in and out like entrances and exits on a freeway was the same woman who just six months before had laughed gaily and danced at my wedding.

Ruth Kramer Ziony,
"Scream of Consciousness"

one-third of Americans now living eventually will have cancer and that cancer will affect three out of four families.[2] Although the rate of "cure" (meaning a patient has no evidence of cancer and has the same life expectancy as a person who never had cancer) has been increasing, the mortality rate from cancer has also been rising. Although the amount spent by individual cancer patients for care and treatment is difficult to assess, the American Cancer Society estimates the overall medical costs for cancer at $20 billion annually. It has been estimated that, on average, an American who died of cancer in 1983 had medical expenses of more than $22,000 during the final year of his or her life. In addition, patients are typically faced with loss of earnings; expensive procedures, drugs, and other medical supplies; repeated and sometimes lengthy hospitalization; and prolonged and costly rehabilitation.

Besides the financial expenditures, there are the personal and social costs. Emotional havoc accompanies the discovery that one has a life-threatening illness: mental and emotional anguish, pain and discomfort, fear, a sense of hopelessness, depression and anxiety, feelings of loneliness. The patient's family shares this burden, experiencing the pain of bereavement when the patient cannot be cured.

Society also pays a high price. Public as well as private funds are allocated to programs of research, education, prevention, and care. There are indirect costs to society as well. The patient's relinquishment of employment or other social responsibilities levies additional social costs of decreased productivity and the retraining of workers.

For the patient, fears excited by the prospect of undergoing treatment may compound the anxieties related to the disease itself. Patients with a life-threatening illness may fear the loss of their sexual functioning or attractiveness, either as a direct result of the disease or as a side effect of the treatment. Self-concept is intimately related to sexual identity. Concerns about integrity of the body that are raised by the possibility of disfigurement or a reduction in physical abilities must be considered within the context of a person's whole psychosocial sexual role.

For instance, a man who derives his dense of virility and masculinity from his work role may become sexually dysfunctional if illness precludes continuing his usual employment. A feeling that he is "less of a man" in one area of his life may become generalized to other parts of his life, including his sexual identity. Or a woman whose breast is removed because of cancer may feel she is less of a woman — less able to adequately fulfill her role as a wife or mother, or indeed to function in business or social settings. On the other hand, a patient who has been diagnosed as having a terminal condition may become compulsively preoccupied with sex, feeling that within the limited time remaining it is all the more important to produce offspring or to maximize sexual experiences. Whether problems with sexual identity are manifest in avoidance or in compulsive activity, they can have a tremendous effect on the patient's self-concept and his or her relationships with others.[3]

Few patients are ever completely free of the fear that the disease may someday return, even when a cure is apparently successful. The conflict and stress, and indeed panic, arising from the confrontation with death that a life-threatening illness presents, the adjustments in life style and psychosocial role necessitated by such an illness and its treatment — such experiences are common to most seriously ill patients. Nevertheless, much can be done to alleviate the stress, anxiety, and uncertainty that typically accompany life-threatening illness.

Therapeutic tools — including education, counseling, support groups, and communication skills — can be brought to bear on the experience of life-threatening illness. Gaining information about the disease and its treatment, sharing experiences with others in an atmosphere of mutual support, using counseling services to clarify personal and emotional issues, and developing ways of communicating more effectively with caregivers as well as family members and friends — all these are examples of positive approaches that can be taken in dealing with life-threatening illness. Although these techniques will not necessarily make a serious illness less traumatic, they promote an under-standing that places the crisis in a more affirmative context, making one's experience less confusing and melodramatic, and restoring a sense of personal control over the situation.

Our discomfort and uncertainty about life-threatening illnesses sometimes cause us to turn away from the patient, perhaps out of the best intentions, removing him or her from activities and the kind of social supports that are probably needed more than ever. It's difficult for most of us to feel confident about our ability to relate to someone with a life-threatening illness. What do we say? How ought we to act? This uncertainty may be demonstrated both by excessive sympathy and by obsessive avoidance. Neither response is satisfactory, for ourselves or for the patient.

There are no pat formulas for how to behave. But neither is there any special qualification for being sensitive. Because there is no correct way to behave, we can simply be ourselves, uncertainty and all. Accepting our doubt, our fear, allows us to do what we can, to be with the other person without trying to rely on some special program. To do otherwise results in a kind of partial death for the patient.

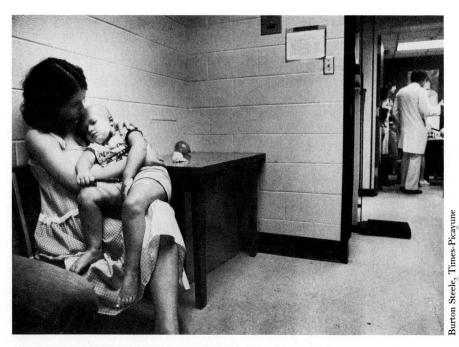

Burton Steele, Times-Picayune

With her seriously ill daughter, this mother waits for the test results that will help determine the next step in care and treatment.

Medical professionals as well as laypersons need to be aware of accommodations that can be made to aid a person with life-threatening illness. Treatment schedules, for example, often can be adjusted so that the patient can continue working or going to school or caring for his or her family. Some medical centers make an effort to schedule chemotherapy for cancer patients early on a weekend so that side effects will be diminished by the beginning of the workweek on Monday. Retraining or modifying job patterns makes it possible for the patient to continue working, and thus maintain a sense of self-worth. It is important for all of us to recognize the impact that life-threatening illness has on the patient. By confronting the reality, we can begin to uncover our fears and cope more creatively with death and dying.

The Experience of Life-Threatening Illness

Imagine one day you wake up and notice symptoms in your body that you associate with cancer. What goes through your mind? Perhaps you just barely admit to yourself the possibility that you're sick. Then you quickly push away such thoughts and go about your day's activities. "After all," you say, "there's no reason to suspect it's anything serious; it's probably just some minor infection."

You forget about it for a while. But, more and more persistently, the symptoms you noticed become more demanding of your attention. "This better not be anything serious," you tell yourself, "I've got too much to do." Yet, part of you recognizes that it really might be serious. You admit your concern, starting to feel a bit anxious about what the symptoms might mean.

So you make an appointment with your doctor, describe your symptoms, submit to an examination, and wait for the results. Perhaps right away, or maybe only after additional tests are ordered, you learn the diagnosis. Your doctor informs you that you have a tumor, a malignancy. Cancer.

Now your thoughts and emotions really become agitated. "What will the doctors do for me? How are they going to treat this illness? What kind of changes will I have to make in my life? Should I postpone the trip we've been planning? What about the pain? What about the treatment? Are there side effects? Can they even cure my kind of cancer? Will I die?"

As your intense drama unfolds, you begin to find ways of coping with this new crisis. Your earlier fears about the symptoms are transformed into concerns about the diagnosis, treatment, and outcome of the illness. You wonder how your life will be affected and what kind of adjustments you will have to make.

As time passes, perhaps you experience a remission: The tumor seems to have stopped growing. The doctors give you optimistic reports. Still, you wonder whether the cancer is really gone for good or just temporarily. You feel like someone in limbo. You're happy that things seem to be going well, but your optimism is mixed with uncertainty and fear. Perhaps after a while you begin to relax and feel less anxious about the cancer's returning. It seems "your" cancer was curable.

On the other hand, you may sooner or later again notice the onset of symptoms. If the cancer is declared incurable, you may fear metastasis, the spreading of the cancer to other areas of your body. Now you wrestle with the

---

I'm forty. So, obviously things happened to me before I came in here. . . . I was married—I had a wife, and I had a son. But my wife divorced me. I was served with the papers the day I went to the hospital for the operation. My son will be twelve this October, I guess. I've never seen him since.

In the beginning, I was bewildered-like. I didn't know what the hell was happening to me. I didn't know what was wrong. And I kept going from doctor to doctor—and getting worse all the time. Slipping and slipping. I was like up in a cloud—and I was cross then. And bitter. I couldn't see why God had made such a big decision on me. I saw my brothers and sisters walking around so healthy-like—and I couldn't understand why it had happened to me and not to them. Things like that. . . . But, after a while, I decided you've got to take what the Lord decides, and make the best of it. . . .

Quoted in Renee Fox,
Experiment Perilous

questions, "Is it going to be painful? What organs will eventually be affected? How long do I have to live?"

This scenario, though in many ways typical, is experienced differently by different patients. Some cancers can be cured by relatively minor forms of treatment. Other cancers persist for a time and then, with treatment, diminish or become stabilized. The prognosis in other cases offers little hope for survival. To whatever degree cancer is perceived as a threat to one's well-being, this scenario is likely to resemble the cancer patient's actual experience and, by extension, the experience of anyone with a life-threatening illness.

Once the disease is judged incurable, the patient's fears may focus on the uncertainty surrounding dying and death. These fears probably have been present from the first, underlying the changing concerns about symptoms, diagnosis, and treatment. Yet when cancer was nothing more than a possibility represented by a particular set of symptoms, attention was directed to what the symptoms might mean. After the diagnosis is learned and as treatment progresses, the fear of death becomes more real, though it is still mitigated by the need to carry out all the various activities that accompany the role of being a patient with a life-threatening illness. Fear is balanced by hope.

As death confronts us squarely, we may yet hope for some last-minute remission, some change for the better that the doctors haven't foreseen. We may fight to the end, thinking, "I've always outwitted the percentages. Why not now?" Or we may cope with the end of life in a very different way, taking as much charge as possible of the remaining time, surrounding ourselves with those closest to us, and accepting our dying. The way each of us copes with dying will likely reflect the ways we've coped with living, the ways we've coped with other losses and changes in our life.

Patterns of Coping with Life-Threatening Illness

The emotional and psychological responses to the confrontation with life-threatening illness have been described by Elisabeth Kübler-Ross on the basis of her work with dying patients.[4] Although these responses do not occur in a static, progressive manner, they may include: (1) denial, (2) anger, (3) bargaining, (4) depression, and (5) acceptance. In an idealized model, an early period of disbelief eventually gives way to some degree of acceptance. A variety of coping mechanisms, however, may be used to prevent a full recognition and acknowledgment of the truth. When confronted by death or loss, a person may respond with avoidance or denial of the truth, or by suppressing or excluding it from consciousness. Setting oneself apart from thoughts or actions that might bring a recognition of the truth — that is, dissociating oneself from it — is another coping mechanism that may come into play when a person faces an unwelcome reality. Bargaining, or attempting to strike a deal with fate or with God, is yet another common response. After the initial responses — "Oh, no, it can't be me! I don't want to hear about it! Those test results must be for someone else; they

"Bloom County," drawing by Berke Breathed, © 1985 by Washington Post Writers Group

got mixed up!" — comes acknowledgment of one's situation: "Yes, I am seriously ill, and I've got to deal with that fact in the best way I can."

Even after the predicament has been acknowledged, however, there is generally considerable anger, vulnerability, and dependency. The anger is often manifest as displaced hostility: "Okay, maybe I could've done something to keep this from happening to me, but, damn it, if it isn't safe, why doesn't the government put a stop to it!" Caregivers often become the object of such displaced hostility. The patient's anger at being ill might be displayed in complaints about food or other aspects of care: "Why can't you fix me a good cup of tea? You know I can't do it for myself!" Such coping mechanisms, difficult and possibly painful for patient and caregiver alike, serve to mask the underlying problem, the confrontation with the illness itself and what it portends.

After a time, many patients come to a greater acceptance of their situation. They are able to explore more dispassionately its inherent issues and possibilities, and they begin to establish productive ways of dealing with the changed

 There are some people who really can't deal with being told the truth about their illness. If you tell them at the wrong time or in the wrong way, it's too devastating for them.

First of all, get to know the patient. Sit down and talk with him, not about his illness particularly, but general topics. Very soon you get a feeling as to whether or not the patient wants to know. There are two groups: those who want to know and don't mind knowing, and those who very plainly don't want to know. There are some patients who have been told they have cancer, hear doctors discussing it, see their charts, and will still turn around and deny that they have cancer. And, of course, that's a gray area. You're not sure if they want to know. If they want to know, tell them. Don't hide the fact.

Quoted from *Death and Dying: The Physician's Perspective*, a videotape by Elizabeth Bradbury

Dear Friends,

In company with our dear Mother Earth, I have arrived at the time of autumn in my worldly life, that time of transition between life and death. Before long, just as the leaves drop from the trees to continue Life's cycle of generation and regeneration, so will my body be shed and become part of the muttering earth. Like the tree gathering in energy to prepare itself for winter, I feel a need to gather energy for the process of dying. Also, I want to share a last celebration with you dear friends. To do this, I have planned a ritual of transition to take place on Sunday, November 3, at 2:30 p.m. here at my home.

I would love it if you can participate with your presence; and if you cannot, I would appreciate your joining us in spirit with loving energy via the ethers that afternoon.

If you can come, please bring a pillow to sit on and a symbolic gift of your energy and blessing for me in this process I am going through--something from nature (rock, shell, feather, etc.); a poem, picture or song; something written or drawn; or whatever you are inspired to bring. Please also bring a casserole, salad or dessert or beverage to contribute to our potluck supper following the ritual.

There is a new joy that is beginning to be realized in me as I acknowledge the prospect of having my spirit float free of my tired body. I look forward to sharing this with you too.

Love and blessings,

Joan Conn

Figure 5-2   *Invitation to a Going-Away Party*
Ritual and companionship can assist in dealing with impending death. This celebration was attended by close friends and family, who said the occasion was an extremely moving experience. Knowing that she would soon die from cancer, Joan created a ritual that involved drawing a line on the floor and, in her weakened condition, she was helped across it by her ex-husband and her children while members of the gathering played music and sang. Although such an event would not be appropriate for everyone, Joan's farewell party aptly reflected her life style and values. She died seven months later.

circumstances of their lives. When ready to discuss these concerns, the patient needs a good listener, someone who can be present without judging or trying to persuade the patient to think or feel otherwise.

If the patient is able to confront the fact of illness and find ways of coping with the eventuality it represents, then chances are he or she will experience some resolution of the crisis. Acceptance does not mean giving up or losing hope; rather, it implies coming to an essentially positive, personally satisfying adjustment. Each such adjustment is unique, determined by such factors as the patient's personality, the kind of helping resources available in his or her environment, and the specific nature of the illness (see Figure 5-2).

These stages of coping with illness should not be thought of as strict categories that occur in a fixed sequence. A variety of emotions — anger, resentment, sadness, acceptance — may be experienced at any part of the process of dealing with illness and the prospect of death. Although there does tend to be movement from initial shock and anger toward eventual acceptance of the situation, a patient who has exhibited great acceptance of his or her death may die raging against the inevitable. Conversely, the angry fighter may find quiet resignation in the final moments of life, dying a peaceful death. Generally speaking, one's style in dying will probably resemble his or her style in living. But the range of adaptive responses to loss or to confronting one's death may vary widely as circumstances change (see Figure 5-3).

Throughout the process of coping with the changes caused by life-threatening illness — from the moment one notices the symptoms and wonders what they mean to the final moments lying in the deathbed anticipating death — hope and honesty exist in a delicate balance unique to each person: honesty to face reality as it is, hope that the outcome is positive. It is interesting to note how the object of hope changes. The initial hope that nothing is really

66—Real Estate Wanted

FORMER President — Major Manufacturing Company, age 56, with possible terminal disease interested in lease purchase of old home. Reasonably large. Farm house with property, condos, land with run down cabin or home in total disrepair. Probably in foothills between Santa Cruz and Castroville. Option period 18 months or final diagnosis — whichever is first. Any remodeling by permission of owner in his name. Will arrive from Seattle on Tuesday evening. Please leave number at Box 9, c/o this newspaper.

Figure 5-3 *Life Change with Life-Threatening Illness: Real Estate Want Ad*
The confrontation with a life-threatening illness may activate desires to accomplish in the present plans that previously had been visualized as occurring in the future.
Source: Register-Pajaronian (Watsonville, Calif.), March 11, 1981.

wrong gives way to hope that there will be a cure. If the disease seems incurable, then one hopes for more time. When time runs out, one hopes for a pain-free and comfortable death, a good death.

Treatment Options

The treatment options for life-threatening illness depend upon the nature of the disease and the patient's particular situation. As new medical technologies become available, treatment options may be drastically changed. Typically, however, medical advances occur gradually, steadily increasing the choices available to patients. For example, among the new technologies for diagnosing heart problems is the *cine CT*, an advancement in computer tomography that takes stop-action photos of the beating heart. This device allows cardiologists to measure and analyze data about the heart's functioning that otherwise could be obtained only through invasive and expensive procedures such as catheterization.[5]

The options available for treatment depend not only on the nature of the disease and the medical technologies available to treat it, but also on decisions made by society at large. The treatment for sudden cardiac death, a subset of coronary heart disease, is a case in point.[6] Of the 1.5 million heart attacks suffered by Americans each year, about three-quarters of the victims are admitted to hospitals where they receive advanced care; of these patients more than 80 percent survive and are discharged. Often, however, a heart attack is the first indication of any coronary problem. The key to life-saving intervention in cases of sudden heart attack and similar emergencies is a rapid and coordinated medical response. In communities that have placed a high priority on providing this kind of response and where emergency personnel are equipped with cardiac care units, fatalities have declined. Such care can be costly, however. Thus, a community's ability or willingness to pay for this kind of care can affect a patient's options for treatment.

Ethical issues must sometimes be resolved before a new therapy can be applied widely. For example, critics of the artificial heart argue that it does not really save patients' lives; it only changes the way they die. Proponents say the artificial heart could extend the lives of many people. Besides ethical issues involving patient care, questions of economics must be considered. With perhaps 35,000 potential candidates for the artificial heart each year in the United States, at a cost of $150,000 per implant, the procedure could add $5 billion to the nation's health bill. Some argue that this money should be used for health education aimed at preventing heart disease; others say that a similar amount is spent by Americans each year on video games.[7]

Current research in cancer treatment suggests major roles for recombinant DNA technology and for "monoclonal antibodies" that can be tailored to attack selected targets on cancer cells. With increased understanding of disease processes and improved diagnostic procedures, there is better "staging" of the disease to determine its precise characteristics and, when appropriate, to apply

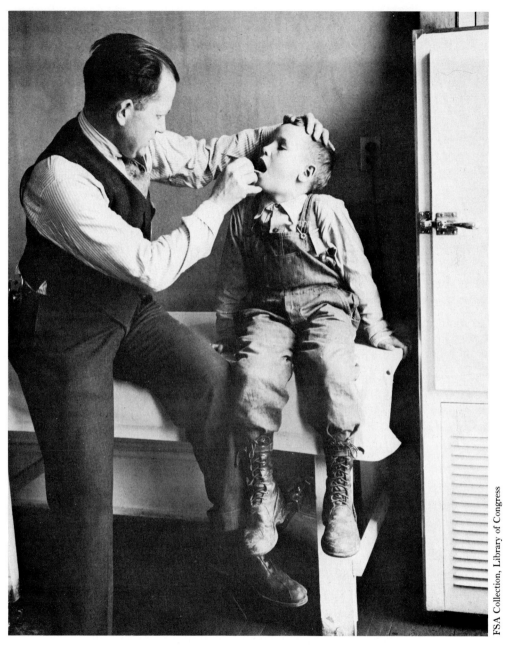

In 1935, medical care in Reedsville, West Virginia, seems less formal than that received in the urban clinics and hospitals of today. Although the practice of medicine has been enhanced by new methods of diagnosis and treatment, most people still believe that the relationship between physician and patient is central to the outcome of an illness.

TABLE 5-1   *Medical Treatment Word List*

Alkylating agents: A family of chemotherapeutic drugs that combine with DNA (genetic substance) to prevent normal cell division.

Analgesic: A drug used for reducing pain.

Antimetabolites: A family of chemotherapeutic drugs that interfere with the processes of DNA production, and thus prevent normal cell division.

Benign: Not malignant.

Biopsy: The surgical removal of a small portion of tissue for diagnosis.

Blood count: A laboratory study to evaluate the amount of white cells, red cells, and platelets.

Bone marrow: A soft substance found within bone cavities, ordinarily composed of fat and developing red cells, white cells, and platelets.

Cancer: A condition in which there is the proliferation of malignant cells that are capable of invading normal tissues.

Chemotherapy: The treatment of disease by chemicals (drugs) introduced into the bloodstream by injection or taken by mouth as tablets.

Cobalt treatment: Radiotherapy using gamma rays generated from the breakdown of radioactive cobalt-60.

Colostomy: Surgical formation of an artificial anus in the abdominal wall, so the colon can drain feces into a bag.

Coma: A condition of decreased mental function in which the individual is incapable of responding to any stimulus, including painful stimuli.

Cyanotic: A blue appearance of the skin, lips, or fingernails as the result of low oxygen content of the circulating blood.

Diagnosis: The process by which a disease is identified.

DNA: Abbreviation for deoxyribonucleic acid, the building block of the genes, responsible for the passing of hereditary characteristics from cell to cell.

Hodgkin's disease: A form of tumor that arises in a single lymph node and may spread to local and then distant lymph nodes and finally to other tissues, commonly including the spleen, liver, and bone marrow.

Immunotherapy: A method of cancer therapy that stimulates the body defenses (the immune system) to attack cancer cells or modify a specific disease state.

Intravenous (IV): Describing the administration of a drug or of fluid directly into a vein.

Leukemia: A malignant proliferation of white blood cells in the bone marrow; cancer of the blood cells.

Lymph nodes: Organized clusters of lymphocytes through which the tissue fluids drain upon returning to the blood circulation; they act as the first line of defense, filtering out and destroying infective organisms or cancer cells and initiating the generalized immune response.

Malignant: Having the potentiality of being lethal if not successfully treated. All cancers are malignant by definition.

Melanoma: A cancer of the pigment cells of the skin, usually arising in a preexisting pigmented area (mole).

Metastasis: The establishment of a secondary site or multiple sites of cancer separate from the primary or original site.

Multimodality therapy: The use of more than one modality for cure or palliation (abatement) of cancer.

T A B L E 5-1 (*continued*)

Myelogram: The introduction of radiopaque dye into the sac surrounding the spinal cord, a process that makes it possible to see tumor involvement of the spinal cord or nerve roots on X-ray.

Oncologist: An internist (specialist in internal medicine dealing with nonsurgical treatment of disease) who has subspecialized in cancer therapy and has expertise in both chemotherapy and the handling of problems arising during the course of the disease.

Parkinson's disease: Degenerative disease of the brain resulting in tremor and rigid muscles.

Prognosis: An estimate of the outcome of a disease based on the status of the patient and accumulated information about the disease and its treatment.

Prosthesis: An artificial structure designed to replace or approximate a normal one.

Regression: The diminution of cancerous involvement, usually as the result of therapy; it is manifested by decreased size of the tumor (or tumors) or its clinical evidence in fewer locations.

Relapse: The reappearance of cancer following a period of remission.

Remission: The temporary disappearance of evident active cancer, occurring either spontaneously or as the result of therapy.

Sarcoma: A cancer of connective tissue, bone, cartilage, fat, muscle, nerve sheath, blood vessels, or lymphoid system.

Subcutaneous cyst: A cyst located beneath the skin; usually benign.

Symptom: A manifestation or complaint of disease as described by the patient, as opposed to one found by the doctor's examination; the latter is referred to as a sign.

Terminal: Describing a condition of decline toward death, from which not even a brief reversal can be expected.

Therapeutic procedure: A procedure intended to offer palliation (abatement) or cure of a condition or disease.

Toxicity: The property of producing unpleasant or dangerous side effects.

Tumor: A mass or swelling. A tumor can be either benign or malignant.

Source: Excerpted and adapted from Ernest H. Rosenbaum, M.D., *Living with Cancer: A Guide for the Patient, the Family and Friends* (St. Louis: C.V. Mosby, 1982).

various therapies in combination. In the management of serious illnesses, emphasis is being placed on individualized treatment. Although different illnesses require forms of treatment specific to each, the options available to patients can be illustrated by focusing on the treatment modalities associated with cancer. (Key terms used in conjunction with the treatment of cancer and other diseases are defined in Table 5-1.)

As a general term, *cancer* encompasses many different types of malignant, or potentially lethal, growths that occur in many parts of the body. Because cancerous cells reproduce in a manner unregulated by the body's normal controls on cell growth, over time there is the possibility of unlimited expansion. First affecting tissues in one part of the body, cancer may spread either by invading adjacent tissues or by *metastasis*, a process whereby diseased cells travel in the blood or lymph system or through body tracts, to more distant parts of the body.[8] Successful treatment of cancer requires the destruction or removal of all cancerous tissue; otherwise, the disease recurs.

A number of therapies — primarily surgery, radiation therapy, and chemotherapy — have been applied to the management of cancer. But none is effective for all of the forms in which cancer may appear in the body. A treatment with a high rate of success with one type of cancer may be ineffective with another. Frequently, a combination of therapies is recommended, each designed to accomplish a particular aim within a comprehensive treatment program. Some treatments of life-threatening illness create the need for adjunctive therapies to counteract the side effects of the primary mode of treatment. As we discuss the various methods of treating cancer, the benefits and disadvantages of each type of therapy will be emphasized, along with its effects on the patient's experience.

Surgery

The greatest percentage of cancer cures have been due to the use of surgery. Indeed, most of the progress in cancer survival has come about because of improvements in surgical techniques and in preoperative and postoperative care, especially in control of infection. At present, surgery has no peer in the cure of cancer, although with some forms of cancer it is not successful.

However, whether used diagnostically or therapeutically to effect a cure, surgery is a target of controversy. Not only do physicians sometimes disagree about its benefits and risks, many people are frightened by the thought of undergoing surgery. Although surgery is a routine modern medical practice — and surgery to remove diseased tissues or organs is one of the earliest types — many people are afraid that, with cancer particularly, one surgical procedure leads to others. Considering the aims of cancer surgery — to keep the disease from spreading — it is true that repeated surgery may be necessary if this mode of treatment is to be followed through. In many cases, surgery has clearly at least extended a person's life, if not altogether effecting a cure.

Many people fear surgery as a violation of the body and the loss of some part of it; often they fear possible disfigurement, disability, or loss of bodily function. In cancer surgery, not only is the organ or tissue with the malignancy removed, but a wide margin of the adjacent tissue, possibly including adjacent organs, may also be removed to prevent the spread of cancer. In the case of breast cancer, for example, radical mastectomy (breast removal) has been a fairly common method of treatment. In radical surgical procedures, even if nearby lymphatic nodes appear normal, they are removed to prevent the persistence of any malignant cells that might cause a recurrence of the cancer if only the primary growth was removed. Such radical techniques have achieved a high percentage of cures in such diseases as breast cancer, although many practitioners are now seeking less disfiguring methods of successfully removing the cancerous tissue.

Another criticism sometimes voiced against surgery involves its use in

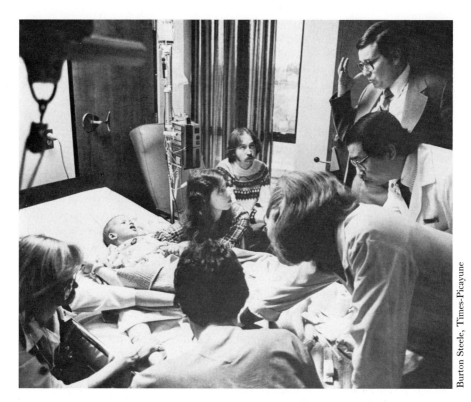

Burton Steele, Times-Picayune

Family members and consulting physicians gathered around the bedside of a seriously ill child discuss the impending brain surgery that everyone hopes will bring a favorable prognosis.

diagnosis. Some argue, for example, that taking a biopsy to detect a cancer in its early stages may contribute to the spread of disease. On the other hand, for surgery to be curative, it must be done before the cancer has spread into organs or tissues that cannot be safely removed. Thus, the advantages of early diagnoses must be weighed against possible risks.

Reconstructive techniques are also important to the overall success of surgery. For example, patients who undergo surgery for cancer of the colon or rectum can now be supplied with relatively simple devices for waste elimination. Improvements in such reconstructive and rehabilitative techniques have lessened the impact of radical surgery on the patient's life style and shortened recovery time.

In addition to the diagnostic and therapeutic uses of surgery already described, surgery is also used in some cases when severe pain is uncontrollable by other methods. Relief is made possible by the severing of nerve pathways that transmit the painful sensations. Also, surgery is important as a preventive measure in some cases. For example, surgery is used to eliminate precancerous conditions in the mouth, chronic ulcers that might lead to cancer of the colon, and certain precancerous polyps in the colon and rectum.

Despite the progress achieved by surgery, however, fewer than 50 percent of cancer patients can be cured by this procedure alone. Therefore, great effort has gone into discovering auxiliary therapies that can be given following surgery.[9]

Radiation Therapy

One of the most widely employed of these auxiliary therapies is *radiation*, which is used to treat more than half of the cancer patients in the United States. The potentialities of radiation for treating cancer were recognized soon after the discovery of radium in 1898. Radiation therapy uses ionizing radiation to destroy cells, thus preventing further cellular division and growth. Radiation affects both normal and cancerous tissues, but since cancer cells usually grow more rapidly than normal cells, they are more seriously damaged. Not all forms of cancer respond to radiation therapy. Some growths and tissues are quite sensitive to radiation; others are relatively resistant.

Many physicians credit radiotherapy with effecting cures for many cancers, although others question whether adequate statistics exist to support this claim. In any event, radiation does seem to be effective in at least slowing the growth of many types of malignancy. Remissions, though sometimes lasting for a year or less, frequently occur after radiation therapy. Even when a cure is not achieved or the growth arrested, however, a palliative effect often occurs, lessening the severity of the symptoms. Cancers of the breast, esophagus, bladder, brain, skin, uterus, larnyx, and tongue are among those commonly treated by radiation therapy. Radiation is often used as an adjunct to surgery for other cancers, such as cancer of the breast or cancer of the bone. It is also used in conjunction with chemotherapy in some cases.

Radiation therapy requires equipment costing many millions of dollars. Indeed, radiology is the most expensive branch of medicine in any institution, and the developmental cost of new technologies is great. Critics contend that these large expenditures divert funds that might be better spent investigating other possibly more effective options. It can also be argued, however, that the development of new instruments, which allow a greater radiation dose to be delivered to deep-seated malignancies without serious skin damage or other discomfort, makes possible the extensive use of radiation therapy in cancer treatment. Computers and radiology are now being wedded into a hybrid technology that allows computer-assisted planning and dose calculation; as these technologies proceed, it is expected that more efficient methods of analyzing data will result in more effective radiation therapies.

A further criticism levied against radiation treatment concerns the possibility of bringing harm to the patient by an increased vulnerability to infections and other maladies resulting from high doses of radiation. Again, this is an area where risks must be weighed against benefits. Although it is reasonable to rely to a large extent on the training and experience of the radiotherapist who must evaluate the various factors relative to a particular malignancy and then plan an optimal program of treatment, it is also prudent for the patient to understand his or her options before embarking on a course of treatment.

Radiation therapy can cause uncomfortable side effects. Most patients who receive radiation therapy are scheduled for frequent, intense treatments, commonly as often as three or four times a week over a period of several months. The radiation dose is prescribed on the basis of the stage of the disease and the patient's ability to withstand the side effects. Nausea, vomiting, tiredness, and general weakness often accompany treatment, and patients undergoing radiation therapy often express dread of additional treatments. Because the side effects are so frequently debilitating, many patients must curtail their activities in order to get necessary bed rest.

Although the successes with radiation therapy tend to be less dramatic than those possible with surgery, its continued achievement of at least moderate successes with many patients makes radiation therapy one of the most commonly practiced methods of treating cancer, either alone or in concert with other modes of therapy. As with surgery, however, radiation by itself is not a cure for most cancers, since the dosage required to eradicate all the cancer cells would also kill the patient.

Chemotherapy

Chemotherapy is the use of toxic drugs to kill cancer cells. It originated from the observation that the toxic effects of mustard gases during World War I included damage to the bone marrow. Following World War II, clinical trials with chemotherapy began and the early results were encouraging. Today, many different chemotherapeutic agents are employed, in various combinations, for treating cancer.[10] Chemotherapy has been called the leading weapon for *increasing* the number of patients who can be cured of cancer. To be effective therapeutically, the dose must be strong enough to kill the malignancy or slow its growth, but not so potent that it might seriously harm the patient. Ideally, a chemical agent of this kind would attack only the cancerous cells in the body without affecting normal, healthy tissue. Unfortunately, no such selective agent has yet been developed.

All the diverse chemotherapeutic agents basically work by blocking the metabolic processes involved in cellular division. Because cancer cells divide more rapidly than do most normal cells, the agents used in chemotherapy are designed to preferentially affect the cancerous cells.

A patient's chemotherapy program is continually evaluated in light of the stage of malignancy and the patient's response to therapy. A typical treatment program might entail six weeks of intensive chemotherapy, followed by a respite from treatment, then another cycle of chemotherapy.

Like radiation therapy, chemotherapy brings discomforting side effects to many, though not to all, patients: loss of hair, sleeplessness, nausea, difficulty in eating and digestion, bleeding sores around the mouth, ulceration and bleeding in the gastrointestinal tract, and various other toxic effects. Sometimes the visible side effects can be quite alarming to the patient's family and friends.

Side effects can be made worse by the patient's anxiety in anticipating additional treatments. At times it is in the patient's best interest to suspend therapy temporarily, allowing him or her time to rest and to regain a sense of equanimity toward therapy. If the patient's condition steadily declines despite the best therapeutic efforts, therapy may be stopped and any future medical efforts concentrated solely on controlling pain and other distressing symptoms: antinausea medications to control sickness, sedatives to induce sleep, and analgesic or narcotic medications to alleviate pain and discomfort.

Whether the particular drug used in chemotherapy is an alkylating agent, which prevents cells from making genetic material (DNA); an antimetabolite or antibiotic, which blocks nucleic acid synthesis; or an alkaloid, which stops cell division and induces other cellular changes, chemotherapeutic agents owe their effectiveness to the fact that they are poison. As a result, they damage normal as well as diseased tissue. In addition, some cancer cells eventually become resistant to the drugs. To overcome these limitations, and because chemotherapeutic agents generally destroy only the portion of the cell population that is currently undergoing division, several drugs that act on cells in different ways are usually administered in combination.

Although chemotherapy does not usually result in a cure, it has been used successfully with some forms of cancer. It has produced long-term, disease-free remissions in many children with acute leukemia, for example, and in many patients with advanced stages of Hodgkin's disease. Some of these patients have been in remission for five years or more and may, in fact, be cured. In certain forms of malignant diseases, such as leukemia, which cannot be treated by surgery, the palliative effects achieved by chemotherapy have allowed patients to lead a comparatively normal, even prolonged, life. Some skin cancers have also responded favorably to applications of certain chemotherapeutic ointments.

Interestingly, chemotherapy appears to be most effective with the less common forms of cancer and least effective with the more prevalent forms — cancers of the breast, colon, and lung. Nevertheless, with many cancers, chemotherapy does bring about a partial or temporary remission or some palliation of symptoms. Often, a more comfortable life, if not a cure, is achieved for the patient.

Other Therapies

Because the most common forms of treatment for cancer — surgery, radiation, and chemotherapy — do not always bring about a cure, patients sometimes pursue experimental or unorthodox therapies that seem to offer hope. Within the medical establishment itself, a perennial search is underway for more effective methods of treating disease; and, as new discoveries are made, the response from patients is often dramatic. When the National Cancer Institute announced the possibility of using Interleukin-2, a protein produced by the immune system, to boost the body's own natural defenses in attacking some forms of cancer, within a week's time the Institute logged over a thousand calls from people wanting to know how to avail themselves or a family member of the new therapy.[11] Although researchers emphasized that the discovery was a "first step" and "not a cure for cancer," many of the callers were desperate and felt they had "nothing to lose" from trying an experimental treatment.

Conventional medical therapies for cancer have helped countless persons back to health, whether briefly or for longer periods. Yet the obvious deficiencies of these therapies—the possibility of unpleasant side effects and varying rates of success—have caused some patients to seek treatments not offered by the medical establishment.

Unorthodox therapies encompass methods of treatment that the medical establishment considers unproven or potentially harmful. Those who advocate such remedies may be branded as quacks and their methods characterized as contemporary editions of Dr. Feelgood's Medicine Show, a form of snake oil medicine that, even if intrinsically quite harmless, diverts patients from conventional medical programs where they might receive more beneficial help.

Most patients prefer orthodox therapies, but others distrust the conventional approach and choose unsanctioned alternatives as their initial course of therapy. Some patients try to find a comfortable balance between medically approved therapies and more innovative approaches. For example, they may follow their doctor's prescription for radiation therapy or chemotherapy while at the same time pursuing techniques, such as biofeedback, meditation, or visualization, designed to mobilize the body's own resources. Many alternative approaches to treatment can be combined with an orthodox medical approach; others cannot, and require a radical departure from conventional medical practices.

What comes to mind when you hear the word *unorthodox*? Not accepted? Outside of the establishment? Ineffective? Nontraditional? Unsanctioned? That a supposed cancer cure derives from the pits of apricots or almonds may push the limits of credibility. Yet many of our most common medications are derived from such seemingly unlikely sources. Indeed, such medications—whether in natural or synthetic form—comprise a significant portion of the armamentaria of conventional medicine. Premarin, for instance, a drug that is widely prescribed to relieve menopausal symptoms, comes from *pregnant mares'* urine. Penicillin is naturally produced from molds. Digitalis, prescribed for some heart ailments, derives from the plant foxglove. The active ingredient of common aspirin is close kin to a substance found in the bark and leaves of the white willow. Clearly, the source of a proposed medicinal substance ought to concern us less than the question, Does it work?

Some of the methods banned from use in established medicine are unproven simply because of lack of research to determine their possible validity.[12] Still, lack of scientific evidence is no testimony to a therapy's effectiveness. What some of these unproven therapies need is a well-administered research design, by standard scientific criteria, to evaluate them satisfactorily.*

Your Caring Presence: Ways of Effectively Providing Support to Others

1. Be honest about your own thoughts, concerns, and feelings.

2. When in doubt, ask questions:

How is that for you?

How do you feel right now?

Can you tell me more about that?

Am I intruding?

What do you need?

What are the ways you can take care of yourself?

3. When you are responding to a person facing a crisis situation, be sure to use statements such as:

I feel _____

I believe _____

I would want _____

Rather than:

You should

That's wrong

Everything will be ok.

which are statements that may not give the person the opportunity to express his/her own unique needs and feelings.

4. Stay in the present as much as possible: How do you feel RIGHT NOW? What do you need RIGHT NOW?

5. Listening is profoundly healing. You don't have to make it better. You don't have to have the answers. You don't have to take away the pain. It's his pain. He needs to experience it in his own time and in his own way.

6. People in crisis need to know they have decision-making power. It may be appropriate to point out alternatives.

7. Offer any practical assistance that you feel comfortable giving.

8. If the situation warrants it, feel free to refer individual to appropriate agency.

The Centre for Living with Dying

Laetrile

Probably the most famous of the unorthodox cancer therapies is laetrile, synthesized in 1953 by Ernst T. Krebs and his son.[13] Laetrile occurs naturally in about twelve hundred plants, including food plants, found across the face of the earth. The laetrile available commercially is usually derived from the kernels of apricots, peaches, and bitter almonds. Laetrile has been around for a very long time. It has been used for medicinal purposes since ancient times in China, and among the ancient Greeks, Egyptians, and Romans. Arabic physicians are reported to have used it in preparations to treat tumors. Proponents of laetrile argue for its safety by asserting that, out of perhaps as many as 100,000 cancer patients using the drug each month, there are only two or three deaths annually from accidental overdose.

Whether laetrile is effective in treating cancer cannot be unequivocally substantiated at present. In the summer of 1977, the medical establishment announced that laetrile had been proven useless as a cancer cure; but advocates claimed that deficiencies in the research plan had compromised the test results. Critics attribute patient deaths to the use of laetrile, both because of its potentially toxic components and because it substitutes for orthodox therapies. Laetrile is seen as yet another misguided search for a "magic bullet" that will effect a miraculous cure for cancer.

Interferons

Unlike laetrile, interferons are considered by many in the medical establishment to be among the most promising of the unproven therapies. Whereas, from the establishment point of view, laetrile was tested and it failed, research on interferons has only recently gotten underway in earnest. Although it is too soon for a final judgment, many believe that interferons represent an exciting possibility for cancer therapy.

What are interferons? Simply put, they are a family of proteins produced by the body's cells when in the presence of viral infection. Although found in virtually all human cells, interferon is produced in such minute quantities that a teaspoon of purified interferon is worth approximately $250 to $300.[14] It is not entirely clear just how interferons work, although they seem to activate an immunologic response similar to the body's own defenses against disease.

Although preliminary results tend to cast doubt on whether interferons indeed represent a dramatic breakthrough in cancer therapy, there are indications that interferons can beneficially affect some cancers. A small number of companies have begun production of interferons using recombinant DNA technologies of genetic engineering.

At present, interferon therapy is still almost entirely experimental and the results are tentative; however, it seems that interferons may be most effective against relatively small tumors, which are treated in the early, less virulent stages. The medical community's interest in interferons is reflected in a forecast published by the National Academy of Sciences; it notes that the information available thus far about interferon therapy supports the belief that it warrants serious attention, although it is too soon to say where interferons might fit into the total scheme of cancer therapy.[15]

Infection and the Cancer Patient

Because cancer lowers the body's resistance to microorganisms, cancer patients tend to be extremely susceptible to infection. Some believe infection to be the most significant cause of mortality and manifest ill health, or wasting away, in cancer patients.[16] Infection can result from both endogenous, or resident, organisms and exogenous, or external, organisms. All three of the primary modes of treating cancer — surgery, radiation therapy, and chemotherapy — carry risks of infection. While surgery always involves some risk of infection, cancer patients' risk is increased significantly because resistance to infection tends to be lower and because malignancies tend to be conducive to the growth of microorganisms. Radiation therapy and chemotherapy increase the risk of infection because they work by suppressing the body's natural immune system.[17]

Treating cancer patients for infection is often difficult because the use of antibiotics to combat the infection may disturb the balance of normal microbial flora. Those who care for cancer patients need to be aware of the various preventive and therapeutic measures that are available for reducing the threat of infections. That hospitals are poor environments for avoiding infection is an additional argument against unnecessary hospitalization.

Coping Mentally and Emotionally with Life-Threatening Illness

It has long been a truism in medicine that hope and positive attitudes play a key part in the patient's ability to cope with illness. Indeed, some physicians have withheld the facts about a serious illness, fearing that a full, open disclosure might lessen the patient's chances of recovery or survival. However well-intended, this approach may do harm to the patient. When the patient is seen as a passive participant who merely follows the program outlined by the physician, options that rightfully belong to the patient may be subtly taken away. There is a difference between glossing over the facts to protect the patient and giving an account of the situation in a manner that corresponds with the patient's willingness to learn the truth. The second course of action is based on cooperation and a sense of partnership between physician and patient.

The distinction between these two models of how the patient is perceived is important, for it can determine whether or not the patient has available the range of resources that he or she finds necessary for coping with the realities of serious illness. When a patient is treated as a whole person and his or her preferences are respected, a sense of self-worth and dignity is elicited in the patient. He or she is empowered to make choices that demonstrate a sense of purpose resulting from a healthy self-concept.

The capacity to maintain a sense of self-worth, to set goals and strive to meet them, to exercise choice out of an awareness of one's power to meet challenges, to engage in active interactions with one's environment—all of these reflect a "coping potency" that sustains the will to live in the face of death. The goal is not to foster a one-dimensional strategy of coping with or "controlling" death. The goal is to help the patient manage his or her own adaptive responses and to facilitate self-control.

The role of the emotions in influencing physical well-being has received considerable attention in recent years.[18] In his book *The Will to Live*, Arnold Hutschnecker cited his clinical observations to support the thesis that the chief cause of death is illness traceable to emotional disorders. Cardiologists Meyer Friedman and Ray Rosenman established a relationship between certain patterns of behavior and the onset of heart disease, which they reported in their book, *Type A Behavior and Your Heart*. The role of emotional factors in the progress of cancer was dealt with in Lawrence LeShan's *You Can Fight for Your Life*. Oncologist Carl Simonton, in the book *Getting Well Again*, described certain predisposing factors in the development of tumors.

What are some of the common themes in these accounts? They are: loss of sense of purpose in life; inability to express anger or resentment; self-dislike and self-distrust; despairing and hopeless outlook on life; impatience with the pace at which events occur; striving to do more in less time; inability to relax; preoccupation with having, rather than being; inability to forgive; tendency toward self-pity; inability to develop and maintain meaningful relationships; and poor self-image. Taken together, these attitudes and behaviors are characterized by intense stress.

At the Cancer Counseling and Research Center in Dallas, Texas, established in 1974 by oncologist Carl Simonton and psychotherapist Stephanie Mathews Simonton, a variety of techniques are used for treating the emotional and physical aspects of illness.[19] The best known of these techniques is *visualization*. Here, the patient creates a mental state in which he or she takes control of bodily processes by imagining the diseased parts of the body becoming well again. Affirmations that one already exists in a state of wellness and creative fantasies directed toward wholeness are also used to generate a sense of well-being (see Figure 5-4, p. 164). The methods now known as the Simonton approach had their origin in the discovery that cases of spontaneous remission shared a common factor: The patient had viewed himself or herself as being well again. The Simontons' work suggests that the belief systems of the patient, the patient's family, and the physician must all be considered if emotional influences are to help in effecting a cure.

Studies have also been done at the Center on the effects of personality patterns and life histories on the outcome of disease processes. Stephanie Matthews Simonton reports that the stress of chronic depression and low self-esteem is a significant problem for many people with cancer.[20] A major focus of the work at the Center relates to helping patients learn to cope more effectively with the stress in their lives. Often, this means encouraging patients to express their feelings and to give more attention to their own lives. The techniques used at the Center are based on an understanding of the body's own immune response. Simonton says, "We know of no drugs or therapies that are as effective against cancer as the specific antigens an individual's body can create," and she adds, "the mind can affect this immune activity."

Many of the treatment methods developed by the Simontons are now in widespread use both in North America and abroad.[21] In addition to the imaginative techniques practiced at the Center, the Simontons also advocate the use of conventional cancer therapies. With chemotherapy, for instance, the patient visualizes the chemical agent inside the body, working to diminish the cancer and to restore well-being. The patient's responsibility and full participation in the process of disease and cure are stressed; however, patients are urged not to feel guilty about having the disease, but rather to simply become aware of the areas in their lives in which emotional needs have not been adequately satisfied.[22]

Figure 5-4 *Good Cells and Bad Cells: A Child's Drawing*
In this drawing by a child with cancer, the health-giving good cells are
depicted as being victorious over the diseased bad cells. Such imaginative
techniques can be ways of enlisting the patient's internal resources as an
adjunct to conventional therapies.
Source: Center for Attitudinal Healing, *There Is a Rainbow Behind Every Dark Cloud*
(Millbrae, Calif.: Celestial Arts, 1978), p. 71.

Essential to maintaining a positive attitude under the stress of life-
threatening illness is the patient's own self-image. Others who interact with the
patient can be crucial as well. Their expressed fears and misconceptions about
serious illness can have a significant bearing on how the patient perceives both
his or her physical condition and sense of self-worth.

The late Orville Kelly, founder of the support group Make Today Count,
described his response and the reactions of others when he learned that he had
cancer.[23] Kelly's first awareness that something was wrong led him to quit his
job as a newspaper editor and seek a change of climate. Soon afterwards he
discovered a swelling that was diagnosed as a malignancy. Given a prognosis of
from six months to six years to live, Kelly was depressed and contemplated
suicide, fearing that he might become a burden to his family.

Friends and relatives acted uncomfortable in his presence. One woman asked his wife, "How is he?"— despite the fact that Kelly was no more than a few feet away. Though yet alive, he was being subjected to a kind of social death, his full humanity already being written off by uneasy friends and relatives.

Despite his frightening prognosis, Kelly began to realize that in fact he was still alive. He could still love and be loved. No matter how short a time he might have to live, he could make the best of each day. He began talking openly about his feelings, expressing the kinds of concerns experienced by someone with a terminal illness. An article he wrote for the local newspaper elicited such response that it eventually led to the formation of the Make Today Count organization, a support group for the terminally ill that now has chapter meetings throughout the United States and in Canada and Europe.

The purpose of Make Today Count is to offer terminal patients and their families a comfortable and supportive environment where they can feel free to express themselves concerning the impact of life-threatening illness in their lives. These informal meetings are also attended by nurses, members of the clergy, oncologists, social workers, and others who wish to learn about and share the concerns of the terminally ill and their families. Recognizing that none of us is immune to death, the support groups founded by Kelly emphasize the importance of making each day count.

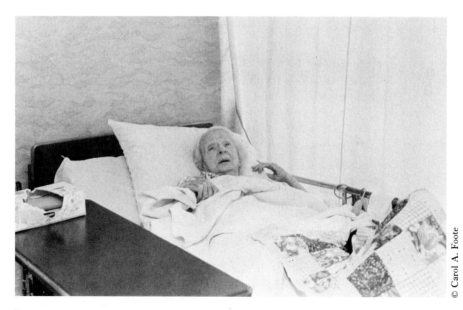

© Carol A. Foote

Being with a loved one who is dying confronts us with the fact of our own mortality as well as the losses associated with that person's death. Even when communication is hampered by physical disability, such times can be precious opportunities for sharing our deepest feelings with someone we love whose presence will be missed in our lives.

Helping a Loved One Who Is Dying

Most of us feel somewhat uncomfortable in the presence of a friend or relative who has been diagnosed with a life-threatening illness. What can we say? It seems that anything we might think of to express our feelings is little more than a stale platitude. So perhaps we stay away or, when visiting, avoid eye contact, shying away from real communication. We let ourselves off the hook while still managing to acknowledge our concern by directing our questions to a member of the patient's family rather than directly to the ill person.

Yet, if we truly love that person, we want to show our concern and to make meaningful human contact. We want to listen, to understand our friend's or relative's concerns, feelings, and thoughts. Perhaps feeling a little foolish and afraid, we may find ourselves wanting to make the situation something other than it is, something more comfortable, less distressing.

It is all right not to know how to respond or what to say. What we can offer is ourselves as we are, with our uncertainty and fear and anxieties. Indeed, we need not *do* anything. Being there for the other person means being sensitive to

There Are Days Now

There are days now
when I can see
the souls of elephants
being towed to heaven;
and the whales, the whales,
those hulls full of sadness!
Soon the trees will be loosed from their moorings
and sail off
like a chorus of Greek Women
rigid with grief.

I am resigned to this,
and yet
with each of their passings
there is a crumbling
along the banks of my bloodstream.
So if I touched you now,
my friend,
how could it be with my whole hand,
the fat resting firm beneath the palm,
and not with a clutch of fingers,
as though I had grabbed you in passing
and were holding on?

Morton Marcus

what is going on in the moment and simply responding as our heart dictates. If we are preoccupied with what we should do or say, or with wondering whether we are going to blunder somehow, our minds are full of confusion. The heart's simplicity is crowded out.

Being with someone who is dying, or who is facing death, we confront our own mortality.[24] It brings us to our senses, and we appreciate just how precious life is and just how uncertain. In that shared humanity, there is a recognition that each of us faces a similar predicament.

In such a context, being with someone who is dying can be a rare opportunity to share the deepest part of ourselves. What is shared may well be anger, frustration, pain, guilt, blame, denial. But there are few opportunities in life to be so vulnerable that we can touch those parts of ourselves usually kept hidden.

Being with someone who is dying does not mean that we must become comfortable, but that we learn to accept our discomfort. We learn that we cannot expect to have all the answers.

Further Readings

David Carroll. *Living with Dying: A Loving Guide for Family and Close Friends.* New York: McGraw-Hill, 1985.

Norman Cousins. *Anatomy of an Illness as Perceived by the Patient: Reflections on Healing and Regeneration.* New York: W. W. Norton, 1979.

Judylaine Fine. *Afraid to Ask: A Book for Families to Share About Cancer.* New York: Lothrop, Lee & Shepard, 1986.

Charles A. Garfield, *Stress and Survival: The Emotional Realities of Life-Threatening Illness.* St. Louis: C. V. Mosby, 1979.

Barney G. Glaser and Anselm L. Strauss. *Awareness of Dying.* Chicago: Aldine, 1965.

Orville E. Kelly. *Until Tomorrow Comes.* New York: Everest House, 1979.

Stephen Levine. *Meetings at the Edge: Dialogues with the Grieving and the Dying, the Healing and the Healed.* Garden City, N.Y.: Anchor Press/Doubleday, 1984.

E. Mansell Pattison. *The Experience of Dying.* Englewood Cliffs, N.J.: Prentice-Hall, 1977.

Leslie Roberts. *Cancer Today: Origins, Prevention, and Treatment.* Washington, D.C.: Institute of Medicine and National Academy Press, 1984.

Ernest H. Rosenbaum. *Living with Cancer.* St. Louis: C. V. Mosby, 1982.

Bernard Schoenberg, Arthur C. Carr, David Peretz, and Austin H. Kutscher, editors. *Psychosocial Aspects of Terminal Care.* New York: Columbia University Press, 1972.

Avery D. Weisman. *Coping with Cancer.* New York: McGraw-Hill, 1979.

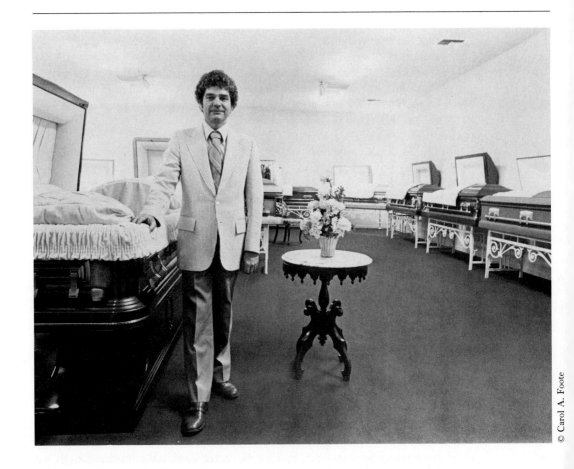

© Carol A. Foote

Familiarity with the choices available in funeral services can help us appreciate our many options, perhaps alleviating some of the stress of making such choices in the midst of crisis. The roles of the funeral director and others who can provide assistance in coping with the practical matters of death may also be better understood.

C H A P T E R 6

Last Rites: Funerals and Body Disposition

A young musician recently described the ceremony he would choose to mark his death: "My body would be cremated and the ashes put into an Egyptian urn. My friends would place the urn on stage at a rock concert and, as the band plays on, everyone will dance and celebrate the changes that we all must pass through eventually."

Some people would find the musician's choice lacking in solemnity. "That's not a funeral," they might say, "it's a party." The friends of the musician, however, might respond that his death style is consistent with his life style. Our personal choices regarding last rites tell something about our attitudes and beliefs about death. The ceremonies that a community enacts to mark the passing of one of its members express, through symbol and metaphor, how death is perceived within that particular cultural or social group.

The musician's funeral, for instance, bespeaks an emphasis on celebrating the joys of life well lived in contrast to expressing the sadness associated with mourning a death. His choice for cremation may reflect the belief that existence is transitory, as if to say, "Life is a passing show. When the movie's over for me, why should I want to preserve my body?" The Egyptian urn in which the ashes are placed may symbolize the musician's hope that in some way he is part of a historical continuity that transcends even death. Each component of the musician's death ceremony reveals something about his concept of death.

A society's attitude toward death, as well as toward the meaning and purpose of life, is usually revealed in its funeral customs. Examining the death customs of the ancient Egyptians, for example, we see a culture preoccupied with acquiring mortuary goods and preparing for the afterlife. A dominant theme in Egyptian religion was belief in life after death. The body was mortal. Yet within it were immortal parts: the *Ba,* a soul or psychic force, and the *Ka,* a spiritual double representing the creative and preserving power of life. At death, the *Ka* flew to the afterlife while the *Ba* lived on in the body.

As the permanent dwelling place of the *Ba,* the body was preserved by mummification and protected by wooden coffins, sometimes placed within stone sarcophagi; and the tomb was built to resemble one's earthly home.[1] If adequate preparations were made, there was no reason to fear death. By providing a home for the *Ba* (often depicted in the form of a bird hovering above the mummy of the deceased), continued enjoyment of the afterlife was ensured. On the other hand, if the *Ba* were destroyed, one would suffer "the second death, the death that really did come as the end." It would be as if the person were annihilated, as if he or she had never come into existence.

For the Egyptians, the body, as the concrete basis of one's individuality and immortality, was required in perpetuity. Preservation of the physical form, either as mummy or as statue, was necessary for survival. Thus, a person was forever attached to the tomb. This relationship between the identity of the

Metropolitan Museum of Art, Rogers/Harkness Funds, 1920

The presence of mortuary goods helped ensure a pleasant afterlife for the ancient Egyptians. Dating from the Eleventh Dynasty, about two thousand years before the present era, this funerary model of a paddling yacht comes from the tomb of Meket-Re.

person and the tomb, which may in some sense be universal, can be found in the feeling of communion with the deceased that one has at graveside.

Likewise, the customary American funeral contains a wealth of information concerning how we think about death in our society. Consider, for example, the practice of cosmetically restoring the corpse to a more or less lifelike appearance. Critics of American funeral practices say that this effort to disguise the face of death perpetuates the tendency to deny death. Some would eliminate not only the questionable practice, but the funeral itself.

Lavish displays for the dead have aroused criticism at least since the time of the Greek philosopher Herodotus in the fourth century B.C. But, as some writers have observed, ours is the first society that apparently wishes to do away with all traces of death by quickly disposing of the corpse. To determine whether contemporary American funeral practices encourage death to be denied rather than accepted, each of us must consider these questions: Who does the funeral serve—the living or the dead? What is the purpose—socially and psychologically—of last rites? What are the essentials?

As we saw in Chapter 2, in some cultures the funeral is primarily a vehicle for preparing the dead to successfully migrate to the after world. If properly carried out, last rites ensure not only safe conduct for the dead but also peace for the survivors. The American funeral is focused on the welfare of the survivors. Socially, the funeral provides a setting wherein the bereaved family is able to make a public statement that one of its members has died. The wider community responds with sympathy and support for the bereaved. Psychologically, the funeral provides a framework within which survivors confront the fact of their loss. By enacting the funeral ritual, survivors begin to resolve the crisis and accept the loss.

What happens, then, when the corpse is removed from the site of death and taken directly for cremation, and the ashes are scattered—all without participation of family or friends? If, as many believe, funeral ceremonies serve an important social and psychological function for survivors, is something significant omitted when last rites are so abrupt? Examining our own feelings about funerals and learning about the available choices can allow us to create alternative ceremonies that reflect a new awareness of death and its meaning in our lives.

Social Aspects of Last Rites

Funeral ceremonies and memorial services are rites of passage that reflect a community's acknowledgment that one of its members has died. Often termed *last rites,* they mark the final transition or passage of an individual in his or her status as a member of the larger social group. Just as a community convenes to commemorate the other major social transitions in a person's life—birth, marriage, and childbirth, for instance—there is a gathering together of the survivors to commemorate the deceased's participation as a member of the community and his or her passage from the group by death.

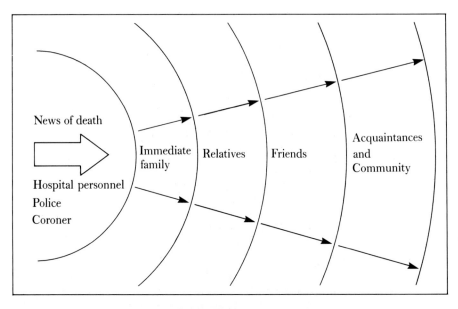

Figure 6-1   *Widening Circles of Death Notification*

Notification of Death

A death occurs. First to learn about it, besides the attending medical team, are usually members of the immediate family. Then, in a gradually widening network, other relatives and friends of the deceased are notified. David Sudnow observed that notification occurs generally in a consistent pattern from the immediate family to the wider community (see Figure 6-1).[2] Those with closest relationships to the deceased are notified first, followed by those with less intimate relationships. Sudnow also discovered that notification of a death generally takes place between persons in a peer relationship. For example, a bereaved mother might first call the child who had been closest to the deceased, and that person then calls the other brothers and sisters. They, in turn, notify more distant kin.

A similar pattern of notification occurs among those who were not directly related to the deceased. For instance, a co-worker or neighbor told about the death notifies others who had a similar relationship with the deceased. This process of notification — taking in a gradually widening circle of relatives, friends, and acquaintances — continues until virtually everyone affected by the death is notified.

Death notification also takes place by means of death notices that appear in the newspaper (see Figure 6-2). We expect death announcements to appear in a timely fashion. When they do not, the results can be upsetting. The following complaint is typical: "The obituary did not appear in the newspaper until the

Beth Blanchette

Beth Blanchette, 22, ill for the past eight years with Hodgkin's disease, died Tuesday at her home in Aptos.

Miss Blanchette, despite or perhaps because of her illness, had volunteered her services in the death and dying program at Cabrillo College, often speaking to classes.

A native of New Hampshire, Miss Blanchette was salutatorian of the class of 1977 at Aptos High School. She continued her education at Cabrillo College and UC-Santa Cruz until her illness made further study impossible.

She leaves her parents, Ron and Patricia Blanchette, of Aptos; a sister, Sarah, of Aptos; a brother, Craig, of Aptos; grandparents, Oliver and Marion Blanchette, of New Hampshire, and close friends, the Donatini family of Aptos.

A memorial celebration of Miss Blanchette's life and death will be held Saturday at 2 p.m. at her home, 2724 Borregas Drive, Aptos.

The family requests donations be sent to the Beth Blanchette Scholarship Fund for a biology student at Cabrillo College, 6500 Soquel Drive, Aptos.

White's Chapel, 138 Walnut Ave. Santa Cruz, is in charge of arrangements.

Figure 6-2 *Newspaper Obituary*
Source: Register-Pajaronian
(Watsonville, Calif.), July 22, 1981.

morning of the funeral. . . . We had a number of calls and letters from people who didn't know about the funeral until it was too late."[3]

When the deceased person is better known, news of the death is broadcast more widely, because it affects more people. Thus, notification about the deaths of public figures is carried out on a grand scale. The death of President John F. Kennedy, for example, was known about by 90 percent of the American people within an hour of its official pronouncement at Parkland Hospital in Dallas.[4]

Human beings feel the need to respond to the death of a significant other. The actual response depends on many factors, including the relationship with the deceased. But obviously, a person not notified cannot respond. The person who hears about the death only after the final disposition of the body may deeply

In an earlier time, when society was more agrarian, the whole community could pause from the daily round and rally to the support of the family at the funeral. In this urban age, however, when families live anonymously and work miles from their bedroom communities, and when approximately 60 percent of the women are in the work force, it is increasingly difficult for people to attend daytime funerals unless the deceased is a close relative. The policy of many companies is to give released time to employees only for the funeral of an immediate family member. Consequently, the tendency is for acquaintances to call at the parlor during evening visitation hours and for only the closest friends and relatives to attend the funeral itself. Many clergy feel this deprives the family of a powerful support system and renders impossible a corporate celebration of the life of the deceased.

Frank Minton, "Clergy Views of Funeral Practice"

regret not having been able to participate in the final ceremonies marking that person's death. This inadvertent exclusion may add to the survivor's shock and make the process of coming to terms with the loss more difficult. The mutual support of the community of bereaved persons is not likely to be as available after the initial period of mourning has passed. Thus, the belatedly notified person may feel alone in dealing with grief.

The process of death notification may also help to set apart the bereaved during the period of mourning. In some societies, the black armband, mourning colors and garb, as well as various other signs and symbols, distinguish the bereaved person from those not in mourning. Those traditional signs of mourning have almost vanished from American life. Yet most people still feel that the bereaved deserve special consideration during their distress.

A woman who became involved in an automobile accident several days after the death of her child said later that she wished she could have had a banner proclaiming her status as a "mother whose child has just died." With no outward symbol of her bereavement, she was subjected, as any of us would be, to the strain of waiting around and filling in seemingly endless accident report forms. Had she lived in a small enough town, the process of notification itself might have set her apart in such a way that the task of completing the paperwork would have been made easier and more convenient.

Though often taken for granted, the process of death notification is important. It can elicit communal support that is usually quite helpful to survivors in dealing with their loss. Notification also provides the impetus for coming to terms with the fact that a significant loss has taken place.

Mutual Support of the Bereaved

When people learn about the death of someone significant to them, they tend to gather together, closing ranks to provide support and comfort in their mutual bereavement. Generally, this emotional and social support is directed primarily toward the bereaved family. When one small child asked her mother why they were going to visit a bereaved family, the mother replied, "It's important for people to know that you care." What we think we can or cannot do for the bereaved family matters less than that somehow we demonstrate our care and concern. J. Z. Young says, "Probably the very act of coming together symbolizes communication. A symbol is a sign that points to some state that is of emotional importance. The very fact of assembly gives reassurance that we are part of a larger whole and the individual life is strengthened thereby."[5]

Those who gather at the home of the bereaved participate in a unique social occasion. Unlike other social interactions, this one is not by "invitation only"; generally speaking, anyone who wishes may come. Some persons stay only a short while, expressing their condolences and then leaving. Others, often relatives or close friends, stay for a longer time, perhaps assisting with the preparation of food, caring for children, helping with funeral arrangements, greeting visitors, or doing whatever else needs doing during the crisis.

Gathering together to support and comfort the bereaved continues throughout the events of the funeral. This unique pattern of social interaction has important psychological implications for the bereaved as well. It serves to corroborate the fact that a loved one has died. It expresses the notion, "Our community of family and friends has undergone a significant change of status; one of our members is dead." The coming together of the community members to support one another confirms the significance of that loss.

Bereavement as Social Change

Death is a change of status for the person who dies, and brings a change of status for the survivors. Recalling our discussion of the LoDagaa in Chapter 2, we know that funeral rituals embody the rhythms of separation and integration. The survivors come together as a community to let go of the dead person, and to acknowledge that their situation is no longer the same. This change of status is sometimes reflected in language, as when we refer to someone as a widow or widower. The use of a special term to designate a surviving husband or wife calls attention to the social and psychological impact of a spouse's death. (Indeed, the reaction to a spouse's death may be so severe that it threatens the survivor's well-being, a situation discussed in Chapter 7.)

Funerals as a Coping Mechanism

Death must be confronted not only within the social setting in which it occurs, but withing the psyche of the bereaved person. While the processes of death notification and visitations are forms of social interaction, they also provide a potent psychological means for coming to terms with a death.

When death occurs, the most immediate need of the survivors is the disposition of the corpse, which involves both a mental process (deciding what is to be done) and a physical activity (carrying out the course of action decided upon). Making arrangements for disposition of the body engages the survivor in a process that helps to reinforce the realization that the deceased is really dead.

Thousands of American citizens joined in the funeral observance honoring the Unknown Serviceman of the Vietnam Era. Here the procession is crossing Memorial Bridge between a Marine honor cordon, on its way to Arlington National Cemetery. Replete with full military honors, the funeral was an occasion for expressing national gratitude and grief in response to the ultimate sacrifice of those who died in the wartime service of their country.

William E. Rosemund, U.S. Army Photo

This gradual realization of the loss can take place whether the survivor simply talks with someone about funeral arrangements or actively constructs the coffin and digs the grave. Surrounding the final disposition of the body is a complex of social, cultural, religious, psychological, and interpersonal factors that determine the ritual form in which this basic task of body disposition is accomplished. The ceremonial dimensions provide significance to the events that lead to the final disposition of the deceased's body.

The American Funeral: History and Criticisms

Are those who provide care of our dead, the funeral directors, doing a satisfactory job? Not everyone would answer affirmatively. Yet the criticisms of American funeral practices have sometimes obscured the fact that most Americans give the funeral service trade positive marks. In a 1979 survey of persons who had recently had to make funeral arrangements, 96 percent said they were either highly satisfied (72 percent) or satisfied (24 percent) with the services they received.[6] Similar results have been reported in other surveys of public opinion, with about nine out of ten Americans rating the performance of funeral homes as good to excellent.[7] Why, then, does there seem to be such a public outcry about contemporary funeral practices, and to what extent are the criticisms justified?

To answer this question, we need to understand how American funeral

 If you have an uncomfortable feeling about funerals, which are the accepted social pattern for confronting death in our culture, if you try to avoid or eliminate them, that might be a sign that you're dealing with major residual death anxiety. That's one of the things that shows up in our culture: the way people delude themselves and retreat from the major therapeutic resources that are provided culturally. There's a notion that if we have a mini-funeral, we'll have mini-grief. But we know that the exact opposite is true.

The more you reduce your emotional acting out at the time of the event, the more you prolong the pain of grief and postpone the therapeutic work of mourning.

That's why in a culture such as ours, where you have an unwise management of grief, you have a very large proportion of illness responses after the death experience. People act it out physically, rather than doing it psychologically or socially. That's a very heavy weight.

But in primitive cultures, such as the aboriginals in Australia, where you have almost a two-week funeral process, where there are all kinds of acting out of deep feelings, you come to the end of that two weeks and a major portion of the grief work has been done, and the survivor is ready to move into the period of resolution through the mourning process, which takes quite a bit longer usually.

Edgar N. Jackson,
from an interview with the authors

practices evolved to the patterns we are familiar with today. Formerly, when families themselves took care of the disposition of their dead, any criticism of their manner of performance would have been superfluous. Nor, of course, was it designed to produce a profit. Disposition was simply a human task to be carried out in a spirit of compassion, kindness, and respect. We may yet have a residual feeling that realizing a profit from performing these services is somehow macabre.

Another consideration arises from our own anxiety about death and our aversion to touching or being in the presence of a corpse. (Such aversion can perhaps be attributed to our unfamiliarity with personal care of the dead: an effect, rather than a cause, of current practices.) Yet when the corpse is of someone we have loved, our aversion may be mixed with guilt; we are pulled in opposing directions, and feel uncomfortable about the dead. We may unconsciously resent the funeral director who handles the body of our loved one. Thus, we feel a confusing range of emotions regarding the dead: aversion, guilt, resentment, affection, and anxiety.

In the early years of our country, lumber was plentiful and people built big houses to shelter their rather large extended families. The family's ceremonial occasions were held within the home. In the 1880s the undertaker was a tradesman, a merchant who supplied the materials and funeral paraphernalia: such items as the casket and carriage, door badges and scarfs, special clothing, memorial cards and announcements, chairs, robes, pillows, gauze, candles, ornaments, and so on — items used to equip the home for the mourning ritual (see Figure 6-3).

By the end of the nineteenth century, however, the undertaker had assumed a much larger role. No longer merely a tradesman who furnished goods to the bereaved family, the undertaker had become a provider of services. He was being asked to take more control and to assume a larger role, actually taking part in the disposition of the dead: laying out the body for the wake, transporting it to the church for the funeral, and finally to the cemetery for burial.

B. WHEATLEY,

CABINET MAKER

AND

GENERAL
FURNISHING UNDERTAKER.

Funerals attended to at all hours.

Alfred Street, near King,

ALEXANDRIA, VA.

Figure 6-3   *City Directory Listing for a Cabinet Maker and Supplier of Funeral Furnishings, circa 1850*

J. C. TAYLOR & SON'S
PATENT IMPROVED ICE CASKETS,
FOR PRESERVING THE DEAD BY COLD AIR.
The Pioneer Corpse Preserver, Over 3,500 in Use.

PRICES AND SIZES:

6 Feet 4 Inches Long, 20 Inches Wide, $60 00. | 4 Feet 10 Inches Long, 17 Inches Wide, $48 00.
5 " 10 " " " 20 " " " 58 00. | 3 " 10 " " " 15 " " " 42 00.

Send for Illustrated and Descriptive Price-List, Containing full Particulars.

FOR SALE AT MANUFACTURERS' PRICES, BY

Paxson, Comfort & Co., 523 Market St., Philadelphia.

Figure 6-4 *Refrigerated Casket Advertisement,* 1881
Undertakers of the 1880s could keep a body for viewing over a longer period
of time by using an ice casket such as the one shown in this advertisement.
When embalming became widespread, these cold-air preservation devices
became obsolete.
Source: Atheneum of Philadelphia Collection; from Paxton, Comfort, and Company,
Undertakers' Supplies Catalog, 1881.

Embalming the dead had gradually come into use in the years after the
Civil War. Vanderlyn Pine mentions that President Lincoln's funeral procession, which traveled from Washington, D.C., to Springfield, Illinois, was a
public event that increased awareness of the new practice of embalming.[8] There
is some evidence that embalming was performed on some of the soldiers killed
during the Civil War, to permit their bodies to be returned home.[9] Other means
of temporarily retarding decomposition of the corpse continued in use, however
(see Figure 6-4).

With the coming of smaller houses and increased urbanization, the place
where the dead were prepared for burial changed: The funeral "parlor" moved
from the parlor of the family home into a room reserved for such use by the
undertaker. The funeral parlor in town then became the substitute for the
ceremonial room that people no longer had in their own home. This one-room
funeral parlor was the forerunner of the present-day funeral home or mortuary.

The last quarter of the nineteenth century in America saw the growth of trade and professional organizations. Also affected by this trend were the undertakers, who by that time had already become "morticians" and were starting to think of themselves as "funeral *directors*." The Funeral Directors' National Association, established in the 1880s — now the National Funeral Directors Association (NFDA) — was among the first of these new trade organizations designed both to promote business and to establish minimum standards for service. Trade publications, such as *The Casket* and *Sunnyside,* provided a means of communication among funeral directors. In 1917 the National Selected Morticians was formed as a limited-membership group dedicated to the ideal of service. A more recent organization, the National Foundation of Funeral Service, was formed in 1945, to conduct research, establish a comprehensive library of funeral service information, and sponsor an institute providing professional education for funeral directors. Today, most states require that funeral directors be certified by state licensing, and all states require that embalmers be licensed.

The American funeral has been criticized on several grounds, from general objections to what a funeral represents to criticisms of particular funeral practices. Bertram Puckle's *Funeral Customs: Their Origin and Development,* published in 1926, was of the first type, being a general polemic against the lavish concern for the dead, which was not unique to American funeral practice, but common to care of the dead in human societies generally. To Puckle the funeral represented a vestige of the superstitious fear of the dead characteristic of the pagan and the primitive.

In 1959 LeRoy Bowman, in *The American Funeral: A Study in Guilt, Extravagance, and Sublimity,* documented the commercialism and conspicuous display connected with funerals while investigating the social and psychological value of funerals. Bowman concluded that contemporary funeral practices were overlaid with such ostentation that the fundamental meaning and dignity of the funeral rite had all but disappeared. The American funeral, he said, "appears to be an anachronism, an elaboration of early customs rather than the adaptation to modern needs that it should be."[10] To avoid the potential for exploitation associated with the materialistic features of contemporary practices, Bowman urged Americans to become more aware of the essential social, psychological, and spiritual functions of funeral rituals.

To Bowman, the funeral director was not a professional, but a tradesman, often selling wares that were unnecessary and unwanted.[11] The function of the funeral director, Bowman said, should be to help the family fulfill its own wishes. In this, Bowman urged considerably more flexibility in our last rites. "The uniformity of present usage should give way to individually adapted procedures, whatever they may be."[12] A balanced and sober inquiry, Bowman's book continues to have value to anyone wishing more participation in the design of funeral rituals.

In 1963 two books appeared that helped to bring criticisms about the American funeral to the attention of the public: Jessica Mitford's *The American Way of Death* and Ruth M. Harmer's *The High Cost of Dying*. The messages

The funeral director is caught between ambivalent demands: On the one hand, he is encouraged to disguise the reality of death for the survivors who do not possess the emotional support once provided by theology to deal with it; on the other hand, he is impelled to call attention to the special services he is rendering. Thus, he both blunts and sharpens the reality of death.

Robert Fulton and Gilbert Geis,
"Death and Social Values"

were similar, though somewhat different in tone. Both books cited the economics and the materialism of the contemporary funeral and called for reforms.

Mitford said that conventional funeral practices were not only bizarre, but morbid. In our attempt to disguise and prettify death, we make it more grotesque. She took issue with the euphemisms employed to soften the reality of death: the metamorphosis of coffins into "caskets," hearses into "coaches" or "professional cars"; flowers become "floral tributes," and cremated ashes are "cremains." The corpse, meanwhile, lies in state in the "slumber room." The undertaker, now a "mortician" or "funeral director," offers the solid-copper "Colonial Classic Beauty," replete with a "Perfect-Posture" adjustable innerspring mattress, in a choice of "60 color-matched shades." Within this handsome arrangement, the deceased wears "handmade original fashions" from a "gravewear couturiere" and "Nature-Glo, the ultimate in cosmetic grooming."[13]

Mitford's satiric criticisms sparked considerable concern among those in the funeral trade, who saw it as a serious threat to their economic well-being. The book also increased the public's awareness of alternatives, such as memorial societies. Above all, Mitford's indictment of what she considered to be unscrupulous practices being perpetrated on an unsuspecting public led to a widespread reexamination of the American way of death, both within the funeral trade itself and in society at large. Once the initial furor lessened, most funeral directors began to respond to the criticisms in a reasonable and cooperative way; many worked earnestly to offer a wider range of choices in funeral service. A 1967 survey of funeral directors by Robert Fulton indicated a trend toward more individualized services offered by the funeral trade.[14]

According to a study of clergy attitudes toward funeral directors, the experiences of members of the clergy with funerals and with funeral directors were on the whole positive.[15] Still, some clergy members expressed reservations about the level of protection from occasional inappropriate practices — although few recalled personally unpleasant experiences. Cautious, somewhat critical reservations were expressed more frequently about funeral practices in urban areas, where more funeral establishments are operated by bureaucratic corporations, than in rural locales or small towns, where funeral directors tend to be the owner-operators of a single funeral home.

Some clergy members have voiced concerns about the expanding role of funeral directors into areas that previously came under the jurisdiction of the religious community. In earlier times the clergy fulfilled a significant role in dealing with the bereaved family and in making preparations for the disposition of the corpse. Now funeral services are seldom held in churches, having been moved to the chapels that are part of the modern funeral establishment. Many clergy would like to reverse this trend, particularly in the case of funerals for their church members.[16] Although many clergy do advocate simpler and less costly funerals, even those most critical of present practices did not fault funeral directors for a lack of professional integrity.

A 1979 study by Kalish and Goldberg, conducted for the Federal Trade Commission (FTC) as part of its investigation into funeral practices, sampled community attitudes toward funeral directors.[17] It was found that a substantial majority approved of present funeral practices. In general, respondents said they were shown an adequate range of caskets, understood what was included in the price, and received sufficient information to make a satisfactory decision. Most believed that the funeral director had been helpful in selecting the kind of service desired, without deprecating less expensive caskets or services. Indeed, they expressed the view that the funeral director had helped them keep costs down. Very few believed there was any attempt to manipulate the purchase of funeral services by taking advantage of their grief.

Kalish and Goldberg concluded that most people believed the requirements to be stipulated in the proposed rules of the Federal Trade Commission were already being met or were not needed.[18] How to account, then, for the horror stories? If the relatively few complaints voiced to the FTC were extrapolated to the larger community, there could be tens of thousands of people who experienced problems with funeral services. There is a widespread feeling that funeral directors could be in a position to take advantage of their customers since the activities and costs of funeral services are unfamiliar to most people. The funeral industry is viewed as a "mystery business," about which the average person knows little. Thus, despite what appears to be general satisfaction with funeral service, there is also some concern about whether one would know if he or she were being ripped off.[19]

Perhaps largely because of this concern, the Federal Trade Commission implemented its "Trade Regulation Rule on Funeral Industry Practices" in 1984. The Funeral Rule, as it is called, stipulates that funeral providers give detailed information about prices and legal requirements to persons who are arranging funerals. It requires disclosure of itemized price information, both over the telephone and in writing. Misrepresentations about the disposition of human remains are prohibited, as are certain unfair practices, such as embalming for a fee without prior permission, requiring customers to purchase caskets for a direct cremation, or making the purchase of any funeral good or service conditional on the purchase of any other funeral good or service.[20]

Looking back at the debate between those who claimed that abuses existed and the funeral service industry, with its response that such abuses were the

"Now, Mr. Barlow, what had you in mind? Embalmment of course, and after that incineration or not, according to taste. Our crematory is on scientific principles, the heat is so intense that all inessentials are volatilized. Some people did not like the thought that ashes of the casket and clothing were mixed with the Loved One's. Normal disposal is by inhumement, entombment, inurnment or immurement, but many people just lately prefer insarcophagusment. That is *very* individual. The casket is placed inside a sealed sarcophagus, marble or bronze, and rests permanently above ground in a niche in the mausoleum, with or without a personal stained-glass window above. That, of course, is for those with whom price is not a primary consideration."

Evelyn Waugh, *The Loved One*

Library of Congress

The funeral has traditionally been a time when family and friends come together to pay respects and to say farewells. It is a time of mutual support for the bereaved and of tribute to the deceased. The display of flowers surrounding this coffin bespeaks the affection felt for the deceased while she was alive and the sense of loss at her absence from the community.

exception, perhaps both sides were right. It would seem that most funeral directors are honest and sensitive to their customers' needs, and public attitudes generally confirmed satisfaction with funeral service practices even before the FTC's rule. Yet the exceptions may have been sufficiently numerous and widespread to warrant governmental regulation.

Selecting Funeral Services: Awareness and Alternatives

The purchase of funeral services is a transaction unique in commerce. Most people give it little or no thought until they find themselves in the midst of an emotional crisis. When arrangements for funeral services are made during a time of crisis and confusion, the customer is confronted with the need to make an on-the-spot decision about a purchase that cannot be returned. Caskets do not bear a notice saying, "Return in thirty days if not completely satisfied." Once made, the decision is final. Lack of information, coupled with lack of any forethought about funerals or body disposition, may lead to decisions that will be regretted later. For instance, unaware that a casket is not required for a body that is to be cremated, the bereaved may be inclined to buy the best available, thinking that there is no real alternative.

The choices involved in selecting funeral services tend to be quite different from those involved in other purchases. When purchasing a new car, for example, you can shop around and test-drive various makes and models. If you encounter a salesperson who uses high-pressure techniques, you can either submit to such tactics or walk away: You have a clear choice. Yet, rarely do the emotional conditions in which funeral services are purchased allow for such coolheadedness or presence of mind that the bereaved can simply walk away and go elsewhere to compare prices. In some localities, there may be only one mortician to serve the entire community. Even in the best of circumstances, the customer may be hard put to find suitable alternatives. When a death has already occurred, it can be too late to start investigating the options.

Our choice of the last rites with which we want to mark the passing of a loved one is influenced by family preferences and traditions, religious beliefs, and community customs. The funeral is a setting for private sorrow and public loss in which the burden of grief is reduced by sharing with others. It effects the disposition of the corpse while acknowledging that indeed a life has been lived. As a consequence, many believe that a funeral ought to be consistent with the life style of the deceased in order to bring about psychological closure for the survivors. The typical American funeral may fail to meet people's needs in precisely this respect: It may bear little resemblance to the deceased's style when living.

The funeral is a statement from the family to the wider community: "We have lost someone, and we are grieving." Ideally, it is a personal statement based on felt needs and values. Unfortunately, the funeral may become an occasion for an expensive or lavish display as survivors attempt to assuage guilt or to compensate for some unresolved conflict with the deceased. Spending a huge sum of money on a funeral, under such circumstances, may thwart the real purpose of last rites: namely, to acknowledge publicly that a member of the community has died, and to effect closure on that person's life for the bereaved. The purpose of the funeral can be realized whether it is garnished with diamonds and rubies, or with poetry and a song.

Funeral Service Charges

As in other areas of our lives, today we are paying closer attention to the financial concomitants of death. Funeral establishments now provide customers with a cost-analysis of their services, enabling the customer to choose those elements best suited to closure of the deceased's life.

The National Funeral Directors Association has distinguished four categories of charges that together make up the cost of a conventional American funeral.[21] The first category includes the services provided by the funeral director and mortuary staff, the use of mortuary facilities and equipment, and the casket and related funeral merchandise selected by the customer.

The second category pertains to the actual disposition of the body. Depending on the method of disposition chosen, this can include the purchase of a gravesite and costs for opening and closing the grave; or, if above-ground entombment is chosen, the cost of a mausoleum crypt; or, if the body is cremated, the cost of cremation and the subsequent interment, entombment, or scattering of the cremated remains, as well as the cost of an urn to hold the ashes, if desired.

The third category is made up of costs related to memorialization, which may include a monument or marker for the grave, or, for cremated remains, a memorial niche in a columbarium with an inscription or plaque.

The fourth category involves miscellaneous expenses either paid directly by the family or reimbursed to the undertaker. These may include a clergy member's honorarium, the use of limousines and additional vehicles (if not included in the funeral services category), flowers, notices of the death that appear in newspapers, and transportation outside the local area.

In summary, then, the total cost for the final disposition of the deceased includes funeral service charges, body disposition costs, memorialization expenses, and miscellaneous or supplemental expenses.

Until recently, the funeral director's portion of these expenses might be quoted to customers in a variety of ways. The most widespread form of pricing, and the simplest, was the single-unit method: A single price was quoted for a standard funeral; the specifics of the service and the total price depended upon the type of casket selected. A more expensive casket thus would become the centerpiece of a correspondingly more ornate and elaborate ceremony.

As consumers wanted more detailed information about costs, many funeral directors turned to functional or multi-unit pricing: A separate price would be quoted for each of the several components of the total service provided. For example, using a bi-unit method of pricing, there would be one charge for funeral services and another for the casket. Tri-unit pricing further breaks out

TABLE 6-1 *Funeral Rule Itemization Requirements*

Forwarding of remains to another funeral home [1]
Receiving remains from another funeral home [1]
Direct cremation [1,2]
Immediate burial [1]
Transfer of remains to funeral home
Embalming [3]
Other preparation of the body
Use of facilities for viewing
Use of facilities for funeral ceremony
Other use of facilities [4]
Hearse
Limousine
Other automotive equipment
Acknowledgment cards
Casket prices [5]
Outer burial container prices [6]
Charge for professional services of the funeral director[7]

1. Any fee for professional services must be included in the price quoted for this item.

2. If a provider offers direct cremations, consumers must be allowed to provide their own container if they desire, as long as it meets state or crematory requirements. Also, if direct cremations are offered, the provider must make available either an unfinished wood box or alternative container for consumers who request it. A disclosure to this effect must be included in conjunction with the price for direct cremations.

3. In addition to the quoted price for enbalming, there must be an affirmative disclosure stating, in part, that "except in certain special cases, embalming is not required by law."

4. Other facilities might include, for example, a tent and chairs for a graveside service.

5. Casket prices must be disclosed either on the General Price List or on a separate Casket Price List.

6. Prices for Outer Burial Containers may be listed on the General Price List or on a separate price list. Also, a disclosure must be made to the effect that "in most areas of the country, no state or local law requires you to buy an outer burial container; however, many cemeteries ask that you have such a container so that the grave will not sink in. Either a burial vault or a grave liner will satisfy these requirements."

7. As noted above, charges for services entailed in forwarding and receiving remains, direct cremations, and immediate burials are not involved here, since the FTC rule requires that service costs be included in the prices for those items. The fee for professional services may be listed separately from other items, or it may be included in the price of caskets. Whichever method is chosen by a funeral provider, a disclosure to that effect must appear on the General Price List.

costs by quoting one charge for the funeral director's services, another for the use of facilities and equipment, and a third for the casket. As you can see, multi-unit pricing methods exemplified the trend toward itemizing funeral costs in ever greater detail.

With the advent of the Federal Trade Commission's "Funeral Rule" in 1984, itemized price information became a requirement for *all* funeral providers.[22] The rule requires, at minimum, that prices be itemized for seventeen specified goods and services, if those items are offered by the funeral provider (see Table 6-1). These goods and services must be specified on the provider's General Price List, which has been called "the keystone of the Funeral Rule," so that customers can compare prices or choose only those elements of a funeral they want. It is important to note that the FTC requirements do not prohibit funeral directors from also offering package funerals, as discussed earlier.

"Doonesbury" drawing, © 1986 by G. B. Trudeau, Universal Press Syndicate

Although the average cost of all funerals conducted in America can only be estimated, a 1984 survey of 671 firms revealed that the average charge per funeral in this sample was $2247. Among these firms, the charges for individual funerals ranged from a low of $100 to a high of $23,560.[23] With over 2 million Americans dying each year, the annual expenditure for funerals in the United States is estimated to be about $4.5 billion, with the federal government's share of these expenses, in the form of veterans' and other benefits, at over $500 million a year. Most of this money goes to the approximately 20,000 firms currently providing funeral services to Americans. Although most of these firms are operating as small businesses, taken in the aggregate disposition of the dead in America is clearly big business.

When criticized for what some have called the high cost of dying in America, funeral directors point out that they have significant operating costs which must be recovered. Personnel, equipment, and facilities are kept available to the public twenty-four hours a day. Indeed, a timely response to the family's call is a matter of professional pride to most funeral directors—a sign of willingness to assist the bereaved in a time of crisis.[24]

Typically, the funeral business resides in a rather large, possibly colonial-style building, the floor plan of which may be adapted or designed especially for its function as a funeral home. Ronny Turner and Charles Edgley argue that funerals can be compared to a theatrical presentation, with certain activities taking place, as it were, offstage.[25] The backstage area, hidden away from the public's gaze, is where the body is prepared by embalming and application of cosmetics for its eventual role in the funeral drama. There is generally no hint of these backstage regions to those who enter by the front door. Turner and Edgley describe the funeral chapel as "a model of theatrical perfection" that might well "make a Broadway star envious." Usually arranged in such a way that there are several entrances and exits, it "may be served by back doors, halls, tunnels, and passageways that lead from the preparation room without ever trespassing frontstage areas."

Funeral directors regard themselves as professionals who provide services to people who are in crisis. While it has become fashionable to criticize the funeral director for taking on the role of a "grief therapist," the fact is that many funeral directors consider this function essential to meeting the needs of the bereaved. Many participate in seminars and courses designed to impart counseling skills specifically for working with bereaved persons.

Comparing the Costs

Comparing the costs of competing funeral establishments may be difficult even when costs are itemized. Different funeral providers do not always offer the same goods and services, and they may choose different methods of presenting prices. Thus, the comparison shopper may be trying to compare what seems like apples and oranges, with confusing results. Nevertheless, it is useful to distinguish among the charges that may be assessed. (As you read the following discussion of funeral goods and services, you may find it useful to refer to the sample prices given in Table 6-2.)

Charge for Professional Services

Essentially, this is a basic charge for the services provided by the funeral director and his or her staff. It is payment for arranging the funeral, consulting with family members and clergy, directing the visitation and funeral ceremony, and preparing and filing necessary notices and authorizations related to body disposition. This latter service may include filing the death certificate and certain claims for death benefits.

The fee for professional services covers a pro-rata share of the overhead expenses required to maintain facilities and staff around the clock. The method of arriving at this charge is, of course, left to the discretion of each funeral provider, and it varies according to a number of factors, including the clientele served and the prices charged by competitors.

Cemetery or crematory services, flowers, and placement of newspaper notices are generally not covered in this basic service charge. Those items are usually billed separately, and there may be a charge for the funeral director's services in purchasing such items on the customer's behalf.

According to the Funeral Rule, if direct cremation or immediate burial is chosen, any fee charged for professional services must be *included* in the price quoted for those methods of disposition. Similarly, this fee must be included in prices quoted for forwarding remains to another funeral home or receiving remains from another funeral home.

As an alternative method of pricing, the FTC rule allows funeral providers to incorporate a fee for professional services into the prices of caskets. When casket prices include a fee for professional services, however, a description of those services must be placed on the casket price list.

Intake Charges

This is the charge for transporting the remains from the place of death to the mortuary. There may be a surcharge for a nighttime pickup to cover additional costs of staff.

T A B L E 6-2   *Sample Funeral Service Prices*

Forwarding of remains to another funeral home	$550
Receiving remains from another funeral home	$445
Direct cremation	
with container provided by purchaser	$460
including alternative container	$500
including cloth-covered wood casket	$758
Immediate burial	
with container provided by purchaser	$430
including cloth-covered wood casket	$728
including oak-finished pine casket	$1,228
Transfer of remains to funeral home	$50
($50 additional for nighttime transfer)	
Embalming	$125
Other preparation of the body	
Cosmetology	$45
Hairstyling	(included)
Dressing and placing remains in casket	$45
Disinfection and sanitation (preparing for closed-casket funeral)	$85
Use of facilities for viewing (per day)	$50
Use of facilities for funeral ceremony	
Chapel	$200
Smaller stateroom	$125
Other use of facilities	
Staff conducting graveside service	$50
Scattering cremated remains at sea or in mountains	
Holding remains (per day) (applies only to immediate burial or	
cremation when body is not embalmed)	$15
Hearse	$70
Limousine	$45
Other automotive equipment	$40
Acknowledgment cards (box of 25)	$10
Memorial folders or prayer cards (first 100)	$25
(Add $10 for every additional 100)	
Register book	$15
Burial clothing	$72–$103
Cremation urns	$10–$298
Casket prices	$298–$6,395
Outer burial container prices	$50–$1,500
Charge for professional services	$375

Embalming

Nowhere in the United States is embalming required by law, except in certain circumstances. Yet embalming is such an accepted mortuary practice in America that hardly anyone questions it. Embalming involves removing the blood and other fluids in the body and replacing them with chemicals to disinfect and temporarily retard deterioration of the corpse. This procedure is usually considered a practical necessity when a body will be viewed. With few exceptions, however, the new FTC rule requires that mortuaries obtain express permission to embalm from the family in order to charge a fee for the procedure.[26] Furthermore, the price list must include the following disclosure next to the price for embalming:

> Except in certain special cases, embalming is not required by law. Embalming may be necessary, however, if you select certain funeral arrangements, such as a funeral with viewing. If you do not want embalming, you usually have the right to choose an arrangement which does not require you to pay for it, such as direct cremation or immediate burial.

Embalming laws vary from state to state. In Connecticut, for instance, embalming is required only when a body is to be transported across state lines by common carrier (bus, train, plane, or commercial vehicle). In Kentucky, embalming is not mandatory under any circumstances. The District of Columbia requires that a body be embalmed only when death results from communicable disease. In Louisiana, a body must be embalmed if it is held longer than thirty hours before final disposition. California requires embalming only when the body is to be transported by common carrier. In summary, then, according to the specific requirements of each state, special circumstances involving transportation, disease control, and the final disposition of the body may make embalming mandatory.[27]

If refrigeration is available, a mortuary may offer the alternative of storing a body for a short time without embalming. A refrigerated, unembalmed body will remain relatively preserved for about three days, although some mortuaries stipulate that they will not hold an unembalmed body for longer than forty-eight hours. The cost of refrigeration is likely to be somewhat less than for embalming.

Some mortuaries have a combined charge for embalming and body preparation; others itemize each of the procedures involved in readying a body for viewing and for the funeral. Thus, in addition to embalming charges (or, if embalming is not done, in lieu of such charges), separate fees may be charged for each of the procedures performed in the preparation room.

Other Body Preparation Charges

Body preparation includes minimal antiseptic hygiene procedures, such as washing the body. One funeral establishment lists separate charges for embalming; for cosmetology, hairstyling, and manicuring; and for dressing the body, placing it in the casket, and composing it for viewing.

Casket Prices

Of all funeral costs, many people feel that the most important is that of the casket, because of its symbolic and emotional value in honoring the deceased. The customer is faced with a wide range of options, and, whereas many other items of the funeral service are based on a standard fee, the price of a casket is highly variable. The latitude in choice ranges from inexpensive cardboard containers all the way to solid mahogany, copper, or bronze caskets costing thousands of dollars. Depending on the socioeconomic status of their clientele, most funeral homes can provide a variety of caskets in a wide range of prices. Since funeral homes are free to determine their own methods of pricing their caskets, the customer may discover that a casket selling for $1000 in one funeral home costs twice as much in another. This price difference may be due to a higher markup designed to increase the profit margin; or, as mentioned earlier, it may result from the fact that the funeral provider has chosen to include the fee for professional services in the casket price rather than charging it separately.

Because of this variability, prices of caskets can be discussed here only in general terms, with the aim of understanding the types and qualities of caskets available. A relatively inexpensive conventional casket could range in cost between roughly $300 and $900. These caskets are typically made of plywood and covered with cloth and contain a mattress that is likely to be made of straw covered with an acetate sheet.

At the next pricing level, refinements appear. Although these are also made of wood, they may be covered with copper or bronze sheathing. Gasketed steel caskets are available at prices ranging from about $1000 to several thousand dollars. The mattress, too, exhibits refinements, being constructed with springs, over which is a layer of foam rubber and a covering of acetate material. In this range, some caskets are available with sealer devices designed to ensure an airtight environment within the casket. (Although this is a solace to some people, any additional protection is debatable; indeed, critics contend that such devices actually hasten decomposition.)

The price tag on a top-of-the-line casket ranges upwards to $10,000 or more. For this sum, one obtains a casket constructed of mahogany, copper, or bronze, and fitted out with all the accoutrements of the casket manufacturer's art. Deluxe models feature an adjustable boxspring mattress that can be tilted to enhance the display of the corpse.

Marketing analysis indicates that the gasketed steel casket is most popular with Americans. Based on the number of caskets shipped to funeral directors, this type of casket holds a 44 percent share of the market, trailed by nongasketed steel (19.1 percent), cloth-covered (17.5 percent), hardwood (13.4 percent), copper or bronze (2.3 percent), and stainless steel caskets (0.8 percent).[28]

Our choices for displaying and disposing of the dead are regulated less by the force of law than by custom and by ignorance of alternatives. For example, many people are surprised to learn that there is no law requiring a body destined for cremation to be placed in a casket. Most crematoria require only that the body be delivered in a rigid container. Most mortuaries can provide a cardboard box, which suffices for this purpose, at a small charge. The FTC rule now prohibits funeral providers from telling consumers that state or local law requires them to purchase a casket when they wish to arrange a direct cremation (that is, a cremation that occurs without formal viewing of the remains or any visitation or ceremony with the body present). For firms that do arrange for direct cremations, the rule stipulates that the following disclosure be made to customers:

> If you want to arrange a direct cremation, you can use an unfinished wood box or an alternative container. Alternative containers can be made of materials like heavy cardboard or composition materials (with or without an outside covering), or pouches of canvas.

Finally, as regards caskets, the FTC rule requires funeral providers to supply customers with a list of the prices and descriptions of available caskets. This may be handled in one of two ways, either on the General Price List or on a separate Casket Price List.

Facilities Charges

The use of a visitation or viewing room is a common component of most funerals. In the itemized listing of prices, the funeral director may use whatever method of pricing is preferred or follow common practice for that particular area. For example, various settings in the funeral home might be listed along with the charges for each by day, half day, or hour. Similarly, if a funeral ceremony is held at the mortuary chapel, a charge for the use of that facility will be specified by the funeral provider. When other facilities are made available to customers (for example, a tent and chairs for graveside services), the charges for their use must be stated on the funeral provider's price list.

Vehicles

As with other aspects of funeral service, mortuaries may follow quite different price schedules for the use of vehicles. According to the FTC rule, charges for the use of a hearse, limousine, or other automotive equipment must be itemized separately on the General Price List. Sometimes additional vehicles are requested for the use of pallbearers, family members, or other participants, such as clergy. A "flower car" may be used to transport floral arrangements to the cemetery. If a motorcycle escort is desired, there will be a charge for each escort.

Outer Burial Container Prices

If outer burial containers are offered by the funeral home, their prices must be listed, either separately or on the General Price List. In addition to listing prices, the following disclosure must be made:

> In most areas of the country, no state or local law makes you buy a container to surround the casket in the grave. However, many cemeteries ask that you have such a container so that the grave will not sink in. Either a burial vault or a grave liner will satisfy these requirements.

Since many funeral homes do not sell burial vaults or grave liners, this item may not appear on the price lists of the mortuaries in your area. Further information about the types of outer burial containers is given in our discussion of burial and entombment costs later in this chapter.

Miscellaneous Charges

Under this category, we include charges for goods or services provided directly by the funeral home as well as those obtained from outside sources on behalf of the customer. This latter category could include such "cash-advance" items as floral arrangements and newspaper notices. The customer may be billed for the actual amounts of the items, or the funeral provider may add a surcharge for arranging these cash-advance items. If an additional charge is made, a notice to that effect must be shown on the General Price List.

Acknowledgment cards are specifically mentioned by the FTC rule as needing to be itemized if the funeral provider sells those items or performs the service of filling out and sending them for customers.

Other items that come under the heading of miscellaneous costs include any fees or honoraria for pallbearers, an honorarium for the clergyperson who conducts the funeral service, and the cost of any burial garments purchased from the mortuary.

Direct Cremations and Immediate Burials

Not all funeral homes offer direct cremations and immediate burials to consumers, although the number of those that do is increasing. These methods of body disposition occur without formal viewing of the remains or any visitation or ceremony with the body present.

If direct cremation or immediate burial is offered by a funeral home, the charge — including the fee for professional services — is shown on the General Price List. When direct cremation is selected, the customer must be given the option of providing the container or of purchasing an unfinished pine box or alternative container (such as canvas pouch, or a box made of cardboard, plywood, or composition material). Similarly, for immediate burials, the customer has the option to provide a container or purchase a simple casket, such as one made of wood and covered with cloth.[29]

Body Disposition

Think for a moment about the manner you would choose for the disposition of your body after you die. When Americans are asked their preferences, responses usually fall into one of three categories: burial, cremation, or donation to science. Corpses must be disposed of because of sanitary considerations, though it is unlikely that a person's choice of method would be influenced by that fact. It is more likely that preferences result from social, cultural, and philosophical reasons. Although bodies can be disposed of in ways other than the three mentioned, most of us would probably consider them improper.

The decomposition of the body is hastened in some societies by washing

U.S. Navy Photo

Burial at sea is a naval tradition the world over, particularly during times of war.
Here the body of a seaman is committed to the deep during burial services aboard
the USS Ranger in 1963.

the flesh from the bones when the corpse is partially decomposed and then retaining parts of the body as a memorial. In other societies the body is left to the elements, and generally decomposes quite rapidly (except in very dry, desert climates, where the heat removes the moisture from the body, acting thereby to preserve it). Some Indian tribes of the American plains constructed platforms on which the corpse was left exposed to the effects of the sun, wind, and rain. In some societies, the remains of the dead are consumed by birds of prey or other animals. In India, for example, one can still view the Towers of Silence on Bombay's fashionable Marabar Hill, where the Parsi community disposes of its dead by leaving corpses to be devoured by vultures. As followers of Zoroaster, they regard earth, fire and water as sacred, not to be defiled by the dead. Their beliefs are not shared, however, by the residents of high-rise luxury apartments whose windows look out upon what they consider an improper and grotesque method of body disposition.

Burial can be in a single grave dug into the soil or entombment in a multitiered mausoleum. The phrase burial at sea might connote a corpse slid ceremonially off the side of a ship or a corpse placed inside a boat set aflame and

Assume that we are confronted with the dead body of a man. What disposition shall we make of it? Shall we lay it in a boat that is set adrift? Shall we take the heart from it and bury it in one place and the rest of the body in another? Shall we expose it to wild animals? Burn it on a pyre? Push it into a pit to rot with other bodies? Boil it until the flesh falls off the bones, and throw the flesh away and treasure the bones? Such questions provoke others which may not be consciously articulated, such as: "What do men generally think this body is?" And, "What do they think is a proper way of dealing with it?"

Robert W. Habenstein and William M. Lamers,
The History of American Funeral Directing

then set adrift. Cremation causes rapid dissolution of the body by intense heat and has been carried out by means ranging from a simple wood fire to sophisticated electric retorts.

Another method of body disposition is donation to science. The person who chooses this method may gain satisfaction from the notion that a contribution is being made to the advancement of knowledge: "My body will serve a useful function even after I'm gone." However, most medical schools and similar institutions usually have an adequate supply of cadavers, making donation an option that may be difficult for most people to exercise.

Elmer Ruiz: Gravedigger

Not anybody can be a gravedigger. You can dig a hole any way they come. A gravedigger, you have to make a neat job. I had a fella once, he wanted to see a grave. He was a fella that digged sewers. He was impressed when he seen me diggin' this grave—how square and how perfect it was. A human body is goin' into this grave. That's why you need skill when you're gonna dig a grave.

The gravedigger today, they have to be somebody to operate a machine. You just use a shovel to push the dirt loose. Otherwise you don't use 'em. We're tryin' a new machine, a ground hog. This machine is supposed to go through heavy frost. It do very good job so far. When the weather is mild, like fifteen degrees above zero, you can do it very easy.

But when the weather is below zero, believe me, you just really workin' hard. I have to use a mask. Your skin hurts so much when it's cold—like you put a hot flame near your face. I'm talkin' about two, three hours standin' outside. You have to wear a mask, otherwise you can't stand it at all. . . .

The most graves I dig is about six, seven a day. This is in the summer. In the winter it's a little difficult. In the winter you have four funerals, that's a pretty busy day. . . .

continued

continued from previous page

The grave will be covered in less than two minutes, complete. We just open the hoppers with the right amount of earth. We just press it and then we lay out a layer of black earth. Then we put the sod that belongs there. After a couple of weeks you wouldn't know it's a grave there. It's complete flat. Very rarely you see a grave that is sunk. . . .

I usually tell 'em I'm a caretaker. I don't think the name sound as bad. I have to look at the park, so after the day's over that everything's closed, that nobody do damage to the park. Some occasions some people just come and steal and loot and do bad things in the park, destroy some things. I believe it would be some young fellas. A man with responsibility, he wouldn't do things like that. Finally we had to put up some gates and close 'em at sundown. Before, we didn't, no. We have a fence of roses. Always in cars you can come after sundown. . . .

A gravedigger is a very important person. You must have hear about the strike we had in New York about two years ago. There were twenty thousand bodies layin' and nobody could bury 'em. The cost of funerals they raised and they didn't want to raise the price of the workers. The way they're livin', everything wanna go up, and I don't know what's gonna happen.

Can you imagine if I wouldn't show up tomorrow morning and this other fella—he usually comes late—and sometimes he don't show. We have a funeral for eleven o'clock. Imagine what happens? The funeral arrive and where you gonna bury it? . . .

There are some funerals, they really affect you. Some young kid. We buried lots of young. You have emotions, you turn in, believe me, you turn. I had a burial about two years ago of teen-agers, a young boy and a young girl. This was a real sad funeral because there was nobody but young teen-agers. I'm so used to going to funerals every day—of course, it bothers me—but I don't feel as bad as when I bury a young child. You really turn. . . .

This grief that I see every day, I'm really used to somebody's crying every day. But there is some that are real bad, when you just have to take it. Some people just don't want to give up. You have to understand that when somebody pass away, there's nothing you can do and you have to take it. If you don't want to take it, you're just gonna make your life worse, become sick. People seems to take it more easier these days. They miss the person, but not as much.

There's some funerals that people, they show they're not sad. This is different kinds of people. I believe they are happy to see this person—not in a way of singing—because this person is out of his sufferin' in this world. This person is gone and at rest for the rest of his life. I have this question lots of times: "How can I take it?" They ask if I'm calm when I bury people. If you stop and think, a funeral is one of the natural things in the world. . . .

I believe I'm gonna have to stay here probably until I die. It's not gonna be too bad for me because I been livin' twelve years already in the cemetery. I'm still gonna be livin' in the cemetery. (Laughs.) So that's gonna be all right with me whenever I go. I think I may be buried here, it look like.

Quoted in Studs Terkel, *Working*

A few years ago, cryonics became attractive to some people. Cryonics is a method of subjecting a corpse to extremely low temperatures — in effect, keeping the body frozen — until some time in the future when it is envisioned that medical science will have advanced to a point where the body could be resuscitated. Thus, strictly speaking, this is not a method of body disposition in the sense used so far. Although most people view cryonics more as a curiosity than as a realistic alternative to conventional methods of body disposition, it is a practice that has a small number of dedicated adherents.

From the burials of prehistoric cave dwellers to cryonics, human beings have practiced a wide range of alternatives for disposing of the dead. What does your own preference tell you about your attitudes and beliefs about death?

Burial and Entombment Costs

The prices for cemetery plots vary widely among cemeteries and often according to location within a cemetery. The cost of a burial plot is generally about $500, although one can spend more than $5000 or less than $100. (In one small rural cemetery, limited to the township's residents, a burial plot can be purchased for $25.) In addition, although burial vaults are not required by law, most cemeteries require that the casket be placed inside a grave liner or vault to support the earth around and above it. A grave liner costs about $200 to $300, a vault about $300 to $450, although some types of vaults designed (but not guaranteed) to seal out moisture cost substantially more.

The cost of entombment in a mausoleum or outdoor crypt generally ranges from about $1500 to $3000, although again prices vary considerably. The most expensive crypts are typically those at eye level, with the least expensive crypts at the top and bottom.

Whether burial or entombment is chosen, additional charges are levied for opening and closing the grave or crypt. These charges range from about $75 to $350, largely depending on the area of the country.

Memorials and Endowment Costs

A bronze or stone grave marker is likely to cost upwards of about $200. The average cost for a simple, flat-on-the-ground grave marker is about $250, the

---

 Requiem

Under the wide and starry sky
Dig the grave and let me lie
Glad did I live and gladly die
    And I laid me down with a will.

This be the verse you grave for me
Here he lies where he longed to be
Home is the sailor, home from the sea
    And the hunter home from the hill.

Robert Louis Stevenson
(his epitaph)

name plate for a mausoleum crypt somewhat less. More elaborate memorials can cost from a few hundred to many thousands of dollars.

Most cemeteries also assess a "perpetual care cost" or endowment to subsidize upkeep of the cemetery. These costs range upwards of $100 and may be quoted as part of the cost for burial or entombment.

Cremation Costs

In the United States, the practice of cremation extends back into the nineteenth century (cremation had long been practiced by the original inhabitants, of course). In Europe, the practice is considerably older, going back at least to the Bronze Age. Cremation is the most common method of body disposal in such countries as India and is required by law in Tokyo and (except for rural communities with no crematories) also in China.

Although a relatively small percentage of Americans choose to be cremated, it is a method of body disposition that is growing in acceptance. In 1985, there were reportedly 277,900 cremations, which means that this method of body disposal was selected in about 13.5 percent of the total number of deaths for that year. The number of crematories in the United States grew to 847 by 1985, up from 567 just ten years previously. By the year 2000, it is projected that cremation will become the method of body disposition in nearly one-quarter of all deaths in the United States, a proportion that Canada reached in 1985.[30]

The laws regulating the disposition of cremated remains vary among states and localities. For example, until recently a California law prohibited the scattering of ashes by private citizens. If violated, the person scattering the ashes could be charged with a misdemeanor, punishable by a fine or imprisonment; if two or more persons participated, it was considered a conspiracy, and a felony could be charged against them. This law has been removed from the books.

The process of cremation involves subjecting the corpse to extreme heat, approximately 2000 to 2500 degrees Fahrenheit. In the United States, natural gas is the most commonly used fuel. An average-size body takes about one and one-half hours to be reduced to ashes weighing from five to seven pounds.[31] Cremated remains can be buried in a cemetery plot, placed in a columbarium niche, interred in an urn garden, kept by the family, or scattered at sea or on land, in accordance with state and local laws.

The Cremation Association of North America, founded in 1913, encourages memorialization in conjunction with cremation, just as with traditional burials. Urns to hold cremated remains can be purchased at prices from about $25 to $300, though a substantially more expensive urn can be purchased if the customer wishes. If the ashes are to be entombed, columbaria niches (a small vault in which the urn is placed) are available, with the cost depending on the size and location of the niche.

Recent American concern with conventional funerals has brought a rising interest in alternative modes of body disposition, such as cremation. The advent of memorial and cremation societies exemplifies this trend. Typically, these

Edward C. and Gail R. Johnson

A coffin is about to be placed inside the retort at this crematory in Japan. The remains of the deceased will be reduced by fire to a few handfuls of ashes and bits of bone.

societies aim to provide body disposal services to members at a lower cost by contracting with a mortuary or crematorium to provide services based on a volume purchase. In many communities across the country, conventional funeral providers now compete with such organizations, thereby increasing the range of options available to customers.

As with other areas of funeral service since the FTC rule, the customer is usually able to select exactly the services he or she wants. Whereas the conventional mortuary offers a wide range of services related both to the funeral and to the disposition of the body, the typical memorial or cremation society's services deal solely with disposition of the remains. Whether provided by a conventional mortuary or a cremation society, the cost of cremation is generally about $500 to $600, although the services provided for this cost may be broken out separately. The largest of the cremation societies, the Neptune Society, offers a package at a cost of about $500, which includes picking up the body, completing the paperwork, cremating the body, and scattering the ashes.

Some cremation societies offer a choice concerning the extent to which the customer takes responsibility for the disposition of the body, as in the following example. If the society simply picks up the body from the place of death, holds it temporarily while the family takes care of the necessary arrangements and paperwork, and then delivers the body to the crematory, a charge of $250 is

▲ *Top view*   ▼ *Detail of lid interior*

Figure 6-5   *Three Views of a Child's Coffin*

Top view: When the wooden coffin constructed by the family and friends had been completed, the surviving child ran his hand over the surface and voiced his approval but said that it "needs something more." He gathered his marking pens and began to ornament the coffin with drawings. The inscriptions on the outer surface of the lid show the child's interest in identifying by name and by picture the fact that this coffin was built for his brother. His own participation in the making of the coffin is also connoted by the inclusion of his name and by the demonstration of his newly developed skills with the use of numerals and letters.

Detail of lid interior: In this detailed closeup of a portion of the interior lid, viewed from left to right, one can see a chrysalis—indicating a transition from

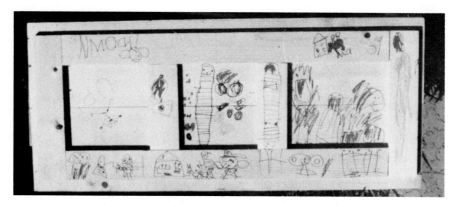

Interior of lid

caterpillar to butterfly — along with some of the younger brother's favorite television characters: Big Bird, Oscar the Grouch, and the Cookie Monster.

Interior of lid: In contrast to the matter-of-fact inscriptions placed on the outer surface, the inside of the coffin lid is filled with representations of experiences, events, and objects that brought joy into the life of the child's younger brother. Many of the dead child's favorite activities, such as listening to the stereo with headphones and sitting on a horse at grandma's house, are depicted. The surviving child depicts himself as sad because of his brother's death, yet also as happy because of the shared experiences he enjoyed with his brother. It is interesting to note the degree of detail and the variety of images placed on the interior of the coffin lid.

assessed. If the family wants the society to take care of the arrangements and paperwork, the cost increases to $395. In either case, the cremation itself costs an additional $120, which is paid to the crematory. There are additional charges for a container if one is wanted or needed ($48) and for scattering the ashes at sea ($60).

In some instances, cremation and memorial societies provide an option allowing family and friends to attend the scattering of the ashes. Generally, however, the advent of these organizations is indicative of a minimalist approach to funerals and body disposition that appeals to a comparatively small, but significant and growing, number of people in the United States. The service provided by cremation and memorial societies is clearly meeting a need felt by many people. Indeed, as mentioned, similar options are now offered by many conventional funeral providers. With the institution of the FTC's Funeral Rule, it has become easier to compare the costs of funeral and body disposition services among competing establishments. In most cases, a telephone call is all that is necessary to obtain relevant pricing information for your own locality.

Making Meaningful Choices

William Lamers has defined the funeral as "an organized, purposeful, time-limited, flexible, group-centered response to death."[32] If this definition is indeed applicable to the modern way of dealing with the dead in America, then what are we to make of the juxtaposition of styles of funeral service? Memorial societies, cremation societies, conventional forms of funeral ritual; criticisms leveled against the funeral service trade and the funeral itself — is there any one, right set of values to guide memorializing the dead and providing for the needs of the survivors?

Probably not. Each of us has to make up his or her own mind. If funeral rituals provide closure on the deceased's life for survivors and allow for the rhythms of separation and integration, then what happens when the social elements are largely lacking, as in the "take-out-and-cremate" practices of the cremation societies? Are the psychological issues resolved satisfactorily? Many would say no, yet there is a paucity of hard data to establish the conventional funeral as the most effective vehicle of psychological resolution.

Edgar Jackson says funeral directors receive more expressions of gratitude from the people they serve than do those in any other helping profession. The funeral director is there at a time when the family is experiencing an acute crisis. The immediate response and help in sorting out the events of the days following the death of a loved one provide stability and reassurance for the bereaved family.[33] Robert Fulton corroborates this view, adding that funeral directors are in a unique position to assist the bereaved and are potentially a valuable part of the community's mental health resources and helping network.[34]

In a pluralistic society such as ours people find different ways of dealing meaningfully with death. There is a fine line between taking charge and delegating care of the dead. Some may never want to assume greater responsibility for caring for their dead loved ones; others will choose a more active role. However, unless we become aware of the alternatives available to us, we may never be involved with last rites that are meaningful for ourselves or others.

The experience of a couple whose young son was killed in an automobile accident is illustrative. They planned no formal funeral ceremony. They intended that the body would simply be cremated and the ashes scattered over the ocean. On the day before the body was released from the coroner for cremation, they were experiencing the acute grief that comes with such a sudden and intimate loss. They were having difficulty coming to terms with their emotions and the loss of their son.

Someone suggested they could direct their energy into building a coffin for their son. Soon, friends and members of the family, including the father and the five-year-old brother of the child who was killed, were busily engaged in the task of constructing a coffin. Later they voiced relief at being able to "do something" (see Figure 6-5 on page 200). For the participants, building the coffin became a meaningful way to honor the dead child as well as a means of working through some of their own feelings, allowing them to get a better handle on their experience. This, then, is the real value of learning about and considering our options: finding the response that is meaningful to us personally.

The social support that accompanies meaningful ritual need not be limited to the period immediately following a death. In traditional Hawaiian culture, for example, the bereaved community would hold a memorial feast on the first-year anniversary of the day of death for any person — man, woman, child, even a newborn baby. For the extended family group, this was "one of the three greatest occasions, the others being the feasts of rejoicing for the first-born and the marriage festival."[35] Although this occasion was called the *'aha'aina waimaka* or "feast of tears," because it was for everyone who had shed tears out of respect and love for the deceased, it was really "a happy occasion, a joyful reunion of all who had previously shed tears together." As one participant described it, "There was drinking, eating, singing and dancing. We had a *lu'au* when all the grief was done."

Further Readings

Consumer Reports. *Funerals: Consumers' Last Rights.* New York: W. W. Norton, 1977.

Earl A. Grollman, editor. *Concerning Death: A Practical Guide for the Living.* Boston: Beacon Press, 1974.

Robert W. Habenstein and William M. Lamers. *The History of American Funeral Directing.* Milwaukee: Bulfin Printers, 1962.

Robert W. Habenstein and William M. Lamers. *Funeral Customs the World Over.* Rev. ed. Milwaukee: Bulfin Printers, 1974.

Paul Irion. *A Manual and Guide for Those Who Conduct a Humanist Funeral Service.* Baltimore: Waverly Press, 1971.

Edgar N. Jackson. *The Christian Funeral: Its Meaning, Its Purpose, and Its Modern Practice.* New York: Channel Press, 1966.

Ernest Morgan. *Dealing Creatively with Death: A Manual of Death Education and Simple Burial.* 10th ed. Burnsville, N.C.: Celo Press, 1984.

Vanderlyn R. Pine. *Caretaker of the Dead: The American Funeral Director.* New York: Irvington Publishers, 1975, 1985.

Vanderlyn R. Pine, editor. *Acute Grief and the Funeral.* Springfield, Ill.: Charles C. Thomas, 1976.

Joe Marquette, UPI/Bettmann Newsphotos

Grief encompasses a wide range of emotions in survivors. Bereavement is often a time of turning inward, of clutching to the reminders of the deceased and to the memories they evoke.

CHAPTER 7

Survivors: Understanding the Experience of Loss

We are all survivors. At some time in our lives we have all experienced loss. Reflect for a moment on something — material or nonmaterial — that you have recently lost. You may recall the loss of a job, a friend's moving away, misplacing an important letter, having to replace a favorite piece of clothing, the death of a pet, any number of things. Whether such losses seem big or small, they are a fact of life for everyone.

Endings are another way to think about loss: The end of summer vacation, turning thirty, graduating from school, leaving a familiar neighborhood, confronting the prospect of retirement — all these endings typify changes that arise in the course of living, changes that often occasion feelings of grief. Some writers call such experiences "little deaths."[1] As you recall some of the "little deaths" in your own life, you can begin to notice the ways in which you have responded to loss. Shock, disbelief, resentment, sadness, and relief are natural reactions. Generally, the more valuable or emotionally charged an experience or relationship, the greater a person's reaction to its loss.

Not everyone has experienced the loss that occurs with death, but everyone has experienced losses of some kind. As you read these words, you are alive. You are a *survivor* of the many changes that have taken place in your life up to the present moment. Keeping this fact in mind as you learn about bereavement, grief, and mourning can provide you with a perspective that will increase your awareness of the issues related to surviving the death of someone close to you.

Perspectives on Grief

For many people, grief has negative connotations. They say, "Oh, don't talk about that subject, it's too depressing," or "I'd rather just think positive thoughts, not dwell on all that negativity." But research in death and dying, by expanding our knowledge of survivorship, allows us a more encompassing and accurate picture of what grief and mourning represent in human experience. Among the most impressive facts is the weight of historical precedent, the vast continuity, the essential unity, in the human experience of bereavement, grief, and mourning. (Recall, for example, the figure in Chapter 2 of the Stone Age burial scene: A Neanderthal family stands beside the gravesite of a family member, mourning their loss.)

Death touches our lives not only when close friends or family members are affected. Death is almost constantly before us through dramatic portrayals and news reports in the mass media. Technology now has the potential to make us all instantaneous survivors. When Egyptian President Anwar el-Sadat was assassinated in October 1981, news of the event was flashed around the world almost instantaneously. Stunned television viewers watched in disbelief as news footage was repeatedly broadcast showing the terrorist attack that came as the Egyptian political leader sat reviewing a military parade in Cairo.[2] The mass suicide in Guyana in 1978 turned national attention to issues of mortality and bereavement for months afterward. Similar reactions occurred in the wake of the space shuttle *Challenger* disaster in 1986.

Bereavement, Grief, and Mourning

The word most often associated with loss by death is grief. We hear that someone is bereaved, is grieving, or has "grief work" to do. We say that the person is mourning. A look at how we define bereavement, grief, and mourning can be instructive in understanding what it means to be a survivor.

Bereavement comes from a root word meaning shorn off or torn up — as if something had been suddenly yanked away. The word thus conveys a sense of a person's being deprived, of having something stripped away against one's will, of being robbed. Bereavement signifies a force that comes from outside as a violent, destructive action taken against us. Obviously, if we think about

Working through our endings allows us to redefine
our relationships, to surrender what is dead
and to accept what is alive,
and to be in the world more fully to face the
new situation.

Stanley Keleman,
Living Your Dying

Comparing the extent and form of emotional responses to announcements of death in various circumstances, I found a considerable amount of variability. On some occasions there was no crying whatever; the doctor's mention of the death was responded to with downward looking silence. On other occasions, his utterance "passed away" or "died" spontaneously produced hysterical crying, screaming, moaning, trembling, etc. . . . In numerous instances I have seen men and women tear at themselves, pulling their hair, tugging at their garments, biting their lips.

David Sudnow,
Passing On: The Social Organization of Dying

bereavement only as a violent event, our understanding will be different from that of the person who defines bereavement as a change that is cyclical and natural, a normal event in human experience. Thus considered, bereavement can be defined simply as the event of loss.

Grief is a person's emotional response to the event of loss. Like bereavement, grief has usually been thought of in negative terms: heartbreak, anguish, distress, suffering — a burdensome emotional state. Yet grief can be considered as the *total* emotional response to loss. Among the full range of emotions that might be present in a survivor's grief are not only sorrow and sadness, but also relief, anger, disgust, and self-pity. Limiting our definition of grief reduces the chances of accepting all of the emotions that may be present.

Mourning is the process of incorporating the experience of loss into our ongoing lives. This process deals with the questions: How does one carry on? How does one survive in the face of a particular change, or change in general? Mourning is also the outward acknowledgment of loss (as is reflected in such remarks as "That family is in mourning and they aren't going out socially. The father died recently"). Social groups define certain behaviors as appropriate for making known the fact that a person is mourning.[3] In Western culture, for example, conventional forms of mourning behavior have included wearing black armbands or clothes of subdued colors and, if the deceased was a public figure, flying the national flag at half-mast. Following the death of George Washington, Congress led the nation in a thirty-day period of mourning, during which some citizens wore black bands on which were stamped in white letters the inscription that appeared on the President's coffin plate: "General George Washington — Departed this life on the 14th of December, 1799."[4] In some places in the world, widows commonly dress in black for many years following the death of a spouse, outwardly acknowledging their loss and their mourning.[5]

In the United States today, mourning behavior is generally much less formal than among some other cultures, or than it was in our past. Because we lack rigorous social definitions of what constitutes appropriate mourning behavior, sometimes there is conflict between conventional notions of mourning and the ideas of the deceased or the survivors, as the following anecdote illustrates.

A young girl recently wrote to a syndicated advice columnist about a "sweet sixteen" party that her dying father had asked the family to celebrate for her, even if the party should occur on the day of his funeral. The girl said she had not felt like having a party, but the family decided to honor the promise to her father. So the party was held two days after her father's death, and it turned out to be a valuable experience for everyone who attended. A problem arose, however, when several relatives became horrified because, in their model of the world, conducting a party was in no way appropriate behavior for a time of mourning.

Although it is possible to establish guidelines for evaluating behavior related to survivorship, it should be recognized that a broad spectrum of mourning behaviors is appropriate. Thus, the student of death and dying will find it useful to suspend judgment about such behavior.

The Experience of Grief

The questions asked most frequently about grief concern the attempt to define *normal* grief and mourning. How long should a person grieve? How old should a child be to attend a funeral or memorial service? What kinds of behavior are appropriate during a period of mourning?

To frame adequate answers to such questions we need to take account of many factors, including personality and values, social and cultural influences, and the relative importance of the deceased to the survivor. These factors affect the duration of grief, the physical and psychological responses, and the disruption of and subsequent reorientation to satisfactory life patterns. As with most attempts to define a norm, a definition of what constitutes normal grief and mourning will allow for wide latitude according to time, place, circumstances of the death, and the particular survivor's experience.

Duration of Grief

Some researchers suggest that the more intense experience of grief, immediately following a loss by death, usually lasts about four to six weeks.[6] During the first year of bereavement, however, the survivor may experience the anniversaries, birthdays, holidays, and other special occasions that previously had been shared with the deceased in ways that involve coming to grips with the deceased's absence.

The period of depression and acute grief following a loss usually lasts no longer than several months.[7] But the period of mourning, the time of gradually accepting the loss and reorienting one's life without the deceased, may continue through the first year of bereavement, sometimes longer. Prolonged grief is described not so much in terms of duration, but in terms of its effect on the survivor. Severe problems with sleeplessness or loss of appetite that persist beyond six months or so may be symptomatic of difficulties in coping with grief.[8] Medical complaints such as ulcerative colitis, rheumatoid arthritis, or asthma may manifest in cases of prolonged grief. It is possible to restore

Edward V. Gillion

© Albert Lee Strickland

The nineteenth-century Romantic view of death is reflected in the Lawson memorial, which characterizes both the devotion of the bereaved to the deceased and the belief that loving relationships continue beyond the mortal framework of the human lifespan.

Contemporary memorial stones often reflect a similar emphasis on the unending love felt by survivors for the deceased and on the faith that bonds forged during a person's lifetime can remain strong despite death.

abnormal grief reactions to normal through the use of therapeutic means, even years after the death.[9]

With a major loss such as death, the survivor's overwhelming experience is the sense of finality. For this reason, and because the loss is so important, the survivor may experience a recurrence of grief for that loss at various times throughout his or her lifetime, although with decreasing intensity and frequency. Nevertheless, certain incidents that arise naturally in daily life will again bring to mind that what once was is no more. In *The First Year of Bereavement,* Gerald Caplan describes how this understanding of grief has replaced earlier formulations which postulated that widows normally complete the psychological work of mourning for their dead husbands by four to six weeks after the death.[10] It is now recognized that, although most widows are not actively mourning after the turmoil of the first one to three years, the loss nevertheless remains a part of them, and feelings of grief never cease entirely.

In our own lives we can recognize the recurrence of mourning for earlier losses. We may mourn the loss of childhood and its experiences. A woman told about visiting her parents after some years of living on her own. One day, while poking around in the attic, her mother opened a trunk and pulled out a collection of dolls that had belonged to the daughter when she was a child.

Seeing the dolls elicited feelings of grief for the childhood that was now lost to the past. She said, "I looked at those dolls and their tiny clothes, and I got in touch with the loss of that time in my life when my mother had taken care of me and had made clothes for my dolls. There I was, sitting in the attic, just bawling."

Each of us has undoubtedly experienced similar situations in our own lives. Some event, picture, place, melody, or other stimulus has provoked feelings of grief related to something or someone no longer present in our lives. In a landmark study of grief published in 1944, "The Symptomatology and Management of Acute Grief," Erich Lindemann identified three primary tasks necessary for satisfactorily *managing* grief: first, letting go of the deceased, accepting the fact of the loss; second, adjusting to a life without the deceased; third, forming new relationships.[11] Although the grief may be acute only briefly, the feelings associated with a loss may recur at various times and in varying intensity throughout our lives.

Symptoms of Grief

The research done by Erich Lindemann and others has provided a fairly detailed picture of the range of somatic symptoms, or body reactions, that may be present with normal grief.[12] Somatic disturbances can include tightness of the throat, choking, shortness of breath, the need for frequent sighing, an empty feeling in the abdomen, muscle weakness, chills, and tremors. These bodily sensations may be accompanied by intense mental distress: tension, loneliness, and anguish.

The survivor's perceptions may be disorganized. Events may seem unreal, sensory responses undependable and erratic. The survivor may describe periods of hallucination or even euphoria. During such times, the survivor may experience a heightened perceptual and emotional sensitivity to persons and events in the immediate environment. It is common for survivors to be preoccupied with images of the deceased.[13] Often, survivors appear to be highly irritable or even hostile. They sometimes talk incessantly about the deceased. Or they may seem to talk about everything but their confrontation with loss and the circumstances of the death. They may also show a general restlessness.

In addition to feelings of sadness, longing, loneliness, and sorrow, there may be feelings of guilt or anger. The survivor may feel anger and outrage at the apparent injustice of the loss, and tremendous frustration and a sense of

All that day I walked alone. In the afternoon I looked for a church, went into a cafe, and finally left on the bus, carrying with me more grief and sorrow than I had ever borne before, my body in tatters and my whole life a moan.

Oscar Lewis,
A Death in the Sanchez Family

Bereaved persons in most cultures may dream that a beloved person has come back. In the early stages of bereavement, this, as well as hallucinating the dead, is a normal manifestation of grieving. However, Hawaiians usually see the dead in dreams more often, for more reasons, and for longer periods after a death than do, for example, Western Caucasians. In modern Western culture, when dreams (or hallucinations) of the dead continue too long, they are usually symptoms of pathological grief: the process or "work" of grieving has not progressed through the normal stages.

For the Hawaiian who is emotionally close to his ethnic roots, such prolonged dreaming or envisioning of the dead may or may not be a sign of blocked grief work. In the Hawaiian tradition, the dead do return: in dreams and visions, in sensations of skin, in hearing the voice or smelling the perfume or body odor of the one who has died.

The difference between what is culturally normal and what may be pathological is only partly spelled out by the dream content. We must also know what is going on in the life and family life of the dreamer; we must know how much and what kind of emotion the dream aroused. Especially, we must know what were the relationships in life between the one who died and the survivor who dreams.

Mary Kawena Pukui, E. W. Haertig, and
Catherine A. Lee, *Nana I Ke Kumu (Look to the Source)*

impotence at the inability to control events. As survivors, we may feel that if we could arrange the world more to our liking, we would not have included loss as part of the human experience.

The symptoms and behaviors appropriate to normal grief clearly make up a broad range of responses. But no particular survivor will necessarily experience all of them, nor must all be present if grief is to be considered normal. If a person has mental images of the deceased and says, "Oh no, I shouldn't be thinking like this," this denial can create additional conflicts and greater difficulties in coming to terms with loss. In contrast, if a survivor is aware that many kinds of feelings are acceptable, the experience of grief is likely to be much more easily managed.

When loss occurs, the usual patterns of conduct are disrupted. People stop doing the things they ordinarily do. Their actions may be so unlike their usual behavior that an outsider, or even an acquaintance, might judge it bizarre or aberrant. In an early study of grief, "Mourning and Melancholia," Sigmund Freud addressed this concern from the psychoanalytic perspective.[14]

Although grieving behavior may be quite different from a person's usual behavior, Freud said, normal grief is not a pathological condition, nor is its presence a cause for medical treatment. Grief is the normal reaction to loss. When the bereaved perceives that the love object no longer exists, grief arises, along with a defensive demand to withdraw libido (energy) from the object to which it had been attached. This demand may meet with opposition, causing the survivor to temporarily turn away from reality in an attempt to cling to the

Theorist	Onset ◄ – – – – – – – – – – – – · GRIEF · – – – – – – – – – – – ► Resolution						
Gorer	Shock		Intense grief work			Reestablishing physical and mental balance	
Kavanaugh	Shock	Disorganization	Volatile emotions	Guilt	Loss and loneliness	Relief	Reestablishment
Raphael	Shock, numbness, disbelief		Separation pain		Psychological mourning process	Reintegration	
Weizman and Kamm	Shock, disbelief, denial		Undoing	Anger		Sadness	Integration
Worden	Accepting the reality		Experiencing the pain		Adjusting to a changed environment	Withdrawing and reinvesting emotional energy	

Figure 7-1   *Grief Models by Theorist*

lost object. Normally, the libido eventually becomes detached from the love object, and the ego (personality) becomes free of its clinging attachment to the deceased.

Studies have led to the conclusion that acute grief possesses the qualities of a definite syndrome, with both psychological and somatic symptomatology.[15] However, the signs of grief may either appear immediately or be delayed; they may even appear to be absent. Symptoms may be distorted, exaggerated, or highly variable — differing among individuals and according to circumstances.

Phases of Grief

In an attempt to understand and delineate the various processes associated with grief, researchers have devised a number of models that present these processes within a framework involving a theory of stages (see Figure 7-1).[16] Some models postulate three stages, others seven or ten. To outline the stages of grief work in this manner seems to suggest a linear progression from the first stage, through the second, and so on, until the process has been completed. Although this notion might provide comfort to those who wish to evaluate a survivor's journey toward reintegration after loss, it is important to place these theories in their intended context.

The theories concerning stages of grief represent an effort to specify various aspects of a process that occurs in highly individualistic ways. Thus, although models of grief can be very helpful in increasing our understanding, we should not try to superimpose a particular structure on the actual grief experience of a particular survivor.

Geoffrey Gorer has divided grief work into three stages.[17] The first stage is a fairly brief period of *shock*, usually lasting from the time the survivor learns of the death until the final disposition of the deceased's body. During this period the survivor is often occupied with the activities surrounding the body of the deceased, such as arranging for burial or cremation, and sorting out the deceased's personal and family affairs. This is traditionally the time when sympathy cards arrive and the survivor accepts the condolences of friends and relatives.[18]

The second stage is a period of *intense grief work.* Varying considerably among survivors, this stage generally lasts from several weeks to a few months. During this period the bereaved's attention is withdrawn from external events, and many of the physiological symptoms associated with intense grief may be present. For example, the survivor may experience restlessness and disturbed sleep, perhaps with dreams in which the deceased figures prominently. Lack of appetite and weight loss are also common during the second stage. Paradoxically, at a time when grief is often most intense, the survivor usually receives relatively little support from family, friends, or the community or by way of formal rituals, for the funeral, memorial service, and the like have already passed. This stage is often a time when the bereaved is left alone with his or her grief.

The third and final stage in Gorer's model is a period of *reestablishing physical and mental balance;* the survivor is no longer constantly experiencing acute physical or emotional turmoil at the knowledge of being bereft. Sleep and appetite return to normal, and the survivor is again an interested participant in the outside world.

Social institutions and customs may perform a valuable service to the survivor during the initial period of grief, the stage of intense shock.[19] The presence of family and other social groups and the need to actively attend to the various details of the funeral and disposition of the body may help to define the role and behaviors expected of survivors at a time of crisis.

The regimen provided by the activities of this period is often in marked contrast to what occurs afterward. Typically, after the final disposition of the deceased's body, friends and family disperse, leaving the bereaved largely on his or her own to find adequate ways of coping with the loss. Yet much of the intense grief work takes place just when support systems are most lacking. As survivors, and as caring persons, we should remember that a lack of support at this crucial time can limit opportunities for the bereaved to express feelings of grief, with the possible result that these feelings are suppressed and normal readjustment is delayed or thwarted.

Another person who has contributed to our understanding of grief is Robert Kavanaugh, who postulates seven stages in the process of mourning.[20] As with Gorer's theory, Kavanaugh's first stage is characterized by *shock,* which may be manifest in disbelief and denial. In his outline, each of the stages is a distinct emotional state, though not necessarily separate; as he says, "they invariably intertwine and overlap."

Kavanaugh describes the second stage of mourning as *disorganization,* which he likens to being stranded in the middle of a fast-flowing stream while water and debris rush about the motionless and helpless bereaved person. The third stage is one of *volatile emotions,* which suggests the image of boiling water,

Grief may indeed range the gamut. It may be shrill and maniacal; it may be subdued and reflective; it may be philosophical. The recording of grief and of the response to it, of the sadness that is virtually physiological and is certainly deeply mysterious in its fullest psychological character, serves, as Aristotle and the later students of tragic cartharsis have suggested, as a kind of purgation, as a means of releasing the terrible suppressed tensions, fears, anxieties, deeply fearsome in their potential for still greater unknown effect. Identifying the full range and depth of the symptoms must always come first, must be the basis on which understanding, management, and assimilation of grief into the totality of living rests.

Morris Freedman, "Notes on Grief in Literature"

intermittently giving off steam, like a volcano, while at other times appearing relatively dormant. Subsequent stages are characterized as periods of *guilt;* a sense of *loss and loneliness* as needs and dependencies that previously were met by the deceased become apparent; *relief* that the pain is subsiding as attachment diminishes, bringing a new freedom to the bereaved's life (which, Kavanaugh adds, may be difficult to admit to others); and *reestablishment,* as the bereaved person moves ahead with his or her life.

In the model of grief described by Beverly Raphael, the first response when a loved one dies is *shock, numbness, and disbelief.*[21] This initial response fades as the bereaved moves through the funeral rites and the reality of the death is gradually acknowledged. *Separation pain* marks the period following the funeral. During this time the bereaved experiences intense yearning for the person who has died. Then, as the finality of the loss is accepted, the bereaved begins to review and sort through all the bonds and "bits" of interaction that built the relationship. During this *psychological mourning process,* there is an intense reexperiencing of the whole history of the relationship, and the bonds of attachment are slowly relinquished. At first, the world seems disorganized and chaotic; eventually, as the bonds of the relationship are undone, there is a sense of *reintegration* with the world and the emotions are "freed for reinvestment in life once more."

Savine Gross Weizman and Phyllis Kamm describe a five-phase model of grief.[22] During the first phase, the dominant response to loss is one of *shock, disbelief, and denial.* Confused and bewildered by the impact, the bereaved may feel vulnerable and seek protection by isolation and withdrawal. The second phase in this model is termed *undoing,* "a process in which the mourner attempts to undo the calamity in order to make everything as it was before." Fantasies of alternatives that would have prevented the death are characteristic of this phase. The bereaved may blame himself or herself, feeling somehow responsible for the death. Guilt may be felt about one's actions toward the deceased. This is a time of "if onlys" and "what ifs," as the bereaved comes to terms with issues of responsibility and power relating to changing the reality that is: The person is dead.

Anger is the characteristic emotion of the third phase. The object of anger may be the deceased loved one ("How could you abandon me?"), God ("How could you let this happen?"), or the situation itself ("How could this happen to me?"). This anger may be displaced toward persons in one's environment, such as family members or friends.

In the fourth phase, as the reality of the death begins to be absorbed, the predominant feeling becomes one of *sadness*. Feelings of longing, disappointment, and hopelessness also mark this phase. Weizman and Kamm characterize the fifth phase, *integration,* as one in which "the reality becomes part of you." Although sadness doesn't disappear completely and may be stimulated when a reminder or memory is especially poignant, it recedes into the background. The present concerns of life become the foreground on which the bereaved focuses.

Notice the similarities and differences in the various models of grief presented here. What elements seem central to the process of successfully facing a loss and resolving the grief? Keeping in mind that these models represent an outline or synthesis of the responses that may be experienced when we are confronted with a loss, the *tasks* of mourning described by William Worden may prove helpful in putting all of them into perspective.[23]

The first task of mourning, says Worden, involves *accepting the reality* of

© Albert Lee Strickland

This tombstone in a Canadian cemetery records the brief lives of twin sisters and bears silent witness to the loss felt by survivors.

the loss. Even when a death is anticipated, the reality may be difficult to accept fully. "Denying the facts of the loss," says Worden, "can vary in degree from a slight distortion to a full-blown delusion." The second task involves *experiencing the pain* of grief. This includes both the physical pain that may be experienced as well as the emotional and behavioral pain of loss. As Worden says, "Not everyone experiences the same intensity of pain or feels it in the same way, but it is impossible to lose someone you have been deeply attached to without experiencing some level of pain."

The third task involves *adjusting to a changed environment* in which the deceased is missing. It may take considerable time to make this adjustment, especially when a relationship was of long duration and exceptional closeness. Often, the many roles fulfilled by the deceased in one's life are not fully realized until after the loss occurs. Finally, the fourth task of mourning involves *withdrawing emotional energy* from the relationship that has ended so that the energy can be reinvested. Worden remarks that people sometimes have difficulty with this task, either because of a feeling that it somehow involves a dishonoring of the deceased's memory or because they fear investing emotional energy into another relationship that could also end in loss. The successful completion of this final task of grieving is hindered when the bereaved holds onto past

---

 A Letter from the Canadian Prairie

Heather Brae, Alberta
January 12, 1906

Miss Jennie Magee
Dear Sister:

You will be surprised to hear from me after so many years. Well I have bad news for you. My Dear little wife is Dead and I am the lonelyist Man in all the world. She gave Birth to little Daughter on the 27th of December three Days after she went out of her mind and on the 7th of January she took Pnumonia and Died about half past three in the afternoon. We buried her tuesday afternoon in a little cemetary on the Prarry about 15 miles from here. I am writing to you to see if you will come and keep house for me and raise my little Baby. I would not like to influence you in any way as I am afraid you would be lonely when I have to go from home as I will now and again. You are used to so much stir in the city. I have 400 acres of Land and I have 9 or ten cows and some hens. If you come you can make all you can out of the Butter and eggs and I might be able to Pay you a small wage . . . Write and let me know as soon as Possible what you think about the Proposition. I am writing to the rest tonight to let them know the bad news. I think this is all at Present from your affectionate Brother.

William Magee

Linda Rasmussen, Lorna Rasmussen,
Candace Savage, and Anne Wheeler,
A Harvest Yet to Reap: A History of Prairie Women

attachments and refuses to form new ones. This task may be the most difficult of all. Yet to leave it undone is be stuck in a condition of not loving. The completion of mourning involves the recognition that, although one does not love the deceased person any less, there are also other people to be loved.

Because the descriptions of stages seem to suggest an orderly progression, one may be tempted to think that he or she should move through these stages much like walking, from step 1 to step 2 to step 3, and so on — all in a very neat and clearly delineated fashion, spending so much time in one stage, then moving on to the next stage. The model of grief as a process that can be distinguished by specific stages is an aid to comprehending how grief functions and its effect on survivors. But we need not mistake the map for the territory. Although the description of stages is useful in defining certain aspects of grief that may be encountered by a survivor, the actual experience of grief and mourning will probably resemble a series of dance steps more than it does a cross-country walk.

When you recall a loss in your life, you may remember the elements of shock, intense emotions, and becoming reestablished, but not in such a clear one-two-three sequence of mutually exclusive states. Sometimes it may have felt as if all the feelings were present at once. Part of you may have been feeling shock while another part was calm. We are capable of experiencing many emotions, even conflicting ones, at the same time.

The Mortality of Bereavement

To be a survivor is to experience not only symptoms of physical disease but dis-ease of a psychological and social nature as well. We have already enumerated some of the observable symptoms that may arise in the body with the onset of grief: tightness of the throat, loss of appetite, difficulty in breathing, and a host of others.[24] These body responses constitute one aspect of the biology of grief.

However, there is another aspect of the biological response to grief that can have far more serious consequences for the survivor. W. D. Rees and S. G. Lutkins examined the mortality of bereavement and found that the death rate among survivors during the first year of bereavement was nearly seven times that of the general population.[25] And research by Arthur C. Carr and Bernard Schoenberg has shown that some chronic diseases have a higher incidence among the recently bereaved.[26] These diseases include cancer, tuberculosis, ulcerative colitis, asthma, obesity, rheumatoid arthritis, congestive heart failure, leukemia, and diabetes. In a recent study conducted by Marvin Stein at Mount Sinai School of Medicine, diminished immune response was found among a group of widowers during the first few months following bereavement.[27] Although no direct cause-and-effect link has been established between bereavement and the onset of disease, the statistical evidence suggests that reaction to loss can contribute to the epidemiology of certain diseases, especially those related to stress.

Hans Selye's studies point to the existence of an acute alarm reaction, or mobilization of the body's resources, in situations of high emotional stress.[28] According to Selye, the alarm reaction is a "generalized call to arms" of the body's defenses, and it manifests itself in various physiological changes that prepare the organism to cope with the agent or situation that elicited the alarm reaction. If this reaction is not followed by some form of adaptation or resistance to the agent eliciting it, severe damage or even death can ensue. The stress associated with bereavement appears at times to aggravate a physical condition that may have been latent, causing symptoms to become manifest or to develop more rapidly. Stress is a component of the grief process that can play a crucial role in the survivor's ability to cope with loss.

One researcher, George Engel, compiled a number of case reports indicating a relationship between stress and sudden death.[29] He then classified the various stressful situations into eight categories, four of which can be considered as either a direct or an indirect component of grief and mourning: (1) the impact of the death of a close person, (2) the stress of acute grief, (3) the stress that occurs with mourning, and (4) the loss of status or self-esteem following bereavement.

On first thought, loss of self-esteem may not seem to be corollary of experiencing bereavement. Guilt, however, tends to lower self-esteem, and guilt is a common component of grief. Consider the bereaved person who says, "If only I had tried harder, if I had done something differently, my friend might not have died." In addition, situations in daily life may work to lower a survivor's self-esteem following the death of a spouse, close friend, or family member. For instance, a widower who used to attend social functions with his spouse may find that he is now left off the guest list. A widow may decline invitations or avoid situations that she considers activities for couples. The financial status of the bereaved person often changes. If self-worth has been dependent on a certain income level, then less money and tighter finances may lower self-esteem. The loss of status enjoyed because of a deceased spouse's professional or community standing can have a similar effect.

It has been recently documented that stress lowers the body's immunological resistance to certain types of disease. Jerome F. Fredrick has pointed out that a single virus, known as the Epstein-Barr virus, is the causative agent in two quite dissimilar diseases:[30] mononucleosis, a relatively benign ailment that can usually be cured with treatment and bed rest; and lymphocytic leukemia, a life-threatening illness with a high fatality rate.

Antibodies to Epstein-Barr virus have been found in over 90 percent of individuals by the time they reach ten years of age.[31] It has been theorized that stress produces biological changes that can depress the natural immune mechanism, allowing the virus to manifest as disease.[32] It may be that the degree of stress and the ability to deal with stress determine whether a person develops mononucleosis, a relatively mild disease, or the much more serious lymphocytic leukemia.

During the fifteenth century, grief was one of the legal causes of death that could be listed on death certificates. Researchers such as Colin Murray Parkes have looked into the question of whether one can indeed die of a "broken heart."[33] Studies verify that some survivors, especially during the first year of bereavement, do have a higher incidence of some diseases.[34] The ways that grief and related stress affect specific processes in the body are now being explored with great interest by medical researchers. Perhaps we will soon agree with the people of the fifteenth century that it is not so far-fetched to include "grief" and "a broken heart" among the causes of death.

When stress is not dealt with adequately, disease can result. The determinant, however, is not so much the presence of stress as the ability to cope with it.[35] How a person copes with catastrophic losses — such as the death of a spouse, close friend, or family member — tends to be consistent with how that person copes with the everyday stresses and small losses of daily living. It is important, therefore, to be aware of stress and its potentially harmful effects, and to take constructive steps to manage the level of stress in one's life.

Variables Influencing Grief

Just as no two persons are alike, no two experiences of grief are alike. The circumstances of a death, the personality and social roles of the bereaved, his or her relationship with the deceased — these are among the factors that influence the nature of grief. An understanding of these factors can provide not only knowledge about the processes of grief, but also clues about why some deaths seem especially devastating to survivors.

Robert Fulton has shown that a major influence on the experience of grief is whether the circumstances of a death classify it as a *high-grief* or *low-grief* death.[36] A high-grief death is characterized by the intense emotional and physical reactions to loss usually associated with normal grief; a low-grief death, although emotionally affecting, is less devastating, and thus the reaction to loss is less severe and the bereaved is able to cope more readily with the loss. The death of a child is often cited as the classic example of a high-grief death, whereas the death of someone in old age, someone we think of as having lived a long and varied life, is likely to be a low-grief death. It is the circumstances of a particular death and its effect on a particular survivor, however, that really determines whether the emotional response is of high or low grief. The survivor's age may also be a determining factor, as we will see in Chapters 8 and 9. For example, the death of a parent may be more catastrophic to a young child or an adolescent than to a grown child who had moved away from home.

The experience of grief also varies according to the amount of social support available. For instance, after the death of an unborn child, whether through miscarriage or induced abortion, a survivor is likely to receive little support from the social conventions that comfort other survivors in their grief. Often, no funeral or other ceremony is observed, and the loss may not be acknowledged at all by the larger community. Thus, the usual processes that allow a survivor to confront a loss and to take leave of the deceased are greatly hampered. The kinds of losses we are considering here relate to what Kenneth

Many people believe the death of a young child to be the most heartrending of all bereavement experiences — what researchers term a high-grief death, because it tends to elicit a tremendous sense of loss.

Doka terms *disenfranchised grief;* that is, grief experienced in connection with a loss that is not socially supported or acknowledged through the usual rituals.[37] When grief is disenfranchised — either because the significance of the loss is not recognized or because the relationship between the deceased and the bereaved is not socially sanctioned — the person who has suffered the loss is given little or no opportunity to mourn publicly. When a high-grief death is treated by society as if it were not a significant loss, the process of adjustment is more difficult for survivors.

The Survivor's Model of the World

A survivor's experience of loss and grief is conditioned to a large extent by his or her model of the world; that is, by his or her perception of reality and judgment about how the world works. In considering how a person's model of the world applies to the experience of bereavement, of particular importance are four factors that have been identified by Edgar Jackson as conditioning a person's emotional reaction to bereavement.[38]

The first factor is the individual's personality. Personality, of course, influences how we relate to life experiences generally: Some people seem to ride easily over large bumps, but may receive quite a jolt from a small shock; for others, the situation is reversed. In this respect, self-concept is an important determinant of how a person responds when death occurs. An immature, dependent personality will be more vulnerable to the loss of a person in whom a large amount of emotional capital has been invested. Such an investment may represent an attempt to compensate for feelings of personal inadequacy by projecting part of one's self-identity onto another person. When bereavement occurs, more of this projected self is involved in the loss. The person with greater self-esteem and a stronger self-concept is not so prone to such overcompensation, and grief is likely to be less devastating.

The second conditioning factor identified by Jackson is social roles, which provide the framework wherein the survivor tries to cope with grief. Again, it is the way in which a person incorporates social roles into his or her model of the world that influences the response to death. This response is determined in part by answering the question, What does society say should be a particular survivor's response to death in general or to a particular death? A soldier in combat is expected to perform his duties despite any personal feelings of grief or loss when comrades die. Among some primitive societies a widow knows in advance what kind of behavior is expected, and the members of her society gather to ensure that grief is expressed in quite specific ways. In most modern societies, on the other hand, people generally have greater freedom to determine for themselves what kinds of behavior are appropriate. Even so, the social and cultural environment is important in defining a person's grief and mourning.[39]

The third factor that conditions a grief reaction is the survivor's perception of the relative importance of the deceased.[40] Was the deceased an important person in my life? Will my life be changed greatly by this death? The deaths of family members and close friends usually cause the deepest grief, but the deaths of others who have been significant in our lives can also cause strong grief reactions. Most Americans grieved for the deaths of President John F. Kennedy, Robert Kennedy, Martin Luther King, and the *Challenger* astronauts, even though the vast majority had never met any of them personally.[41] A similar outpouring of national grief occurred when Abraham Lincoln was killed by an assassin's bullet.

The fourth conditioning factor identified by Jackson is the person's value structure; that is, the relative worth assigned to different experiences and possible outcomes. For example, we sometimes hear people say something like, "Of course, his wife misses him terribly, but she is also relieved that he is no longer enduring such pain and suffering." In other words, the knowledge that her husband's suffering is over helps mitigate her grief at his death. Jackson cites an example of a husband who, knowing that he will soon die from a terminal illness, prepares with his wife for the time when he will not be present to help manage their financial affairs. Again, the value that this couple placed on being prepared was a conditioning factor relative to their experience of facing the husband's dying and the wife's subsequent grief. In a more general way, a value structure that allows death an appropriate place in a person's philosophy of life can be significant in determining how he or she experiences loss and grief.

Mode of Death

How a person dies affects a survivor's grief. The type of death — be it natural, accidental, or a suicide — influences the grief experience, as does the survivor's previous experience with that type of death.[42] Some researchers believe that if a death has been anticipated, perhaps as a result of chronic illness, it is generally not as difficult to deal with as one that occurs suddenly, without warning. Prior knowledge of an impending death allows a survivor to contemplate its circumstances before it actually occurs, perhaps alleviating some of the pain of grief.[43] Others disagree, arguing that anticipatory grief does not diminish the grief experienced after the loss occurs.[44] There is perhaps no simple resolution of this question, but there is general agreement that shock is more intense and overwhelming when death is unanticipated and sudden.

Consider the various ways in which people die. We think of the aged grandmother, dying quietly in her sleep; the young child pronounced DOA after a bicycle accident; the chronically ill person dying a lingering death; the despondent executive who commits suicide. Our minds can provide us with many such examples — powerful, heart-wrenching images. Each mode of death, each set of circumstances in which death occurs can uniquely affect the survivor's ability to integrate the loss.[45] For example, consider some of the qualities that are unique to suicide.

Survivors are often left with a numbing feeling of, "Oh, my God, he did it to himself!" That someone has willingly chosen to end his or her life adds an element of personal confrontation, a stark reminder not only of our mortality but that each of us could choose to terminate our own physical existence.

The impact of a suicide upon survivors usually intensifies feelings of guilt and blame. If someone close to us was in such pain that he or she chose suicide, we may be burdened with the question, "Why didn't I see the predicament and do more to help in coping with the problems?" We may blame ourselves in some way for that person's death. What did we do that may have worked to

The other day I heard the father of a boy who had committed suicide say, "Everyone has a skeleton in their closet. But the person who kills themselves leaves their skeleton in another's closet." The grief and guilt that arise in the wake of suicide often leave a legacy of guilt and confusion. Each loved one wracks the mind and tears the heart questioning, "What could I have done to prevent this?"

Stephen Levine, *Who Dies? An Investigation of Conscious Living and Conscious Dying*

precipitate the decision to commit suicide? How could we have prevented the death? Why didn't we hear the cry for help before it was too late?

Besides guilt and self-blame, the survivor may direct strong feelings of anger and blame toward the suicide for not bearing up under the stress and strain of life: "I'm not copping out on life. Why did they?" Suicide is seen as the ultimate affront, the final insult — one that, because it cannot be answered, compounds the survivor's frustration and anger.

Furthermore, a suicide is typically unexpected. Its suddenness and surprise can only magnify the survivor's sense that death was wrong or inappropriate. Like the death of a child, a death by suicide goes against the grain of our intrinsic belief that people should live on into old age. The death of a child or a suicide, then, may leave the survivor with an additional, burdensome feeling that the death was premature.

Persons who have survived a disaster in which others were killed also have special concerns in grieving.[46] They have become survivors twice over — survivors of a catastrophic event that could have ended their own lives, and survivors of the deaths of others, perhaps friends or relatives. In studies of survivors of the Holocaust, researchers often found a deep sense of guilt about having survived the camps and the torture while others were not as fortunate.[47] Although there is evidence that such feelings tend to be intensified by disasters or events such as the Holocaust, this sense of guilt at still being alive can affect any survivor.

If the deceased was a victim of homicide, anger and fear may become the survivor's predominant emotions. For a time, the world may be experienced as dangerous, filled with perverted and cruel people, an unsafe place. As with a suicide or the death of a young child, the suddenness and apparent injustice of the circumstances of death affect the grief experience.

Relationship of Survivor to Deceased

The experience of bereavement is profoundly influenced by the relationship between the deceased and the survivor. Think for a moment about the various kinds of relationships in your life. As you name them, you will notice that a variety of labels come to mind — parents, children, pets, neighbors, co-workers, teachers, friends, and lovers. The *form* of a given relationship is one of the

This portrait of the Saltonstall family, painted in 1611 by David Des Granges, provides a record of living family members and their relational links with the deceased, whose influence is still felt. The husband and father, Sir Richard, is portrayed as if standing at the bedside of his dead wife whose arm reaches toward their two children. Seated in the chair and holding her baby, the newest member of the family, is Sir Richard's second wife, whom he married three years after the death of his first wife.

David Des Granges, Tate Gallery, London

factors determining a survivor's experience of grief. The death of a family member or other close relative, for example, will probably require a greater adjustment than the death of a co-worker or neighbor. But the outward form of relationship is not the sole determinant of a survivor's experience of grief.

Whatever the outward form may be — kin, friend, neighbor, or mate — relationships vary according to the degree of intimacy involved, the perception of each other's roles, the expectations of the other person, and the feelings about the quality of the relationship itself. In Bali, for example, family members and other kin are rarely referred to by their *personal* names, but rather by the *degree of relationship,* thus placing emphasis on the social roles. In our culture, most people do refer to siblings and other relatives by their personal names, yet how many refer to a parent by his or her given name?

A person's relationship with his or her parents may reflect the socially defined roles of "parent" and "child" more than feelings of friendship or personal intimacy. For some, however, a parent may occupy additional roles of business associate, neighbor, and close friend. These differing roles and expectations are likely to result in a very different experience of grief when that parent dies.

As we see, then, a number of factors influence whether a particular relationship is *central* or *peripheral* to a person's life. A death involving someone central to the survivor's life generally will be much more affecting than the death of someone felt to be on the periphery. The degree of relationship, level of intimacy, and the roles and expectations associated with the relationship all influence whether we categorize a particular relationship as central or peripheral to our lives.

Larry Bugen has proposed a theory about the grief experience that relates a survivor's relationship to the deceased (categorized as central or peripheral) with the survivor's *belief* about the circumstances of the death (whether preventable or unpreventable) to predict the severity of the grief response. In other words, a survivor's attachment to the deceased and his or her sense of the appropriateness of the death will generally determine the response. For example, given a *central* relationship between the survivor and the deceased and the belief that the death was *preventable,* one would expect the grieving process to be both intense and prolonged. On the other hand, if the survivor had a *peripheral* relationship with the deceased and believed that the death was *not preventable,* one might expect the grieving process to be mild as well as relatively brief.[48]

Ambivalence is another factor influencing relationships and subsequent grief. Such feeling about the quality of a relationship, reflecting a push-pull struggle between love and hate, may be subtle or dramatic. Perhaps no relationship is entirely free of ambivalence or questions about its quality. But when feelings of ambivalence are intense and prolonged, grieving can be complicated by unresolved emotions.

Unfinished Business

Unfinished business can be aptly termed "business that goes on after death." Something remains incomplete at the time of death. The content of unfinished business, how it is handled, and how the survivor is affected by it all have an impact on the experience of grief. Unfinished business can be thought of in one or both of two ways relative to its effect on survivors: First is the fact of death itself; second is the relationship between deceased and survivor. As to the first, perhaps an earlier death of a parent, child, sibling, or someone else close continues to be a vivid reminder of the survivor's uncertainty and fears about death. Regardless of an individual's particular beliefs or values, the more finished is the business of death — that is, the more comfortable the survivor feels about it — the easier it will be to accept death and to cope with grief and mourning. If a person rails against death, denying it and refusing to accept it, the experience of grief is more likely to be difficult and perhaps prolonged.

Accepting death, giving it a place in our lives, allows us to be finished with otherwise unresolved issues about death itself.

Second, and probably more crucial in alleviating the stress and pain of grief, is the unfinished business between the deceased and the survivor. Something in the relationship was left incomplete — perhaps some long-standing conflict was never resolved during the deceased's lifetime, and now the survivor feels it is too late. Such unfinished business can include things that were and were not said, things done or not done. Unfinished business may give the survivor feelings of unfulfillment. The work of Elisabeth Kübler-Ross and others points up the importance of finishing business between the person who is dying and his or her survivors. Open and uninhibited discussion at the time of an impending death can yield significant benefits both for the person who is dying and for the survivor.

Persons who have experienced the death of someone close often say that the things left unsaid or undone seem to come back to pain them, to give them bad times in the night. The sense of never being able to resolve the conflicts left by unfinished business is what amplifies the suffering. Consider the image of a son standing over his father's grave saying, "If only we had been closer, Dad. We ought to have taken more time to visit each other."

It may be possible to resolve some unfinished business even after the person's death by working through such unresolved experiences with the help of various techniques of counseling and therapeutic intervention. But it is easier and clearer to work toward resolving unfinished business daily, in all our relationships and especially our intimate ones. Perhaps the key to taking care of unfinished business is forgiveness: accepting the situation as it is.

Deathbed promises constitute a particular kind of unfinished business, and they affect more people than we might at first imagine. Imagine the classic scene in which the person who is dying elicits some promise from the survivor to perform some particular action after the person dies. Most survivors agree to enact the promise, whether or not they really want to comply with the deathbed request. Thus, a deathbed promise can later cause considerable conflict for the survivor, who may be torn between fulfilling the promise and taking a contradictory course of action. Some people carry through a deathbed promise and find it to be a gratifying choice; others find that a deathbed promise needs to be reevaluated in the light of their own wishes and circumstances.

Intellectual Versus Emotional Responses

When there is a marked difference between the survivor's emotional and intellectual responses to death, and the survivor believes that only one response can be right, the result is conflict. To expect the head and the heart to react the same to loss is unrealistic; there will probably be disparity between feelings and thoughts. Many different emotions will be felt, and many different thoughts, during the process of working through grief. By allowing them all and withholding judgment as to the rightness and wrongness of particular emotions or thoughts, the survivor is much more likely to experience grief as healing.

One must give oneself permission to experience feelings of loss. Survivors often have rigid rules about what kind of feelings can be expressed in grief, and when — such as where and when it is acceptable to be angry, or to open to the pain and release an intense outburst of sadness.

Permission to have and express feelings is of immense importance in dealing with the issues of survivorship. Intellectually, we may think, "How can I be mad at someone for dying?" Yet anger may indeed be a component of grief; consider the example of someone who died because of driving while intoxicated, or of the suicide. On the other hand, anger may be present even if death was seemingly unavoidable and beyond the victim's control. One young mother told of walking past a photograph of her recently deceased child and noticing, amid the grief and pain, a small voice within her blurting out, "Brat! How could you die and leave me as you did!" In a purely intellectual sense, we might be tempted to think this mother's behavior quite out of place. How could she be angry at her child for dying? Yet that sense of rage, that frustrated anger, is typical in the experience of survivors.

Survivors must permit themselves to experience those feelings, to feel anger at the person for having died and anger at themselves for not having been able to prevent the death — indeed, giving themselves permission to experience all the feelings that arise. Thus, they need not judge themselves as uncaring or bad.

An Elegy on the Death of John Keats

Ah, woe is me! Winter is come and gone,
But grief returns with the revolving year;
The airs and streams renew their joyous tone:
The ants, the bees, the swallows reappear;
Fresh leaves and flowers deck the dead Seasons' bier;
The amorous birds now pair in every brake,
And build their mossy homes in field and brere;
And the green lizard, and the golden snake,
Like unimprisoned flames, out of their trance awake.

Alas! that all we loved of him should be
But for our grief, as if it had not been,
And grief itself be mortal! Woe is me!
Whence are we, and why are we? of what scene
The actors or spectators? Great and mean
Meet massed in death, who lends what life must borrow.
As long as skies are blue, and fields are green,
Evening must usher night, night urge the morrow,
Month follow month with woe, and year wake year to sorrow.

Percy Bysshe Shelley, "Adonais"
(excerpt)

Advice for the Bereaved

Realize and recognize the loss.
Take time for nature's slow, sure, stuttering process of healing.
Give yourself massive doses of restful relaxation and routine busy-ness.
Know that powerful, overwhelming feelings will lessen with time.
Be vulnerable, share your pain, and be humble enough to accept support.
Surround yourself with life: plants, animals, and friends.
Use mementos to help your mourning, not to live in the dead past.
Avoid rebound relationships, big decisions, and anything addictive.
Keep a diary and record successes, memories, and struggles.
Prepare for change, new interests, new friends, solitude, creativity, growth.
Recognize that forgiveness (of ourselves and others) is a vital part of the healing
    process.
Know that holidays and anniversaries can bring up the painful feelings you thought
    you had successfully worked through.
Realize that any new death-related crisis will bring up feelings about past losses.

                                                    The Centre for Living with Dying

Coping Mechanisms for Survivors

From the dawn of human consciousness, survivors have made use of a variety of activities, rituals, and social institutions for help in coping with the fact of loss. We have seen in previous chapters how funeral rites and other ceremonies surrounding disposition of the body have served this purpose by providing an orderly and acceptable framework for dealing with the initial shock of loss. However, because the process of coming to terms with a loss continues beyond the brief period taken up with such rituals, many survivors seek additional sources of support for adequately coming to terms with their loss.

In the past, much of this support was provided within the family and the close-knit community of friends and relatives. With changes in the patterns of social life, such as smaller families and greater geographic mobility, some of these traditional sources of support may be unavailable or insufficient to meet the particular needs of survivors. Thus, many bereaved persons have sought support by sharing their concerns with others who have had similar bereavement experiences. Such survivor support groups extend communal support beyond the initial period of the funeral rites and provide supportive resources that may be otherwise lacking in the survivor's milieu.

In addition to funeral rituals and survivor support groups, coping mechanisms for survivors include gaining an understanding of how best to proceed with the practical management of life's affairs. We will look briefly at how each of these coping mechanisms for survivors can aid in the process of coming to terms with bereavement and grief.

Accordion player Graham Jackson, at the funeral of President Franklin Delano Roosevelt, is a poignant example of how bereaved persons often express their loss in public as well as in private.

Edward C. Clark, Life Magazine, © 1945 Time Inc.

Funerals and Rituals

Funeral rituals can help provide a sense of closure on the deceased's life and thereby aid integration of the loss into the ongoing lives of survivors. Sociologist Glenn Vernon notes that such rituals typically represent an opportunity for a "controlled expression of anger and hostility, and also for a lessening of guilt and anxiety."[49] The role of the wake among traditional Hawaiians illustrates Vernon's remarks. Everyone in the *ohana,* or extended family, came to the wake, including children. With each new arrival, a relative would say — as if telling the dead person — "Here comes Keone, your old fishing companion," or "Tutu is coming in now; remember how she used to massage you when you were sick." The mourners then addressed the dead, recalling their memories and perhaps describing their feelings of abandonment, even scolding the deceased for dying. A fishing companion might exclaim, "What do you mean, going off when we had planned to go fishing! Now who will I fish with?" Or a

The upper middles would probably drink themselves silly at the funeral. Although a few years ago this would have been frowned on. When my husband in the sixties announced that he intended to leave £200 in his will for a booze-up for his friends, his lawyer talked him out of it, saying it was in bad taste and would upset people. The same year his grandmother died, and after the funeral, recovering from the innate vulgarity of the cremation service when the gramophone record stuck on 'Abi-abi-abi-abi-de with me', the whole family trooped home and discovered some crates of Australian burgundy under the stairs. A rip-roaring party ensued and soon a lower middle busybody who lived next door came bustling over to see if anything was wrong. Whereupon my father-in-law, holding a glass and seeing her coming up the path, uttered the immortal line: 'Who is this intruding on our grief?'

Jilly Cooper, *Class*

wife might say, "You had no business to go. You should be ashamed of yourself. We need you."[50]

Although these customs were not consciously planned to vent grief, they nevertheless facilitated it. The practice of scolding the corpse, for instance, provided an opportunity for survivors to vent hostility toward the dead who had abandoned them. What a contrast to the Western cultural notion that one should "not speak ill of the dead," which may deny feelings of anger toward the deceased.[51]

Of course, not all funeral rituals are alike. Some survivors express their grief with intense fervor, others adopt a nearly stoic expression of grief. In one culture funerals are occasions for weeping and wailing, even literally "tearing one's hair out," magnifying the emotional response to provide catharsis; another culture emphasizes keeping emotions subdued, not demonstrating grief, not breaking down.[52] But, whatever its particular characteristics, as a culturally condoned vehicle for expressing grief behavior, the rituals that surround death serve to facilitate closure by offering survivors a social framework for coping with the fact of death.

Survivor Support Groups

Survivor support groups are becoming increasingly important to help survivors cope with grief and mourning by sharing concerns and empathy with one another. Such groups are based upon the concept of *perceived similarity*. Members of a group usually have experienced similar losses and meet together to support one another as they work toward understanding and integrating those losses into their lives. Probably the best known of these groups are the many organizations of widows (often known as widow-to-widow groups) within which widows can congregate to share their experiences of being a woman alone, and to encourage one another in coping with the death of a spouse. Other support groups exist as well, each ministering to the needs of a particular group of survivors.

Just as survivor support groups differ in their emphasis, they also differ in approach and methodology. Some are composed entirely of peers, whereas others are facilitated by a trained professional or lay counselor. In some groups meetings resemble an encounter session, the rule being to accept and express feelings. Others function more as social groups, simply providing a place for the survivor to come and be with others who have had similar experiences.

Practical Management of Life's Affairs

A prevalent belief in our culture is that it is important for survivors to take a hand in the practical management of their everyday affairs as soon as possible following bereavement. In fact, it often seems to be suggested that how well the survivor is managing grief can be measured by how well he or she is managing the daily concerns of life.[53]

The survivor must deal with the impact of change, possibly affecting every detail of life: The family unit is different; the social realities have changed; there are legal and financial matters that require attention. The survivor must face these issues and answer the question, "How can I make the adjustment in each of these areas?" Because the loss of someone close brings tremendous change, it is helpful if, in the management of life's affairs, the survivor limits the number of other changes that occur at the same time.

Bereavement as an Opportunity for Growth

Survivors are better able to cope if they are aware that death and bereavement can be an opportunity for growth. This perspective allows movement toward resolving the loss. One can begin to reformulate the loss, thus freeing up energy that had been bound to the past. As John Schneider says, "There is a change in perceptual set from focusing on limits to focusing on potential; from coping to growth; and from problems to challenges."[54] The tragic event of the loved one's death is reformulated in a way that offers new opportunities. The reframing of this experience can carry over into other areas of a person's life, so that beliefs and assumptions that were once limiting may be reassessed with greater self-confidence and self-awareness. The process of resolving loss and working through grief provides incentives that make possible significant life changes.

In this way, the loss is transformed. The intensive focus on self-awareness

So each shall mourn, in life's advance,
Dear hopes, dear friends, untimely killed;
Shall grieve for many a forfeit chance,
And longing passion unfulfilled.

William Makepeace Thackeray,
"The End of the Play"

Pam Price, UPI/Bettman Newsphotos

Family members leave the church after attending the funeral of a son and brother. As a focus of familial and community support for the bereaved, the funeral ceremony performs a unique function among the social rituals devised to mark significant events in the lives of members of a community.

gives way to a new sense of identity in which the loss is placed within a context of growth and life cycles. Grief becomes a unifying rather than alienating human experience, and the lost relationship is viewed as changed, but not ended. Transforming the loss involves integrating what was lost into one's own life energies. Being a survivor may allow changes in beliefs and values,

TABLE 7-1 *Factors Influencing the Integration of Loss*

Expressing feelings about loss	Denial of loss
Relief	Blame
Replacement	Anger
Recognizing loss	Fear
Acceptance	Hope
Passage of time	Rewriting the script
Withdrawal/detachment	Unfinished business
Ritual	Communication style
Family involvement	Guilt
Relationship	Resistance
Sorting out experience	Ritualistic behavior
Assuming responsibility	Role playing

understanding about death and about life, that might not otherwise have been possible (see Table 7-1).

Death is a community event. Death does not end the survivor's membership in family, community, or nation. Attitudes toward the dead are largely a continuation of the natural affections and styles of relationship that hold for the living in any given culture. Bereavement, grief, and mourning are complementary threads in the fabric of life, part of the warp and weft of human experience.

A survivor's response to death is complex, encompassing a multitude of personal, family, and social factors. It is influenced also by the circumstances surrounding the death. By becoming aware of the vast range of responses that can be present in the experience of loss and grief, we increase our choices for dealing with loss. By understanding the issues involved in survivorship, we offer ourselves greater opportunity to cope successfully with loss and to use the experience of loss as a means of becoming more fully human.

Further Readings

C. S. Lewis. *A Grief Observed.* New York: Seabury Press, 1961.

Edgar N. Jackson. *The Many Faces of Grief.* Nashville: Abingdon Press, 1977.

Marian Osterweis, Fredric Solomon, and Morris Green, editors. *Bereavement: Reactions, Consequences, and Care.* Washington, D.C.: National Academy Press, 1984.

Colin Murray Parkes and Robert S. Weiss. *Recovery from Bereavement.* New York: Basic Books, 1983.

Lily Pincus. *Death and the Family: The Importance of Mourning.* New York: Vintage Books, 1974.

Therese A. Rando. *Loss and Anticipatory Grief.* Lexington, Mass.: Lexington Books, 1985.

Beverly Raphael. *The Anatomy of Bereavement.* New York: Basic Books, 1983.

Judy Tatelbaum. *The Courage to Grieve: Creative Living, Recovery and Growth Through Grief.* New York: Harper & Row, 1982.

Roberta Temes. *Living with an Empty Chair: A Guide Through Grief.* Amherst, Mass.: Mandala, 1977.

J. William Worden. *Grief Counseling and Grief Therapy: A Handbook for the Mental Health Practitioner.* New York: Springer, 1982.

A child feels the death of a parent or other close family member or friend as deeply as do adult survivors of a close death. This young girl finds solace and a means of coming to terms with the death of her father by bringing a favorite drawing to the gravesite and spending some time alone with her thoughts and memories of her father and what his loss represents in her life.

CHAPTER 8

Death in Children's Lives

Change is pervasive in the lives of children. Families move and the children leave their familiar playmates, their neighborhood, their school, the people and places they have come to know and to which they feel an attachment. A parent may say, "But, dear, it's only for a year," or, "We'll come back to visit next summer." To the child, however, a year or next summer may seem a very long time indeed. Such concepts may lie outside the young child's familiar frame of reference. Change can represent a very real loss for the child.

Changes in family relationships — divorce or separation, for instance — may be experienced as a kind of death. The child senses that the known relationship has changed, but exactly what kind of relationship the future may hold is uncertain and possibly bewildering. Even though such changes may not connote the sense of finality that adults reserve for death, the child may experience a lingering uncertainty, a kind of "little death." Separation from one's parents is usually painful for a child whether the separation is due to death, divorce, or some other reason. [1]

Change is also experienced as older brothers and sisters grow up and move away from home. As the composition of the family changes, the child is faced with the need to adjust to new and unfamiliar situations. Perhaps the child delights in the change insofar as it means he or she now enjoys the thrill of having one's own room. On the other hand, with the departure of an older sibling, the child may be losing an advocate or a confidant who provided support and understanding. Change often brings both gains and losses.

An addition to the family, a new baby brother or sister, is a change that the child may experience with both excitement and trepidation. The new family member may represent an intrusion upon the child's place in the family, a loss of attention from parents and other family members. Yet the child may also enjoy the adventure and the more mature responsibilities that accompany change.

Changes like all those given require readjustments in the child's life. The child's world is filled with such "little deaths." In addition, a child may encounter more significant losses: the death of a brother or sister, a parent, or a friend; or confrontation with an illness that threatens his or her own life. As much as we may wish it could be otherwise, children also are exposed to events of change and loss, experiences of bereavement and grief. In this chapter, we examine issues of life-threatening illness and bereavement as they affect children, as well as the means for helping children cope with these experiences of change and loss in their lives.

Major Causes of Death in Childhood and Adolescence

The most difficult death for many people to face is the death of a child. Death is often viewed as appropriate only when it comes in old age, at the end of a person's lifespan. That death may occur during childhood, that a person's lifespan may be brief, is generally not easy to accept. Confronting the death of a child tends to uncover our uneasiness about death in a more dramatic way than when death is seen as the culmination of a long life. Yet the fact that death can end a child's life underscores the truth that no one is immune to death.

To our predecessors, the death of an infant or a child was not so uncommon. Although such deaths did not go unmourned, they were not seen as inappropriate. Today, because of the tremendous reduction in infant and child mortality, we are inclined to consider a child's death as quite unfair and inappropriate.

With the dramatic decline in deaths from infectious diseases, the relative importance of injury has increased. As the most prominent cause of death during the first half of the human lifespan, injury has been characterized as "the last major plague of the young."[2] When we review the main causes of death among children aged one to fourteen years, we find that accidents top the list, followed by cancer, heart disease, homicide, and suicide. For persons aged fifteen to twenty-four, the leading cause of death is again accidents, followed by suicide, homicide, cancer, and heart disease. (The incidence of suicide and homicide among young persons is discussed in Chapter 13.)

Of all the deaths resulting from accidents in the age groups just mentioned, a significant number involve motor vehicles. Many of these accidents further involve the use and abuse of alcoholic beverages, which have been found to influence not only motor vehicle accidents but other types of accidents as well. The importance of injury as the leading cause of death and disability of children and young adults in America is resulting in a growing recognition that the magnitude of the problem deserves a coordinated program of public education and research. Injury can be devastating to a young person, emotionally as well as physically. Even when death is not a result, injury can involve significant losses. If a person feels that he or she played a role in the events that led to the disability or death of a friend or other loved one, guilt may predominate among the emotions experienced after the loss. Moreover, because accidents occur suddenly and unexpectedly, allowing no time to prepare for the outcome, their aftermath is often especially shocking and devastating to survivors.

Children with Life-Threatening Illness

Although more children and adolescents die from injuries received in accidents than from the effects of disease, the situation confronting the child with a life-threatening illness is one of special poignancy. Perhaps we feel, justifiably or not, that an accident is something that just "happens" and is, therefore, unpreventable, whereas we expect medicine to provide a cure for disease. In this section, we turn our attention to the ways children perceive their direct experience with life-threatening illness and how they cope with that reality in their lives.

The Child's Perception of Illness

The terminally ill child's inquisitiveness about dying may be painful for a parent to adequately confront. The child's desire to understand his or her illness and its prognosis may be met with silence. Despite this silence, however, children are often able to interpret the behavior of those around them in order to gain insight into their condition.

In her study of a children's ward, Myra Bluebond-Langner observed that children typically were able to guess their condition by interpreting how people behaved toward them.[3] These children, most of whom were between the ages of three and nine, could assess the seriousness of their illness even though no one had told them that they were very sick or that they were going to die. Although the children sometimes discussed their illnesses with their peers, they refrained from doing so with adults.[4] Apparently perceiving that the topic made adults uncomfortable, the children on the ward talked about the taboo topic among themselves, much as children discuss other forbidden topics, out of range of an adult's hearing.

Bluebond-Langner also observed that the children's interpretations of their

When I am dead, and laid in grave,
And all my bones are rotten,
By this may I remembered be
When I should be forgotten.

On a girl's sampler, 1736

conditions changed over time; the illness was first perceived as acute, then chronic, and finally fatal. Similarly, medications were first "healing agents," then "something that prolongs life." As their perception of drugs progressed from something that was "always effective" to "effective sometimes" to "not really effective at all," their behaviors toward taking medication changed likewise.[5] The children generally knew a great deal about the world of the hospital, its staff and procedures, and the experiences of leukemic children. Most were aware of the condition of other children, making comments like "Jeffrey's in his first relapse" and noticing when other children died. Again, they shared these experiences among themselves. Although many children did not know the proper name for their disease, they typically exhibited considerable knowledge about its treatment and prognosis.[6]

Fears and Anxieties

Most researchers who have studied seriously ill and dying children report that the sick child's primary concern is related to fears of pain and separation. The three main sources of stress for hospitalized dying children can be summarized as: (1) separation from the mother (or mother figure), (2) painful or traumatic procedures, and (3) the deaths of other children. Development of the concept of death at successive stages of childhood (discussed in Chapter 3) is reflected by the sequence of major concerns experienced by the sick child. For example, children under five years old tend to be most distressed by separation from the mother. Children in the middle group, roughly ages five to nine, tend to be most concerned about the discomforting and possibly disfiguring effects of the disease and related medical procedures. The older child is more likely to experience anxiety caused by awareness of other children's deaths.[7] These findings are essentially consistent with the developmental model: Separation anxiety is typical of the young child; a personification of death, with fears about mutilation and pain, becomes predominant during the middle years of childhood; and the older child's anxieties resulting from the deaths of other children correspond to a more mature understanding of death as final and universal.[8]

In the Hospital

Illness separates the child from the people and the surroundings that are familiar and loved. Besides physical pain, there may be anguish resulting from the child's inability to engage in the activities and pursuits of healthy children. The sick child often misses school, is restricted from playtime activities, and becomes enmeshed in a more or less alien world of hospitals and medical paraphernalia.

Even when a child has grown somewhat accustomed to life in and out of the hospital, new forms of treatment and new medical settings may be unfamiliar and upsetting. Change of routine may bring added fears and anxieties. As the illness changes, the child's need to deal with new, unfamiliar doctors and other medical personnel may be quite disturbing. This reaction may

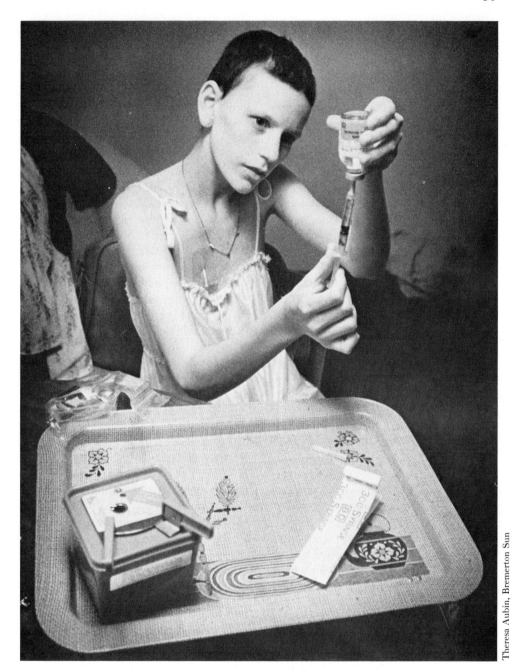

Theresa Aubin, Bremerton Sun

Adolescents and older children with life-threatening illnesses may take on increasing responsibilities for their daily treatment regimes. Here, a young cancer patient flushes her venous access catheter, the route used to administer chemotherapy, which must be cleaned nightly.

occur regardless of how friendly the hospital setting is or what efforts are made by the staff to create a special environment for sick children.[9]

Thus, parents and health care personnel must continually be preparing a child to deal with new aspects of illness and hospitalization. As nursing educator Donna Juenker points out, "Each time a child returns to the hospital he is literally a different person. He is at a wholly new stage of development with correspondingly different fears and expectations.[10]

The Child's Coping Mechanisms

The seriously ill child is not simply a passive participant in the medical and social circumstances surrounding the illness. A child may experience psychosocial concerns related to absence from school, changes in family patterns, the threat of increased dependency on others, and the financial or emotional strain on his or her family. Medical concerns may relate to the visibility of the illness, physical discomfort, and the symbolic significance attached to the part of the body affected. How a child perceives the illness and the manner in which he or she responds to it depends on such factors as age, the nature of the illness and its treatment, family relationships, and past experience.

Like everyone else, the sick child makes use of various coping mechanisms in order to deal with the anxiety and confusion that accompany life-threatening illness. Of course, the child's age and developmental stage determine the possible level of awareness and the kinds of coping mechanisms that are available. Yet even a very young child may exhibit a surprisingly wide range of resources for coping with the threat of death.

Children with life-threatening illnesses often use distancing strategies to limit the number of persons with whom they have close relationships. This reduces the risk of a distressing interaction because there are fewer opportunities for such an occurrence. A child may select from the total situation only those aspects or those persons that he or she finds least threatening. In this way, the child attempts to construct as safe and secure an environment as possible within the circumstances.

At various times, a child may avoid stress by attempting to deny the reality of the situation, or by withdrawing from a potentially stressful situation. The child may cope with a painful procedure by rationalizing that it will help to effect a cure. Or the painful treatment may be balanced in the child's mind by making a deal that allows some desire to be fulfilled once the pain is endured. For example, a child may ask, "After I get my shot, can I play with my toys?" Some children cope by regressing to a pattern of behavior that reflects a less-demanding, more-comfortable time in their lives. For example, a child may regress to the use of baby talk or "forget" his or her toilet training.

Sublimation or goal substitution may be an effective means for the child to cope with the infringements of a serious illness. For example, a child who is prevented by illness from engaging in a competitive sport may find a substitution for the desired activity by playing board games with other children in a highly competitive fashion.

These and other coping mechanisms enable the child to deal with the uncomfortable and frightening aspects of the illness. Donna Juenker says, "Through experience every child develops his own strategies of coping with stress. These mechanisms range from complete escape or denial to temporary regression to a positive restructuring of the stressful situation into manageable dimensions."[11] The manner in which a child copes with his or her illness depends not only on its circumstances, but also on the child's perception of its meaning and consequences.

Children as Survivors of a Close Death

Nearly all parents would wish to spare their children the pain of bereavement. Sometimes rather grand attempts are made to minimize the effects of a loss when it occurs in a child's life. The death of a pet, for example, may be swiftly followed by its replacement with another animal. At best, such a course of action has limited usefulness because death is a fact of life that eventually cannot be ignored. A more constructive approach when such losses occur is to help the child explore his or her feelings about death and develop an understanding of death that is appropriate for his or her ability to comprehend.

In this section, the bereaved child's expression of grief is examined, with particular emphasis on the child as survivor of the death of a parent or sibling.

The Bereaved Child's Experience of Grief

Children are capable of experiencing grief. A bereaved child may experience the same kind of physical and emotional symptoms as adults, including lack of appetite, insomnia, nightmares, and nausea. Although children tend to exhibit considerable resiliency in coping with tragedy, adults can nevertheless contribute by being willing to listen to the child's expressions of mourning and to communicate and demonstrate support for the child's well-being.[12]

Although a child's response to loss is similar in many respects to that of adults, a particular child's experience will reflect the influence of such factors as age, stage of mental and emotional development, patterns of interaction and communication within the family, closeness of relationship with the person who has died, and previous experiences with death.

Significant differences may be observed between children of the same age in their abilities to comprehend death and cope with its effects on them as survivors. For example, one five-year-old might appear quite devastated by the death of a parent. Another child of the same age and in similar circumstances might seem comparatively unaffected. The first child may put forth intense effort in trying to come to terms with the loss. The second child, on the other hand, may seem satisfied with the brief explanation that "Daddy's gone and he won't ever be coming back." Which of these children do you believe exhibits the healthier response to loss?

As you may have guessed, such a question is inappropriate, because not enough is known about each child to allow framing an adequate reply. Suppose, however, that the first child's pattern of coping involves a period of acute grief, succeeded by a satisfactory resolution of the loss. Suppose, further, that the second child's indifference is only transitory, a temporary state of mind that is succeeded by a protracted and possibly difficult process of coming to terms with the death, a process that may continue into adolescence or even adulthood before the loss is satisfactorily resolved. As this example suggests, it is not always possible to rely on appearances to assess how well a child is coping with loss.

A child may cope with the pain of a loss by selectively forgetting, or by reconstructing reality in a more desirable and comfortable way. For example, a child may not recall how frightened he was by the sight of a sibling lying in a hospital bed surrounded by awesome medical paraphernalia, or the memory of a protracted illness that included long stays in the hospital may be reconstructed so that it seems as if the sibling was only away from home briefly for a few tests. The forgotten details or the reconstructed images allow the child to think about the experience without being overwhelmed with painful memories. On the other hand, as Richard Lonetto states, "An actual death experience for the child also can stimulate the development of more mature concepts about death that do not follow a prescribed pattern."[13] So, although it is reasonable to expect that age and cognitive development affect a child's response to loss, many other variables are at work, not least of which are the attitudes exhibited by the significant adults in the child's life.

The Death of a Pet

Often, a child's first experience with death involves a pet, a situation that is not surprising considering that there are some 48 million dogs, 27 million cats, and 25 million birds kept as pets in the United States.[14] When a pet dies, parents may wonder how best to help their child cope with the loss. Should one try to minimize the child's loss? Or should the death be seen as a natural

---

Suddenly the feeling that this was all just a dream ended. Christopher was angry. It wasn't fair. Why did that dumb man have to hit Bodger?

"I ought to run *him* over with a truck."

"Oh, honey, Bodger ran right in front of him. The man didn't have time to stop."

They took Christopher home to bed where he relived the accident over and over in his mind. He tried to pretend that the truck had missed the dog, or that he hadn't called and Bodger had stayed on the other side. Or he pretended that they hadn't left the dirt road where there were hardly ever any cars. Or that they had stayed home and waited.

But the bad dream always rolled on out of his control until the moment when Bodger was lying in the road.

Carol and Donald Carrick, *The Accident*

opportunity for the child to consider what death means and to explore his or her feelings about the loss?

One mother described the responses of her daughters to the deaths of a new litter of baby rabbits.[15] Upon learning the news, the seven-year-old burst into tears and howled, "I don't want them dead." The five-year-old at first stood silently and then asked to call her father at work. She told him, "If you had been here, Daddy, you could have been the rabbits' doctor," reflecting a belief, appropriate for her age, that it should have been possible somehow to save the baby rabbits or restore them to life. Later, when the children began to dig a grave to bury the dead rabbits, the seven-year-old stopped crying for the first time since learning the news, while the five-year-old kept repeating, "The baby rabbits are dead the baby rabbits are dead," in a monotone.

In the days following the rabbits' deaths, the girls asked many questions. The seven-year-old was particularly interested in questioning a family friend who was a widow about her dead husband. How often did she think about him and why did people have to be taken away from those who loved them, she wanted to know. The five-year-old, meanwhile, continued to mourn silently until her mother encouraged her to express her feelings. Then she began to sob. Finally, she said, "I'm glad I'm only five, you only die when you're old."

The younger child's first concern was for herself, the fear that she herself could die. The older child, on the other hand, worried about the durability of relationships. Although each child had a distinctive response to the loss, both children showed a need to be close to their parents during the days following the deaths of the rabbits, and they told the story of the rabbits' deaths again and again as they dealt with their experience.

Of course, it is not just children who are affected by the death of a pet. A woman describes the reaction of her husband to the death of Iggy, a desert iguana.[16] When the iguana died, she reported that her husband "cried throughout the shoebox burial in the backyard." He was crying "for every pet he had ever loved and lost," he said.

Attachments between humans and pets can be very strong. Yet mourning the loss of a pet sometimes elicits ridicule. Some may say that the bereaved pet owner is overreacting. After all "it was only an animal, a mere pet." Those who counsel individuals who are grieving over the loss of a pet, however, emphasize that feelings should be expressed by adults as well as children. As for replacing a pet, time should be allowed to mourn the loss before a new animal is acquired. This may take weeks or months, perhaps longer. The bonds of attachment to the pet that has died may jeopardize a healthy transition of affections to another animal if the natural process of grief has been prematurely curtailed or ignored.

A sign of the increasing attention given to mourning the loss of a pet can be seen in growth of pet cemeteries. The International Pet Cemetery Association reports a total of 400 pet cemeteries in the United States, with the oldest dating back to the 1800s.[17] The appropriateness of grief over the death of a pet has also been acknowledged by veterinarians. A major greeting card company recently introduced sympathy cards expressing condolences with respect to the loss of a

Jack Delano, FSA Collection, Library of Congress

Children can feel strong attachment to their pets. Involving a child in the experience of a pet's death through ritual or discussion provides a means of coping with the loss.

Small boy. 'Where do animals go when they die?'
Small girl. 'All good animals go to heaven, but the bad ones
go to the Natural History Museum.'

Caption to drawing by E. H. Shepard, *Punch,* 1929

pet. When the bond between a pet and its owner is broken by death, the significance of that loss is increasingly recognized as a natural occasion for mourning, by adults as well as children.[18]

The Death of a Parent

Of all the deaths that can be experienced in childhood, the most affecting is generally considered to be the death of a parent. A parent's death is perceived as a loss of security, nurture, and affection — a loss of the emotional and psychological support upon which the child could formerly rely.

Because the relationship between parent and child is seldom free from conflict, whether or not openly exhibited, a parent's death may also elicit feelings of guilt. What child has not at some time directed angry thoughts — "I wish you were dead!" — toward his or her parents? Recalling such feelings, the bereaved child may feel responsible somehow for the parent's death.

Sometimes feelings of guilt result from what the child imagines to be actions that in some way contributed to a parent's death. For example, a child whose parent died of a terminal illness might remember particular instances

George Willard became possessed of a madness to lift the sheet from the body of his mother and look at her face. The thought that had come into his mind gripped him terribly. He became convinced that not his mother but someone else lay in the bed before him. The conviction was so real that it was almost unbearable. The body under the sheets was long and in death looked young and graceful. To the boy, held by some strange fancy, it was unspeakably lovely. The feeling that the body before him was alive, that in another moment a lovely woman would spring out of the bed and confront him, became so overpowering that he could not bear the suspense. Again and again he put out his hand. Once he touched and half lifted the white sheet that covered her, but his courage failed and he, like Doctor Reefy, turned and went out of the room. In the hallway outside the door he stopped and trembled so that he had to put a hand against the wall to support himself. "That's not my mother. That's not my mother in there," he whispered to himself and again his body shook with fright and uncertainty. When Aunt Elizabeth Swift, who had come to watch over the body, came out of an adjoining room he put his hand into hers and began to sob, shaking his head from side to side, half blind with grief. "My mother is dead," he said. . . .

Sherwood Anderson, *Winesburg, Ohio*

Figure 8-1   *A Four-Year-Old's "I Am Mad at You" Drawing*
Following the death of his father, a four-year-old has depicted his father saying, "Donovan, I am mad at you." Notice that the father is portrayed as being bald due to chemotherapy treatments. Whereas baldness is an accurate representation of the father's appearance, the absence of arms reflects the child's emotional perception of the situation. Arms reach out; they hug and enfold; they are a common means by which human beings express affection for one another. In the later stages of the father's illness, the pain was so great that he was unable to gather the child into his arms. The child's experience of this has been depicted in his drawing. Also notice that the drawing shows the father's body facing the viewer, yet his feet are drawn at an angle as if they are walking off the page. Again, the drawing reflects the child's experience, this time showing the father's movement out of his life. Importantly, the child's mother used the occasion of this drawing an an opportunity to talk with the child about his present feelings regarding his father's death.

when she was noisy and her sick parent needed rest. "Perhaps if I had been less noisy," the child thinks, "Mom would have gotten well." As proof of this imagined connection between the child's behavior and the parent's death, the child may cite the fact that "Mom went away and never came back to us." Such feelings are typical of the responsibility that children may assume as they try to understand their experience of a close death.

The child's experience of himself as a survivor may also give rise to feelings of guilt or uncertainty. A drawing made by a four-year-old whose father died of leukemia illustrates this (see Figure 8-1). Some time after his father's death, as the child was playing with his pencils and drawing paper, he asked his mother how to spell various words. Attracted by the child's activity, his mother noticed that he had drawn a picture of his father. In the drawing the father was saying to the child, "I am mad at you!" Surprised at this depiction of her husband's anger toward her son, the mother asked, "Why should your father have been mad at you?" The child explained, "Because you and I can still play together and Dad can't be with us anymore." Amid the confusing feelings resulting from his father's death, the child was attempting to come to terms with the fact of his own survivorship.

Now, in working with this child as a survivor, his mother had done a very wise thing. She said, "Tell me about this picture." In other words, she began to ask specific, open-ended questions that would elicit descriptions of the child's feelings. By doing this, she was able to respond directly to the child's concerns.[19]

The Death of a Sibling

Unlike a parent's death, a sibling's death rarely represents a loss of security for the surviving child. Still, the effect of such a close death may increase the surviving child's sense of vulnerability to death, especially when siblings are close to one another in age. The surviving child may experience a variety of responses to the death of a sibling. Perhaps the brother or sister was a protector, a caregiver as well as a playmate. The surviving child may be sad that this unique relationship has ended, worried that the protection and care given by the sibling is no longer available, and yet relieved or even pleased that, with the sibling's absence, he or she is now more the center of attention in the family. Such a mixture of emotions may produce guilt and confusion in the child who is trying to come to terms with the death of a sibling.

The young child looks to his or her parents for help in understanding the significance of the sibling's death and in coping with its effects on the family and surviving child alike. The parents' methods of coping play a large part in determining how the surviving child copes.

It sometimes happens that the parents' response to a child's death sets into motion dysfunctional family patterns that impair the surviving child's ability to cope. Such dysfunctional responses may range from resentment of the surviving child to an attempt to recreate in that child some of the qualities of the deceased child. The surviving child's feelings of rejection may be further complicated by feelings of guilt concerning a sibling's death.

Obviously, this scenario describes a "worst case" situation. Yet such parental responses may be present to some degree even among families that seem to be coping very successfully with the loss of a child. As a parent tries to come to terms with the experience of a child's death, he or she may unintentionally minimize contact with the surviving child. The living child may be a painful reminder of the child now lost. On the other hand, a parent may become overprotective of the surviving child.

© Karen Saltzman

Siblings enjoy a special relationship, one conjoining both rivalries and mutual affection and love. The death of a brother or sister thus severs a unique human relationship. The surviving child may feel the loss more intensely because of an identification with the deceased brother or sister. The surviving child recognizes that he or she is also not immune to dying at an early age.

The bereaved child must be given opportunities to acknowledge and express his or her feelings of bereavement. Feelings of guilt as well as sadness need to be explored and resolved in a loving and supportive atmosphere. When a child expresses guilt, one can ask, "What would it take to forgive yourself?" An open exploration allows the child to find personally satisfying ways of coping with a loved one's death.

A surviving child's feelings of guilt may be related to normal sibling rivalry. The sister at whom I angrily yell, "I hate you!" in the morning may be lying dead at the morgue in the afternoon, the victim of a bicycle accident. To a young child, the coincidence of anger directed toward a person and that person's subsequent death may be viewed as a cause-and-effect relationship.

A child's assumption of responsibility may be characterized by a preoccupation with the "should haves." One five-year-old whose younger brother was run over by a truck while they were outside playing told his mother later, "I should have. . . . I should have." He saw himself as his younger brother's protector, responsible for his safety. His mother asked him, "You should have what?" He replied, "I just should have!"

His mother then asked, "What do you mean, you 'should have'?" The boy answered, "I should have looked, I should have known, I should have — ": a flood of "should haves" about being his brother's guardian and protector. Taking the child into her arms, his mother said, "I understand, honey. Daddy's got the 'should haves.' Mommy's got the 'should haves.' We all have them. It's okay to have them. And it's okay to know that everybody could have done something differently, and that they *would* have if they'd had a choice."

When a sibling dies, the surviving child usually tries to fit together what he or she has understood about death up to that time with what is observable in the present. For instance, if a child believes that death is something that happens in old age, and then experiences the death of a younger brother, how can the child reconcile the difference between concept and experience? The primary means by which a child constructs a bridge between earlier notions about death and present reality is simply to observe how parents and significant others respond to bereavement and express grief. Also important in resolving the conflict between the concept and the experience of death is the parent's ability to listen to the child's concerns and to help fit the experience to the child's ability to comprehend the meaning of death.

That allowing a child to participate in the family's experience helps the child cope with crisis is aptly demonstrated in a drawing by the five-year-old who saw his younger brother killed by a truck. The drawing represented "the day my brother was killed"; the point of greatest stress was shown to be the period of time when he was left at a neighbor's house while his parents were at the hospital (see Figure 8-2). Even more frightening than seeing the wheel of the truck roll over his brother's head was the feeling of being left alone, being separated from the rest of his family, not knowing what was happening with his parents and his younger brother.

This child's parents not only encouraged the child to express his feelings,

Figure 8-2   *A Five-Year-Old's "Crooked Day" Drawing*
In this drawing of "The Crooked Day," a five-year-old boy depicts his experience of the events that transpired on the day his brother received fatal injuries in an accident. Contrary to what might be assumed about this drawing, the places on the line where the greatest stress is indicated occurred after the accident itself. The sharp dip in the line at the lefthand side of the drawing represents the accident; the point at which the line crosses back on itself denotes the time when the surviving child was left with a neighbor while his parents were at the hospital with his brother. This was a period of uncertainty and confusion, and the child was angry about not being with the other members of his family. The point at which his parents returned and informed him of his brother's death is indicated by the vertical slash marks, which were literally stabbed onto the paper. The jagged line connoting the remainder of the day represents the emotional upheaval that occurred as the child and his parents together focused their attention on coping with the initial shock of their loss. Importantly, the drawing ends with an upward slanting line that is indicative of an essentially positive attitude — the child's ability to deal constructively with his experience of loss. This drawing demonstrates that even a simple artistic expression, such as a line depicting the chronology of events, can reveal a wealth of detail about a child's experience of a traumatic event such as death.

they also sought out community resources as an added support for coping with tragedy. Just as the child's work with spontaneous drawings helped bring to light his disturbance at being left out, the parents gained support by sharing their experience with others who had survived similar experiences, as well as by making use of the therapeutic resources in the community.

Helping Children Cope with Change and Loss

As we have seen, change sometimes brings painful experiences into a child's life. The death of a parent or sibling is a significant loss, as is a personal confrontation with life-threatening illness. How can a parent — or any caring person — help a child who must come to terms with the experience of loss? In the aftermath of a close death, what kind of assistance can be offered to a bereaved child? How do family patterns and styles of communications influence a child's ability to cope with change and loss?

Consider what it feels like for an adult to face the terminal illness or death of someone close. Now, how does this person explain these painful circumstances to a child? Because of the nature of the crisis, perhaps coupled with notions about a child's limited ability to understand, the child's feelings and concerns may be inadvertently dismissed or ignored. Even an adult who recognizes the child's interest or need to know may be uncomfortable about exposing the child to what might be painful and disturbing news. Adults are often concerned that knowing the truth might cause a child more harm than good.

Actually, a child's natural curiosity makes the option of withholding information unlikely to succeed. In any event, simple concern for the child's feelings dictates that he or she be included in matters affecting emotional well-being. Still, as Erna Furman points out, adults often find it difficult to talk to children about death until they have had some time to sort out their own feelings and thoughts.[20]

Children seem to cope more easily with their feelings about a close death or the serious illness of a family member when they are allowed to participate in the unfolding experience of grief and bereavement. When they are excluded, or when their questions go unanswered, the resulting uncertainty in the child's mind may generate additional anxiety, confusion, and pain. Sharing the reality of what is happening allows a child to begin to understand and cope with the experience.

Being sensitive to a child's natural inquisitiveness and concern about death and dying does not mean that one should overwhelm the child with excessive detail, nor does it mean talking down to the child as if he or she were incapable of comprehending at all. Rather, it implies an openness in responding to the child's concerns within the context of his or her ability to understand. In talking to a child about death or some other crisis, it is important to keep the explanation simple, to stick to basics, and to verify what the child has understood.

Although a child's experience of change and crisis is similar in some respects to an adult's, there are also significant differences. These differences in a child's manner of perceiving, experiencing, and coping with change need to be considered by parents and others who wish to be helpful to children in crisis.

Guidelines for Sharing Information

Recognizing that children differ and that their methods of coping with loss may differ, it is possible to suggest guidelines that parents and others can use to advantage. First, it is necessary to acknowledge and accept the child's feelings. Crying, for instance, is a natural response to the loss of someone significant. Admonishing a fearful child to "Be brave!" or "Be a little man and buck up!" denies the validity of the child's spontaneous emotion.

Second, to help a child cope with loss, the adult must strive, as much as possible, to answer the child's questions honestly and directly. Explanations

The Lesson

'Your father's gone,' my bald headmaster said.
His shiny dome and brown tobacco jar
Splintered at once in tears. It wasn't grief.
I cried for knowledge which was bitterer
Than any grief. For there and then I knew
That grief has uses—that a father dead
Could bind the bully's fist a week or two;
And then I cried for shame, then for relief.

I was a month past ten when I learnt this:
I still remember how the noise was stilled
In school-assembly when my grief came in.
Some goldfish in a bowl quietly sculled
Around their shining prison on its shelf.
They were indifferent. All the other eyes
Were turned towards me. Somewhere in myself
Pride, like a goldfish, flashed a sudden fin.

Edward Lucie-Smith

should be truthful to the facts, and should be as concrete as possible. Don't overwhelm the child with information that is beyond his or her developmental level.

Religious beliefs can be an important part of a family's understanding of death. If so, it is only natural that parents will want to share these beliefs with their children. But the child deserves to be told that these are *beliefs*. Care should be taken to express such beliefs in a manner that does not lead to misunderstanding or confuse the child. An adult's religious concepts of an afterlife, for example, may be quite different from what the listening child is able to understand. A child who is told that "God took Daddy to be with him in heaven" may not feel very kindly toward a being who could be so capricious and inconsiderate of the child's feelings.[21] Similarly, fairy tales, metaphors, and the like should be avoided or else used with care. Young children tend to take such explanations of death literally.

Foremost among the guidelines for helping children cope with crisis is a willingness to listen. Sometimes we assume that our own experience of the world is shared by others. In fact, though, each of us perceives the world uniquely. Understanding another person's experience requires the art of listening. The aim is to discover what the other person thinks, feels, and believes: What does he or she think is important about this situation? What are the person's concerns, fears, hopes, and anxieties? If a need for support or assistance is expressed, then what specific kind of help is being asked for?

These questions are especially important in the case of children. Sometimes children are required to be "unseen and unheard," thus thwarting their natural tendency to explore and grapple with the emotions and thoughts generated by change. Particularly when it disrupts familiar patterns of living, change can result in much confusion and conflict, creating a tangle of emotions and thoughts that is difficult to sort out. Paying attention to a child's behavioral changes is a way to gather information about his or her experience of crisis. Helping a child to know what is happening can go a long way toward helping the child arrive at a basis for coping with change.

When children are asked about their experiences with crisis, many say that the most difficult times came when they did not know what was actually happening. A child whose diagnosis of life-threatening illness was withheld from her by her family said later, "We'd always done everything with each other knowing what was going on. Suddenly that was different. That scared me more than what was happening to my body. It felt like my family was becoming strangers."[22] A sudden change in family communication patterns can be alarming to a child, actually heightening anxiety about the crisis itself.

Even in families that encourage openness, crisis may precipitate break-downs in communication, as the following story illustrates: A young girl whose mother refused to discuss her illness told a hospital staffer, "I know I'm going to die. I want to talk to Mother, but she won't let me. I know she's hurting, but I'm the one who's dying." When told of this conversation by the staff member, the girl's mother replied angrily, "She wouldn't be thinking of dying if you hadn't made her talk about it."

As the communication between mother and daughter continued to deterio-rate, the daughter became increasingly withdrawn. Still refusing to allow her daughter to discuss her feelings about the illness, the mother let her communica-tion style finally degenerate into baby talk: "Her doesn't feel goody today. . . Her doesn't want to talk."[23]

Clearly, the communication style exhibited by this mother and daughter is unlikely to help either of them cope with the predicament. Lack of openness means that the needs for affection and reassurance of both mother and daughter are not being met satisfactorily.

We can picture communication styles occupying a continuum that ranges from encouraging the child's participation in all facets of the crisis to trying to keep reality hidden from the child. The best gauge of a child's readiness to be informed about a potentially painful situation is the child's own interest, usually expressed through questions. Using the child's own questions as a guide, straightforward and honest answers can be given without burdening the child with facts irrelevant for his or her understanding of the situation. Above all, the child needs to be reassured that he or she is loved.

Using Books as Tools for Coping

One way for adults to explore the subject of death with children is through books. In recent years, publishers have brought out an increasing number of children's books concerned with dying, death, and bereavement. Of the more

Lament

Listen, children: Anne shall have the keys
Your father is dead.   To make a pretty noise with.
From his old coats   Life must go on,
I'll make you little jackets;   And the dead be forgotten;
I'll make you little trousers   Life must go on,
From his old pants.   Though good men die;
There'll be in his pockets   Anne, eat your breakfast;
Things he used to put there,   Dan, take your medicine;
Keys and pennies   Life must go on;
Covered with tobacco;   I forget just why.
Dan shall have the pennies
To save in his bank;   Edna St. Vincent Millay

than 150 books for children and young adults dealing with these topics, about two-thirds are works of fiction featuring death or dying as a primary theme.[24].

Books for children deal with various losses involving significant relationships, including parents, grandparents, siblings, other relatives and friends, as well as pets. A book can even be found dealing with the seldom-seen topic of the death of a child's mother.[25] Bibliotherapy — that is, the use of books as an aid to coping — can facilitate communication between an adult and a child and create an opportunity to talk about feelings and experiences. For example, a four-year-old whose father has died can view a picture book such as *Everett Anderson's Good-Bye,* which depicts a young boy's feelings about his father's death, and be encouraged to talk about his or her own feelings.[26] An adult might ask, "What else do you think someone like Everett might do or say when feeling angry about his father's death?"

The therapeutic value of reading books describing how a protagonist successfully faces death is not limited to younger children. Stories can suggest additional choices for readers of any age, adults as well as children. In situations wherein death has recently occurred or is expected, the selection of an appropriate book may give adults and children an opportunity to begin talking about each other's experiences (see Figure 8-3).

When a Family Member Has a Life-Threatening Illness

When a member of the child's family is seriously ill, family routine will be disrupted. If the family's style of communication is closed, or if a child is kept from learning the truth about a parent's or sibling's illness, the well child may become confused as to the reasons for changes in the family's usual patterns of interaction. It may seem to the child that he or she is rejected, left out of family activities, or ignored for no apparent reason. The well child may wonder, "Why are my parents so nice to my sister, but they ignore me all the time!" or "Geez, I get into trouble about every little thing while my brother gets off scot-free no matter what he does!"

BIBLIOGRAPHIES

Joanne E. Bernstein. *Books to Help Children Cope with Separation and Loss.* New York: R. R. Bowker, 1977.

Hannelore Wass and Charles A. Corr, editors. *Helping Children Cope with Death: Guidelines and Resources.* Washington, D.C.: Hemisphere, 1982.

BOOKS FOR CHILDREN

Chana Byars Abells. *The Children We Remember.* New York: Greenwillow, 1986. Combines text and photographs from the Yad Vashem Archives to chronicle the story of Jewish children during the Holocaust.

Alice Bach. *Waiting for Johnny Miracle.* New York: Harper & Row, 1980. The story of a teenager's experience with cancer and the emotional reactions of the patient, her family, and her friends.

Marion Dane Bauer. *On My Honor.* New York: Clarion, 1986. The story of a boy's feelings of guilt over the role he played in the death of his best friend.

Joanne Bernstein and Stephen Gullo. *When People Die.* New York: E. P. Dutton, 1977. An explanation of the feelings and behaviors associated with grief.

Eve Bunting. *The Empty Window.* New York: Frederick Warne, 1980. The young protagonist's experiences with and reactions to a dying friend.

Eve Bunting. *Face at the Edge of the World.* New York: Clarion, 1985. A boy reflects on his friend's last week of life to discover why he committed suicide.

Eve Bunting. *The Happy Funeral.* New York: Harper & Row, 1982. The funeral of a child's Chinese-American grandfather.

Leo Buscaglia. *The Fall of Freddie the Leaf: A Story of Life for All Ages.* Thorofare, N.J.: Charles B. Slack, 1982. The passage of a leaf through the seasons.

Mary Carey. *A Place for Allie.* New York: Dodd, Mead, 1985. A girl comes to terms with her father's death and her mother's resulting concerns with security.

Carol Carrick. *The Accident,* illustrations by Donald Carrick. New York: Seabury/Clarion, 1976. A young child copes with the death of a pet.

John B. Coburn. *Anne and the Sand Dobbies: A Story About Death for Children and Their Parents.* New York: Seabury Press, 1964. A father answers the questions of his son who has lost both his dog and his younger sister.

Eleanor Coerr. *Sadako and the Thousand Paper Cranes,* illustrations by Ronald Himler. New York: Putnam, 1977. The story of a Japanese girl's illness and death from leukemia resulting from the Hiroshima bomb, her courage, and the memorial to her by her classmates and community.

Miriam Cohen. *Jim's Dog Muffins,* illustrations by Lillian Hoban. New York:-Greenwillow/William Morrow, 1984. A friend and a teacher help a boy cope with the loss of his dog.

Elizabeth Corley. *Tell Me About Death, Tell Me About Funerals,* illustrations by Philip Pecorado. Santa Clara, Calif.: Grammatical Sciences, 1973. Information about funerals is presented in a comforting manner to a girl whose grandfather has died.

Tomie DePaola. *Nana Upstairs and Nana Downstairs.* New York: Penguin, 1978. A boy learns to face the eventual deaths of his grandmother and great-grandmother.

Elfie Donnelly. *So Long, Grandpa.* New York: Crown, 1981. A Viennese boy learns to cope with the illness and death of his grandfather.

Carol J. Farley. *The Garden Is Doing Fine.* New York: Atheneum, 1975. A girl learns to accept the reality that her father is dying.

continued on next page

Figure 8-3 *Books for Helping Children Cope with Loss*

Barbara Girion. *A Tangle of Roots.* New York: Charles Scribner's Sons, 1979. A mother's sudden death and the daughter's readjustment following the loss.

Charlotte Graeber. *Mustard,* illustrations by Donna Diamond. New York: Macmillan, 1982. A young boy deals with the increasing infirmity and eventual death of a cat that had been part of the family since before he was born.

Earl Grollman. *Talking About Death: A Dialogue Between Parent and Child.* Boston: Beacon Press, 1976. A nonfiction explanation about death.

Bernice Hogan. *My Grandmother Died,* illustrations by Nancy Munger. Nashville: Abingdon, 1983. A young boy learns to cope with the finality of his grandmother's death by maintaining his memories of her.

Lyn Littlefield Hoopers. *Nana.* New York: Harper & Row, 1981. A grandmother's death.

Nancy Jewell. *Time for Uncle Joe.* New York: Harper & Row, 1981. Memories of a deceased uncle.

M. E. Kerr. *Night Kites.* New York: Harper & Row, 1986. A teenage boy grapples with the discovery that his older brother is dying of AIDS.

Jill Krementz. *How It Feels When a Parent Dies.* New York: Knopf, 1981. A photographic essay with children's descriptions of their experiences.

Matthew Lancaster. *Hang Tough.* New York: Paulist Press, 1985. The experiences of a ten-year-old boy dying of cancer.

Madeleine L' Engle. *A Ring of Endless Light.* New York: Farrar, Straus & Giroux, 1980. A teenage girl copes with experience of loss, grief, and terminal illness by discovering underlying spiritual and moral dimensions.

Eda LeShan. *Learning to Say Goodbye: When a Parent Dies.* New York: Macmillan, 1976. Nonfiction.

Gloria H. McLendon. *My Brother Joey Died,* photographs by Harvey Kelman. New York: Simon & Schuster, 1982. The issues surrounding a sibling's death as told from the perspective of a nine-year-old.

Miska Miles. *Annie and the Old One,* illustrations by Peter Parnall. Boston: Little, Brown, 1971. The story of a Navajo girl's efforts to prevent the inevitable by unraveling each day's weaving on a rug whose completion she fears will bring her grandmother's death.

Jane Mobley. *The Star Husband,* illustrations by Anna Vojtech. New York: Doubleday, 1979. This adaptation of a Native American myth affirms the natural cycle of life, death, and rebirth.

Herbert Neiberg and Arlene Fisher. *Pet Loss: A Thoughtful Guide for Adults and Children.* New York: Harper & Row, 1982.

Linda Peavy. *Allison's Grandfather,* illustrations by Ronald Himler. New York: Charles Scribner's Sons, 1981. A young child reflects upon her friend's grandfather's death.

Joan Phipson. *A Tide Flowing.* New York: Atheneum, 1981. A boy finds means to cope with crises despite his mother's death and his father's rejection.

Elizabeth Richter. *Losing Someone You Love: When a Brother or Sister Dies.* New York: G. P. Putnam's Sons, 1986. The experience of sibling loss as related in interviews with young people.

Ann Rinaldi. *Term Paper.* New York: Walker and Company, 1980. A father's sudden death and a child's subsequent feelings of responsibility for the death.

continued on next page

Anne Warren Smith. *Sister in the Shadow*. New York: Atheneum, 1986. During a summer job as a mother's helper, a young girl is confronted by the effects of an earlier experience of crib death on the family's patterns and relationships.

Sara Bonnett Stein. *About Dying: An Open Family Book for Parents and Children Together*. New York: Walker and Company, 1974. A story about death comprised of parallel texts providing basic information for children and supplemental information for adults.

Susan Varley. *Badger's Parting Gifts*. New York: Lothrop, Lee and Shepard, 1984. The story of an old dog's dying and the grieving of those who loved him.

Judith Viorst. *The Tenth Good Thing About Barney,* illustrations by Erik Blegvad. New York: Atheneum, 1971. A boy thinks of the ten best things about his pet cat who has died.

Isle-Margret Vogel. *My Twin Sister Erika*. New York: Harper & Row, 1976. The death of a sibling.

E. B. White. *Charlotte's Web,* illustrations by Garth Williams. New York: Harper & Row, 1952. This classic story describes the grief experienced at the death of a close friend — Charlotte, a spider — and the continuing of life through her offspring.

Paul Zindel. *The Pigman's Legacy*. New York: Harper & Row, 1980. The memory of a dead friend.

Charlotte Zolotow. *My Grandson Lew*. New York: Harper & Row, 1974. Lew learns the value of memories of his deceased grandfather.

Charlotte Zolotow. *If You Listen*. New York: Harper & Row, 1980. A mother reassures a child of her father's love.

Although openness is an important condition for helping a child to cope with the crisis, once again explanations must be suited to the child's cognitive abilities. For example, a very young child whose parent is seriously ill might be told simply that "Mommy has an ouch in her tummy which the doctors are trying to fix." A school-age child, on the other hand, might be given a more complex explanation to the effect that the parent needs medical treatment because something is growing in her stomach that doesn't belong there.

A child who is aware of a parent's or sibling's illness will probably feel anxiety, which may be manifest in various ways. For example, a child may be angry because "Mommy isn't here," yet feel guilty because of imagined notions about "causing the illness." To help balance these conflicting feelings, the child can be urged to participate in comforting the sick person in ways that are appropriate for the child. A child might pick a bouquet or make a small drawing as a gift. This allows the child to affirm and express feelings of love and kindness despite possible feelings of anger or guilt.

Siblings who feel neglected because the family's attention is devoted more and more to a sick brother or sister may resent the adjustments they have to make in their lives. Again, the well child can be helped to balance conflicting emotions by being allowed to become a participating family member who is given information about the crisis and encouraged to be part of the process of

Mark Boster, AP/Wide World Photos

These young girls pay a final visit to a slain classmate, who died at age twelve because of a senseless act of violence. Feelings of grief may be mixed with feelings of dread and fear, the recognition that death can come at any time and to anyone, regardless of age. Whether caused by an abrupt act of violence or by prolonged illness, the experience of death in children's lives may elicit this awareness of mortality.

dealing with the sibling's illness. When the child is included in these ways, there is a greater likelihood that family communication will be maintained and that the family routine will seem much more normal. Although children cannot be protected from the reality of death, their experiences of it can be made less traumatic when they receive sensitive, caring support from those closest to them.

Support Groups for Children

Many of the organizations dedicated to providing support during the crises of serious illness and bereavement have an emphasis on caring for all members of a family, including the children. The Compassionate Friends, for instance, not only provides support to bereaved parents, but has related programs that are designed to help their surviving children cope with the loss of a sibling. Other support groups, such as the Center for Attitudinal Healing, have a primary focus on the ill child, although typically there are auxiliary programs involving other family members. Organizations such as these may be local or national in extent.[27]

Another type of support organization for children with life-threatening illness involves volunteers, numbering from a few individuals to several hundred, who seek to grant the wishes of children with a limited prognosis. The Sunshine Foundation, founded in 1976, along with the Brass Ring Society and the Starlight Foundation, both formed in 1983, are examples of such organizations.[28] Through the efforts of such groups, children and their families may be given the opportunity to take a vacation together or to fulfill some other wish that otherwise seemed impossible.

Community support represents an important adjunct to the family's own support system. Organizations like those mentioned can aid not only the child who is seriously ill or bereaved, but also the parents and other adults who are experiencing corresponding losses.

Further Readings

Myra Bluebond-Langner. *The Private Worlds of Dying Children.* Princeton, N.J.: Princeton University Press, 1978.

John Bowlby. *The Making and Breaking of Affectional Bonds.* London: Tavistock, 1979.

Center for Attitudinal Healing. *There Is a Rainbow Behind Every Dark Cloud.* Millbrae, Calif.: Celestial Arts, 1978.

Charles A. Corr and Joan N. McNeil, editors. *Adolescence and Death.* New York: Springer, 1986.

Erna Furman. *A Child's Parent Dies: Studies in Childhood Bereavement.* New Haven, Conn.: Yale University Press, 1974.

Robert A. Furman. "The Child's Reaction to Death in the Family," in *Loss and Grief: Psychological Management in Medical Practice,* edited by Bernard Schoenberg et al., pp. 70–86. New York: Columbia University Press, 1970.

Jo-Eileen Gyulay. *The Dying Child.* New York: McGraw-Hill, 1978.

Helen Rosen. *Unspoken Grief: Coping with Childhood Sibling Loss.* Lexington, Mass.: Lexington Books, 1985.

John E. Schowalter et al., editors. *The Child and Death.* New York: Columbia University Press, 1983.

Holding their dead baby, this Harlem couple finds comfort in the sharing of their memories and their grief as they acknowledge the death of their firstborn child. Of all the losses that can be experienced during adult life, most people feel that the death of a child is the most painful.

CHAPTER 9

Death in the Lives of Adults

*J*ust as human development does not stop with childhood's end, the patterns of coping with loss continue to evolve throughout a person's lifespan. Even when the circumstances of bereavement are outwardly similar, a person's response to loss depends on many factors, not least of which is age. Although the *event* of a parent's death, for example, may occur during childhood or adulthood, the *experience* will differ at each developmental period. Furthermore, adult life entails losses that happen only during maturity. The death of a spouse occurs in the context of marriage, the death of a child in the context of family and the childbearing and childrearing years.

If we define stress as any stimulus that requires an organism to adapt, surviving the death of someone close to us clearly fits within that framework.[1] Thus, loss can be viewed as a type of environmental stress affecting human beings. Although the death of a loved one is the most obvious loss we are likely to experience, stress also results from losses that occur in connection with other major life changes — such as marriage, divorce, the birth of a child, moving to a new home, graduation from school, or getting a new job. Just as we can associate distinct developmental tasks and abilities with children of varying ages, so, too, there are distinctive phases and transitions of adult life.

Psychosocial Stages of Adulthood: A Developmental Perspective

In Chapter 3, we discussed the first five stages of psychosocial development proposed by Erik Erikson; namely, those pertaining to the years of childhood and adolescence. The last three stages of psychosocial development, according to this model, occur during adulthood. As in childhood, each stage of adult life requires a particular developmental response, and each stage builds upon previous ones.

Young adulthood, the first of these adult stages, is represented by the conflict between intimacy and isolation. This stage involves various forms of commitment and interaction, including sex, friendship, cooperation, partnership, and affiliation. Because mature love takes the risk of commitment, as contrasted with the self-absorbed and self-reflective love of adolescence, the death of a loved one may be most devastating during this stage and the next.[2] In a study of losses experienced by college students, more than three-quarters involved the loss of a significant other either by death or by separation resulting from the end of a friendship, the dissolution of a love relationship, or divorce.[3]

The next psychosocial stage, says Erikson, is *adulthood*, which involves the crisis of generativity versus stagnation. This stage is characterized by a widening commitment to take care of the persons, things, and ideas one has learned to care for. This emphasis on care helps explain why the death of a child is so painful. Symbolically and actually, a child's death is opposed to the nurturant psychosocial task of adulthood.

When we reach the stage of *maturity*, the eighth and final stage of the life cycle, according to Erikson, the turning point or crisis to be resolved is that of integrity versus despair. Viewing all the developmental phases as connected, with each building on the ones before, the crisis of this stage is especially powerful. This last phase is marked by the end of our "one given course of life." Successfully negotiating this last developmental task gives us the strength of wisdom, which Erikson describes as "informed and detached concern with life itself in the face of death itself."[4]

Loss Experiences in Adulthood

Keeping this developmental perspective in mind, the rest of this chapter will focus on specific loss experiences occurring during adult life. You may find it useful to consider the losses that have occurred in your own life, both as a child and as an adult. How have they differed, and in what ways are they similar? Have others responded to your experiences of loss in supportive ways? What coping mechanisms were you able to bring into play to move through the experience successfully? Questions of this kind can form the framework for examining typical losses in adult life.

Individual Differences in Meaning of Death and Coping Styles

In the study of losses experienced by college students, it was found that events some students considered to be major losses—such as course failure,

Mickey Sanborn, U.S. Air Force Photo

Among the most poignant losses that can be experienced in adult life are those related to war. The Vietnam Veterans' Memorial in Washington, D.C., is a focal point for coping with the grief of individual as well as national losses. For many who fought the war, as well as for other survivors, the effects are pervasive and felt daily. Here, visitors reflect on the names of individuals engraved on the face of the black wall of the Memorial, following its official dedication in November 1982.

Last Words

Goethe's mother (1808): (To a servant girl bringing an invitation to a party) "Say that Frau Goethe is unable to come, she is busy dying at the moment."

Beethoven (1827): "I shall hear in Heaven."

Hegel (1831): "Only one man ever understood me . . . And he didn't understand me."

Palmerston (1865): "Die, my dear Doctor? — That's the last thing I shall do!"

Gertrude Stein (1946): "What is the answer?" After a short silence she laughed and added, "Then what is the question?"

Gide (1951): "I am afraid my sentences are becoming grammatically incorrect."

The Oxford Book of Death, edited by D. J. Enright

---

death of a pet, or suspension of a roommate from school — were viewed by others as less significant. This disparity does not mean that students in the first group were wrong, that their losses weren't so important after all. Neither does it indicate that the other students were insensitive and unfeeling. It does underscore the fact that a person's *interpretation* of loss, its personal meaning in his or her own life, determines its relative significance.[5]

The aspects of death that make us fearful or anxious also differ among individuals. For instance, even though a butcher and a funeral director are both involved in jobs with death-related implications, they may each feel comfortable with their own, but not the other's, work.[6] Similarly, the attitudes a person has toward the prospect of his or her own death reflect individual differences, and these attitudes change within the same person over the course of life. If death seems a remote possibility, an event not expected to occur for many years, the thought may cause little alarm or concern. When a medical checkup reveals the presence of a life-threatening illness, however, the response may be quite otherwise. The meaning of death is also usually interpreted differently as a person ages. Failing health, for example, is among the reasons given by some aged persons for preferring death to continued existence (see Table 9-1).[7] Although, as a group, the old appear to fear death less than do younger people, individual differences remain important throughout the lifespan.

In addition to interpreting the significance of losses and the meaning of death in distinctive ways, individuals use various ways of coping. Variability in coping styles — from acceptance to drug intoxication — was noted as one of the most revealing features of student reactions to loss in the study mentioned. Social support, especially talking about the loss with others, was typically important in resolving grief. Successfully handled, the experience of loss can result in meaningful learnings and positive changes of attitude.

TABLE 9-1 *Some Reasons Given by Aged Persons for Accepting Death*

Death is preferable to inactivity.

Death is preferable to the loss of the ability to be useful.

Death is preferable to becoming a burden.

Death is preferable to loss of mental faculties.

Death is preferable to living with progressively deteriorating physical health and concomitant physical discomfort.

Source: Adapted from Victor W. Marshall, *Last Chapters: A Sociology of Aging and Dying* (Monterey, Calif.: Brooks/Cole, 1980), pp. 169–177.

Think about the experiences of your life and those of other adults you know. Notice the range of losses that come to mind. Some of these losses may be associated with the major causes of death among adults. Among the middle-aged, for instance, violent deaths from accidents, suicides, and homicides take a significant toll; for the older population, death usually results from weakened physiological defenses.

Aging and the Incidence of Loss

Although many illnesses and disabilities are most common among persons in the seventh or eighth decade of life or older, the probability of dying steadily increases as we grow older. Aging doesn't begin at age fifty, or age sixty-five, or age eighty-five. Already, at this very moment, we are all aging.

Besides the experience of nearing our own death, the usual order of nature dictates that our experiences of others' deaths also increase as we grow older. Children become seriously ill, and some die. Relationships come to an end, suddenly or perhaps over a longer period due to chronic illness. Growing older also increases the chances that an individual will experience the death of his or her parents, and, conversely, that a parent may experience the death of an adult child. Eventually, we may find it impossible to care adequately for ourselves. Moving out of our own home to live with others or, more likely, with strangers

"Bloom County," drawing by Berke Breathed, © 1984 by Washington Post Writers Group

sharing the surroundings of institutional care may bring a loss of virtually everything familiar acquired over a lifetime. We now turn to these losses that occur in adult life.

Parental Bereavement

What is different about a child's death from that of an adult? What comes to mind when you think about a child being diagnosed as terminally ill? What makes the death of a child a high-grief death? To most of us, the death of a child connotes the unfinished, the untimely loss of a life that was presumed to have a potential for longevity. Perhaps the parents envisioned the child playing on the local youth soccer team, graduating from school, getting married, raising children — all the various milestones and occasions that comprise a sense of continuity into the future. These plans and hopes for the child's life are ended by death. The usual expectation is that a child will outlive his or her parents. A child is expected to carry something of the parent into the future, even after the parent's death. In this sense, a child's very existence grants a kind of immortality to the parent, and this is taken away when the child dies.

If parenting is defined as the task of raising a child to the age of self-sufficiency, a bereaved parent may feel that he or she has failed. The special interdependency between parent and child makes the death of a child a deep experience of loss. With parents whose child has died, mourning may be focused on issues of parental responsibility.[8] People generally define parenting as protecting and nurturing a child until he or she can act independently in the world. If mourning parents hold such a definition, the death of a child may be experienced as the ultimate lack of protection and nurture, the ultimate breakdown and failure in being a good parent.

Such feelings about the parental role of safeguarding a child are universal, and parents expend considerable effort in seeking to guarantee a child's safety and welfare. Among the Cree of North America, for example, infants were often given "ghost-protective" moccasins to wear. Holes were cut in the bottom of the moccasins as a means of protecting the baby against the threat of death. If the spirit of an ancestor appeared and beckoned, the infant could refuse to go, pointing out that his or her moccasins "needed mending."[9]

In counseling bereaved parents, clinicians often note the presence of a kind of "general chaos" in the lives of the couple. Frequently, a directionlessness sets in, part of a pervasive sense that both parents have been robbed of a past and a future. The prevailing attitude may be one of "do it now." Sexual acting out is not uncommon during parental bereavement.[10] As individuals, the parents may have very different grieving styles, which leave each of them feeling isolated and unsupported by the only other person in the world who shares the magnitude of the loss. The attitudes and behaviors of parents after a child's death often reflect the reality of feeling overwhelmed, which can help us to understand why the incidence of divorce is high among bereaved parents.

Most of these issues of parental bereavement span the life cycle. They are present for forty-year-old parents and for eighty-year-old parents. They are experienced by parents of grown-up children as well as by parents of babies. A parent's fantasies and plans can be just as strong for an unborn infant as for an older child. But to understand completely the nature of parental bereavement and the range of losses involved, both the age of the parent and the age of the child are significant. A sixty-five-year-old divorced or widowed mother may feel considerable loss of security when her thirty-five-year-old child dies suddenly. One such woman said repeatedly: "He was going to take care of me when I got old; now I have no one." Whether or not her son would have indeed taken on the responsibility she imagined, his death represented the loss of *her* plan. Plans for both the parent and the child are over.

Pregnancy Loss and Perinatal Death

Pregnancy represents a major life transition for adults.[11] The expected result is the birth of a viable, healthy baby. Miscarriage, induced abortion, stillbirth, and neonatal death are not the expected outcomes of pregnancy.[12] Self-esteem suffers when a parent feels unable to complete the act of sexual reproduction. Blame for this failure can be turned inward as well as directed outward. Questions about the cause of the tragedy abound: Was it that glass of wine, the aspirin, or, as one mother asked in desperation, "Was it the nutmeg I put on my oatmeal?" The most inconsequential actions may be evaluated in this manner.

Anger is a common response of the newly bereaved parents. Physicians, nurses, and other health personnel are blamed. Anger toward the other parent may include the accusation, "You never wanted this baby anyway!" Anger can be focused upon the baby itself, resulting in confusing emotions for the parents. After all, parents may ask themselves, what kind of person could be angry at an innocent infant? Yet anger of this kind is a valid response to such a loss. As one woman said of her stillborn daughter, "Why did she just drop in and out of my life? Why did she bother coming at all?" The emotional response can also include auditory or kinesthetic hallucinations, sometimes continuing sporadically for months and even years. A baby cries in the night, waking parents from sleep; the baby kicks inside the womb, yet there is no pregnancy, no live child.

Postpartum depression may be intensified. In the absence of a baby, the mother must cope with continued physical reminders, such as the onset of lactation. One bereaved mother said, "I wanted to go to the cemetery and let my milk flow onto my daughter's grave." At the same time, a father may feel culturally constrained to "be brave" to provide support to the mother who is, after all, recuperating physically as well as emotionally. Thus, a father's need to grieve may not be met, and his emotions may remain below the surface until long after the event.

With the loss of a child during pregnancy, well-intentioned family members and friends may minimize the death in an effort to console the bereaved parent. People say, "You're young; you can have another baby," unaware that such a comment, though possibly true, is inappropriate. No other baby will replace the one who has just died. Advice such as this is especially difficult for those couples who postpone having children until after establishing careers as they may feel an added constraint of time that compounds the experience of loss.

Many clergy and health professionals do realize the importance of some form of leavetaking (such as funerals) when pregnancy loss occurs, particularly in cases of perinatal death (that is, fetuses born after twenty to twenty-eight weeks of gestation). But individuals who experience a loss caused by miscarriage or abortion may not receive the same degree of public acknowledgment or social support.

Miscarriage

Fifteen to 20 percent of all conceptions result in a spontaneous abortion, commonly referred to as a *miscarriage*.[13] Many people assume that a loss during the early stages of pregnancy evokes feelings of disappointment, though not grief. To parents who dream of their baby even before its conception, however, miscarriage can be especially painful and confusing. Anticipation experienced during pregnancy can be both positive and negative, and this ambiguity is a source of doubt and guilt when the pregnancy ends with miscarriage. A parent may ask, "Didn't I want this baby enough?"

When a series of miscarriages occurs, grief can be further compounded. Women who have this experience express shock at being labeled "habitual aborters." Insinuations that their miscarriages result from psychosomatic problems can compound the feeling of being betrayed by their bodies. Another remark heard by parents is that miscarriage is simply "Nature's way" of weeding out genetic anomalies. To the grieving parents, this is no consolation to the fact that it was *their* baby Nature decided to sort. Platitudes of any kind that minimize or deny the loss actually experienced are, at best, unhelpful.

Parents may have difficulty identifying their loss precisely or making sense of what has happened.[14] One young mother's grief was complicated after a miscarriage early in her pregnancy because she had no remains to be buried. "I didn't know where my baby was," she said. She was able to begin resolving her grief when she returned to the hospital and asked for the remains of her baby.

 "My husband was understanding but couldn't know what this did to my whole sense of myself," said Karen following her miscarriage. "After months of my moping and lack of interest, he wondered if I wasn't prolonging things and overreacting. I started resenting him for having escaped the full emotional burden of the loss. It was a difficult time for us. I think it is impossible for a man to understand miscarriage on anything but an intellectual level."

Rochelle Friedman and Bonnie Gradstein,
Surviving Pregnancy Loss

Taking them home, she buried them in her backyard. She takes comfort in looking out the window and knowing her baby is there.

Finally, even though a miscarriage may have occurred many years ago, grief for the unborn baby can reappear during other significant life events; for example, at the birth of a subsequent child or the onset of menopause. A particular marker, such as reaching age forty or age sixty-five, can reawaken feelings of grief.

Induced Abortion

Even when the decision for an abortion is based on information about the baby's health, this choice can be a source of conflict adding to the parents' grief. Many genetic diseases can now be identified by tests during the early phases of pregnancy; and, when the results are unfavorable, terminating the pregnancy may seem the best or only choice. Some tests can be done only well into the pregnancy, after the mother has already felt the baby moving. The predominant feature of this type of loss is guilt, and there is little social support, including support groups, available to help. Parents who decide in favor of a therapeutic abortion fear that no one will understand their "choice" and that they will be judged harshly. Couples who terminate pregnancies may face not only the death of a particular baby, but also the possibility of a childless future; biological considerations or genetic risk may preclude the choice to conceive again. Caring and sensitive counseling for couples who face this tragedy is often an essential element in helping them cope with their grief.

Elective abortion, when considerations other than fetal health are involved, also represents a loss that may be difficult to grieve. The repercussions of such decisions may not be felt until later. One woman, who had chosen to abort a pregnancy as a young adult because she and her husband felt their relationship could not withstand the added pressures of raising a child at that time, experienced considerable remorse later when she and her husband found themselves unable to have other children. "That may have been our only chance," she lamented. When losses of this kind occur, individuals may experience subsequent pregnancy loss as "retribution" for an earlier abortion.

Furthermore, persons who are significant in one's life may not sanction the act, or they may not recognize that a loss has occurred. Kenneth Doka points out how the differing viewpoints concerning abortion may place the bereaved in a dilemma: Those who believe a loss occurred may not sanction the act, whereas those who sanction the act may not recognize that grief in response to the perceived loss needs to be expressed and legitimized. As with other forms of disenfranchised grief, the problems of grieving may be exacerbated when the usual sources of solace and social support are not available or helpful.[15]

Stillbirth

"Instead of giving birth, I gave death," said a mother whose daughter died in childbirth. Instead of a cradle, there is a grave; instead of receiving blankets, there are burial clothes; instead of a birth certificate, there is a death certificate. The world is turned upside down, the confusion endless.

It is important that the newly bereaved parents acknowledge their child's birth. Rather than whisking away the stillborn infant as quickly as possible, many hospitals encourage the parents to see and hold their baby. Working through the experience of grief is facilitated by acknowledging the reality of the baby's life and death. When the parents are involved only to the extent of signing the death certificate, the aims of healthy grieving are thwarted. Support groups dealing with issues of pregnancy loss encourage hospitals to make use of information packets that include a "Certificate of Stillbirth," which acknowledges the birth as well as the death of the child. Linking objects, such as a lock of hair, a photograph, and the receiving blanket, can provide immense support to parents, if not at first, then later when they want to hold to every precious memory.[16]

Neonatal Death

When a baby is born alive but with life-threatening disabilities due to prematurity, congenital defects, or similar causes, the ensuing period of waiting for a seriously ill baby to die can be a nightmare for parents. Frustration and a sense of futility may be overwhelming as surgery or other interventions are attempted and fail. These feelings can be especially severe when the hospital has no facility where the parents can be with their baby, even if only briefly.

Sometimes a baby born with one or more life-threatening conditions embarks on a life-or-death struggle that lasts weeks. Parents may be confronted with the need to work through ethical choices that could result in their baby's death.[17] During this time, the cost of medical care to keep the baby alive and comfortable is rising astronomically. After the baby dies, the parents may feel resentment toward the hospital and its staff for having gone through such an ordeal only to be billed later for the medical expenses.

In circumstances involving a critically ill newborn, *any* decision may haunt parents. They may ask themselves over and over whether they made the right choice. Often, letting the baby die is the only choice. As one young neonatologist remarked, "One of the most difficult and important things for me to learn was to hand over the baby to the parents so it could die in their arms."

Loss of the "Perfect" Child

When a child is born with disabilities, such as congenital deformities or mental retardation, parents can find it difficult to accept the reality that the child is not as they had wished for and dreamed about. Coming to terms with this loss is not easy. In such instances, parents need to grieve for lost expectations. Coping means finding ways to help themselves and their child lead the most productive lives possible under the circumstances.

Small Son

They have gone.
The last mourner,
the last comfort,
last cliche.

I wrap a pillow
in your blanket.
Lie burying my face
to hold your fading
milk sweet smell.

The silence swells.

I run

to where the stand
of saplings wait
for clearing.

Chopping, slashing,
small limbs
dragged and pulled
and piled for burning.

I turn away
consumed,
the taste of ashes
in my mouth.

Maude Meehan

Sudden Infant Death Syndrome

Although it is not, strictly speaking, in the category of pregnancy loss, Sudden Infant Death Syndrome (SIDS) carries with it many of the same consequences in terms of bereavement. SIDS victims are usually under the age of one year; the death is sudden, and often comes at night. Parents are left angry, and often with a tremendous amount of guilt. Although medical researchers now have some indication of possible causes, SIDS remains largely unexplained. The suddenness of death, the age of the child, and the uncertainty about the cause of death all combine to make such a death a high-grief experience for survivors.[18]

In the past, the parents of an infant whose death was attributed to SIDS were often subjected to criminal investigation. Concerns about child abuse prompted law enforcement officials to question whether the parents might be responsible. Investigation into SIDS deaths is now generally handled with greater sensitivity, partly as a result of information disseminated by support groups concerned with SIDS and the effects of misdirected questioning and accusations on grieving parents. Still, parents who survive the death of a child due to SIDS often quesion themselves just as sternly, wondering if the death was in any way due to something they did or to something they left undone; could it have been prevented in some way?[19]

The Critically Ill or Dying Child

For the parent whose child is critically ill or dying, the experience represents many losses. Many of the issues discussed in connection with pregnancy loss, neonatal death, and the death of an infant also pertain to the death of an older child or adolescent. The meaning of such a death is more complex, however, because the relationship between parent and child has been of longer duration with a correspondingly larger store of memories. A child may represent many different things to a parent. As Beverly Raphael reminds us, a child is "a part of the self, and of the loved partner; a representation of generations past; the genes of the forebears; the hope of the future; a source of love, pleasure, even narcissistic delight; a tie or a burden; and sometimes a symbol of the worst parts of the self and others."[20]

A parent's attachment to a child begins before birth. As experiences are shared, the bond between parent and child takes on an increasing complexity. As a child becomes increasingly his or her own person during the years of childhood and adolescence, the relationship between parent and child at times may include feelings of ambivalence, no matter how strong the bonds of affection and love. The emotional complexity of this relationship can make the threatened loss or death of a child an especially difficult type of bereavement.

When a child's life is threatened by illness, it affects the entire pattern of family life. Parents and siblings are all involved in coping with the fact of the illness, which gradually becomes integrated into overall family patterns. When the prognosis of the disease is death, the impact of such an announcement is likely to be devastating, setting into motion a need to adapt to the unpleasant reality.

Patterns of Family Involvement

Added to the physical isolation that accompanies illness, as the child grows closer to death there is often a psychic separation, a distancing from the child by parents, relatives, and even members of the health care team. For the dying child, this psychic distancing can be the most severe pain of all.

If the significant adults in the child's life find it increasingly difficult to witness the physical disintegration caused by the disease, they may wish to avoid situations that could elicit painful feelings. Visits with the child may become shorter and less frequent. Sometimes, parents exhibit their unwillingness to discuss the reality of the situation by taking long absences from the child's room or by keeping their interactions with the child as brief as possible. They may create excuses for interruptions when the situation becomes too painful, or may avoid altogether any topics related to the child's illness. In these and similar ways, parents can subtly signal their limits about what they feel comfortable discussing with the child.

Established family patterns also play an important part in determining the kind of emotional and psychological support that is provided for the dying child. Members of an extended family, with a large network of relatives, may be able to pace themselves, arranging visits to the hospital on a schedule that allows support for the child to be shared in such a way that no one is physically or emotionally overwhelmed. Members of a smaller family, on the other hand, may be unable to spend as much time with the child as they would like. Parents who work, for example, may want to be with the child more and yet have to earn

The overwhelming grief of parental bereavement is expressed in the soft-ground etching Überfahren *(Passing Over), by Käthe Kollwitz, whose art became a means of working through her own sorrow following the death of a child. The dead child is carried by adults bent with the burden of grief; other children look on.*

money to cover medical expenses. Perhaps whatever action is taken, the resulting neglect of its opposite will bring feelings of guilt at "not having done enough."

A family's communication patterns also shape how parents and other family members relate to a child's illness. Few families can sustain complete openness to the reality of a child's terminal illness throughout what may possibly be a very lengthy process from diagnosis of the disease to the child's death. Indeed, usually the illness itself varies in the intensity of debilitating or disrupting symptoms. At times, the sick child may function quite normally and the routine of special medical care becomes simply another aspect of family life. At other times, the disease may require that the family deal very specifically with the changes in the child's condition. Most families have to learn how to adjust to the fluctuations between hope for recovery and acceptance of terminal illness while always supporting the child in the best way possible.

In observing family interactions that occur in response to life-threatening illness, Glaser and Strauss noted four basic ways in which individuals establish the context of awareness with regard to the dying patient.[21] These modes or contexts of awareness include both the content and the style of interpersonal communication about death. It will be instructive to consider briefly each of these patterns of awareness and communication.

In the *closed awareness* context, the dying person does not recognize that death is impending, although other persons may know. In general, closed awareness does not allow for communication about the illness or the probability of death.

In the *suspected awareness* context, the patient suspects that the prognosis is death, but is not told so by those who know. The dying person may try to confirm or deny these suspicions by testing family members, friends, and medical personnel in an effort to elicit information known by others but not openly shared with the patient. Despite others' secrecy, however, the patient may observe that the illness is severely disrupting the family's usual style of relating, and may sense others' fearfulness or anxiety about his or her condition, thus confirming the suspicions in the patient's mind.[22]

The *mutual pretense* context can be likened to a dance in which the participants sidestep a direct confrontation about the patient's condition. Typically, this involves complicated, though usually unspoken, rules of behavior designed to sustain the illusion that the patient is getting well. With mutual pretense, everyone — the patient included — recognizes the fatal prognosis, but all act as if the patient will recover. In her study of dying children, Bluebond-Langner found that mutual pretense was generally practiced right to the end, despite any violation of the unspoken rules that might have disclosed the child's true condition.

Underlying mutual pretense is the notion that everyone should strive to avoid "dangerous" or "threatening" topics, such as details of the child's disease and prognosis, the child's appearance, medical procedures, another child's illness or death, and future plans and events. Obviously, this eliminates from discussion a considerable portion of the child's current experience.

The pattern of mutual pretense usually begins early; subtle signals are communicated between parents, caregivers, and the child that the method being used to cope involves pretending that things are really normal. Thus, caregivers may substitute "possible WBC disease" — a shorthand reference to white blood cells — for the more explicit "fourth-stage leukemia."

If something happens that threatens to break the fiction and disclose the reality of the situation, the parties to mutual pretense simply act as if the threatening event did not occur. Various distancing strategies may be called upon to preserve the illusion that the child is not seriously ill — most often by avoiding any interaction that threatens disclosure of the truth. Children may respond to the risk of disclosure by becoming angry or withdrawn; adults may excuse themselves by saying they need to go out for a smoke or a walk or to make a phone call. In the short term, such strategies can be useful ways of coping with a difficult and painful situation.

Glaser and Strauss's fourth designation, the context of *open awareness*, describes the situation in which the likelihood of death is acknowledged and discussed. Such openness does not necessarily make death easier to accept, but it does offer the possibility of sharing support in ways that would not otherwise be available.

During Bluebond-Langner's study of dying children, she saw only two families who eventually moved into a context of open awareness with a dying child. This observation is important, especially for those who wish to understand or work with dying children and their families, because it contrasts with what typically occurs in the case of terminally ill adults.[23] With adults, there generally comes a point when mutual pretense is dropped as the truth becomes apparent, thus creating the possibility of adopting a more open style of interaction.

In working with adults, Glaser and Strauss found that the awareness context is a crucial element in determining the interaction among staff, family,

---

 Last year, a fourteen-year-old boy who suddenly collapsed on the street was rushed to our hospital emergency room. Even though there were no clinical signs of life, at least six physicians frantically attempted resuscitative measures. In the hallway outside the emergency room, I came upon two stunned parents who were standing absolutely alone. None of the physicians wanted to leave the dramatic scene to obtain a history, let alone provide any solace. I did not want to either, the boy was dead (possibly from a cardiac conduction defect — even the autopsy later was unrevealing); but I forced myself to sit down in an adjoining room and listen while they talked of their hopes and their son's aspirations. I am used to talking with parents whose children die of sudden infant death syndrome; this was different and I was overwhelmed. Afterward, I went to my office and cried. I later thought that I should have let my interns and residents witness me cry to learn that professionalism does not preclude expression of human feeling.

Abraham B. Bergman, "Psychological Aspects of Sudden
Unexpected Death in Infants and Children"

and patient. As new information is presented to the patient or to family members, the awareness context may change. For example, a context of closed awareness or mutual pretense may prevail throughout a succession of medical procedures. Then, perhaps with the news of yet another series of tests or treatment program, the illness may be acknowledged as life threatening. At that point, the awareness context may shift from closed or suspected to open.

Caring for the Terminally Ill Child

Perhaps one of the clearest messages to come out of the current interest in death and dying is the need to redefine the meaning of caregiving for patients whose prognosis is death. It is essential that caring for the terminally ill child take into account not only physical needs but also emotional and psychological needs as well. (In addition, the child's family needs to be embraced by the system of health care.)

Often, seriously ill children need what Thesi Bergmann and Anna Freud call "mental first aid" to help them cope with their thoughts and emotions.[24] Such mental or emotional first aid may simply mean comforting the child and being supportive through a difficult or painful procedure. On the other hand, a child who is severely disturbed by his or her illness may require a more substantive technique of intervention to successfully deal with anxiety, guilt, anger, and other possibly conflicting or unresolved emotions. Whereas some children seem to cope with traumatic experiences without requiring much outside help, others may need considerable support to cope successfully with relatively minor crises. Whatever the case, working with children requires a flexible approach.

Richard Lonetto points out that attempting to protect a child from confronting disturbing feelings may result in even greater anxiety and conflict. A child who feels unsupported or unsure about what is happening may experience fantasies that are more frightening than the truth.[25] An atmosphere of support and encouragement in which the child and the parents feel free to express their fears and concerns can help to alleviate anxiety as well as diminish the child's feelings of separation and loneliness.

As much as possible, family members can be encouraged to participate in the child's care. Although professional caregivers are equipped by training and experience to provide for the child's medical needs, a parent's special expertise lies in the nontechnical aspects of child care. Activities such as bathing the child, helping the child get dressed, assisting at meal times, tucking the child in at night, and providing emotional support are all tasks wherein a parent can be involved to the benefit of everyone concerned.[26]

Confronting the Reality That a Child Is Dying

To move from avoidance to acceptance in confronting the reality of a child's terminal illness requires that those persons close to the child agree to be honest with themselves and with others. A decision must be made to be candid, but with compassion and kindness toward everyone affected by the child's illness.

Truth without compassion may be destructive. Compassionate communication of truth acknowledges the reality in a spirit of loving kindness.

Bluebond-Langner noticed that the families that dealt with a child's illness with open awareness were those in which the parents did not derive their personal identities solely from their role as parents.[27] In other words, although parenting was an important part of their lives, it did not constitute the totality of their self-image, which encompassed other significant accomplishments and values as well. Thus, even though they were in the midst of a painful and frustrating predicament, their own survival was not an issue.

Creating a context of open awareness does not make the situation easier or mean that one will cope more successfully. At times, it may become more difficult, because the option to distance oneself from the experience by avoiding or denying it is less available. However, open awareness is not a condition that is static and unchanging; there may be a shift from comparative openness to being closed or to mutual pretense, depending upon the intensity of the immediate experience and the ability or desire of the persons involved to cope with that reality.

Congruency of — that is, agreement between — beliefs and actions is an important determinant of how a crisis is experienced. The more your beliefs and actions are congruent, the more likely you are to cope successfully with a crisis. Suppose, for instance, that in your value system a style of pretense is seen as a useful way to deal with situations that are threatening or discomforting, and that such a style of communication is typical of your family's interactions. Then pretense may be an effective means of coping with painful circumstances such as those surrounding a dying child. Suppose, on the other hand, that you value openness and honesty, and your family has always been scrupulously honest with one another. If a child is dying, yet everyone is pretending that the crisis really doesn't exist, that the child is getting well, then your anxiety is likely to be made even more unbearable by the conflict between your beliefs and actions.

Crisis, though unsettling and painful, is also an opportunity for turning one's attention to the essentials of life and relationship with others. Dr. Jerome Schulman, a child psychiatrist whose interviews with families in crisis are reported in his book *Coping with Tragedy*, concludes that some persons who are confronted by the reality of a seriously ill child not only survive, but grow from the experience: "Rather than simply coping — in the sense of merely surviving — many parents and children respond to a severe illness by making a more mature reevaluation of their lives and achieving a truer vision of what counts. Their lives become more significant, more basic, more meaningful. They live one day at a time . . . but they learn to make each new day more enriching."[28]

The Death of an Adult Child

Although there is scant research on parental bereavement in situations involving the death of an adult child, Beverly Raphael points out that the "older parent who experiences the death of an adult child is likely to be deeply disturbed by it."[29] Even though there is likely to be a degree of separation between an adult child and his or her parent, the parent's grief may be intense. Such a death may be difficult for the bereaved parent to resolve. Indeed, it has been suggested that the death of an adult child may be the most difficult of all griefs. The death is not only "untimely," as are deaths of children generally, but may result in a form of "survivor guilt" particularly distressing for parents.[30] For a young or middle-aged adult to die while his or her parents live on seems unnatural. It goes against the proper order of things.

The older parent who survives the death of a middle-aged child may also suffer the loss of a caregiver. The child represented a source of comfort and security that is now gone. Parental bereavement also can be complicated by a parent's sense of "competing" with the child's spouse for the role of "most bereaved." In situations where all of those who have been bereaved by the child's death need and seek comfort, who has priority in receiving the attentions of others? Sometimes the loss of an adult child results in circumstances that require parents to assume care of their grandchildren. Meeting such an unforeseen need may be emotionally disruptive as well as economically difficult. The death of an adult child, happening as it does "out of sequence" and unexpectedly, can present an especially difficult form of parental bereavement.

Peer Support Groups for Specific Parental Bereavements

Many kinds of support groups exist to give help and information to parents who are coping with the serious illness or death of a child. One such group, Compassionate Friends, is directed primarily to the needs of parents who have experienced the death of a child.[31] A group known as the Guild for Infant Survival is composed of parents who have lost children to "crib death" or Sudden Infant Death Syndrome (SIDS).[32] Another group, Candlelighters, is made up of parents of children with cancer. From a child's initial diagnosis with cancer, through his or her treatment and long-term survival or death, there are specific programs for the child, his or her parents, and other family members. These programs range from offering emotional support in coping with the reality of childhood cancer to providing practical information for dealing with problems related to treatment, nutrition, interruption in school attendance, disruption of family patterns, and so on.[33]

Besides providing emotional support for the grief experienced at the loss of a child, some organizations for bereaved parents also engage in political advocacy designed to remedy the circumstances that precipitated the death. Examples of these peer support groups for parental bereavement include Mothers Against Drunk Driving and Parents of Murdered Children. The grief resulting from losses such as those reflected in the names of these two organizations is often complicated by the circumstances that surrounded a child's death. These circumstances may include intrusions on the family's grief by media coverage of the event as well as criminal investigation and judicial proceedings.

Spousal Bereavement

Of all the transitions in the life cycle, the death of a spouse is considered the most disruptive crisis. The ties between two persons in a marital relationship are usually so closely interwoven that the death of one partner "cuts across the very meaning of the other's existence."[34] Although we know it is likely that one spouse will die before the other and that the survivor will be left to carry on alone, such thoughts are kept in the background. The pressing activities of daily life occupy our attention until one day the possibility becomes a reality that can't be ignored.

The aftermath of a spouse's death has been described as follows: "Everyday occurrences underscore the absence of your mate. Sitting down to breakfast, or dinner, opening mail, hearing a special song, going to bed, all become sources of pain when they were formerly sources of pleasure. Each day is full of challenges and heartbreaks."[35] Although a spouse's death always requires an adjustment from being a couple to being single, the transition may be especially hard for the survivor who is also a parent. With children to care for, there is an added burden of making a transition to single parenthood.

Factors Influencing Spousal Bereavement

Of all the death experiences in adulthood, the loss of a spouse has been most often and intensively studied.[36] Most research has focused on a relatively brief time span following bereavement; studies of enduring effects are comparatively rare. Thus, questions remain: How common are cases of severe difficulties among widows and widowers, and how long do such problems usually last? It is not easy to tease out the various factors that contribute to problems in coping with the death of a spouse. Financial problems and adjusting to living alone clearly play a role. Three major factors, in addition to those discussed in Chapter 7, seem to affect the outcome of spousal bereavement: the survivor's patterns of interaction with the deceased, age, and gender.

The patterns of intimacy and interaction between spouses form an important determinant of how the loss of a partner will be perceived by a survivor. Whereas one couple derives primary satisfaction from shared activities, another

When a man to whom you have been married for more than thirty years dies, a piece of you that you will never know again goes out the door with him. Sitting dry-eyed in a chair watching the rescue-squad men load him onto the stretcher and strap him in, I was mercifully numb. Yes, I said obediently, I would await a call from the coroner; yes, his doctor could be reached at the hospital; yes, I would be all right alone.

And then they were wheeling him out the door, casting uneasy backward glances at me. Thirty years of being us was suddenly transformed into just me.

Elizabeth C. Mooney, *Alone: Surviving as a Widow*

Mr. and Mrs. Andrew Lyman, Polish tobacco farmers living near Windsor Locks, Connecticut, exemplify some of the qualities that contribute to a close relationship. When such a bond is severed by death, the effect is felt in every area of the survivor's life.

prefers separateness. In some relationships, the focus is on children; in others, the adult partners take precedence. The patterns of a relationship are in a constant state of flux, as the partners themselves develop and as circumstances change over time. Thus, the loss of a mate can have many different meanings.

Consider, too, the difference in outlook between a young couple, married only a short time, and an older couple whose lives have been shared for many years. Although the death of a spouse may occur at any time, it occurs most

> your hair is falling out,   and
> you are not so beautiful:
> your eyes have dark shadows
> your body is bloated;   arms covered with
>   bruises and needlemarks;
> legs swollen and useless . . .
>   your body and spirit
> are weakened with toxic chemicals
> urine smells like antibiotics,
>   even the sweat
> that bathes your whole body
>   in the early hours of morning
> reeks of dicloxacillin   and methotrexate.
>
>   you are nauseous all the time
> i am afraid to move on the bed
> for fear of waking you   to moan
> and lean over the edge
>   vomiting into the bag
>
>   i curl up fetally
>   withdraw into my dreams
> with a frightened back to you . . .
>   and i'm scared
>   and i'm hiding
> but i love you so much;
> this truth does not change . . .
>   years ago,
> when i met you, as we were falling in love,
> your beauty attracted me:
>   long, golden-brown hair
> clear and peaceful green eyes
> high cheekbones   and long smooth muscles
>   but you know—and this is true—
> i fell in love with your soul
>   the real essence of you
> and this cannot grow less beautiful . . .

continued

continued from previous page

> sometimes   these days
> even your soul is cloudy
>   i still recognize you
>
> we may be frightened
>   be hiding our sorrow
> it may take a little longer
> to acknowledge the truth,
> but i would not want to be   anywhere else
>   i am here   with you
> you can grow less beautiful to the world
>   you are safe
>   i will always love you.
>
> A young widow

often among older couples, after the children are grown and perhaps have children of their own, and after other transitions common to the later years of life, such as retirement, have been experienced. Spousal bereavement in old age may follow a lifetime of mutual commitment and shared experiences. In contrast, a young couple just setting out to build a world together is engaged in an "ongoing creative dialogue which, in turn, defines the mature love relationship."[37] When one of the partners dies, the survivor is left alone to reconstitute previously shared aims. Although an older person must also come to terms with such a loss and reorganize his or her life accordingly, the reevaluation of aims and goals is not likely to be as thoroughgoing. During the years from youth to old age, a person's standard of living and overall quality of life are also likely to change, thus affecting the meaning and reality of loss. Finally, youth and age involve differing expectations about mortality.

Age is a factor in the coping styles of widows and widowers as well.[38] Although bereaved spouses of all ages report depressive symptoms during the first year of bereavement, younger people apparently experience more physical distress and they tend to rely more on drugs to counter this distress than do older persons. On the other hand, aged persons may have health problems that were neglected while they cared for an ailing spouse. In the first year following the loss of a mate, there appear to be increases in the morbidity and mortality rates of widows and widowers, with aged persons particularly at risk.[39] While caring for a dying spouse, the survivor's ties to the outside world may have been curtailed, thus increasing feelings of loneliness following bereavement.

Relief following the death of a spouse, although little discussed, is an emotion experienced by many widows and widowers who have cared for an ailing spouse over a long period of time or when the death prevents further suffering for the deceased. Less socially accepted, or even acknowledged, is relief experienced when a mate's death is welcomed as the end to an unsatisfactory relationship.

Although spousal bereavement involves experiences that are common to both men and women, it also elicits distinct behaviors related to culturally sanctioned gender roles. In one culture, a widower might avoid crying publicly since to do so would be viewed as "weak" and shameful. A widower in another culture, however, might express his grief through many tears and loud crying since not to do so would suggest a "weakness" in ability to love.

Spousal bereavement can be devastating for either sex, and individuals who have lived out traditional sex roles may find the transition especially hard. Learning to manage unfamiliar role responsibilities in the midst of grief can be a formidable task, intensifying feelings of helplessness. The widow who has never written a check or the widower who has never prepared dinner is confronted not only with grief at the loss of a loved one, but also with major role readjustments. New skills must be learned simply to manage the needs of daily life.

Both widowers and widows appear to have a less happy and exciting life than their married counterparts. But adverse effects appear to be more prevalent among widowers, perhaps because those who have lived out traditional sex roles find it difficult to manage the domestic matters that previously had been left to the now-deceased spouse. Widowers also may be less likely than widows to seek help from others, again a trait that may be associated with a traditional sex role. As Judith Stillion points out, men who care for an ailing partner over an extended period of time may be at a disadvantage in coping with the onset of normal physical and psychological problems of bereavement if "their socialization prohibits them from asking for help, showing strain, or even, in some instances, recognizing and discussing their feelings with helping professionals."[40]

Gender also influences the experience of spousal bereavement in another way. Because women statistically live longer than men, it is estimated that three out of every four married women will be widowed at one time or another. Of the 13.2 million widowed persons living in the United States, 11 million are widows.[41] Those widows who want to remarry may be faced not only by social pressures but with a situation wherein there are few eligible men. One study found that widowers were significantly better adjusted than were widows, even when such factors as income, level of education, age, and amount of forewarning of death were considered.[42] To account for this, three reasons were suggested: First, women have tended traditionally to shape their identities around their husbands, whereas this has not been true of men in our culture. Second, the fact that men tend to die earlier than women and that men who survive their wives tend to marry women younger than themselves decreases the likelihood that women will remarry; knowing this, widows are less optimistic about their chances of future intimacy than widowers. Third, widows are often concerned about making decisions and handling finances alone, as well as about their physical safety and their children.

© Carol A. Foote

Of America's more than 1 million nursing home patients, women outnumber men by about three to one. The majority are white, widowed, and disabled. Few have visitors and only about 20 percent return home; the vast majority will die in the nursing home.

On the other hand, some have suggested that widowhood is less difficult for women than retirement is for men. This is because there are many other widows with whom to share leisure time and activities, so that a woman's status actually increases with widowhood, whereas a man's status decreases at retirement. In a society that is increasingly mobile, and in which the conventional social supports (such as the extended family) may be disappearing, the elderly widowed may be at a particular disadvantage. Education and social class appear to "play a major role in the way in which a widowed woman reconstructs her identity and her world after the death of her husband."[43]

Difficulties experienced in adjusting to the death of a spouse are influenced both by the grieving process and by attendant role changes. Understanding the effect of these processes can lead to the availability of better social support mechanisms designed to alleviate the stresses of spousal bereavement.

"Widow" is a harsh and hurtful word. It comes from the Sanskrit and it means "empty." I have been empty too long. I do not want to be pigeon-holed as a widow. I am a woman whose husband has died, yes. But not a second-class citizen, not a lonely goose. I am a mother and a working woman and a friend and a sexual woman and a laughing woman and a concerned woman and a vital woman. I am a person. I resent what the term widow has come to mean. I am alive. I am part of the world.

If fate had reversed its whim and taken me instead of Martin, I would expect him to be very much part of the world. I cannot see him with the good gray tag of "widower." He would not stand for it for one moment. And neither will I. Not anymore.

But what of love? The warmth, the tenderness, the passion I had for Martin? Am I rejecting that, too?

Ah, that is the very definition of bereavement. The love object is lost. And love without its object shrivels like a flower betrayed by an early frost. How can we live without it? Without love? Without its total commitment? This explains the passionate grief of widowhood. Grief is as much a lament for the end of love as anything else.

Acceptance finally comes. And with it comes peace. Today I carry the scars of my bitter grief. In a way I look upon them as battle stripes, marks of my fight to attain an identity of my own. I owe the person I am today to Martin's death. If he had not died, I am sure I would have lived happily ever after as a twentieth-century child wife never knowing what I was missing. . . .

But today I am someone else. I am stronger, more independent. I have more understanding, more sympathy. A different perspective. I have a quiet love for Martin. I have passionate, poignant memories of him. He will always be part of me. But—

If I were to meet Martin today. . . ?

Would I love him?

I ask myself. Startled. What brought the question to my mind. I know. I ask it because I am a different woman.

Yes. Of course I would. I love him now. But Martin is dead. And I am a different woman. And the next time I love, if ever I do, it will be a different man, a different love.

Frightening.

But so is life. And wonderful.

Lynn Caine, Widow

Social Support for Widows and Widowers

Adjustment to the loss of a spouse can be mediated to a great extent by social support systems. Relationships with friends, neighbors, and family appear to result in lower levels of loneliness and worry and higher feelings of usefulness. Maintaining relationships with nonrelatives appears to be especially important, since friendships are based on common interests and life styles. Family relationships, in contrast, may pose a potential psychological threat to the widowed elderly since they contain elements of "role reversal" between the adult child and the aging parent that suggest or demand dependency from the aged widow or widower.[44]

Perhaps the most valuable resource for the recently widowed is contact with peers; that is, other widows or widowers who can serve as role models during the subsequent period of adjustment. In this way, the new widow has a role model from whom to learn how to be a widow.[45] Successful contact of this kind can make other intervention unnecessary. The widowed person acting as role model does not try to minimize the painful or difficult feelings of grief. Rather, exposed to the helper's accepting attitude, the newly widowed person learns to live with these feelings and to gain perspective on them. Many such groups now include widowers as well, and separate widower-to-widower support groups also exist. Those who have taken part in such support groups generally report that the experience was beneficial.

The Death of a Parent

The death of a parent usually represents the loss of a long-term relationship that has nurtured and provided much support to the surviving child. The love between parent and child is associated with such qualities as unconditional and absolute; parents are often described as "completely accepting" and "always there when the chips are really down, no matter what." Thus, a parent's death confronts the surviving child with issues peculiar to that relationship.

Any death can remind us of our own mortality, but the death of a parent may force upon a person the realization, perhaps for the first time, that he or she has become an adult. When parents are alive, they usually provide moral support for their children; there is a sense that if real trouble comes a child can call on his or her parents for at least psychological comfort. For many people, these feelings provide a great sense of security. With a parent's death, that security is diminished or no longer available. The bereaved child may feel there is no one who would answer a call for help unconditionally. With the knowledge of his or her own transitory nature may come feelings of insecurity and fear of being alone.

There is some evidence that the death of our parents results in a "developmental push," which "may effect a more mature stance in parentally bereaved adults who no longer think of themselves as children."[46] When both parents have died, there is a subtle role change for the adult child, who no longer has his or her parents to "fall back on," even if only in one's imagination. One woman who had survived the deaths of both her parents said that, although she knew that friends and other family members loved her and cared about her, she felt that the love from her parents was unique, unconditional, and irreplaceable.

The death of a mother is considered a harder loss to sustain than the death of a father. This may be due partly to a mother's traditional status as the primary nurturing caregiver. Another reason, however, may lie in the fact that, statistically, fathers die before mothers. Thus, when the mother dies, her death

We have been so long accustomed to the hypothesis of your being taken away from us, especially during the past ten months, that the thought that this may be your last illness conveys no very sudden shock. You are old enough, you've given your message to the world in many ways and will not be forgotten; you are here left alone, and on the other side, let us hope and pray, dear, dear old Mother is waiting for you to join her. If you go, it will not be an inharmonious thing . . . As for the other side, and Mother, and our all possibly meeting, I *can't* say anything. More than ever at this moment do I feel that if that *were* true, all would be solved and justified. And it comes strangely over me in bidding you goodbye how a life is but a day and expresses mainly but a single note. It is so much like the act of bidding an ordinary good night. Good night, my sacred old Father! If I don't see you again — Farewell! a blessed farewell!

Your

William

William James, to his father, Henry James, Sr., during the latter's final illness in 1882

represents the loss of having "parents," and the bereaved adult child may experience reactive grief over the death of the other parent as well.

The typically low level of grieving associated with the death of a parent during adult life is sometimes related to the fact that the adult child is generally involved in his or her own life and feelings of attachment have been largely redirected toward others, such as spouse and children. Nevertheless, the loss of a parent may continue to have an impact as the bereaved child recalls the relationship that had existed.

Illness and Aging

The expectations most people have about aging or being old differ from the actual experience. Young adults typically expect problems among older people to be more serious than they are for those who experience them. We often tend to group together people over a wide age range without regard to their differences. The stereotyped image of an aged person is marked by such outward signs as dry and wrinkled skin, graying hair, baldness, failing eyesight, loss of hearing, stiff joints, and general physical debility.[47] But, as Judith Stillion points out, aged persons tend to be more individually distinct than any other segment of the population, at least until death is imminent, because they have had more years to create unique life histories. Thus, "human beings are more alike at birth than they will ever be again."[48]

The image of what it means to be old is also changing among the old themselves. As the culminating phase of a human life, the period of old age or maturity is an appropriate time to focus on the developmental tasks specific to that part of the human journey. Hannelore Wass suggests that older persons are entitled to become familiar with information about the processes of human

While There Is Time

I carry the folding chair
for my mother
I carry the shawl
the large straw hat
to shield her from the glare
She leans her small weight
on my arm   Frail legs unsteady
feet now cramped with pain

Each day we sit for hours
at the ocean   The sun is hot
but she is wrapped and swathed
her hands are icy cold
they hide their ache
beneath the blanket

Her eyes follow the
movement that surrounds us
the romp of children
flight of gulls
the strong young surfers
challenging the sea

When the visit is ended
when my mother leaves
I will burst from the house
run empty-handed to the beach
hold out my arms
and swoop like a bird
my hands will tag children
as I pass

I will run and run
until I fall
and weep
for the crushed feet
the gnarled fingers
for her longing
I will run for both of us

Maude Meehan

development and aging and with the subject of dying and death.[49] Practical death education for aged persons could include discussions of patients' rights, the right to die, emotional support groups, legal matters, and funerals. Within this context of death education for the aged, Wass suggests six broad goals:

1. Learning about physiological, psychological, and social processes and aspects of dying
2. Learning about attitudes toward dying and death
3. Learning to come to terms with the reality of one's own mortality
4. Learning to live with the fact of death
5. Learning to help a dying or bereaved family member or friend
6. Learning to cope with loss and bereavement

With improvements in nutrition and health care, the debilitating effects of aging are being steadily pushed toward the end of the human lifespan (see Figure 9-1). Although the maximum *lifespan* has remained relatively static at about eighty-five to ninety years of age, *life expectancy* has steadily increased, with the result that most indviduals now enjoy comparatively good health and active life styles until nearly the time of death.

Still, the cumulative effect of these physical, mental, and cultural factors related to aging is that the older person eventually experiences loss on a daily

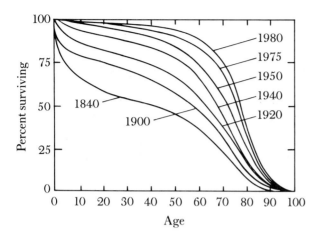

Figure 9-1 *Survival Curves, 1840–1980*
Notice that the progressive elimination of premature death due to disease increasingly approaches the "rectangular curve" that would occur in the absence of any premature death. *Source:* James F. Fries and Lawrence M. Crapo, *Vitality and Aging: Implications of the Rectangular Curve* (San Francisco: W. H. Freeman, 1981), p. 70.

basis. These losses may include diminished physiological functions, changes in self-esteem, inability to continue as a materially productive member of society, and an increasing helplessness and vulnerability in all aspects of life.

Chronic and Debilitating Illnesses

The most obvious of these losses are those that occur in connection with the diseases common to the second half of life. These diseases include atherosclerosis, hypertension, and stroke syndrome, which are often found in interrelationship, each condition influencing the onset of the others. *Atherosclerosis,* a buildup of fatty deposits in the arteries that eventually constricts the flow of blood, has been singled out as a nearly universal health problem posing a barrier to any appreciable prolongation of life. *Hypertension,* or high blood pressure, frequently accompanies or contributes to a variety of other illnesses, and it can lead to death from stroke or heart failure. *Strokes* are caused by a sudden blocking or rupture of the cerebral arteries, thereby interfering with the circulation of the blood in the brain. Even when a stroke is not fatal, its aftermath may include loss of memory, defects in speech, emotional problems, paralysis, or loss of control over bodily functions. Although conditions precipitating these illnesses may begin at an early age, the threat to well-being is generally cumulative, thus increasing the likelihood of ill effects as one gets older.

Some cancers also have age-specific mortality rates. Cancers of the lungs, breast, or cervix, for example, are more frequent at younger ages, whereas cancers of the stomach, intestinal tract, prostate, skin, or kidney are more common among aged persons.

In addition to the major causes of death — diseases of the heart, cerebrovascular disease, and cancer — other illnesses may either be fatal or, if not, result in severe, incapacitating losses. Arthritis and rheumatism, for example, although

The worst fear of people who are at risk for Huntington's disease is that they will eventually get the disease and life will become meaningless for them. For most people, death itself is not nearly as fearful as the possibility of years of meaningless suffering. . . .The meaning of life is not, after all, the same for everybody. It varies from person to person according to a multitude of circumstances. And for each person it varies from day to day, even from hour to hour. The meaning of life constantly changes but *never ceases to exist*. It exists even in suffering. Often it exists especially in suffering. That is fortunate, because suffering is an inevitable part of life.

Dennis H. Phillips, *Living with Huntington's Disease:*
A Book for Patients and Families

seldom identified as causes of death, can nevertheless be debilitating and limit normal activities.

Degenerative diseases such as Alzheimer's and Parkinson's also bring specific losses in their wake, as do hereditary diseases such as Huntington's and amyotrophic lateral sclerosis (ALS). When Alzheimer's disease affects a middle-aged or an old person, for example, there are losses not only for the affected individual but also for family and friends who can no longer relate in the same way to the person they once knew. As the husband of one Alzheimer's patient said, "My wife is standing next to me, but she's not really there; what's standing there is a memory." As the most common form of neurological illness, Alzheimer's affects an estimated 2 million adults in the United States. Although most persons with the disease are over age sixty-five, Alzheimer's has been found in patients who are in their late twenties. Along with progressive destruction of memory, Alzheimer's symptoms include declines in learning, attention, and judgment; disorientation in time and space; difficulty in finding words and communicating; and changes in personality. It has been estimated that, when the involvement of family members is taken into account, perhaps 12 million people in America are touched by Alzheimer's disease, which has been

It is hard for me to speak of the regression that I watch. At first, there was a groping to express herself, along with the intense frustration at her every attempt. And then her moments of expression became less frequent, until eventually the struggle stopped. This disease has invaded her brain to such a depth that a state of passivity and helplessness has set in. One scene that is forever impressed on my memory took place in my apartment a little over two years ago. My mother was unable to achieve the simple motion of entering a room to sit in an armchair. She fearfully clung to the door frame, her eyes darting back and forth from chair to door, door to chair. Ultimately, she remained at the door until help came. Today, two years later, I wish I could at least see her standing unassisted.

Princess Yasmin Khan, daughter of Rita Hayworth

called the "silent epidemic."[50] Thus, the psychological aspects of the disease result in a multitude of losses.

The physiological signs of aging itself may be accompanied by *psychological disorders,* such as emotional distress (sometimes resulting from stressful and anxiety-provoking conditions) and disorders related to personality, mood, and depression, as well as *psychosomatic symptoms* affecting such physical processes as sleep, appetite, bowel movements, and fatigue. The old may also exhibit a variety of neuroses, psychoses, and brain syndromes. Each of these conditions, in varying degrees and according to their seriousness, involves significant change, transition, and loss.

Besides specific diseases, a variety of dysfunctions can have an impact upon the older person's quality of life. For instance, sensory and cognitive impairments may result in loss of hearing or sight, or in a diminished sense of taste and smell. Oral and dental problems may make eating difficult, with the result that nutrition suffers, thus compounding the cycle of poor health. Deficient reaction times and psychomotor responses may increase the chance of accidents. Although any of these illnesses or disabilities could represent a significant loss by itself, a number of these conditions may be present at once.

Consider for a moment the effect of even a relatively minor injury on your usual functioning. As you think about the limitations this injury poses, you may gain insight into what multiple losses may mean in the lives of those who experience them. Such limitations clearly involve confrontations with loss: What was once possible is now gone.

Because patients with debilitating diseases such as those discussed require long-term care to manage the symptoms associated with the disease, there is also a significant impact on families. As a result, support programs for both patient and family members have developed, including home care, day care, respite care, patient groups, family groups, dedicated nursing home units, and other group living facilities. The issues that arise in the context of caring for persons with chronic and debilitating illnesses are perhaps most pronounced in situations that involve the very old.

Caring for the Chronically Ill and Aged Adult

Listen to conversations about care of the chronically ill and the old. Notice how many times individuals describe the need for care in language like this: "She couldn't live by herself so her son took her in," or "He was failing and had to be placed in a nursing home." A question like, "What will we do with Dad when he is too old to manage by himself?" reflects both genuine concern and inadvertent disregard for the aged relative. It is perhaps not surprising, in light of remarks like these, that many aged persons report feelings of being put away, taken in, done to, and otherwise manipulated, their integrity ignored. What is the reality?

Historically, the family has been a haven for ill and aged relatives. Some families do care for aged members of the household, and a high value is placed on such care by some cultural groups. Although many chronically ill and aged persons do live in their own homes or with their families, a significant number require more assistance than they or their family members can provide. Public assistance and concern has grown as families increasingly find it difficult to provide for ill and aged relatives. In the United States, social service programs on behalf of the aged can be traced to the Depression of the 1930s and passage of the Social Security Act of 1935. It was not until 1950, however, with enactment of the Old Age Assistance Act, that the first federal program designed specifically to relieve problems among the aged was implemented. Following implementation of the Medicare and Medicaid programs in the mid-1960s, widespread federal assistance became an accepted means of providing care for America's elderly. The question of how to provide adequate, as well as economical, care for the aged is of increasing public concern. These issues become ever more important as the expectation of life increases, resulting in greater numbers of aged persons in society (see Figure 9-2). Already, the cost of Social Security and other social service programs is a matter of intense public debate.

Institutional and Community Programs of Care

The types of institutions in which older people find themselves are of several types. *Domiciliary care homes* provide custodial care to residents who need minimal supervision in a sheltered environment and who are able otherwise to take care of their own needs. For persons with more serious illnesses or disabilities who need medical attention, there are *personal care homes*. Depending on whether residents can manage their own medical regimes, these facilities may or may not provide nursing care. Retirement communities and residential hotels or apartments generally fall into these two categories, which comprise about one-fourth of the institutional choices available.

Skilled nursing facilities, offering either intermediate or comprehensive levels of care, furnish round-the-clock nursing services based on personal need, as well as medical and dietary supervision. Such institutions may operate as extended care or convalescent facilities associated with a general hospital or they may be independent facilities that admit residents without prior hospitalization.

Alternatives to institutional care, which at least some aged persons can benefit from, also exist. These programs are not available in all areas, nor can

In Europe the availability of domiciliary homes for the elderly goes back to sixteenth-century "alms houses" for the indigent old in England and on the continent. During the Middle Ages, care of the elderly was sporadic, generally perceived of as a moral obligation of the church. In England, the Poor Law of 1601 settled the responsibility of caring for the poor and infirm on the shoulders of each community.

Jon Hendricks and C. Davis Hendricks, *Aging in Mass Society*

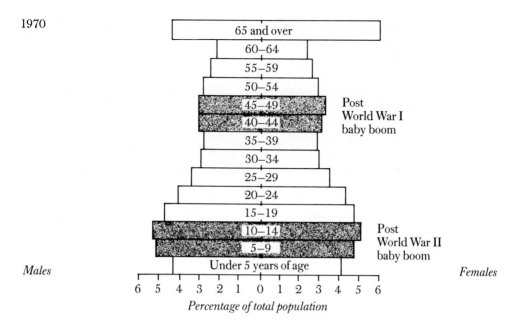

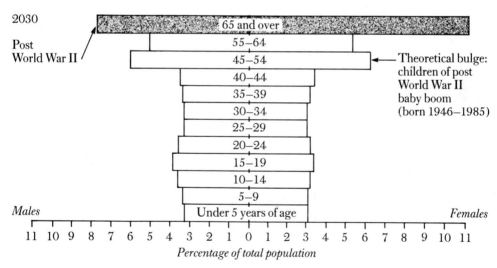

Figure 9-2 *Population Pyramids*

Population pyramids for the years 1970 and 2030 show a dramatic increase in the number of persons ages sixty-five and over in the coming decades, as well as the ratio between males and females in this and other age groups.

Source: Judith Stevens-Long, *Adult Life,* 2nd ed. (Palo Alto, Calif.: Mayfield, 1984), p. 10. Based on D. Decker, *Social Gerontology* (Boston: Little, Brown, 1980), and Leon F. Bowmer, "America's Baby Boom Generation: The Fateful Bulge," *Population Bulletin* 35 (1980): 29–33.

© Albert Lee Strickland

There are a variety of options for care of the frail elderly. The wide veranda and rocking chairs of the "rest home," however, are fast disappearing from the American scene.

they always provide the degree of support required. Nevertheless, they demonstrate that it is possible to provide care in ways that maintain an appropriate balance between support and independence. *Home health care,* for example, assists persons who are able to continue living in their own homes. Depending on the resources available in a community, this assistance may be provided by one or more agencies and in a variety of ways, ranging from medical and nursing visits to preparation of meals, help with exercise and other maintenance needs, and simple (but important) visitation. It is estimated that as many as 40 percent of aged persons now living in institutions could remain in their own communities, in familiar surroundings, if adequate home health care services were available to them.

Day hospitals and *elder daycare centers* represent another form of alternative care for the aged. Although the specific services provided depend upon local resources, typical services include health maintenance, financial and general counseling, meals, and other services designed to increase independence, such as housekeeping, shopping, and transportation.

Halfway between institutionalization and independent living is a new form of care known as *congregate housing*. This is usually a large residence with individual apartments or a series of structures within a small neighborhood. The distinguishing feature of this form of care is its organizational structure, which, like a series of concentric circles or graduated steps, provides the particular level of care needed by each resident. In such a community, some individuals are essentially living independently, preparing meals in their own apartments or eating in the dining room when they wish. In this way, they enjoy a sense of security, knowing that help is available when it's needed, without giving up their independence.

Losses Through Institutionalization

Institutional care is depersonalizing. Despite the best intentions on the part of staff members, the emotional needs of residents may suffer. Residents may be deprived of their personal property along with their sense of self-concept and integrity. Rules and regulations, which seem unavoidably to increase depersonalization, abound. Even a cherished picture of a loved one may find no place in the resident's room: not the bed stand (that's for bed pans), not the wall (patients are frequently moved); so where? Often the answer is, "Nowhere." Gerontologists — those who study the aged and the processes of aging — have found that the "psychological railroading" associated with highly routinized environments can lead to *institutional neurosis,* the symptoms of which include "a gradual erosion of the uniqueness of one's personality traits so that residents become increasingly dependent on staff direction for even the most mundane needs."[51]

Although institutional care must be oriented toward providing adequate, efficient services to residents — often including extensive medical care — there is general agreement that much could be done to increase flexibility. Favoring institutional expediency over the unique needs of residents cannot be justified.

Institutional Care for the Frail Elderly

The older a person is, the more likely he or she is to become institutionalized. Despite the image of aged persons being "dumped" in a nursing home by uncaring family members, this is rarely the reality. On the contrary, families may delay obtaining adequate care for their elders because of reluctance to face the need for more intensive care than they can provide at home. Institutionalization is often viewed as the ultimate personal failure for both the aged person and his or her family. Perhaps two-thirds of the elderly view institutions as the least desirable alternative possible, "a sort of confession to final surrender, a halfway stop on the route to death."[52] When institutional care becomes the only

TABLE 9-2   *Steps in Choosing a Nursing Care Facility*

1. Make a list of local facilities offering the type of services needed.
2. Find out whether the facilities are licensed and certified.
3. Visit the facilities.
4. Prepare a checklist of desirable features and evaluate each facility in light of the needs of the person who would be moving in.
5. Determine the costs.
6. Make your decision.

Source: Adapted from Colette Browne and Roberta Onzuka-Anderson, editors, *Our Aging Parents: A Practical Guide to Eldercare* (Honolulu: University of Hawaii Press, 1985), pp. 204–209.

reasonable course open to the family of an aged relative, a more satisfying outcome is made possible when necessary information is gathered before a decision is made for a particular facility (see Table 9-2). In the coming years, our prospects for the future also include changes in the patterns of disease as well as the technology of health care. New alternatives to both institutional and home-based care for the aged will be explored. And, perhaps most important, we will continue to see and create new social attitudes about being old.

Further Readings

Pamela T. Amoss and Stevan Harrell, editors. *Other Ways of Growing Old: Anthropological Perspectives*. Stanford, Calif.: Stanford University Press, 1981.

Stanley Brandes. *Forty: The Age and the Symbol*. Nashville: University of Tennessee Press, 1985.

Colette Browne and Roberta Onzuka-Anderson, editors. *Our Aging Parents: A Practical Guide to Eldercare*. Honolulu: University of Hawaii Press, 1985.

Committee on an Aging Society. *Health in an Older Society*. Washington, D.C.: National Academy Press, 1985.

Rochelle Friedman and Bonnie Gradstein. *Surviving Pregnancy Loss*. Boston: Little Brown, 1982.

Mark Jury and Dan Jury. *Gramp*. New York: Penguin, 1976.

Ronald J. Knapp. *Beyond Endurance: When a Child Dies*. New York: Schocken, 1986.

Louis E. LaGrand, *Coping with Separation and Loss as a Young Adult.* Springfield, Ill.: Charles C. Thomas, 1986.

Elizabeth C. Mooney. *Alone: Surviving as a Widow*. New York: G.P. Putnam's Sons, 1981.

Marty Richards et al. *Choosing a Nursing Home: A Guidebook for Families*. Seattle: University of Washington Press, 1985.

Harriet Sarnoff Schiff. *The Bereaved Parent*. New York: Crown, 1977.

Jerome L. Schulman. *Coping with Tragedy: Successfully Facing the Problem of a Seriously Ill Child*. Chicago: Follett, 1976.

Judith M. Stillion. *Death and the Sexes: An Examination of Differential Longevity, Attitudes, Behaviors, and Coping Skills*. Washington, D.C.: Hemisphere, 1985.

David D. Van Tassel, editor. *Aging, Death, and the Completion of Being*. Philadelphia: University of Pennsylvania Press, 1979.

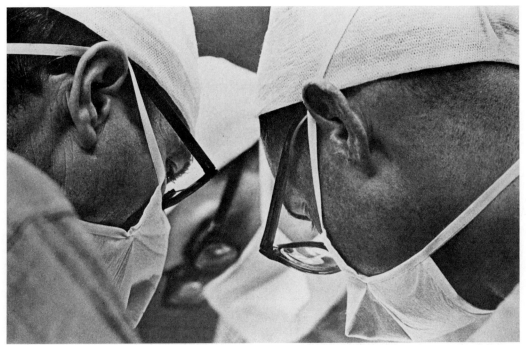

W. Eugene Smith. Center for Creative Photography, University of Arizona, © Heirs of W. Eugene Smith

*At the Hospital for Special Surgery physicians use medical techniques
that call for teamwork and expertise. Life-sustaining interventions made
possible by advances in medical technologies require physicians and
society as a whole to consider difficult issues of medical ethics.*

CHAPTER 10

Medical Ethics: Dying in a Technological Age

Grandpa was born before Henry Ford put his first automobile on the road, and he died shortly after Neil Armstrong set his foot on the moon. From Michigan to outer space, he experienced an unprecedented advance in the technological capacities of our society. At the time of his death, he was surrounded by technological innovations. The canvas-topped, hand-started two-seater car he hand-built in 1922 had been replaced by a factory-built vinyl-topped, four-door automatic, with power steering and power brakes. A retired auto worker, he had begun to question the consequences that the automobile brought to the quality of his life. If he had been conscious just before his death, he might have talked about the consequences that the machines sustaining his life brought to the quality of his death.

What are the ethics of caring for the dying in a technological age? Advances in biomedical technology have presented us with new and frequently confusing choices. Open heart surgery can repair defects that once were fatal. When repair is not possible, replacement of the defective organ may be. In the United States there are more than 100 medical centers where major organ transplants are regularly performed.

The most common of these are kidney transplants, which many thousands of people have received, some of them continuing to function for well over two decades. Skin transplantation, or grafting, too, has been carried out successfully thousands of times. Cornea transplants, replacing the outer lens of the eye, have achieved notable success in more than

The Oath of Hippocrates

I swear by Apollo the physician, and by Aesculapius [god of medicine], Hygeia [goddess of health], and Panacea [goddess of healing], and all the gods and goddesses, that, to the best of my ability and judgment, I will keep this oath and agreement: to regard my teacher in this art as equal to my own parents; to share my living with him and provide for him in need; to treat his children as my own and teach them this art if they wish to learn it, without payment or obligation; to give guidance, explanations, and every other kind of instruction to my own children and those of my teacher, and to students who subscribe to the Physician's Oath, but to nobody else.

I will prescribe treatment to the best of my ability and judgment for the benefit of my patients and will abstain from whatever is harmful or pernicious. I will give no poisonous or deadly medicine, even if asked to, nor make any such suggestion; neither will I give any woman a pessary to produce an abortion. I will both live and work in purity and holiness. I will not operate, not even on patients suffering from the stone, but will leave this to specialists who are skilled in this work. Into whatever houses I enter, I will make the patient's good my principal aim and will avoid all deliberate harm or corruption, especially from sexual relations with women or men, bond or free. Whatever I see or hear about people, whether in the course of my practice or outside it, if it should not be made public, I will keep it to myself and treat it as an inviolable secret.

While I abide by this oath and never violate it, may all people hold me in esteem for all time on account of my life and work; but if I break this oath, let the reverse be my fate.

10,000 patients. Good results have been obtained from transplants of bone marrow, pancreas, lung, and liver as well. The most dramatic of transplant operations, the heart transplant, has been performed well over two hundred times, though the success rate has not matched the early promise.

Margaret Mead said that the great advances in medicine came about because physicians have taken seriously the Hippocratic obligation to keep people alive.[1] But the practice of this worthy maxim can sometimes lead to confusing consequences. The average person might reject the notion that there is an obligation to keep people alive in certain instances, as when a person is maintained in a hopelessly comatose condition, or when a physician feels bound by duty to keep a deformed baby alive.

Advances like bypass grafts, intra-aortic balloon pumps, membrane oxygenators, new drug therapies, sophisticated and innovative surgical techniques, and supersensitive monitoring devices offer us medical interventions for sustaining life that were unimaginable until recently. The technologies, which now have such an overwhelming impact on the way we die, may present the greatest challenge ever faced by people as they confront the prospect of their own or another's death.

Most deaths in modern societies are anticipated, the result of a malady that may linger months or even years. At any given time, perhaps 1 million of us have an irreversible, debilitating ailment that is ordinarily expected to result in death. Yet even such chronic diseases are being actively combatted. Now that infectious diseases of the past have been largely controlled, the medical community is waging war against the diseases that are killing us today.

The human organism can often be kept going despite the cessation of normal heart, brain, respiratory, or kidney function. When medical technologies spare patients' lives and enable them to resume more or less normal functioning, the results are gratifying. But, paradoxically, the very technologies designed to prolong our lives may prolong our dying as well. Should a person who is dying of widespread cancer be sustained artificially or perhaps even be repeatedly resuscitated, all while in great discomfort and pain and with no hope of ever returning to a normal existence? When life is sustained artificially, though the person shows no signs of personality or consciousness and there is no chance of recovery, ethical questions arise.

When death mercifully does come in such instances, who or what finally "dies"? Put another way, what in fact is "death"? When does it occur? Until quite recently, cessation of breathing and heartbeat was death. In our time, the definition of death is less certain.

Better health care, improved sanitation practices, proper nutrition, reduction in infant mortality and deaths in early childhood, and other such factors have contributed both to the expectation of a longer lifespan and to enhanced well-being generally. Assuming that you represent the statistically average person, you can look forward to living for a total of about seventy-three years. Following a typical progression, your death will probably occur in an institutional setting: a hospital or similar facility offering care for terminal patients.

The social and technological advances that have brought about improved health care and greater choices in medical services have also resulted in questions concerning how best to make use of these choices and improvements. When these questions impinge upon the ethical realm of decision making, the choices can be difficult for individuals and for social institutions alike. Indeed, questions involving moral values and ethical judgments are among the most difficult that are addressed in a discussion of death and dying.

To place these issues within their current context, it is useful to reflect upon the topics discussed in preceding chapters. Historical developments; patterns of coping with death in other cultures; the process by which we learn about death in childhood; the patterns of bereavement, grief, and mourning; options available for caring for the seriously ill; and the characteristics associated with life-threatening illness—all these aspects of death and dying provide a framework for considering the ethical issues involved.

Truth Telling and the Terminal Patient

If you were diagnosed as having a life-threatening illness, would you want to know about it? Some people answer quickly: "Of course, I want to know about everything that's going on with me!" Others answer as readily: "If there's any way that I could be spared the truth, I'd rather not know that I'm about to die." Whatever our response, it's likely to be conditioned by the attitude that we assume in the more casual situations of our daily lives. Our life style influences our death style. A perennial fighter against the odds and a person who believes that "ignorance is bliss" and shuns stress are likely to have very different responses to terminal illness.

Surveys indicate that most people would want to be told if they were diagnosed with a life-threatening illness. Yet the questions of *when* and *how* they should be told are often difficult to answer. Physicians must present such news in a way that serves the best interests of each patient. Factors of personality, emotional constitution, and capacity for continued function under stress must be considered anew in each instance. Although consultations with other physicians or with other members of the health team may assist the primary physician who must inform the patient, there are few guidelines. Most doctors are guided by their experience.

A diagnosis of life-threatening illness affects not only the patient but also members of the patient's family. Indeed, sometimes it is a member of the family who learns the truth first. Those who know then have a burden of responsibility, for they must decide what to tell the patient.

Most physicians now feel a responsibility to inform a patient about the facts of his or her life-threatening condition, and they try to do so sensitively and in appropriate ways. But this has not always been the case. A study conducted in the 1950s revealed that most doctors at that time demonstrated a "strong and general tendency to *withhold* this information."[2] None of the doctors surveyed reported having a policy of telling every patient. When they did inform patients, their descriptions of the disease were usually couched in euphemisms. They might tell a cancer patient that he or she had a "lesion" or a "mass." Some used a more precise description such as "growth," "tumor," or "hyperplastic tissue." But often the description was couched to suggest that the cancer was benign. Adjectives were used to temper the impact of the cancer diagnosis. The tumor was "suspicious" or "degenerated." Treatment was advised because the tissue was "precancerous" or the tumor was "in the early curable stage."

In short, these physicians phrased their descriptions in the most general terms while still eliciting the patient's cooperation in the proposed course of treatment. Some of the factors that motivated the physicians in this early study are just as important today. Many physicians seem to fear that knowledge of the actual prognosis may adversely affect the patient's ability to cope with the illness. Thus, they believe they are acting in the patient's best interest by minimizing the patient's sense of the threat of the illness. Doctors generally believe that it is crucial to give reassurance and support to the patient, to make sure that patient maintains hope.

Nevertheless, the overall climate of truth telling among physicians has changed markedly in recent decades. With the coming of a greater general freedom to discuss death, a terminal patient is more likely to learn the truth about his or her illness, and to learn sooner, than usually happened in the past.

Despite doctors' greater forthrightness, the full extent of an illness may not be disclosed until the patient or a family member exhibits a readiness to be told.

Although the general facts of an illness may be disclosed voluntarily by the physician, details that might be depressing news to the patient are generally withheld unless the patient takes the initiative. The most direct way of expressing the desire to receive such information is to ask questions.

Informed Consent to Treatment

The relationship between patient and physician implies the existence of a contract whereby each party agrees to perform certain acts designed to achieve the desired results. Fundamental to the contract are self-determination and informed consent. Just as we have the right to choose a physician according to our own preferences and wishes, we have the right to self-determination regarding the proposed plan of treatment. We can concur with it or reject it. In practice usually we simply rely on the physician's judgment, accepting the diagnosis of an illness and acceding to the proposed course of treatment; we follow the doctor's advice and expect a more-or-less speedy recovery. We see our doctor to obtain medication to cure the flu or to mend a broken arm and give relatively little thought to considering various alternatives for treatment. The etiology, or cause, of the disease or injury generally concerns us less than obtaining relief from its symptoms.

More complex, however, is the question of the patient's consent to treatment when the illness is serious or even life threatening. Not only has life-threatening illness vastly greater consequences for the patient, but the physician's role is fraught with greater ambiguity. Frequently, several different treatment plans are available, each with its own set of potential risks and benefits. Medical practitioners may be uncertain about what might be the most promising treatment. Too, with diseases like cancer, the side effects of surgery, radiation, and chemotherapy may be as frightening or as discomforting as the disease itself.

Clearly, then, the patient's *informed consent* to a plan of treatment is crucial. Informed consent is based on three principles: First, the patient must be competent to give consent. Second, consent must be given freely and voluntarily. Third, consent must be based on an adequate understanding of what is involved in the treatment program. Ideally, the physician informs the patient about the risks of the proposed therapy, about alternative methods of treatment, and about the likely outcome of undertaking no treatment.

The antecedents of informed consent go back hundreds of years in English common law and also can be seen in the context of medical treatment since the beginning of this century. Although the phrase "informed consent" did not achieve legal definition until 1957, the doctrine of informed consent has been recognized in case law or statute in nearly all American jurisdictions. The President's Commission for the Study of Ethical Problems in Medicine noted that "the legal doctrine of informed consent imposes on physicians two general duties: to disclose information about treatment to patients and to obtain their consent before proceeding with treatment."[3]

Nurse: Did they mention anything about a tube through your nose?

Patient: Yes, I'm gonna have a tube in my nose.

Nurse: You're going to have the tube down for a couple of days or longer. It depends. So you're going to be NPO, nothing by mouth, and also you're going to have IV fluid.

Patient: I know. For three or four days, they told me that already. I don't like it, though.

Nurse: You don't have any choice.

Patient: Yes, I don't have any choice, I know.

Nurse: Like it or not, you don't have any choice. (laughter) After you come back, we'll ask you to do a lot of coughing and deep breathing to exercise your lungs.

Patient: Oh, we'll see how I feel.

Nurse: (emphasis) No matter how you feel, you have to do that!

President's Commission for the Study of Ethical Problems in Medicine and Biomedical and Behavioral Research, *Making Health Care Decisions: A Report on the Ethical and Legal Implications of the Patient-Practitioner Relationship*

Decisions about medical care involve values and goals as well as methods and behavior. The values underlying informed consent include serving the patient's well-being and respecting his or her right to self-determination. To make these values a reality, attention must be paid not only to the patient's capacity to make decisions about his or her care, but also to the communication process between patient and practitioner.

Although it has substantial foundations in law, the doctrine of informed consent is essentially an ethical imperative. It cannot be equated with "reciting the contents of a form that details the risks of particular treatments," but involves instead a "process of shared decision-making based upon mutual respect and participation." Because people differ in their attitudes toward autonomy and choice relative to medical care, the process of informed consent must be flexible. Despite this variability, however, informed consent is "ethically required of health care practitioners in their relationships with all patients, not a luxury for a few."

Although a survey conducted for the Commission found "a universal desire for information, choice, and respectful communication about decisions," many people have only a vague notion of informed consent. When asked, "What does the term *informed consent* mean to you?" 21 percent of those surveyed said they did not know. About half said that informed consent meant "agreeing to treatment" or "letting the doctor do whatever is necessary or best." Only 10 percent mentioned having information about risks, and less than 1 percent mentioned being told about alternatives.

Among physicians, about half described informed consent as "generally informing patient about condition and treatment," while somewhat fewer added that it included "disclosing treatment risks to patient." Only 14 percent mentioned telling patients about treatment alternatives.

Informed consent requires that patients *and* caregivers be prepared for shared decision making. Despite a tradition emphasizing the individual's right to self-determination, medical practitioners from the time of Hippocrates have frequently been skeptical of this sentiment. Hippocrates' advice to physicians includes the admonition to do one's duties "calmly and adroitly, concealing most things from the patient while you are attending to him" and to reveal "nothing of the patient's future or present condition."

Informed consent becomes increasingly important when medical care is provided by teams of highly specialized professionals whose responsibilities may be defined less by the overall needs of the patient than by particular diseases or organ systems. There may be no single individual charged with responsibility for the entire care of the patient, no one with whom the patient is familiar to turn to for information, advice, and comfort. The threat such a situation poses to the patient's autonomy cannot be remedied by "formal disclosure of remote risks on informed consent forms." Nor can legal prescriptions alone ensure or enforce compliance with the ethical imperative of informed consent.

Although some have argued that patients cannot understand medical information relevant to their health care, about half of the physicians surveyed by the Commission reported that 90–100 percent of their patients could understand most aspects of their condition and treatment, if sufficient time and effort were given to explanation. Another third said that 70–89 percent of their patients could understand. The Commission noted that "questions of patient capacity in decisionmaking typically arise only when a patient chooses a course — often a refusal of treatment — other than the one the health professional finds most reasonable."

Although coercive treatment is rare, caregivers can — unwittingly or not — exert undue influence on patients by means of subtle or overt manipulation. The Commission remarked that "a good deal of routine care in hospitals, nursing homes, and other health care settings is provided . . . without explicit and voluntary consent by patients." Once the patient is in a health care institution, cooperation with those who provide such routine care is generally expected. The tacit communication may be that the patient has no choice.

Thus, communication can determine whether informed consent is present. When medical information is presented by caregivers, the facts and possible outcomes must be tailored to facilitate a discussion attuned to the needs, capabilities, and emotional state of a particular patient. In the Commission's survey, 97 percent of the public said "patients should have the right to all available information about their condition and treatment that they wish," with 94 percent reporting that they would "want to know everything." When asked who could judge best the amount of information that should be divulged, however, the public's responses were nearly evenly divided between patient (45 percent) and physician (44 percent). About three-quarters of the doctors said they felt it was their responsibility to make sure patients were fully informed, while 19 percent said the responsibility was shared between doctor and patient.

When the physicians were asked about how they treated the issue of informed consent, slightly more than half (56 percent) said they always discussed their diagnosis and prognosis with patients and another 42 percent said it was their usual practice. When asked what they would tell a patient who had a fully confirmed diagnosis of advanced lung cancer, however, only 13 percent said they would give a straight statistical prognosis. A third said they would tell the patient that they didn't know how long he or she might live, "but would stress that it could be for a substantial period of time"; 28 percent would say that they "couldn't tell how long, but would stress that in most cases people live no longer than a year"; and 22 percent would "refuse to speculate on how long the patient might live." Thus, although it appears that physicians generally do disclose information to patients about diagnosis and prognosis, they may not divulge as much as some patients would like, particularly when the information involves placing an expectation on the amount of time a patient has remaining to live.[4]

To the degree that a proposed course of treatment is elective, the outcome uncertain, and the procedure experimental, the patient's informed consent becomes correspondingly more important. For example, the drawing of a blood sample is a widely known and commonplace procedure and entails little risk to the patient. Consequently, we do not expect to receive a detailed explanation of it or of any risks when we roll up our sleeve for the insertion of the needle. However, a complicated surgical procedure, one that involves a nearly equal proportion of risks and benefits, makes the matter of the patient's informed consent crucial.

Unfortunately, the ideal of informed consent is not always easy to attain. In some cases, it may be difficult to clearly determine what constitutes sufficient information on which the patient can base a decision. Too, patients differ in how much they want to be told. Some patients take an active role in their treatment, even suggesting to their physician alternative methods of treatment; they are eager to receive a full disclosure of the medical facts, and insist on understanding the various options. Other patients prefer simply to follow the program outlined by their doctor; they do not want to know about potential risks or the percentage of failures.

Patients devise different strategies for coping with their illnesses; full disclosure may be a help to some patients, a hindrance to others. This difference can present a dilemma to the medical practitioner. Required to obtain the patient's informed consent before proceeding with treatment, the physician must also be sensitive to the patient's preferences for the amount and kind of information given.

The issues surrounding informed consent will undoubtedly be among the chief concerns of medical practitioners for some time. Physicians must safeguard themselves against the threat of malpractice suits that may arise when patients do not adequately understand the possible consequences of a course of treatment. The great advances in medical care have simultaneously raised our

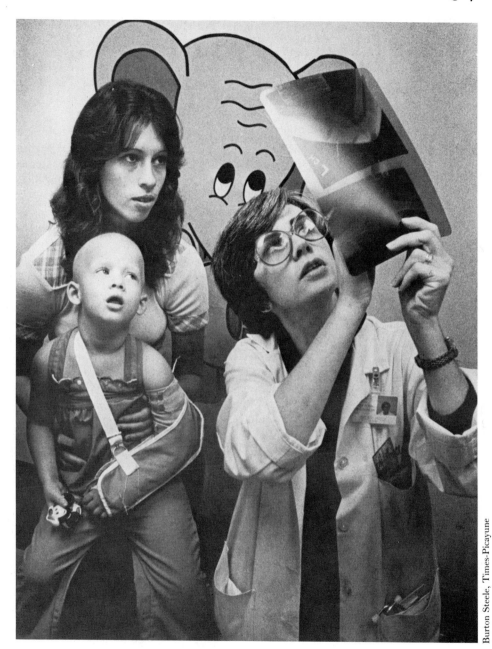

Informed consent is a fundamental ethical principle in medicine. Even fairly routine procedures, such as mending a small fracture, may become complicated when the patient is leukemic, as is this child: Alternatives must be weighed more carefully before a course of treatment is chosen.

expectations of what can be achieved and made medical practices more esoteric — a paradoxical situation, given that the patient must sufficiently understand the medical realities to make informed decisions about the proposed plan of treatment.

Choosing Death: The Decision Not to Prolong Dying

Some persons argue that everyone should have the *legal* right to die, regardless of whether that option is exercised. In earlier times, the Hippocratic obligation of the medical practitioner was interpreted to mean, "Thou shalt not kill, but needst not strive officiously to keep alive." More recently, however, the slogan of the medical practitioner had become, in effect, "Keep the patient alive at all costs." The conflict of conscience engendered by the modern technological marvels of the hospital not only affects the dying and their relatives, it also presents a burdensome paradox to the physician. What is the moral balance between preserving life and preventing suffering? More and more, people are concerned about the *quality* of lives that are saved by technology.

Patients themselves often make last-ditch attempts to end their lives. Some of them, Joseph Fletcher says, "swallow Kleenex to suffocate themselves, or jerk tubes out of their noses or veins, in a cat-and-mouse game of life and death which is neither merciful nor meaningful."[5] The traditional deathbed scene has been largely replaced by institutional dying. Sedated or comatose, the patient is surrounded by an array of machinery and tubes, less a whole human person than an objectified extension of technology. The implicit contract between a patient and physician makes the question of how to deal with such cases extremely difficult. The medical staff is duty bound to render beneficial treatment to the patient. But what constitutes the best care in such cases? Should life be preserved regardless of circumstance? Can a doctor *allow* a patient to die and be judged moral? Such questions are central to the debate concerning *euthanasia* — that is, an "easy" or painless death — a term applied to the intentional ending of a person's life when he or she is suffering from an incurable and painful disease.

Glanville Williams is among those who argue that euthanasia is indeed morally permissible when it prevents an even greater cruelty — that is, it is crueler to prevent someone who is in pain and wishes to die from obtaining the release offered by death. Williams believes that both the patient and the physician ought to have liberty to pursue the course indicated as in the patient's best interests, given his or her terminal condition.[6]

Critics respond by emphasizing the dangers that might arise if euthanasia became an acceptable policy. Objections include the potential difficulty of obtaining a patient's clear consent, the risk of incorrect diagnosis, and the uncertainty regarding whether a new development might have come in time to offer a cure. Finally there is the "wedge" argument: One should not permit acts that, although possibly moral in themselves, might eventually pave the way for acts that would be immoral. If we permit euthanasia in cases of irreversible terminal illness today, then, so the argument goes, perhaps tomorrow we will

When I was a junior physician in a hospital, we were once called urgently to the bedside of a lady of ninety. The nurse had used the term "cardiac arrest"—the old lady's heart had stopped (as hearts are apt to do, around ninety!). But because the cardiac arrest alarm was raised, I and the other houseman launched into a full-scale resuscitation. With violent drugs injected directly into the heart, blasts of electric current through her chest, noise and chaos, she had anything but a peaceful death. On reflection we realized that all this had been inappropriate, but nothing in our medical student training gave us any guide. Indeed once the emergency is in the air, there is not time to weigh up the pros and cons. The decision is rarely a doctor's anyway, because usually the only person on the scene when an emergency occurs is a nurse—probably a relatively junior one if it is night time—and she decides whether or not to resuscitate. Needless to say, it is a very courageous nurse who decides not to. Once things have started, it is very difficult for the doctor when he arrives to stop everything, particularly if the patient is showing signs of reviving.

Richard Lamerton, *Care of the Dying*

extend the practice on a wider, less justifiable scale. Allowing terminal patients to die would possibly lead to more questionable acts motivated by caprice and whim.[7]

As in other areas of our relationship with death, the American attitude toward dealing humanely with persons who are diagnosed as irreversibly, terminally ill is ambiguous. On the one hand, both human consideration and medical ethics require that we preserve and sustain life. Our laws reflect this goal, and they provide substantial penalties for anyone who hastens another's death. Yet, in practice, deciding between saving a life and allowing a person to die is not always as clear as these distinctions might suggest. When we hear of someone who is hopelessly ill and in a coma, kept alive by sophisticated equipment that sustains breathing and heartbeat, we may question whether such a heroic attempt to preserve life is appropriate. There is a pervasive feeling that when a person is without hope of ever regaining consciousness or any semblance of normal human activity, he or she should be allowed to die in peace.

Most physicians and health personnel who work with the dying would agree. A patient whose case is utterly without hope may be designated "Code 90," or "DNR" (Do Not Resuscitate), or "CMO" (Comfort Measures Only), each a message to the hospital staff that, should death appear to be imminent, extraordinary life-saving measures should not be applied. Efforts are directed toward easing pain and making the patient as comfortable as possible until death comes.

In general, when a hopelessly ill or comatose patient is near death, three options can be considered: (1) active treatment to forestall death; (2) active intervention to terminate life; and (3) passive management, a middle course involving neither extraordinary life-saving measures nor active hastening of death.

A physician might follow any of these three courses of treatment, depending on the circumstances of a particular case. Active intervention to willfully terminate life is rare, however. More likely, the physician must decide to pursue either active intervention involving extraordinary measures, or passive management, providing only ordinary, essential means of treatment. Ordinary, essential care includes the use of proven therapies that are maximally effective with minimal danger.[8] Extraordinary measures, on the other hand, often involve a significant risk, and the results are usually unpredictable. They are designed to sustain life artificially until the patient's own restorative powers can take over.

Of the studies undertaken by the President's Commission, none received greater public response than the report on issues of foregoing life-sustaining treatment. "Today, for almost any life-threatening condition, some intervention is capable of delaying the moment of death," the Commission said. "Matters that were once the province of fate have now become a matter of human choice."[9] Antibiotics, nursing support, artificial feeding procedures, and home physical therapy, as well as respirators, kidney machines, and other technologies of modern medicine are examples of therapies that sustain life. Foregoing life-sustaining treatment means doing without a medical intervention that would be expected to extend a patient's life. It includes noninitiation of treatment as well as discontinuation of an ongoing treatment.[10]

Ethical questions about the "right to die" have become prominent since the landmark case involving Karen Ann Quinlan. On April 15, 1975, at age twenty-one, she was admitted to the intensive care unit of a New Jersey hospital in a comatose state. Soon her vital processes were being artificially sustained via a mechanical MA-1 respirator. When she remained unresponsive, in a so-called "persistent vegetative state" with no known hope of recovery, Karen's parents asked to have the respirator disconnected so that nature might take its course. This request was opposed by the medical staff responsible for Karen's care, and their refusal resulted in a suit before the New Jersey Superior Court to determine who should have the right to act on Karen's behalf: her parents or the medical staff. Although the Superior Court ruled in favor of the medical staff, keeping Karen on the respirator, this decision was overturned by the Supreme Court of New Jersey in March of 1976.[11] Artificial respiration was discontinued and Karen was eventually transferred to a nursing care facility where she died in June 1985 at age thirty-one. Karen Ann Quinlan became a focus for the issues of "death with dignity," and discussion of these issues has not ended with her death.

Recently, families of comatose patients in a number of states have sought and obtained court rulings allowing removal of artificial feeding tubes. In Florida, for example, a District Court of Appeals noted that artificial feeding is similar to other extraordinary means of sustaining life, such as the respirator. It ruled that the right of privacy includes the right to remove nasogastric tubes from persons who are in persistent vegetative states with no prospect of regaining cognitive brain function. In a unanimous decision, the court said that when the use of medical technologies results in a situation where all that remains is the forced function of bodily processes, including artificial sustenance of the body itself, "we

Assistance in providing nutrition to chronically ill and dying patients ranges from help with eating, as seen here in the case of these nursing home residents, to total reliance on artificial feeding. The issue of artificially providing nutrition to comatose, hopelessly ill patients is one of the newest ethical issues in medicine.

recognize the right to allow the natural consequences of the removal of those artificial life-sustaining measures."[12] Concurrence in such decisions is reflected in a policy announced by an ethics panel of the American Medical Association stating that artificial feeding and the infusion of water can be stopped in cases of irreversible coma.

Ethical issues involving forced feeding of noncomatose patients became prominent in the California judiciary when the decision of Elizabeth Bouvia, a quadriplegic, to refuse such treatment was upheld by the state Supreme Court. The ruling said that mentally competent, informed patients have the right to refuse any medical treatment, including life support provided by mechanical or artificial means. This historic ruling allowing Elizabeth Bouvia to refuse forced feeding has been hailed by some as a victory for individual liberties; others call it "legal suicide."

Who should make decisions about foregoing life-sustaining treatment? There is general agreement that decisions about health care rest with competent patients. Still, a patient's choices may be limited on moral or legal grounds. In the final report of its studies, the President's Commission emphasized the importance of: (1) respecting the choices of individuals who are competent to decide to forego even life-sustaining treatment; (2) providing guidelines and procedures for making decisions on behalf of patients who are

A number of years ago, before all the discussion about defining brain death and maintaining life on a respirator and so on, a patient of mine, a young pregnant woman at term, suddenly developed extremely high blood pressure. Then she had a stroke and the baby's heartbeat stopped, so we supported her by artificially maintaining blood pressure and other vital functions, including breathing. But she had had a complete brain death immediately. And she had lost the baby. We got an EEG [electroencephalogram], and it was completely flat. We repeated it twenty-four hours later, and again it was completely flat.

It was the worst tragedy I've ever seen, because in just a few minutes she was gone and the baby was gone—just within moments. I talked with her husband, her mother, and her father. (Now, this was long before the issues surrounding definition of death had become so contentious that the lawyers got involved.) I told them that the thing to do was turn off the machine. Just as I had not read about all this, they as a family had not read about it. It seemed quite logical to me.

So we picked a time when we were going to do it, and they all came and waited outside the door. I told them again what I was going to do, and they said to go ahead and do it. I went in and turned off the machine. The nurse and I watched her, and in five minutes her pulse rate had stopped. I think this is the proper way to handle this sort of situation when brain death is involved. I think it has a negative effect to continue life support systems for weeks and months. It was a tragedy, and given the tragedy, what options do you have? Continue the life support system or don't continue it. To me, there's no argument whatsoever to continue the life support system.

Quoted from *Death and Dying: The Physician's Perspective,* a videotape by Elizabeth Bradbury

unable to do so on their own; (3) maintaining a presumption in favor of sustaining life; (4) improving the medical options available to dying patients; (5) providing respectful, responsive, and supportive care to patients for whom no further medical therapies are available or elected; and (6) encouraging health care institutions to take responsibility for ensuring that adequate procedures for decision making are available for all patients.[13] Probably no other topic of death and dying generates as much debate as do the ethical issues related to the hopelessly ill.

Allowing to Die: The Special Care Nursery

The ethical issues that arise from the dilemma of whether to sustain life or to allow death are perhaps most sensitively realized in the case of infants. As we saw in Chapter 1, throughout this century and especially within the past few decades, the mortality rate among infants and children has been reduced, largely through advances in both the knowledge and techniques of neonatal care. In hospitals with specialized infant intensive care units, for instance, the neonatal mortality rate is roughly half that of hospitals not having such special care nurseries.

The special care nursery, with the crucial difference it can make in an infant's chances of survival, is an innovation in medical practice that virtually everyone would applaud. Unfortunately, some of the infants whose lives are spared will never be capable of living what is considered a normal human life. They may suffer from cardiopulmonary ailments or brain damage, or they may be handicapped by some congenital malformation. Formerly, such dysfunctional conditions in infancy would almost surely have resulted in death. Now that many such infants survive because of the specialized care they receive, we are confronted by ethical questions concerning the quality of their lives and the guidelines that should be operable in determining whether or not medical intervention is the best course of action.

Should the life of an infant with intestinal blockage be spared by surgical intervention? What if the infant is brain-damaged or severely retarded? Is the answer always "Yes, life should be saved," or does the answer change according to circumstances?

Consider the following case: An infant was born with his entire left side malformed, with no left eye, and practically without a left ear; his left hand was deformed, and some of his vertebrae were not fused. Being also afflicted with a tracheo-esophageal fistula (an abnormality of the windpipe and the canal that leads to the stomach), he could not be fed by mouth. Air leaked into his stomach instead of going to the lungs, and fluid from the stomach pushed up into the lungs. One doctor commented, "It takes little imagination to think there were further internal difficulties as well." In the ensuing days, the infant's condition steadily worsened. Pneumonia set in; his reflexes became impaired; and, because of poor circulation, severe brain damage was suspected. But despite the seriousness of all these factors taken together, the immediate threat to his survival, the tracheo-esophageal fistula, could be corrected by a fairly easy surgical procedure.

The debate began when the parents refused to give their consent to surgery. Some of the doctors treating the child believed that surgery was warranted and took the case to court. The judge ordered surgery, ruling that "at the moment of live birth, there does exist a human being entitled to the fullest protection of the law. . . . The most basic right enjoyed by every human being is the right to life itself."[14]

In another case, which provides some contrasts to the one just cited, the mother of a premature baby overheard the doctor describing her infant as having Down's syndrome with the added complication that the intestines were blocked. Ordinary surgery can correct this kind of blockage; without correction, the child cannot be fed and will die. The mother felt that "it would be unfair" to her other children if a retarded child were brought into the home. Her husband supported this decision, and they refused their consent for surgery.

One of the physicians argued that the degree of mental retardation in children with Down's syndrome cannot be predicted, though generally their IQ is in the 50–80 range; and, in the physician's words, "They're almost always trainable. They can hold simple jobs, and they're famous for being happy children. They're perennially happy and usually a great joy." When further complications do not appear, a long life can be anticipated.

However, the hospital staff did not seek a court order to override the parents' decision against surgical intervention. As a result, the child was placed in a side room and, over the following eleven days, it starved to death.[15]

The differences between these two cases are instructive. The severely malformed infant in the first case seemed to have less chance of survival or of living a normal life than the afflicted infant in the second example. Yet the hospital staff in the first case chose to seek a court order granting treatment, whereas the staff at the second hospital chose to abide by the parents' wishes even though the child could probably have been saved. However, the decision by the latter medical staff was not an easy one. Staff members expressed considerable uneasiness and strain regarding the child's lack of treatment.

Commenting on the second case, James Gustafson argues that the child's right to life was not adequately explored, either by the physicians or by the parents. From the doctors' point of view, once the decision was made not to proceed with the operation, the child became terminal, and thus further means of sustaining life were unwarranted. Gustafson, however, argues that the subsequent withholding of ordinary means of treatment was in actuality an *extraordinary* nonintervention.

Whatever our feelings may be about the decisions just described, a distinction between cases involving infants and those involving terminal cancer patients is worth noting. In the case of the terminal patient with a prolonged illness, Gustafson says, "All procedures which might prolong life for a goodly length of time are likely to have been exhausted." But, in cases involving infants, the withholding of treatment results from a "decision not to act at all."[16]

The difficulties inherent in making decisions about the medical care of seriously ill newborns were highlighted in the study by the President's Commission. While affirming that parents should have the power of decision in most instances, the Commission also stated that medical institutions should pursue the best interests of an infant "when those interests are clear."[17] Using as an example the situation of an otherwise healthy Down's syndrome child whose life is threatened by a surgically correctable condition, the Commission said that such an infant should receive surgery since he or she would benefit. While stating that therapies expected to be futile need not be provided, the Commission added that, even in cases when no beneficial therapy is available, all parties concerned should act to ensure the infant's comfort.

Public attention to these issues was stimulated in 1983 when the Department of Health and Human Services (HHS) published rules that required hospitals to post signs near delivery rooms and nurseries stating: "Discriminatory failure to feed and care for handicapped infants in this facility is prohibited by federal law."[18] Included on the notice was a toll-free number for a 24-hour HHS "hotline" that could be called anonymously if someone believed an infant was being denied food or customary care.

A particularly controversial feature of the government's plan was the creation of "Baby Doe squads," which were to immediately begin an investigation at any hospital where an infraction of the HHS rule was suspected. During the four weeks that the hotline was in operation, more than 400 calls were logged, four of which were considered serious enough to warrant sending out a Baby Doe squad. In no instance was a violation found, although the presence of investigators did upset some parents, who were unsure why their infant had become the focus of an investigation.

The government's drastic steps to set up procedures allowing for intervention in situations involving disabled infants resulted from the case of an infant, known as "Baby Doe," who had been born with Down's syndrome and a blockage of the digestive tract. His parents refused to allow surgery to correct the blockage, no judicial intervention ensued, and the infant died. Subsequently, HHS was instructed by President Reagan to invoke a section of the Rehabilitation Act prohibiting discrimination against the handicapped in the future.

Shortly after the rules had gone into effect, a federal judge concluded that HHS had acted improperly by ignoring well-established standards for rulemaking and showing a lack of consideration for the rule's effects on medical staff, parents of critically ill infants, and the infants themselves, whose quality of care could be affected by the disruptive presence of a Baby Doe squad. Although the HHS subsequently proposed two revisions of the "Baby Doe" rule, in June 1984 the controversial regulations were struck down by a federal judge who said they were invalid and unlawful. This ruling was affirmed by the Supreme Court in 1986. These judicial decisions repudiated the government's argument that disabled infants were protected by provisions of the Rehabilitation Act. The courts said that Congress had not intended the act to apply to medical treatment involving infants.

Meanwhile, the Department of Health and Human Services took a new tack. It published regulations based on the Child Abuse Prevention and Treatment Act, which had recently broadened the definition of child abuse to include the withholding of "medically indicated treatment" from disabled infants with life-threatening conditions. Under the new regulations, treatment could be withheld when it would be ineffective in "ameliorating or correcting" an infant's life-threatening condition, when it would only prolong dying, or when an infant is irreversibly comatose. The new rules provide for state and local government action in Baby Doe cases, with the aim of making federal intervention unnecessary.

Ethical questions arise not only from decisions to withold treatment, but also from decisions to provide treatment. In October 1984, doctors at Loma Linda University transplanted a baboon heart into an infant known as "Baby Fae." They hoped the transplant would provide a "bridge" pending the availability of a human heart. Although the infant had been born with a congenital heart malformation that is usually fatal within the first month of life, the decision to implant the baboon heart elicited criticism from other physicians and medical ethicists, who called it "wishful thinking" to believe that the

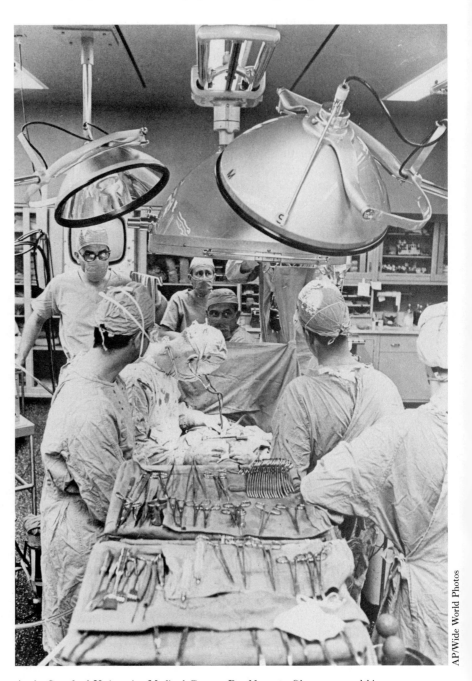

At the Stanford University Medical Center, Dr. Norman Shumway and his colleagues perform open-heart surgery. Advances in transplantation procedures and related medical therapies make such operations more feasible, yet they also raise questions that are difficult, at times quite painful, to resolve.

infant's relatively immature immune system would not reject such a cross-species transplant. Even critics acknowledged, however, that the transplant team did demonstrate that such a procedure is technically feasible and might be appropriate in some cases as a "bridge" when a human heart is unavailable and other medical options are absent.[19]

Organ Transplantation

Of recent innovative medical techniques for saving patients formerly considered hopeless, probably the best known is the transplantation of human organs. In some cases — kidney and skin transplants, for example — the donor is a living person. Donor and recipient may even be members of the same family. The transaction involved in the gift of an organ from one's own body for transplanting into the body of another can generate feelings of altruism and a sense of pride. In a very real way, such a gift allows another person to live.

Yet the donor's decision may also involve feelings of masochism or guilt. Perhaps a donor feels "backed against the wall" by other family members who want the transplant operation to take place. At the same time, the potential recipient of an organ may experience conflict concerning the transaction. The recipient may feel guilty that another person has to give up an organ, to the possible jeopardy of the donor's health; there may be anxiety about the outcome: "What if we all put ourselves through this procedure and my body rejects the donated organ? I'll feel responsible for ruining someone else's life, and we'll all be losers." Thus, both donor and recipient may have mixed feelings. Generally, the medical team responsible for the transplant operation tries to make sure that the psychological issues are resolved just as successfully as those related to the physiological concerns.

When a living donor is unavailable, or when the needed organ — a heart, for example — cannot be removed from a living human being, an alternative must be found. The organ may be removed from the body of someone who agreed before death to allow organs to be taken for transplantation. Sometimes the deceased's next of kin give permission. As with living donors, intense feelings can surround the decision to give a gift of such importance to another human being.

Because fewer organs are donated than are needed, physicians must choose among prospective recipients. Thus, the physician or the medical team becomes a "gatekeeper." Once a prospective recipient has been certified as physically suitable for a transplant, other factors are considered. Emotional stability, age, and the ability to withstand stress all influence the chances of achieving a successful outcome.[20] The ideal candidate for a transplant is a patient whose condition is deteriorating despite the best conventional medical treatment available, and for whom a transplant offers a reasonable likelihood of recovery — in other words, someone who is likely to die in the absence of radical intervention. Thus, the alternative — death — makes the risks associated with a transplant procedure acceptable.

Because organ transplantation has become an important part of current

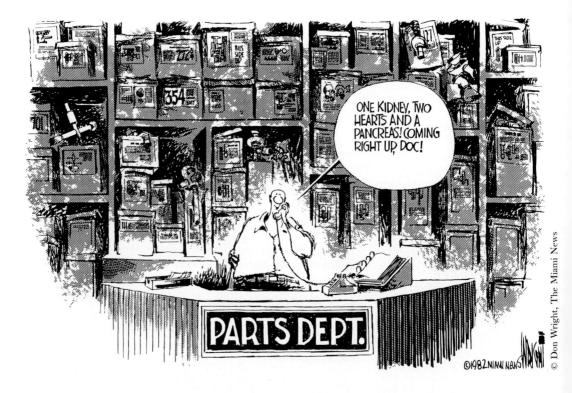

ONE KIDNEY, TWO HEARTS AND A PANCREAS! COMING RIGHT UP, DOC!

PARTS DEPT.

© Don Wright, The Miami News

medical interventions, there is a constant need for replacement body parts—liver, kidney, heart, and so on. Many of these organs come from cadavers. The practice of medicine now routinely includes the transplantation of organs from the body of a person who has been declared dead into the body of a living person who can continue to receive the lifegiving benefits of the transplanted organ. But even if some transplant procedures have become relatively routine, they have caused some quite dramatic changes in the way we think about death—in particular, the moment of death.

Consider the issues that arise in connection with heart transplants: Someone is critically afflicted with a heart that no longer performs adequately to sustain life; if there is to be a replacement for the defective organ, it must come from another human being—one who has died because, obviously, a living person cannot donate a heart. The issue becomes complicated by the fact that a replacement heart cannot itself be damaged. It cannot, in effect, be "dead." Thus, to provide a viable heart for transplantation requires nearly split-second timing, as well as an extremely precise definition of death.

Current medical technologies allow doctors to maintain the viability of body organs by sustaining certain physiological functions in the body of a person who has been declared dead. The determination of death in such cases proceeds from methods of defining death that were only recently formulated.

The Need for a New Definition of Death

On the face of it, the definition of death might seem quite obvious: A person dies, is dead, and the corpse is disposed of. But as soon as someone asks, "What do you mean by 'a person dies'?" the whole matter begins to unravel. What at first may seem simple turns out to involve an amazing complexity. Indeed, there are many historical accounts of persons being thought dead who in fact were in a state that only mimicked biological death.

Not too many years ago, one could hear horror stories about bodies lying in a morgue coming back to life, as it were, and startling the bereaved family, not to mention the mortician. A state of unconsciousness, perhaps, or an extreme slowing of body functioning had resulted in the appearance of death. To provide a safeguard against the threat of being buried alive, some people gave instructions that their bodies be placed in coffins with bells or some other attention-getting device that the "corpse" could activate even after burial should consciousness return after a mistaken determination of death (see Figure 10-1).

Think for a moment. When would you consider yourself to be dead? How would you know that death had occurred in someone else? The answers to these questions range from the definite, "when decay and putrefaction have set in," to those more difficult to put into practice: "when I can no longer take care of myself." A person using the first method for making a determination of death would hardly be pleased to be judged dead by the standards of the second.

The present concern with defining death is, of course, much more sophisticated. It takes into account complex scientific data. Although we still must make determinations of death from observable indications that life has ceased, these observable signs can be interpreted differently, depending on how death is defined. In other words, how we define death establishes the empirical procedures to be used in making a determination that a person has died. To better understand the issues relating to defining and making a determination of death, some writers distinguish five levels at which decisions are made with respect to the death of a human being: First, a conceptual understanding of what constitutes death must be established; second, general criteria and procedures for determining that a person has died must be selected; third, these criteria must be applied in a particular case to determine if the patient meets the criteria; fourth, if the criteria are met, the person is pronounced dead; and fifth, the death is attested on a certificate of record.[21]

The Traditional Signs of Death and the New Technology

Historically, the death of the human organism has been ascertained by the absence of heartbeat and respiration. With the cessation of these vital signs, and as the cells and tissues of the body die, certain advanced signs of death become evident: the lack of certain reflexes in the eyes, the fall of body temperature to that of the environment (algor mortis), the purple-red discoloration of parts of the body as blood settles (livor mortis), and the rigidity of skeletal muscles (rigor

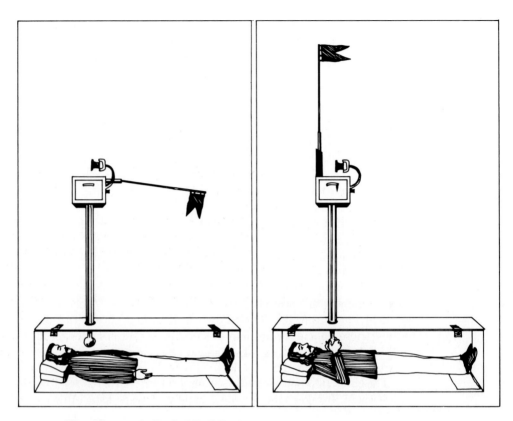

Figure 10-1   *Coffin Bell-Pull Device*
To prevent premature burial in cases of doubtful death, devices such as this French "life-preserving" coffin were invented and patented. If activated, the box above the ground opened to let in air and light, the flag raised, a bell rang, and a light came on to signal that the buried person was still alive. The person who had been mistaken for dead could also call out, and his or her voice would be amplified by the device. The fear of being buried alive stemmed from the period of great plagues and epidemics when, in the hasty disposition of the dead, a mistaken determination of death might result from a state of illness that only mimicked death.

mortis). Even today, most deaths are determined by the absence of these vital signs.

However, with the advent of respirators and other sophisticated devices to sustain these vital processes artificially, the traditional means of determining death have become inadequate. That is, by these traditional criteria an organism may be termed alive on the basis of artificially maintained breathing and heartbeat although the patient is in an irreversible coma and there is no brain wave activity. Thus, the current reexamination of the criteria for determining death has focused attention on defining human death on the basis of brain death — or, in some instances, cerebral death: cessation of activity in a part of the brain, the cerebrum. Stated briefly, the present medical definition of death describes a state in which the heart has stopped beating, breathing has ceased, and brain wave activity (as determined by electroencephalogram, or EEG) has ceased.

As pointed out in an editorial in the British medical journal *Lancet,* the problem of defining brain death arises only when a patient is put on a respirator and is thus sustained artificially; indeed, the editorial stated rather bluntly that the resulting dilemma about brain death is therefore of the doctor's own making.[22] In fact, the dilemma is one that relates to a host of medical, legal, ethical, moral, and religious concerns. The debate about new definitions of death and how they should be applied has become a public policy issue of interest to both professionals and laypersons, much like the debate over nuclear armaments. Like the nuclear debate, the history of which can be traced to a particular event — the development of the atomic bomb — so can the debate concerning how death should be defined and determined: the development of the respirator. Thus, the current situation is the result of a technological innovation. Clyde Nabe says:

> Technology seldom presents itself in a value-free way. There are usually trade-offs involved; the respirator saves lives and allows many human beings to continue productive lives that would otherwise be lost. But it also presents us with situations wherein we are uncertain we are dealing any longer with a human life; the morality of continuing to respirate a body that may or may not be a human being is unclear.[23]

Rather than replacing the traditional clinical means of diagnosis — pulse, heartbeat, and respiration — the new criteria for determining death supplement them, being applicable to instances that arise from the new technology. The widespread use of organ transplantation procedures has been an important impetus to recent efforts to arrive at a new definition of death. In many cases, transplanted organs are taken from donors who have suffered brain death but whose heartbeat and breath are maintained artificially. With regard to organ transplantation, two issues are central; (1) determining when death can be said to have occurred, and (2) deciding when it is permissible to remove the deceased's organs. Even when the second of these issues is not relevant to a particular patient's situation, however, the determination of death can still present a dilemma. As the *Lancet* editorial emphasized, once a patient is placed on devices that artificially sustain vital functions, a variety of complex medical, legal, and ethical questions may impinge on how death is defined.[24]

If alternative definitions of death are to be assessed, the distinction between clinical death and cellular death must be understood. As we have seen, *clinical death* is determined by a set of criteria that are imposed on a particular array of vital signs (such as blood flow and breathing). Thus, when a patient's breathing or heartbeat stops — even if temporarily, as during certain surgical procedures —

it can be said that the patient was clinically dead during the time these vital functions had ceased. However, it can be argued that when the state of cessation of vital functions is reversible, it would be imprecise or unwarranted to term such a cessation clinical death.

Cellular death, on the other hand, refers to a process that is gradual and that involves complex variables, including such vital signs as blood flow and breathing, but also encompassing physiological processes within the body's cells. Once the process of cellular death is well underway, the body's major systems and organs have begun an irreversible process of deterioration. The breakdown of these metabolic processes — the sum of which we call life — results in a loss of these organic functions — that is, death. We have already seen how, as death progresses at the cellular level, such phenomena as algo mortis, livor mortis, and rigor mortis occur in the body.

Cellular death may affect some organs of the body, causing irreversible breakdown, while other organs of the body are sustained by artificial means. As Robert Veatch points out, "It is now possible to manipulate the dying process so that some parts of the body cease to function while other parts are maintained indefinitely."[25] This ability of modern medicine to alter the natural sequence and process of cellular death has brought about a need to redefine the physiological meaning of death and to institute new procedures for making a clinical determination of death.

Conceptual and Empirical Criteria

What is death? How can it be determined that a person has died? These questions, though closely related, involve separate issues that must be distinguished. As Clyde Nabe points out, to untangle the complexity of these issues, we must "make plain the distinctions between the *clinical criteria* for determining when death has occurred, and the *decision* as to what *constitutes* death, and what we mean by 'death.'"[26] Definitions of death involve conceptual issues; methods of making a determination that death has occurred involve empirical and procedural issues.

Veatch has outlined four levels that must be addressed in the inquiry concerning the definition and determination of death.[27] The first level involves formally defining *death,* an essentially conceptual or philosophical endeavor. Veatch supplies a formal definition: "Death means a complete change in the status of a living entity characterized by the irreversible loss of those characteristics that are essentially significant to it." This definition encompasses the deaths not only of human beings but also of nonhuman animals, plants, cells, and indeed can even be understood metaphorically as applying to a social phenomenon such as an organization or a society or culture. Nonetheless, as Veatch says, "It is clear at least that death is a dramatic change in the status of the entity."

To give content to this formal definition, we must address Veatch's second level of inquiry, again a conceptual or philosophical question: What is so essentially significant about life that its loss is termed *death*? Some answers have included the flow of vital bodily fluids (breath and blood, for example), the soul, and in more recent definitions, consciousness. We will examine each of these in greater detail shortly.

The third level distinguished by Veatch concerns the question of the *locus* of death: Where in the organism should one look to determine whether death has occurred? With this question, we move from conceptual issues to an empirical enquiry — although the answer to this question depends upon the conceptual basis used to define death.

At Veatch's fourth level of inquiry the criteria of death must be formulated: In other words, what technical tests must be applied at the locus to determine if an individual is living or dead?

To summarize these four levels: We must first establish a general definition of death; then give that definition content by stating what is essentially significant about the change of status from life to death; then locate where in the organism one can observe the signs of this change; and finally describe the tests that should be applied to determine whether a person is alive or dead. Veatch believes that it is the confusion of these four levels that has confounded much of the current debate and efforts to establish new standards for determining death.

Four Approaches to the Definition and Determination of Death

Veatch then identifies four "plausible approaches" to defining and determining death. Whereas the formal definition of death applies to all of these approaches, the subsequent levels of inquiry — that is, those involving a particular concept of death, the locus of death, and the criteria for determining death — are distinctive for each approach. Each approach relates death to a loss: the first, of the flow of vital fluids; the second, of the soul by the body; the third, of the capacity for bodily integration; the fourth, of the capacity for social interaction. As you read about each approach, you can see how death is determined in accordance with the way it is defined.

Irreversible Loss of Flow of Vital Fluids

The first approach pertains to the cessation of the flow of vital bodily fluids. With this conceptual·understanding of death, one looks to the heart, blood vessels, lungs, and respiratory tract as the locus of death. To determine whether an individual is alive or dead, one would observe the breathing, feel the pulse, and listen to the heartbeat. The modern methods of electrocardiogram and direct measurement of oxygen and carbon dioxide levels in the blood could be added to these traditional tests, because these more sophisticated tests nevertheless focus upon the same loci and criteria for determining death.

This approach of defining death is adequate for making a determination of death in most cases even today. When vital functions are artificially sustained by machines, however, no unambiguous determination of death can be made by this definition. For instance, a patient is connected to a heart-lung machine that keeps the vital fluids of blood and breath flowing through the body. According to this definition, the patient is alive. If the patient is disconnected from the machine, these vital functions cease and, by this definition, the patient is dead. Yet during open-heart surgery, these circulatory systems are interrupted — making it possible to consider the patient clinically dead under this definition. But we know the patient is not dead, because such temporary cessation is simply part of the surgical procedures.

The ambiguity of this first approach to defining death results from defining death on the basis of physiological criteria that, although intimately related to life processes, do not seem to constitute the most significant criterion for identifying human life.

Irreversible Loss of the Soul by the Body

In the second approach to defining death — one used in many cultures worldwide and from time immemorial — the criterion is the presence or absence of the soul in the body. Within this framework, as long as the soul is present, the person is alive; when the soul leaves, the body dies. Indeed, some traditions define death in precisely this way. The *Tibetan Book of the Dead,* for example, presents the view that life is terminated in a series of gradual steps, from a state of life to the state we call death. Christian theologians and other religious ethicists also grapple with this question.

This second conceptual definition of death, then, involves the irreversible loss of the soul by the body. The locus of the soul has not been scientifically established (nor has its existence), although some believe the soul is related to the breath or the heart, or perhaps, as did the seventeenth-century philosopher René Descartes, to the pineal body, a small protrusion from the center of the brain. Thus, for those who hold this concept, the criteria for determining death would presumably involve some means of ascertaining death at the particular locus where the soul is thought to reside. For example, if the soul is thought to be coincident with the breath, then absence of breath would indicate the loss of the soul and, hence, death.[28]

To most persons living in modern, urban-technological societies, in which secular beliefs are prominent, this approach to defining death is simply not relevant. Our first difficulty would be to adequately define the soul. Even if this difficulty could be surmounted, we would need some way to ascertain whether the soul was present or absent at a given time. Moreover, this definition of death forces an examination of whether death occurs because the soul departs from the body, or, conversely, whether the soul departs from the body because death has occurred. In other words, does the soul "animate" the body, giving it life, or do the physiological processes of vitality in the body provide a vessel wherein the soul resides? Such questions may elicit fascinating speculations, but they bear little relevance to the dilemmas posed by modern medical practice in a scientific age.

Irreversible Loss of the Capacity for Bodily Integration

In the third approach, death can be defined as the irreversible loss of the capacity for bodily integration. A human being is seen as a "complex, integrated organism with capacities for internal regulation [through] highly complex homeostatic feedback mechanisms."[29] This approach is more sophisticated than the first, because it refers not simply to the traditional physiological signs of vitality in the body (the flow of breath and blood), but to the more generalized capability of the body to regulate its own functioning.

This definition at least partly resolves the ambiguity of the first definition, for a determination of death would not be made merely because a person's physiological functioning was being maintained by a machine. On the other hand, a determination of death would be made when the organism itself was no longer capable of bodily integration. In other words, artificial life support would not constitute the determining factor; rather, only with the *irreversible* loss of the capability for bodily integration would a determination of death be made.

The locus for such a determination is currently considered by clinicians to be the central nervous system — more specifically, the brain. The determination of death that results from this definition is often characterized as "brain death" (although this term is somewhat misleading because it focuses attention on the death of a part of the organism, not the whole organism).

One of the most notable efforts to establish criteria for determining death by this definition is that of the Harvard Medical School Ad Hoc Committee to Examine the Definition of Brain Death. This committee identified four essential criteria for brain death; (1) lack of receptivity and response to external stimuli; (2) absence of spontaneous muscular movement and spontaneous breathing; (3) absence of observable reflexes, including brain and spinal reflexes; and (4) absence of brain activity, signified by a flat electroencephalogram (EEG).[30] Notice that these criteria incorporate the traditional means of determining death — heartbeat and blood flow. Procedures for applying these criteria have been adopted widely, particularly when the traditional means of determining death prove inconclusive. The criteria have been demonstrated to be valid for predicting the complete and irreversible loss of brain activity; the use of the Harvard criteria has not resulted in anyone being erroneously pronounced to be in an irreversible coma.[31] In a number of states, the main features of the Harvard criteria have been passed into law.

Irreversible Loss of the Capacity for Social Interaction

Although the Harvard criteria have gained wide acceptance, some believe they are too conservative; that is, they are criticized as too broad to specify what is essentially significant about human life. For example, Veatch argues that it is the higher funciton of the brain, not merely "reflex networks that regulate such things as blood pressure and respiration" that define the truly essential characteristics of a human being. Thus, the fourth approach to defining death emphasizes the capacity for consciousness and social interaction. The implicit premise of this aproach is that for a person to be fully human, not only must certain biological processes operate, but the social dimension of life — consciousness — must be present. Being alive implies the capacity for conscious interaction with one's environment and with other human beings. By this approach, when the capacity for social interaction is irreversibly lost, a determination of death would follow.

Using this approach, where should one look to determine whether an individual is alive or dead? Although the locus of consciousness as defined above is not absolutely established at present, and further neurophysiological studies are needed, current scientific evidence points to the neocortex, the outer surface of the brain, where processes essential to consciousness and social interaction are located. If the supposition proves correct, it is possible that the EEG alone would provide an adequate measure for determining death.

Any criteria employed under this fourth definition would be more selective than those used to fit the other definitions in current use. Consequently, a person considered dead by the criteria derived from the fourth definition could be considered alive by the heart-and-lung criterion of the Harvard committee — as Veatch says, a possibly false-positive diagnosis.

At present there is no consistent public policy for determining whether a person is alive or dead. Rather, various definitions and criteria are in use, each reflecting a particular concept of death and criteria for recognizing its occurrence. Public discussion on these matters is needed if we are to develop policies that reflect the pluralism within American society rather than a single mandate. As Veatch says, "If I am to be pronounced dead by the use of a philosophical or theological concept that I do not share, I at least have a right to careful due process."[32] Such due process in the definition and determination of death can come about only through responsible decisions that set public policy.

Modern medicine raises a thicket of difficult social and ethical issues. We have grown used to seeing members of the medical community try to resolve them in the courtroom. Sometimes they're there as expert witnesses, sometimes as defendants in malpractice suits. At other times they come seeking the protection of a judicial ruling, for example, on the circumstances in which a gravely ill patient has "the right to die" and "heroic" life support can be withdrawn. Once in a while it's a criminal matter. . . .

Moral uncertainties will continue to abound in medicine. No hospital rule book can do justice to the ambiguous circumstances in which lower-level line staff must translate institutional policy to humane practice. This is true, incidentally, not only for a licensed practical nurse at the bottom of a hospital pecking order, but for a policeman or social worker or a member of a dozen other occupations whose members deal daily with humanity's most painful contradictions. This is often underrespected, underpaid, emotionally draining work with impossibly complex multiple objectives: How simultaneously to follow a rulebook, get the job done and be humane?

Excerpts from an
editorial in the *Boston Sunday Globe*,
November 8, 1981

Legislation Defining Death

The responsibility of determining whether or not death has occurred in a particular case usually rests with the attending physician. Yet, as we have just seen, the philosophical and moral issues that impinge so greatly on deciding exactly what is meant by death must concern everyone. The definition of death touches upon many aspects of social life. Criminal prosecution, inheritance, taxation, treatment of the corpse, and mourning are all affected by the way society "draws the dividing line between life and death."[33] Many states have recognized that the traditional definition of death — that is, the cessation of the flow of vital bodily fluids — is sometimes inadequate in the present technological setting.

In 1970, Kansas became the first state to adopt brain-based criteria for determining death. A number of other states subsequently adopted similar statutes. Because the Kansas-inspired statute contained dual definitions of death (one based on cessation of vital functions and the other on brain functions), it did not provide a unitary description of death and therefore was criticized as potentially confusing.

In 1972, Alexander Capron and Leon Kass proposed an improvement on the Kansas statute that related the two standards for determining death.[34] This proposal was governed by the following five principles:

> (1) The statute should concern the death of a human being, not the death of cells, tissues, or organs, and not the "death or cessation of his role as a fully functioning member of his family or community." (2) It should move incrementally, supplementing rather than replacing the older cardiopulmonary standards. (3) It should avoid serving as a special definition for a special function such as transplantation. (4) It should apply uniformly to all persons. (5) It should be flexible, leaving specific criteria to the judgment of physicians.

With various modifications this proposal was adopted by several states. The proposal was criticized by some, however, because it did not address the issues raised by organ transplantation procedures; that is, it did not require at least two physicians to participate jointly in determining death, nor did it stipulate that the physician who pronounces death not be a member of the medical team seeking organs for transplantation. Capron and Kass responded to this criticism by asserting that transplant considerations ought to be dealt with in separate legislation dealing specifically with that subject, such as the Uniform Anatomical Gift Act.[35]

Another model statute was proposed in 1975 by the American Bar Association. It was designed to provide a definition of death "for all legal purposes." This proposal virtually ignored traditional cardiopulmonary criteria for determining death, focusing instead on the "irreversible cessation of total brain function." As with the earlier statutes, the ABA proposal, verbatim or with modification, was adopted by a number of states. These proposals were followed in 1978 by the Uniform Brain Death Act and, in 1979, by a model

---

Uniform Determination of Death Act

1. [*Determination of Death.*] An individual who has sustained either (1) irreversible cessation of circulatory and respiratory functions, or (2) irreversible cessation of all functions of the entire brain, including the brain stem, is dead. A determination of death must be made in accordance with accepted medical standards.

2. [*Uniformity of Construction and Application.*] This act shall be applied and construed to effectuate its general purpose to make uniform the law with respect to the subject of this Act among states enacting it.

Figure 10-2   *Uniform Determination of Death Act*
Source: President's Commission for the Study of Ethical Problems in Medicine and Biomedical and Behavioral Research, *Defining Death: A Report on the Medical, Legal and Ethical Issues in the Determination of Death* (Washington: Government Printing Office, 1981), p. 73.

proposed by the American Medical Association. Several states adopted statutes based upon either one or more of the proposed models or their own individual standards for determining death.

Finally, in 1981, the statute recommended by the President's Commission, known as the Uniform Determination of Death Act, was adopted by Colorado and Idaho, making them the first states to do so (see Figure 10-2). This proposal was designed to be broadly acceptable, thus easing the enactment of uniform law for defining and determining death throughout the United States. It has been widely endorsed by political and professional groups, including the American Bar Association and the American Medical Association, both of which approved the proposal as a substitute for their own earlier models. Recommending enactment of uniform statutory law, the Commission also said decisions about such a law should be left to the individual states, rather than imposed by the federal government.

According to the report of the Commission, the Uniform Determination of Death Act "addresses the matter of 'defining' death at the level of general physiological standards rather than at the level of more abstract concepts or the level of more precise criteria and tests," because these change over time as knowledge and techniques are refined. Since irreversible circulatory and respiratory cessation will be the obvious and sufficient basis for diagnosing death in the vast majority of cases, the statute acknowledges that fact by setting forth the basis on which death is determined in such cases; namely, that breathing and blood flow have ceased and cannot be restored or replaced.[36] When a patient is not supported on a respirator, the need to evaluate brain functions does not arise.

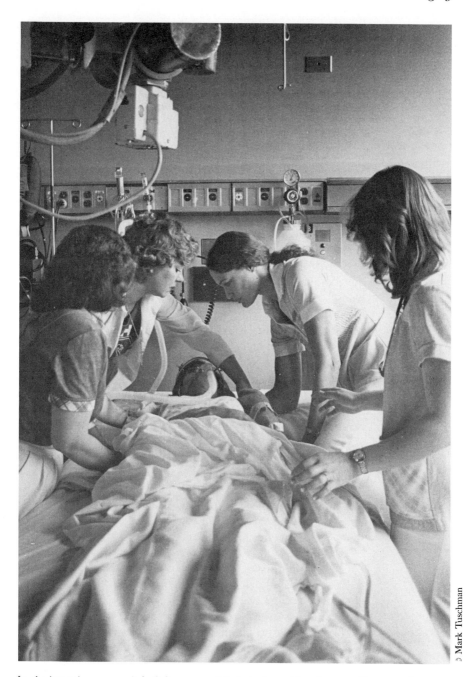

In the intensive-care unit both human and technical considerations combine to make necessary the evaluation of ethical questions regarding the meaning of life and death.

The Commission also said that a statutory definition of death should be kept separate and distinct from any provisions concerning organ donation and the termination of life-sustaining treatment. In contrast to most of the earlier proposals, which stated that a person would be "considered dead" when the criteria were met, the language of the Uniform Determination of Death Act is clearer and more direct. It states simply that a person who meets the standards set forth in the law "is dead."[37]

Confusion about the definition of death has arisen, the President's Commission said, "because the same technology not only keeps heart and lungs functioning in some who have irretrievably lost all brain functions but also sustains other, less severely injured patients." The result has been a "blurring of the important distinction between patients who are *dead* and those who are or may be *dying*." The Commission concluded that "proof of an irreversible absence of functions in the entire brain, including the brainstem, provides a highly reliable means of declaring death for respirator-maintained bodies."[38] Irreversible loss of functions of the whole brain is generally the result of: (1) direct trauma to the head, such as from a motor vehicle accident or gunshot wound, (2) massive hemorrhage into the brain from a ruptured aneurysm or from complications of high blood pressure, or (3) anoxic damage from cardiac or respiratory arrest or severely reduced blood pressure.[39]

The Commission argued that it would radically change the meaning of death to expand our definition to include persons who have lost all cognitive functions but still are able to breath spontaneously.[40] Death is an absolute and single phenomenon, the Commission said. Thus, even terms such as "brain dead" are misleading. When brainstem functions remain — for example, when respiration occurs naturally but there is no cognitive awareness — the condition of such a patient can be described as "persistent vegetative or noncognitive state." (This was the case with Karen Ann Quinlan, cited earlier.) Although one may observe involuntary movements and unassisted breathing in a person's body, the lack of higher brain functions indicates an absence of awareness of self and the environment. Sustained by medical and nursing care, including artificial feeding through intravenous or nasogastric tubes and antiobiotics to fight recurrent infections, such patients may survive for years without a respirator.[41]

The Commission emphasized a "whole brain" formulation in preference to a definition based on functions of the so-called "higher brain." In doing so, it cited the nearly universal acceptance of the "whole brain" concept by both the medical community and the general public. A "higher brain" formulation, on the other hand, would require agreement on the meaning of personhood, a concept that does not enjoy such consensus. If "personhood" is made to depend on a certain state of awareness or consciousness, then the severely senile or retarded individual could be excluded. Likewise, according to some proposed definitions, a person whose higher brain functions have been permanently damaged but whose lower brain continues to function might lack the qualities of "personhood." Yet such individuals are alive, not dead. At the present level of understanding and technique, said the Commission, "the 'higher brain' may well exist only as a metaphorical concept, not in reality."[42]

The rise of modern medical technologies has created a need to define more specifically the locus of death when the traditional criteria prove insufficient to make a determination of death. Despite considerable progress toward a working definition of death, our legal definitions are sometimes inadequate when applied in certain circumstances that arise during the process of dying. In short, our guidelines for determining death will require further refinement as we fashion public policy with regard to prevalent medical practices.

Yet perhaps the precise moments of both our entry into and exit from life will prove to be elusive. The search for scientific criteria that allow a definite determination of death may provide ever more precise, but not absolute, definitions. This is not to suggest that the search is futile. But ultimately there is no alternative to the human responsibility for making ethical decisions on matters of life and death in circumstances of fundamental ambiguity.

Further Readings

Tom L. Beauchamp and Seymour Perlin, editors. *Ethical Issues in Death and Dying*. Englewood Cliffs, N.J.: Prentice-Hall, 1978.

Leslie F. Degner and Janet I. Beaton. *Life-Death Decision Making in Health Care*. Washington, D.C.: Hemisphere, 1986.

Renee C. Fox. *Experiment Perilous: Physicians and Patients Facing the Unknown*. Philadelphia: University of Pennsylvania Press, 1974.

Renee C. Fox and Judith P. Swazey. *The Courage to Fail: A Social View of Organ Transplants and Dialysis*. Chicago: University of Chicago Press, 1974.

Rasa Gustaitis and Ernle W. D. Young. *A Time to Be Born, A Time to Die: Conflicts and Ethics in an Intensive Care Nursery*. Reading, Mass.: Addison-Wesley, 1986.

Frank Harron, John Burnside, and Tom Beauchamp. *Health and Human Values: A Guide to Making Your Own Decisions*. New Haven, Conn.: Yale University Press, 1983.

Albert R. Jonsen, Mark Siegler, and William J. Winslade. *Clinical Ethics: A Practical Approach to Ethical Decisions in Clinical Medicine*. New York: Macmillan, 1982.

Jay Katz and Alexander M. Capron. *Catastrophic Diseases: Who Decides What? A Psychosocial and Legal Analysis of the Problems Posed by Hemodialysis and Organ Transplantation*. New York: Russell Sage Foundation, 1975.

Stanley Joel Reiser, Arthur J. Dyck, and William J. Curran, editors. *Ethics in Medicine: Historical Perspectives and Contemporary Concerns*. Cambridge, Mass.: MIT Press, 1977.

Earl E. Shelp. *Born to Die? Deciding the Fate of Critically Ill Newborns*. New York: Free Press, 1986.

Roberta G. Simmons, Susan D. Klein, and Richard L. Simmons. *Gift of Life: Social and Psychological Impact of Organ Transplantation*. New York: Halsted Press/Wiley, 1977.

Robert M. Veatch. *A Theory of Medical Ethics*. New York: Basic Books, 1981.

William J. Winslade and Judith Wilson Ross. *Choosing Life or Death: A Guide for Patients, Families, and Professionals*. New York: Free Press, 1986.

This drawing by William A. Rogers, Reading the Will, *humorously depicts some of the emotional responses heirs may experience during probate. Besides issues involving wills and probate, the judicial system touches on many other aspects of death and dying; these range from trying homicide cases to settling questions involving the continuance of life support to a hopelessly comatose patient.*

The Law and Death

*F*rom the relative simplicity of filing a death certificate to the settling of a complicated estate, the law and legalities impinge upon our experiences of death and dying. In some cases, laws serve to increase our options; in other cases, they restrict them.

We examine first the legalities involved in the so-called living will, or natural death directive, and then the process of organ donation as formalized by the Uniform Anatomical Gift Act. Both of these legal developments are directly related to the material covered in the previous chapter on ethical decisions in medicine.

We then examine administrative and institutional concerns, such as the death certificate, the role of the coroner and the medical examiner, and the procedures involved in autopsies. We also discuss how these reflect societal interests in the circumstances surrounding and following death. The remainder of the chapter deals with making a will, probating an estate, paying estate and inheritance taxes, and claiming insurance and other death benefits.

Living Wills

In a *living will,* also known as a natural death directive, a person requests that medical heroics be avoided when death is imminent, that life-sustaining devices and extraordinary medical procedures not be used when there is no realistic chance of recovery. The living will is partly a way to protect physicians from accusations of malpractice and from civil liability

Editor: If the governor signs the bill currently before him, this will become the first state to legalize suicide.

I believe this measure is immoral, bizarre, and tainted with Mephistophelian connotations.

Legislators, at all levels, should legislate laws pertaining only to life, as we know it. Death, in any manner, is nature's absolute domain, and no one should attempt to trespass on that domain.

I trust the governor is wise enough and sane enough to veto the bill presently lying heavily and cadaverously on his desk.

Editor: We have explored this bill and its implications in death and fully support the right of an individual, who wishes to do so, to be allowed to make a legally recognized written directive requesting withdrawal of life-support systems when these procedures would serve no purpose except to artificially delay the moment of death.

We reiterate our belief in the basic human right of an individual to control his destiny. We have communicated our support of this bill to the legislature and to the governor.

Editor: This bill, and all other natural-death or death-with-dignity bills, is based on a faulty premise. For when we react to tubes, oxygen and other paraphernalia, our concern is with daintiness, not dignity.

Dignity is the quality of mind having to do with worth, nobility, and forbearance. The dying, with the help of the living, can have dignity—no matter what functions of control are lost.

Instead of unplugging and abandoning our dying patients, we should work to achieve truly compassionate care for them in hospices like those in London, England, and New Haven, Connecticut.

Editor: No physician is required by law to use extraordinary means of preserving life, and none has ever been convicted for failing to do so.

So the real purpose of death-with-dignity or natural-death bills must be to set the stage for letting doctors take positive action: giving lethal injections or denying ordinary means of care to patients who may be handicapped or burdensome to society.

We must be suspicious of any trend which offers death as a solution to problems, no matter how heart-rending those problems may be.

Editor: The bill allowing an adult of sound mind to refuse extraordinary life-preservation measures reaffirms for me the value of life. Life is active choosing toward greater fulfillment and reduced suffering, not the beating of a heart in a pain-wracked and hopeless body. This bill is a public and legal recognition of that principle.

Figure 11-1   *Letters in Response to Proposed Living Will Legislation*

or criminal prosecution when they follow a patient's directive and has achieved widespread notice in a relatively brief time. As the letters in Figure 11-1 indicate, however, the use of such a document is not free of controversy.

Whereas opponents argue that living wills are a step toward society's acceptance of active euthanasia, possibly leading to abuses such as arbitrarily withdrawing nutrition from patients thought to be close to death, proponents believe living wills safeguard the rights of patients to determine the manner of their own dying.

Some form of legislation relative to living wills has been enacted in most states.[1] Such legislation typically stipulates that a living will can be executed at any time by an adult and that it remains in force—unless amended by the signer—for a specified period of years (in one instance, for five years; in another, for seven). In some cases, before a living will is presumed to be valid, a person must be declared a "qualified patient" (that is, he or she must be in a terminal condition) before executing the directive. Otherwise, the attending physician will not be bound by the directive and may consider other factors—such as information from the patient's family and the nature of the illness, injury, or disease—before deciding whether the directive should be implemented.

In many states living wills are not always legally binding. There may be few, if any, guarantees to ensure that a patient's wishes will be carried out. Thus, whether the wishes expressed in a living will or natural death directive are followed may depend largely upon the policies of a given health care institution and standard practices within a community or jurisdiction.

Uncertainty about the projected course of an illness or a disease may cause doctors to be wary of committing themselves to the declaration that a patient is hopelessly terminal. Too, a patient having reached such a stage may not be capable of signing a natural death directive or of ensuring that its provisions are followed. Indeed, the implementation of a natural death directive may depend largely on the nature of the relationship between patient and physician and on the physician's willingness to abide by the patient's wishes.

Although there is growing interest in making such options available when the severity of an illness or injury allows no reasonable chance of recovery, at present a person may encounter difficulties in formalizing this choice. In some instances, an individual's written personal statement to his or her physician expressing specific wishes may be more reliable than a particular form. In effect, the natural death directive may be less a directive than a request.

Recognizing this limitation, California enacted legislation in 1985 providing for a Durable Power of Attorney for Health Care (see Figure 11-2). An individual can now complete a document that *does* have the force of law in the state of California. This document allows a person to designate an agent who is empowered to make health care decisions, particularly with respect to the withholding or withdrawal of life-sustaining treatment. An agent must act consistently with a patient's wishes as specifically stated in the document itself or as otherwise made known. In addition, a court may take away the agent's power to make decisions if he or she: (1) authorizes any illegal act; (2) acts contrary to the patient's known desires; or (3) where those desires are not known, does anything clearly contrary to the patient's best interests.

Unless revoked orally or in writing by the person making it, the Durable Power of Attorney for Health Care is effective in California for seven years from the date of its execution; and, if the person is unable to make health care decisions at the end of that period, the power of attorney remains in force until he or she can make such decisions. This California statute is an indicator both of the evolving nature of living will legislation and of support for the idea that

---

Statement of Wishes

TO MY FAMILY, MY PHYSICIAN, AND MY ATTORNEY:

If the time comes when I can no longer take part in decisions for my own future, let this statement stand as my wishes.

If there is no reasonable expectation of my recovery from physical or mental disability, I request that I be allowed to die and not be kept alive by artificial means or heroic measures. Death is as much a reality as birth, growth, maturity, and old age — it is the one certainty. I do not fear death as much as I fear the indignity of deterioration, dependence, and hopeless pain. I ask that drugs be mercifully administered to me for terminal suffering even if they hasten the moment of death.

This request is made after careful consideration. Any physician or any other person following these wishes shall be released from any liability whatever as a result of following said wishes.

Dated: _____

Signature: _____

Figure 11-2   *Statement of Wishes for Optional Use with California's Durable Power of Attorney for Health Care*

individuals should be permitted to make decisions about their own health care even as they approach death.

Organ Donation

The Uniform Anatomical Gift Act, enacted in some form in all fifty states, provides for the donation of the body or specific body parts upon the death of the donor.[2] Although today fewer cadavers are needed for medical education, organs and body parts are needed for transplantation. Many organs are needed, and many people are gratified that by donating an organ they will help others even after their own death.

Organs can be donated by completing a form such as the uniform donor card (see Figure 11-3). A donor may specify that only certain body parts or organs are available for donation or may state that any needed organs or body parts may be taken. Besides specifying how one's body may be used after death, the donor may also specify the final disposition of his or her remains once the donation has been effected.

Although the Uniform Anatomical Gift Act is a legal instrument, the deceased's wishes are sometimes thwarted by strong objections from a prospective donor's family. A hospital is not likely to take the donated organ if the

---

UNIFORM DONOR CARD

OF_____
                    Print or type name of donor

In the hope that I may help others, I hereby make this anatomical gift, if medically acceptable, to take effect upon my death. The words and marks below indicate my desires.

I give: (a) —— any needed organs or parts
         (b) —— only the following organs or parts

_____
                Specify the organ(s) or part(s)

for the purposes of transplantation, therapy, medical research or education;

         (c) —— my body for anatomical study if needed.

Limitations or
special wishes, if any: _____

Signed by the donor and the following two witnesses in the presence of each other:

_____   _____
    Signature of Donor   Date of Birth of Donor

_____   _____
      Date Signed   City & State

_____   _____
        Witness   Witness

This is a legal document under the Uniform Anatomical Gift Act
or similar laws.

For further information consult your physician or

National Kidney Foundation
315 Park Avenue South, New York, NY 10016

Figure 11-3 *Uniform Donor Card*
Source: National Kidney Foundation.

family adamantly disagrees with the deceased's wishes. Thus, as with other posthumous provisions, one should discuss plans to make an organ donation with family members to determine their feelings.

Although the success achieved with organ transplants has given hope to the seriously ill, it has also created a waiting list of patients seeking donor organs. In some states, legislators are attempting to increase the availability of scarce organs. In 1986, California joined New York and Oregon in *requiring* general acute care hospitals to ask families for permission to uses needed organs when a patient dies. Other states are considering similar legislation. These laws require hospitals to develop a protocol for identifying potential organ and tissue donors and to notify and cooperate with organ procurement centers when organs have been donated. At or near the time of death, a hospital must ask the deceased's family whether the deceased was an organ donor; and, if not, the family must be informed about the option to donate organs and tissues. The hospital protocol, according to the law, should "encourage reasonable discretion and sensitivity to the family circumstances" in discussing organ donation with surviving family members.

The National Organ Transplant Act, enacted by Congress in 1984, provides for a nationwide organ-sharing network designed to help coordinate the matching of donated organs with potential recipients. Interest in such a network was stimulated by reports of American kidneys being exported and sold despite the need for such organs in this country and by the potential for abuses resulting from commercialization of donated organs. As the proposed organ-sharing network is envisioned, a computer will be used to match organ donations with waiting transplant recipients and a system developed to track the status of all donated and transplanted organs in the United States.[3]

The Death Certificate

On the face of it, the document used to certify the facts of death seems quite straightforward, a concise summary of the pertinent data regarding the deceased and the mode and place of death. As Edwin Shneidman and others have shown, however, this seemingly simple document has much broader implications than one might at first imagine.[4]

Although death certificates vary from state to state, most follow the general format outlined by the United States Standard Certificate of Death. In addition to its value and purpose as a legal document that affects disposition of property rights, life insurance benefits, pension payments, and so on, the usefulness of the death certificate extends to such diverse matters as aiding in crime detection, tracing genealogy, and gaining knowledge about the incidence of disease and other aspects of physical and psychological health.

Death certificates, says Shneidman, should reflect both a private and a public function. Certification of death ought to be concerned with the facts of death, not only as experienced by the person who died but also as experienced and accounted for by witnesses. The typical death certificate now in use (see Figure 11-4) provides for noting only four different *modes* of death: accidental, suicidal, homicidal, and natural. As Shneidman points out, the *cause* of death isn't necessarily the same as the *mode* of death. For example, if a death were caused by asphyxiation due to drowning, should such a death be classified as an accident, a suicide, or a homicide? Any of these modes might apply.

Underlying these basic distinctions between mode and cause is the more complex issue of untangling the intentions and subconscious factors, the states of mind and actions, that may have contributed, directly or indirectly, to the death. For instance, if an intoxicated person jumps into a swimming pool with no one else present and drowns, is the death accidental or suicidal? Does it make a difference to the answer whether the impetus for alcohol abuse resulted from emotional distress and feelings of despondency?

Or what is the mode of death if the cocktails were served by a too-generous hostess? What if the person serving the excessive alcohol were also an heir of the person who dies? Obviously, intentions can be far more complex than allowed for by the relatively elementary distinctions concerning mode and cause of death now listed on most death certificates. A pilot study was done in Marin County, California, to assess the conventional classifications of mode of death as well as the lethality of the deceased's intention. The study revealed that some deaths classified as natural, accidental, and homicidal were also precipitated by the deceased's own actions; the deceased had lethal intentions against himself or herself.

The Coroner and the Medical Examiner

Most deaths in the United States result from disease. In such cases, usually the physician attending the patient at the time of death completes and signs the

CERTIFICATE OF DEATH
STATE OF CALIFORNIA

STATE FILE NUMBER				**LOCAL REGISTRATION DISTRICT AND CERTIFICATE NUMBER**		

DECEDENT PERSONAL DATA

1A. NAME OF DECEDENT—FIRST | 1B. MIDDLE | 1C. LAST | 2A. DATE OF DEATH (MONTH, DAY, YEAR) | 2B. HOUR

3. SEX | 4. RACE | 5. ETHNICITY | 6. DATE OF BIRTH | 7. AGE | IF UNDER 1 YEAR MONTHS / DAYS | IF UNDER 24 HOURS HOURS / MINUTES

8. BIRTHPLACE OF DECEDENT (STATE OR FOREIGN COUNTRY) | 9. NAME AND BIRTHPLACE OF FATHER | 10. BIRTH NAME AND BIRTHPLACE OF MOTHER

11. CITIZEN OF WHAT COUNTRY | 12. SOCIAL SECURITY NUMBER | 13. MARITAL STATUS | 14. NAME OF SURVIVING SPOUSE (IF WIFE, ENTER BIRTH NAME)

15. PRIMARY OCCUPATION | 16. NUMBER OF YEARS THIS OCCUPATION | 17. EMPLOYER (IF SELF-EMPLOYED, SO STATE) | 18. KIND OF INDUSTRY OR BUSINESS

USUAL RESIDENCE

19A. USUAL RESIDENCE—STREET ADDRESS (STREET AND NUMBER OR LOCATION) | 19B. | 20. NAME AND ADDRESS OF INFORMANT—RELATIONSHIP

19C. CITY OR TOWN | 19D. COUNTY | 19E. STATE

PLACE OF DEATH

21A. PLACE OF DEATH | 21B. STREET ADDRESS (STREET AND NUMBER OR LOCATION)

21C. CITY OR TOWN | 21D. COUNTY

CAUSE OF DEATH

22. DEATH WAS CAUSED BY: (ENTER ONLY ONE CAUSE PER LINE FOR A, B, AND C) | 24. WAS DEATH REPORTED TO CORONER?

IMMEDIATE CAUSE (A) | APPROXIMATE INTERVAL BETWEEN ONSET AND DEATH | 25. WAS BIOPSY PERFORMED?

CONDITIONS, IF ANY, WHICH GAVE RISE TO THE IMMEDIATE CAUSE, STATING THE UNDERLYING CAUSE LAST | DUE TO, OR AS A CONSEQUENCE OF (B) | DUE TO, OR AS A CONSEQUENCE OF (C) | 26. WAS AUTOPSY PERFORMED?

23. OTHER CONDITIONS CONTRIBUTING BUT NOT RELATED TO THE IMMEDIATE CAUSE OF DEATH | 27. WAS OPERATION PERFORMED FOR ANY CONDITION IN ITEMS 22 OR 23? OPERATION / DATE

PHYSICIAN'S CERTIFICATION

28A. I CERTIFY THAT DEATH OCCURRED AT THE HOUR, DATE AND PLACE STATED FROM THE CAUSES STATED. I ATTENDED DECEDENT SINCE (ENTER MO. DA. YR.) I LAST SAW DECEDENT ALIVE (ENTER MO. DA. YR.) | 28B. PHYSICIAN—SIGNATURE AND DEGREE OR TITLE | 28C. DATE SIGNED | 28D. PHYSICIAN'S LICENSE NUMBER

28E. TYPE PHYSICIAN'S NAME AND ADDRESS

INJURY INFORMATION

29. SPECIFY ACCIDENT, SUICIDE, ETC. | 30. PLACE OF INJURY | 31. INJURY AT WORK | 32A. DATE OF INJURY—MONTH, DAY, YEAR | 32B. HOUR

33. LOCATION (STREET AND NUMBER OR LOCATION AND CITY OR TOWN) | 34. DESCRIBE HOW INJURY OCCURRED (EVENTS WHICH RESULTED IN INJURY)

CORONER'S USE ONLY

35A. I CERTIFY THAT DEATH OCCURRED AT THE HOUR, DATE AND PLACE STATED FROM THE CAUSES STATED. AS REQUIRED BY LAW I HAVE HELD AN (INQUEST-INVESTIGATION) | 35B. CORONER—SIGNATURE AND DEGREE OR TITLE | 35C. DATE SIGNED

FUNERAL DIRECTOR AND LOCAL REGISTRAR

36. DISPOSITION | 37. DATE—MONTH, DAY, YEAR | 38. NAME AND ADDRESS OF CEMETERY OR CREMATORY | 39. EMBALMER'S LICENSE NUMBER

40. NAME OF FUNERAL DIRECTOR (OR PERSON ACTING AS SUCH) | 41. LOCAL REGISTRAR—SIGNATURE | 42. DATE ACCEPTED BY LOCAL REGISTRAR

STATE REGISTRAR

A. | B. | C. | D. | E. | F.

VS-11 (1-78)

Figure 11-4 *Certificate of Death in Use in California*
Source: California Department of Health Services, Vital Statistics Branch.

death certificate. When death is sudden or occurs in suspicious circumstances, the cause of death must be determined by a coroner or medical examiner. Suspected homicides and suicides are investigated, as are accidents, deaths that occur on the job, deaths that occur in jails and other government institutions, deaths that occur in hospitals or similar facilities when negligence is suspected or the death was unexpected, and deaths that occur at home when there is no attending physician who is able to sign the death certificate attesting to the cause of death.

The cause of death is determined by use of various scientific procedures,

© Carol A. Foote

When death occurs under suspicious or uncertain circumstances, the coroner or medical examiner usually directs an investigation to determine the cause of death. If foul play is suspected, a police or sheriff's department investigation is undertaken.

possibly including an autopsy, toxicology and bacteriology tests, chemical analyses, and other studies that are necessary to arrive at adequate findings. The results of such a postmortem examination may play a crucial role in court cases or insurance settlements. Too, the outcome of such proceedings may be important not only to law enforcement agencies but also to the families involved: Whether a death is due to foul play, negligence, suicide, accident, or natural causes can have a significant emotional effect on survivors. Unlike autopsies performed as part of medical training or at a family's request, investigations that come under the purview of the coroner or medical examiner are required by law.

It should be noted that usually the coroner is an elected official and the medical examiner is most often appointed. The major difference between these two positions, however, has to do with training. Whereas the coroner may not need any special background or training, the medical examiner is a qualified medical doctor, generally with advanced training and certification in forensic pathology (that is, the application of medical knowledge to questions of law). In addition to responsibilities for investigating the cause of death in questionable circumstances, the medical examiner often plays a key role in community health programs such as suicide prevention, drug abuse education, and research.[5]

The office of coroner developed in England approximately 800 to 900 years ago. Coroners were originally referred to as "crowners," the name deriving from the fact that they were officially appointed by the Crown to represent the King's interests in the investigation of violent, unexplained, and suspicious deaths, and more importantly, in the disposition of any personal or real property that became available under the existing laws following a homicide or suicide. The Latin word for crown is *corona*, and hence in later years the name of the office came to be called coroner.

> Cyril H. Wecht, "The Coroner and Death"

Autopsies

An *autopsy* can be defined as a postmortem examination of a corpse to determine the cause of death or to investigate the extent and nature of changes caused by disease. An autopsy may be performed for legal or official reasons, or as part of a hospital's teaching or research program. Those hospitals that aspire to achieve and maintain official status as teaching institutions must carry out a relatively high percentage of autopsies. In such hospitals, autopsies are used to confirm diagnosis, train doctors, and conduct research. In the United States, the number of autopsies has dropped to about 14 percent of all deaths. This relatively low rate severely limits the number of studies that could result in medical benefits.

Sometimes, the deceased's family will request an autopsy to determine whether genetic or infectious conditions led to death or to help resolve questions about possible malpractice. Except when required by law, an autopsy can be performed only after the next of kin's consent is obtained.[6]

When death occurs in suspicious circumstances or is related to a suspected criminal act, an autopsy is often required by law. The autopsies ordered in such instances are generally conducted under the supervision of the coroner or medical examiner.

Laws Regulating Body Disposition

In most states the deceased's next of kin are responsible for disposition of the body. When the deceased has provided for donation of the body or body parts, the final disposition of the remains is often left to the discretion of the hospital, medical school, or other medical institution that has possession of the body. Even in these instances, however, the next of kin is usually able to have a say in the final disposition of the remains once the medical purposes have been achieved.

The responsibility of the next of kin to arrange for the final disposition of the body is circumscribed by laws governing the manner in which disposition may be effected. For example, some communities have enacted ordinances

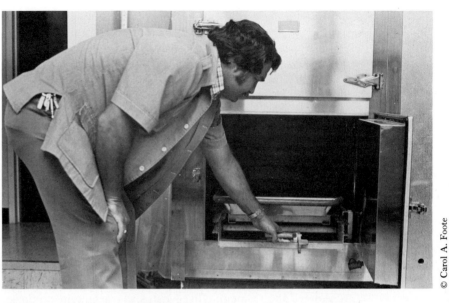

© Carol A. Foote

When a coroner's preliminary investigation reveals the need to scientifically determine the cause of death, the corpse is brought to the morgue, where it is held until an autopsy can be performed.

The autopsy, or medical examination to determine the cause of death, is conducted under the coroner's direction when the circumstances of a death are violent, suspicious, or unexplained, or when a death is medically unattended and a doctor is unable to certify the cause of death. All homicides, accidents, and suicides come under the coroner's or medical examiner's jurisdiction.

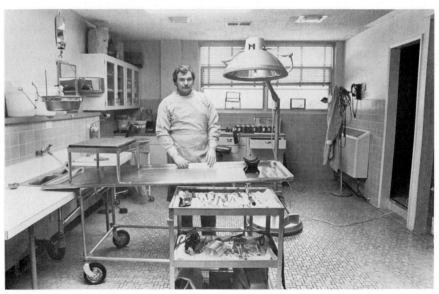

© Carol A. Foote

prohibiting burial of a corpse within city limits. Although the general policies regulating body disposition are more or less uniform throughout the United States, laws and ordinances do vary among states and localities. Some of these differences as regards the practice of embalming are discussed in Chapter 6 in connection with funerals and body disposition.

Wills

A legal document expressing a person's intentions and wishes for the disposition of his or her property after death, the *will* is a valuable tool for planning one's estate and for conveying property to one's beneficiaries. Conferring a kind of immortality on the *testator* (the person making the will), a will can be thought of as the deceased's last words; as such the will can become a focal point for powerful emotions, embodying as it does the testator's feelings and intentions toward his or her survivors.

Many people think of a will as simply a tool for financial planning, perhaps overlooking its important comforting effects for testator and survivors. Barton Bernstein, a lawyer who has written widely on this point, says that the attorney who assists in drawing up a will and in executing it can perform a valuable service in helping survivors to deal with bereavement and to handle their affairs during the period of mourning.

Many terminally ill patients and their families seek the help of counselors and other mental health professionals as a means of exploring their fears, uncertainties, and conflicts as well as devising a plan to meet the prospects that lie ahead. Bernstein believes that lawyers should be included as part of that interdisciplinary team. Otherwise, although the help obtained from such professionals can be a tremendous aid in clarifying concerns, opening communication channels, and enhancing interpersonal relationships, the task of planning for a future that will not include the dying family member may be neglected.

"What would you like for breakfast, Jack?" I asked my son-in-law on Sunday, the day after the funeral.

"A fried egg, over," he replied.

Such a simple thing. Yet, I'd never fried an egg.

Oh, we often had them on weekends; but my husband was the breakfast cook, while I dashed up and down the steps putting clothes in the washer, running the vacuum, and all the other tasks always awaiting a working wife.

I stood there, the frying pan in one hand, the egg in the other.

How many times in the future would I find myself standing the same way? How many things had I never done? How many things had I taken for granted?

Maxine Dowd Jensen,
The Warming of Winter

The death of a major breadwinner can be especially devastating. Bernstein points out that estate planning not only can optimize survivors' financial security but also helps ensure peace of mind to survivors and to the terminally ill person, who can be confident that his or her affairs have been put in order. Additionally, the service of a lawyer may be effectively used to ensure that the dying person's wishes regarding organ donation or the terms of a natural death directive are carried out.[7]

In cases of terminal illness, when death follows expected medical probabilities there are three basic legal stages.[8] The first stage involves long-range planning, in which the terminally ill person arranges his or her legal and financial affairs for the eventuality of death. During the second stage, which occurs shortly before death, the survivors gather pertinent legal papers, obtain sufficient funds to cover immediate expenses, and notify the attorney and insurance representative so they will be ready to make a smooth transition of the deceased's legal and financial affairs. Also at this time, if the dying person intends to make an anatomical gift, the appropriate medical personnel are alerted.

In the third stage of legal activity, which follows the family member's death, preparations for burial are made, the will is delivered to an attorney for probate, and various other legal and financial professionals come into the picture. The effort that went into planning is now rewarded in the survivors' greater sense of security and certainty that affairs have not been left to chance. The survivors can confront their loss without the distraction and worry of a complex legal and financial entanglement.

Definitions and Elements of Wills

The right or privilege to determine how one's property will be distributed following death is not available in all societies, nor is it without limitations. Whereas in some countries the government automatically assumes control over the settlement of a person's affairs, in the United States the individual has much more liberty in determining how property will be distributed. Still, depending on the laws of a particular state, enforcing and carrying out the provisions of a

And in a decade or two or more when death taps at the door, your estate may be far larger than you now envisage. It may be so already. One tends to think in terms of a few principal segments of one's estate. For purposes of planning, your "estate" includes everything of monetary value: your home and other real estate; all bank and savings accounts; usables including *objets d'art* and hobbies, such as a stamp collection; your carefully planned investment portfolio; life insurance; rights under a pension plan, if you enjoy that umbrella; as well as growing protection from social security. All must be arranged so as to afford maximum benefit to the beneficiaries.

Paul P. Ashley, *You and Your Will*

will may be restricted by circumstances that affect one's heirs. For example, someone may try to avoid willing anything to his or her spouse, but if the will is contested it may be overturned by a court. Some statutes require that dependent children be provided for in the will. Sometimes a court overrules provisions made in a will. The rule of thumb is that anything in a will that clearly conflicts with ordinary standards of social policy may be abrogated or made invalid if the will is contested.

The person who makes a will must have the mental capacity to understand the nature of the document and the consequences of signing it. He or she must understand the nature and extent of the property being bequeathed by the will and be able to identify the persons who, by convention, ought to be considered when making a will, whether or not they actually become beneficiaries. Given these conditions, and in the absence of any significant delusions, the testator is said to be of sound mind, capable of executing a legal will. State laws generally specify a minimum age at which a person can make a legal will — usually eighteen, though in several states as young as fourteen — and various other requirements, such as the presence of witnesses and execution of the document in a proper form.

In addition to standard information such as the testator's identification and a declaration that the document constitutes the person's last will and testament (along with a statement revoking previous wills, if applicable), a will may include information regarding the property to be distributed, the names of children and other heirs, specific bequests and allocations of property, as well as information concerning the establishment of trusts, the granting of powers to a trustee and/or guardian, other provisions for disposition of property, and payment of taxes, debts, and expenses of administration. An *executor* of the will, a person who will see that the provisions in the will are carried out properly, is named, and an attestation clause, which is signed by the persons witnessing the testator's making of the will, is included. Not all these items are necessarily part of every will, nor is a will limited to the items listed here. For instance, an additional provision may delineate how property is to be distributed when simultaneous accidental deaths occur. Many wills contain a provision spelling out the lines of succession should the primary beneficiary die before the estate can be settled.

Most attorneys encourage people making their wills to involve spouses in the process to prevent problems that can arise when each spouse makes out a will separately or without the other's knowledge. When survivors find out after the testator's death that things are not as expected, an added burden of pain and confusion makes coping with the death that much more difficult. There is no requirement, however, that one's spouse be involved in the making of a will.

Keeping in mind these general principles regarding wills, we now proceed to an examination of various types of wills and some of the nuts-and-bolts issues that pertain to making a will. A *holographic will* is one written entirely by the hand of the person signing it. Some states do not recognize holographic wills as valid, and those that do generally have stringent conditions for such a document to be deemed valid. Therefore, a holographic will should not be considered a substitute for a formally executed will.

Subject to even stricter requirements, and thus even less desirable, is the *nuncupative will,* which is made orally. Indeed, many states do not recognize a nuncupative will, or do so only under extremely limited circumstances. A few states admit an oral will if the person makes it in fear of imminent death or expectation of receiving mortal injuries, and the peril does result in death. A nuncupative will may also be valid when made by a soldier or sailor engaged in military service or by a mariner at sea; in these instances, the individual need not be in immediate peril. Generally, an oral will must be witnessed by at least two persons who agree to attest that the will is indeed a statement of the testator's wishes. Because of the limitations, however, and because it is not valid in all state jurisdictions, a nuncupative will is not recommended.

The Formally Executed Will

The *formally executed will* is the conventional document used for specifying a person's wishes for the distribution of his or her estate after death (see Figure 11-5). If carefully and sensitively prepared, it not only has sufficient clarity of purpose and expression to withstand a court's scrutiny, but can help ease the burden and stress on survivors while demonstrating the testator's affection for those who were close during life.

There is more than one type of formally executed will. The *mutual will,* which contains reciprocal provisions, is used by many husbands and wives who wish to leave everything to the other spouse with no restrictions. Such a will says, in effect, "I leave everything to my spouse." However useful for many people, the mutual will has a potential disadvantage in that it limits the range of choices that are available when a will is executed individually.

The *conditional will,* another type of formally executed will that is useful in some circumstances, states that certain actions will take place provided that a specified future event occurs. For example, suppose a potential beneficiary is living in an institution and is incapable of self-care, but there is a reasonable chance of recovery within a few years. A testator might want to bequeath money or property to that person, but make receipt contingent upon the person's recovery. With a conditional will, the money or property could be held in trust for that person until the conditions specified in the will have been satisfied. Although such a will can be appropriate under certain circumstances, some estate planners recommend against making a conditional will because of the difficulty of stipulating with exactitude the nature of events and circumstances that might occur in the future.

To make a formally executed will, it is usually necessary to consult an attorney. A comprehensive review of an estate may require that various records and other information be gathered.[9] During the meeting with the attorney, the nature of the property and the testator's wishes for its distribution are discussed.

Many of the legal issues surrounding death can be clarified with the help of a competent attorney who is versed in the options available to clients.

Several meetings may be required to carefully plan and consider the ramifications of various alternatives.

Once the will's content is finally determined and its provisions set, the attorney has it typed and an appointment is made for its formal execution. On that occasion, two (in some states, three) disinterested persons are brought in to serve as witnesses, the will is reviewed, the testator acknowledges that the document is his, and signs it. Although preparation of the will may involve weeks or even months of thoughtful consideration and planning, the actual signing can take less than five minutes. Once the will is signed and witnessed, the testator is assured that the distribution of the estate according to his or her wishes is protected by a valid legal document.[10]

Codicils

A will is not unchangeable. It can be revoked and replaced by a new will or amended. An amendment to a will is called a *codicil*. Amending a will is a means of adding new provisions without having to rewrite it entirely. For instance, a testator who, after the will has been executed, acquires valuable property, such as an art collection, might want to make a specific provision for the new property without disturbing other parts of the estate plan. A codicil,

Will of Tomás Antonio Yorba

In the name of the Holy Trinity, Father, Son, and the Holy Ghost, three distinct persons and one true God, Amen.

1st Clause. Know all [men] who may read this my last will and testament: that I—Tomás Antonio Yorba, native born resident of this department of California, legitimate son of Antonio Yorba and Josefa Grijalva—being sick, but, by divine mercy, in the full enjoyment of my reason, memory and understanding, believing, as I firmly do, in all the mysteries of our holy Catholic faith, which faith is natural to me, since I have lived in it from my infancy and I declare that I want to live in it as a faithful Christian and true Catholic, trusting that, for this reason, his divine Majesty will have mercy on me and will pardon all my sins, through the mysteries of our Lord Jesus Christ and the intercession of his most holy mother, who is my protector and benefactress in these my last moments, so that together with my guardian angel, with St. Joseph, my own name's saint, and all the other saints of my devotion and all the other hosts of heaven, they will assist me before the grand tribunal of God, before which all mortals must render account of their actions—make and decree this my last will and testament as follows, in ordinary paper because of lack of stamped paper.

2nd Clause. Firstly, I commend my soul to God who created it, and my body to the earth, from whence it was fashioned, and it is my wish that I be buried in the church of the Mission of San Gabriel in the shroud of our father St. Francis, the funeral to be according to what my executors and heirs consider that I deserve and is befitting.

3rd Clause. Item: In regard to the expenses of the funeral and masses, these should be drawn from the fifth of my estate, according to the disposition of my executors, and I leave the residue of this fifth to my son Juan.

4th Clause. I declare that with respect to my debts, my heirs and executors should collect and pay any legal claims that may turn up or be due according to law. Item: I declare to have been married to Doña Vicenta Sepúlveda, legitimate daughter of Don Francisco Sepúlveda and Doña Ramona Sepúlveda, of this neighborhood, by which marriage I had five children named: (1) Juan; (2) Guadalupe, deceased; (3) José Antonio; (4) Josefa; (5) Ramona. The first being 10 years old, the second died at the age of three, the third six years old, the fourth four years old, and the fifth two years old. Item: I declare to have given my wife jewels of some value as a wedding present, but I do not remember how many, nor their value; but they must be in her possession, since I gave them to her. Item: According to my reckoning I have about 2,000 head of cattle, 900 ewes and their respective males, three herds of about 100 mares and their stallions, and three donkeys; about 21 tame horses, 7 tame and 12 unbroken mules; and lastly, whatever cattle, horses or mules may turn up with my brand which may not have been legally sold. Item: I declare to have the right—through inheritance from my father—to part of Middle Santa Ana and Lower Santana, known to be of the Yorbas. I have in Middle Santa Ana an adobe house, its roof being part timber and part thatched, consisting of 18 rooms, including the soap-house. Item: I declare that I have two vineyards with wooden fences which are now planted with bearing vines and some fruit trees; also a section of enclosed land.

5th Clause. I declare that it is my wish to name as executors and guardians of my estate, first, my brother, Don Bernardo Yorba, and second, Don Raimundo Yorba, by joint approval, to whom

continued

continued from previous page

I give all my vested power, as much as may be necessary, to go in and examine my property for the benefit of my heirs in carrying out this will, and I grant them the power to procure another associate [executor] to expedite its due execution, whom I consider appointed as a matter of course, granting him the same authority as those previously named.

6th Clause. I name as my heirs my children and my wife, in the form and manner indicated by the laws, following the necessary inventory.

7th Clause. In this my last will, I annul and void whatever will or wills, codicil or codicils, I may have previously made, so that they may stand nullified with or without judicial process, now and forever, since I definitely desire that the present testamentary disposition be my last will, codicil, and final wish, in the manner and form most legally valid. To this effect I beg of Don Vicente Sanchez, Judge of 1st *instancia*, to exercise his authority in probating this will

To which I, the citizen Vicente Sanchez, 1st constitutional Alcalde and Judge of the 1st *instancia* of the city of Los Angeles, certify; and I affirm that the present testamentary disposition was made in my presence, and that the testator, Don Tomás Antonio Yorba, although ill, finds himself in the full command of his faculties and natural understanding, and, to attest it, I do this before the assistant witnesses—the citizens Ramon Aguilar and Ignacio Coronel—the other instrumental witnesses being the citizens Bautista Mutriel and Mariano Martinez; on the 28th day of the month of January, 1845. The testator did not sign because of physical inability, but Don Juan Bandini signed for him.

Figure 11-5 *Historical Will*

Social custom plays a significant part in the making of a will. The will of Don Tomás Antonio Yorba, dating from the period of Mexican rule in California, presents an illuminating contrast to the modern will with its emphasis on the distribution of the testator's property. Although Yorba's estate was among the largest of the time—consisting of a Spanish land grant of 62,000 acres known as the Rancho Santiago de Santa Ana in Southern California—only a small fraction of his will relates to matters affecting the distribution of the estate to his heirs.

Source: Huntington Library. Translation by H. Noya.

which is executed in the same manner as the original will, would accomplish that objective. Whether or not one has added amendments to a will, every will should be reviewed periodically to determine if changed circumstances call for revising the will.

Revoking a Will

When the addition of codicils makes the will unwieldy or potentially confusing, it is time to review the entire will and make a new one. States vary in their requirements for legally revoking a will. Generally, the testator's *intent* to revoke the will must be demonstrated; the accidental burning of a will, for instance, does not imply revocation. On the other hand, if someone turns up with an earlier will, it may be difficult to prove that it was revoked if a subsequent will does not explicitly do so. When in doubt about the validity of a will, seek competent legal advice.

Probate

The process by which an estate is settled and the property distributed is called *probate*. During the course of probate the validity of the will is proved; an executor or administrator of the estate is appointed; the necessary matters for settling the estate are carried out; and, with the probate court's approval, the decedent's property is distributed to the beneficiaries. If the deceased left a valid will, property is distributed in accordance with its terms. If there is no will, the probate court usually names an administrator and the property is then distributed according to the laws of intestate successson that hold sway in that particular state.

Probate lasts an average of nine to twelve months, though it may last a considerably longer or shorter time according to circumstances and the complexity of the estate. Essentially, the probate period allows time for the deceased's affairs to be resolved, debts and taxes paid, arrangements made to receive monies due the deceased at the time of death, and finally distribution of the deceased's property. Notices to creditors are generally published in newspapers so that claims outstanding against the estate can be paid prior to distribution of the property to beneficiaries. In addition, the period of probate includes an opportunity for any interested persons to contest the validity of the will.

The Duties of the Executor or Administrator

Someone has to be responsible for carrying out all the steps necessary to settling an estate through probate. A person named in the will to do so is called an *executor,* if a man, or, if a woman, *executrix*. In the absence of a will, or if no executor is named in one, or if the named person is unable to act, the court appoints an *administrator,* or, if a woman, *administratrix,* to settle the estate.

Whether an executor or an administrator, the person must generally meet

 The clock wound by Elizabeth still ticked, storing in its spring the pressure of her hand.

Life cannot be cut off quickly. One cannot be dead until the things he changed are dead. His effect is the only evidence of his life. While there remains even a plaintive memory a person cannot be cut off, dead. A man's life dies as a commotion in a still pool dies, in little waves, spreading and growing back towards stillness.

John Steinbeck, *To a God Unknown*

certain minimum requirements stipulated by the law of the state in which probate occurs. If the court believes the executor named by the testator is capable of doing the job, the choice is usually approved. When an administrator is to be appointed, state law requires the drawing up of a preferential list of candidates. Assuming that the necessary qualifications are met, the order of preference typically begins with the spouse of the deceased and continues successively through the deceased's children, grandchildren, parents, siblings, more distant next of kin, and a public administrator.

Once approved by the court, the executor takes an oath to perform all duties faithfully. Some states require the posting of a bond to protect beneficiaries from any potential mismanagement of the estate during the probate period. Once these legalities are in order, then the actual job of settling the estate begins.

The prospective executor's or administrator's first duty is to notify interested parties of the testator's death. This is typically accomplished by placing a notification of death in appropriate newspapers (see Figure 11-6). Such a notice serves three purposes: (1) It announces that someone is ready to prove the will of the decedent; (2) it acknowledges that someone is petitioning

---

**NOTICE OF DEATH OF
LEE D. WILLIAMS
AND OF PETITION TO
ADMINISTER ESTATE
Case Number: 11111**

To all heirs, beneficiaries, creditors, contingent creditors, and persons who may be otherwise interested in the will or estate of LEE D. WILLIAMS.

A petition has been filed by JANE DOE, in the Superior Court of Santa Cruz County requesting that JANE DOE be appointed as personal representative to administer the estate of the decedent.

A hearing on the petition will be held on March 22, 1982, at 8:30 a.m. in Dept III, located at 701 Ocean Street, Santa Cruz, California 95060.

IF YOU OBJECT to the granting of the petition, you should either appear at the hearing and state your objections or file written objections with the court before the hearing. Your appearance may be in person or by your attorney.

IF YOU ARE A CREDITOR or a contingent creditor of the deceased, you must file your claim with the court or present it to the personal representative appointed by the court within four months from the date of first issuance of letters as provided in section 700 of the California Probate Code. The time for filing claims will not expire prior to four months from the date of the hearing noticed above.

YOU MAY EXAMINE the file kept by the court. If you are a person interested in the estate, you may file a request with the court to receive special notice of the filing of the inventory of estate assets and of the petitions, accounts and reports described in section 1200 of the California Probate Code.

s/ JOHN P. SMITH
Attorney for the Petitioner

JOHN P. SMITH
9999 Pacific Avenue
Santa Cruz, CA 95060
March 7, 9, 14

Figure 11-6
Newspaper Notice to Creditors

to be appointed by the court to begin probate; and (3) it gives notice of the death to creditors so that any outstanding claims against the estate can be submitted for settlement.

The executor makes an inventory of the estate, including all personal and real property owned by the decedent. Names and addresses of all beneficiaries are compiled. If the deceased had a safe deposit box, its contents are inventoried. Bank accounts, stocks, bonds, and other assets are similarly inventoried, as are the contents of the deceased's home. In practice, certain personal property may be excluded from the inventory, though the general principle is "when in doubt, include it in the inventory." When a surviving spouse is the estate's primary or sole heir, the inventory of personal and household goods can be less meticulous, though items that have special worth, such as paintings, jewelry, and antiques, are specified.

At the same time, important papers are gathered, including insurance policies, deeds, bank passbooks, Social Security and pension information, military service records, and other documents that will require review and possibly action. Several copies of the death certificate are obtained to facilitate claims for payment of insurance benefits and the like.

The executor is also responsible for properly managing the estate pending its final disbursement to heirs. He or she may choose to open a bank account in the name of the estate so that all income and expenses can be accounted for accurately. Tax returns may need to be filed on behalf of the decedent and the estate. The executor may be charged with paying an allowance to the surviving spouse or to minor children for their support during the perod of probate. If the decedent was in business or was a stockholder in a corporation, the executor must skillfully execute a smooth transition that benefits the estate. Similarly, if rental properties are part of the estate, they must be managed until the estate is settled.

Because settling an estate frequently involves complex legal matters, many testators appoint an attorney to be executor. An executor or administrator who is not knowledgeable in the law usually enlists the aid of an attorney to make certain that legal requirements are satisfied. It should be recognized that both the executor or administrator and the attorney are entitled to compensation for their services to the estate. These fees are usually a percentage of the value of the estate's assets, the percentage being computed according to fee tables established by state legislatures.

After all the information is compiled about payments due the estate and claims against it, the executor or administrator takes the necessary steps to have the debts paid and to receive monies due. Questionable claims are submitted to the court for determination of validity. If an estate's funds are not sufficient to pay all creditors, disbursement is usually made according to guidelines established by state law. Tax returns are filed and the appropriate payments are made.

Finally, a schedule for distributing the estate's property to the beneficiaries is prepared and submitted for the approval of the probate court. Once the court's approval is obtained, the property is distributed, a final accounting is prepared for the court's review, and receipts are obtained to certify that the distribution has been made correctly. Assuming that everything has been carried out properly, the court then discharges the executor or administrator. The estate is settled.

Avoiding Probate

Because probate involves delays and can sometimes be expensive, many people try to avoid it. Books purporting to explain how to avoid probate appear from time to time on the bestseller lists, demonstrating the widespread appeal of this kind of financial advice. Sensible, legal steps can be taken to avoid or at least minimize probate costs. For example, a husband and wife may own their house and other assets in joint tenancy, a form of property ownership that allows a spouse to take full legal possession of the property upon the other's death without probate.

Some approaches to avoiding probate, however, can have serious pitfalls, particularly the do-it-yourself approach taken without obtaining qualified legal counsel. Suppose, for example, that an elderly couple would like their house to go to their grandson after their deaths. Intending to avoid probate, they might visit a local stationery store, purchase the appropriate form to file a change of ownership, add the grandson's name to the property deed, and record this document with the county recorder. So far, so good. But now suppose that several years later they decide to sell the house, or they change their minds about making the grandson their beneficiary and want to remove his name from the deed. To make this desired change, they must obtain the grandson's signature, much as if he were "selling" his right of ownership in the house. Placing a minor's name on a deed may require going into court and requesting that a legal guardian be appointed to act on behalf of the minor should a change of ownership be desired.

Joint bank accounts, also sometimes used to avoid probate, can create similar difficulties. Because each person has full rights of ownership of the account, either is permitted to withdraw money without the other's permission — or even knowledge. To forestall this potential problem, banks sometimes recommend that funds be kept in a so-called Totten trust, by which a person deposits money under his or her own name as *trustee* for another person. Thus, as long as the trustee is alive, no one else can get into the account; upon the trustee's death, the funds go to the recipient named in the trust. Another alternative (much like the Totten trust for money accounts) involves setting up a trust, so that one person holds property in trust for another. In some instances a couple may even hold their own property in trust for themselves or an individual may hold property in trust for himself or herself. But, again, such devices should not be established without an understanding of all the possible ramifications.

Such examples notwithstanding, avoiding probate is still a worthwhile endeavor, but one that is likely to present difficulties if ventured into too simplistically. Given careful consideration and the benefit of competent legal and financial advice, many options are available for setting up one's estate so that the chance of probate is minimized or eliminated. It may be possible, for instance, that certain assets can be protected from probate even though others cannot. Arranging that fewer assets fall under probate can make procedures less complex and briefer. Such actions may offer significant savings of legal fees and erstwhile probate costs. However, all such plans to avoid or minimize probate should be adopted only after careful consideration.[11]

Laws of Intestate Succession

It is estimated that seven out of ten Americans die without leaving a will. Perhaps so many of us fail to make a will because death makes us uncomfortable. Or perhaps, overwhelmed by busy-ness, we neglect this aspect of financial planning with the questionable excuse that we are not yet at the age when death is statistically probable. Considering the consequence that can result when one dies *intestate* — that is, without a will — we would do well to give this matter more than passing thought.

Of those persons who die intestate, possibly some believed that their heirs would be adequately served nevertheless; others, quite likely, simply never gave making a will any serious consideration. Few circumstances justify not making a will, no matter how inconsequential the total value of an estate may seem.

One of the chief reasons for making a will is to assure that property will be disbursed according to one's wishes. In the absence of a will, property is distributed according to general guidelines established in state law. The state generally tries to accomplish what it believes the deceased would have done had he or she actually made a will. The laws that dictate the disbursement of property, the care of minor children, and all the matters that pertain to settling the estate reflect society's ideas of fair play and justice. Thus, the values of society, rather than the deceased's personal values, determine the outcome.

If any heirs are minors, their share of the estate will be held in trust for them, and their guardian, even when it is the surviving parent, may be forced to periodically report to the court on management of the children's trust. Suppose that both parents are killed simultaneously in an accident. In the absence of a will, the care of the children and the management of their assets placed in trust by the state might be delegated to persons with whom the parents would have been less than pleased. The complications that may arise from dying intestate make a solid argument for taking steps to execute a will.

To handle the affairs of the estate, the court appoints an administrator — usually the surviving spouse. This seems not too different from what might have occurred had the decedent left a will naming an executor. However, whereas an

When it comes to divide an estate, the politest men quarrel.

Ralph Waldo Emerson,
Journals (1863)

executor is permitted to act more or less independently in the management of the estate provided that he or she acts prudently, the court-appointed administrator may be required to obtain the court's approval before proceeding with sensible and necessary decisions. When an estate is sizable or is otherwise complex, the difference between management of the estate by an executor and management by the court-appointed administrator may be significant.

Although the laws of intestate succession differ among states, some general patterns prevail. In community-property states, for example, any property held in common goes automatically to the surviving spouse. If there are no children, separate property also goes to the surviving spouse. When there is only one child, the estate will probably be divided equally between child and surviving spouse. If there is more than one child, usually one-third of the estate goes to the surviving spouse and the remaining two-thirds is divided equally among the children.

If there is no surviving spouse, property is divided among the children; if no children, disbursement is made to the deceased's parents; if they are not living, property is likely to be divided among the deceased's surviving siblings; if there are none, the estate may be divided among the late siblings' children. In attempting to settle an estate, the court will make a determined effort to locate surviving heirs. If none can be found, however, the proceeds from the estate go to the state.

This outline provides a general idea of how the laws of intestate succession apply, though states do differ in their approach. In some states, for example, if there are no children, the estate is divided equally between the surviving spouse and the deceased's relatives, including his or her parents, siblings, and the children of siblings. In some instances, one scheme of disbursement is followed in dividing personal property and another in dividing real property.

Because the laws of intestate succession are designed to protect the interests of the surviving spouse and children of the deceased, some people find it convenient to let the state decide how their property is distributed after death. The major flaw in this view, however, is that the decisions made by the state may be quite other than those the person would have made. It may happen, for example, that a needy spouse receives inadequate funds while distant relatives enjoy a windfall. Or the assets held in trust for minor children and by the surviving spouse may make sound financial management difficult, placing an unnecessarily heavy burden on one's survivors. Paul Ashley observes that the distinction between intestate succession and distribution according to the terms of a formally executed will is fundamental: Who would you rather have make the rules and decide the outcome of your estate — the legislature and public officials, or you, the testator?[12]

Estate and Inheritance Taxes

Estate and inheritance taxes have the same rationale as other forms of taxation: the redistribution of wealth. Equality of opportunity is a cornerstone of

American society, and taxation is seen as a method of breaking up concentrations of wealth and providing greater economic benefits for a greater number of citizens. Although there may be dissent about *how* wealth is thus redistributed, it is presumed that there is consensus among the American people about the desirability of redistribution. Nevertheless, few people enjoy paying taxes, and many feel that so-called death taxes are among the most abhorrent.

Others find estate and inheritance taxes less repugnant than income taxes, however, because the beneficiaries of an estate may have contributed little or nothing toward its accumulation. It can also be argued that it is more reasonable for the government to step in to take its share at the time of a person's death, rather than to exact its due while the person is living by taxing his or her income. A case can even be made for the philosophical view that inheritance taxes should be 100 percent: "Empty we come into the world, empty we leave." But this notion goes against the grain of human nature. Many people take pleasure from the thought that something of oneself is being left behind for others' enjoyment; such a bequest confers a sort of immortality on the giver. In addition, it might be argued that an excessively high inheritance tax removes the incentive to work and build for the future, making such a tax detrimental to the national economy.

Estate Taxes

The estate tax, imposed by the federal government, is not a tax on property, but rather a tax paid on the *transfer* of property from the decedent to his or her beneficiaries. Estate taxes are assessed on the total value of the taxable estate transferred upon an individual's death. Like individual income tax returns, estate taxes are calculated on the basis of assets less allowable deductions. The estate's assets are those items included on the inventory taken by the executor or administrator, and the value of these assets is generally determined by court-appointed appraisers. Once the gross value of an estate is determined, the next step involves computing allowable deductions. Typical deductions include expenses incurred during a terminal illness; funeral costs; administrative expenses; debts, mortgages, and liens against the estate; net losses that occur during administration of the estate; charitable and public bequests; the marital deduction (discussed in the next section); and several categories of tax credits, if applicable to a particular estate.

The Marital Deduction

First enacted in 1948, the *marital deduction* was designed to extend to everyone in the United States the same opportunity for tax savings that had been provided to those living in community-property states. Whereas earlier laws placed a limit on the deduction allowed on transfers of property between spouses, current law provides an unlimited marital deduction. This means that no tax need be paid on the death of the first spouse if the entire estate is left to the surviving spouse. In some cases, however, particularly those involving large

Chronicle Features, 1984

"The Far Side," drawing by Gary Larson, Chronicle Features

3-9 Larson

"Aaaaaaaa! . . . It's George! He's taking it with him!"

estates, it may not be advantageous to use the unlimited marital deduction since it is designed to allow a *postponement* of tax until the death of the surviving spouse, not an *avoidance* of tax.[13]

Historically, although the marital deduction did provide an opportunity to avoid taxation on transfers of estates between spouses, it limited a testator's freedom of choice with respect to the distribution of his or her estate. Now a married person can create a Qualified Terminable Interest Property (QTIP) trust that provides the tax benefit and allows the testator to control the ultimate disposition of the property. All income earned by property in a QTIP trust must be paid to the surviving spouse. The testator also specifies who will receive the trust assets upon the death of the surviving spouse. Taxes on the QTIP property are determined as of the date of death of the surviving spouse. If a testator wants to distribute property differently — to provide a bequest to children, for example — the tax savings of the marital deduction do not apply. Thus, some people choose to incur larger taxes as a trade-off for retaining greater control over how an estate will be distributed.

Gifts

One way to lessen estate taxes is through lifetime gift giving. As a result of the Economic Recovery Tax Act of 1981, the annual gift tax exclusion was increased to $10,000 per donee. With gift splitting, spouses can transfer up to $20,000 per year, per donee, without incurring a tax liability. These amounts can be given to as many people as the donor wishes, whether related or not; and the giver pays no gift tax and the recipients pay no income tax. Such giving of gifts reduces the size of the estate on which estate taxes are assessed.

In addition, the Economic Recovery Tax Act abolished the "three year contemplation of death" rule (which said that gifts made during the three years before death were part of the decedent's taxable estate), except for life insurance policies and certain gifts with "strings attached"—that is, gifts requiring the recipient to satisfy some condition.

Although no one is advised to make gifts that might jeopardize the giver's own financial security, some estate planners contend that those who wish to provide benefits to donees could make much greater use of this annual exclusion for gifts. Not only do tax advantages accrue from such gift giving, but the giver experiences the pleasure of giving and the recipient's pleasure at receiving the gift.

Inheritance Taxes

Whereas estate taxes are levied by the federal government, inheritance taxes are imposed by the states. Taxation rates and regulations vary among the states. Inheritance tax has generally been smaller than the federal estate tax. However, many estates now exempt from federal estate taxes may remain subject to state inheritance taxes.

Inheritance taxes are levied according to the relationship between the decedent and the beneficiary: As the relationship grows more distant, the exempt amount is decreased and the tax rate on the excess is increased.

Some states tax insurance benefits, others do not, and yet others provide exemptions calculated according to the relationship of the named beneficiary to the insured. Some states have made efforts to abolish inheritance taxes. Information about the specific inheritance tax rates and regulations that apply in your state can be obtained from a local attorney, the state's inheritance tax department, or reference books such as *The World Almanac*.

Trusts

A *trust* can be defined simply as the holding of property by one person for the benefit of another. The many kinds of trusts constitute extremely valuable tools of estate planning. One of the most common forms of trusts involves arranging for the financial security of minor children. Trusts are also set up to provide funds for college or similar expenses.

Although we usually think of trusts as a financial planning tool that benefits others, it is possible to set up a trust for oneself. In fact, the person making the trust can serve as both its trustee and beneficiary. A *living trust,* for example, can be established whereby a husband and wife hold their property in trust for themselves. Such a trust differs from a *testamentary trust,* which becomes effective upon the testator's death.

One wise use of the living trust is to provide funds for medical care in the event that the trustor is unable to act in his or her own behalf because of senility or some other incapacity. One instance of the wisdom of planning before need is described by Paul Ashley. An eighty-year-old man established a living trust, designating his attorney to handle his affairs if he should not be able to do so himself. Shortly after setting up this trust, the man suffered a stroke that incapacitated him for nearly three years, making it impossible for him to conduct necessary business and financial transactions. Because he had had the foresight to institute a living trust for just such a contingency, he and his wife were assured of receiving every care and comfort that could be made available during the term of his disability.[14]

Trusts can be designed to serve many different kinds of purposes. Trusts are often an excellent means to avoid or minimize the complexity and duration of probate procedures, thus saving time and money. Because the optimal use of trusts requires careful consideration and awareness of available alternatives, it is best to first consult an attorney who is qualified to undertake this kind of financial planning.

Life Insurance and Death Benefits

Whereas less than half of us have arranged for someone to handle the affairs of our estate following our death, and less than one-third of us have made a will, most of us own some type of life insurance. It is estimated that perhaps over 90 percent of the American populace have insurance, though the average amount per policyholder is about $30,000.

Policies and Considerations

Life insurance offers a convenient and relatively inexpensive means of providing at least a basic estate for our beneficiaries after we die. It may represent a fairly small portion of a comprehensive estate, or the major portion of a smaller estate. The distinguishing feature of life insurance in estate planning is that it offers a means whereby many people join together to share a potential risk that each could not bear alone.[15] Insurance plans can be designed in a wide variety of ways and to suit many purposes. Some policies are part of a total investment portfolio that can be drawn upon during the insured's lifetime. Other policies provide for benefit payments only after the death of the insured. Table 11-1 presents a glossary of insurance terms.

The insurance company generates its profit from carrying out the administrative duties that are necessary in bringing together the large number of

TABLE 11-1   *A Brief Glossary of Life Insurance Terms*

Beneficiary: The person (or other entity, such as an institution or a charitable organization) named to receive the proceeds of a life insurance policy that are payable at the death of the insured.

Endowment: A life insurance policy that provides for the payment of the face amount of the policy after a specified number of years, or at a specified age of the insured, or to the beneficiaries of the insured at his or her death.

Face amount: The amount of insurance protection under a given policy as stated on the first page, or face, of the agreement; this amount may be increased by dividends or decreased by loans against the policy.

Group life insurance: An insurance agreement covering a group of people, often the employees of a company or, in some cases, the members of a voluntary-membership organization; the premiums may be paid either exclusively by the employer or jointly by the employer and employees.

Insured: The person whose life is insured under the terms of an insurance agreement, often the person who takes out the policy.

Life insurance policy: A written agreement between an insurance company and the insured that provides for payment of a stipulated sum of money to the beneficiary or beneficiaries named in the policy or to the estate of the deceased upon the death of the insured.

Nonparticipating policy: A policy on which no refunds or dividends are paid and which bears a relatively low guaranteed premium.

Paid-up policy: An insurance policy on which no further payments are due and under which there remain outstanding benefits as provided by the terms of the policy.

Participating policy: An insurance policy in which the insured shares in the distribution of dividends resulting from the surplus earnings of the insurance company.

Premium: The amount paid to an insurance company by the insured in exchange for the benefits provided under the terms of the policy.

Underwriter: The insurer, or a person acting on behalf of the insurer, who accepts and classifies the life insurance risk; also, the person who solicits insurance as an agent of the insurer and who assumes the obligation on behalf of the insurer by signing the insurance agreement.

participants required for such a cooperative venture. Broadly speaking, there are two kinds of life insurance companies. A *mutual* company is owned by the policyholders and is managed by a board of directors chosen by the policyholders. After administrative expenses are paid, the profits from operating the firm are returned to policyholders in the form of dividends. A *stock* company, on the other hand, is owned by a comparatively small number of persons, its stockholders. Generally, the policies written by a stock company are nonparticipating; that is, no dividends are paid to those who are insured by the company. Instead, profits are shared by the company's stockholders. Usually, insurance premiums are lower with a stock company, though when dividends paid over a period of time are taken into account, one may find that insurance costs are ultimately less with a mutual company.

The two major types of insurance policy are *term* and *whole life*. Term insurance provides protection for a stated period of time and expires without value if the insured survives longer than the stated period. The duration of term insurance is usually from about five to twenty years, depending upon the need for such temporary protection. A whole life policy, on the other hand, continues throughout the insured's lifetime. Upon the death of the insured, the policy provides for payment of the stated amount of insurance as increased by any dividends that have been retained and reduced by any loans against the policy. (Whole life insurance is also called ordinary life and straight life.) Each of these types of insurance, term and whole life, has features that make it attractive in accomplishing one's financial goals. As with other aspects of financial planning, the role of insurance in building one's estate is best considered with professional assistance.

Aimed at informing the public about survivor benefits available through Social Security, this poster addresses an age group that may give little consideration to the possibility of a spouse's death and its financial consequences.

To be confident that the advice you receive is competent and impartial, it is probably wise to compare the insurance programs offered by several companies. Companies licensed to sell insurance must conform to state laws regulating insurance practices. The designation CLU (for Chartered Life Underwriter) is awarded to agents who complete a college-level course of study in insurance and financial planning. Any reputable agent can provide you with the names of clients who may be able to help you assess the services provided by the agent's company.

Those who favor including insurance as part of estate planning argue that life insurance may offer some advantages not available from other forms of investment. For example, unlike some other assets, life insurance benefits are not subject to attachment by creditors. Too, benefits usually become available immediately following death, unlike assets that must be processed through probate. Thus, insurance benefits can have important psychological and emotional value as well. Such funds may provide relief and a sense of security to a surviving spouse and other dependents during the period immediately after bereavement. Knowing that money is available to cover anticipated expenses may help to reduce the stress associated with this period of crisis.

Some advisors, however, urge survivors to be careful that funds from insurance policies are not spent too hastily or without due consideration. If the proceeds are sufficient, it may be advisable to place them in a savings account where they can draw interest until they are needed. A hasty or ill-informed decision concerning how insurance benefits are spent may ultimately increase the survivor's stress rather than alleviating it. Issues like this, so important for the well-being of one's survivors, need to be carefully considered during the making of a comprehensive financial plan and will.

Other Death Benefits

Many survivors qualify for various lump-sum and income benefits from government programs and institutions such as Social Security and the Veterans Administration. The amount of such benefits usually depends upon the survivor's eligibility for such programs and the payment schedule in effect when benefits are claimed. The dependents of Civil Service employees may be entitled to similar benefits.

To obtain current information about any of these government death-benefit programs, one can call or write the government bureau administering them. It is important to realize that a person entitled to benefits under one or more of these programs will receive such benefits only if a claim is filed. Moreover, delays in filing may result in a loss of benefits.

Actions taken by a survivor may also affect eligibility to receive government benefits. For example, a spouse who remarries or has income that exceeds specified limits may lose entitlement to Social Security benefit payments. A well-conceived and adequate estate plan will include consideration of benefits that may accrue from government programs such as those mentioned as well as benefits that may be due from employee or union pension programs. Further,

Burial in a national cemetery, such as the Black Hills National Cemetery in South Dakota, is a benefit made available to veterans who have served in American military forces during wartime. Such cemeteries have been established across the United States. Other death benefits for veterans include a lump-sum payment to help defray burial expenses and, under certain circumstances, direct payments to survivors.

© Albert Lee Strickland

some states have passed laws requiring that a surviving spouse and any dependent children be given the choice of continuing group health insurance policies which were held by the deceased spouse. Having an understanding of such benefits and knowing how to get them can help alleviate feelings of anxiety and vulnerability that may accompany bereavement.

Further Readings

George J. Annas. *The Rights of Hospital Patients: The Basic ACLU Guide to a Hospital Patient's Rights*. New York: Avon Books, 1975.

Paul P. Ashley. *You and Your Will: The Planning and Management of Your Estate*. New York: New American Library, 1977.

Joseph M. Belth. *Life Insurance: A Consumer's Handbook*. 2nd ed. Bloomington: Indiana University Press, 1985.

Robert N. Brown, Clifford D. Allo, Alan D. Freeman, and Gordon W. Netzorg. *The Rights of Older Persons: The Basic ACLU Guide to an Older Person's Rights*. New York: Avon Books, 1979.

Charles F. Hemphill, Jr. *Wills and Trusts: A Legal and Financial Handbook for Everyone*. Englewood Cliffs, N.J.: Prentice-Hall, 1980.

Charlotte Kirsch. *A Survivor's Guide to Contingency Planning*. Garden City, N.Y.: Anchor Press/Doubleday, 1981.

William J. Moody. *How to Probate an Estate: A Handbook for Executors and Administrators*. Rev. ed. New York: Cornerstone Library, 1977.

Oceana Publications, Inc. *How to Make a Will, How to Use Trusts*. 4th ed. Dobbs Ferry, N.Y.: Oceana Publications, 1978.

Frank Smith. *Cause of Death: The Story of Forensic Science*. New York: Van Nostrand Reinhold, 1980.

The thermonuclear warhead presents a new kind of encounter with death; such warheads, and such encounters, have become pervasive since the first detonations of atomic weapons during World War II. This ominous mushroom cloud rises from a surface blast at Enewetak Island in 1952. Today's nuclear devices are many times more powerful.

CHAPTER *12*

Environmental Encounters with Death

*T*he essayist E. B. White said, "To confront death, in any guise, is to identify with the victim and face what is unsettling and sobering."[1] Though we are often insulated from death in modern societies, we nevertheless encounter it in many different guises. In news reports and our entertainment, death is a staple item. Consciously or not, we risk subtle, and sometimes dramatic, encounters with death as we engage in our life's pursuits — on our jobs and in our recreational activities. Fatal accidents and disasters are yet other experiences in which the human tragedy of death may be encountered. Violence, war, and nuclear catastrophe, which threaten us not only as persons but as a society also, overshadow and influence many of our plans and activities. Is it surprising, then, that this inventory of potential encounters with death contributes to the high incidence of stress, which affects so many people and becomes yet another potential threat to life?

Mostly, we ignore or give only passing thought to these encounters with death. Seldom do we contemplate death in a way that shakes us emotionally or gives us pause. Yet our environment furnishes us with opportunities for encountering death at almost every turn. In Chapter 1 we saw how the mass media — newspapers, television, movies — as well as art, literature, and music all present images that can affect our own attitudes toward death. In subsequent chapters we examined other encounters with death, such as life-threatening illness and surviving the deaths of others close to us. Here we look at some of the encounters with death that pertain in various degrees to life in modern societies. Some, such as natural disasters, have been part of human experience since life began; others, such as the nuclear threat, represent a wholly new dimension of our encountering death in life.

Risk Taking

The images communicated by the media and other forms of popular culture can influence the kinds of risks we are willing to take in our lives. Often, risks accompany the actions we take in pursuit of the "good life." Indeed, all life involves risk, though the degree of risk we are willing to assume is typically subject to our personal choices concerning how we live our lives.

Think about your own life. What kinds of risk do you face in your employment, your leisure activities, your style of living in general? Are any of the risks life threatening? Do you take "calculated" risks? Can you exercise choice about assuming these risks, or do some seem to be unavoidable?

In some areas of our lives we can exercise considerable choice about the nature and degree of risk that affects us. For example, smoking, drinking, taking drugs, and driving habits typically involve risks that can be controlled. Similarly, we can usually exercise choice in our occupation and recreational activities.

The risks associated with various jobs are sometimes quite dramatic, involving dangers that most people, given a choice, would very likely avoid. Such occupations come readily to mind: for example, explosives expert, high-rise window washer, movie stuntperson, test pilot, as well as police officer and fire fighter. Such a list could be continued almost indefinitely. We might add scientists and researchers working with hazardous materials, mine workers,

I stared in a horrified trance as a figure appeared, frozen in the air for the briefest moment, its arms outstretched above its head as if in utterly hopeless supplication. Then it continued its relaxed, cart-wheeling descent, with only the thundering crashes attesting to its frightening impacts on the rock. It disappeared into a gully.

"Don't look!" I screamed to my wife, who was, of course, as helplessly transfixed as I was. And the sounds continued. After a time, the figure came into view at the base of the gully and continued down the pile of rubble below. My last view of it is frozen in time. The figure's arm was curled easily over its head, and its posture was one of relaxation, of napping. It drifted down that last boulder field like an autumn leaf down a rippling brook. Then it disappeared under the trees, and only the pebbles continued to clatter down the rock. Suddenly it was very, very still.

I looked down to Debby and had to articulate the obvious: "That was a man," I said quietly, numbly.

William G. Higgins, "Groundfall"

electricians, heavy-equipment operators, and farmworkers using toxic pesticides. As you add your own examples to this list, notice whether they involve the risk of sudden death — as from an explosion or a fall from a high-rise building — or of long-term exposure to hazardous conditions. Some jobs involve health risks that are identified only after many years of continual exposure to the harmful condition.[2]

An occupation may increase the risk of death by increasing the worker's level of stress. No doubt all work involves stress; whether stress becomes a threat to the worker's health, however, depends on both the nature of the work and the worker's attitude. A U.S. government report, *Work in America,* states, "Satisfaction with work appears to be the best predictor of longevity — better than known medical or genetic factors — and various aspects of work account for much, if not most, of the factors associated with heart disease."[3]

Death can also be encountered in our recreational activities and sports — mountain climbing, parachuting, scuba diving, motorcycle racing, and the like. Some people might characterize such activities as thrill seeking, though this term may suggest motives that some participants in these activities would not ascribe to themselves. Often, part of the pleasure derived from such activities is the fact that there is an element of risk; thus, an opportunity to test limits and develop confidence in the ability to accept the risk and deal positively with fear. On the other hand, the thrill may come from successfully achieving the goal of the particular activity. Mountain climbers, for instance, might willingly accept the risk because climbing provides both physical conditioning and the aesthetic pleasure of reaching the heights and surveying the expanse of uncluttered nature.

Although mountain climbing involves obvious risks, two different climbers may relate to these risks in vastly different ways. One may begin the climb with an attitude of abandon that could only be characterized as foolhardy or death defying. The other may devote many hours to obtaining instruction, preparing equipment, conditioning for the climb, and asking advice from more experienced climbers before deciding to set foot on a mountain. In short, steps can be taken to minimize the risks. An activity, then, may be attractive to some persons *because* of its inherent risks, whereas others accept the risks as inseparable from the other attractive features of the activity.

No one is immune to risks. At home, on the job, or at play the risk of death confronts us in one way or another. After a classroom discussion about the risks involved in various activities, one student said, "It seems we're coming around to the point that everything we do involves risks. You could even stab yourself with your knitting needle!" Perhaps, but usually when we consider activities involving risk, we think of pursuits about which there is a direct acknowledgement of the risk. The possibility of falling backward from a rocking chair while knitting strikes most people as less risky than, say, driving a formula race car or embarking on a Himalayan expedition.

Sometimes the risks we face are not known. More often, we can exercise

To keep from tumbling through space at 125 miles per hour, this mile-high skydiver spreads his arms and legs to control his freefall before opening his parachute. Although risks are ever present in our lives, we expose ourselves to many of them by personal choice.

UPI/Bettmann Newsphotos

options that allow us to control or manage the element of risk. What automobile driver has not chosen at some time to drive just a bit faster in order to arrive at the destination sooner? Accident statistics, as well as common sense, tell us that exceeding the speed limit increases the risk. Yet one makes a trade-off; the added risk is exchanged for the expected benefit of arriving at the destination sooner.

A death resulting from a high-risk sport or similar activity may have a special impact upon other individuals who engage in the same activity. In addition to the impact upon those who are involved most immediately (for example, persons who had rented equipment or given instruction to the deceased), the death also affects the larger community of participants in the sport by challenging "the underlying assumption of the sport that careful, cautious practice insures safety."[4] To cope with this challenge, and with the death itself, rumors may circulate that the deceased failed to take necessary precautions or followed an unwise or ill-considered course of action. These rumors may represent an attempt to fit what has happened into a manageable scheme and to mitigate any feelings of guilt about having been unable to prevent the death. As a means of coping with such a death, this tendency to "blame the victim" may facilitate the resolution of grief and allow the participant to feel comfortable continuing the activity despite the risks.

Accidents

Accidents are the third most common cause of death among the total population in the United States and the *leading cause* of death among persons ages forty-five and younger. According to the National Research Council's Committee on Trauma Research, more than 140,000 Americans die in car wrecks, fires, and other mishaps every year.[5] Another 80,000 people suffer permanently disabling brain or spinal cord damages from injuries received in accidents. Although the health care cost related to accidents is about $100 billion, only two cents of each dollar spent for federal health research goes for injury studies. It has been suggested that the problem of accidents and resulting injuries warrants a coordinated research and information-gathering effort as part of the Centers for Disease Control in Atlanta.

Often, accidents are viewed as happening by "chance" or because of "fate" or "bad luck." From that view, it follows that little if anything can be done to prevent accidents. But the definition of an accident as an event that occurs "by chance or from unknown causes" can be refined, as the dictionary reflects, to encompass the understanding that an accident may indeed be "unavoidable," or it may result from "carelessness, unawareness, or ignorance." Thus, accidents are typically events over which individuals do have varying degrees of control. For example, suppose a gun is brought into the household. The presence of the gun increases from zero the chance that there may be an accidental firing of the weapon. Of course, such an accident may never happen. But if a gun were *not* in the home, there would be *no* chance of an accidental firing.[6]

In other words, the choices we make affect the probabilities of various kinds of accidents. It is an established fact that drivers who have been drinking tend to take greater risks than do sober drivers. It has also been determined that a driver's judgment and performance are inversely related to the amount of alcohol imbibed, whereas a driver's tendency to overrate his or her driving abilities is directly related to amount imbibed. The effect of alcohol on driving is evident in the fact that, statistically, about half the drivers involved in accidents are under the influence of alcohol.

Are such accidents the result of mere chance or fate? If not, then steps can be taken to reduce the probability of such accidents. Unfortunately, the notion that accidents are chance events contributes to the neglect of such problems as drinking and driving. A better understanding of accident causes — one that considers such factors as carelessness, lack of awareness, and neglect — might well result in constructive actions toward the prevention of these kinds of accidents.

Sometimes we call certain persons *accident prone* because they seem to become involved in accidents with an unusually high frequency. Although the term is often used jocularly, there is not sufficient evidence to scientifically define a personality type that would be described as accident prone. However, certain known factors can affect the type of accident that may occur and the individual's probability of being involved in an accident. Such accident proneness is usually based on factors such as age and experience.[7]

For example, insurance rates reflect the degree of risk of motor vehicle accidents: Policies cost more for both the young driver and the elderly driver. A large percentage of accidental deaths among teenagers results from their use of the automobile. Because the elderly also incur an increased risk, it is interesting to compare the reasons. The young driver's increased risk results largely from inexperience and youthfully impulsive driving habits. The elderly person's increased risk, on the other hand, is due to slower reaction time and physical impairments that make driving more hazardous.

When accidents of all types are considered, adolescent and young adult males are at greatest risk. It is unclear whether the high accident rate for this age group and sex reflects this group's greater willingness to assume risks (to assert masculinity, perhaps?) or the cultural attitudes that tend to encourage males more than females to engage in risky activities.[8]

So far we have emphasized intrinsic factors that influence accidents — that is, factors having to do with a person's own physical and mental qualities. Another set of factors — extrinsic factors, or conditions that exist within the environment — also influences the occurrence of accidents. Unsafe conditions present in the environment are sometimes called "accidents waiting to happen." Often such conditions are the result of negligence or of ignorance about the threat they pose to safety. For example, say a swimming pool is left unattended and easily accessible to young children; if a toddler happens by and falls into the pool and is drowned, the owner of the pool might be judged negligent.

Typically, unsafe conditions in the environment reflect the attitudes and value systems of the person or group responsible, or of society as a whole. For instance, a landlord who refuses to correct unsafe conditions on the tenant's premises apparently does not value others' safety. Accidents caused by drunk driving occur because of choices made by both the drinking driver and society. Societal neglect is also partly responsible for many of the fire disasters that occur in the United States. Fire safety remains a serious national problem, though actions could be taken to improve unsafe conditions that contribute to fire deaths.

Examples like these could be multiplied many times over in various areas of environmental health and safety. Indeed, it seems that unsafe conditions are ubiquitous. It would be naive to believe that the risks we encounter could be eliminated completely. Still, in many areas of our lives, risk can be minimized (see Figure 12-1). The lack of attention — perhaps one should say the lack of resolve — to take the necessary steps toward correcting unsafe conditions

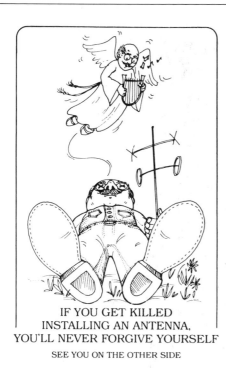

WHEN YOU'RE INSTALLING YOUR CB BASE STATION OR TV ANTENNA, TAKE THIS ADVICE OR YOU COULD BE IN FOR THE SHOCK OF YOUR LIFE!

1.

When raising any antenna —
either CB or television —
make certain that the antenna
and its support cables or guy wires
cannot fall into or contact power lines.

2.

Never place your ladder next to
electric wires leading to your home.

3.

If you're installing a rotor,
be sure that it won't turn the antenna
around into nearby power lines.
Make sure the power lead is grounded.

4.

Support cables should be
well secured at both ends and
should be insulated according to
manufacturer's instructions.

IF YOU GET KILLED
INSTALLING AN ANTENNA,
YOU'LL NEVER FORGIVE YOURSELF

SEE YOU ON THE OTHER SIDE

Figure 12-1   *Antenna Hazard Warning*
The threat of death may be used to warn consumers and employees of risks to safety. Here, the threat of death is presented with a touch of humor, being represented as a transition to an angelic state complete with stereotypical harp.
Source: Pacific Gas & Electric Company.

prompts Robert Kastenbaum and Ruth Aisenberg to ask: "How negligent must a society be before its 'accidental' deaths are tantamount to homicide?"[9]

Disasters

Some encounter death from disaster vicariously, through news reports. Others vividly recall disaster as a frightening event, occurring suddenly and bringing destruction and loss. For everyone, the possibility of disaster is a constant threat, the end result of a sequence of events that ultimately leads to catastrophe.

Disaster can be defined as a life-threatening event that affects many people within a relatively brief period of time, bringing sudden and great misfortune.

Disasters result from natural phenomena — floods, earthquakes, and other "acts of God" — as well as human activities. Included in the latter category would be fires, airplane crashes, chemical spills, and nuclear contamination.

In the United States, the incidence of disasters has increased in recent years. One reason for this increase is that more than half the U.S. population now lives within fifty miles of the coastline, an area that in the West is vulnerable to fires, floods, earthquakes, and landslides, and in the Southeast is prey to storms, hurricanes, and tornadoes. The growth in population and the rise of industrialization have themselves brought increased exposure to disasters related to human activities; for example, fires, explosions, and chemical pollution.

These factors have increased the risk of disaster worldwide. In 1984, the world's worst industrial accident occurred when gaseous methyl isocyanate escaped from Union Carbide's pesticide plant in Bhopal, India, bringing death to 2,500 people residing near the plant. The unprecedented magnitude of this accident was followed by what was reported to be the largest human-caused, mass disaster lawsuit ever, with claims totaling more than $100 billion in damages.

In recent years, an increasing number of disasters have been related to environmental pollution, as happened in Bhopal. The accidental contamination of livestock feed with the chemical PBB in Michigan and the emergency shutdown of the nuclear reactor at Three Mile Island are other examples.[10] In 1986, radioactivity was released over a large area of eastern and northern Europe when a nuclear power plant at Chernobyl in the Soviet Union exploded and suffered catastrophic failure, an accident termed the worst in the history of nuclear power generation. Dangerous levels of radiation contaminated the area surrounding the plant, causing death and serious injury and damaging the food supply. The proliferation of technology requires that attention be given to the potential for such catastrophes.[11]

Although communities can decrease the risk of injury and death by taking measures designed to lessen the impact of a potential disaster, the effects of a disaster are difficult to anticipate fully. In September 1985, a devastating earthquake hit Mexico City, without warning, killing almost 10,000 people. Previously, the city had enacted building codes that accounted for the possibility of low-frequency earthquake waves associated with the ancient lake beds on which Mexico City is built. But these codes did *not* include a specification for the number of shaking cycles that buildings should be constructed to withstand, a factor that seismologists later determined contributed to the large number of fatalities.[12]

People often submit themselves to the risk of disaster because of considerations that make the risk acceptable. Employment opportunities, for example, may prove the deciding factor. Perhaps many people who live in areas where disaster is a likely event rationalize the danger, if they give it any thought at all, as simply "playing the percentages."

Adequate warnings of an impending disaster can save lives. Yet necessary

Charlie Palmer, UPI/Bettmann Newsphotos

Flowers placed by survivors adorn the coffins of victims who perished in an early New Year's Day fire in Chapais, Quebec. Survivors of a disaster often experience its traumatic effects for a long time after.

information may be withheld because of greed or political expediency, or simply because of uncertainty about the nature and extent of the threat, or because of concern about causing panic.

The tragedy that followed the eruption in 1902 of the Mt. Pelee volcano, on the island of Martinique, in the West Indies, is particularly instructive of how information that could warn potential disaster victims is sometimes mismanaged with disastrous consequences. The officials of the nearby community of St. Pierre were alerted to the likelihood that the volcano would erupt. But, concerned that the population would panic if notified and thus thwart their plans for an upcoming local election, the St. Pierre officials withheld any warning of the danger from the populace. As a result, virtually the entire population of the small community was incinerated. When news of an impending disaster is managed in such a way, it demonstrates what Robert Kastenbaum describes as the "enormously powerful threat [of] a tightly controlled information network."[13] The May 1980 eruption of Mount St. Helens provides an instructive comparison. Even though this eruption was larger, only sixty lives were lost compared with 30,000 casualties resulting from the eruption of

Mount Pelee. This dramatic difference is attributable to adequate warnings of the hazard and timely establishment of a restricted zone of access.[14]

An incident at the Enrico Fermi atomic reactor, near Detroit, in 1966 illustrates how modern technology may compound the difficulties of making sound judgments in the face of a potentially widespread disaster. Reports indicate that the malfunction of the reactor system presented the threat of mass deaths. Yet workers, though informed that a problem existed, were told that it posed no hazard. Commenting on this incident, Kastenbaum says, "The nature of the situation made it very difficult for officials to provide accurate information even if they did not have misgivings about admitting the full scope of the threat." The experts themselves were confused and unsure about what might happen next or what to tell the community. As a result, "many of the communications were vague and contradictory, as might be expected in such a situation."[15]

Even with an adequate warning system and a reliable, efficient information network, people do not always respond to such threats in a prudent fashion. Just as some people ignore the risks associated with smoking or drug abuse, individuals may feel they are immune to disaster. Predictions of natural disasters are often met with the response: "I've never been affected before. Why should I start worrying now?" The same attitude is exhibited when persons who learn of a chemical spill or a fire nearby decide to travel to the disaster area for a closer look.

What can be done when disaster strikes? What kind of help is needed in its aftermath? Imagine the situation: People are injured, some are missing, others are dead. Homeless survivors are likely to be in a state of shock and uncertainty about the whereabouts of loved ones and about the future. Each type of disaster, of course, creates particular problems that need attention.

Meeting the immediate needs of survivors — providing food and shelter, caring for medical needs, and restoring vital community services — is essential. Yet even as attention is given to responding to these immediate needs, the emotional needs of survivors should not be neglected (see Figure 12-2). Ministering to these might include forming a missing person group to help alleviate the anxieties of survivors who are worried about the safety of relatives. Locating and caring for the dead is also an important aspect of helping survivors cope with the trauma of disaster. The comment of one relief agency worker, "It doesn't really make too much sense to dig up the dead and then go and bury them again," reveals an unfortunate ignorance of the human emotions that surround disposition of the dead.[16] Perhaps what survivors of a disaster need most is compassion.[17]

When a storm dumped 20 inches of rain in one night on a coastal community in California in 1982, residents awoke the next morning to the news that twenty-two people had been killed, more than a hundred families had lost their homes, and another three thousand homes had been severely damaged. Within a few days, an impromptu organization was set up to help survivors deal with the psychological trauma of their losses. Known as Project COPE

Chevron National Travel Card
P.O. Box 5010, Concord, CA 94524
Phones: California (800) 642-0262, Alaska, Hawaii (800) 227-1642, All Other States (800) 227-1306

```
WE'VE HEARD ABOUT THE PROBLEMS THAT HAVE HIT
YOUR AREA BECAUSE OF THE SEVERE WEATHER, AND
WE SINCERELY HOPE YOU HAVE NOT BEEN
PERSONALLY AFFECTED.

HOWEVER, IF CIRCUMSTANCES HAVE DISRUPTED YOUR
ROUTINE, WE WANT YOU TO KNOW WE ARE READY TO
HELP YOU BY EXTENDING MORE TIME TO PAY YOUR
ACCOUNT.

PLEASE CALL US AT TOLL FREE (800)642-0262, OR
DROP US A NOTE IN THE ENCLOSED POSTAGE PAID
ENVELOPE IF WE CAN ASSIST.

IT'S THE LEAST WE CAN DO TO SHOW OUR
APPRECIATION FOR YOUR BUSINESS AND CONFIDENCE
IN CHEVRON.

                        SINCERELY,

                        J.L. CARL

JANUARY 18, 1982   MANAGER, TRAVEL CARD SERVICES
```

Figure 12-2   *Disaster Letter from Chevron*
Even a computerized corporate response to the disruption of normal living
patterns can assist and comfort survivors as they cope with the devastation
wrought by a natural disaster.

(Counseling Ordinary People in Emergencies), it provided immediate counseling to disaster victims and coordinated the services of more than a hundred mental health professionals.[18] Counselors found that people who had lost loved ones or property were experiencing grief reactions heightened by the sudden, capricious nature of their losses. Some who had lost only material possessions felt guilty for mourning the loss of property when others had lost family members. Some felt guilty for surviving the disaster. Those made homeless by the storm felt isolated and alone. There were feelings of anger at bureaucratic delay and toward uncooperative insurance companies and government agencies. Many of the victims felt anxious, vulnerable, and depressed. In some cases, old problems reemerged related to personal or relationship issues.

COPE set up programs to respond to each of these problems. Survivors were reassured that their reactions were not unusual and helped to recognize that their grief was legitimate. Victim support groups brought together individuals who could understand and listen to one another's concerns. Counselors helped survivors sort out their priorities so they could begin solving problems created by the disaster. Skills were shared to help victims channel their anger constructively. Emergency crews and relief workers were not left out. It was recognized that individuals who come to the aid of victims (including those who counsel the victims) are also vulnerable to the emotional impact of a disaster. With its comprehensive response to the psychological needs of survivors, COPE was cited as a model of providing mental health care to disaster victims.

We cannot eliminate the encounter with death that accompanies disaster, but we can take steps to reduce its impact, preserve life, and demonstrate compassion for survivors. And we can implement, when possible, procedures to warn of impending disasters.

In 1721, the novelist Daniel Defoe wrote *A Journal of the Plague Year,* a fictional account of the Great Plague of 1665 that had devastated London. Drawing upon published accounts and his recollection of tales heard during childhood, he vividly depicted the horror of a plague-stricken city and the terror of its helpless citizens, confronted by a tragedy they could not comprehend. What prompted Defoe to write, in 1721, about a plague that had taken place almost two generations earlier? He knew that a plague again threatened to sweep across Europe, a plague that could cause death and destruction on the scale of the Great Plague of 1665. Defoe wrote to alert a largely indifferent populace to the threat so that precautions could be taken and the catastrophe averted. (Fortunately, the plague of 1721 was far less virulent than had been anticipated.)

Today we no longer fear the Black Death, but when disaster strikes, the effects are no less serious for its victims and survivors. Too often, warnings come too late or go unheeded. Perhaps death seems something that happens only somewhere else, to someone else. Yet in a subtle though pervasive way, those of us now living are confronted by a plague of sorts that is no less threatening than the more easily distinguishable plague of Defoe's time. Indifference to the modern forms of plague — violence, war, nuclear catastrophe, environmental pollution — can only increase the likelihood of an encounter with disaster.

Violence

Violence, one of the most potent of our encounters with death, can affect our thoughts and actions even though we ourselves have not been victimized. Potentially, if not in actuality, all of us are its unsuspecting victims. Interpersonal violence is now officially recognized as a public health problem, as evidenced by the establishment of a new governmental office, the Violence Epidemiology Branch at the Centers for Disease Control, charged with studying assaultive behavior and homicide.[19] The most threatening of violent acts are those that occur without apparent cause, when the victim is selected seemingly at random, thus heightening anxiety at the possibility that violence could unexpectedly confront anyone.[20]

Think about the bystander killed during the commission of a robbery or the victim of what seems a senseless and brutal attack by a mass murderer. Recently, in California, a number of murders were committed by someone whom the police dubbed the Trailside Killer, because the killings occurred along several popular woodland trails. A woman who usually jogged every morning along one of these trails expressed feelings of being personally threatened because these violent acts had taken place "so close to home." In an area where she had previously felt safe and secure, she now felt fearful. Although she had no direct experience of the killings, she was nevertheless victimized by the violence because it occurred in her own familiar environment.

Another woman described a potential encounter with death that began innocently enough when she answered a knock on her door. Recognizing a former schoolmate whom she hadn't seen in a long time, she invited him in and they began to chat. She began to feel somewhat uneasy, though she could not say why. About two months later, however, she heard on the news that her visitor had been arrested and was subsequently convicted for the brutal murders of several young women. These murders had been committed around the time of his unexpected visit. Recalling the experience, this woman commented, "I sometimes wonder how close we may be to death at times and just not realize it. It seems we really never know."

During the period when the murders of young black children were occurring in Atlanta, Georgia, a television report showed one of the city's playgrounds, which was devoid of activity even on Memorial Day. Ordinarily, it would have been bustling with the laughter and spirited activities of children and their families. The fear of violence shaped people's behavior in response to the potential threat of yet more killings of Atlanta's children. Violence had become a fact to be reckoned with.

The possibility of encountering violence seems to be increased by the anonymity and isolation characteristic of much of modern life. Feelings of connectedness to others can generate a sense of safety and security. In small towns and close-knit neighborhoods there is often a community concern that tends to make random violence less likely. The modern landscape seems to provide fewer of such societal mechanisms. Living life in comparative isolation from our neighbors, many of us experience little comfort from the thought that violence might be averted by warnings or that help is available when a threat becomes real.

Some people believe that violence is endemic in American society. The fact that there were often few legal restraints during the great westward expansion gave rise to attitudes that promoted arbitrary justice and encouraged people to do whatever survival seemed to require, be it inside or outside the law. The treatment of the Native American nations, as well as the history of slavery and prejudice against black Americans, is replete with acts of violence. When such historical examples are combined with current statistical analyses of violence, some argue that American society has in many ways fostered the notion that violence can solve one's problems.[21]

Community standards of morality and justice play a major role in determin-

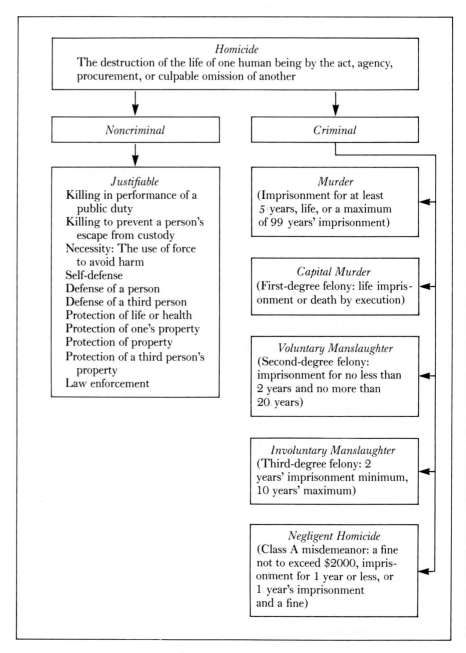

Figure 12-3   *Schematic View of Texas Homicide Statutes*
Source: Vernon's Texas Codes Annotated: Penal Code, 1974. From Henry Lundsgaard,
Murder in Space City: A Cultural Analysis of Houston Homicide Patterns (New York:
Oxford University Press, 1977), p. 213.

ing how the act of killing is assessed by a society and by its legal-political-judicial system. As Figure 12-3 illustrates, homicide — the killing of one human being by another — is separated into the two categories: lawful and unlawful. These categories may encompass additional distinctions.

Thus, although a murder is necessarily a homicide, a homicide is not always a murder. The circumstances surrounding a particular killing, the relationship between the killer and the victim, and the killer's motivation and intention are all considered in how an act of homicide is assessed within the American judicial system.

In a study of more than 300 killings that occurred in a major American city in 1969, it was found that more than half of the suspects were released before reaching trial.[22] To comprehend the reasons why many homicide cases are never brought to trial, it is necessary to look at how the circumstances of a homicidal act influence its investigation, and how the judicial processes determine whether an accused killer is brought to trial.

The medical-legal investigation of an act of homicide generally includes three components: (1) an autopsy to determine the official cause of death; (2) a police investigation to ascertain the facts and gather evidence pertinent to the killing; and (3) various judicial and quasi-judicial procedures, carried out by the district attorney's office and the court system, to determine whether there is sufficient cause to bring a case to trial.

Fundamental to this investigation is the acknowledgment that homicide is an interpersonal act. That is, it involves a relationship between the killer and the victim: They may have had close domestic ties, being members of the same family or otherwise related; they may have been friends or associates; or they may have been strangers. In a 1969 study, summarized in Table 12-1, Henry Lundsgaarde found that "the closer, or more intimate, the relationship is between a killer and his victim, the less likely it is that the killer will be severely punished for his act."[23] In other words, killing a stranger was more likely to result in a stiff penalty than would killing a friend or family member.

The response of the criminal justice system to acts of homicide reflects cultural attitudes about killing and what constitutes appropriate punishment.[24] Basing its standards on cultural attitudes, the criminal justice system in a particular community sets about its task of determining whether an act of homicide is lawful or unlawful. If lawful, the killer is released and the case is closed. If unlawful, a further determination is made as to whether the killing in question was an act of murder, manslaughter, or negligent homicide — and there are various degrees of criminal intent within each of these categories as well.[25]

What are the cultural assumptions by which an act of homicide is judged? Lundsgaarde's research showed that "the legal outcome for a person who kills his wife's lover is . . . very different from the outcome for a person who combines killing with theft, robbery, or similar criminal or antisocial acts."[26] Society is reluctant to become involved in matters that fall within the domain of the family, even when they involve violence. This situation reflects a desire to avoid

T A B L E 12-1   *Three Major Killer and Victim Relationships Expressed in Reference to Final Case Disposition*

Case disposition	Relatives (Percent)	Friends/Associates (Percent)	Strangers (Percent)
Offender deceased	3.90	4.41	
No bill ⎫			
No charge filed ⎬	40.26	36.77	23.64
Nolle prosequi ⎭			
Dismissed	3.90	2.94	1.82
Not guilty	6.49	4.41	3.64
Probation	10.39	8.82	7.27
Death penalty			9.09
Outcome undetermined	10.39	2.94	3.64
Charge pending	2.30		7.27
Life sentence	1.29	2.94	1.82
Sentenced	20.78	36.77	41.82
Total	100.00	100.00	100.00

Source: Excerpted from Henry Lundsgaarde, *Murder in Space City: A Cultural Analysis of Houston Homicide Patterns* (New York: Oxford University Press, 1977), p. 232

interfering in family matters because a close relationship is believed to involve its own set of mutual responsibilities and obligations—its own "code of justice," if you will—that provides social sanctions for acts that occur within the relationship. In contrast, "the killer who chooses a stranger as his victim overtly threatens the preservation of the social order."[27]

To put it another way, an individual who kills a stranger is not likely to be constrained by personal concern for the victim. Thus, society devotes its attention to acts of homicide that threaten the preservation of law and order within the larger society.[28] Killings that occur within the family unit or between persons who know one another tend to be viewed as less of a threat to society at large.

The American system of criminal law places considerable emphasis on motivation and intention, factors that tend to be uncertain and hard to define. Their analysis is based largely on presumptions about human behavior that derive from custom and social convention.

There are some who believe that violence is "contagious" in modern American society.[29] This reasoning can be developed along several lines: First, it may be that a violent society creates an environment in which psychotic individuals are encouraged to act out their antisocial behaviors in more harmful ways than they might if alternative ways of releasing such potentially violent tendencies were available. Second, each violent incident may spawn others, thus spreading the contagion of violence. Third, some believe that if an act of violence is not properly resolved, it will be repeated. With regard to this last point, a "proper resolution," according to Fredrick Wertham, is "for society to

"We have a responsibility to the victims of crime
and violence. . . . It is a responsibility to put away
childish things, to make the possession and use
of firearms a matter under-taken only by serious
people who will use them with the restraint and
maturity that their dangerous nature deserves -
and demands."

Robert F. Kennedy,
July 11, 1967

© U.S. Conference of Mayors   1620 Eye Street N.W.   Washington, D.C. 20006   Design: Tom Ocken

Designed by Tom Ocken, © U.S. Conference of Mayors, Yanker Poster Collection, Library of Congress

*Looking down the barrel of a handgun, the viewer is pointedly confronted by
the possibility of death in this poster designed to increase public awareness of
the pervasive threat represented by the widespread possession of firearms.*

make clear what it wants. Society must say, *No, this we will not tolerate,*" and this must be affirmed and upheld by a judicial process that emphasizes accountability for one's acts.[30]

Capital Punishment

Is capital punishment, then, the strong statement that is needed? In theory at least, capital punishment — which has been termed "planned, timed dying" — is supposed to serve a twofold purpose: (1) to punish the offender, and (2) to have a deterrent effect on potential offenders.[31]

Most researchers agree, however, that capital punishment is not an effective deterrent to murder. According to Glenn Vernon,

> Investigations into the ineffectiveness of the death penalty as a deterrent to murder revealed that some murderers were so busy with other things during the events preceding the murder that they simply did not think of the death penalty, and that others were interacting with their victims in such an extremely emotional manner that the consequences of their murderous acts were not even taken into account.[32]

Kastenbaum and Aisenberg state that the more likely influence of capital punishment on death by violence is to increase its frequency, because it reinforces the notion that killing can solve problems.[33] The greatest risk for the potential murderer, they contend, is not the risk of execution, "but the risk of being killed by the police, the intended victim, or some bystander."[34]

If capital punishment is an ineffective deterrent to murder, then what alternatives are available to society? A possible approach to criminal justice is suggested by Lundsgaarde. Comparing our present system with early Anglo-Saxon and English law and with many non-Western legal systems as well, he notes that "modern criminal law has completely transformed the ancient view of homicide as a wrong against a victim and his family to its modern version that views homicide as an offense against the state."[35] The modern tendency is to view crime as a social problem.

Lundsgaarde states that the separation of civil and criminal law — more specifically, the separation of personal obligation and criminal liability — essentially eliminates the killer's liability to the *victim as person*. Instead, the liability is viewed as violence against the public at large. Somehow restoring an element of civil liability for violent acts — say, by some form of victim compensation program, perhaps — might more effectively deter homicidal behavior and violent crimes than do present arrangements.

In seeking ways to reduce the level of violence in society, it may be useful to consider some factors that tend to prevent violent behaviors. Even if some individuals might have a greater innate potential for violence or aggressive behavior, how that potential is expressed depends to a significant extent on environmental influences. Kastenbaum and Aisenberg suggest that implementation of the following guidelines can lessen the potential for violence:[36]

1. Avoid the use of prejudicial, dehumanizing, or derogatory labels, whether applied to oneself or to others.
2. Avoid or eliminate conditions that underlie dehumanizing perceptions of oneself or others.
3. Promote communication and contact between potential adversaries, emphasizing similarities and common goals rather than differences.
4. Refrain from using physical punishment as the primary means of discipline.
5. Champion the good guys.
6. Teach children that violence is not fun, cute, or smart. Emphasize that they are responsible for their behavior.
7. Identify and foster the human resources that can provide alternatives to violence. For example, promote sharing among children, and encourage then to think before engaging in impulsive and possibly hostile actions against others.
8. Reduce the attractiveness of violence in the mass media.

Courting Death

Victims, too, sometimes play a part in encouraging violent acts against themselves. Indeed, some homicide inspectors have concluded that the victim is not always as innocent as is generally thought. Consider the example of a husband who has been repeatedly threatened by his angry wife wielding a loaded revolver. His response to this threat is, "Go ahead, you might just as well kill me." What can be said about his role as a victim in such circumstances?

Kastenbaum and Aisenberg cite another such incident: A daughter, overhearing her parents arguing, tried to intercede, but was told by her mother, "Never mind, honey; let him kill me." After the daughter left the house to seek assistance, her father obtained a revolver from another room and shot and killed the girl's mother.

Investigators have found that, during domestic strife, wives have made statements like, "What are you going to do, big man, kill me?" coupled with dares like, "You haven't got the guts." Kastenbaum and Aisenberg remark that such statements "strike us as combining elements of seduction and lethality." At least in some cases, they conclude, there are indications that the victim not only seemed to be "asking for it," but was the one actually responsible for escalating the conflict to the level of physical violence.[37]

Dysfunctional Strategies

Even a brief discussion of homicide and lethal behaviors points up society's frequent ambivalence. Whereas violence makes up much of our entertainment, violence in real life is generally condemned. Yet society seems uncertain about how to stem the tide of violence. The judicial system often appears to function arbitrarily. The notion that violence between individuals is an acceptable means of solving problems or achieving goals makes recourse to violence easier to

TABLE 12-2   *Factors Favoring Violence*

Anything that physically or psychologically separates the potential killer from the victim. For example, the use of a gun leads to a concentration on the means (pulling the trigger) rather than the end result (the death of a person). Psychological separation occurs when the victim is perceived as fundamentally different from oneself.

Anything that permits the killer to define murder as something else, such as "making an example of the victim," "making the world safe for democracy," "implementing the final solution," or "exterminating the terrorists."

Anything that fosters perceiving people as objects or as less than human. This happens when victims become "cases," "subjects," or "numbers," as well as when the killing occurs from a distance as with high-altitude bombing or submarine warfare.

Anything that permits one to escape responsibility by blaming someone else: "I was just carrying out orders."

Anything that encourages seeing oneself as debased or worthless: "If I'm treated like a rat, I might as well act like one. What have I got to lose?"

Anything that reduces self-control or that is believed to have this effect: alcohol, mind-altering drugs, hypnotism, mass frenzy, and the like.

Anything that forces a hasty decision or that does not permit time for "cooling off." That is, a situation may force one to decide to shoot or not to shoot with no opportunity for deliberation.

Anything that encourages a person to feel above or outside the law: The notion that rank, prestige, wealth, or the like makes it possible for one to "get away with murder."

Source: Adapted from Robert Kastenbaum and Ruth Aisenberg, *The Psychology of Death: Concise Edition* (New York: Springer, 1976), pp. 291–294.

tolerate. The victim, too, in many cases, seems to play a crucial role in his or her own demise. Violence, which threatens us all in various ways, results at least partly from social patterns as well as social problems.

These patterns and problems often reveal the presence of "dysfunctional strategies," factors that increase the likelihood of violence rather than prevent it. Kastenbaum and Aisenberg use the term *psychic maneuvers* to describe the factors that have been determined to facilitate murder and other homicidal acts.[38] Their listing of these factors is summarized in Table 12-2. You might review this list three times. First, think about how each of these psychic maneuvers might function in your own life. Note that they do violence to ourselves and others even when they function far more subtly than the overt act of homicide. Second, note how these psychic maneuvers function within society, how they contribute to antagonisms between individuals and between groups. The third time, consider how each of these psychic maneuvers represents a dysfunctional strategy that is typically found in the conflicts and wars between nations.

War

Within the context of ordinary human interaction, our moral as well as legal codes stand in strict opposition to killing. War abrogates the conventional sanctions against killing by substituting a different set of conventions and rules about moral conduct. In war, killing is not only acceptable and necessary, but possibly heroic. The expectation that one will kill and, if necessary, die for one's country is a concomitant of war. Human life becomes a low-priority item in the prevailing value system. As Arnold Toynbee says, "The fundamental postulate of war is that, in war, killing is not murder."[39]

In Dalton Trumbo's classic antiwar novel, *Johnny Got His Gun,* we find a veteran "without arms legs ears eyes nose mouth" who devises a means of communicating with the outside world by "tapping out" messages on his pillow with his head. He asks to be taken outside, where he can become an "educational exhibit" to teach people "all there was to know about war." He thinks to himself, "That would be a great thing to concentrate war in one stump of a body and to show it to people so they could see the difference between a war that's in newspaper headlines and liberty loan drives and a war that is fought out lonesomely in the mud somewhere, a war between a man and a high explosive shell."[40]

Think for a moment about your responses when you hear or read about war. What kinds of images are evoked when you think about combat, the bomb, Hiroshima, disarmament, the Nazi Holocaust, kill ratios, Vietnam? Reflect on your own personal experiences and the experiences of those close to you. What makes the encounter with death in times of war different from other encounters with death?

War is sanctioned by society as a legitimate means of achieving some desired goal — say, defending the national interest or protecting the homeland. Nevertheless, as Glenn Vernon says, "confrontation with wartime killing may be one of the most difficult experiences of those who have been taught to avoid killing."[41]

To put aside the ordinary rules of moral conduct, war activates a special set of conventions designed to make it psychologically possible for individuals to go against the grain of what they have learned about right and wrong. As long as the combatant "keeps more or less faithfully to the recognized rules," Toynbee says, "most of humankind have been willing to alter their moral sense in such a way as to regard the killer in war as 'being righteous.' "[42] As Vernon puts it, "Human behavior is relative to the situation, and given the right situation man can be taught or can learn to kill: whereas given other situations quite different behavior patterns are followed."[43]

A Vietnam veteran, writing about his combat experiences, says, "Changes in personality and mood are rooted in the special climate of the combat zone. These mutations evolve in such a wily fashion that the person who undergoes them is not aware of the alterations himself."[44] This is the crux of the matter. The conventions of war are mind- and personality-altering. It is possible to debate the ethical issues involved in war, its demands on citizens, the meaning of patriotism, and so on, arguing whether or not killing in wartime is intrinsically different from what would be defined as murder under other circumstances. The result is the same; the logic, the intention differs.

Col. Rex L. Dively, Signal Corps Photo

At Buchenwald, near Weimar, Germany, a few of the dead are piled in a yard awaiting burial following the invasion by the Allies. Starvation and disease due to unsanitary living conditions, as well as the incessant torture of prisoners, caused an average of two hundred deaths each day at this infamous Nazi concentration camp.

Here is an account of a soldier's first encounter with death on the battlefield:

> Stone dead, he was. Eyes wide open, staring at nothing. A thin veneer of blood curling at the corner of his lips. Two gaping holes in his chest. Right leg half gone. My first combat fatality. A lifeless body where only moments before a heart beat its customary seventy pumps in one orbit of the minute hand. It is one thing to hear about death; to watch it happen is quite another. I went over to the nearest tree and vomited my guts out.[45]

By his next experience of combat death, however, he questioned whether he was becoming callous and unfeeling: "I was becoming impervious to the

The third plane came in, skimming the treetops, engine screeching. Two napalm canisters spun down from the Skyhawk's bomb rack into the tree line, and the plane pulled into a barrel-rolling climb as the red-orange napalm bloomed like an enormous poppy.

"Beautiful! Beautiful!" I said excitedly. "They were right on 'em."

The napalm rolled and boiled up out of the trees, dirty smoke cresting the ball of flame. The enemy mortar fire stopped. Just then, three Viet Cong broke out of the tree line. They ran one behind another down a dike, making for the cover of another tree line nearby. "Get 'em! Get those people. Kill 'em!" I yelled at my machine-gunners, firing my carbine at the running, dark-uniformed figures two hundred yards away. The gunners opened up, walking their fire toward the VC. The bullets made a line of spurts in the rice paddy, then were splattering all around the first enemy soldier, who fell to his knees. Letting out a war whoop, I swung my carbine toward the second man just as a stream of machine-gun tracers slammed into him. I saw him crumple as the first Viet Cong, still on his knees, toppled stiffly over the dike, behind which the third man had taken cover. We could see only the top of his back as he crawled behind the dike. What happened next happened very quickly, but in memory I see it happening with an agonizing slowness. It is a ballet of death between a lone, naked man and a remorseless machine. We are ranging in on the enemy soldier, but cease firing when one of the Skyhawks comes in to strafe the tree line. The nose of the plane is pointing down at a slight angle and there is an orange twinkling as it fires its mini-gun, an aerial cannon that fires explosive 20-mm bullets so rapidly that it sounds like a buzz saw. The rounds, smashing into the tree line and the rice paddy at the incredible rate of one hundred per second, raise a translucent curtain of smoke and spraying water. Through this curtain, we see the Viet Cong behind the dike sitting up with his arms outstretched, in the pose of a man beseeching God. He seems to be pleading for mercy from the screaming mass of technology that is flying no more than one hundred feet above him. But the plane swoops down on him, fires its cannon once more, and blasts him to shreds. As the plane climbs away, I look at the dead men through my binoculars. All that remains of the third Viet Cong are a few scattered piles of bloody rags.

Philip Caputo, *A Rumor of War*

death of my fellow soldiers, and, in addition, I was negating the possibility of my own . . . demise."[46]

A Vietnam veteran explains:

Social context is much more important than most people realize. We pretty much live within the boundaries of one social context. If you lived in a different society, you would consider a different set of behaviors as normal. What's bewildering and frightening in the combat situation is how quickly "normal" can change.[47]

Each of us experiences differences in our behavior according to the social context. How we behave among family members is likely to be different from how we behave among strangers or business associates. Sometimes these

During World War II, the Russian poster (left) *directed the message to Soviet troops: "Soldier of the Red Army, SAVE US" (note the swastika on the bayonet), and the American poster* (right) *appealed to citizens at home to buy bonds to provide financial support for the war effort. Though both posters suggest the threat of death to women and children, unlike the Americans the Russians were faced with the reality of German troops invading their homeland.*

differences reveal the presence of contradictory values. Usually, such contradictions remain subtle and rarely meet head on. The contradictory values that exist for the soldier in combat, however, require what the veteran just quoted calls

> . . . a much more total schizophrenia. When you're there you don't really remember what it's like to come back into the social context of a society where killing is abhorrent. And, when you come back home, you don't really remember the context of the combat situation, except perhaps in your nightmares.[48]

When a society reflects on its participation in war, it often speaks in terms of patriotism, the heroism of fighting for one's country, the need to defend the things that are held dear. When we listen to the words of those who have lived through combat, however, we often hear a very different kind of value system at work. We hear about individuals fighting for their lives or fighting because they had no alternative. Heroic intentions and patriotic feelings may be the rationale

Rites of Passage

. . . As a psychiatrist who has worked with Vietnam veterans, I know all too well the long-term effects of wartime traumas. Ten and fifteen years after the events, there remain nightmares, fears, depression and, most fundamentally, failures of loving in veterans of combat. The timelessness of the unconscious does not bend to political realities. National treaties mark the beginning, not the end, of the psychic work of mastery.

Primitive societies intuitively knew the value of cultural ceremonies that marked the end of hostilities. Rites of passage were provided for the soldiers and the society to make the transition from the regression of combat to the structure of integrated living. These rituals acknowledged and sanctioned the otherwise forbidden acts of war. They thanked the soldier for his protection, forgave him his crimes and welcomed him back to life.

Our failure to provide such a cleansing for our warriors and ourselves has left our culture struggling for closure. It has as well made the task of intrapsychic mastery so much more difficult for the individual soldier.

Harvey J. Schwartz, M.D.

for donning the uniform, but in combat the emphasis is likely to be on survival.[49]

This is an issue that most of us would prefer to avoid. We do not want to hear what combat is really like, the reality of being in a situation where ordinary standards of conduct are turned topsy turvy and killing another human being becomes necessary and accepted behavior. The bravado and heroics of war may fascinate us. The reality is more difficult to face.

War is dehumanizing and depersonalizing. Lifton and Olson liken Vietnam to Hiroshima in that both events reflect the progression of modern technological warfare, which results in "unseen victims suffering and dying without ever having met their opponents."[50] Although the Vietnam war was reported extensively in the daily news, the veteran's experience of it is still incomprehensible to most Americans: "The veterans of the Vietnam war have much to teach us about our culture and ourselves. We sense in their words and in their experience something that must be faced. As survivors of that experience, they confront us with truth at its source."[51] However, for the most part, returning Vietnam veterans have been viewed "not as heroic warriors, but rather as the unfortunate agents of a policy of death which no one has understood."[52]

"Technological alienation" has been termed the "most characteristic feature of the twentieth-century war machine."[53] It was not until World War I that warfare began to involve civilians on a large scale. Toynbee remarks that the Western world was horrified, during the Spanish Civil War, by the German aerial bombing of the Basque town of Guernica on April 26, 1937, an action that indiscriminately slaughtered civilians of both sexes and of all ages.[54] But by World War II, civilian victims outnumbered military casualties. Early warfare had limits: The bow and arrow, the bullet from the gun, even the aerial bomb had limited destructive and death-dealing effects. With the advent of the atomic bomb, unleashed on Hiroshima on August 6, 1945, the conventional limits of warfare were radically altered.[55]

During the aerial bombings of World War II, the peak of destruction was exemplified by the mass deaths in Dresden, Hiroshima, and Nagasaki. Gil Elliot says:

> By the time we reach the atom bomb, the ease of access to target and the instant nature of macro-impact [large-scale destruction] mean that both the choice of city and the identity of the victim have become completely randomized, and human technology has reached a final platform of self-destructiveness. . . . At Hiroshima and Nagasaki, the "city of the dead" is finally transformed from a metaphor into a literal reality.[56]

Such an image, whether metaphor or reality, is not easy to contemplate. Hiroshima symbolizes the horrible destruction made possible by the world's arsenal of atomic weapons. It is noteworthy that Dalton Trumbo's veteran, who asked to be allowed to become a living exhibit of the ravaging, destructive effects of war, was denied his request because "he was a perfect picture of the future and they were afraid to let anyone see what the future was like."[57]

The Nuclear Threat

Since 1945, the growth of the nuclear weapons arsenal has brought about a likelihood of an encounter with death of unprecedented proportions.[58] With the exception of the bombs dropped on Hiroshima and Nagasaki, this encounter has been more a threat than a reality. Still, the fact that nuclear weapons might be used, with little or no warning, has shaped our lives in ways both subtle and dramatic. A study of high school students indicates that young people are deeply affected by the threat of nuclear war; many are doubtful about the future and about their own survival.[59]

Our visions of what war would be like if fought with atomic weapons are reflected in its changing portrayal in movies. During the first decade after World War II, the bomb was typically portrayed as an instrument for keeping the peace. Beginning in 1959, however, with Stanley Kramer's *On the Beach,* and continuing to the present with movies such as *Dr. Strangelove, Fail Safe,* and *War Games,* moviegoers have seen atomic weapons portayed as something to be feared. In November 1983, more than 80 million Americans — the third largest audience of any dramatic program in television history — watched *The Day After,* a movie depicting the hypothetical aftermath of an atomic attack on Lawrence, Kansas. Before it aired, the movie had stimulated public debate about whether it should be viewed by children and whether it would be propaganda for a nuclear freeze. As for the movie's influence, it was found that virtually no shift occurred in viewers' attitudes toward defense policy or nuclear

We know, as surely as we know that we are alive, that the whole human race is dancing on the edge of the grave. Yet most of us believe in our hearts that it can never really happen — just as we do not really believe we are going to die . . . It is not a pleasant thought, but it cannot be ignored: the game of war is up, and we are going to have to change the rules if we are to survive. During the last two years of World War II, over one million people were being killed *each month*. If the great powers go to war with each other just once more, using all the weapons they now have, a million people will be killed each minute. Technology has invalidated all our assumptions about the way we run our world.

There is a terrifying automatism in the way we have marched straight toward scientific total war over the past few centuries, undeterred by the mounting cost and the dictates of reason and self-interest. We *do* know what is going to happen, and we are frightened, but we do none of the seemingly obvious things that might let us alter our course away from oblivion. We resemble a column of intelligent lemmings, holding earnest meetings to denounce the inequity of cliffs during halts in the march. Everybody agrees that falling off cliffs is a bad idea, many have noticed that the cliff edge is getting steadily closer, and some have come to the heretical conclusion that the column's own line of march is causing this to happen. But nobody can leave the column, and at the end of each halt it sets off again in the same direction.

Some generation of mankind was eventually bound to face the task of abolishing war, because civilization was bound to endow us sooner or later with the power to destroy ourselves. We happen to be that generation, though we did not ask for the honor and do not feel ready for it. There is nobody wiser who will take the responsibility and solve this problem for us. We have to do it ourselves.

Gwynne Dyer, *War*

war. Nor was there any significant change in viewers' feelings about their own political effectiveness with respect to arms reduction and disarmament.[60] In analyzing this surprising lack of effect on public attitudes, researchers suggested that, even though the film may have demonstrated that the aftermath of nuclear war is a prospect that demands our attention, it offered no cogent argument about the causes of nuclear war, nor did it provide a sense of the individual's capacity to have a role in preventing it.[61]

The watershed moment for any discussion of nuclear war must be the bombing of Hiroshima. The bomb fell near the center of the city, and its explosive force, heat, and radiation immediately engulfed all of Hiroshima:

> Within a millionth of a second of the atomic bomb explosion over Hiroshima, the temperature of the blast center was several million degrees centigrade. A millisecond later, a 300,000° C sphere formed, sending out a tremendous shock wave. The wave, losing energy as it expanded, was powerful enough to break windows 15 kilometers from the hypocenter.[62]

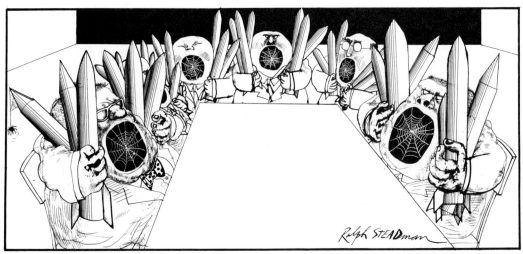

"Disarmament Talks," © 1987 Ralph Steadman, Swann Collection, Library of Congress

Besides the physical devastation caused by the bomb, Lifton says "the most striking psychological feature of this immediate experience was the sense of a sudden and absolute shift from normal existence to an overwhelming encounter with death."[63] For the survivors of Hiroshima, the awesome effects of the atomic bomb initiated "an emotional theme within the victim which remains with him indefinitely: the sense of a more-or-less permanent encounter with death."[64]

Currently, it is estimated that over 50,000 nuclear weapons are deployed in twenty-four countries and their dependencies.[65] Modern weapons technology has progressed to the point that a missile can carry its strategic nuclear warhead a distance of 6000 miles in less than half an hour, and hit within a few hundred feet of its target.

The impact of even a small or limited nuclear attack would be enormous. Although some believe the consequences might be endurable — because they would be on a scale comparable to previous wars and epidemics — the Office of Technology Assessment of the United States Congress has estimated that the number of deaths could be as high as 20 million persons, and "the effects of nuclear war that cannot be calculated are at least as important as those for which calculations are attempted."[66] Scientists now believe that the aftermath of nuclear war could include further devastation in the form of a *nuclear winter* brought about by large-scale climate changes resulting from the use of nuclear weapons. Thus, even for survivors of a nuclear holocaust, the long-range effects could be catastrophic.

Both the potential destructiveness of nuclear weaponry and the cost of building such weapons are mind boggling. How can one grasp the significance of the fact that the present worldwide stockpile of nuclear weapons represents something like one million times the destructive power of the Hiroshima bomb? Or that the two world superpowers invest over $100 million per day toward upgrading their nuclear arsenals?[67]

T A B L E 12-3   *Avoiding the Truth About Nuclear War*

Some commonly used defense mechanisms to avoid facing the truth about nuclear warfare:

Intellectualization: Using knowledge and technical understanding to distance oneself from the facts.

Dogmatism: Maintaining a closed system of beliefs to avoid facts that might be unsettling.

Rationalization: The "ubiquitous defense," exemplified by statements like, "The President knows more about how to prevent nuclear war than we do," or, "Nuclear warfare is such a terrifying possibility that no country will ever actually resort to it," or, "Whatever happens will be God's will."

Displacement: An unconscious process by which substitute objects displace the real source of threat. For instance, the superpatriot's concerns about "the enemy" may displace anxieties about the threat to one's own survival represented by nuclear war.

Isolation: Divorcing fact from feeling. One might think about or discuss nuclear war while suppressing the feelings that follow from the possibility of annihilation.

Denial: Ignoring or dismissing facts that would cause pain or anxiety if perceived objectively.

Source: Adapted from Lester Grinspoon, "Fallout Shelters and the Unacceptability of Disquieting Facts," in *The Threat of Impending Disaster,* edited by George H. Grosser et al. (Cambridge, Mass.: MIT Press, 1965), pp. 123–126.

Despite its magnitude — indeed, its omnipresence — people still find it possible to deny the nuclear threat: first, because the geographical distance between the weapons and their potential victims makes the threat seem remote, and, second, because nuclear warfare is so different from conventional warfare. Yet, although these factors increase our psychological distance from the nuclear threat, the delivery time for such weapons is decreasing. Lester Grinspoon explains that denial is used to cope with the nuclear threat because "people cannot risk being overwhelmed by the anxiety which might accompany a full cognitive and affective grasp of the present world situation and its implications for the future."[68] Table 12-3 describes some of the ways people use to avoid facing the truth about nuclear war.

Another kind of threat associated with the production of nuclear weapons has only recently begun to achieve widespread notice. Exposure to radioactivity in connection with the production and testing of nuclear weapons is perhaps a less dramatic threat than that of nuclear warfare, but its effects are no less disastrous. It is estimated that since 1945 over 1200 nuclear tests have been conducted in various parts of the world.[69] Between 1948 and 1963, nearly 300,000 American soldiers were exposed to low-level radiation during the hundreds of tests sponsored by the military and the Atomic Energy Commission.[70] Now the incidence of leukemia among these veterans is reported to be more than twice the national average, although so far the government has disallowed any connection between their exposure to radioactivity and the onset of cancer.

Clearly, nuclear warfare represents a threat to each of us. Lifton and Olson write:

*Observer-participants in the Army's exercise "Desert Rock VI" huddle
in trenches and attempt to protect themselves seconds before the
detonation of an atomic device at Yucca Flats, Nevada, in 1955.*

U.S. Army Photo

I grew up during the Depression; everything in the country had stopped; there was no work, the factories were cold and empty. People daydreamed about what this country was going to be like when it got going again — the kind of houses people would live in, the kind of cars they would drive, the kind of vacations they'd take, the kind of clothes they'd wear, and all that — and it was a dream for their descendants. I don't find anybody now who gives a damn about what kind of world their grandchildren are going to inherit . . .

All the ads tell you that your own life is short, enjoy it while you can: buy this right now, start drinking really good wines, just take a really swell vacation, drive a really fast car, do it right now. I think it's much more absorbing to plan a world for our grandchildren, but there are no ads that invite you to do that. In a way, the threat of the Bomb may be a boon to wine merchants, restaurateurs, manufacturers of fancy automobiles, salesmen of condos in Aspen. It's all going to blow up — that's part of the sales message.

Kurt Vonnegut, quoted in *Publishers Weekly*

Nuclearism is a peculiar, twentieth-century disease of power. We would do well to specify it, trace its roots, and see its connection with other forms of religious and immortalizing expression. . . . It yields a grandiose vision of man's power at a historical time when man's precarious sense of his own immortality makes him particularly vulnerable to such aberrations.[71]

An economic and military analyst, reporting in 1980, states that "for the eighth year in a row, world military expenditures increased faster than the rate of inflation."[72] During the 1960s and 1970s, few areas of the world escaped the impact of war. The threat to survival represented by nuclear weapons has been equivalent to a more or less constant encounter with death for four decades.[73]

President Dwight Eisenhower, in 1956, said:

We are rapidly getting to the point that no war can be won. War implies a contest; when you get to the point . . . that the outlook comes close to the destruction of the enemy and suicide for ourselves . . . then arguments as to the exact amount of available strength as compared to somebody else's are no longer the vital issues.[74]

Stress

We see violence, homicide, war, nuclear catastrophe clearly as causes of death. Yet a more subtle condition, stress, can be just as much a threat to our well-being. Many researchers believe that stress plays an important role in such characteristically modern ailments as hypertension (high blood pressure), heart disease, and cancer. Increased susceptibility to such ailments may result when prolonged stress wears down the body's defenses.

Although the term *stress* in popular usage means different things to different people, it can be defined as any influence that disturbs the natural equilibrium of the body. In the early 1900s, a Harvard physiologist, Walter Cannon, demonstrated that certain emotional responses to stress, such as fear or rage, prepare the body for what is called the "fight-or-flight" response: intense action designed to return the organism to a state of equilibrium, or homeostasis. Thus, stress results when a situation demands that some adjustment or adaptation be made. This adaptation in turn causes certain physiological changes designed to meet the stressful demand.

Hans Selye, perhaps the foremost investigator of stress, defines it as "the nonspecific response of the body to any demand."[75] According to Selye's formulation, any stimulus — whether physical or emotional, pleasant or un-pleasant — can elicit the same physiological response. In his medical practice, Selye noticed that patients exhibited certain patterns of behavior that were strikingly similar regardless of the particular ailment that caused them to seek medical attention. Selye's theory of stress developed from his curiosity about what was behind this pattern of "just being sick." He found that the body's response to a threatening stimulus, or *stressor,* involved three stages: First, the stressor provokes the body to an immediate alarm reaction. Next, the body marshalls resistance to the stressor. Finally, if stress persists, resistance breaks down and a state of exhaustion ensues.

All of us experience the alarm reaction as we respond to the changing events of our lives. If the stressor is minor and lasts only briefly, the body's defensive mechanisms subside and functioning quickly returns to normal. If the stressor persists or is more intense, the body's adaptive mechanisms continue to function at an elevated level to resist stress. Eventually, the mechanisms are exhausted and vital functions are depleted. Some believe that these debilitating effects occur when stress is so extreme that the emotions elicited activate certain hormonal responses in the body; the result is a lowering of the body's resistance to disease.

It is this psychosomatic nature of stress — the ability of emotional and mental states to influence physical changes — that is of particular interest to researchers. Stress is a natural part of human existence; with the quickening pace of change experienced by most people today, however, the role of stress as an agent for good or ill in the body has become increasingly important. Some believe that the nature of stress has changed markedly since the turn of the century. Whereas in earlier times stress was primarily related to such environmental conditions as the need to obtain food, shelter, and warmth, today stress is related to such factors as more complex life styles, rising expectations, and inner discontent. Thus, the psychological factors influencing stress have become predominant.

Table 12-4 shows a rating scale devised by Drs. Thomas Holmes and Richard Rahe to measure the perceived impact of various life-change events in terms of the degree of social readjustment required. Much as a sound of known loudness can be used as a benchmark for comparing the intensity of other sounds, Holmes and Rahe used marriage — giving it a value of 50 — as a point of

T A B L E 12-4   *The Social Readjustment Rating Scale*

Life Event	Mean Value
1. Death of spouse	100
2. Divorce	73
3. Marital separation from mate	65
4. Detention in jail or other institution	63
5. Death of a close family member	63
6. Major personal injury or illness	53
7. Marriage	50
8. Being fired at work	47
9. Marital reconciliation with mate	45
10. Retirement from work	45
11. Major change in the health or behavior of a family member	44
12. Pregnancy	40
13. Sexual difficulties	39
14. Gaining a new family member (e.g., through birth, adoption, oldster moving in, etc.)	39
15. Major business readjustment (e.g., merger, reorganization, bankruptcy, etc.)	39
16. Major change in financial state (e.g., a lot worse off or a lot better off than usual)	38
17. Death of a close friend	37
18. Changing to a different line of work	36
19. Major change in the number of arguments with spouse (e.g., either a lot more or a lot less than usual regarding child-rearing, personal habits, etc.)	35
20. Taking out a mortgage or loan for a major purchase (e.g., a home, business, etc.)	31
21. Foreclosure on a mortgage or loan	30
22. Major change in responsibilities at work (e.g., promotion, demotion, lateral transfer)	29
23. Son or daughter leaving home (e.g., marriage, attending college, etc.)	29
24. In-law troubles	29
25. Outstanding personal achievement	28
26. Wife beginning or ceasing work outside the home	26
27. Beginning or ceasing formal schooling	26
28. Major change in living conditions (e.g., building a new home, remodeling, deterioration of home or neighborhood)	25
29. Revision of personal habits (dress, manners, association, etc.)	24
30. Troubles with the boss	23
31. Major change in working hours or conditions	20
32. Change in residence	20
33. Changing to a new school	20
34. Major change in usual type and/or amount of recreation	19
35. Major change in church activities (e.g., a lot more or a lot less than usual)	19
36. Major change in social activities (e.g., clubs, dancing, movies, visiting, etc.)	18

continued

TABLE 12-4, *continued*

Life Event	Mean Value
37. Taking out a mortgage or loan for a lesser purchase (e.g., for a car, TV, freezer, etc.)	17
38. Major change in sleeping habits (a lot more or a lot less sleep, or change in part of day when asleep)	16
39. Major change in number of family get-togethers (e.g., a lot more or a lot less than usual)	15
40. Major change in eating habits (a lot more or a lot less food intake, or very different meal hours or surroundings)	15
41. Vacation	13
42. Christmas	12
43. Minor violations of the law (e.g., traffic tickets, jaywalking, disturbing the peace, etc.)	11

Source: T. H. Holmes and R. H. Rahe, "The Social Readjustment Rating Scale," *Journal of Psychosomatic Research,* 11 (1967): 213–218.

comparison for evaluating the perceived impact of other life-change events. In their study of subjects representative of a cross-section of socioeconomic and demographic groups, Holmes and Rahe found virtual agreement about the relative intensities of various life events. The life events shown in Table 12-4 are listed in decreasing order of intensity as based on the "mean value" comparisons assigned to them by participants in the study.

Significantly, Holmes and Rahe found a correlation between the frequency of life-change events and the onset of illness. People who became sick had generally experienced an increasing number of stressful life changes in the preceding year.[76]

Take a few minutes to review the stress scale to determine how many of these events you have experienced during the past year. Stress is a normal part of human life, but when a large number of stress-producing events occur within a brief period, or elicit a high level of stress, there is a greater likelihood that stress may become overwhelming. As you review the changes in your own life that required readjustment, would you give them the same ranking as did the participants in Holmes and Rahe's study?

Personality and life style are other factors that many researchers believe play a major role in the onset of certain diseases. For example, the incidence of duodenal ulcers is apparently higher among persons who are uneasy about expressing intense emotions like anger. Although emotional dysfunction is the sole cause of few diseases, it may exacerbate the physical causes of a great many diseases, such as asthma, allergy, disorders of the skin, digestive disorders, and tuberculosis.

Among the most significant findings relating stress to illness is the linking of heart disease to what cardiologists Meyer Friedman and Ray Rosenman have characterized as *Type A behavior.*[77] Type A behavior is typified by extreme competitiveness, rapidity of thought and action, and consciousness of dead-lines. This pattern of living

> increases the amount of stress hormones, adrenaline and noradrenaline, made by the body's sympathetic nervous system. These stress hormones raise the level of free active fat in the blood to prepare the body for physical exertion which, in the modern urban environment, seldom comes. As a result, the now redundant free fatty acids are laid down in the walls of blood vessels as neutral fats and cholesterol. When the coronary arteries have been narrowed by a critical amount, a final stressful episode makes the blood supply to the heart insufficient for its needs, often due to blocking of one of the heart's arteries by the formation of a blood clot on the roughened vessel wall.[78]

The end result of this process can be catastrophic for the Type A individual: The heart either stops beating because of an insufficient supply of blood to its muscular walls or the part supplied by the blocked artery is painfully damaged.

Before 1900, there was comparatively little heart disease. Most researchers date the marked increase in heart disease from the twentieth century, with the greatest increase occurring since the 1940s. Many believe that the epidemic levels of heart disease in the developed countries can be traced to the effects of life styles that derive from high technology and affluence. Among the most consequential factors of this life style are cigarette smoking, rich and fatty foods, and physical inactivity. The relationship between life style and the onset of heart disease has been confirmed in findings generated from a study of the residents in the small Massachusetts town of Framingham, which began in 1948. This important study — officially titled the Framingham Heart Disease Epidemiology Study — has singled out stress as the most pervasive of all risk factors for heart and circulatory disease, noting that stress often influences other risk factors as well, such as cigarette smoking and overeating.

In the view of many researchers, another disease influenced by stress is cancer, which some believe might be more appropriately relabeled one of the "diseases of maladaptation."[79] Although the link between stress and cancer is not conclusively proved as yet, many believe that the personality type that is especially prone to cancer is characterized by loneliness, self-containment, and an inability to express emotions.

It is important to recognize that stress does not invariably lead to bodily deterioration and death. Any change is stressful and creates tension within the individual. But the *presence* of stress is less a determinant of potential problems than the manner in which a person *copes* with stress.[80] Understanding how stress works and its effect on the body is the first step toward coping more effectively with stress. As Dr. Jean Tache says,

> In each one of us lies dormant a primeval man who in certain situations is aroused and imperiously takes command of the personality. Given the ancient problem-solving options available to him — fight or flight, both requiring physical activity — he can hardly come up with satisfactory solutions to modern problems, for they require reflection, negotiation, and compromise.[81]

When the alarm reaction becomes habitual, such that the body's stress responses are called upon to function at a heightened level much of the time, the result is likely to be illness. "It is not that the ancient way of doing things is not useful," Tache adds, "it is that this biological vestige is mobilized too often in circumstances where it need not be, given the high price it exacts in terms of health and well-being."[82]

Dr. Selye advises that people learn how to deal with stress "without distress."[82] How can this be accomplished in light of the levels of stress commonly experienced by people today? First, Selye recommends that each person find the maximum level of stress that he or she is comfortable with, and that situations that exceed this level be avoided when possible. For example, it may be possible to limit the number of stressful changes that occur at a given time in one's life. Also, situations that elicit potentially harmful levels of stress can be managed in such a way that one makes a positive use of stress rather than succumbing to its negative effects. The stress that may accompany taking a test, for example, can be used to generate mental alertness and preparedness rather than anxiety about the outcome.

Regular physical exercise is another means of coping with stress. Physical exertion provides an outlet for the physiological responses associated with the stress encountered in daily life. In addition, relaxation techniques — such as biofeedback and meditation — offer a means of dealing with stress that many researchers believe can have tremendous usefulness for modern people.[84] Finally, the symptoms of stress can be a signal that we need to reexamine our patterns of living. One medical scientist states that about half of the people living in modern societies have "blood pressure sufficiently elevated to result in increased mortality."[85] This hypertension can be recognized as an indicator of personal and social problms that need to be confronted and corrected, rather than simply treated with drug therapies or other techniques while the root causes are ignored.[86]

Look again at Table 12-4, the social readjustment rating scale devised by Holmes and Rahe. Note that items ranked as most stressful have in common the element of loss: loss of loved ones, relationships, freedom, well-being, self-esteem. Such losses are inherent in the encounters with death discussed in this chapter. Stress, then, is a concomitant of the encounter with death and loss. Disturbing news, risk taking, accidents, violence and homicide, war and the potential for nuclear catastrophe — these encounters with death affect us in our daily lives.[87] Sometimes the encounter is subtle, sometimes it is stressful, calling into action our physiological defenses against threat. The failure to find adequate means of coping with these encounters with death and the stress of modern living represents a threat to the survival of the society as well as the individual.

Further Readings

Nancy H. Allen. *Homicide: Perspectives on Prevention.* New York: Human Sciences Press, 1980.

Committee on Trauma Research, National Research Council. *Injury in America: A Continuing Health Problem.* Washington, D.C.: National Academy Press, 1985.

Bruce L. Danto, John Bruhns, and Austin H. Kutscher, editors. *The Human Side of Homicide.* New York: Columbia University Press, 1982.

Terrence Des Pres. *The Survivor: An Anatomy of Life in the Death Camps.* New York: Pocket Books, 1977.

Mary Douglas and Aaron Wildavsky. *Risk and Culture: An Essay on the Selection of Technical and Environmental Dangers.* Berkeley: University of California Press, 1982.

Japan Broadcasting Corporation, editors. *Unforgettable Fire: Pictures Drawn by Atomic Bomb Survivors.* New York: Pantheon Books, 1981.

Robert Jay Lifton. *Home from the War: Vietnam Veterans: Neither Victims nor Executioners.* New York: Basic Books, 1985.

Alan Monat and Richard S. Lazarus, editors. *Stress and Coping: An Anthology.* 2nd ed. New York: Columbia University Press, 1985.

Dorothy Nelkin and Michael S. Brown. *Workers at Risk: Voices from the Workplace.* Chicago: University of Chicago, 1984.

Beverly Raphael. *When Disaster Strikes: How Communities and Individuals Cope with Catastrophe.* New York: Basic Books, 1986.

Al Santoli. *Everything We Had: An Oral History of the Vietnam War by Thirty-Three American Soldiers Who Fought It.* New York: Random House, 1981.

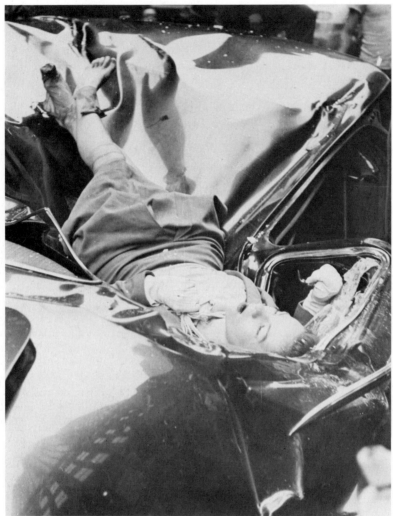

After plummeting eighty-six floors from the observation deck of the Empire State Building — visible in the metallic reflection at lower left — this young woman lies dead, the victim of suicide.

C H A P T E R *13*

Suicide

Statistics indicate that nearly 30,000 Americans a year choose to end their lives by suicide. Suicide is the second-ranked cause of death for all males ages fifteen to twenty-four.[1] It is estimated that more than 750,000 people in the United States are seriously affected by someone else's suicide each year.

Many experts believe that the official statistics grossly understate the actual number of suicides, perhaps even by half. Edwin Shneidman, one of this country's foremost suicidologists, explains why official understatements may occur: "Because of religious and bureaucratic prejudices, family sensitivity, differences in the proceedings of coroner's hearings and postmortem examinations, and the shadowy distinctions between suicides and accidents — in short, the unwillingness to recognize the act for what it is — knowledge of the extent to which suicide pervades modern society is diminished and distorted."[2]

Most people have at some time in their lives at least fantasized about the possibility of committing suicide. Such thoughts are not uncommon during childhood and adolescence, and they may crop up from time to time in later life as well. Typically, such thoughts occur as a kind of "trying out" or "testing" of the notion, rather than as a serious consideration of the suicidal act.

It is perhaps not too disturbing to fantasize about suicide in our innocent daydreams. But expressing or discussing such thoughts often causes embarrassment

Thurs July 10
1:35PM

My Darling Wife.
This afternoon I am going to make a 3rd attempt at bringing my turbulent life to an end. I hope that it is successful.

I dont know what I want from this world of ours, but you see I am due to go soon anyway. My mother died at 60 ish as did her brothers and father. Also Alf has gone now.

Please dont get Margaret to come over here. – but you go as planned It will do you good. Put the Bungalow on the market and have a sale of the chattels. Then buy a smaller one.

The field will have vacant pos in Nov if you want to sell that

The wills are in the safe.

My love to you, Margaret, Michael and Janice.
I love you all – you have been so good to me

Tommy   X.X.X.X.X.
             XX.X.X.X.X.

Dial Police 999
Also Bill   891459.

IT IS NOW 2.00 PM Tommy xx.

Figure 13-1 *Suicide Note and Report of Death*
Even when a newspaper account is as detailed as this British report (facing page), the facts of suicide as described in the newspaper may reveal very little of the intense human factors — the personal and social dynamics — that precipitated the suicidal act.

Retired man's suicide

A HYTHE man aged 64 killed himself because he could not stand old age, an inquest heard yesterday.

Retired maintenance engineer Aubrey Heathfield Aylmore, who lived at Forest Front, Hythe, was found dead in his car by his wife.

The inquest heard that Mrs. Heathfield Aylmore had been to a WI meeting and returned home an hour later than planned.

She found her husband's body in the garage with a length of hose pipe running from the exhaust into the car.

A note was found in which Mr. Heathfield Aylmore said that this was his third suicide attempt and that he wanted to "put an end to my turbulent life."

Dr. Richard Goodbody, consultant pathologist, said cause of death was asphyxia due to carbon monoxide poisoning.

Coroner Mr. Harry Roe said that Mr. Heathfield Aylmore had been depressed at the thought of growing old.

or discomfort, dealt with by forced humor, uneasy laughter, or a cerebral intellectuality that distances us from the threat of mortality that suicide represents. We attempt to mask our discomfort at the awesome fact that each of us has the power to choose whether or not we continue to exist (see Figure 13-1).

Death is usually conceived of as something that "happens" to an individual, an event over which a person has little or no conscious control. "Why," it is asked, "would someone willingly end his or her own life?" The idea of doing so may seem inexplicable, yet there are many reasons why a person might try. Think for a moment about why a person would choose to die. What are some of the reasons that might cause a person to voluntarily end his or her own life.?

Suicide is often ascribed to the person's despondency about a particular set of circumstances. Such a description leaves much unanswered, however. Suicide has many different causes, and it is useful to investigate more specifically the factors that can influence a person to commit suicide. Suicide may result from feelings of dissatisfaction with "society," or from frustration at perceiving oneself as "different" from others. It may be an escape from mental or emotional pain. The decision to commit suicide can derive from a variety of emotional factors, including feelings of shame, guilt, despair, loneliness, anger, fear, frustration, or the desire for revenge. Suicide may seem to offer the only escape, the only means of changing an untenable situation.

In thinking about some of the factors that can influence a person to commit suicide, you may find yourself thinking, "There's nothing that could cause me

TABLE 13-1   *Four Definitions of Suicide*

Suicide is . . .

The act or an instance of taking one's own life voluntarily and intentionally, especially by a
   person of years of discretion and of sound mind. (*Webster's New Collegiate
   Dictionary*) [a]

Self-killing deriving from one's inability or refusal to accept the terms of the human
   condition. (Ronald W. Maris) [b]

All behavior that seeks and finds the solution to an existential problem by making an
   attempt on the life of the subject. (Jean Baechler) [c]

The human act of self-inflicted, self-intentioned cessation. (Edwin Shneidman) [d]

   [a]Used by permission. From *Webster's Ninth New Collegiate Dictionary,* © 1986 by Merriam-Webster Inc.,
Publishers of the Merriam-Webster® Dictionaries.
   [b]Ronald W. Maris, *Pathways to Suicide: A Survey of Self-Destructive Behaviors* (Baltimore: Johns Hopkins
University Press, 1981), p. 290.
   [c]Jean Baechler, *Suicides* (New York: Basic Books, 1979), p. 11.
   [d]Edwin S. Shneidman, editor, *Death: Current Perspectives,* 2nd ed. (Palo Alto, Calif.: Mayfield Publishing Co.,
1980), p. 416.

to think seriously about ending my own life." To those who believe they have
the resources to deal effectively with the exigencies or demands of life, suicide
may seem a radical solution indeed. Yet suicide is a complex human behavior,
one that involves a diversity of self-destructive intentions. Thus, our first step
toward understanding the dynamics of suicide must be to develop a working
definition of suicide that provides a framework for organizing this complexity
into more manageable form.

Comprehending Suicide

   In beginning to think about the reasons why a person would decide to
voluntarily end his or her own life, it soon becomes evident that suicide can be
studied on the basis of the apparent cause or purpose of the suicidal act, the
individual and cultural meanings attached to suicidal behaviors, and the
particular population segment affected by suicide. The definitions of suicide in
Table 13-1 will help us establish a comprehensive working definition that is
useful for all of these approaches.

   Notice that each definition emphasizes certain aspects of suicidal intention
and behavior. Although the basic dictionary definition provides a good starting
point for understanding suicide, it is somewhat vague. As you review these
definitions, pay particular attention to how each explains the dynamics of
suicide. Ask yourself: What kinds of human behavior does the definition
include? Is suicide a specific act or a process? What is the context of suicide? For
example, Ronald Maris's definition focuses on the cause or rationale for suicide.
French social scientist Jean Baechler's definition emphasizes suicide as a means
of resolving problems. Notice how suicide is defined as a behavior rather than as
a specific act. As a response to an existential problem, suicide relates to the

individual's total experience of a situation, the inner as well as outer dimensions. Notice also that behavior that involves "making an attempt on the life of the subject" may be immediate or long term. Thus, alcoholism might be considered a suicidal behavior inasmuch as it reflects the alcoholic's attempt to solve an existential problem by making use of something that, over time, can have disastrous and possibly fatal consequences.

Shneidman's definition emphasizes the factors of intention and action, and the concept of ending one's conscious existence. From your perusal of these definitions, you can see that suicide involves thoughts about death (that is, the wish to be dead) as well as certain actions or behaviors to carry out that intention. With this functional understanding of suicide in mind, we are prepared to examine the dynamics of suicide as conceptualized in two complementary theories.

Two Models of Suicide

The modern study of suicide has followed two main lines of theoretical investigation: (1) the sociological model, which has its foundation in the work of nineteenth-century French sociologist Emile Durkheim; and (2) the psychological model, based on the work of the psychoanalyst Sigmund Freud. Each of these theories offers a coherent framework, developed from direct observations of human behavior, within which to understand suicide.

Richard Cory

Whenever Richard Cory went down town,
    We people on the pavement looked at him:
He was a gentleman from sole to crown,
    Clean favored, and imperially slim.

And he was always quietly arrayed,
    And he was always human when he talked;
But still he fluttered pulses when he said,
    "Good-morning," and he glittered when he walked.

And he was rich—yes, richer than a king—
    And admirably schooled in every grace:
In fine, we thought that he was everything
    To make us wish that we were in his place.

So on we worked, and waited for the light,
    And went without the meat, and cursed the bread;
And Richard Cory, one calm summer night,
    Went home and put a bullet through his head.

Edwin Arlington Robinson

The Social Context of Suicide

The sociological model, as its name implies, focuses on the relationship between the individual and society. Individual behavior is considered in its social setting and within the group dynamics that influence it. Ronald Maris states the Durkheimian view thus: "An integrated social situation is one in which individuals are strongly attached to society's governing rules by a sense of moral obligation or structural independence, or both."[3] Within this social context, then, suicide is viewed as the result of a disturbance in the ties between the individual and society. When there is some imbalance or upset with respect to this relationship, the potential for suicidal behavior increases. From this premise, Durkheim postulated three types of suicide: anomic, egoistic, and altruistic. Each is related to a particular kind of interplay between the society and the individual.

Anomic suicide occurs when the relationship between an individual and the society is suddenly shattered as a result of some trauma or catastrophe. When this happens, the usual standards of social conduct are weakened; the person is in a state of *anomie*. Because of these broken ties the individual experiences anxiety, disorientation, isolation, and loneliness. The anomic event could be a severe loss — the loss of a job, the amputation of a limb, the death of a close friend or family member. Indeed, any sudden and disruptive change — whether it is perceived as positive or negative — might precipitate an anomic suicide. Durkheim suggested that even sudden wealth might stimulate suicide if the person felt unable to cope with his or her changed status and new opportunities. Calling attention to the particular disruptions caused by divorce and by economic hardship, Durkheim argued that anomic suicide is a chronic condition of modern societies.

Egoistic suicide occurs when an individual's mental energies are concentrated on the self to such an extent that the societal sanctions are ineffective. Because of inadequate integration between the individual and the family or other social groups, the suicidal individual has little concern for the community. Thus, society's demands that its members not kill themselves does not deter the egoistic suicide. Persons who are disenfranchised or who live at the fringes of

 Suicide Note Written by a Divorced Woman, Age 61

You cops will want to know why I did it, well just let us say that I lived 61 years too many.

People have always put obstacles in my way. One of the great ones is leaving this world when you want to and have nothing to live for.

I am not insane. My mind was never more clear. It has been a long day. The motor got so hot it would not run so I just had to sit here and wait. The breaks were against me to the very last.

The sun is leaving the hill now so hope nothing else happens.

society may feel no compulsion to heed life-affirming values because they do not experience themselves as meaningfully related to the wider community; society may be perceived as faceless and uncaring. In this sense, anomie and egoism may reinforce each other. In Durkheim's view, when an individual is detached from social life and his or her own goals become predominant, the person's own personality takes precedence over what might be called the collective personality. The egoistic suicide represents "the special type of suicide springing from excessive indivualism."[4]

Altruistic suicide, the third category in Durkheim's typology, refers to suicides that result from an excessive integration between the individual and the society. In this case, the group's values predominate over the individual's. *Seppuku,* the ritual disembowelment practiced by the samurai in feudal Japan, and *suttee,* the voluntary immolation of a Hindu widow on her husband's funeral pyre practiced in precolonial India, are examples of altruistic suicide. A modern instance of altruistic suicide occurred on November 20, 1978 in Jonestown, Guyana, when more than 900 persons met their death in what has been called the largest mass suicide in history. At a previously little-noticed jungle clearing, which had been the communal settlement of the followers of the Reverend Jim Jones, many of the victims drank cyanide-laced fruit punch and families died together in one another's arms. In hypnotic tones from his throne above the crowd, Jones urged community members to drink the poison.[5] The customs of the social group influenced the individual's decision to commit suicide.

For more than 900 Americans who left their home to join a religious fanatic called the Reverend Jim Jones, death came in the jungles of Guyana with these comforting words from the man who engineered the largest mass suicide the world has witnessed:

> What's going to happen here in a matter of a few minutes is that one of those people in the plane is going to shoot the pilot. . . . So you be kind to the children and be kind to seniors, and take the potion like they used to in Ancient Greece, and step over quietly, because we are not committing suicide—it's a revolutionary act.
>
> Everybody dies. I haven't seen anybody yet didn't die. And I like to choose my own kind of death for a change. I'm tired of being tormented to hell. Tired of it. (Applause)

A few cultists protested. Some women screamed. Children cried. Armed guards took up positions around the camp to keep anyone from escaping:

> Let the little children in and reassure them. . . . They're not crying from pain, it's just a little bitter-tasting. . . . Death is a million times more preferable to spend more days in this life. If you knew what was ahead of you, you'd be glad to be stepping over tonight . . . quickly, quickly, no more pain. . . . This world was not your home. . . .

Here the tape runs out. The sound stops before the report of the pistol that killed Jim Jones, presumably fired by his own hand.

Robert Ramsey and Randall Toye, *The Goodbye Book*

We see, then, that between society and the individual there are two forces: Integration, the bond between the individual and the group; and regulation, the coercive power of the group over the actions of the individual. Anomic suicides result when the regulative function of social sanctions are ineffective. Egoistic suicides result when the integrative bond between society and the individual is weak. Altruistic suicides result when the level of integration and regulation is strong, and circumstances stimulate the individual to commit suicide in order to conform to the values of the social group.

The Mental and Emotional Dynamics of Suicide

The psychological model focuses on the dynamics of the individual's mental and emotional life. This model originated in Sigmund Freud's theory of self-destruction. In contrast to the Durkheimian view, which looks to external events for an explanation of suicide, the Freudian model concentrates on the unconscious processes within the individual mind or personality. Within this intrapsychic realm there are motivations of which the individual is unaware, but that exert a nonetheless powerful influence on behavior.

According to the psychological model, under conditions of enormous stress, the intrapsychic pressures impelling a person toward self-destruction may increase to the point that they overwhelm the defense mechanisms of the ego, or self. There follows a regression to more primitive ego states characterized by powerful forces of aggression. Even with these aggressive forces mobilized, however, the fundamental urge toward self-preservation militates against the ego's acquiescence to its own death.

Thus, another psychodynamic process comes into play. Freudian theory states that the psychological process of identifying oneself with an admired object (that is, another person) characteristically involves a high degree of ambivalence, such that, according to circumstances, feelings of love may alternate with feelings of hate: "The *conscious* feelings for the object often reflect one half of the ambivalence, while the other half is kept unconscious, though nonetheless powerful in the individual's mental life."[6]

These psychodynamics are applied to suicide as follows: When the self is frustrated, the aggressive component of the ambivalence is directed against the internalized person — that is, the internal "image" of the person with whom the self has formed an identification. This completes the mental circuit, as it were, so that it is not the self against which aggression is directed, but rather the

Suicide Note Written by a Married Man, Age 45

My darling,

May her guts rot in hell—I loved her so much.

Henry

Romeo and Juliet also embody another popular misconception: that of the great suicidal passion. It seems that those who die for love usually do so by mistake and ill-luck. It is said that the London police can always distinguish, among the corpses fished out of the Thames, between those who have drowned themselves because of unhappy love affairs and those drowned for debt. The fingers of the lovers are almost invariably lacerated by their attempts to save themselves by clinging to the piers of the bridges. In contrast, the debtors apparently go down like slabs of concrete, apparently without struggle and without afterthought.

A. Alvarez, *The Savage God*

object of the ambivalent identification. Suicide does away with the source of frustration by eliminating the internalized object that is ambivalently loved and hated. Thus, in the psychoanalytic model, suicide is linked with homicide. As Edwin Shneidman says, "Psychodynamically, suicide can be seen as murder in the 180th degree."[7]

Although frustration, hostility, and aggression are central to the psychological dynamics of suicide, other factors may also be present, including guilt, anxiety, and dependency, as well as feelings of helplessness, hopelessness, and abandonment. Karl Menninger noted that suicide involves strong, unconscious hostility combined with a lack of capacity to love others. Internal as well as external conditions can contribute to the crisis that precipitates suicide.

Most suicides are carried out in what might be characterized as a very "iffy" way. That is, an analysis of suicidal behavior reveals the presence of conflicting forces that compete for the greater share of the person's mental energies. Thus, in the psychological model *ambivalence* is a characteristic of suicide. At issue is the will to live versus the will to die. Erwin Stengel says, "Most people who commit acts of self-damage with more or less conscious self-destructive intent do not want either to live or to die, but to do both at the same time—usually one more than the other."[8] Ambivalence refers to this wanting to have it both ways.

Ambivalence toward suicide can be considered in several ways. First, as already suggested, the suicidal individual is likely to experience simultaneously a wish to live and a wish to die. The balance between these opposing polarities may be delicate, with an otherwise minor incident tipping the scales one way or the other. In addition, ambivalence can refer to a situation in which one of these forces is stronger than the other, though the weaker one nevertheless continues to affect the person's behavior. Thus, it represents the possibility that the situation could change if certain circumstances come into play. Stengel says, "Most suicidal acts are manifestations of risk-taking behavior. They are gambles. The danger to life depends on the relationships between self-destructive and life-preserving, contact-seeking tendencies, and on a variety of other factors, some of which are outside the control of the individual."[9]

Considered as an act of communication, suicide aims to force a change. Somehow, the suicidal person's situation is such that he or she no longer wishes to continue living in it. Notice, however, that the person is not necessarily completely intent upon committing suicide. For most suicides, the goal is not death but the eradication of some problem; suicide seems a means of accomplishing that goal. Much suicidal behavior represents a desperate cry for help, a message to the effect that "something has to change in my life; I can't go on living this way."[10]

Among the valuable insights developed from the psychological model of suicide are the following:

1. The *acute* suicidal crisis is of relatively brief duration; that is, it lasts hours or days rather than weeks or months—though it may recur.
2. The suicidal person is likely to be ambivalent about ending his or her life. Plans for self-destruction are generally accompanied by fantasies that rescue or intervention will occur before the fatal act is completed.
3. Most suicidal events are *dyadic:* They involve both the victim and a significant other in some way.

These insights have been usefully applied in constructing a better understanding of suicide and in instigating methods of suicide prevention and intervention.

Each of the two major theories of suicide—the sociological and the psychological models—is an important step toward increased understanding of the patterns of suicidal behavior. Although each model has its roots in a particular methodology, current theories of suicide generally draw upon both in an effort to devise a comprehensive general theory of suicide. For the layperson as well as the professional, the insights from these investigations increase understanding and aid in the process of alleviating the dysfunctional factors that influence suicidal behaviors.

Types of Suicide

Many classification schemes have been applied to suicide in attempts to better comprehend its personal and social meanings (see Table 13-2). A useful starting point is an outline presented by Edwin Shneidman and Norman Farberow, which includes four categories of suicidal behavior: (1) surcease suicide, (2) psychotic suicide, (3) cultural suicide, and (4) referred suicide. In classifying suicides according to these four psychological labels, Shneidman and Farberow analyzed suicide notes to determine the reasoning of the suicidal person that led to the fatal act. The implications of this attempt to grasp the "logic of suicide" is that "if one knew the lethal modes of reasoning and the suppressed premises (or beliefs) which lead to a deadly conclusion, then one might have effective clues to use in the prediction and prevention of suicide."[11]

TABLE 13-2   *Meanings of Suicide*

Some Cultural Meanings of Suicide

Suicide is sinful: A crime against nature, a revolt against the preordained order of the universe.

Suicide is criminal: It violates the ties that exist, the social contract between persons in a society.

Suicide is weakness or madness: It reflects limitations or deviancy ("He must have been crazy" or "He couldn't take it").

Suicide is the Great Death, as in *seppuku, suttee,* and other culturally approved forms of ritual suicide.

Suicide is the rational alternative: The outcome of a "balance-sheet" approach that sizes up the situation and determines the best option.

Some Individual Meanings of Suicide

Suicide is reunion with a lost loved one, a way to "join the deceased."

Suicide is rest and refuge: A way out of a burdensome and depressing situation.

Suicide is getting back: A way of expressing resentment and revenge at being rejected or hurt.

Suicide is the penalty for failure: A response to disappointment and frustration at not meeting self-expectations or the expectations of others.

Suicide is a mistake: The attempt was made as a cry for help and was not intended to be fatal, but there was no rescue or intervention and the outcome was death.

Source: Adapted from Robert Kastenbaum, *Death, Society, and Human Experience,* 2nd ed. (St. Louis, Mo.: C. V. Mosby, 1981) pp. 239–255.

Surcease Suicide

Surcease suicide is attempted with the desire to be released from pain, emotional or physical. For example, a person with a painful terminal illness who wishes to escape further suffering may perceive suicide as a way to do so. To some, suicide represents a rational way out of an unfortunate predicament. This type of suicide is sometimes called "rational suicide" because the reasoning used — death will provide surcease from pain — conforms to normal logic. Others refer to this type of suicide as "auto-euthanasia," self-administered mercy killing.

Is choosing to die in such circumstances properly termed suicide, or is it more appropriately termed *euthanasia,* the "good" or "easy" death? Organizations such as the British group Exit provide information about suicide methods to people who feel that their only real choice is to bring about their own death, as painlessly as possible. Suicide is viewed by some as the natural right of a patient who is dying from a painful illness.[12] Furthermore, the patient choosing to end his or her life already faces the prospect of imminent death, a fate over which he or she has no control except to determine the moment and character of the act of dying.

Notice your own feelings about the distinction between euthanasia and suicide. To many, the difference involves the kind of pain from which the person desires release. In this sense, euthanasia relates primarily to surcease from physical pain. Suicide, on the other hand, is generally thought of as escape from emotional or mental pain. With suicide, the person determines to end his or her existence because somehow life seems too great a burden to bear any longer. Suicide is generally considered an act of violence, whereas euthanasia is more likely to be considered a benevolent act that ensues from a decision made by the patient and perhaps is enacted with the consent of loved ones.

Some people, however, would find such a distinction between suicide and euthanasia odious. Which of these terms, for example, would be applied to the self-inflicted death of an elderly widower who was bereft of family and friends and was facing economic distress and a generally bleak future?[13] Suicides that result from the desire for surcease from pain — whether physical or emotional — are seen by some as a failure of society to adequately respond to the needs of persons in distress. They ask: Does the presence of physical or emotional pain make suicide a truly logical choice, or do more reasonable alternatives exist? Analgesics and sedatives can provide freedom from physical pain; companionship and other therapeutic means can alleviate emotional suffering. However, when these forms of treatment are not available, or when they are perceived as inadequate, a decision may be made to end suffering by taking action to cause one's death.

Psychotic Suicide

Psychotic suicide results from the impaired logic of the delusional or hallucinatory state of mind associated with clinically diagnosed schizophrenia or manic-depressive psychosis. The victim may try to eradicate the psychic malignancy or punish himself or herself by self-destruction, even though there is no conscious intention to die. The patient cannot make use of the normal human faculties of rationality that would separate these conflicting aims. Shneidman and Farberow point out that to treat the psychotic's suicidal impulses one must first treat the psychosis and only later the suicidal tendencies.

Cultural Suicide

Cultural suicide results from the interactions between self-concept and cultural beliefs about death. In medieval Japanese society, ritual suicide, called *hara-kiri* or *seppuku,* was culturally accepted, even demanded, in certain circumstances, especially among the warrior, or samurai, class. Occasions when suicide might seem the only socially acceptable course for a samurai included disgrace in battle or the death of a lord, as well as the desire to make a public statement of one's disagreement with a superior. In such cases, *seppuku* or ritual suicide became the necessary act for an honorable warrior, and specific instructions pertained to the manner in which the suicidal act was to be performed.[14]

Similarly, until modern times, certain castes in India were expected to practice *suttee,* which called for the wife of a nobleman to throw herself upon his funeral pyre. Such self-immolation was condoned by the prevailing religious

AP/Wide World Photos

Flames engulf the body of a Buddhist monk, Quang Duc, whose self-immolation before thousands of onlookers in downtown Saigon was a protest against alleged persecution of Buddhists by the government of South Vietnam.

and cultural beliefs, and a widow's reluctance to perform this ritual suicide would meet with social disapproval. Indeed, a reluctant wife might find herself "helped" onto the burning pyre.

Cultural suicide does not always involve an acceptance of social norms, as already alluded to in the case of samurai who committed seppuku as a means of protesting policies of their superiors. Within the recent past, suicide as protest came to public attention during the Vietnam war, when Buddhist monks committed suicide by self-immolation to protest governmental policies.

Referred Suicide

Referred suicide includes those suicides that are likely to come most readily to mind for most people. This type of suicide results from a destructive logic, such that the victim "confuses the self as experienced by the self with the self as experienced by others." In other words, the victim's self-concept is confused with imaginings of what others think about him or her. The victims of referred suicide tend to feel lonely, helpless, and fearful; they typically experience

Suicide Note Written by a Single Woman, Age 21

My dearest Andrew,

It seems as if I have been spending all my life apologizing to you for things that happened whether they were my fault or not.

I am enclosing your pin because I want you to think of what you took from me every time you see it.

I don't want you to think I would kill myself over you because you're not worth any emotion at all. It is what you cost me that hurts and nothing can replace it.

difficulties in establishing and maintaining meaningful personal relationships. These problems with self-identity, coupled with an inability to feel comfortable relating to others, often involve the victim's self-perception as a failure.

To understand the dynamics of this type of suicide, it is useful to consider the analogy of referred pain, which is defined as pain that is experienced at some distance from its actual source. An injury in the elbow, for example, may be experienced as pain in the little finger; an inflammation of the liver is often experienced as pain in the shoulder. Just as this phenomenon is characterized as referred pain, the root causes of referred suicide are likewise only indirectly related to the end result: death by suicide. Whereas surcease and cultural suicides involve a comparatively straightforward logic between intention and action, the logic of referred suicide is ambiguous. The decision to end one's life is not based on a dispassionate assessment of the situation, but results instead from anguish and confusion about one's options.

Self-concept is an important factor. The failure to perform to expectations or according to certain role definitions sometimes provokes the crisis of self-concept that ultimately leads to suicide. The expectation may be related to something outside the individual ("If I can't be a good enough daughter to please my parents, I give up!"), or it may be related to inward feelings of frustration ("Everybody thinks I'm doing okay, outwardly, but I feel rotten").

Suicidal behaviors may arise from the loss of meaning in one's life. Even after significant successes, a person may feel, "Now what?" The accumulation of successes one after another may appear to be a Sisyphean effort, a continual struggle for achievement but with little sense of accomplishment. Or perhaps the person feels that all that can be accomplished has been: There is nothing more to be gained. Like Alexander the Great, after "conquering the world," one may feel there is nothing to strive for, no reason to live. Suicide may seem the logical response to the loss of one's self-image as the successful conquering hero. Conversely, success may be accompanied by a feeling that "if this is what success is all about, it's not worth the effort."

Stress, competition, aggressiveness, and inability to balance conflicting demands can exist in personal as well as professional life. An orientation toward "super-achievement" often results from taking on more responsibilities than one is truly comfortable with, and the ensuing stress eventually becomes overwhelming. The sense of personal failure can be lethal.

Other Dynamics of Suicide

The four types of suicide – surcease, psychotic, cultural, and referred – represent basic conditions that can precipitate suicidal actions. This listing could be expanded in various ways. For example, we could delineate a category of suicides relating to a "poetic" or "romantic" attraction to death, suicides that exhibit a fascination with the "mystique" of death, especially self-willed death. Death may be approached as a lover to be courted. The poet Sylvia Plath wrote: "I will marry dark death, the thief of the daytime."[15] The novelist Ernest Hemingway and the poets Anne Sexton and Hart Crane are other examples of writers whose fascination with death possibly played a lethal role in their ultimate suicides.

Do such suicides reflect a conscious choice to experience the ultimate, a desire to embrace the mystery of death, of nonbeing? Or do such suicides result from more ordinary frustrations and experiences? Although death is sometimes romanticized in their writings, the suicides of writers and other artists seem to be characterized by such frustrations as affect the lives of all of us. Failure to find meaning in life and problems with relationships are common threads. As someone said, "The death of love evokes the love of death."

Another dynamic that may have an effect on the incidence of suicides is that of suggestibility or imitation. Although reports of suicides in the media have sometimes been blamed for triggering more suicides, studies generally have not found such an effect.[16] Nonetheless, the idea that suicide can be contagious has a long history. Following the publication of Goethe's *The Sorrows of Young Werther* in 1774, for instance, youthful suicides were frequently attributed to the book's influence.[17]

Whether or not attention to suicide in a book, movie, or newspaper report can stimulate an increase in the suicide rate, there is no question of the importance of the overall sociocultural environment. A study of suicide among Micronesian males during a twenty-year period dating from 1960 confirmed the

---

 Suicide Note Written by a Single Man, Age 51

Sunday 4:45 PM   Here goes

To who it may concern

Though I am about to kick the bucket I am as happy as ever. I am tired of this life so am going over to see the other side.

Good luck to all.

Benjamin P.

occurrence of an "epidemiclike" increase.[18] Within the islands of Micronesia, this period was marked by rapid sociocultural transformation, as traditional styles of living gave way to reliance upon a cash economy and modern forms of education, employment, health services, and technology. In studying suicide among Micronesians, investigators reconstructed events leading up to a suicide. Such a review — which is designed to determine the thoughts, feelings, and actions of the deceased — is known as a *psychological autopsy*. Information is pieced together by interviewing the victim's friends and relatives as well as other members of the community. Using these techniques, a significant number of linkages among suicides were found, including two or three suicides occurring among a small circle of friends over several months. There were also cases of suicidal acts in reaction to the suicide of a friend or relative and "suicide pacts" among two or more persons. Taken together, these phenomena pointed to the existence of a "suicide subculture" wherein suicide begat suicide. In an environment characterized by a general familiarity with and acceptance of the *idea* of suicide, suicide became "a culturally patterned and partly collective response" to personal dilemmas and problems.

Subintentional Suicide

Subintentional suicide can be viewed as yet another type of life-threatening behavior. As defined by Edwin Shneidman, "The subintentioned death is one in which the person plays some partial, covert, subliminal, or unconscious role in hastening his own demise."[19] Although not usually defined as suicide by official reporting methods, this mode of death does not fit precisely into such categories as natural or accidental either. As we saw in a previous chapter, there may be a subintentional factor influencing the onset of some illnesses. Similarly, the investigation of homicide cases sometimes turns up evidence that points to a subintentional factor resulting in the victim's taking certain actions or behaving in some way that served to provoke his or her death at another's hands.

Some of the fatal events reported as accidents occur because the victim chose to take an unnecessary and unwise risk. We might call such behavior careless or imprudent, but probing deeper we might find such accidents to be the logical and unavoidable end result of a pattern of behavior that conforms to the definition of subintentional suicide.

In addition to subintentional death, Shneidman delineates two other characteristic patterns of death-related behaviors: intentioned and unintentioned. Table 13-3 presents an outline of these three patterns. Notice that within each of these categories a person might exhibit a variety of attitudes and behaviors regarding death. As you review this table, ask yourself: Where do I stand on this list? What does that say about my own regard for life and death?

Childhood and Adolescent Suicide

Although the overall suicide rate in the United States has remained fairly constant in the recent past, a significant shift has taken place among certain age

T A B L E 13-3   *Patterns of Death-Related Behavior and Attitudes*

Intentioned Death: Death resulting from the suicide's direct, conscious behavior to bring it about. A variety of attitudes or motives may be operative:

The *death seeker* wishes to end consciousness and commits the suicidal act in such a way that rescue is unlikely.

The *death initiator* expects to die in the near future and wants to choose the time and circumstances of death.

The *death ignorer* believes that death ends only physical existence and that the person continues to exist in another manner.

The *death darer* gambles with death, or, as Shneidman says, "bets his life on a relatively low objective probability that he will survive" (such as by playing Russian roulette).

Subintentioned Death: Death resulting from a person's patterns of management or style of living, although death was not the conscious, direct aim of the person's actions:

The *death chancer,* although in many ways like the death darer, may want higher odds of survival.

The *death hastener* may expedite his or her death by substance abuse (drugs, alcohol, and the like) or by failing to safeguard well-being (for example, by inadequate nutrition or precautions against disease or disregard of available treatments).

The *death facilitator* gives little resistance to death, making it easy for death to occur, as in the deaths of patients whose energies, or "will to live," are low because of their illness.

The *death capitulator* is one who, usually out of a great fear of death, plays a subintentional role in his or her own death, as may a person upon whom a so-called voodoo death has been put, or as may a person who believes that someone admitted to a hospital is bound to die.

The *death experimenter* does not consciously wish to die, but lives on the brink, usually in a "befogged state of consciousness" that may be related to taking drugs in such ways that the person may become comatose or even die with little concern.

Unintentioned Deaths: Death in which the decedent plays no significant causative role. However, various attitudes toward death may shape the experience of dying:

The *death welcomer,* though not hastening death, looks forward to it (as might an aged person who feels unable to manage adequately or satisfactorily).

The *death accepter* is resigned to his or her fate; the style of acceptance may be passive, philosophical, resigned, heroic, realistic, or mature.

The *death postponer* hopes to put death off for as long as possible.

The *death disdainer* feels, in Shneidman's words, "above any involvement in the stopping of the vital processes."

The *death fearer* is fearful, and possibly phobic, about anything related to death; death is something to be fought and hated.

The *death feigner* pretends to be in mortal danger or pretends to perform a suicidal act without being in actual danger, possibly in an attempt to gain attention or to manipulate others.

Source: Adapted from Edwin S. Shneidman, *Deaths of Man* (New York: Quadrangle Books, 1973), pp. 82–90.

groups. Until the late 1960s, suicide rates generally increased directly with age, with the lowest suicide rates among the young and the highest among the aged. Now, however, a decrease in the rate among older persons has been offset by an increase among adolescents and young adults. Suicide is in second place, following accidents, as a leading cause of death among persons ages fifteen to twenty-four.[20] More than 5,000 young people age twenty-four and under commit suicide each year in the United States.

Moreover, most suicidologists are convinced that the actual number of suicides among young people is considerably underreported. The suicide rate among children and adolescents might be much higher than current statistics indicate if accidents were carefully examined for intent. Further, "given the stigma against suicide in our society, it is reasonable to assume that some of the childhood deaths such as those resulting from running in front of cars or plastic bag suffocation might not be accidental but intentional."[21]

The ratio of completers to attempters also appears to be higher for young people than for older people. For people in general and those in the older age group, the ratio is probably between 5:1 and 10:1, whereas for adolescents it may be as high as 25:1 or 50:1. There may be as many as 250,000 young people

Unable to earn a living by writing and too proud to accept food offered to him by his landlady, this seventeen-year-old killed himself by taking poison. Painted in 1856 by Henry Wallis, The Death of Chatterton *depicts an adolescent suicide that was precipitated by crisis arising out of the developmental transition from child to adult.*

Henry Wallis, Tate Gallery, London

TABLE 13-4 *Some Possible Causes of Youthful Suicide*

Low self-esteem and poor self-image
Sense of lack of control over one's life
Early separation from parents
Excessively high parental expectations
Devaluing of emotional expression
Lack of effective relationships with peers
Pressure for achievement and success
Increased use of drugs and alcohol

Source: Adapted from William C. Fish and Edith Waldhart-Letzel, "Suicide and Children," *Death Education* 5 (1981), pp. 217–220; and from Michael Peck, "Youth Suicide," *Death Education* 6 (1982), p. 33.

attempting suicide in the United States each year and perhaps a million or more children moving in and out of suicidal crises, thoughts, and episodes.[22] Ten percent of the children in any public classroom may be considered at risk. Suicide attempts are being made (or perhaps *recorded*) at younger ages than in the past. Since the risk for completed suicide is higher among those who have previously attempted suicide, particularly during the first years following an attempt, young people who have attempted suicide remain with the high-risk age group for a longer period of time.[23] Although young children do exhibit suicidal behavior and even kill themselves, it is difficult to apply the label "suicide" when a child has yet to form a mature concept of death. Nevertheless, children as young as nine or ten do threaten, attempt, and commit suicide.[24]

Factors Influencing Youthful Suicide

Although suicides among adolescents share some characteristics in common with suicides among older persons, specific dynamics affect children and adolescents (see Table 13-4). In an early study, researchers noted five major motivational factors influencing children's suicide: (1) the desire to escape from a difficult situation; (2) the attempt to assert independence or to punish persons who "interfered" with the child; (3) the effort to gain attention and affection; (4) the wish to achieve reunion with a deceased loved one; and (5) spite.[25]

More recently, researchers have been probing the question of how increases in suicide and homicide among the young are related to such factors as: (1) violence in the media, especially television; (2) the easy availability of lethal weapons, which can change youthful posturing into deadly warfare; (3) the moral legacy of Vietnam; (4) drug and alchohol abuse; and (5) an apparent nationwide acceptance of more violence in our lives.[26] Some suicidologists see a correlation between violence and suicide among the young: As acts of violent aggression have increased, there has been a corresponding increase in suicide.

In a survey of risk factors relative to suicidal behavior in children and adolescents, both early developmental experiences and current environmental situations were cited. Besides aggression and family violence, these factors included depression, parental suicidal behavior, and family losses.[27] In addition, it has been shown that parents and others who work with young people should pay particular attention to youngsters who have recently lost a parent or who suffer from learning disabilities related to hyperactivity, perceptual disorders, or dyslexia, since these characteristics also seem to involve a greater risk for suicide.

The postwar baby boom is another factor mentioned as contributing to the increase in self-destructive behavior among young people. Many see a relationship between a rise in youthful suicides and the pressures and overcrowding experienced by a large cohort of "baby boomers" passing through the violence-prone years of childhood. This factor, coupled with lack of employment opportunities and other economic factors, has brought about significant life-style and behavioral changes in the experience of the generation now moving up through adolescence and young adulthood. The result may be too many young people wanting too many things that are not available, thus increasing their feelings of anonymity and alienation.

The upheavals in family life during the last few decades are also viewed as an important influence on suicidal behavior among the young. New life styles within the family setting may be increasing the pressures upon all family members. Some researchers call for special attention to the needs of children whose parents divorce. Because divorce is so prevalent among American families, however, it has not been clearly established as a cause of suicide. Still, economic pressures and increased mobility add to the sense of upheaval and lessened security of family patterns. Young people sometimes respond to these changes with uncertainty, fear, and anger. Suicide may seem a way of imposing some control over events that are beyond one's ability to influence effectively. Much suicidal behavior is linked with a life style without goals, direction, or substance. Commenting on the values of the home, the family, and parenting, Michael Peck says that many adolescents "describe what might best be called a narcissistic do-your-own-thing upsurge among parents," with the result that youngsters grow up with "little clear-cut guidance, confused or absent values, and a sense of floating along in time without direction."[28]

Youthful suicide also exhibits characteristics related to gender. For example, the rate of *completed* suicide for boys is reported to be about four times higher than for girls, even though girls *attempt* suicide nearly three times as often. One reason for this may lie in the methods used: Girls tend to take pills or slash wrists, whereas boys tend to use less equivocal means, such as guns. This difference also may stem from a social milieu in which girls are given greater permission to verbalize their feelings, whereas "boys seem to be more driven to desperate measures with finality."[29]

Categories of Youthful Suicide

One of the categories used to describe youthful suicides is that of the *loner personality type,* which typically emerges at around age fourteen and builds to a high potential for suicide in the later teens. Another category is made up of *depressed* youngsters who act out their depression in harmful, disruptive, or illegal ways, sometimes involving alcohol or drug abuse. The category of *psychotic suicide* also affects young people.

Crisis suicide represents perhaps less than 15 percent of all youthful suicides. The typical pattern here is that of an adolescent who reaches a point in his or her life involving sudden traumatic changes, such as the loss of a loved one or the loss or threatened loss of status in school. In response, the young person may exhibit sudden and dramatic changes in behavior, possibly including loss of interest in things that were previously important, hostile and aggressive acts (in a previously placid youngster), or signs of confusion, disorganization, and depression.

The final category of youthful suicide to be discussed is that of persons for whom suicidal behavior is a form of communication, the classical *cry for help*. This is a person who becomes suicidal when the usual ways of expressing feelings of frustration are blocked. This category of suicidal behavior is associated more frequently with attempters and threateners than with persons who commit suicide. There is often no history of suicidal behavior, and the lethality of the attempt is generally low. Peck says: "The ultimate purpose of the behavior, in a post hoc analysis, seems to be to clear the way, to open up, to break through the barriers, so that the significant others will know how desperate or how unhappy the person feels."[30] Despite this underlying goal of opening up communication and the usually low order of lethality of the suicidal behavior, death may result nonetheless, even if unintentionally. It is important for everyone concerned to recognize that a serious problem exists and to make efforts toward increasing communication and proposing remedies. Too often, this kind of low-lethality suicidal behavior is met with defensive hostility or with attempts to minimize its seriousness and make it seem unimportant. When this attitude persists, the risk of suicide increases along with the possibility that the next attempt will be lethal.

Furthermore, a child or adolescent may fail to fully recognize the danger inherent in his or her self-destructive actions. Adolescence is typically a time of "testing the limits." Sometimes such teenage flirtations with death exemplified as "playing chicken" prove to be more than was bargained for. More obviously suicidal behaviors, such as cutting one's wrists or taking a drug overdose, may be engaged in as a means of gaining attention or of expressing frustration, without full recognition of their potential for causing death. Or such suicidal behaviors may be engaged in with a kind of lackadaisical attitude about the possible outcome. Whatever the motive, however, the outcome can be just as deadly.

Contemplating Suicide

In most groups of classroom size, one or two persons have at some time contemplated suicide. Perhaps such thoughts were momentary flashes — "What would it be like if I weren't alive?" or "If I killed myself, it would solve all my problems" — which were soon replaced by more constructive methods of coping. Imagine for a moment the progression of thoughts of someone seriously considering suicide.

Assume first that in an untenable situation suicide seems the only recourse, or at the least an option to be considered further. The next step might involve formulating some means of killing oneself. At this point the means have not been actually acquired, but various possibilities are given consideration.

Many people have reached this stage — perhaps through mere fantasizing, or perhaps with serious intentions. For some, the shock of recognizing that one is harboring such thoughts is enough to force a decision toward a more life-affirming alternative. For others, once the means of suicide is decided upon, the next step toward suicide is taken, a step that greatly increases the level of lethality with regard to suicidal intention.

This stage involves actually acquiring the means to kill oneself, thus setting into motion the logistics that make suicide a real possibility. As at the earlier steps in this sequence, a change of mind is still possible, and a different solution can be sought. Otherwise, the final step in the suicidal progression comes into play: actually using the means that have been acquired to commit the suicidal act.

These steps toward lethality have been described as occurring in a definite sequence, but to the person involved the process may be experienced as anything but logical and orderly. In actuality, suicide typically involves a complex array of conflicting thoughts and emotions. The predominant experience may be one of confusion. Still, recognizing the particular steps that must be taken to carry out the suicidal act is useful for understanding both the amount of sustained effort involved in completing a suicide and the many decision points at which a change of mind or outside intervention is possible.

Choice of Method

Once a decision is made to commit suicide, a choice must be made concerning the means to be used (see Figure 13-2). Sometimes a particular method of suicide is chosen because of the image it represents to the suicidal individual. One might imagine drowning as a dreamy kind of death, a merging back into the universe. Or one might associate an overdose of sleeping pills with the death of a movie star. Whatever one's image of a particular method, the reality is likely to be quite different. Some persons who overdose on drugs do so expecting a quiet or peaceful death. The actual effects of a drug overdose are often far from peaceful or serene.

Sometimes a particular method of suicide is chosen for its anticipated impact on survivors. A person who wants survivors to "really pay for all the grief they caused me" might select a means of suicide that would graphically communicate this rage. Someone who did not want to "make a scene" might choose a method imagined as being less shocking to one's survivors.

Experience and familiarity also influence the choice of suicidal method. For example, an experienced hunter well acquainted with rifles might be inclined to turn to such a weapon for suicide because of its accessibility and familiarity.

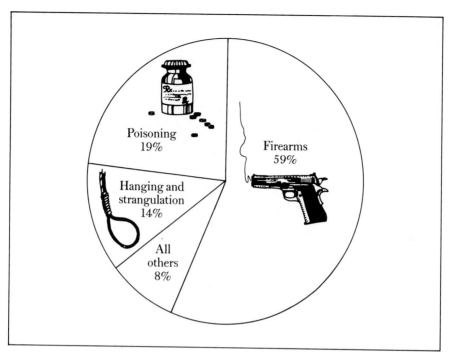

Figure 13-2 *How Americans Commit Suicide*
Source: National Center for Health Statistics, *Vital Statistics of the United States.*

Someone who understands the effects of various drugs might use them to concoct a fatal overdose.

In short, the choice of suicidal method reflects the experience and state of mind of the person choosing it. It may be a spontaneous choice using whatever lethal devices are readily at hand. Or it may be the result of considerable thought and even research. Either way, the choice of suicide method often reveals significant information about the state of mind that led to the attempt.

The process of making this choice can be likened to making the travel arrangements for a cross-country trip. A person wanting to travel from the West Coast to the East Coast must consider the various kinds of transportation available — automobile, train, airplane, and so on. Some of these are quite rapid; others are relatively slow and deliberate. For example, once you board an airplane and it lifts off the runway, there is no opportunity to change one's mind and disembark before touching down at the scheduled destination. On the other hand, someone bicycling from coast to coast would have innumerable opportunities to decide upon a different destination.

Similarly, some methods of committing suicide offer little hope of changing one's mind after the lethal act is initiated. Once the trigger is pulled on a revolver placed next to one's skull, for example, there's virtually no possibility of

Käthe Kollwitz, Library of Congress

Despair, a common component of many suicides, is starkly depicted in this lithograph, Nachdenkende Frau, *by Käthe Kollwitz. If the potential victim's warning signals are observed by persons who take steps to provide crisis intervention, the suicidal impulses may be thwarted.*

altering the likelihood of a fatal outcome. On the other hand, the would-be suicide who cuts her wrists or takes an overdose of drugs *might* have time to alter an otherwise fatal outcome by deciding to seek medical help. The potential for death, if help is not forthcoming, may be as great as that of the gunshot wound to the head, but there would generally be a greater possibility of intervention. There is, then, an order of lethality among methods used in the suicidal act.

Order of Lethality

The various methods used in suicide attempts are not necessarily equivalent in potential lethality. Some methods carry a greater statistical risk of lethality than others. In the following listing, eleven methods of attempting suicide are ranked from most to least lethal. Any of these methods is potentially a killer. Ranking is by probability of death from use of the method.[31]

Order of Lethality

1. Gunshot
2. Carbon monoxide
3. Hanging
4. Drowning
5. Plastic bag (suffocation)
6. Impact (jumping from a high place)
7. Fire
8. Poison
9. Drugs
10. Gas
11. Cutting

Although each method is potentially fatal, how it is applied influences the degree of lethality. For instance, a bullet into the head or the heart is more likely to kill than a gunshot wound to other parts of the body. Likewise, with the least lethal item on this list, cutting, the depth of cut and the location of the wound are significant determinants of the outcome.

Generally, persons who use the most lethal methods in their suicide attempts and are unsuccessful have a lower risk of future suicide attempts than do those who use the less lethal methods. In other words, the person who survives a self-inflicted gunshot wound is less likely to try suicide again than someone who unsuccessfully used a plastic bag. In the following list, methods are ranked according to the statistical probability that those who used them unsuccessfully will attempt suicide again.

Relationship Between Order of Lethality and Repeated Suicide Attempts

1. Plastic bag
2. Carbon monoxide
3. Drowning
4. Gas
5. Poison
6. Gunshot
7. Impact
8. Cutting
9. Drugs
10. Hanging
11. Fire

Perhaps coming very near death somehow purges the suicidal individual of the wish to end his or her life. Persons admitted to intensive care as a result of suicide attempts show a relatively low rate of repeat attempts. The highest rate of repeat suicide attempts is among those who received no treatment for their injuries.

It should be kept in mind that these statistics reflect general patterns of suicidal behavior. And although such statistics are useful for those involved in suicide intervention and treatment programs, they cannot be used as a reliable means for predicting the behavior of a particular individual.

> ### Resume
>
> Razors pain you;
> Rivers are damp;
> Acids stain you;
> And drugs cause cramp.
> Guns aren't lawful;
> Nooses give;
> Gas smells awful;
> You might as well live.
>
> Dorothy Parker

Suicide Attempts

A useful distinction in studying suicidal behavior is the difference between *attempted* suicide and the *fait accompli*. Most studies indicate that for every eight persons who attempt suicide, one succeeds.[32] Some suicidologists believe that there are two fairly distinct populations among those who engage in suicidal behavior: the *attempters* (who tend toward repeated, unsuccessful attempts) and the *completers* (whose first attempt typically succeeds). They believe that attempters and completers may have quite different aims with regard to their suicidal acts.[33]

At least some failed suicides aim to make a kind of dramatic statement that is a cry for help. The suicide attempt says: "I am deadly serious, and you'd better pay attention!" This communication may be directed inward to oneself or outward to others. The person states the need for a significant change in his or her life.

Of course, some suicide attempts fail not because of the person's intention to fail, but rather, perhaps, because of some outside intervention or because of some error of execution — for example, an intended drug overdose fails because too little or the wrong kind of drug was taken. Some people who survive a suicide attempt look upon their continued existence as a second chance or a "bonus life." This is frequently true of those who *meant* to die. They often exhibit more positive values and more constructive attitudes in their relationships with others than they did before their unsuccessful suicide attempt.

Although there is considerable evidence to support the view that some suicides are meant to fail and others are meant to succeed, one should nevertheless be careful about assigning a particular attempt to one or the other of these categories: An attempt meant to fail may succeed; one meant to succeed may fail. It is not correct to assume that a failed suicide attempt was meant to fail and is only a gesture. Suicidal behavior is life threatening; it can be lethal whether intended to be or not. Psychological autopsies of some suicide victims reveal that they quite likely intended that their attempt would be stopped short of death, but help did not arrive in time. Suicide attempts should always be taken seriously.

Suicide Notes

Suicide notes have been called "cryptic maps of ill-advised journeys."[34] Although it is often assumed that nearly all suicides leave notes behind for their survivors, in fact only about one-quarter of suicides write a final message.[35] As at least a partial record of the mental state of suicides, such notes are of immense interest to the suicidologist. Imagine yourself in circumstances that would lead to your writing a suicide note. What kinds of things would you want to say in your last words to your survivors?

Actual suicide notes represent a wide variety of messages and intentions. Some notes explain to survivors the decision to commit suicide. Others express anger or blame. Conversely, some notes emphasize that the writer's suicide was "no one's fault." The messages in suicide notes range from sweeping statements of the writer's philosophy or credo regarding suicide to extremely detailed listings of practical chores that will need attention after the writer's death. For example, one note instructed survivors, "The cat needs to go to the vet next Tuesday; don't miss the appointment or you'll be charged double. The car is due for servicing a week from Friday."

Suicide notes may include: expressions of love, hate, shame, disgrace, fear of insanity, self-abnegation, feelings of rejection; explanations for the suicidal act or defenses of the right to take one's life; disavowal of any survivor's responsibility for the suicide; instructions for distributing the suicide's property and possessions. Genuine suicide notes typically display dichotomies of logic, hostility toward others mixed with self-blame, the use of particular names and specific instructions to survivors, and a sense of decisiveness about suicide. A theme of many is that of an intense love-hate ambivalence toward survivors, as expressed succinctly in the following suicide note:[36]

> Dear Betty:
> I hate you.
> Love,
> George

This example of ambivalence also points up the dyadic nature of suicide — here involving husband and wife. Suicide notes often provide clues about the intentions and emotions that led the person to suicide, but they rarely tell the whole story — and they often raise more questions than they answer. The message of a suicide note may come as a surprise to survivors who previously had no hint of the person's feelings there expressed.

Suicide notes often have a significant effect on survivors. Whether the final message is one of affection or of blame, survivors have no opportunity to respond. In this sense, suicide represents the ultimate last word.

Suicide Note Written by a Married Man, Age 45

Dear Claudia,

You win, I can't take it any longer. I know you have been waiting for this to happen. I hope it makes you very happy, this is not an easy thing to do, but I've got to the point where there is nothing to live for, a little bit of kindness from you would of made everything so different, but all that ever interested you was the *dollar*.

It is pretty hard for me to do anything when you are so greedy even with this house you couldn't even be fair with that, well it's all yours now and you won't have to see the Lawyer anymore.

I wish you would give my personal things to Danny, you couldn't get much from selling them anyway, you still have my insurance, it isn't much but it will be enough to take care of my debts and still have a few bucks left.

You always told me that I was the one that made Sharon take her life, in fact you said I killed her, but you know down deep in your heart it was you that made her do what she did, and now you have two deaths to your credit, it should make you feel very proud.

Good By Kid

P.S. Disregard all the mean things I've said in this letter, I have said a lot of things to you I didn't really mean and I hope you get well and wish you the best of everything.

Cathy—don't come in.

Call your mother, she will know what to do.

Love,
Daddy

Cathy don't go in the bedroom.

Suicide Prevention, Intervention, and Postvention

Many believe that there is little reason to be optimistic about the prospect of preventing suicide or eliminating it from the repertory of human behaviors. To do so, society would have to eradicate the sources of human unhappiness and dissatisfaction. Efforts to create a social environment that is conducive to the successful pursuit of happiness must necessarily fall short of perfection. Interpersonal problems and social pressures thwart the achievement of universal happiness and satisfaction. This is not to say that efforts to ameliorate human suffering are completely unavailing, only that they are inherently limited.

More successful in reducing the incidence of successful suicide is life-saving *intervention*. Whereas suicide prevention aims to eliminate suicide, the goal of suicide intervention is to reduce the lethality of the individual suicidal crisis. Although in practice many suicide intervention programs operate under the name of "suicide prevention centers," such programs make use of the theories and techniques common to crisis intervention. Their emphasis is on providing short-term care and treatment to persons in a suicidal crisis in order to reduce its inherent lethality, thus reducing the risk of suicide.

Finally, suicide *postvention* (a concept formulated by Shneidman) is primarily assistance given to the suicide victim's survivors — family members and other loved ones. The bereaved survivors have special needs, for they often experience feelings of guilt and self-blame, which need to be adequately confronted. When these feelings are not attended to properly or are mismanaged, they increase the likelihood of dysfunctional relationships and other difficulties in the lives of suicide survivors.

In the early 1960s there were fewer than a half-dozen suicide crisis centers in the United States; by the late 1970s there were more than two hundred. The 1980s have seen the rise of suicide crisis centers and hotlines focusing on specific groups. For example, the severe economic crisis affecting American farmers and ranchers led to the establishment in Montana of a suicide hotline for people in rural areas.[37] The typical suicide prevention center operates primarily as a telephone-answering center with around-the-clock availability to persons in crisis. The services provided are mainly designed to serve as a short-term resource for persons contemplating suicide. The caller's anonymity is respected, and the caller's expressed need of help is unquestioningly accepted. Staff members — some of them professionals, many of them volunteers who have been given special training — make use of various techniques to reduce the suicidal caller's stress.

As the incidence of suicide and the problems associated with it have increased, some suicide intervention centers have expanded their services to encompass treatment for a broad range of self-destructive behaviors. For example, at the Los Angeles Suicide Prevention Center, the crisis telephone hotline is now complemented by a variety of counseling and community services. Low-cost counseling is available for potential suicide victims as well as for the survivors of a friend's or relative's suicide. Clinics have been instituted to provide treatment for depression and drug abuse. Community-based programs for former offenders who have been released back into society and for troubled youths also have been implemented to assist individuals in overcoming destructive behaviors. The activities of the Los Angeles Suicide Prevention Center exemplify the understanding of suicide as a subset of a larger class of self-destructive behaviors, all of which require attention if tragedy is to be averted.

Helping the Suicidal Person

A number of commonly held beliefs, or myths, have grown up about suicide and about the kind of person who is likely to commit suicide. Unfortunately, many of these beliefs, being false, are possibly harmful, for they have the effect of depriving the suicidal person of needed help. As you review

TABLE 13-5   *Myths and Facts About Suicide*

Myth: People who talk about suicide do not commit suicide.

Fact: About three-quarters of those who attempt suicide communicate their intentions to others, as hints, direct threats, or self-destructive actions or preparations for suicide. Often, these cries for help go unheeded by friends, family members, co-workers, or health care personnel.

Myth: Improvement in a suicidal person means the danger has passed.

Fact: A severely depressed person is likely to be at greatest risk when seemingly on the upswing. Improvement may be necessary before the person can take the steps to carry out the suicidal intention. Many suicides occur within three to six months following apparent improvement. Thus, an apparently positive change in mood could be a danger signal: Making the decision to carry out the suicidal act can be exhilarating and freeing; the person feels, "Ah, now that I've made the decision, I no longer have to agonize about what I'm going to do." This apparent relief can be misinterpreted by others, who may believe the crisis has passed.

Myth: Once a suicide risk, always a suicide risk.

Fact: The pattern of suicidal crisis resembles a bell curve; the peak of crisis is generally brief. The simultaneous conjunction of the thought of killing oneself, possession of the means to complete the act, and the inability to receive help or intervention is a more-or-less unusual set of circumstances. If intervention occurs, the suicidal person may well be able to continue leading a productive life, putting suicidal thoughts behind.

Myth: Suicide is inherited.

Fact: Suicide does not "run in families" in the sense of being a genetically inherited trait. However, surviving the suicide of a loved one may create beliefs about suicide that influence one's subsequent behavior. For example, fear that one has a greater potential for suicide may create a self-fulfilling prophecy. In this sense, the suicide of a family member may provide an excuse, or make it easier, to use suicide as a means to escape a difficult situation.

---

the listing of fallacies about suicide given in Table 13-5, notice which ones you may have believed or unconsciously incorporated into your assumptions about suicide.[38]

If a person says, "I feel like killing myself," that statement should not be taken lightly or brushed aside with the quick response, "Oh, well, you'll probably feel better tomorrow." To the person in crisis, there may seem little hope of a "tomorrow" at all. It is important to pay attention to the message being communicated. Similarly, responding to such a statement with a provocation — "You wouldn't be capable of committing suicide!" — or with a tone of moral superiority — "I don't want to hear such immoral and unhealthy talk!" — may be damaging, deepening rather than alleviating the suicidal crisis. A response that provides only a litany of the "good reasons" why the person should not commit suicide may also offer little practical assistance to the person in crisis.

More helpful is listening carefully to exactly what the person in crisis is

T A B L E 13-5, *continued*

Myth: Suicide affects only a specific group or class of people.

Fact: Suicide occurs among all socioeconomic groups and persons with widely divergent life styles. Related to this myth is the notion that suicide affects only the poor or the disadvantaged. In fact, suicide seems to occur more frequently among those who apparently have "the best of everything." Social integration is a more important determinant of suicidal behavior than socioeconomic class.

Myth: Suicidal behavior is insane.

Fact: Although suicidal actions usually reflect unhappiness and dissatisfaction with one's situation, the planning and carrying out of suicide usually require careful reasoning and deliberate judgment. True, some suicides are mentally ill. On the other hand, in some cultural contexts, suicide represents the rational acceptance of a socially demanded act of self-sacrifice. Although suicide notes typically reveal considerable ambivalence about the act, many notes reveal considerable lucidity about the writer's intentions.

Myth: Suicidal people are fully intent on dying.

Fact: Most suicides are undecided about continuing to live or ending their lives. In their ambivalence, they may gamble with death, leaving the possibility of rescue to fate. Although about 5 to 10 percent of suicide attempters do ultimately commit suicide after previously unsuccessful attempts, the vast majority do not. Thus, an attempted suicide may be unsuccessful without necessarily being a "failure." More likely, it is meant to signal that social or interpersonal needs are not being satisfactorily met and that the person wants a change.

Myth: The motive for a particular suicide is clearly evident.

Fact: People often try to establish a quick "cause" for suicide, attributing it to the loss of money, disappointment in love, or some other immediate condition. Deeper analysis often uncovers a lengthy sequence of self-destructive behaviors leading up to the act of suicide itself. The apparent "cause" may be simply the final step of a complex pattern of self-destructive acts.

---

communicating; the tone and context of statements should reveal to the sensitive listener something about the communicator's real intent. Often, remarks about suicide are made in an offhand manner: "If I don't get that job, I'll kill myself!" Perhaps the remark is a figure of speech, much as in the possibly joking statement, "I'll kill you for that!" There is a tendency to discount such statements in American culture, where "talk is cheap," and "actions speak louder than words."[39] When a suicidal threat is intended seriously, however, it deserves to be taken seriously. To do otherwise is to fall prey to the myth that "talking about suicide means the person will not really go through with it."

These less than helpful tendencies can be counteracted by knowledge of the patterns of suicidal behavior, and by the ability to distinguish facts from fallacies. Another way to assist the person in crisis is to become acquainted with the community crisis intervention resources that are available.

Perhaps most important, become aware of your own attitudes about life, death, and suicide. When working with someone who is struggling with

Suicide Note Written by a Married Man, Age 74

What is a few short years to live in hell. That is all I get around here.

No more I will pay the bills.

No more I will drive the car.

No more I will wash, iron, & mend any clothes.

No more I will have to eat the leftover articles that was cooked the day before.

This is no way to live.

Either is it any way to die.

Her grub I can not eat.

At night I can not sleep.

I married the wrong nag-nag-nag and I lost my life.

W.S.

To the undertaker

We have got plenty money to give me a decent burial. Don't let my wife kid you by saying she has not got any money.

Give this note to the cops.

Give me liberty or give me death.

W.S.

suicidal thoughts, you should recognize that no one can take *ultimate* responsibility for another's decision to end his or her life. Doing what can be done without trying to assume total responsibility may be difficult when one's inclination is to preserve life, yet only so much can be done to assist another person in crisis.

In the short term, it may be feasible to keep someone from taking his or her life. Constant vigilance or custodial care of some kind may be available to prevent suicide during a brief period of intense suicidal crisis. But the decision to assume responsibility for preventing someone else's suicide over a prolonged period is extremely difficult to implement. How much responsibility one feels comfortable about assuming for another person must be feasible and consonant with the particular situation. A terminally ill man dying in great pain said to his wife: "You'd better keep my medication out of reach, because I don't want to keep up this struggle any longer." The wife was forced to decide whether she could take responsibility for his choice of either continuing to live with pain or ending his life by an overdose. After much soul searching, she concluded that, although she had great compassion for his predicament and did not want him to suffer, she could not assume the responsibility for safeguarding his medication, doling out one pill at a time, constantly fearful that he might locate the drugs and attempt suicide anyway.

Not taking responsibility does not mean that one must go to the opposite extreme, expressing such an attitude as, "Well, if you're going to kill yourself, then get it over with!" Although one should recognize that there are inherent limits to how much one person can protect another from that person's own self-destructiveness, one can at the same time provide life-affirming care and compassion.

The suicidal person is probably experiencing considerable ambivalence about acting on his or her thoughts of suicide. The suicidal person may seem

Graffiti

I find a snapshot
buried in my father's drawer.
A picture of the grandfather I never knew.
Small, stooped yet dignified he stands
beside my brother's wicker pram
surrounded by his family.
My mother tells the story, hidden in the past
of the last time she saw him.
She was big with child, and so allowed to sit
while his two daughters served the sons
who gathered at the table.
Grandma who reigned as always at the head
arranged the seating of those sons
not in the order of their age
but of the weekly wage they earned
and without question brought to her.

I learn that you, mild gentle man
never at home in the new language, the new land,
subdued by failure, each passing year withdrew
further into old world memories, and silence.
Rising that evening from the table, as usual
scarcely noticed as you went to lie down
on your narrow bed, there was no sign, no signal.
Only that as you passed, you bent
with a shy unaccustomed show of tenderness
to murmur "*Liebchen*" and to kiss my mother's head.
She tells me that I leaped and struggled in her womb
when from your room you shattered silence
with a shot. Your life exploding
sudden messages across blank walls in bursts of red.

Maude Meehan

Stanley Forman, Boston Herald American

Once a person is this close to the suicidal act, the chance of a successful intervention is usually slight. Fortunately, in this dramatic instance intervention was successful.

intent on succeeding at suicide while hoping to fail. It is important to sustain or stimulate that person's desire to live. Plans for self-destruction are likely to proceed apace with fantasies or plans for rescue. The person who happens to be cast in the role of helper in such a drama can try to affirm the individual's beliefs that there are choices other than suicide.

One way to help persons in crisis is to help them discover what about themselves *can* matter, however small or insignificant it may seem. It is important that something be found that matters *to the person*. A useful way to elicit this information is to ask the person to think of something he or she has found valuable about himself or herself in the past. Once it has been found, ask the person what the possibilities are of continuing that sense of value into the present.

Asking the person what is useful, what he or she needs in order to feel valuable and worthwhile, may be a matter of survival. Some people do not survive; others can, with assistance from others and commitment from themselves. The sustaining motivation to survive cannot come from without; it has to be generated from within the person's own experience. In the short term, external support can help to ensure survival during the peak period of crisis. But one should be skeptical of the notion that one person can sustain another person's will to live over the long term.

Suicidal thoughts and behaviors indicate a critical loss of a person's belief that he or she is someone who matters. The feeling that nothing matters, in the sense that one's life is in complete disarray, is not by itself the stimulus for suicide. More important to suicidal thoughts and behaviors is the person's belief that "*I* don't matter." As we have seen, those two streams of thought in combination — the sense that the external situation is unsatisfactory and that one does not matter enough to improve it — can lead to death by suicide.

Further Readings

A. Alvarez. *The Savage God: A Study of Suicide.* New York: Random House, 1971.

Margaret Pabst Battin. *Ethical Issues in Suicide.* Englewood Cliffs, N.J.: Prentice-Hall, 1982.

Albert C. Cain, editor. *Survivors of Suicide.* Springfield, Ill.: Charles C Thomas, 1972.

Jacques Choron. *Suicide.* New York: Charles Scribner's Sons, 1972.

Fred Cutter. *Art and the Wish to Die.* Chicago: Nelson-Hall, 1983.

Norman L. Farberow, editor. *Suicide in Different Cultures.* Baltimore: University Park Press, 1975.

Larry Gernsbacher. *The Suicide Syndrome: Origins, Manifestations, and Alleviation of Human Self-Destructiveness.* New York: Human Sciences, 1985.

Corrine Loing Hatton and Sharon McBride Valente, editors. *Suicide: Assessment and Intervention.* 2nd ed. Norwalk, Conn.: Appleton-Century-Crofts, 1984.

Lee A. Headley, editor. *Suicide in Asia and the Near East.* Berkeley: University of California Press, 1983.

Herbert Hendin. *Suicide in America.* New York: W.W. Norton, 1982.

Syed Arshad Husain and Trish Vandiver. *Suicide in Children and Adolescents.* New York: SP Medical & Scientific Books, 1984.

Norman Linzer, editor. *Suicide: The Will to Live vs. the Will to Die.* New York: Human Sciences, 1984.

Karl Menninger. *Man Against Himself.* New York: Harcourt, Brace & World, 1938.

Seymour Perlin, editor. *A Handbook for the Study of Suicide.* New York: Oxford University Press, 1975.

David K. Reynolds and Norman L. Farberow. *Suicide: Inside and Out.* Berkeley: University of California Press, 1976.

Louis Wekstein. *Handbook of Suicidology: Principles, Problems, and Practice.* New York: Brunner/Mazel, 1979.

*The corpse placed on the funeral pyre, these men prepare to light the
cremation fire. Cremation has been a traditional practice in India, where
Hindus believe that "even as the person casts off worn-out clothes and
puts on others that are new, so the embodied Self casts off worn-out
bodies and enters into others that are new."*

CHAPTER 14

Beyond Death/After Life

*D*eath—and then what?

Some people have a ready answer to this perennial question:"When you're dead, you're dead—that's it!" or, "You go through a transition and take birth in another body," or, "After you die you go to heaven," or, "Your body is buried until the end of time when it's resurrected and you live again." Each of these responses reflects a particular understanding of the meaning of human existence. Beliefs about life after death occupy a broad spectrum, from the notion that death spells the end, to the notion that the "soul" or "self" lives on after death in some fashion.

Lately there have been signs of tremendous interest in the possibility of survival after death. Books on the subject appear on bestseller lists, and magazines boost circulation by reporting yet more "proof" that life continues beyond the death of the body. Perhaps much of the current excitement about life after death is a faddish preoccupation with what seems a fascinating possibility. But the underlying concern about "What happens after I die?" has occupied the attention of human beings since the dawn of consciousness.

This concern with immortality is cut from the same cloth as questions about the meaning of life and the corollary, "How, then, should one live?" Responses to these questions reflect a person's values and beliefs about human experience and the nature of reality. Our philosophy of life influences our philosophy of death. Conversely, how we perceive death and what meaning we give it affect the way we live.[1]

Most of us would agree with Socrates that "the unexamined life is not worth living." Such self-investigation includes the discovery of what one believes about death and its consequences. Ambivalence about the issue of survival after death is aptly described in an anecdote related by Bertrand Russell: A woman whose daughter had recently died was asked what she thought had become of her daughter's soul. She replied, "Oh, well, I suppose she is enjoying eternal bliss, but I wish you wouldn't talk about such unpleasant subjects."[2]

Concepts of Death and Immortality

Exploring your beliefs about immortality may not result in an easier acceptance of death — nor should it necessarily.[3] But it can provide a more coherent philosophy of life and death, making possible a congruence between hopes and perceptions. In this chapter we explore the meaning of mortality by investigating some of the ways that cultures ancient and modern, Eastern and Western, have answered the question, "What happens after death?" The answers voiced by ancient thinkers as well as the theories put forward by present-day researchers provide grist for the mill of our own contemplation about this ultimate human concern.

Age-Old Beliefs About Afterlife

The notion that life continues on in some form after death is one of the oldest concepts held by human beings. As we saw in Chapter 2, the burial practices of the Neanderthals reflect some form of belief about an existence beyond the grave. In some of these early gravesites, archeologists have uncovered skeletons that were bound by hands and feet into a fetal position, perhaps suggestive of beliefs about "rebirth" into other forms of existence following death.

It may not be possible for us living today to know precisely the beliefs that influenced the behaviors of our ancient ancestors. We can surmise something of their world view, however, by studying the artifacts from these and other preliterate cultures. We know, for instance, that in many such societies death represents a change of status for the deceased, a transition from the land of the living to the land of the dead. Neither alive nor dead in the modern sense of those terms, the deceased members of a clan or community still affected the living. Elaborate rituals were performed to moderate the potentially harmful

Every time an earth mother smiles over the birth of a child, a spirit mother weeps over the loss of a child.

Ashanti saying

influence of the departed and to provide occasions when the whole community — living and dead — could join in celebration of their essential unity and common destiny. The dead are both honored and feared as long as they remain within the memory of the living community.

Some form of judgment is a key feature of most beliefs about what follows death. Among the various concepts of afterlife among traditional Hawaiians, for example, was the belief that a person who had offended a god or who had harmed others would suffer eternal punishment. Such an unworthy soul became a wandering spirit, "forever homeless, forever hungry."[4] The ancestor-gods had the power to punish or reward the released spirit, or even to send it back to the body. Misfortune also could result when a person had neither loving relatives to care for the corpse, nor the guardianship of family ancestor-gods who help souls find their way to the world of spirits. Thus, those who had lived worthily were welcomed into eternity, whereas those who had done misdeeds in life, without repenting for or correcting them, were punished. The reward for living a good life was eternity with those closest to the family-loving Hawaiian: one's own ancestors.

To understand the conciousness from which such a view of immortality arises, the notions of self that have developed in Western cultures during modern times must be put aside momentarily. Against the emphasis on individual identity and the self, imagine a mentality in which group identity is all-encompassing. The family, the clan, the people — these social groups represent the loci of communal consciousness within which the thoughts and actions of the individual are subsumed. Thus, these age-old beliefs convey less a concern with individual survival than a desire for the continuation of the community and its common heritage. Having shared in the life of the group, the individual participates in its ultimate destiny, a destiny that can transcend even death.

Death and Resurrection in the Hebrew Tradition

Considered as a whole, the books of the Bible do not provide a systematic theology of death or of the afterlife. Death is not ignored, but the biblical literature reflects a progression of ideas developed over a long period of history. The story told in the Bible is of a people whose concerns were centered on a common destiny. Individuals were seen as actors in an unfolding drama, and its denouement was foretold in the promises made by their God, Yahweh.

As the patriarch Abraham lay dying, his last thoughts were for the continuation of his progeny so that these promises could be realized in the ultimate unfolding of history. Abraham's vision is reiterated by the biblical writers as in one circumstance after another they affirm the destiny of the clan and of the nation of Israel. By contributing to this common destiny, the righteous person never ceased to be part of the continuing story of the people as a whole.

Within this context, however, the picture of death and what follows is not monochromatic. As the expression of Judaic thought changed over time, there

The platform burial of a Tahitian chief is depicted in this drawing by William Hodges, made during Captain Cook's second voyage to the South Pacific in the 1770s.

In a world populated by unseen spirits who could exert their influence for good or evil upon the living, the death of a chief or other important person occasioned a spectacular display of grief, which was presided over by a chief mourner (right). Usually a priest or close relative of the deceased, the chief mourner wore an elaborate costume of pearl shells and the feathers of tropic birds. Rattling a pearl shell clapper and brandishing a long wooden weapon inset with sharks' teeth, the chief mourner was accompanied by other weapon-carrying men who could strike anyone in their way, thus helping ensure that funeral rites were carried out in a manner that would offend neither the living nor the dead.

"There is always hope for a tree:
    when felled, it can start its life again;
    its shoots continue to sprout.
Its roots may be decayed in the earth,
    its stump withering in the soil,
but let it scent the water, and it buds,
    and puts out branches like a plant new set.
But man? He dies, and lifeless he remains;
    man breathes his last, and then where is he?
The waters of the sea may disappear,
    all the rivers may run dry or drain away;
but man, once in his resting place, will never rise again.
    The heavens will wear away before he wakes,
    before he rises from his sleep."

Job 14:7–12, *The Jerusalem Bible*

were corresponding developments in how mortality and its meaning were understood. In the biblical story of Job's encounter with adversity and death, the human situation is described quite bleakly: "As a cloud fades away and disappears, so a person who goes down to the grave will not come up from it."[5] This resignation toward death is echoed in the other Wisdom books — including Proverbs, Ecclesiastes, and some of the Psalms — which present the thought of the ancient Hebrew sages on the question of human destiny. Righteous conduct is advised because it leads to harmony in the present life, not because it offers a chance of gaining future rewards for the individual.

Between the time of Job and the time of the prophets there was gradual change from resignation to hopefulness in the face of death. In the apocalyptic, or visionary, writings of prophets such as Daniel and Ezekiel we see the strands of thought that eventually are woven together in the notions that describe the resurrection of the body. Daniel envisions a future in which the "sleeping" dead will awaken, "some to everlasting life, some to everlasting disgrace."[6] Those developments in Judaic thought are related to a sharpened sense of the importance of the individual. Even so, resurrection is still understood primarily in communal terms. The apocalyptic vision is still centered on a time when the people of Israel will be restored to their promised destiny.

The idea of the resurrection of the body is an important development in Hebrew thought. By influencing Christian theology as well, it has maintained its influence to the present. Developing over a long period of history, this view of survival after death "consists in the belief that, at the end of time, the bodies of the dead will be resurrected from the grave and reconstituted."[7]

In the main, this new doctrine did not alter the essential understanding in Hebrew psychology of the human person as an undivided psychophysical entity. Although the breath or spirit was sometimes identified with the principle of vitality that is common to all forms of conscious life, there was no intrinsically immortal element that could be distinguished from the total person. As Wheeler Robinson wrote, "The Hebrew idea of personality is an animated body, and not an incarnated soul."[8] In other words, it is not as if the soul *takes* a body, but rather that the body *has* life. This understanding is quite different from the ancient Greek notion that in some way the soul survives the death of the body. In the Hebrew understanding of personhood, such concepts as body or soul cannot be abstracted from the essential integrity of the human person. It is within this context that notions about the resurrection of the body developed in later Hebrew thought.

In the life of the Hebrew people, the characteristic theme concerns the importance of faith — faith in the people of Israel as a community with a common destiny, and faith in Yahweh, whose promises will be realized in the unfolding of the divine plan. The consensus expressed by the biblical writers would seem to be: "Our present existence is of God; if there is life hereafter, it will also be God's gift. Thus, what need is there for anxiety about death? What matters is to live righteously and to ensure the well-being and survival of the community." The enduring concern of the Judaic tradition is that one should not lose sight of the tasks at hand.

Yet as ideas about the resurrection of the body developed alongside an increasing emphasis on the individual, it is possible to discern the glimmerings of a latent dualism. This dualism of body and soul would eventually become manifest in the early centuries of the present era, when Christianity came under Hellenistic influence.

Hellenistic Concepts of Immortality

Among the ancient Greeks, or Hellenes, there were differing views of what conditions might be after death. For most, however, the afterworld was not an attractive prospect. The realm of the dead was generally pictured as a shadowy place, inhabited by bloodless phantoms. It is perhaps not surprising, therefore, that death seems to have elicited feelings of despair.

Yet the ancient Greeks of the Hellenistic Age did not perceive death in the same way that many people do today. They were preoccupied with communal, not individual, concerns. In the Athenian democracy, for instance, what mattered was the survival of the *polis,* the corporate existence of the city-state.

 For the whole world is the sepulchre of famous men, and it is not the epitaph upon monuments set up in their own land that alone commemorates them, but also in lands not their own there abides in each breast an unwritten memorial of them, planted in the heart rather than graven on stone.

Thucydides, *The Peloponnesian War*

Speak not smoothly of death, I beseech you, O famous Odysseus. Better by far to remain on earth the thrall of another . . . rather than reign sole king in the realm of bodyless phantoms.

Homer, *The Odyssey*

Personal immortality was important only inasmuch as it affected the survival of the community.

Within this context, an individual could hope to achieve social immortality by fulfilling the responsibilities of citizenship; that is, by performing actions directed toward the common good. Heroic acts are remembered by the community. Thus, the hero achieves a renown that extends beyond a single lifetime.

Of course, some people sought more than just symbolic immortality. Greater assurances of happiness beyond death could be had by participating in one of the mystery religions, cults whose origins are clouded in the mists of prehistory. Those willing to dedicate themselves to the rites of purification prescribed by the priests of the mystery cult could exchange the dire picture of the afterworld for the more promising one of an idyllic future in paradise.

Among the pre-Socratic philosophers, speculation about the afterlife generally conformed to the popular beliefs of their culture. Most conceived of life and death as aspects of an ever-changing, eternal flux — and they believed that the soul was the vital principle that continued in some fashion after death. But they generally did not believe that the soul survived as a distinct entity, as the personality or self of a particular individual. To many early Greek thinkers, whatever continued beyond death merged with the stuff of the universe.

Pythagoras and his followers believed that one's conduct during life determined the destiny of the soul after death. Pythagoreans believed that, with discipline and purification, transmigration of the soul, successive rounds of births and deaths, led to eventual union with the Divine or Universal Absolute. These beliefs were not what most Greeks of that time held, but rather drew upon the Orphic mystery religions of earlier Greece going back to the ancient cult of

Become accustomed to the belief that death is nothing to us. For all good and evil consists in sensation, but death is deprivation of sensation. And therefore a right understanding that death is nothing to us makes the mortality of life enjoyable, not because it adds to an infinite span of time, but because it takes away the craving for immortality. For there is nothing terrible in life for the man who has truly comprehended that there is nothing terrible in not living.

Epicurus, *Letter to Menoeceus*

> . . . he who has lived as a true philosopher has reason to be of good cheer when he is about to die, and that after death he may hope to receive the greatest good in the other world. . . . For I deem that the true disciple of philosophy . . . is ever pursuing death and dying; and if this is true, why, having had the desire of death all his life long, should he repine at the arrival of that which he has been always pursuing and desiring?
>
> Plato, *Phaedo*

Dionysos. The idea that a person's conduct could influence the soul's existence in the afterlife contrasted with the predominant view that postulated a rather indistinct immortality in which all participated regardless of their actions. In any event, the ideas expressed by Pythagoras would eventually find a wider following in somewhat altered form during the pre-Christian era, and the connection between conduct aad immortality would be further refined during the early centuries of Christianity.

With Socrates there are signs of a shift from a social immortality predicated on the life of the community, to the possibility of personal survival after death. Precisely what Socrates believed in this regard is unclear, although he seems to have favored the notion that the individual soul would survive after the death of the body. He describes his sense of anticipation at the prospect of communion with the spirits of the great in the afterworld. But he also describes death as *either* eternal bliss *or* dreamless sleep.[9]

In the *Phaedo* Plato advances a number of "proofs" that the soul is eternal and is released from the body at death. Thus, the concept of immortality of the soul—an idea that pervaded Orphic thought in ancient Greece and that Pythagoras and Socrates favored—was further refined in Plato's writings. The dualism of body and soul is emphasized, and their respective fates are distinguished from one another: "The body is subject to corruption because it is mortal. . . . The soul, however, is immortal and not subject to death."[10]

For Plato and many of his successors, death gained in importance. The recollection of death as the common fate of humankind could be used as a means of concentrating on the eternal verities. Death could be a reminder of the importance of choosing wisely how to live in the present life. These thoughts are echoed by the Roman Stoic, Marcus Aurelius, who lived in the second century of the present era. "The constant recollection of death," he said, "is the test of human conduct."[11]

Christianity: Death, Resurrection, and Eternal Life

The New Testament, like the later books of the Old Testament, emphasizes the ultimate hope of resurrection of the body as a promise of God that will be realized at the end of time. Jesus himself seems to have been little concerned with speculations about the afterlife. Rather, his message focused on the

This scene from Dante's Divine Comedy *shows the guide Charon ferrying worthy souls up the River Styx toward Paradise. Unable to reach the heavenly kingdom, the unworthy, immersed in the river, struggle in despair.*

impending arrival of the Kingdom of God and the corresponding need for righteousness. The notion of the soul's immortality, which implies a dualistic view of the human person, is foreign to the biblical understanding, which postulates the human individual as a unity.

Nevertheless, the ideas of resurrection that had been developing for some time in the Judaic tradition became radically transformed in the minds of early Christians. The New Testament writers could proclaim that death was vanquished by Christ's resurrection. Death, a universal human experience as a result of Adam's fall from grace, is no longer inevitably the enemy.[12] The life, death, and resurrection of Jesus becomes the new model of reality for believers, heralding the possibility of eternal life for everyone. Whereas previously resurrection was to occur communally, to the people, Ninian Smart says, "here there was the resurrection of a particular person here and now, and not in the consummated future."[13] Christ was the prototype of the salvation available to all those who would share in his resurrection. Importantly, the coming of the Kingdom of God was anticipated as a glorious event that would happen in the very near futrue. Eternal life was, so to speak, just around the corner.

With Jesus no longer in their midst, and as the small group of Christians began to reframe their expectations about when the Kingdom of God would happen, the notions about resurrection also began to undergo some change. In the writings of Paul there is an attempt to resolve some of these problems of death, afterlife, and the events foretold for the end of time. Resurrection can be understood in several ways. It is a special kind of bodily existence, different from historical existence. But it can also be understood as having a symbolic or spiritual meaning. Resurrection implies a participation in the Kingdom of God, a participation that is assured by righteousness and faith. Milton Gatch says:

> The fundamental elements of the tradition — the lack of distinction between body and spirit and the overriding concern not with the destiny of an individual but with that of the People — are carefully maintained to the absolute exclusion of either the dualistic and metaphysical or the political notion of immortality which the Hellenistic Age had inherited from fifth-century Greece.[14]

Even so, the Hellenistic notion of a cosmic dualism, which postulated the soul as immortal, a part of the human person that existed in a disembodied state after death, was a persistent and pervasive influence on early Christian thought. During the formative period of the early Church there was constant interplay between the Hebrew traditions and the intellectual heritage of Greco-Roman culture. Gatch says about this period:

> The notion of resurrection and of the restoration of an elect people continued to be prominent. But the idea of a disembodied afterlife for the soul was also current and led to the conception of some sort of afterlife between the separation and the reunion of soul and body. From a picture of death as the inauguration of a sleep which would last until the divinely instituted resurrection, there emerged a picture of death as the beginning of quiescence for the body and of a continued life for the soul, the nature of which remained more or less undefined.[15]

Behold, I show you a mystery; We shall not all sleep, but we shall all be changed. In a moment, in the twinkling of an eye, at the last trump: for the trumpet shall sound, and the dead shall be raised incorruptible, and we shall be changed. For this corruptible must put on incorruption, and this mortal must put on immortality. So when this corruptible shall have put on incorruption, and this mortal shall have put on immortality, then shall be brought to pass the saying that is written, Death is swallowed up in victory. O death, where is thy sting? O grave, where is thy victory?

I Corinthians, 15

Despite the resistance of the early Church fathers to these pagan concepts, gradually there developed a greater emphasis on the destiny of the individual soul. With this, there developed a greater concern about the potential consequences of an individual's conduct during life. By the third or fourth century, Church doctrine exhibited a greater willingness to accommodate the notion that punishment for misconduct could take place during an intermediate period between death and resurrection.

By the thirteenth century, in the writings of Dante and Thomas Aquinas, the original biblical concept is almost completely subordinated to the Greek notion of dualism and its attendant concept of the soul's immortality. Some of the consequences that these changes had in people's attitudes and behaviors relative to death and dying are discussed in Chapter 2. The interplay between these contrasting concepts is illustrated by an observation made by Stephen Vicchio of two tombstone inscriptions, dating from the colonial period, found in New Haven, Connecticut.[16]

On the first tombstone, the inscription reads, "Sleeping, but will someday meet her maker." The second is inscribed, "Gone to his eternal reward." The first inscription reflects an understanding that postulates the resurrection of the body, an event that will occur at some time in the future. The second is based on the concept of the immortality of the soul, which continues to exist even though

Go Down, Death—A Funeral Sermon

Weep not, weep not,
She is not dead;
She's resting in the bosom of Jesus.
Heart-broken husband—weep no more;
Grief-stricken son—weep no more;
Left-lonesome daughter—weep no more;
She's only just gone home.

James Weldon Johnson

the body dies. As Vicchio points out, the difference between these two tombstone inscriptions is particularly incongruous when you consider that these two individuals were married to each other and are buried side by side in this New England cemetery. Yet, one of them is "sleeping," while the other is "gone."

In these colonial tombstone inscriptions we see a curious example of how these essentially disparate ideas could coexist in time. Indeed, the visitor to such early American cemeteries is struck by the significant changes in attitudes toward death that occurred during a very small span of years.

Today, each of these notions — resurrection or immortality — has its own adherents. For some, the distinction is vital. But many others give little thought to either the distinction or the necessary logic that follows from each of these conceptual understandings. Until fairly recent times, most people living in the Western world could find adequate answers to the enigma of death by relying upon the teachings of the Christian creeds. In the modern world our understanding of death has been altered radically. The religious consciousness of the Apostle Paul — for whom the subjugation of death was a reality demonstrated by Christ's resurrection — now seems an anachronism to many people. Death has been secularized, divorced from its mythic and religious connotations.[17]

The secularization of death has not done away with concerns about what happens afterward. But the underpinnings for the traditional beliefs no longer carry the same weight in a culture that emphasizes the need for empirical verification. Theological or philosophical discussions about the afterlife seem to many to resemble the famous debate about the number of dancing angels that will fit on the head of a pin. Yet vestiges of these concepts remain lodged in the modern consciousness.

Judaism and Christianity both present a linear picture of human history. Both traditions describe a progression of events that begins with creation and eventuates in the resolution of the cosmic story at the end of time. Such an orientation to human experience naturally leads to an interest in eschatologies — pictures of the ultimate state, doctrines of the last things. From the wellsprings of the Judeo-Christian tradition and Hellenistic ideals of progress, the Western world has predominantly framed its beliefs about what happens after death in a historical context that is oriented toward the future. For most of its past, the Western view has been that human beings live a single life; that the soul survives death, perhaps in a disembodied state; that at some future time each soul will be judged; and that, depending upon one's conduct during earthly existence, the aftermath will be either hellish torment or heavenly bliss.[18]

The Place of Death and Immortality in Eastern Thought

The Western approach to experience tends to be dualistic. Experiences are analyzed as being *either* this *or* that. The Western thinker typically makes distinctions, points up contrasts, establishes differences. Within this context, life is opposed to death, death is the enemy of life; life represents affirmation, death negation. Death is "evil," life "good."

The Egyptian papyrus of Hunefer depicts the Hall of Judgment and the Great Balance where the deceased's soul is weighed against the feather of truth. Beneath the scales the Devourer of Souls awaits the unjust while Horus is ready to lead the just to Osiris, the lord of the underworld, and to a pleasurable afterlife.

In the cultures of the East, on the other hand, the characteristic mode of thought emphasizes the integrity of the whole rather than the differences between constituent parts. It seeks to discover the unity that underlies apparently contradictory phenomena. Whereas Western thought distinguishes between "either/or," Eastern thought subsumes such distinctions within a holistic "both/and" approach. In place of the dualistic view of reality typical of Western thought, the corresponding Eastern mode of thought characteristically reflects the position that such apparent dualisms are merely illusory aspects of an essentially undivided reality.

This unitary view of reality is reflected in many of the sacred texts of the East. The *I Ching,* or *Book of Changes,* for instance, postulates a world of experience that is constantly being transformed. Life and death are manifestations of a constantly changing reality. Like the symbol of the *Tao,* these contrasting aspects of reality interpenetrate one another. Death and life are not seen as mutually exclusive opposites, but rather as complementary facets of an underlying process. We see this process in the inexorable cycles of birth, decay, and death. Like a pendulum moving through its arc, the completion of one cycle heralds the beginning of another.

> Though it will die soon
> The voice of the cicada
> Shows no sign of this.
>
> Bashō

Everything in the phenomenal world exhibits this pattern of constant arising and passing away. Through their observations of this process, the sages of the East developed the concept of reincarnation or transmigration — the notion that life and death are complementary aspects of a continuing process. For some, reincarnation is understood as a physical reality: "I will take birth in another body following the death of my present body." Others deny this physical, materialist understanding of reincarnation, saying that there is, in fact, no "I" to be reborn. What we identify as "I" or "self" is an insubstantial, everchanging process.[19]

Hindu Theologies of Death and Rebirth

One of the distinguishing features of Hinduism is the belief in the transmigration of souls; that is, the passing at death of the soul from one body or being to another. In the *Bhagavad-Gita* Krishna tells Arjuna:

> For death is a certainty for him who has been born,
> and birth is a certainty for him who has died.
> Therefore, for what is unavoidable thou shouldst not grieve.[20]

Individual souls, or *jivas,* transmigrate through a succession of bodies. This process is termed *samsara,* which refers to "passing through" a series of incarnational experiences. What links these experiences together is *karma,* which can be roughly defined as the moral law of cause-and-effect. The thoughts and actions of the past determine the present state of being; and, in turn, present choices influence future states. This karmic process can be interpreted as pertaining to the ever-changing flow of moment-to-moment experience, as well as to the successive rounds of deaths and rebirths. As each moment conditions the next, karma sustains this reincarnational flow of being.

Yet, according to Hinduism, the workings of karma provide only a partial description of reality. Underlying the apparent separateness of individual beings is a unitary reality. Just as the ocean can be imagined as composed of innumerable drops of water, undifferentiated being is manifest in human experience in the form of an apparently separate self. Huston Smith expresses the Hindu perception this way: "Underlying man's personality and animating it is a reservoir of being that never dies, is never exhausted, and is without limit in awareness and bliss. This infinite center of life, this hidden self or *Atman,* is no less than *Brahman,* the Godhead."[21]

Difficulty and suffering arise in human experience, Hinduism says, because of not recognizing the true nature of existence; namely, that the relationship between *Atman* and *Brahman* is essentially one absolute identity. Instead, we see ourselves as separate from this essential unity. We hold to our cherished self-concepts—"my" life, "my" self—ignoring the reality in which all such notions are illusory and substanceless. Our attachments to these concepts of "self" as separate and distinct cause us suffering in the present life and perpetuate the endless wheel of births and deaths, the wheel of *karma*.

To escape this fate, Hinduism teaches that we need to become free of the illusion of separate selfhood, with its attendant pain. A liberated being is one who recognizes that life and death transcend such mistaken notions of self-identity, and thereby becomes free of the conditioning effects of karma. The *Bhagavad-Gita* says:

> Worn-out garments are shed by the body:
> Worn-out bodies are shed by the dweller.[22]

The goal is to transcend the conditioned realm of birth and death, to put a stop to the persistent effects of *karma*.

To be free of death means letting go of attachments to the phenomenal world, releasing the grasp on the false distinctions of a separate self and its unceasing desires. Death is inescapable, a natural corollary of conditioned existence. What is born passes away. Yet for the person "whose consciousness has become stabilized by the insight that it is the very nature of things to come-to-be and pass-away," there is no "occasion either for rejoicing over birth or grieving over death."[23]

To loosen the bonds of attachment, Hinduism offers various aids in the form of rites and practices that can assist in the awakening to truth. Some of these methods emphasize paying close attention to the processes that surround death. For example, one practice involves attending to the transitory and ever-changing nature of one's own body, observing its inexorable progress toward decay and dissolution, its constant transformation, moment to moment. Another practice involves imagining one's death and the ultimate fate of the body, its return to elemental matter in the grave or on the funeral pyre. Some of these meditation practices occur in the presence of a dead body or at burial or cremation grounds. Death becomes a clear reminder of the everchanging flow of *karma,* a reminder that there is nothing to hold to, no permanence, no solid self. By confronting one's own mortality, one becomes reoriented toward the transcendent dimensions of reality. The death of the separate self is the letting go of conditioned existence, "the death that conquers death."[24]

The Buddhist Understanding of Death

Zen master Dōgen, founder of the Sōtō Zen sect in Japan, said, "The thorough clarification of the meaning of birth and death—this is the most important problem of all for Buddhists."[25] Although there is considerable variety in Buddhist practices and beliefs—as there is in the Hinduism that served as the background of Siddhartha Gautama's experience of awakening to become the

The cosmic dance of the Hindu deity Shiva, an ever changing flow of creation and dissolution, embodies the fundamental equilibrium between life and death, the underlying reality behind appearances.

Thus shall you think of all this fleeting world:
A star at dawn, a bubble in a stream;
A flash of lightning in a summer cloud.
A phantom, an illusion, a dream.

> Buddha,
> *The Diamond Sutra*

Buddha — death holds a central place in the teachings of Buddhism. And although its meaning may be variously interpreted by different sects and schools, the ultimate goal for Buddhists is *nirvana,* which literally means "extinction" — as when a flame goes out if deprived of fuel. It is the "unconditioned state beyond birth and death that is reached after all ignorance and craving have been extinguished and all karma, which is the cause of rebirth, has been dissolved."[26]

Buddhism denies the existence of a permanent, unchanging self or substantial soul that transmigrates intact from one life to the next. What we call "self" is really nothing more than a process of continuous change with no permanence. Everything is transitory and impermanent (*anicca*), in continual unease and unrest (*dukkha*), and substanceless (*anatta*).[27] *Karma* can be understood as the universal principle of causality underlying the constant stream of psychophysical events. Dōgen says, "Life constantly changes, moment by moment, in each of its stages, whether we want it to or not. Without even a moment's pause our karma causes us to transmigrate continuously."[28]

From the Buddhist perspective there are two kinds of death: continuous and regular. Continuous death is the "passing show" of phenomenal experience, constantly arising and passing away, moment by moment. Regular, or corporeal, death pertains to the physical cessation of vital body functions at the end of a lifetime.

There is no "self" to survive after death or to be reborn, yet *karma* transmigrates to the next moment of arising into being. This transmigration can be likened to impressing a seal onto wax or mud, or to the transfer of energy in a game of billiards when the cue ball strikes the cluster of balls, creating new energy events. As Philip Kapleau, an American teacher of Zen Buddhism, says, "Rebirth does not involve the transfer of a substance, but the continuation of a process."[29]

Like Hinduism, Buddhism teaches that it is necessary to renounce the desires and cravings that maintain the delusion of a separate self. When all attachments are dropped, the wheel of *karma,* the incessant round of birth-decay-death, is given no further fuel. How does one awaken to this reality, to *nirvana?* Dōgen says, "Simply understand that birth and death are in themselves nirvana, there being no birth-death to be hated nor nirvana to be desired. Then, for the first time you will be freed from birth and death."[30]

Before we were born we had no feeling; we were one with the universe. This is called "mind-only," or "essence of mind," or "big mind." After we are separated by birth from this oneness, as the water falling from the waterfall is separated by the wind and rocks, then we have feeling. You have difficulty because you have feeling. You attach to the feeling you have without knowing just how this kind of feeling is created. When you do not realize that you are one with the river, or one with the universe, you have fear. Whether it is separated into drops or not, water is water. Our life and death are the same thing. When we realize this fact we have no fear of death anymore, and we have no actual difficulty in our life.

Shunryu Suzuki, *Zen Mind, Beginner's Mind*

The paradox of Dōgen's statement about birth-death and the importance of using death as a means of awakening to truth is echoed in the words of the Zen master Hakuin, who is known as the reviver of the Rinzai sect, the other great Buddhist lineage in Japan. For those who wish to investigate their true nature, Hakuin advised meditation on the word *shi,* the character for death. To do this, he suggested a koan: "After you are dead and cremated, where has the main character [the chief actor or one's 'original face'] gone?" Hakuin wrote:

> Among all the teaching and instructions, the word *death* has the most unpleasant and disgusting connotations. Yet if you once suddenly penetrate this "death" koan, you will find that there is no more felicitous teaching than this instruction that serves as the key to the realm in which birth and death are transcended, where the place in which you stand is the Diamond indestructible, and where you have become a divine immortal, unaging and undying. The word *death* is the vital essential that the warrior must first determine for himself.[31]

Guides to After-Death States

A person who by religious persuasion perceives death as an opportunity for awakening to truth is naturally interested in influencing the character of the after-death state and the next incarnation. According to W. Y. Evans-Wentz, "Buddhists and Hindus alike believe that the last thought at the moment of

Your essence was not born and will not die. It is neither being nor nonbeing. It is not a void nor does it have form. It experiences neither pleasure nor pain. If you ponder what it is in you that feels the pain of this sickness, and beyond that you do not think or desire or ask anything, and if your mind dissolves like vapour in the sky, then the path to rebirth is blocked and the moment of instant release has come.

Bassui, Zen Buddhist, comforting a dying person

death determines the character of the next incarnation."[32] Writings like the *Bardo Thödol,* or *The Tibetan Book of the Dead,* as it is better known in the West, are intended to direct the thought processes of the dying person during the transitional period of life-death-rebirth.

The passing from one stage of the after-death experience to another can be likened to the process of birth. Moving through first one *bardo* state to another, "the Knower [that is, the principle of consciousness, or the experiencer] wakes up out of one swoon or trance state and then another, until the third Bardo ends."[33] The term *bardo* can be translated as "gap" or "interval of suspension" and is usually taken to mean the state between birth and death.[34] The *Bardo Thödol* offers counsel on how to use these experiences — some terrifying, some benign — to awaken to a more enlightened incarnation. Although acknowledging that these experiences after death are likely to appear quite real to the *bardo* traveler, the text emphasizes that the deities or demons encountered are simply apparitions, the experiencer's own projections.[35]

Although the *Bardo Thödol* and similar texts are commonly thought to be designed to be read as a person experiences the process of dying, they have a broader application as well. Indeed, such texts can serve as a guide for the living as well as the dying. As Chögyam Trungpa says, the *Bardo Thödol* deals with "the principle of birth and death recurring constantly in this life"; thus, these writings refer not only to the interval after death, but also to the situation encountered by the living, for "the bardo experience is part of our basic psychological make-up."[36]

As to the states described in the *Tibetan Book of the Dead,* they are intermediate states of consciousness. They do not represent ultimate or transcendent perfection, but rather further steps on the way. Nevertheless, the period immediately following death is considered to be an especially opportune time for gaining insight. The priest at a Buddhist funeral, for example, speaks directly to the deceased, expounding on the teachings that can awaken the intermediate being to the true nature of existence. Philip Kapleau says, "The funeral and subsequent services thus represent literally a 'once in a lifetime' opportunity to awaken the deceased and thereby liberate him from the binding chain of birth-and-death."[37]

Near-Death Experiences: At the Threshold of Death

Lately, contemporary reports of personality survival after death have generated considerable public interest as well as scientific inquiry. Stories of persons who have come back from the edge of death describe fascinating glimpses of a paranormal, or scientifically unexplainable, order of existence beyond the observable universe. Some interpret these near-death experiences, or NDEs, as indicating that the human personality survives death; others believe that the phenomena experienced by such near-death survivors represent a psychological response to the stress of facing a life-threatening danger.

NDEs: A Composite Picture

Significantly, although researchers differ in their interpretations of near-death experiences, their studies reveal a strikingly similar picture of such phenomena.[38] Let us imagine what might be experienced during an overwhelming encounter with death, resulting perhaps from an accident or from a life-threatening illness or acute medical crisis. Perhaps, almost beyond awareness, you hear a voice saying that you're not going to make it, you're going to die.

It's like a dream, but somehow the experience seems more real than ordinary waking consciousness. Vision and hearing are extremely acute; sensory perceptions are heightened. You experience your thought processes as clear, rational. Yet you no longer seem tied to a body. As you become aware of this feeling of disconnectedness, you notice yourself separate from the body, floating free. From a corner of the room, you look down at the body below and recognize it as your own.

Perhaps you feel a little lonely, drifting in space, yet there is a sense of calm, a serenity that was rarely if ever experienced in the body. All the usual constructs of time and space seem irrelevant, unreal. As you feel yourself moving farther away from the once-familiar world of your now-dead body, you enter a darkness, a tunnel, some transitional stage in your journey.

At this point you notice a light, more brilliant than any imagined during your earthly existence, beckoning, drawing you onward, its golden hues heralding your approach to the other side.

Perhaps now you experience the whole of your previous life in the body, a nearly instantaneous matrix of flashbacks, impressions of your former life, events, places, people: your life reviewed and projected on the transparent screen of consciousness.

You enter the light, glimpsing a world of unimaginable and unspeakable brilliance. A loved one greets you, or perhaps you become aware of Jesus or Moses or another being of light and ineffable grace. Only now you realize that you cannot enter fully into this light, not yet, not this time.

Dimensions of Near-Death Experiences

For most people who have experienced such phenomena as those encountered in your imaginary journey, the return to the body is a blank. Others report feeling a jolt or becoming aware of pain upon return to consciousness in the body. Many emerge from their experience with a greater appreciation of life, a determination to make better use of the opportunities presented to them. Typically, they feel more self-confident, more able to cope with the vicissitudes of life. Loving relationships become more important and material comforts less important. Researcher Kenneth Ring says that the typical near-death experiencer "has achieved a sense of what is important in life and strives to live in accordance with his understanding of what matters."[39]

Our imaginary, composite picture of a near-death experience incorporates a number of elements that are in fact only rarely experienced. Whereas 60 percent

In Hieronymous Bosch's portrayal of the Ascent into the Empyrean — the highest heaven in medieval cosmology — the soul, purged of its impurities, approaches the end of its long journey and union with the Divine.

of the respondents in Ring's sample experienced feelings of peace and well-being, 37 percent experienced themselves as separate from their bodies, 23 percent experienced the entry into a dark tunnel or transitional stage, 16 percent experienced seeing a bright light, and 10 percent experienced themselves actually entering the light, though only for a "peek" into their unearthly surroundings.[40] Ring found that NDEs resulting from illness were more likely to be complete — to have all of these characteristic core elements — than were NDEs resulting from accidents. On the other hand, over half the accident victims experienced panoramic life review, compared to only 16 percent of the respondents whose experiences were related to illness or attempted suicide.[41]

The encounter with a "presence" — a loved one or other personage — is sometimes linked to the decision to return, to terminate the experience. Some near-death experiencers believe that this decision is made for them, others that they arrived at this decision themselves. Usually, the decision to return is related in some way to unfinished business or responsibilities that the person believes must be attended to before his or her death.

In broad outline, the description provided in our imaginary near-death experience is typical of reports in the literature. Stephen Vicchio has identified four core elements that appear to be characteristic of NDEs: The person (1) hears the news of his or her death; (2) departs from the body; (3) encounters significant others; and (4) returns to the body.[42]

What are we to make of these experiences? How should the data regarding NDEs be interpreted?

Interpreting Near-Death Experiences

Near-death experiences are clearly a fascinating field of inquiry. To some they suggest (or confirm) hoped-for possibilities. Others view NDEs as a fertile field for research into the nature of human consciousness. To yet others NDEs illustrate the remarkable psychodynamic processes that surface when annihilation of the self is threatened. Although the general features of NDEs tend not to be matters of dispute, such experiences can elicit widely divergent interpretations.[43]

For the early Hawaiians, their observations of *apparent* death, or persons who had "left the body prematurely," were interpreted in accordance with beliefs about the ancestor-gods. On each island, there was a special promontory overlooking the sea; this was the *leina,* or leaping place, of the soul or spirit on its journey to the realm of the ancestors. If, on its way to the *leina,* a soul was met by an ancestor-god and sent back, the body would revive. Otherwise the ancestor-god would lead it safely to and over the *leina;* once beyond that hurdle, the soul was safe with the ancestors.[44] Notice that a specific place was designated as the point of transition between life and death.

For various reasons (often, though not always, having to do with a person's behavior), an ancestor-god might delay a soul's acceptance into eternity. For instance, if a person died before his or her earthly work was done, the ancestor-god conducted the soul back to the body. "Sometimes when it is not yet time to die," reports Mary Pukui, "the relatives [ancestors] stand in the road and make you go back. Then the breath returns to the body with a crowing sound, *o'o-a-moa*." After such a person had been fully restored to life, he or she took a purifying bath and was welcomed back into the family.

Albert Heim, a Swiss geologist and mountain climber, is considered to have been the first investigator to systematically gather data on near-death experiences.[45] Working at the turn of the century, Heim interviewed some thirty skiers and climbers who had been involved in accidents resulting in paranormal experiences. Heim's subjects experienced such phenomena as detachment from their bodies and panoramic memory, or life review. These characteristics of near-death experiences have since become familiar to researchers in this area.

The data compiled by Heim were subsequently interpreted by psychoanalytic pioneer Oskar Pfister, who explained these experiences as being caused by shock and depersonalization in the face of impending death. In other words, when a person's life is threatened, psychological defense mechanisms may come into play, creating the phenomena associated with NDEs. The psychological approach initiated by Pfister continues to be elaborated by a number of present-day researchers.

The researchers believe that NDEs can be explained satisfactorily without hypothesizing life after death. Such explanations include suggestions of a possible connection between NDEs and dream states, hallucinations, side effects of pharmacological agents, and various neurophysiological causes. The psychological model described by Russell Noyes and Roy Kletti posits that defensive reactions lead to depersonalization in the face of mortal danger. Their model is perhaps the most comprehensive explanation of this type offered thus far. According to this model, NDEs can be broken down into three stages: resistance, life review, and transcendence. The first stage, *resistance,* involves recognition of the danger, fear of it and struggle against it, and finally acceptance of death as imminent. This acceptance, or surrender, marks the beginning of the second stage, *life review.* As the self is detached from its bodily representation, panoramic memories occur, often in almost simultaneous succession, appearing to encompass a person's entire life. This experience of life review is often related to a sense of affirmation of the meaning of one's existence and its integration into the universal order of things. The third stage, *transcendence,* evolves from the increased detachment from one's individual existence and is marked by an increasingly cosmic or transcendental consciousness replacing the more limited ego- or self-identity.

Noyes suggests that experiences such as calm detachment, heightened sensory awareness, panoramic memory, and mystical consciousness represent the ego's protective response when confronted by its own demise.[46] In other words, the threat of death can set into motion various psychological processes that provide an escape for the ego, the experiencing self. Because these processes dissociate the experiencing self from the body, the threat of death is perceived as being a threat only to the *body,* not to the "self" that is doing the perceiving.

It is wonderful that five thousand years have now elapsed since the creation of the world, and still it is undecided whether or not there has ever been an instance of the spirit of any person appearing after death. All argument is against it; but all belief is for it.

James Boswell, *Life of Johnson*

In contrast to researchers such as Noyes and Kletti, another group has followed the lines established in the late nineteenth century by parapsychologists. These investigators believe that to adequately understand NDEs one must be willing to go beyond the usual methods of scientific inquiry. In short, the researchers must be prepared to accept the possibility, which is not scientifically verifiable, that NDEs are what they seem to be — that is, experiences of states of consciousness that transcend the death of the body. Thus, such researchers tend to accept anecdotal reports of NDEs at face value, and try to construct a model of reality that will account for such experiences.

In his recent book, *Heading Toward Omega,* Kenneth Ring places near-death experiences within the framework of an "emergent form of consciousness" reflecting an evolutionary trend.[47] Near-death experiences, he says, are lessons about the nature and meaning of human existence. They teach us that the *appearance* of death is not at all like the *experience* of death. In studying the aftereffects of NDEs, Ring found that the experience induced significant value changes. At their core, NDEs are deep spiritual experiences that accelerate spiritual development. For many, the result of a near-death experience seems to be a positive personal transformation, sometimes dramatically so, with the feeling of being a different person. This difference is manifested in a new appreciation of life and concern for others. Materialism and worldly success become less important than the quest for the meaning of life. Perhaps most interesting, many respondents report planetary visions, glimpses into alternative global futures, often involving scenarios that depend upon actions human beings take in the present. These prophetic visions do not involve simply the possibility of a future "golden age." On the contrary, the general scenario of these visions is one of catastrophic disturbances in both the social and natural environment. Nuclear war is often mentioned, along with worldwide economic collapse and other such disasters. In short, these visions portray what is termed a "planetary near-death experience," ultimately resulting in the dawn of "a new era in human history marked by human brotherhood, universal love, and world peace."

Ring says that the deeper meaning of this scenario, one involving a source of hope, can be seen only by changing our perspective, focusing not on the individual but on the collective. In this sense, NDEs may represent an evolutionary thrust toward higher consciousness for all humanity. Thus, people who have experienced NDEs may be a "bridge to the next step in our destiny as a species." When enough people have experienced the transformation that occurs in connection with an NDE, a "critical mass" will be reached, one that will transform society and culture as a whole. Indeed, according to this view, the current interest in death and dying is itself a signpost pointing to an understanding of physical existence as merely one aspect of life. In this interpretation, therefore, those who have experienced NDEs are our "messengers of hope," bringing us the news that we need not fear death.

Personal accounts of the kind just discussed, regardless of their interest, are of inherently limited scientific value. Yet researchers into paranormal phenomena must rely upon such anecdotal evidence while closely adhering to scientific reporting methods. For example, Ian Stevenson at the University of Virginia is compiling detailed case histories of persons whose experiences are suggestive of reincarnation.[48] As with Ring's studies of NDEs, this work is significant because of its emphasis on reliable documentation. A Gallup poll conducted during the early 1980s showed that about two-thirds of all adult Americans answered "yes" to the question, "Do you believe in life after death?"[49] Only one-fifth, however, thought that life after death would be proven scientifically.

Of course, those approaching the question of survival after death with their minds already made up in the affirmative have no difficulty finding corroborative evidence. One book, for example, begins with the assertion that "human beings survive physical death," which is supported by accounts of apparitions, hauntings, out-of-body experiences, deathbed visions, resuscitations, possession experiences, reincarnation claims, and mediumistic communications or "accounts from the realm beyond death."[50] Another book is a 562-page compilation of excerpts from religion and mythology and statements from a multitude of individuals that affirm the case for reincarnation and immortality.[51]

Such works are interesting, and they have a place in any thoroughgoing investigation into the subject of personality after death. However, it is unlikely that they accomplish much more than to confirm the preconceptions of the already decided.

A more objective approach is reflected in the work of Karlis Osis and Erlendur Haraldsson, whose reports of cross-cultural studies of near-death experiences are widely valued.[52] Osis and Haraldsson conclude that the evidence from NDEs strongly suggests life after death. In their view, "Neither medical, nor psychological, nor cultural conditioning can explain away deathbed visions."[53] One of the points put forward in support of this conclusion is the observation by some researchers that in some deathbed visions there are apparitions that are contrary to the experiencer's expectations. Osis and Haraldsson mention "apparitions of persons the person thought were still living, but who in fact were dead," as well as apparitions that do not conform to cultural stereotypes, as with dying children who are "surprised to see 'angels' without wings."[54]

Arguments and counterarguments have been put forth in favor of each of these basic approaches to the phenomena of NDEs. Casting a critical eye on this

Drawing by Henry Martin, from TV Guide®, © 1978 Triangle Publications

'While on the operating table my heart stopped beating and I died.
At that moment, Merv, I learned there was a life after life and a chance
for a best selling book based on this discovery, and a hit movie
based on the book, and TV guest shots to plug the movie, and commercials
generated by TV appearances and...'

ongoing debate, Stephen Vicchio observes that "much of the literature is philosophically unsophisticated, relying too heavily on metaphysical explanations, while ignoring or disregarding alternative explanations."[55] Indeed, the issues could be much clarified by an understanding of the theological and philosophical antecedents of the present theories formulated to explain such experiences.

Near-death experiences are real, for some persons do have them. The question is how they should be interpreted. We have already discussed two models.

The first model postulates that death is the destruction of the personality. Near-death experiences are explained as resulting from some dysfunction of the brain or nervous system, or as resulting from the ego's defensive reaction to a life-threatening situation. Thus, what are perceived as visions of an after-death existence actually arise from "memories already stored in the brain" that "express desires, expectations, and fears of the individual, as well as beliefs characteristic of his culture."[56]

The second model postulates that near-death experiences indicate survival after death. Death is seen as the "transition to another mode of existence."[57] According to this hypothesis, the experiences of incorporeal entities and the glimpses of postmortem states of being result from extrasensory perception of objective phenomena. In other words, they are what they seem to be: experiences of life after death.

Each model of NDEs offers an explanation about "how the world works." One's own model of reality is likely to favorably dispose a person toward one or the other of these interpretations of near-death experiences. Furthermore, there remains a third approach to understanding the significance of NDEs, namely, the possibility that both propositions are valid: There is life after death; but also NDEs are a psychological phenomenon whereby the personality is radically altered as it negotiates the passage from one state to another. Perhaps near-death experiences engage an order of reality that is not contained fully within either of these models.

In considering how to interpret reports of near-death experiences, one should remember that, indeed, these are *near-death* experiences, not, strictly speaking, experiences after death. The reality that such experiences open to investigation may turn out to be much vaster than, and quite different from, what we suppose if we consider them only as glimpses of "another world." As we will shortly see in our discussion of psychedelic experiences, the matrices for such experiences may lie within the depths of human consciousness.[58] It should also be noted that many people experience clinical death and after being resuscitated simply have nothing to report.

As Robert Kastenbaum cautions, one needs to be careful of a too-ready acceptance of the "fantastic voyage" implied by most life-after-death accounts because "there is the potential for real pain, real suffering, real errors in judgment that increase the jeopardy of ourselves and our loved ones."[59]

> The happily-ever-after theme threatens to draw attention away from the actual situations of the dying persons, their loved ones, and their care givers over the days, weeks, and months preceding death. What happens up to the point of the fabulous transition from life to death recedes into the background. This could not be more unfortunate. The background, after all, is where these people are actually living until death comes.[60]

Finally, three points expressed by Charles Garfield, after extensive work with the dying, should be considered:

1. Not everyone dies a blissful, accepting death.
2. Context is a powerful variable in such altered-state experiences as those involving hypnosis, meditation, psychedelics, and schizophrenia. It may be that a supportive environment for the dying person is an important factor in

determining whether the outcome is a positive altered-state experience for the dying.

3. The "happily ever after" stance toward death may represent a form of denial when what is really needed by the dying is a demonstration of real concern and real caring in their present experience.[61]

Whatever the beliefs that one may hold about life after death, as Garfield says, "Let us have the courage to realize that death often will be a bitter pill to swallow."[62]

Death in the Psychedelic Experience

The death-related experiences resulting from the use of LSD (lysergic acid diethylamide) and other psychedelic — that is, mind-manifesting or mind-opening — substances may shed light on our inquiry into the question of personality survival after death. From its earliest clinical applications, LSD was seen to have far-reaching implications for our understanding of death and human consciousness.

In the early 1960s, Eric Kast of the Chicago Medical School began pioneering studies of the analgesic effects of LSD on patients suffering intense pain.[63] Besides relieving the symptoms of physical pain and discomfort, LSD therapy also diminished emotional symptoms, such as depression, anxiety, tension, insomnia, and psychological withdrawal. LSD seemed to accomplish these impressive results by altering the patient's learned response to pain — that is, the patient's anticipation of pain based on past experiences. By becoming free of this conditioning, the patient was oriented to the present and thus able to respond to the sensations actually experienced rather than to an image of pain that had grown more and more discomforting over time.[64]

Perhaps even more significant than the diminution of physical symptoms, however, was the change of attitude toward death and dying. Following the psychedelic experience, patients often showed a greatly diminished fear of death and less anxiety about the life-threatening implications of their illness. This transformation of the concept of death is attributable to the transcendental nature of the psychedelic experience:

> Dying persons who had transcendental experiences developed a deep belief in the ultimate unity of all creation; they often experienced themselves as integral parts of it, including their disease and the often painful situations they were facing.[65]

As a result of LSD therapy, many patients exhibited a greater responsiveness to their families and their environment. Their self-respect and morale were enhanced, and they showed a greater appreciation of the subtleties of every-day life.

The encouraging results of these early studies inspired others to initiate programs offering psychedelic therapy for dying patients.[66] Eventually, the data from these studies — and from studies of the phenomena associated with

LSD-assisted therapy in other contexts — formed the basis for a comprehensive theory of LSD therapy drawn from a new model of the human unconscious. That LSD induced such transcendental experiences in randomly selected subjects was considered strong evidence that "matrices for such experiences exist in the unconscious as a normal constituent of the human personality."[67]

Although LSD was first synthesized in 1938 by the Swiss chemist Albert Hoffman, its chemical action on the brain is still not completely understood.[68] However, its psychedelic properties — that is, its amplifying and catalyzing effects on the mind — are well documented. From the earliest studies, researchers noticed that LSD appeared to activate "unconscious material from various deep levels of the personality."[69] Of particular importance is what Stanislav Grof describes as the "shattering encounter" with certain critical aspects of human existence: birth, decay, and death.[70] This recognition of one's own mortality is often accompanied by an agonizing existential crisis.

According to Grof, this "deep realization of the vulnerability and impermanence of humans as biological creatures" has two important consequences: First, it initiates a profound emotional and philosophical crisis that forces the individual to seriously question the meaning of existence and his or her values in life. Second, it opens areas of religious and spiritual experience that seem to be intrinsic to the human personality and independent of the individual's cultural or religious background.[71] Grof says that even "uncompromising atheists" become interested in the spiritual quest after confronting these experiences during an LSD session.

Like the phenomena discussed in connection with near-death experiences, the psychedelic experience typically contains elements that are not scientifically explainable. Grof and Halifax note that "subjects unsophisticated in anthropology and mythology experience images, episodes, and even entire thematic sequences that bear a striking resemblance to the descriptions of the posthumous journey of the soul and the death-rebirth mysteries of various cultures."[72] As with NDEs, the psychedelic experience often results in a significantly altered outlook on the meaning of life and death.[73] The tranformations observed following LSD sessions with a transcendental emphasis often include dramatic changes in the experiencer's hierarchy of values. "Having experienced death and rebirth and/or feelings of cosmic unity," Grof says, "LSD subjects tend to

Death and life, usually considered to be irreconcilable opposites, appear to actually be dialectically interrelated. Living fully and with maximum awareness every moment of one's life leads to an accepting and reconciled attitude toward death. Conversely, such an approach to human existence requires that we come to terms with our mortality and the impermanence of existence.

Stanislav Grof and Joan Halifax,
The Human Encounter with Death

put less emotional emphasis on the past and future and show an increased appreciation of the present."[74] He adds:

> An individual who has a transcendental experience develops an entirely new image of his or her identity and cosmic status. The materialistic image of the universe in which the individual is a meaningless speck of dust in the vastness of the cosmos is instantly replaced by the mystical alternative. . . . This is a drastic change of perspective and it has far-reaching consequences for every aspect of life.[75]

Although there are many parallels between **LSD** experiences and NDEs, this apparent similarity should not be construed as necessarily confirming one or another interpretation of the data. Either of the interpretive models discussed in connection with NDEs — that is, the psychological explanation or the postulation of personality survival after death — could be applied to the **LSD** phenomena. Or a wholly different explanation might be offered for each of these orders of experience. Nevertheless, some researchers believe that the data resulting from such paranormal experiences — however induced — suggest that the nature of human consciousness is not fully comprehended in the currently accepted theories of Western science.[76] As Stanislav Grof says, "Reality is always larger and more complex than the most elaborate and encompassing theory."[77]

Beliefs About Death: A Wall or a Door?

In the final analysis, then, what do afterlife experiences or NDEs, and other paranormal experiences, reveal concerning the perennial question of human personality survival after death? Is death the joyful and ultimately fulfilling experience it seems to be from survivors' reports of near-death experiences? Or are such experiences only psychological projections, wish-fulfilling fantasies that

Our normal waking consciousness, rational consciousness as we call it, is but one special type of consciousness, whilst all about it, parted from it by the filmiest of screens, there lie potential forms of consciousness entirely different. We may go through life without suspecting their existence; but apply the requisite stimulus, and at a touch they are there in all their completeness, definite types of mentality which probably somewhere have their field of application and adaptation. No account of the universe in its totality can be final which leaves these other forms of consciousness quite disregarded. How to regard them is the question—for they are so discontinuous with ordinary consciousness. Yet they may determine attitudes though they cannot furnish formulas, and open a region though they fail to give a map. At any rate, they forbid a premature closing of our accounts with reality.

William James,
*The Varieties of Religious Experience:
A Study in Human Nature*

serve to mask the terror of confronting one's own demise? What shall we believe about survival after death?

Clyde Nabe has characterized the two basic philosophical perspectives regarding death as follows: Death is either a *wall* or it is a *door*.[78] As we have seen, in the first view, death is the "disorganization of the functional structure of the matter which is a particular human body," and thus is the "cessation of all possibility for the person who dies." In short, death is a *wall,* not a door. In the second perspective, the possibility arises that "what is real need not necessarily be equated with what is material," thus the dissolution of the body need not be viewed as necessarily resulting in the dissolution of the human person. In other words, death is a *door,* not a wall.

We can imagine many variations on these two basic positions regarding what happens at death. Indeed, the doctrines of various religions and the explanations offered for paranormal experiences of death are just such variations. For example, stating the Christian perspective, we could say that death appears to be a wall, but at some time in the future — at the Resurrection — it turns out to have been a door. The Hindu concept of reincarnation would suggest that death is a door, not a wall. Buddhists might respond that death is both a door and a wall, and is neither. The conventional psychological explanation of NDEs might seem an argument in favor of the position that death is a wall that is experienced as a door. The transpersonal and parapsychologies, on the other hand, might suggest that the door and the wall are simply alternative ways of experiencing the same reality.

The absolute certainty that death is a complete and definitive and irrevocable annihilation of personal consciousness, a certainty of the same order as our certainty that the three angles of a triangle are equal to two right angles, or contrariwise, the absolute certainty that our personal consciousness continues beyond death in whatever condition (including in such a concept the strange and adventitious additional notion of eternal reward or punishment) — either of these certainties would make our life equally impossible. In the most secret recess of the spirit of the man who believes that death will put an end to his personal consciousness and even to his memory forever, in that inner recess, even without his knowing it perhaps, a shadow hovers, a vague shadow lurks, a shadow of the shadow of uncertainty, and, while he tells himself: 'There's nothing for it but to live this passing life, for there is no other! ' at the same time he hears, in this most secret recess, his own doubt murmur: 'Who knows? . . . ' He is not sure he hears aright, but he hears. Likewise, in some recess of the soul of the true believer who has faith in a future life, a muffled voice, the voice of uncertainty, murmurs in his spirit's ear: 'Who knows? . . . ' Perhaps these voices are no louder than the buzzing of mosquitoes when the wind roars through the trees in the woods; we scarcely make out the humming, and yet, mingled in the uproar of the storm, it can be heard. How, without this uncertainty, could we ever live?

Miguel de Unamuno, *The Tragic Sense of Life*

It is important to recognize that what we believe about death and the afterlife can influence the actions we take when a person nears death. For example, if we take the materialist view, seeing death as a wall, we may insist that life-sustaining efforts be carried out to the end. On the other hand, if we conceive of continued consciousness after death, we might prefer to use the last hours of our life on earth preparing for a transition into another mode of existence. As Nabe says, "How we respond to the death of someone else, and to our own death, is thus dependent on much broader philosophical questions."[79]

Beliefs about what happens after death may offer comfort and solace to the dying and to their survivors as well. The person who believes that death is the end may feel reassured that suffering experienced in life will end at death. Another person may be comforted by the belief in personality survival after death. By understanding our own beliefs about death, we are able to "care more adequately for each other when death — wall or door — comes to those we love."[80]

Further Readings

Paul Badham and Linda Badham, editors. *Death and Immortality in the Religions of the World.* New York: Paragon House, 1986.

S. G. F. Brandon. *The Judgment of the Dead: The Idea of Life After Death in the Major Religions.* New York: Charles Scribner's Sons, 1967.

James P. Carse. *Death and Existence: A Conceptual History of Human Mortality.* New York: John Wiley & Sons, 1980.

Jacques Choron. *Death and Western Thought.* New York: Macmillan, 1963.

Sylvia Cranston and Carey Williams. *Reincarnation: A New Horizon in Science, Religion, and Society.* New York: Julian Press, 1984.

R. C. Finucane. *Appearances of the Dead: A Cultural History of Ghosts.* Buffalo, N.Y.: Prometheus Books, 1984.

Stanislav Grof and Christina Grof. *Beyond Death: The Gates of Consciousness.* New York: Thames and Hudson, 1980.

Murray J. Harris. *Raised Immortal: Resurrection and Immortality in New Testament.* Grand Rapids, Mich.: Eerdmans, 1985.

Frederick H. Holck, editor. *Death and Eastern Thought: Understanding Death in Eastern Religions and Philosophies.* Nashville: Abingdon, 1974.

Philip Kapleau, editor. *The Wheel of Death: A Collection of Writings from Zen Buddhist and Other Sources on Death-Rebirth-Dying.* New York: Harper & Row, 1971.

Morton T. Kelsey. *Afterlife: The Other Side of Dying.* New York: Paulist Press, 1979.

Hans Kung. *Eternal Life? Life After Death as a Medical, Philosophical, and Theological Problem.* Garden City, N.Y.: Doubleday, 1984.

Jung Young Lee. *Death and Beyond in the Eastern Perspective: A Study Based on the Bardo Thodol and the I Ching.* New York: Gordon and Breach, 1974.

Stephen Levine. *Who Dies? An Investigation of Conscious Living and Conscious Dying.* Garden City, N.Y.: Anchor Press/Doubleday, 1982.

Frank E. Reynolds and Earle H. Waugh, editors. *Religious Encounters with Death: Insights from the History and Anthropology of Religions.* University Park, Pa.: Pennsylvania State University Press, 1977.

Jack Riemer, editor. *Jewish Reflections on Death.* New York: Schocken Books, 1974.

Arnold Toynbee et al. *Man's Concern with Death.* New York: McGraw-Hill, 1968.

Emily Vermeule. *Aspects of Death in Early Greek Art and Poetry.* Berkeley: University of California Press, 1979.

Photojournalist W. Eugene Smith's children appear in his 1946
photograph, "The Walk to Paradise Garden," the first taken by Smith
after two years of inactivity and numerous operations to make him sound
again after multiple wounds received in the Pacific during World War II.
Smith said he was determined that his first frame successfully "speak of a
gentle moment of spirited purity in contrast to the depraved savagery I
had raged against with my war photographs."

The Path Ahead: Personal and Social Choices

*D*eath may be devalued, even denied for a time, but it cannot be eluded. In our relationship with death, we are both survivors and experiencers. In previous chapters we have seen that there can be many different attitudes toward death and dying. Death may be seen as an ever-present threat, or as a benign catalyst, provoking us to greater awareness and creativity in life. Death may seem the ignominious end to even the best of human accomplishment, or it may be seen as a welcome respite from life's sufferings. Death holds many meanings.

One student in a death and dying class said, "Confronting death has put me in touch with life." Acknowledging the impact of death in our lives can awaken us to the preciousness of life. This insight can lead to a greater appreciation of the relationships in one's life. Learning about death can also bring insights concerning the death of old notions of self, as one grows beyond limited concepts of "who I am."

Death education is inseparable from the whole of human experience. The study of death and dying touches on the past, the present, and the future. It takes account of individual acts as well as customs of entire societies. The study of death and dying leads naturally to the arena of political decision, and it ultimately brings us to choices of an emphatically personal nature. Death education is germane to the sphere of social relationships as well as the confrontation with mortality that comes in the most private, personal moments of solitude and introspection.

I say, "Why should a spirited mortal feel proud, when like a swift, fleet meteor or fast-flying cloud, man passes through life to his rest in the grave?" They've asked me, "How do I feel?" I told them that there's nothing to it; you do things the way they ought to be done. I don't see anything to be proud about. It's pretty difficult for a man to feel proud when knowing as he does the short space of time he's here and all paths, even those of our greatest glory, lead but to the grave. So it is very difficult to feel proud when Death says this. You're here today and gone sometimes today.

"A Very Long Conversation with
James Van Der Zee at the Age of Ninety-One,"
in *The Harlem Book of the Dead*

Think about your own relationship to death. What place does death have in your life? What kinds of meanings does death hold for you? Are death and dying compartmentalized in a category all their own, or are they part of a larger fabric of human experience?

In this final chapter we touch upon some of the ways in which what we learn about death impinges on individual and social experience. Rather than providing answers, our aim will be to stimulate inquiry, to raise questions, to speculate about the path ahead.

The Value of Exploring Death and Dying: New Choices

Taking a course or reading a book about death and dying offers an opportunity to take death "out of the closet" and examine it from many perspectives. Possibly you are making new choices in your life as a result of your personal exploration of death. Reflecting on the study of death and dying, one student remarked, "The thought of death had always created a lot of fear; now I find that there's something very fascinating about exploring my own feelings about death and the way that society relates to death." Often, the study of death brings insights into past experiences in one's life. One woman said, "I see now what a big part denial and mutual pretense played in my family's experience of death; the subject of death had really been taboo." Another said, "I was surprised to find how many events in my own life had carried the same kind of emotional impact as a death. Divorce, separation, illness, disappointment — all meant coping with grief, loneliness, fear, and sadness in much the same way as when dealing with a death."

As you think about the various topics covered in this book, what do you notice concerning your understanding of death? Has learning about death and dying expanded your perspective or altered your attitude toward death? Do the terms *death* and *dying* elicit the same patterns of thought and emotion as when you began your study?

"When I used to think about my own death," a student remarked, "I used to slam the door, thinking of all the things I still wanted to do in my lifetime.

Now, I've become a bit more calm, a bit more balanced about it." Another said, "Before I got involved in studying death, I was really uptight about death and dying, especially my own death, even though I haven't had many personal encounters with death. Now I feel that facing my own death is not as difficult, really, as being a survivor of other people's deaths."

Studying death and dying does not necessarily resolve the question, "Why death?" We are born and we die: We face the prospect not only of our own death, but of surviving the deaths of loved ones. For some, investigation of death and dying allows a more accurate perception of what anyone can do to protect or be responsible for another. A parent said, "I've learned something about letting go where my children are concerned. No matter how much you might wish it were otherwise, you can never protect your loved ones from everything."

Responding to this awareness, one student said, "I learned how important it is to appreciate people while you've got them." Becoming aware of death can focus attention on the importance in relationships with others of taking care of unfinished business, saying the things that need to be said, and not being anxious about those things that do not. As one student expressed it, her study of death and dying had impressed upon her a sense of "the precariousness of life."

Recognizing that the preciousness of the human situation is revealed not only in major changes — such as those brought about by death — but also in the less noticed changes experienced in daily life, one can choose to be attentive to the things and persons that are most highly valued.

 I attended your Dealing with Death and Dying class May 10 and 11. You excused me at 1:00, May 11, so that I could go to a function that I needed to attend. I agreed to write notes on an article on cancer to compensate for the class time that I'd miss.

At the same time I was driving home from the class, my Mother was admitted to a Midwestern hospital for internal bleeding due to her accelerated cancerous condition. I left the Bay Area soon after and arrived in Iowa to deal with the reality of death.

Comments on the article don't seem as important to me, now, as some other comments I'd like to make. They concern the necessity of dealing with death and dying.

Had it not been for your class, I would have had more severe problems dealing with all the things death causes us to deal with. The openness of the people in class helped me work through some of the pain I was experiencing as I knew that my Mother didn't have long to live. The class helped me during the time the mortician sat with us and helped us work out the business details, and it helped me through the Midwestern Protestant wake. I was helped as I remembered to make sure that we got what we wanted and were allowed to say our good-byes in ways we wanted. I was able to help my family think clearly about the needs they had so that after Mother was removed from us, we would not say "if only."

A student in a Death and Dying class

Think about the personal and social implications of death and dying. Have your previous opinions on such issues as euthanasia, funerals and body disposition, and war been confirmed? Or have they changed as a result of your studies?

As more people willingly confront issues surrounding death and dying, and examine the options for themselves, changes are occurring throughout society. Examples are the establishment of such helping mechanisms as hospices and suicide intervention programs, as well as other support groups that aid individuals and families in crisis. As death is subjected to a less fearful scrutiny, there is movement — individually and as a society — toward gaining the knowl-

---

Ukiyo-E

What explanation is given for the phosphorus light
That you, as boy, went out to catch
When summer dusk turned to night.
You caught the fireflies, put them in a jar,
Careful to let in the air,
Then you fed them dandelions, unsure
Of what such small and fleeting things
Need, and when
Their light grew dim, you
    Let them go.

There is no explanation for the fire
That burns in our bodies
Or the desire that grows, again and again,
So that we must move toward each other
In the dark.
We have no wings.
We are ordinary people, doing ordinary things.
The story can be told on rice paper.
There is a lantern, a mountain, whatever
    We can remember.

Hiroshige's landscape is so soft.
What child, woman, would not want to go out
Into that dark, and be caught,
And caught again, by you?
Let these pictures of the floating world go on
Forever, but when
This light must flicker out, catch me,
Give me whatever a child imagines
To keep me aglow, then
    Let me go.

    Siv Cedering

edge that can be helpful in dealing with death intelligently and compassionately.

For some, the close examination of death brings insights that help to dissipate or resolve long-held feelings of guilt or blame attached to grief about a loved one's death. The encounter with death that comes through study can open up new and creative possibilities that result in an easier, more comfortable relationship with others and with life itself. The study of death and dying can help to put previously unsettling experiences into perspective.

The notions that may be present at the beginning of a personal exploration of death and dying are expressed in the following statement:

> When I first began to recognize the seriousness of death and dying, I fled from it in fear, although I didn't realize what I was doing. Emotionally, it was harder than I had expected. But I learned that people do survive their losses, and I now know why they are called 'survivors.' I also learned a lot about myself, not all pleasant. A lot of my learning occurred amidst avoidance and trepidation. I thought about things that I had neglected for a long time . . . all my old concepts of death, shadowed in images of hells and old horror movies.

For one man who had felt frustrated, resentful, and guilty about his brother's death twenty years earlier, the study of death provided an opportunity to open up unexpressed and unresolved grief about a number of close family deaths. As the "stored tears" began to be expressed, he summed up the benefit of his exploration of death: "It feels so good to get rid of that ache."

For some, the study of death and dying brings benefits related to professional concerns as well. One nurse said: "When death occurs on the ward, people often think, 'Oh, well, you're a nurse; it shouldn't bother you.' But it does. . . . I really miss the patient; it's a real loss." A ward clerk in a hospital emergency room described the new and more helpful choices she could make use of in relating to survivors:

> My desk is in the same area with the survivors of an ER [emergency room] death. I used to feel a pain right in the pit of my stomach, wondering what to say to them. I thought I should be able to comfort them in some way, that I should somehow offer them words of wisdom. But now I don't feel that way. I've learned how important it is to simply listen, to be supportive just by being there, instead of trying to find some words that will magically make it all go away.

Others find the study of death and dying academically intriguing. The avenues of exploration into other cultures or into one's own society opened up through such study can be a rapid means of gaining insight into what is essential about a society's values and concepts. Learning about the meaning of death in feudal Japan, for example, provides the student of Japanese culture an appreciation that goes beyond the aesthetic or historic approach to cross-cultural understanding. Concepts about what constitutes a "good" death or about immortality reveal a great deal about the tenor and form of a culture's daily life as well as its highest achievements. Death is at the core of human experience.

Cultural attitudes toward death are reflected in such societal applications as

© Carol A. Foote

Culture and individual personality shape our attitudes toward death. What we understand of death and what meanings we ascribe to it become significant to the extent that we construct a meaningful relationship with the experience of death and dying in our lives. This grave marker expresses a memorialization that is consonant with the life styles of both the deceased and her survivors.

social programs for the aged and medical care of the dying. The willingness of a society to engage in activities that pose risks for the well-being of its citizens also demonstrates something of the consensus with regard to the value of human life. Funeral customs reflect a society's attitudes toward death and intimate relationships. Investigating a society's relationship with death makes available a wealth of information to the person with an inquiring mind and an interest in discerning the larger patterns of belief and behavior.

Societal Applications of Death Education

What kinds of cultural values may be acquired or refined by a greater willingness to think and talk about death, and with what effect on society as a whole? How will our contemporary exploration of death affect the dilemmas of medical ethics? For example, do life-sustaining technologies prolong life or only delay death? A willingness to speak plainly about death and to face the implications of public policy decisions that relate to death can assist a society in sorting out such value-laden issues. Similarly, an awareness of the needs of the dying, coupled with knowledge about the available options for meeting those needs, can bring about improvements in America's health care system. Such an undertaking would require informed participation by citizens from all walks of life.

Shifting to another area of public policy, the experiences of the Vietnam era altered the perceptions of many people with regard to what constitutes the national interest in matters of defense and foreign affairs. Some have sought out knowledge about death and dying to help resolve disturbing personal and social issues raised by American involvement in Vietnam. Experiences such as the Vietnam war can also affect more general attitudes toward death by causing us to examine previously unquestioned assumptions.

A few years ago, the student of death and dying would have found it quite difficult to locate even a single volume on the subject of death in the local bookstore. Today many bookstores have a separate section on death. Some of the books on the shelves are bestsellers. Such books include personal accounts of individuals and families coping with terminal illness and survivorship, as well as essays and anthologies written by professional thanatologists. There are books for children, too, both nonfiction and stories with themes relating to death.

Death education is becoming part of the schools' curriculum; teachers use such real-life experiences as the death of a classmate or the assassination of a world leader to help students better learn about death. Elementary school teachers are seeking, and finding, educational materials that present death in ways accessible to children's understanding.

One result of this interest in death and dying is that many of us are examining the subconscious cultural message that death is "bad." The western and the detective story give us a modern version of the morality play in which the villain dies and the hero lives. Now we are beginning to acknowledge that death and failure are not necessarily synonymous, that the meaning of death lies beyond such distinctions. However, our attitudes toward death have only just begun to change. There are frequent reminders that death remains a taboo and fearful topic for many people. Take a death-and-dying course or read a book such as this one and quite likely someone will ask, "Why would you want to take a class about death?" or "Why in heaven's name would you be reading about death?"

One student said, "Sometimes I feel there's too little space in our society for a person to scream, to cry, to shout, to sing, to touch, to be human." Death evokes all these aspects of human behavior. Yet the person who is experiencing grief over the loss of a loved one may find it difficult to express these natural emotions. Dr. Elisabeth Kübler-Ross and others advocate the institution, in hospitals and other such settings, of a "grief" or "screaming" room: a room set aside not only for letting out the intense emotions of loss and bereavement, but also for physicians and other caregivers to engage in open discussions with patients and family members.

Much has been accomplished. The topic of death has become more acceptable. Themes related to death are explored through drama and fiction and in various other ways to a greater extent, and more seriously, than was thought possible just a few years ago. Health care professionals have made strides toward instituting programs and policies that acknowledge a place for the dying. Educators have developed curricula and the sensitivity necessary for offering instruction to persons who are interested in expanding their knowledge and understanding of death and dying.

Specialized training programs for professionals whose duties bring them into frequent contact with dying and bereaved persons also have become part of death education. These professionals frequently become witnesses of human tragedy in the line of duty. They are present in crises involving death and are called upon to comfort victims and survivors. Thus, besides the skills needed to carry out their primary role, they are also expected to bring sensitivity and expertise in human relations to their dealings with the public. The stress that results from being on the scene when tragedy occurs takes a further emotional toll in their own lives. The image of the police officer, emergency medical technician, or firefighter who "keeps it all in" and never shows his or her emotions is being changed by the recognition that such a strategy is stressful and, in the end, psychologically and physically harmful. Seminars and training

Death is not the ultimate tragedy of life. The ultimate tragedy is depersonalization— dying in an alien and sterile area, separated from the spiritual nourishment that comes from being able to reach out to a loving hand, separate from the desire to experience the things that make life worth living, separated from hope.

Norman Cousins, *Anatomy of an Illness*

Recently my seven-year-old son hopped in my lap and we watched the evening news together. The concluding line of a report on environmental pollution was a quote from U.N. scientists predicting that in twenty years the world would be uninhabitable. As the TV switched to a Madison Avenue jingle designed to encourage us to purchase a non-greasy hair tonic, my son turned to me with a terribly small voice and asked: "Dad, how old will I be when we all die?"

Robert D. Barr, *The Social Studies Professional*

programs that recognize the special needs of these professionals are now being offered in many communities. Death education, "in advance of experiencing the deaths of others," can identify the range of emotional responses that are likely to be encountered, and, through previous contemplation and analysis of their own mortality, these professionals can become better prepared to deal not only with their own feelings but with the feelings of others as well.[1]

There is also a growing freedom for individuals and families to make choices that are personally satisfying, rather than feeling they must conform to some preconceived social norm. For example, just as the 1960s saw more personal creativity in the design of wedding ceremonies, we are beginning to see a similar creativity with regard to matters of death and dying.

Death has come a considerable distance out of the closet into the light of public attention. It is difficult to assess to what extent this increased awareness is the result of what appears to be a pervasive dread concerning the future.[2] The threat of large-scale nuclear warfare has brought death into the consciousness of many people. Some believe that the threat of death on a massive scale now comes not only from the possibility of nuclear catastrophe, but also from widespread environmental pollution, the deadly poisoning of our environment. The accidental poisoning of livestock feed in Michigan a few years back characterizes the kind of risk to which individuals are exposed, but which they feel unable to control. Many people are angry about what they perceive as the precedence of profit over people, yet they feel powerless to affect the situation.[3]

How has this confrontation with death changed the way we think and feel about death? If these threats are as real as they seem, what is it about our attitudes toward death that stops us from truly confronting such threats?

Confronting the meaning of death in social as well as personal contexts may alter our political consciousness. The student of death and dying is likely to be more aware than others of the social issues that involve death. He or she will have an appreciation of the reality represented by newspaper headlines that report death in statistical and dramatic terms. Hazards to public safety — often expressed in tedious analyses of risks versus benefits — take on an added dimension for the person who has explored the human impact of death and dying.

The person who has examined the manner in which death — real death —

> Could it be . . . that one reason why the study of death has emerged as one of the dominant concerns of our time is to help us to become globally sensitized to the experience of death precisely because the notion of death on a *planetary scale* now hangs, like the sword of Damocles, over our heads? Could this be the universe's way of "innoculating" us against the fear of death?
>
> Kenneth Ring, *Life at Death*

impinges on such issues as nuclear disarmament, environmental pollution, and crime in the streets begins to consider them in a new light, with greater understanding and concern. The issues that confront us are not amenable to easy answers. The adage that there are two sides to every question is perhaps nowhere more evident than with regard to death-related issues.

Consider, for example, the debate over a person's right to die and the demand prevalent in our society that life be sustained. Medical technologies are opening new areas of ethical concern. Such technologies are part of a cultural milieu with characteristic attitudes toward death and dying. Reporting and supportive systems are now in place in many localities to facilitate organ transplantation at the moment of the donor's death. In this one area of medical ethics alone, many questions are being dealt with, questions about the medical-legal definition of death and the issues related to keeping a person alive on life support systems.

New Directions in Death Education

Despite (or perhaps because of) the rapid acceptance of death education, a clear sense of continuity and common tradition has not fully developed. Given the proliferation of death education courses and the variety of death awareness programs offered to the public, the subject matter of death education and standards for measuring outcome are still being defined. Although this issue is perhaps most pressing for those in academic settings, it applies also to persons working as teachers, counselors, and in related capacities within the community.

The question of accountability in death education has been difficult to address, partly because such education is conducted in a variety of settings, often with differing methodologies and goals. For example, should the aim of death education be to *alleviate* discomfort and anxiety about dying and death? If acceptance of death is thought to be a superior posture to denial, then efforts must be made "to assess the validity of such notions, despite the difficulties involved in such measurement."[4] Death education is both humanitarian and scientific, thus caring must be combined with objectivity.

Much research remains to be done to address adequately even the most fundamental concerns of thanatology. Robert Fulton recently pointed out, for example, that there seems to be a fixation on nineteenth-century hydrostatic models of grief, which postulate a certain volume of grief that must be poured out. Too, the "work" of mourning is generally conceived of in linear terms, as a step-by-step progression, rather than as a dynamic process of "unraveling the skein of grief."[5] We still know very little about how physiological processes of the brain affect the experience of grief. It may be, suggests Fulton, that the "anniversary reaction," commonly experienced by the bereaved is a manifestation of the associative nature of brain function. Such findings from brain research have yet to be applied to our understanding of dying and death. Related to this area of study is an apparent link between mourning and creativity, which is little understood.

Similarly, in caring for the dying, paternalism may replace advocacy if answers are proposed before the necessary questions have been asked. If such care is to occur within the context of a patient's free choice and beliefs about death, we should be wary of presuppositions that derive from the caregiver's personal perspective or preferences instead of unbiased and informed appraisal.[6] A caregiver who places a high value on resolving conflicts as part of preparing for endings may unintentionally demand, expect, or wish that his or her patients do the same. Our understanding of the phenomena related to dying and death can grow only when we take into account the interplay between theory and application in constructing an adequate knowledge base.

As the shape of death education, counseling, and care continues to evolve into a unified discipline, there has been a call for a global perspective. Although personal and private experiences related to dying and death are indeed central to thanatological study and practice, the global dimensions of death — war, violence, the nuclear threat, environmental catastrophe — are increasingly of concern to those in the field. Fulton has suggested that the comparative lack of firsthand experience with death, combined with the pervasive threat of nuclear annihilation, may cause people to exhibit a fascination with *anything* related to death. This fascination is frequently manifested more as a kind of necrophilia — as displayed in some contemporary novels and films — than as a healthy capacity to cope with mortality.

Death in the Future

As we look to the future, what questions about death and dying will increasingly demand our attention both as individuals and as a society? In the remaining years of this millennium, we will continue to see an ever-growing older population. It is estimated there will be 2.6 million deaths annually by the year 2000, an increase of about one-third over the present number. Care of the dying is likely to be big business as corporations expand their role as surrogate caregivers for the aged and dying.

Imagine what death will be like fifty or one hundred years from now. Extrapolate from present realities and current possibilities. Think back over the key issues discussed in previous chapters. What are some of your speculations about what our relationship to death will be by the middle years of the twenty-first century?

For example, ask yourself to imagine the kind of rituals or ceremonies surrounding the dead several decades from now. Writing about the rapid pace of social change among South Pacific societies, Ron Crocombe remarks upon the trend in these societies of reducing the time spent on each funeral, marriage, birth, and other such occasion of community celebration, as well as diverting such activities from day to night and weekday to weekend. "Most traditional social rituals took more time than can be spared today," he says, "both because there are many more things to do, and because each person is doing different things."[7] Although our own value judgments may determine how we spend our time, such decisions are rarely made independently of social norms and practices. For instance, if a work schedule makes it difficult to attend a midweek funeral, we may be reluctant to insist on having time off. As our notions about how time should be used change, thereby affecting our attitudes and behaviors relative to death, what kinds of funeral practices and services might evolve to correspond to these changes?

As for disposition of the corpse, will there be enough land to continue the practice of burials? Some have suggested that we may see the substitution of high-rise cemeteries, cities of the dead towering above the landscape of the living. Although it is unlikely that current funeral practices will disappear completely within the foreseeable future, changes in methods of arranging for and conducting last rites will undoubtedly occur as consumers exercise new choices. An example of this change can already be seen in some areas of the country as casket dealers set up shop to make their wares available to the public independently of conventional funeral establishments.

In coping with the death of a loved one, what types of social services will be available? Few could have foreseen the rapid rise of specialized support groups and activist organizations such as "Parents of Murdered Children" and "Mothers Against Drunk Driving," to name but two of the groups that provide a forum for the issues and a focus for the grief resulting from particular types of bereavement. What other developments in bereavement, grief, and mourning may take place in the coming years?

Besides support groups for the bereaved, the recent past also has seen an increase in the importance of counseling or therapy following bereavement. In the future, might there be "grief clinics" available on call for emergencies? Would these clinics — much like present health institutions — send out reminders for patients or clients to come in for a bereavement checkup before the anniversary date of a significant death? Bereavement counseling is already acknowledged for its value, especially when circumstances make coping with a death difficult. Such counseling, however, is not yet widely available.[8] With a greater openness in talking about death and acknowledging its place in our lives, there may come a time when professional assistance in dealing with grief is the norm.

What diseases will frighten us and endanger our survival if the currently

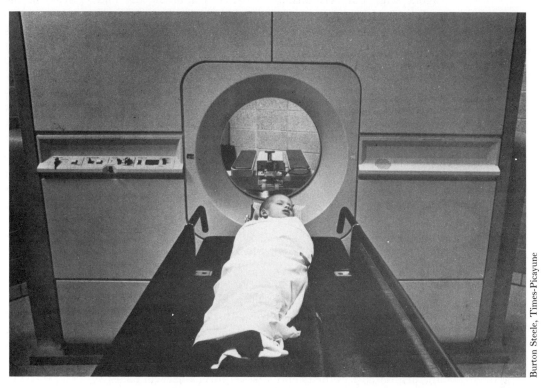

Extrapolating from current medical technologies, we can foresee only faintly the questions and decisions about death and dying that the children of the future will face.

Burton Steele, Times-Picayune

threatening diseases, such as cancer and heart disease, become matters of routine prevention or cure? What change do you imagine will occur within even as short a period as the next decade? In earlier chapters, we discussed the rapid pace of medical advances in diagnosis and treatment. The prognosis for a given disease or category of patients may change from very poor to exceptionally good within the span of a few years with new discoveries and techniques. During the same period, on the other hand, life-threatening diseases that were previously unrecognized or even nonexistent may present new threats. As a case in point: Who could have foreseen the frightening implications of AIDS? Virtually nonexistent a few short years ago, this disease has assumed proportions comparable to the great plagues of the Middle Ages in terms of public fear and uncertainty. When Elisabeth Kübler-Ross proposed opening a hospice for infants and children with AIDS, the nearby community called an emergency meeting to prevent such a move. Can we anticipate that new diseases and threats, as yet undescribed and unknown, will cause similar hysteria in the future?

It is difficult to imagine a time when *no* disease or illness will be life threatening. Yet we have already lived through many technological advances that make possible the sustaining of life beyond any measure conceivable by earlier generations. What technological advances will be commonplace for sustaining life in the coming decades? The mechanical heart, though still a subject of controversy, has become a reality. The future we envision may include "off-the-shelf" replaceable body parts that will sustain life when conventional methods prove futile. In the coming years, organ transplantation may give way to organ substitution. If there is indeed a "bionic" human in our future, what values should guide the use of such innovative, life-sustaining technologies, and who will decide?

In Damon Knight's science-fiction story, "Masks," a man who has suffered physically devastating injuries is repaired with functional artificial body parts. But his mechanically sustained life causes him to question what constitutes a living human being.[9] Another area of speculation is the development of techniques for accurately predicting the time of a person's death. This theme is explored in Clifford Simak's "Death Scene" and in Robert Heinlein's "Lifeline."[10] In different ways both stories seem to suggest that the moment of one's death may be better left unknown. Although such explorations in speculative fiction are typically located in the future, in a setting different from our own, and often incorporate elements of fantasy, the themes investigated refer to present possibilities and current dilemmas of moral choice.

When members of the "baby boom" generation reach retirement age in the first decades of the twenty-first century, what will their lives be like? What changes are likely to occur in the health care system? What will be the quality of life — and of dying? In her story "Golden Acres" Kit Reed envisions a future in which the administrators of an institution for the aged, called Golden Acres, make life-or-death decisions about the aged inmates in order to make room for new arrivals.[11] Golden Acres provides everything for its residents, except the possibility of living out their lives in the ways they wish. Reed's story focuses on a resident who refuses to acquiesce in society's overwhelming neglect of its aged members. As the protagonist describes it, Golden Acres is "a vast boneyard."

Can death be vanquished by technology — or by some other means? A

 I was sitting by myself. The hotel had cleared. A little old lady came in, so I asked her to sit with me. And she told me her life. She had lived for twelve years in hotels. All she had was in this one little room. She had a daughter. She said her daughter wrote twice a week, but her daughter lived at a distance. She went into quite some detail, and I think it hit me then, harder than it ever had, that some day that might be me!

A student in a Death and Dying class

recent magazine article carried the startling message that "You needn't d
The author urges people to do away with the mistaken notion that death r
naturally follow life. Instead, he says, death can be avoided by employing cer
breathing techniques and dietary practices like those used by Indian yogis, who
are reported to continue living indefinitely. Is death becoming obsolete?

Living with Death and Dying

What *personal* value is derived from thinking about and exploring the
many meanings of death? As you think about the various perspectives covered
in your study of death and dying, take a moment to assess the areas that seem of
particular value to you. What insights developed from examining how death is
related to in other cultures? How do the insights gained from study about death
and children relate to your own death experiences as a child or as an adult?
What about your risk-taking behaviors? What aspects of your life style involve
risking death? What do they tell you about your attitudes toward death? In sum,
ask yourself: What have I learned that can be helpful to me as a survivor of
others' deaths — and in confronting my own death?

The study of death and dying engages both the cognitive faculties and the
emotions. What effect does your awareness of death have on the quality of your
relationships with family members, friends, and others? Does an awareness of

---

My Death

"Death is our eternal companion,"
don Juan said with a most serious
air. "It is always to our left, at
an arm's length. . . . It has always been
watching you. It always will until
the day it taps you."

Carlos Casteneda

My death
looks exactly like me.
She lives to my left,
at exactly an arm's length.
She has my face, hair, hands;
she ages
as I grow older.

Sometimes, at night,
my death awakens me

or else appears in dreams
I did not write.
Sometimes a sudden wind
blows from nowhere,
& I look left
& see my death.

Alive, I write
with my right hand only.
When I am dead,
I shall write with my left.

But later I will have to write
through others.
I may appear
to future poets
as their deaths.

Erica Jong

"the precious precariousness of life" prompt a greater sensitivity toward your own and others' needs and compassion for others?

Humanizing Death and Dying

Many people are encouraged by what they see as the increasing openness about and humanizing of death in American society. There are signs that the circumstances surrounding death are being brought back into the personal control of the individuals and families who are closest to a particular death.

However, some question whether this apparent openness toward death might be illusory. Some believe that when death becomes, for example, a topic of casual discussion on television talk shows, our discomfort with the reality of death is betrayed. They ask whether we are not minimizing or devaluing death, trying to acheive a kind of "death without regrets."

As some thanatologists and persons who care for the dying emphasize, death — real death — is not necessarily what it seems to be in our rosy-colored projections and fantasies about the good death. In the urge to humanize death and dying, to accept death, might there also be a more subtle form of denial?

In one sense, none of us is able to "humanize" death. Death is already intensely human. We can work to balance our fears with openness, our anxieties with trust. We can begin to understand the dynamics of bereavement and grief, to make room for loss and change in our lives and in the lives of others.

Death need not be misconstrued as something foreign to our self-interest, a foe to be fought valiantly to the bitter end. But in gaining an easier familiarity with death, we must also be alert to the danger of becoming too casual about it. We may find we have confronted only our *image* of death, not death itself. There are many signs of an increased casualness toward death in modern society. One example is the increasing number of death notices, bearing the announcement, "No services are planned." The decision to forgo last rites may be made by the deceased before death: "I want my body disposed of quickly and cheaply; I don't want to trouble anyone."

Yet few people die without survivors who are affected by the loss. Is death a solitary or a communal event? Can I say that my death is "my own"? Or is death an event whose significance ripples outward to touch the lives not only of friends and loved ones, but also the lives of casual acquaintances and even strangers in ways little understood? What is the desired balance between the individual and the social connotations of death?

It is again becoming possible to exercise some control over the manner of one's dying and death. For some, this means choosing to die at home, with family members making a place for the dying person within the household. Some are making space in the home to hold a wake following the death of a loved one, taking time to be with the body, encountering the loved one's death in a personal and immediate way.

As with these examples, a greater knowledge of one's choices allows the possibility for more meaningful and personally satisfying decisions concerning death and dying.

© Carol A. Foote

The contemplation of death and its meaning will determine how we and our children think about and behave toward death in the decades ahead.

Defining the Good Death

There is no single definition of what constitutes a *good* death. In ancient Greece, to die young, in the fullness of one's creative energies, was considered to be exceptional luck. In our society, on the other hand, death at a young age is considered a misfortune; the death of a person just embarking on an independent life or of someone in the prime of life seems a great tragedy.

The good death can be defined in many ways. Take a moment to think about how you might define it. Consider the various factors — age, mode of death, surroundings, and so on — that would enter into your concept of a good death. Is your concept the same for yourself and for others?

Some may question whether there can be any such thing as a good death. "Death is never good," they might say, "It can only cause pain and sadness." A more useful concept, perhaps, is of the *appropriate* death. What makes some deaths seem more appropriate than others? Our answers are influenced by cultural values and by the social context of death. Avery Weisman has enumerated some of the conditions that define an appropriate death in most modern societies.[12]

First, an appropriate death is relatively pain free; the suffering of the dying is kept to a minimum. The social and emotional needs of the dying person are met to the fullest extent possible. There is no impoverishment of crucial human resources. Within the limits imposed by disabilities, the dying person is free to operate effectively as an individual and to enjoy mobility and independence. In addition, the dying person is able to recognize and resolve, as far as possible, any residual personal and social conflicts. The person is allowed to satisfy his or her wishes in ways that are consistent with the situation and with his or her self-identity and self-esteem.

As death approaches, the dying person is allowed to freely choose to relinquish control over various aspects of his or her life, turning over control to persons in whom confidence and trust have been placed. The dying person also may choose to seek out or to relinquish relationships with significant others. In other words, the person chooses a comfortable level of social interaction.

Weisman points out that to achieve an appropriate death we must first rid ourselves of the notion that death is *never* appropriate. This belief, he says, acts as a self-fulfilling prophecy: We shut ourselves off from creating the possibility of a more appropriate death.

For an appropriate death to be possible, the dying person must be

---

The Angel of Death

The Angel of Death is always with me—
the hard wild flowers of his teeth,
his body like cigar smoke
swaying through a small town jail.

He is the wind that scrapes through our months,
the train wheels grinding over our syllables.
He is the footstep continually pacing through our chests,
the small wound in the soul,
the meteor puncturing the atmosphere.
And sometimes he is merely a quiet between the start of an act
and its completion,
a silence so loud
it shakes you like a tree.

It is only then you look up from the wars,
from the kisses,
from the signing of the business agreements;
It is only then you observe the dimensions
housed in the air of each day,
each moment;

continued

continued from previous page

only then you hear the old caressing the cold rims of their sleep,
hear the middle-aged women in love with their pillows
weeping into the gray expanse of each dawn,
where young men, dozing in alleys,
envision their loneliness to be a beautiful girl
and do not know they are part of a young girl's dream,
as she does not know that she is the dream in the sleep
of middle-aged women and old men,
and that all are contained in a gray wind
that scrapes through our months.

But soon we forget that the dead sleep in buried cities,
that our hearts contain them in ripe vaults,
We forget that beautiful women dry into parchment
and ball players collapse into ash;
that geography wrinkles and smoothes like the expressions on a face,
and that not even children
can pick the white fruit from the night sky.

And how *could* we laugh while looking at the face
that falls apart like wet tobacco?
How could we wake each morning
to hear the muffled gong beating inside us,
our mouths full of shadows, our rooms filled with a black dust?

Still,
it is humiliating to be born a bottle:
to be filled with air, emptied, filled again;
to be filled with water, emptied, filled again;
and, finally, to be filled with earth.

And yet I am glad that The Angel of Death is always with me:
his footsteps quicken my own,
his silence makes me speak,
his wind freshens the weather of my day.
And it is because of him
I no longer think
that with each beat
my heart
is a planet drowning from within
but an ocean filling for the first time.

Morton Marcus

Death can be viewed as a burden or as a blessing. Its meaning changes as circumstances change and as our understanding evolves toward new recognitions of its place in our lives.

protected from needless, dehumanizing, and demeaning procedures. The person's preferences about pain control and consciousness, and about the extent of solitude or gregarious interaction desired, should be respected. "An appropriate death," Weisman says, "is a death that someone might choose for himself—had he a choice."[13]

The death of Charles Lindbergh reveals many of the features of an appropriate death as defined by Weisman.[14] Lindbergh was diagnosed in 1972 as having lymphoma. Until he died two years later, he continued living an active life, traveling and promoting the cause of conservation. When chemotherapy became ineffective, Lindbergh made arrangements for his eventual burial on his beloved island of Maui, in the Hawaiian islands. As his condition worsened,

Lindbergh was hospitalized for several months, but the best efforts of his physicians could not alter the consequences of the disease. Lindbergh then instructed that a cabin on Maui be obtained, and he was flown "home to Maui," where, with two nurses, his physician, and his family, he spent the last eight days of his life in the environment he loved.

During this time, he gave instructions for the construction of his grave and for the conduct of his funeral, requesting that people attend in their work clothes. As Dr. Milton Howell, one of Lindbergh's physicians, describes it, "There was time for reminiscing, time for discussion, and time for laughter."

Finally, Lindbergh lapsed into a coma and, twelve hours later, died. In accordance with his wishes, there had been no medical heroics. Dr. Howell says, "Death was another event in his life, as natural as his birth had been in Minnesota more than seventy-two years before."

Postscript and Farewell

The study of death and dying encompasses a wide range of subjects. Learning about death may have immediate, practical consequences. At the conclusion of a course on death and dying, one student said, "It has helped me and my family in dealing with my mother's serious illness." For others, the practical implications may seem less immediate. Yet, as another student expressed it, "I've gained a lot of useful information which may not be applicable to my life right now, but I know now that information and help is available and I didn't know that before."

Many people find that their explorations have consequences for their life that go beyond their previous notions about death and dying. One student said, "To me, this study has focused on more than just death and dying; it has dealt with ideas and with living, like a class on philosophy." Another student expressed the value of her death explorations as having, "expanded my faith in the resilience of the human spirit."

Death education does pertain to the practical and obvious aspects asso-

"Frank and Ernest," drawing by Bob Thaves, © 1984 NEA Inc.

ciated with the individual and social encounter with death. But an awareness of death and dying can bring an added dimension to the experience of living, moment to moment, as well. The remembrance of death can bring us more into the present. It can serve as a reminder of the precious precariousness of life, and the value of compassion in the ordinary as well as extraordinary circumstances of human experience.

Further Readings

James Agee. *A Death in the Family*. New York: Bantam Books, 1969.

Simone de Beauvoir. *A Very Easy Death*. New York: Warner, 1973.

Ernest Becker. *The Denial of Death*. New York: The Free Press, 1973.

Norman O. Brown. *Life Against Death: The Psychoanalytical Meaning of History*. 2nd ed. Middletown, Conn.: Wesleyan University Press, 1985.

Charles A. Corr, Judith M. Stillion, and Mary C. Ribar, editors. *Creativity in Death Education and Counseling*. Lakewood, Ohio: Association for Death Education and Counseling, 1983.

Elisabeth Kübler-Ross. *To Live Until We Say Good-bye*. Englewood Cliffs, N.J.: Prentice-Hall, 1978.

Richard A. Pacholski, editor. *Re-Searching Death: Selected Essays in Death Education and Counseling*. Lakewood, Ohio: Association for Death Education and Counseling, 1986.

David K. Reynolds. *Constructive Living*. Honolulu: University of Hawaii Press, 1984.

Leo Tolstoy. *The Death of Ivan Ilych and Other Stories*. New York: New American Library/Signet, 1960.

Alan Watts. *Death*. Millbrae, Calif.: Celestial Arts, 1975.

Avery Weisman. *The Coping Capacity: On the Nature of Being Mortal*. New York: Human Sciences, 1984.

E P I L O G U E

It's late. I wonder what Death will look like? A drooling ogre? Perhaps an unblinking skull, the Grim Reaper? A veiled mistress with beckoning arms? The standard forms. Or maybe Death will be a polished young man in a three-piece suit, all smiles and sincerity and confidence. What a disappointment that would be. No, I prefer the scythe — no ambiguity, no surrender . . . no dickering. What's that? . . . I hear him. He's here.

"May I come in?"

I nod. It's the young man who left me two days ago to knock on the doors of his neighbors' homes. "Well . . . ?" My breath is shorter than I thought.

He smiles, looks down at his hands, then at me. "Well, I did as you said. It didn't take long before I realized that I wasn't going to find a household that hadn't been touched by death."

"How many did you go to?"

He covers his mouth with his hand a moment, trying to hide his pride, I guess. "All of them."

"All?"

"Every house . . . I'm very stubborn."

We both smile. My wheezing is worse, and he notices. He shows his concern, and I can see that he understands what is happening.

"You're dying, aren't you, old man?"

I close my eyes in answer. When I open them again, he is at my side.

"Is there someone I should get for you? Your family?"

"Gone."

"Some friend?"

"Gone. All gone . . . except for you." The young man nods, then pulls his chair over next to my own. He takes my hand. I rest a moment. "There is

*something you must do for me," I wheeze. "When I'm dead, burn this house and
everything in it, including me."*

"Leave nothing behind?"

*"This is only a filthy old shack. I'm leaving behind the only thing that anyone
really can leave behind . . . the difference I've made in the lives of the people I've
met." I squeeze his hand as best I can. He squeezes back. "Oh . . . and this." I try to
lift the book in my lap—my book. He sees me struggling, and picks it up for me.
"You take this. It's yours." His eyes widen.*

"But I don't deserve—"

*"There isn't time for that now!" He nods, and lays the book on his lap. Good,
that's done. Moments pass. It gets quieter . . . still. I must close my eyes. I witness
again the glory of ten thousand mornings, ten thousand afternoons, ten thousand
nights . . . then they, too, fade. All that's left is the sound of our breathing, and the
wind. Time slows. Time changes. Where is the scythe? The young man's hand leaves
mine and I hear his footsteps recede . . . stop . . . return. He sits down and I feel his
hand on mine. He opens my fingers and lays something cool and light in my palm,
all lace and limbs . . . the ballerina.*

Now I can go.

David Gordon

Notes

CHAPTER **I**

1. "Expectation of Life at Birth," in *Statistical Abstract of the United States 1986* 106th ed. (Washington: Government Printing Office, 1985), p. 68. The provisional 1984 statistics show an expectation of life at birth for the total population of 74.7 years, a record high, with 71.1 years for males and 78.3 for females.

2. "Death Rates by Age, Sex, and Race," in *Statistical Abstract of the United States 1986*, p. 70. For a survey of the reasons behind this increase in life expectancy, see Joan Arehart-Treichel, "Life Expectancy: The Great 20th Century Leap," *Science News* 121 (March 13,1982) : 186 – 188

3. "Deaths and Death Rates," in *Statistical Abstract of the United States 1986*, p. 70. Statisticians consider this figure of 8.6 per 1000 to be uncommonly low and something of an aberration in the death rate. It reflects the significant shift in the age grouping of the American population. The death rate is expected to stabilize at about 10.0 per 1000 by the year 2000.

4. Robert Fulton, "Death, Grief, and Social Recuperation," *Omega* 1:1 (1970): 25.

5. "Mobility Status of the Population," in *Statistical Abstract of the United States 1986*, p. 15.

6. The 1980 census indicates a continued decrease in the number of extended families. While the number of households in the United States increased by 27 percent during the previous decade, the average number of people in each household declined by about 13 percent. See Philip M. Hauser, "The Census of 1980," *Scientific American* 245:5 (November 1981): 61.

7. Improved nutrition has also contributed to a decreased death rate. In the years between World Wars I and II, almost 200,000 cases of pellagra were reported each year in the American South. Today, this disease of dietary deficiency is virtually unknown in the United States.

8. According to one demographic forecast: "Under current U.S. conditions, a newborn American girl can expect to spend nine years of her life as a widow and has a 60

percent chance of dying in that state; for males, the corresponding figures are two years and 22 percent." See National Research Council, *Outlook for Science and Technology: The Next Five Years* (San Francisco: W.H. Freeman, 1982), p. 34.

9. "Resident Population by Age," "Live Births, Deaths, Marriages, and Divorces," and "Death Rates by Age, Sex, and Race," in *Statistical Abstract of the United States 1986*, pp. 27, 56, 70.

10. The issues surrounding the use of such technologies are discussed in Chapter 10.

11. Marsha McGee, "Faith, Fantasy, and Flowers: A Content Analysis of the American Sympathy Card," *Omega* 11:1 (1980–81): 29. Although flowers, appearing on 80 percent of the cards, were the most commonly used symbol, McGee reports that they "seldom appear to be growing"; rather, they seem to "exist suspended in space." Contemporary cards often include images of sunsets or fields with grain or flowers, apparently intending to convey an impression of "peace, quiet, and perhaps a return to nature" (p. 27).

12. *Amy Vanderbilt's Complete Book of Etiquette* (Garden City, N.Y.: Doubleday, 1959), p.136.

13. Mary N. Hall, "Laughing As We Go," paper presented at the Annual Meeting of the Forum for Death Education and Counseling, Philadelphia, April 1985.

14. Ibid.

15. Robert Kastenbaum, *Death, Society, and Human Experience* (St. Louis: C. V. Mosby, 1977), p. 93. Kastenbaum observes, "Thousands of people receive death notices in the newspaper throughout the year, but relatively few are singled out for an obituary."

16. Files of pending obituaries are maintained by most media organizations — wire services, metropolitan newspapers, and network news bureaus — on persons whose deaths would be considered newsworthy. These obituaries are updated periodically so that they can be printed or aired when the occasion demands.

17. Efforts by family members to obtain an obituary instead of the smaller death notice may meet with resistance. To illustrate, the family of a young woman who died of Hodgkin's disease sent her photo and a brief account of her life and accomplishments to their local newspaper. Despite their efforts and the aid of a local funeral director, a newspaper spokesperson maintained that it was against policy to run obituaries instead of death notices in such cases. Neither the photograph nor the biographical sketch was printed by the paper, which frustrated many people in the community who had become acquainted with the young woman's accomplishments despite her illness.

18. Communication scholar Wilbur Schramm says news exists in the minds of men, in the sense that it has less to do with an *event* than it does with how that event is *perceived,* by reporters as well as their audience. From: *Newsletter of the International Communication Association* 13:3 (Summer 1985) : 8.

19. Staff article, "Why Do They React? Readers Assail Publication of Funeral, Accident Photos," *News Photographer* 36:3 (March 1981): 21–23.

20. John L. Huffman, "Putting Grief in Perspective," *News Photographer* 36:3 (March 1981): 21–22.

21. Huffman, "Putting Grief in Perspective," p. 22. Huffman says, "Photographs mirroring and evoking intense emotions can sometimes cause pain and suffering to those pictured and those close to them." The rapid reporting made possible by the current technology of news transmission occasionally alters the usual death notification process. For example, the parents of a boy killed by the Mount St. Helens eruption learned of their son's death when they saw a photograph of his body in the newspaper.

22. On the day Aldous Huxley died, another death was given prominence in the

news — that of President John F. Kennedy. On a less eventful day, Huxley's death would undoubtedly have received considerable news coverage, but on this day it was largely overlooked. In the media, as in our own lives, some deaths take precedence over others.

23. Michael Arlen, "The Cold, Bright Charms of Immortality," from *The View from Highway 1* (New York: Farrar, Straus & Giroux, 1976), pp. 34–68.

24. "Utilization of Selected Media," in *Statistical Abstract of the United States 1986*, p. 545.

25. Although estimates vary, it is said that the average American child has seen between 13,000 and 18,000 deaths on television by the age of twenty-one.

26. A study of religious programs on television found more mention of death and dying (defined as any reference to the process of death and dying, including physical death and the emotional or psychological process of preparing for death) than any other social topic. See Robert Abelman and Kimberly Neuendort, "Themes and Topics in Religious Television Programming," paper presented at the Annual Meeting of the International Communication Association, San Francisco, May 1984.

27. Roger Ebert, film critic of the Chicago *Sun-Times*, "At the Movies," NBC-TV, September 8, 1985.

28. Despite virtually no advertising or regular theatrical distribution, *Faces of Death* (1983) and its sequel (1985) have sold over thirty thousand copies on videotape.

29. Examples include memoirs like Ron Kovic's *Born on the Fourth of July* (New York: Pocket, 1977), Philip Caputo's *A Rumor of War* (New York: Ballantine, 1978), and Tim O'Brien's *If I Die in a Combat Zone* (New York: Dell, 1979), as well as novels like William Turner Huggett's *Body Count* (New York: Putnam, 1973), Robert Roth's *Sand in the Wind* (Boston: Little, Brown, 1973), James Webb's *Fields of Fire* (New York: Bantam, 1979), and John Del Vecchio's *The 13th Valley* (New York: Bantam, 1982). For a survey of the genre, see: John Hellman, *American Myth and the Legacy of Vietnam* (New York: Columbia University Press, 1986).

30. Alvin H. Rosenfeld, *A Double Dying: Reflections on Holocaust Literature* (Bloomington: Indiana University Press, 1980), p. 12. See also Lawrence L. Langer, *Versions of Survival: The Holocaust and the Human Spirit* (Albany: State University of New York Press, 1982), and Terrence Des Pres, *The Survivor: An Anatomy of Life in the Death Camps* (New York: Oxford University Press, 1976).

31. Frederick J. Hoffman, *The Mortal No: Death and the Modern Imagination* (Princeton, N.J.: Princeton University Press, 1964).

32. Lawrence Langer explores this theme in *The Age of Atrocity: Death in Modern Literature* (Boston: Beacon Press, 1978).

33. William Ruehlmann, *Saint with a Gun: The Unlawful American Private Eye* (New York: New York University Press, 1984), p. 9.

34. Hoffman, *Mortal No*, p. 312.

35. See Richard A. Pacholski, "Death Themes in the Visual Arts: Resources and Research Opportunities for Death Educators," *Death Studies* 10:1 (1986): 59–74.

36. Fritz Eichenberg, *Dance of Death: A Graphic Commentary on the Danse Macabre through the Centuries* (New York: Abbeville, 1983).

37. Anita Schorsch, *Mourning Becomes America: Mourning Art in the New Nation* (Philadelphia: Main Street Press, 1976), p. 1.

38. Carla Gottlieb, "Modern Art and Death," in *The Meaning of Death*, edited by Herman Feifel (New York: McGraw-Hill, 1959).

39. Donald J. Grout, *A History of Western Music*, 3rd ed. (New York: Norton, 1980), p. 41. See also Richard A. Pacholski, "Death Themes in Music: Resources and

Research Opportunities for Death Educators," *Death Studies* 10:3 (1986): 239–263. A modern composition, Leonard Bernstein's *Symphony No. 3 (Kaddish),* is based on the Jewish prayer for the dead.

40. The *Symphonie* is notable as the first completely programmatic or "narrative" symphony. See Ethan Mordden, *A Guide to Orchestral Music* (New York: Oxford University Press, 1980), pp. 153–155.

41. Bob Macken, Peter Fornatale, and Bill Ayers, *The Rock Music Sourcebook* (Garden City, N.Y.: Anchor Press/Doubleday, 1980).

42. George S. Kanahele, editor, *Hawaiian Music and Musicians* (Honolulu: University Press of Hawaii, 1979), p. 53.

43. Kanahele, *Hawaiian Music,* p. 56

44. Marguerite K. Ashford, Bishop Museum, Honolulu, personal communication.

45. From a *New York Times* wire service story (March 6, 1978).

46. David E. Stannard, *The Puritan Way of Death: A Study in Religion, Culture, and Social Change* (New York: Oxford University Press, 1977).

47. Octavio Paz, *The Labyrinth of Solitude: Life and Thought in Mexico (New York: Grove Press,* 1961), p. 60.

48. Adapted from Kenneth J. Doka, "The Rediscovery of Death: An Analysis of the Emergence of the Death Studies Movement," paper presented at the Annual Meeting of the Forum for Death Education and Counseling, San Diego, September 1982.

49. Robert Fulton, *Death, Grief and Bereavement: A Bibliography, 1845–1975* (New York: Arno Press, 1976). The 1970s also saw the publication of several excellent anthologies that helped to focus the field of death studies, including Larry A. Bugen's *Death and Dying: Theory, Research, and Practice* (Dubuque, Iowa: William C. Brown, 1979); Herman Feifel's *New Meanings of Death* (New York: McGraw-Hill, 1977); Robert Fulton's *Death and Identity,* rev. ed. (Bowie, Md.: Charles Press, 1976); Edwin S. Shneidman's *Death: Current Perspectives,* now in its third edition (Palo Alto, Calif.: Mayfield, 1984); Peter Steinfels and Robert M. Veatch's *Death Inside Out: The Hastings Center Report* (New York: Harper & Row, 1974); and Hannelore Wass's *Dying: Facing the Facts* (New York: Hemisphere, 1979).

50. Figures reflect the number of English-language publications based on an online search of *Books in Print* (Ann Arbor, Mich: R. R. Bowker, 1985) and the National Library of Medicine's **MEDLINE** files. In addition, between 1970 and 1978, more than two hundred doctoral dissertations were written on topics related to death and dying. See Joseph C. Santora, "Bibliography of Death and Dying: A Guide to Doctoral Dissertations of the 1970s," *Death Education* 3:4 (Winter 1980): 415–423 (A–H), and *Death Education* 4:1 (Spring 1980): 100–109 (I–Z).

51. Dan Leviton, "The Scope of Death Education," *Death Education* 1 (1977):41.

52. Questionnaire, "You and Death," *Psychology Today* (August 1970).

53. The response to the *Psychology Today* questionnaire indicated an attitude toward death (as of 1970) that was fraught with ambiguity. As a topic, death was taboo, yet people wanted freedom to discuss it. People expressed a love for life, yet they also acknowledged that they participated in activities that risked death. Also indicative of the patterns of death in modern society, of the participants who had some experience with death, 43 percent cited the death of a grandparent and 18 percent cited the death of a pet as their earliest experience with death. The questionnaire was returned by some 30,000 readers, breaking the previous record of 10,000 replies to a *Psychology Today* questionnaire on sex, a fact which some researchers felt emphasized a widespread sense of "urgency to talk about death."

54. Kathleen B. Bryer, "The Amish Way of Death: A Study of Family Support Systems," *American Psychologist* 34:3 (March 1979): 255–261.

CHAPTER 2

1. The use of blood-red oxide to decorate corpses is almost certainly the earliest widespread funeral custom. Ore deposits of hematite in the Bomvu (Red) Ridge in Africa are thought to be the oldest mineworks anywhere in the world. Red ochre was mined in Africa by the earliest *Homo sapiens sapiens*. It appeared in Europe in connection with Neanderthal funeral practices, and was used in burials throughout Europe, Africa, Asia, Australia, and the Americas.

If we imagine the earth as a living organism, hematite is analogous to the blood of Mother Earth. Its symbolic properties, therefore, are obvious. The Christian Eucharist involves a similar symbology: the red wine that represents the blood of Christ.

2. Mary Kawena Pukui, E. W. Haertig, and Catherine A. Lee, *Nana I Ke Kumu (Look to the Source),* 2 vols. (Honolulu: Hui Hanai; Queen Lili'uokalani Children's Center, 1972). A study conducted in the 1930s found families still tracing their lineage from ancestors who were viewed as spiritual guardians of their descendants, often interceding in very practical ways. See E. S. Craighill Handy and Mary Kawena Pukui, *The Polynesian Family System in Ka-'u, Hawai'i* (Rutland, Vt.: Charles E. Tuttle, 1972).

3. Ninian Smart, *The Long Search* (Boston: Little, Brown, 1977), p. 231.

4. For discussion of such beliefs and customs in modern Japan, see Robert J. Smith, *Ancestor Worship in Contemporary Japan* (Stanford, Calif.: Stanford University Press, 1974); and Yamaori Tetsuo, "The Metaphorphosis of Ancestors," *Japan Quarterly* 33:1 (January–March 1986):50–53.

5. T. H. Gaster, in James Frazer, *The New Golden Bough* (New York: New American Library, 1964), p. 459.

6. Frazer, *New Golden Bough,* p. 240.

7. Ibid., p. 241.

8. Ibid.

9. Handy and Pukui, *Polynesian Family System in Ka-'u, Hawai'i,* pp. 98–101. About modern practices, Handy and Pukui add: "Today it is just a matter of different relatives 'giving' a name informally; such a name 'given' constitutes a bond, a token of *aloha,* an expression of gratification and mark of pride and esteem."

10. In some cultures—among Jews, for example—names are not bestowed if the namesake is alive.

11. Anita J. Glaze, *Art and Death in a Senufo Vilage* (Bloomington: Indiana University Press, 1981), pp. 150–151.

12. For further study of mythologies relating to the theme of the origin of death the following sources will prove rewarding: Hans Abrahamson, *The Origin of Death: Studies in African Mythology* (New York: Arno Press, 1977); Joseph Campbell, *The Masks of God: Primitive Mythology* (New York: Viking Press, 1959); Jacques Choron, *Death and Western Thought* (New York: Macmillan, 1963).

13. As an oral work, the epic of Gilgamesh probably dates from the middle of the third millennium before Christ. It achieved written form about a thousand years later. The epic relates the odyssey of a king who tries to avoid death. His journey is precipitated by the death of his friend Enkidu. At great peril, Gilgamesh finally obtains a magical plant said to have the power to renew one's youth. But the plant is seized by a serpent and Gilgamesh returns from his quest empty-handed. As the epic concludes, Enkidu appears to Gilgamesh and gives a dreary account of life in the afterworld.

14. Jamake Highwater, *The Primal Mind: Vision and Reality in Indian America* (New York: Harper & Row, 1981), p. 165.

15. Malcolm Margolin, *The Ohlone Way: Indian Life in the San Francisco–Monterey Bay Area* (Berkeley, Calif.: Heyday Books, 1978), pp. 145–149.

16. Vine Deloria, Jr., *God Is Red* (New York: Dell, 1973), pp. 176–177.

17. Ibid., p. 175. The respect for the burial places of the forefathers has led to disputes concerning the artifacts and bones retrieved from these burial sites by archeologists. Displaying such items in museums is at odds with the concern for maintaining the sanctity of the remains of the dead.

18. David G. Mandelbaum, "Social Uses of Funeral Rites," in *The Meaning of Death,* edited by Herman Feifel (New York: McGraw-Hill, 1959), pp. 189–217.

19. Noel Q. King, *Religions of Africa: A Pilgrimage into Traditional Religions* (New York: Harper & Row, 1970), pp. 13–14. Also see, by the same author, *Christian and Muslim in Africa* (New York: Harper & Row, 1971), p. 95.

20. Communion with the "living dead" in traditional African societies can be compared with our own relationships to deceased loved ones. Sometimes an event or stimulus recalls to mind the memory of a person no longer alive. We may pause a moment, reflecting on the qualities that made that person beloved, experiencing again our feelings of affection for him or her. In our reverie, we might say that we feel as if we are "communing" with the deceased. Perhaps afterward we even feel that we have gained some insight, some piece of information, or some direction that is helpful in our lives. Whereas our society tends not to provide the formal rituals to acknowledge or encourage this kind of experience, the essential elements seem to be not unlike those found in traditional African culture.

21. King, *Religions of Africa,* p. 68.

22. Jack Goody, *Death, Property, and the Ancestors: A Study of the Mortuary Customs of the LoDagaa of West Africa* (Stanford, Calif.: Stanford University Press, 1962). This detailed account of LoDagaa customs is a classic of anthropology.

23. Barbara Brodman, *The Mexican Cult of Death in Myth and Literature* (Gainesville: University of Florida Press, 1976). Brodman notes that one of Spain's greatest writers, and a prodigious intellectual, Miguel de Unamuno, expressed the opinion that the term "cult of death" is not precise enough to describe the true purpose of Spanish (and, by extension, Mexican) customs relative to death. He suggests substituting the phrase "cult of immortality" as more apt.

24. Octavio Paz, *The Labyrinth of Solitude: Life and Thought in Mexico* (New York: Grove Press, 1961), p. 54.

25. Additional sources of information about death customs in Mexican daily life are: Ignacio Aguilar and Virginia N. Wood, "Therapy Through a Death Ritual," in *Death and Dying: Theory, Research, and Practice,* edited by Larry Bugen (Dubuque, Iowa: William C. Brown, 1979), pp. 131–141; Patricia Fernandez Kelly, "Death in Mexican Folk Culture," in *Death in America,* edited by David E. Stannard (Philadelphia: University of Pennsylvania Press, 1975), pp. 92–111; Oscar Lewis, *A Death in the Sanchez Family* (New York: Vintage Books, 1970).

26. For a discussion of the death theme in Mexican literature, see Brodman, *Mexican Cult of Death.*

27. Jose Antonio Burciaga, "A Day to Laugh at Death," San Jose *Mercury News,* November 1, 1985.

28. Paz, *Labyrinth of Solitude,* p. 57.

29. Ibid., p. 51.

30. Brodman, *Mexican Cult of Death,* pp. 42–43.

31. Paz, *Labyrinth of Solitude,* p. 53. Mourners are cautioned against shedding too many tears. Excessive grief may make the pathway traveled by the dead slippery, and thus burden them with a tortuous journey as they try to return to the world of the living on this special night of fiesta and communal celebration.

32. Aguilar and Wood, "Therapy Through a Death Ritual," p. 134.

33. Philippe Ariès, *Western Attitudes Toward Death: From the Middle Ages to the Present* (Baltimore: Johns Hopkins University Press, 1974), and, also by Ariès, *The Hour of Our Death* (New York: Alfred A. Knopf, 1981). The material presented here owes much to Ariès's insightful analyses of attitudinal and behavioral changes in Western culture. Except where otherwise noted, material appearing within quotation marks is drawn from Ariès's works. Additional sources used in developing this presentation include T. S. R. Boase, *Death in the Middle Ages: Mortality, Judgment and Remembrance* (New York: McGraw-Hill, 1972); Jacques Choron, *Death and Western Thought* (New York: Macmillan, 1963); Donna C. Kurtz and John Boardman, *Greek Burial Customs* (Ithaca, N.Y.: Cornell University Press, 1971).

34. These paintings, originally in the Cemetery of the Innocents in Paris, were destroyed in the late seventeenth century, but reproductions or copies can be seen in the woodcuts of the Paris printer Guy Marchant. The Flemish artist Hans Holbein the Younger executed a series of drawings on the theme in 1523–26, depicting the skeletal figure of death surprising victims in the midst of their daily life.

In music, the dance of death theme survives in the German *Totentanz,* which dates from the sixteenth century. For more on the dance of death as manifest through music, see Kathi Meyer-Baer, *Music of the Spheres and the Dance of Death: Studies in Musical Iconology* (Princeton, N.J.: Princeton University Press, 1970).

35. For more on this, see Georges Bataille, *Death and Sensuality: A Study of Eroticism and the Taboo* (New York: Walker and Company, 1962).

36. For more on these historical developments, see the following authors: Diana Williams Combs, *Early Gravestone Art in Georgia and South Carolina* (Athens: University of Georgia Press, 1986). James J. Farrell, *Inventing the American Way of Death, 1830–1920* (Philadelphia: Temple University Press, 1980); and "The Dying of Death: Historical Perspectives," *Death Education* 6 (1982):105–123. David E. Stannard, *The Puritan Way of Death: A Study in Religion, Culture, and Social Change* (New York: Oxford University Press, 1977); "Calm Dwellings: The Brief, Sentimental Age of the Rural Cemetery," *American Heritage* 30:5 (August/September 1979):42–55; and, edited by Stannard, *Death in America* (Philadelphia: University of Pennsylvania Press, 1975). Michael Vovelle, "A Century and One-Half of American Epitaphs (1600–1813): Toward the Study of Collective Attitudes About Death," *Comparative Studies in Society and History* 22:4 (October 1980):534–547.

37. Herman Feifel summarizes: "In the Middle Ages man had his eschatology and the sacred time of eternity. More recently, temporal man lived with the prospect of personal immortality transformed into concern for historical immortality and for the welfare of posterity. Today we are vouchsafed neither." See "The Meaning of Death in American Society," in *Death Education: Preparation for Living,* edited by Betty R. Green and Donald P. Irish (Cambridge, Mass.: Schenkman, 1971).

38. Norbert Elias, *The Loneliness of the Dying* (New York: Basil Blackwell, 1985), pp. 12–16, 35–40, 62–64.

39. Ariès says that the trend toward displacing the site of death from the home to the hospital underwent a marked acceleration between the 1930s and the 1950s. The ritual

dimensions of dying have been replaced by a technological process in which death occurs "by a series of little steps," making it difficult to discern the moment of "real death." Ariès adds: "All these little silent deaths have replaced and erased the great dramatic act of death, and no one any longer has the strength or patience to wait over a period of weeks for a moment which has lost a part of its meaning." The fact that some people are now trying to restore some sense of the real dimensions of dying can be seen in the growing interest in the hospice concept, which again focuses attention on the processes of a person's dying.

CHAPTER 3

1. For a current review of the literature, see Mark W. Speece and Sandor W. Brent, "Children's Understanding of Death: A Review of Three Components of a Death Concept," *Child Development* 55:5 (October 1984):1671–1686.

2. Primary sources of information on early research in death and children include: Irving E. Alexander and Arthur M. Adlerstein, "Affective Responses to the Concept of Death in a Population of Children and Early Adolescents," *Journal of Genetic Psychology* 93 (1958): 167–177, reprinted in *Death and Identity,* rev. ed., edited by Robert Fulton and Robert Bendiksen (Bowie, Md.: Charles Press, 1978); Sylvia Anthony, *The Discovery of Death in Childhood and After* (New York: Basic Books, 1972); Robert Kastenbaum, "Childhood: The Kingdom Where Creatures Die," *Journal of Clinical Child Psychology* 3 (Summer 1974): 11–13; Maria H. Nagy, "The Child's View of Death," *Journal of Genetic Psychology* 73 (1948): 3–27, reprinted in *The Meaning of Death,* edited by Herman Feifel (New York: McGraw-Hill, 1959); Paul Schilder and David Wechsler, "The Attitudes of Children Toward Death," *Journal of Genetic Psychology* 45 (1934): 406–451.

3. Speece and Brent, "Children's Understanding of Death."

4. Adah Maurer, "Maturation of Concepts of Death," *British Journal of Medicine and Psychology* 39 (1966): 35–41.

5. A similar experience is described in Robert Kastenbaum and Ruth Aisenberg, *The Psychology of Death: Concise Edition* (New York: Springer, 1976), pp. 12–14.

6. Mark W. Speece, "Very Young Children's Experiences with and Reactions to Death," (unpublished master's thesis, Wayne State University, 1983).

7. Sandor B. Brent, "Puns, Metaphors, and Misunderstandings in a Two-Year-Old's Conception of Death," *Omega* 8 (1977–1978): 285–293.

8. In a subsequent conversation, the father, Dr. Sandor Brent, reported that his son—now a teenager—has no recollection of this death-related experience. Dr. Brent believes that the lack of memory regarding this experience indicates a successfully managed event. (Personal communication.)

9. One of the clearest and most complete surveys of the literature dealing with death anxiety in children (and adults) is James B. McCarthy, *Death Anxiety: The Loss of the Self* (New York: Gardner Press, 1980). A short exposition of the subject can be found in C. W. Wahl's "The Fear of Death," in *The Meaning of Death,* edited by H. Feifel, pp. 16–29. The reader interested in a more technically oriented discussion of the subject is directed to Martin P. Seligman, *Helplessness: On Depression, Development, and Death* (San Francisco: W. H. Freeman, 1975); and to John Bowlby's classic investigations on attachment and loss: vol. 1, *Attachment* (1969); vol. 2, *Separation: Anxiety and Anger* (1973); vol. 3, *Loss: Sadness and Depression* (1982) (New York: Basic Books).

10. McCarthy, *Death Anxiety,* p. 14.

11. Ibid., p. 105: "Death anxiety persists with the emergence of the self and the fear of the loss of the self underlies many aspects of children's developmental problems. . . .

When anxiety is experienced by a child in accomplishing developmental tasks, it may activate the fear of death, and, conversely, the arousal of death anxiety interferes with the mastery of developmental tasks."

12. Ibid., p. 109.

13. Erik Erikson, *Childhood and Society* (New York: W. W. Norton, 1950).

14. Jean Piaget, *The Child and Reality: Problems of Genetic Psychology,* translated by Arnold Rosin (New York: Grossman Publishers, 1973). Also see Jean Piaget, *The Child's Conception of the World* (London: Routledge & Kegan Paul, 1929). A particularly accessible presentation of Piaget's thought is in Mary Ann Spencer Pulaski, *Understanding Piaget: An Introduction to Children's Cognitive Development* (New York: Harper & Row, 1980). Readers wishing a more technical discussion may consult Howard E. Gruber and J. Jacques Vonèche, editors, *The Essential Piaget* (New York: Basic Books, 1977); and Hugh Rosen, *Pathway to Piaget: A Guide for Clinicians, Educators, and Developmentalists* (Cherry Hill, N.J.: Postgraduate International, 1977).

15. From "Jean Piaget," in Richard I. Evans, *The Making of Psychology: Discussions with Creative Contributors* (New York: Alfred A. Knopf, 1976), p. 46.

16. Gerald P. Koocher, "Childhood, Death, and Cognitive Development," *Developmental Psychology* 9:3 (1973): 369–375; and "Talking with Children About Death," *American Journal of Orthopsychiatry* 44:3 (April 1974): 404–411, reprinted in *Death and Dying: Theory, Research, and Practice,* edited by Larry A. Bugen (Dubuque, Iowa: William C. Brown, 1979), pp. 89–97. The first article cited is more technical than the second. Most of the excerpts of children's responses to questions about death in this chapter are taken from the second article. Koocher has also commented on research design criteria where children are concerned in "Conversations with Children About Death," *Journal of Clinical Child Psychology* (Summer 1974): 19–21. A critique of Koocher's research can be found in R. Lonetto, *Children's Conceptions of Death* (New York: Springer Publishing, 1980).

17. Interestingly, researchers found that, of the seventy-five children in Koocher's study group, the mean age of those classified as preoperational was 7.4 years; of those who used concrete operations, 10.4 years; and of those who used formal operations, 13.3 years. See Gerald P. Koocher, "Childhood, Death, and Cognitive Development," *Developmental Psychology* 9:3 (1973): 371.

18. Helen L. Swain, "Childhood Views of Death," *Death Education* 2 (1979): 341–358.

19. For a study of death-related play activities, see Gregory Rochlin, "How Younger Children View Death and Themselves," in *Explaining Death to Children,* edited by Earl A. Grollman (Boston: Beacon Press, 1967), pp. 51–85.

20. Martha Wolfenstein and Gilbert Kliman, eds., *Children and the Death of a President: Multi-Disciplinary Studies* (Garden City, N.Y.: Anchor Press/Doubleday, 1965), especially pp. 217–239.

21. "First Graders Paint a Happy Ending," Associated Press wire story, January 31, 1986.

22. Reported by Richard Lonetto, *Children's Conceptions of Death,* p. 9. Also see W. S. Baring-Gould and C. Baring-Gould, *The Annotated Mother Goose* (New York: Bramwell House, 1962).

23. Gloria Goldreich, "What Is Death? The Answers in Children's Books — From Fairy Tales to Harsh Reality," *The Hastings Center Report* 7:3 (June 1977): 18–20.

24. A. Cordell Perkes and Roberta Schildt, "Death-Related Attitudes of Adolescent Males and Females," *Death Education* 2 (1979): 359–368. For excellent coverage of gender differences in adults as well as children, see Judith M. Stillion, *Death and the*

Sexes: An Examination of Differential Longevity, Attitudes, Behaviors, and Coping Skills (Washington, D.C.: Hemisphere, 1985).

25. Barbara Kane, "Children's Concepts of Death," *Journal of Genetic Psychology* 134 (1979): 141–153.

26. *Newsweek,* May 5, 1980.

27. In addition to the suggestions for further reading listed at the end of the chapter, the following resources can be helpful as background for discussing death-related topics with children: Dan Leviton and Eileen C. Forman, "Death Education for Children and Youth," in *Journal of Clinical Child Psychology* (Summer 1974); Anna W. M. Wolf, *Helping Your Child to Understand Death,* rev. ed. (New York: Child Study Press, 1973); Rose Zeligs, *Children's Experience with Death* (Springfield, Ill.: Charles C Thomas, 1974.)

28. Erik Erikson, *Childhood and Society* (New York: W. W. Norton, 1950), p. 233.

C H A P T E R 4

1. "Hospital Facilities," in *Statistical Abstract of the United States 1986,* 106th ed., (Washington: Government Printing Office, 1985), p. 108.

2. "National Health Expenditures," in *Statistical Abstract 1986*, p. 96. Consumers paid more than half of this per capita cost in the form of direct medical payments and health insurance premiums. Since the advent of the Medicare and Medicaid programs in the mid-1960s, the federal government's share of personal health care expenditures has also increased dramatically. See National Center for Health Statistics, *Health, United States, 1984* (Washington: Government Printing Office, 1984), pp. 144, 146.

3. "Nursing and Related Care Facilities," in *Statistical Abstract 1986*, p. 111.

4. *Health, United States, 1984*, p. 30. Issues specific to health care for the aged are discussed in Chapter 9.

5. It has been suggested that hospitals make available a "grief room" where family members could feel more comfortable expressing their emotions without fear of upsetting hospital routine. Such a facility could also be more satisfactory for meetings between family members and medical personnel than the hospital corridor.

6. In hospitals, a patient's death may be dealt with as an inconvenience that the staff tries to minimize by preventing emotional reactions. Citing the prevalent practice of urging drugs on family members to keep emotional disruption to a minimum, Robert Blauner comments that modern hospitals often tend to exhibit the features of a "mass-reduction system, undermining the subjecthood of its dying patients." See Robert Blauner, "Death and Social Structure," in Robert Fulton et al., *Death and Dying: Challenge and Change* (Reading, Mass.: Addison-Wesley, 1978), pp. 92–97.

7. Elisabeth Kübler-Ross, *On Death and Dying* (New York: Macmillan, 1969), p. 249.

8. Some believe that the high cost of liability suits and malpractice insurance is adversely affecting the availability of medical services as well as the relationship between physician and patient. At some medical schools, the curriculum now includes mock trials designed to familiarize students with the judicial procedures they may encounter after they enter medical practice. To counter the present climate of malpractice suits, attention is being directed to the need for clearer and more complete communication between doctors and patients.

9. A videotape by Elizabeth Bradbury, "Death and Dying: The Physician's Perspective," provides a glimpse into doctors' pesonal feelings about death and treating the terminally ill. Nine physicians from different specialties are interviewed, with scenes

in the intensive-care unit and emergency room, in the 29-minute, ¾″ color videotape, which is available from Fanlight Productions (see *Instructor's Guide*).

10. Eric Cassell writes: "There are two distinct things happening to the terminally ill: the death of the body and the passing of the person." The death of the body is a physical phenomenon, the passing of the person is a nonphysical (social, emotional, psychological, spiritual) one; yet, these aspects tend to become confused.

Depersonalization and abstraction are part of the scientific method from which come the medical innovations we generally consider to be so beneficial. Yet they are also responsible for the criticism that medical care often seems unfeeling, lacking in humanness. Depersonalization is most likely to occur when the disease process is not well understood and medical practitioners display an apparently greater concern about the disease than about the patient. See Eric J. Cassell, "Dying in a Technological Society," in *Death Inside Out: The Hastings Center Report,* edited by Peter Steinfels and Robert M. Veatch (New York: Harper & Row, 1974), pp. 43–48.

Excellent material concerning "social death" can be found in David Sudnow, *Passing On: The Social Organization of Dying* (Englewood Cliffs, N.J.: Prentice-Hall, 1967), and in the seminal work by Barney G. Glaser and Anselm L. Strauss, *Awareness of Dying* (Chicago: Aldine, 1965).

11. The results of LeShan's study have been reported widely. The original source is Margaretta K. Bowers et al., *Counseling the Dying* (New York: Thomas Nelson & Sons, 1964).

12. Robert Kastenbaum and Ruth Aisenberg, *The Psychology of Death, Concise Edition* (New York: Springer, 1976), p. 179. The strategies used by hospital staff in coping with terminal patients are ably summarized in "How the Medical Staff Copes with Dying Patients: A Critical Review" by Richard Schulz and David Alderman, *Omega* 7 (1976): 11–21.

13. William M. Buchholz, "Medical Eschatology: Combined Role for Caregiver and Scientist," *The American Journal of Hospice Care,* (January-February 1985): 22–24.

14. Informed consent may be difficult or impossible to obtain from patients admitted to the emergency room. When a patient is comatose or obviously confused, the decision for treatment must be made by others, either family members or the medical team itself. On the other hand, when a patient retains sufficient awareness of what is taking place, the medical team may still have difficulty ensuring that informed consent has been given.

Some physicians advocate giving the attending physician the power to decide about treatment, virtually ignoring the patient's part in the decision. Others, acknowledging the patient's right of determination, admit that it is often difficult in practice to guarantee informed consent in an emergency.

Sharon H. Imbus and Bruce E. Zawacki describe a model being used at the University of Southern California's Medical Center with patients who are severely burned and whose survival is unlikely. First, patients are transported to the burn center before any narcotics that might interfere with the patient's coherence or mental clarity are administered. An assessment is then made by the medical staff to determine if any precedent exists for survival in such a case. If not, the team then presents the medical facts to the patient, pointing out as gently as possible that no previous patient has ever survived such severe burns and that death is probably imminent. Provided with such information, the patient is allowed to decide whether or not medical heroics should be attempted. See Imbus and Zawacki, "Autonomy for Burned Patients When Survival Is Unprecedented," in *New England Journal of Medicine* 297:6 (1977): 308–311.

15. This account of Dr. Rosenbaum's methods is from his article "Oncology/

Hematology and Psychosocial Support of the Cancer Patient," in *Psychosocial Care of the Dying Patient,* edited by C. A. Garfield, pp. 169–184; also in *A Hospice Handbook: A New Way to Care for the Dying,* edited by Michael P. Hamilton and Helen F. Reid (Grand Rapids, Mich.: Wm. B. Eerdmans, 1980), pp. 19–43.

16. Contact with dying patients is most frequent in intensive and coronary care units, followed by emergency, medical/surgical, and geriatrics units. Contact is least frequent in obstetrics/gynecology, psychiatry, and pediatrics units.

17. If helping is defined as curing, the terminal care nurse is vulnerable to feelings of failure when a patient dies. To avoid such feelings, a nurse may resort to following hospital routine and standardized policies. The desire to avoid being exposed to the patient's pain and encounter with death may be manifest in delays in administering medication, thus adding to confusion and guilt—all symptoms of the conflicting emotions due to uncertainty about what constitutes "proper and correct" involvement with patients. Such uncertainty may be experienced too with regard to feelings of grief arising from a patient's death. These issues for the health care professional, along with appropriate coping mechanisms, are discussed in Marilee Ivars Donovan and Sandra Girton Pierce, *Cancer Care Nursing* (New York: Appleton-Century-Crofts, 1976), pp. 13–24, which also contains valuable information on positive nursing support for the families of terminal patients (pp. 29–39).

18. Jeanne Brimigion, "Living with Dying," Nursing Skillbook, *Dealing with Death and Dying,* 2nd ed. (Horsham, Pa.: Intermed Communications, 1980), pp. 91–96. This article provides an excellent overview of many of the difficulties that may be experienced by nurses who care for the dying, as well as suggestions for correctives that can compensate for lack of communication and other obstacles to effective care for the dying, especially in terms of staff considerations.

19. M. L. S. Vachon, W. A. L. Layall, and S. J. J. Freeman, "Measurement and Management of Stress in Health Professionals Working with Advanced Cancer Patients," *Death Education* 1 (1978), pp. 365–369.

20. Oncologists may also experience stress resulting from the "demand that they find the time to be sensitive to and deal effectively with the psychosocial needs of patients, families, and staff" (ibid., pp. 372–373).

21. In some instances, this kind of education and support has been expanded to include patients and family members.

22. Brimigion's account of the positive steps taken in this nursing home to bring death out of the closet can be taken as a hopeful sign, though unfortunately such instances remain in the minority.

23. Quoted in Donovan and Pierce, *Cancer Care Nursing,* p. 32.

24. In "Confronting Expected Death" (in Nursing Skillbook, *Dealing with Death and Dying,* pp. 63–72) Eileen Renear lists some of the keys to helping meet the family's needs.

Listening: The caregiver can help to facilitate discussion and the therapeutic flow of feelings, being aware of nonverbal as well as verbal modes of communication. Sensitive, caring communication can be an important accompaniment to physical care.

Shared hope: As much as possible, alleviate the family's concern about pain and discomfort. Allow family members to fulfill a role in caring for the patient if they wish. Share information as well as hope.

When death is imminent: This is a special time to emphasize care, both for the patient and for the family. Even if the patient is comatose, he or she can be respected and treated as a person worthy of care and attention. Caregivers can encourage family members to talk to the patient even though he or she is unconscious or otherwise unresponsive. This is also a time to inform family members about procedures being performed and prepare them for what to expect.

After death: As the focus of caregiving turns to meeting the needs of the survivors, the health professional can provide support and help to keep the lines of communication open, being especially watchful for any signs of delayed grief or other symptomatic behaviors. Often simple actions — bringing a cup of coffee, making a phone call, just spending time — can provide a very meaningful demonstration of support and loving affection.

25. This discussion is derived primarily from reports published in *Science* and U. S. Congress, Office of Technology Assessment, *Review of the Public Health Services' Response to AIDS* (Washington: Government Printing Office, 1985).

26. Similar findings were subsequently reported by a team at the Pasteur Institute in Paris, headed by Luc Montagnier. Gallo's lab is also credited with identifying interleukin-2, a hormone that plays a key role in the growth of T cells such as those implicated in AIDS.

27. A measure of premature mortality, "years of potential life lost" (YPLL), points up the effect of the high fatality rate and relative youth of persons afflicted with AIDS.

28. The political and social response to AIDS is discussed in Dennis Altman, *AIDS in the Mind of America* (New York: Anchor Press/Doubleday, 1986). See also *AIDS: From the Beginning,* a collection of articles from the *Journal of the American Medical Association* (Chicago: AMA, 1986); *Mobilizing Against AIDS: The Unfinished Story of a Virus,* prepared by the Institute of Medicine/National Academy of Sciences (Cambridge, Mass.: Harvard University Press, 1986); and Ruth Kulstad, editor, *AIDS: Papers from Science,* 1982–1985 (Washington: AAAS, 1986).

29. Vickie Ong, "Common Hygiene Required to Care for AIDS Cases, Hospital Expert Says," Honolulu *Star-Bulletin & Advertiser.*

30. "Hospital Utilization Rates," in *Statistical Abstract 1986,* p. 110. Better utilization review and discharge planning, as well as limitations placed on the length of hospitalization by third-party payers, may also play a role. In 1983, Congress implemented a prospective payment system that classifies patients by diagnostic-related groups (DRGs) which, in turn, are the basis for reimbursements to hospitals for services provided to Medicare patients.

31. Many of the advances in pain control, particularly in cases of advanced cancer, have been stimulated by the hospice philosophy of terminal care. Considerable progress has been made in both pharmacological and psychological means of controlling pain. See, for example: John J. Bonica and Vittorio Ventafridda, eds., *International Symposium on Pain of Advanced Cancer* (New York: Raven, 1979); Wilbert E. Fordyce, *Behavioral Methods for Chronic Pain and Illness* (St. Louis: C. V. Mosby, 1976); Josephine Hilgard and Samuel LeBaron, *Hypnotherapy of Pain in Children with Cancer* (Los Altos, Calif.: William Kaufmann, 1984); Harry J. Sobel, ed., *Behavior Therapy in Terminal Care: A Humanistic Approach* (Cambridge, Mass.: Ballinger, 1981); Robert G. Twycross and Sylvia A. Lack, *Symptom Control in Far Advanced Cancer: Pain Relief* (Baltimore: Urban & Schwarzenberg, 1983); and M. Zimmermann, P. Drings, and G. Wagner, eds., *Pain in the Cancer Patient* (New York: Springer Verlag, 1984).

32. The description of practices at St. Christopher's are derived largely from "St. Christopher's Hospice" by Thelma Ingles, in Michael P. Hamilton and Helen F. Reid, *A Hospice Handbook: A New Way to Care for the Dying* (Grand Rapids, Mich.: Wm. B. Eerdmans, 1980); pp. 45–56.

33. Quoted in Constance Holden, "Hospices for the Dying, Relief from Pain and Fear," in Hamilton and Reid, *Hospice Handbook,* p. 61.

34. Robert W. Buckingham, *The Complete Hospice Guide* (New York: Harper & Row, 1983), pp. 13–15. This hospice was one of three demonstration programs funded by the National Cancer Institute; the others were in Boston, New Jersey, and Tucson.

35. A current listing of hospices is available from National Hospice Organization, 1901 Fort Myer Drive, Suite 402, Arlington, VA 22209.

36. Buckingham, *Complete Hospice Guide,* ix–x, p. 5. See also Evelyn M. Baulch, *Home Care: A Practical Alternative to Extended Hospitalization* (Milbrae, Calif.: Celestial Arts, 1980); Glen W. Davidson, ed., *The Hospice: Development and Administration,* 2nd ed. (Washington: Hemisphere, 1985); Deborah Duda, *A Guide to Dying at Home* (Santa Fe, N.M.: John Muir Publications, 1982); Anne Munley, *The Hospice Alternative: A New Context for Death and Dying* (New York: Basic Books, 1983); Sandol Stoddard, *The Hospice Movement: A Better Way of Caring for the Dying* (New York: Random House/Vintage, 1978); and Jack M. Zimmerman, *Hospice: Complete Care for the Terminally Ill,* 2nd ed. (Baltimore: Urban & Schwartzenberg, 1985).

37. For developments in children's hospice, see Charles A. Corr and Donna M. Corr, editors, *Hospice Approaches to Pediatric Care* (New York: Springer, 1985).

38. Information about the Shanti Project is drawn primarily from "The Shanti Project: A Community Model of Psychosocial Support for Patients and Families Facing Life-Threatening Illness," in *Psychosocial Care of the Dying Patient,* edited by Charles A. Garfield (New York: McGraw-Hill, 1978), pp. 355–364.

39. Mary-Ellen Siegel, "I CAN COPE with Cancer," *Cancer News* 38:2 (Spring/Summer 1984):10–12.

40. For further information, contact The Elisabeth Kübler-Ross Center, South Route 616, Head Waters, VA 24442.

41. Talcott Parsons, *The Social System* (New York: Free Press, 1951). A more easily accessible discussion can be found in Russell Noyes, Jr., and John Clancy, "The Dying Role: Its Relevance to Improved Patient Care," in *Psychiatry* 40 (February 1977): 41–47; reprinted in *Death and Dying: Theory, Research, and Practice,* edited by Larry A. Bugen (Dubuque, Iowa: William C. Brown, 1979), pp. 301–308.

42. Noyes and Clancy state, "Society reserves the physician's role for the more important restorative functions and . . . jealously guards against inroads upon the physician's time and energy," in *Psychiatry* 40 (February 1977):42.

CHAPTER 5

1. Quoted in Ernest H. Rosenbaum, "Oncology/Hematology and Psychosocial Support of the Cancer Patient," in *Psychosocial Care of the Dying Patient,* edited by Charles A. Garfield (New York: McGraw-Hill, 1978), p. 174.

2. Statistics from the American Cancer Society's *Cancer Facts and Figures — 1984.* Of patients diagnosed with cancer, nearly 40 percent will survive at least five years after beginning treatment. More than 5 million Americans now living have survived cancer, 3 million of them having been diagnosed five or more years ago.

3. Developing from the time of birth, self-concept encompasses our attitudes, beliefs, thoughts, feelings, goals, fears, fantasies, personal history, sense of self-worth, body image, and psychosexual roles. While self-concept is learned, and thus changeable, the least flexible aspects of self-concept are those relating to body-image, sexuality, and work. The presence of terminal illness dramatically affects each of these aspects of a person's self-concept. See Marilee Ivars Donovan and Sandra Girton Pierce, *Cancer Care Nursing* (New York: Appleton-Century-Crofts, 1976), pp. 204–251.

4. Elisabeth Kübler-Ross, *On Death and Dying* (New York: Macmillan, 1969). Edwin Shneidman prefers to describe the process of coping as "a complicated clustering of intellectual and affective states, some fleeting, lasting for a moment or a day or a week, set, not unexpectedly, against the backdrop of that person's total personality, his 'philosophy of life' (whether an essential optimism and gratitude to life or a pervasive pessimism and dour or suspicious orientation to life) . . . an interplay between acceptance and denial, between understanding what is happening and magically disbelieving its reality . . . a deeper dialogue of the total mind, involving different layers of conscious awareness of 'knowing' and of needing not to know." See Edwin S. Shneidman, "Death Work and the Stages of Dying," in Robert Fulton et al., *Death and Dying: Challenge and Change* (Reading, Mass.: Addison-Wesley, 1978), pp. 181–182.

Avery Weisman categorizes the psychological process of dying in three stages: (1) from the time symptoms are noticed until the diagnosis is confirmed, (2) between diagnosis and the final decline, and (3) the stage of final decline. Conflicts and fears concerning self-image, pain, annihilation or loss of self, and alienation or losing others are especially predominant during the second and third stages. The threat to self-esteem is basic. See Avery D. Weisman, *On Dying and Denying: A Psychiatric Study of Terminality* (New York: Behavioral Publications, 1972).

5. "Pictures of the Heart," *Science News* 129 (January 25, 1986):58.

6. Mickey S. Eisenberg, Lawrence Bergner, Alfred P. Hallstrom, and Richard O. Cummins, "Sudden Cardiac Death," *Scientific American* 254:5 (May 1986):37–43.

7. See "FDA May Attach Strings to Artificial Heart," *Science News* 129 (January 4, 1986):4–5; and "Artificial Heart: The Debate Goes On," *Science News* 129 (February 22, 1986):122.

8. *Carcinomas* — that is, cancers of the skin, mucous membranes, and glandular tissues — are more likely to exhibit metastasis than are *sarcomas* — cancers of the connective tissues such as cartilage, muscle, and bone. Examples of carcinomas include cancers of the skin and breast, as well as cancers of the liver, pancreas, intestines, prostate, and thyroid.

9. John Cairns, "The Treatment of Diseases and the War Against Cancer," *Scientific American* 253:5 (November 1985):56. See also, by Cairns, *Cancer: Science and Society* (San Francisco: W. H. Freeman, 1978).

10. Cairns, "Treatment of Diseases and the War Against Cancer," p. 56.

11. Jean L. Marx, "Burst of Publicity Follows Cancer Report," *Science* 230 (20 December 1985): 1367–1368. Cf. Susan FitzGerald, "New Cancer Experiment Spurs Hundreds of Desperate Calls," Knight-Ridder wire story, December 8, 1985.

12. Ralph W. Moss, *The Cancer Syndrome* (New York: Grove Press, 1980). Moss provides an excellent account of the unorthodox therapies, with particular attention to how they have faired in relation to the cancer "establishment."

13. Ibid., pp. 104–122. Moss gives a generally favorable presentation regarding the use of laetrile; for a contrasting view, see Steven Lehrer, *Alternative Treatments for Cancer* (Chicago: Nelson-Hall, 1979), pp. 166–168.

14. Claire Martin, *Cancer News* 39:1 (Winter 1985):2. For a popular account of the discovery of interferons, see Mike Edelhart, with Dr. Jean Lindenmann, *Interferon: The New Hope for Cancer* (Reading, Mass.: Addison-Wesley, 1981).

15. National Research Council, *Outlook for Science and Technology: The Next Five Years* (San Francisco: W. H. Freeman, 1982), pp. 108–109.

16. Nevertheless, this role of infection is "sparsely represented in nursing literature," as Donovan and Pierce point out in *Cancer Care Nursing,* pp. 93–129.

17. For patients undergoing chemotherapy, a number of precautionary measures

have been developed, including antibiotics, multiple transfusions of blood platelets, and the creation of sterile environments to protect against potentially fatal infection.

18. See Arnold A. Hutschnecker, *The Will to Live* (New York: Doubleday, 1954); Meyer Friedman and Ray H. Rosenman, *Type A Behavior and Your Heart* (New York: Alfred A. Knopf, 1974); Lawrence LeShan, *You Can Fight for Your Life* (New York: M. Evans, 1977).

19. Oncologist Carl Simonton and psychotherapist Stephanie Matthews Simonton began developing the methods of treating cancer patients, now known as the Simonton approach, in 1968. For a discussion of the development and application of these methods, see O. Carl Simonton, Stephanie Matthews Simonton, and James Crieghton, *Getting Well Again: A Step-by-Step Guide to Overcoming Cancer for Patients and Their Families* (Los Angeles: J. P. Tarcher, 1978), and Stephanie Matthews Simonton, *The Healing Family: The Simonton Approach for Families Facing Illness* (New York: Bantam, 1984).

20. Stephanie Matthews Simonton, *Healing Family,* pp. 17–19.

21. Ibid., pp. 6, 15. See also O. Carl Simonton and Stephanie Matthews Simonton, "Belief Systems and Management of the Emotional Aspects of Malignancy," *Journal of Transpersonal Psychology* 7 (1975): 29–47, and Dennis T. Jaffe and David E. Bresler, "The Use of Guided Imagery as an Adjunct to Medical Diagnosis and Treatment," *Journal of Humanistic Psychology* 20:4 (Fall 1980): 45–59.

22. Rosenbaum cautions against a too-ready acceptance of the notion: "If I made myself sick, then I can cure myself." Such an attitude may result in a sense of guilt at having the disease in the first place, rather than helping to marshall the positive emotional energies needed to combat the disease. Nevertheless, Rosenbaum frequently recommends methods similar to those employed by the Simontons when he feels they offer a means of increasing the patient's will to live. For example, Rosenbaum sometimes suggests that patients seek out group counseling and other psychiatric support services offered by hospitals, cancer treatment centers, social welfare departments, the American Cancer Society, and others. For Rosenbaum's comments on this topic, see "Oncology/Hematology and Psychosocial Support of the Cancer Patient," in *Psychosocial Care of the Dying Patient,* edited by C. Garfield, p. 28.

23. Orville Kelly, "Making Today Count," in Bugen, *Death and Dying,* pp. 277–283. Founder of the Atomic Veterans' Rights organization, as well as of Make Today Count, Kelly first felt cheated of life, blaming God for his cancer. Later, however, he recognized that the mortality of every generation is ultimately 100 percent. All of us die, and each of us faces the challenge to make each day count, whether or not we live with a terminal diagnosis. Kelly died in 1980.

24. The patient is not the only person to express various "stages" in coping with terminal illness. The family, too, experiences times of denial, anger, guilt, acceptance, and so on. A moving demonstration of a family member's process of coping is related in Ora Prattes, "Family Support in Action," Nursing Skillbook, *Dealing with Death and Dying* (pp. 77–85). Prattes describes how the mother of a seven-year-old with a malignant brain tumor coped, and her interactions with staff—some helpful, some not—during the eighteen months from the diagnosis until the child's death.

CHAPTER 6

1. This section draws upon material from the following sources: "Coffins and Sarcophagi," exhibition notes provided by the Metropolitan Museum of Art, New York; Henri Frankfort, *Ancient Egyptian Religion: An Interpretation* (New York: Harper & Row, 1948, 1961); Manfred Lurker, *The Gods and Symbols of Ancient Egypt* (New

York: Thames & Hudson, 1980); and Barbara Watterson, *The Gods of Ancient Egypt* (New York: Facts on File, 1984). See also: Morris Bierbrier, *The Tomb-Builders of the Ancient Pharaohs* (New York: Charles Scribner's Sons, 1982); John Romer, *Ancient Lives: Daily Life in Egypt of the Pharaohs* (New York: Holt, Rinehart and Winston, 1984); and A. J. Spencer, *Death in Ancient Egypt* (New York: Penguin, 1982).

2. David Sudnow, "Notes on a Sociology of Mourning," *Passing On: The Social Organization of Dying* (Englewood Cliffs, N.J.: Prentice-Hall, 1967), pp. 153–168.

3. *The Knight Letter* (August 1979), p. 15.

4. Ben H. Bagdikian, *The Information Machines: Their Impact on Men and the Media* (New York: Harper & Row, 1971), pp. 39, 59. Also see Bradley Greenberg, "Diffusion of News of the Kennedy Assassination," *Public Opinion Quarterly* 28:225–232.

5. J. Z. Young, *Programs of the Brain* (New York: Oxford University Press, 1978), p. 255.

6. Richard A. Kalish and Helene Goldberg, "Community Attitudes Toward Funeral Directors," *Omega* 10:4 (1979–1980): 335–346.

7. For example, a 1982 survey found that most of the respondents had a preferred funeral home; and, of those who did, 98.3 percent considered it good to excellent; see Amy Seidel Marks and Bobby J. Calder, *Attitudes Toward Death and Funerals* (Evanston, Ill.: Center for Marketing Sciences, Northwestern University, 1982), pp. 79–82. For results and discussion of other surveys, see Robert Fulton, "The Sacred and the Secular: Attitudes of the American Public Toward Death, Funerals, and Funeral Directors," in *Death and Identity,* rev. ed., edited by Robert Fulton and Robert Bendiksen (Bowie, Md.: Charles Press, 1978), pp. 158–172. Also see Robert Fulton, "Death and the Funeral in Contemporary Society," in *Dying: Facing the Facts,* edited by Hannelore Wass (Washington: Hemisphere, 1979), pp. 236–255, esp. pp. 242–248; and Richard A. Kalish and Helene Goldberg, "Clergy Attitudes Toward Funeral Directors," *Death Education* 2:3(1978): 247–260.

8. Vanderlyn Pine, "The Care of the Dead: A Historical Portrait," in *Death and Dying: Challenge and Change,* edited by Robert Fulton et al. (Reading, Mass.: Addison-Wesley, 1978), p. 274.

9. Through World Wars I and II and down to the Korean conflict, battlefield dead were buried in the particular theater of operations in which they had been killed, with a possibility of final disposition to the United States after the end of hostilities. The Vietnam conflict was the first one in which battlefield dead were returned from a foreign battle zone for U.S. burial as a matter of course.

10. Leroy Bowman, *The American Funeral: A Study in Guilt, Extravagance, and Sublimity* (Washington: Public Affairs Press, 1959), vii.

11. Ibid., p. 83.

12. Ibid., p. 148.

13. Jessica Mitford, *The American Way of Death* (New York: Simon & Schuster, 1963), pp. 16–19.

14. Robert Fulton, "The Funeral and the Funeral Director: A Contemporary Analysis," in *Successful Funeral Service Practice,* edited by Howard C. Raether (Englewood Cliffs, N.J.: Prentice-Hall, 1971), p. 229.

15. Kalish and Goldberg, "Clergy Attitudes Toward Funeral Directors," pp. 247–260.

16. Frank Minton, "Clergy Views of Funeral Practice (Part One)," *National Reporter* 4:4 (April 1981):4. The church was favored by 76.6 percent of the Protestant clergy, 96.4 percent of the Roman Catholic clergy, and 97.9 percent of the Orthodox

clergy; this question was not asked of Jewish clergy since, as Minton states, "Jewish funerals, traditionally held in the home, are now usually held in Jewish mortuaries where the directors are familiar with Jewish ritual. Thus, the location of the service is simply not an issue."

17. Kalish and Goldberg, "Community Attitudes Toward Funeral Directors," pp. 335–346.

18. Ibid. pp. 341, 345–346.

19. Marks and Calder, *Attitudes Toward Death and Funerals,* pp. 82–92. Marks and Calder conclude that most people view the funeral director as the key to obtaining satisfactory services, the expert they can turn to during a difficult time. The funeral home and the funeral director are thought of as synonymous, and the funeral director and his or her staff are expected to be, "above all else, constantly attentive, caring, and supportive."

20. Federal Trade Commission, *Compliance Guidelines: Trade Regulation Rule on Funeral Industry Practices,* p. 3.

21. Pamphlet, "What Do You Really Know About Funeral Costs?" (Milwaukee: National Funeral Directors Association, 1974).

22. Federal Trade Commission, *Compliance Guidelines: Trade Regulation Rule on Funeral Industry Practices.* A funeral provider is defined as any person or firm that sells *both* funeral goods *and* funeral services to the public. Thus, a cemetery that sells outer burial containers and grave liners, but does not provide funeral services, is not covered by the Rule.

23. Vanderlyn R. Pine, *A Statistical Abstract of Funeral Service Facts and Figures of the United States, 1984 Edition* (Milwaukee: National Funeral Directors Association, 1984), pp. 7, 62. This includes charges for professional services, use of facilities and equipment, and the casket as selected by the customer. It does not include the cost of an interment receptacle, cemetery or crematory expenses, monument or marker, or miscellaneous items such as clergy honorarium, flowers, additional transportation, burial clothing, or newspaper notices. Since funeral costs vary among regions of the country as well as between rural and metropolitan areas, average costs can be a useful statistical measure, but cannot be used as a guide for what one may expect to pay in his or her own locale.

24. Figures compiled in 1983 by Vanderlyn Pine *(Funeral Service Facts and Figures)* reflect the substantial investment of capital required for a funeral service business. The average investment in facilities, land, and equipment was $201,121. This figure ranged from $114,821 for firms performing less than 100 funeral services per year, to $1,199,303 for firms performing 500 or more services. These figures do not include compensation for employees, other operating expenses, or the investment in merchandise inventory.

25. Ronny E. Turner and Charles Edgley, "Death as Theatre: A Dramaturgical Analysis of the American Funeral," *Sociology and Social Research* 60:4 (1976): 377–392, reprinted in *Death and Dying: Theory, Research, and Practice,* edited by Larry A. Bugen (Dubuque, Iowa: William C. Brown, 1979), pp. 191–202.

26. Briefly summarized, exceptions to this requirement occur when: (1) state or local law requires embalming; or (2) there are "exigent circumstances," such as: (a) when a family member or other authorized person cannot be contacted despite diligent efforts, and (b) there is no reason to believe the family does not want embalming, and, (c) after the body has been embalmed, the family is notified that no fee will be charged if they choose a funeral that does not require embalming.

27. A listing of embalming laws by state, as of 1977, can be found in *Funerals:*

Consumers' Last Rights, by the editors of *Consumer Reports* (New York: W. W. Norton, 1977), pp. 260–268.

28. Casket Manufacturers Association of America, "Nationwide Summary— Estimate of Sales to Funeral Directors, Unit Volume (July–September 1985)." These sales represent more than 1,800,000 casketed deaths out of slightly more than 2 million total deaths occurring in the United States during this period.

29. If a funeral home offers immediate burials but does not offer direct cremations, the FTC rule does not require the firm to make available an alternative container or unfinished wood box, although a funeral director might choose to do so.

30. James M. Weir, "Cremation: Statistics to Year 2000, A Presentation to the Cremation Association of North America," Keystone, Colorado (August 1985), Table 1.

31. The term *ashes* leads some people to believe that the cremated remains will look and feel like wood or paper ashes. In reality, the ashes are composed of pieces of bone, which look and feel like coarse coral sands whose shell-like components are worn by the wind and waves.

32. Quoted in *Concerning Death: A Practical Guide for the Living,* edited by Earl Grollman (Boston: Beacon Press, 1974), and in Raether, *Successful Funeral Service Practice.*

33. Personal communication.

34. Robert Fulton, in *Dying: Facing the Facts,* edited by H. Wass.

35. E. S. Craighill Handy and Mary Kawena Pukui, *The Polynesian Family System in Ka-'u, Hawai'i* (Rutland, Vt.: Charles E. Tuttle, 1972), p. 157. See also: Mary Kawena Pukui, E. W. Haertig, and Catherine A. Lee, *Nana I Ke Kumu (Look to the Source),* vol. 1 (Honolulu: Hui Hanai; Queen Lili'uokalani Children's Center, 1972), p. 139.

C H A P T E R 7

1. Stanley Keleman, *Living Your Dying* (New York: Random House/Bookworks, 1974), p. 5. Elisabeth Kübler-Ross has also discussed the similarities in the responses to losses that occur in daily life and the loss that occurs with death: *On Death and Dying* (New York: Macmillan, 1969), p. 32.

2. For a critique of the mass media's ability to communicate such news rapidly, see Ben H. Bagdikian, *The Information Machines: Their Impact on Men and the Media* (New York: Harper & Row, 1971). The public's reaction to the loss of significant publc figures by assassination is discussed in Harold Cox, "Mourning Population: Some Considerations of Historically Comparable Assassinations," in *Death Education* 4:2 (1980): 125–138.

3. Philippe Ariès, "The Reversal of Death: Changes in Attitudes Toward Death in Western Societies," in *Death in America,* edited by David E. Stannard (Philadelphia: University of Pennsylvania Press, 1975), pp. 134–158. Ariès points out that practices of seclusion began during the Middle Ages and served two purposes: (1) to allow the truly unhappy survivors to shelter their grief from the world and (2) to prevent survivors from forgetting the deceased too quickly. Seclusion enforced on the survivors a period of abstinence from the social relationships and pleasures of life.

4. Mary Caroline Crawford, *Social Life in Old New England* (Boston: Little, Brown, 1914), p. 461.

5. The veiled woman dressed in black, a *mater dolorosa,* arrived on the scene in the nineteenth century as a symbol of seclusion, emphasizing how nearly impossible it was for the living to forget their dearly departed.

6. Studies by C. Murray Parkes, reported in his *Bereavement: Studies of Grief in Adult Life* (New York: Basic Books, 1972), suggest that the pangs of grief are most severe during the first two to five weeks following bereavement. These findings have also been confirmed by Ira O. Glick, Robert S. Weiss, and C. Murray Parkes, *The First Year of Bereavement* (New York: John Wiley & Sons, 1974), with the additional note that the death of a spouse typically results in a reaction that must be measured in years rather than in weeks, even though the most acute reaction occupies a comparatively brief time.

7. Larry A. Bugen, "Human Grief: A Model for Prediction and Intervention," *American Journal of Orthopsychiatry* 47:2 (1977): 196–206. Reprinted in *Death and Dying: Theory, Research, and Practice,* edited by Larry A. Bugen (Dubuque, Iowa: William C. Brown, 1979), pp. 33–45.

8. Bugen also discusses behavior that may occur during prolonged grief, such as keeping the clothing of the deceased and aspiring to the occupation of the deceased. A decision about which behaviors are "abnormal" can be made by those who have had experience with a broad range of grief responses. For example, the mother who visits her child's grave every week may draw comfort from that act. The mother who delivered a stillborn infant at home and who hid its body and has spent the ensuing days dressing it may also receive comfort from that act. But most people would agree that the latter act is an abnormal, if not impractical, way to generate feelings of comfort.

9. Vamik Volkan and C. R. Showalter, "Known Object Loss, Disturbance in Reality Testing, and 'Re-grief' Work as a Method of Brief Psychotherapy," *Psychiatric Quarterly* 42 (1968): 358–374. A more recent article by Vamik Volkan, "A Study of a Patient's 'Re-grief' Work," *Psychiatric Quarterly* 45 (1971): 255–273, discusses changes in concepts and techniques since the introduction of this therapeutic model, especially the use of *linking objects,* that is, inanimate objects that serve as catalysts for grief work.

10. Glick, Weiss, and Parkes, *First Year of Bereavement,* viii. Reporting on a longitudinal study of forty-nine widows and nineteen widowers, none older than forty-five years, it was found that the forces of bereavement and adjustment usually operate over a much longer period, which is more appropriately termed a period of "life transition" than a "life crisis," and that most widows and widowers continued the psychological work of mourning for their dead spouses for the rest of their lives.

11. Erich Lindemann, "Symptomatology and Management of Acute Grief," *American Journal of Psychiatry* 101 (1944): 141–148.

12. In addition to the Lindemann study "Acute Grief," see the following: H. H. Brewster, "Separation Reaction in Psychosomatic Disease and Neurosis," *Psychosomatic Medicine* 14 (1952): 154–160; P. J. Clayton, "The Clinical Morbidity of the First Year of Bereavement: A Review," *Comparative Psychiatry* 14 (1953): 151–157; D. Maddison, "The Relevance of Conjugal Bereavement for Preventive Psychiatry," *British Journal of Medical Psychology* 41 (1968): 223–233; C. M. Parkes and R. J. Brown, "Health After Bereavement: A Controlled Study of Young Boston Widows and Widowers," *Psychosomatic Medicine* 34 (1972): 449–461.

13. Robert E. Neale, *The Art of Dying* (New York: Harper & Row, 1973), p. 73.

14. Sigmund Freud, "Mourning and Melancholia," *Collected Papers,* vol. 4 (New York: Basic Books, 1959), pp. 152–170. This treatise was originally published in 1917.

15. Some of the difficulties in establishing adequate research designs in the area of bereavement syndromes are outlined by Gerald Epstein, Lawrence Weitz, Howard Roback, and Embry McKee in "Research on Bereavement: A Selective and Critical Review," *Comprehensive Psychiatry* 16 (1975): 537–546. Briefly, these difficulties include: (1) lack of consensus on which population to designate as the normal control;

(2) failure to consider demographic factors (e.g. ethnicity, socioeconomic class, religion, marital status, residence); (3) deficiencies in methods of gathering data (e.g., interviews are dependent on the selective memory and responsiveness of the subject).

16. See, for example, Alfred Herzog. "A Clinical Study of Parental Response to Adolescent Death by Suicide, with Recommendations for Approaching the Survivors," *Proceedings of the Fourth International Conference for Suicide Prevention,* edited by Norman L. Farberow (Los Angeles: Delmar Publishing, 1968). Herzog has applied stage theory to the needs of survivors: (1) *resuscitation* (initial shock of the first twenty-four hours), (2) *rehabilitation* (first month to sixth month), and (3) *renewal* (the healthy tapering off of the mourning process from the sixth month on).

Dale Vincent Hardt uses John Bowlby's three stages of mourning in his research reported in "An Investigation of the Stages of Bereavement," *Omega* 9 (1978–1979): 279–285. For John Bowlby's work, refer to his three volumes, *Attachment and Loss* (New York: Basic Books), vol. 1, *Attachment* (1969); vol. 2, *Separation: Anxiety and Anger* (1973); and vol. 3, *Loss: Sadness and Depression* (1982).

17. Geoffrey Gorer, *Death, Grief, and Mourning in Contemporary Britain* (London: Cresset Press, 1965), p. 112.

18. Glenn M. Vernon, *Sociology of Death: An Analysis of Death-Related Behavior* (New York: Ronald Press, 1970), p. 158. Vernon discusses how mourning rites during the period of shock serve to reintegrate the family following the disruption caused by the death of one of its members.

19. Gorer, *Death, Grief, and Mourning,* p. 132.

20. Robert E. Kavanaugh, *Facing Death* (Los Angeles: Nash Publishing, 1972), pp. 107–124.

21. Beverly Raphael, *The Anatomy of Bereavement* (New York: Basic Books, 1983), pp. 33–51.

22. Savine Gross Weizman and Phyllis Kamm, *About Mourning: Support and Guidance for the Bereaved* (New York: Human Sciences Press, 1985), pp. 42–63.

23. J. William Worden, *Grief Counseling and Grief Therapy: A Handbook for the Mental Health Practitioner* (New York: Springer, 1982), pp. 11–16.

24. Lindemann, "Acute Grief," p. 141.

25. W. D. Rees and S. G. Lutkins, "The Mortality of Bereavement," *British Medical Journal* 4 (1967): 13–16.

26. Arthur C. Carr and Bernard Schoenberg, "Object-Loss and Somatic Symptom Formation," in *Loss and Grief: Psychological Management in Medical Practice,* edited by Bernard Schoenberg et al. (New York: Columbia University Press, 1970), pp. 36–47.

27. For an overview of the relationship between the emotions and the body's immune response, see Nicholas R. Hall and Allan L. Goldstein, "Thinking Well: The Chemical Links Between Emotions and Health," *The Sciences* 26:2 (March/April 1986): 34–40.

28. Hans Selye, *The Stress of Life,* rev. ed. (New York: McGraw-Hill, 1976), pp. 36ff.

29. George L. Engel, "Sudden and Rapid Death During Psychological Stress," *Annals of Internal Medicine* 74 (1971). See also Engel, "Emotional Stress and Sudden Death," *Psychology Today,* November, 1977.

30. Jerome F. Fredrick, "Grief as a Disease Process," *Omega* 7 (1976–1977): 297–305.

31. Ibid.

32. Edgar N. Jackson, "The Physiology of Crisis," in his *Coping with the Crises of*

Your Life (New York: Hawthorne Books, 1974), pp. 48–55. Jackson gives a layperson's overview of the physiology of stress.

33. Colin Murray Parkes, "The Broken Heart," in his *Bereavement: Studies of Grief in Adult Life* (New York: Basic Books, 1972).

34. Epstein et al., "Research on Bereavement," *Comprehensive Psychiatry* 16 (1975): 537–546.

35. Current popular writings about stress management indicate an emphasis on surviving the crises of daily life.

36. Robert L. Fulton, "Death, Grief, and Social Recuperation," *Omega* 1 (1978): 23–28.

37. Kenneth J. Doka, "Disenfranchised Grief," paper presented at the Annual Meeting of the Association for Death Education and Counseling, Atlanta, Spring 1986.

38. Edgar N. Jackson, *Understanding Grief: Its Roots, Dynamics, and Treatment* (Nashville: Abingdon Press, 1957), p. 27. In an unpublished interview with the authors, Jackson described how the death of his young son became the impetus for his studies of grief. In effect, his studies of grief were in part a mechanism for coping with, understanding, and coming to terms with the loss. This is an example of how an individual survivor's value system shapes the means of coping with a loss.

39. Richard A. Kalish and David K. Reynolds, *Death and Ethnicity: A Psychocultural Study* (Los Angeles: Ethel Percy Andrus Gerontology Center, University of Southern California, 1976), p. 30. Differences among ethnic groups are noted through interviews with Japanese-Americans, Mexican-Americans, blacks, and Anglos. For example, over half of the Japanese-Americans and Mexican-Americans felt that at least one year (and preferably two or more years) should pass before a widowed spouse remarries. Among blacks and Anglos, only one-fourth of the sample held such a position.

40. Importance may also be considered in terms of similarity to the deceased. A recent study explores the hypothesis that the more similar to the deceased a survivor believes he or she is, the greater is the grief. See Robert J. Smith, John H. Lingle, Timothy C. Brock, "Reactions to Death as a Function of Perceived Similarity to the Deceased," *Omega* 9 (1978–1979): 125–138.

41. Vernon, *Sociology of Death*, p. 149. President John F. Kennedy's death caused widespread grief among the general population, manifested by tears (53 percent), tension (66 percent), sleeplessness (48 percent), and loss of appetite. It is notable that researchers found a tendency for individuals to react to the assassination of the President in terms of personal grief and loss rather than in terms of a more generalized concern for the future or of political or ideological concern.

42. Arlene Sheskin and Samuel E. Wallace, "Differing Bereavements: Suicide, Natural, and Accidental Death," *Omega* 7 (1976): 229–242.

43. Bernard Schoenberg, Arthur C. Carr, Austin H. Kutscher, David Peretz, and Ivan K. Goldberg, eds., *Anticipatory Grief* (New York: Columbia University Press, 1974), p. 4. Also see Lindemann, "Acute Grief," p. 141.

44. Glick et al., *First Year of Bereavement*, p. 14.

45. See, for example, Edwin S. Shneidman, "Postvention and the Survivor-Victim," in *Death: Current Perspectives*, 2nd ed., edited by E. S. Shneidman (Palo Alto, Calif.: Mayfield, 1980), pp. 233–240. The effect of war as a mode of death is explored in Lea Barinbaum's article, "Death of Young Sons and Husbands," *Omega* 7 (1976): 171–175.

46. See, for example, June S. Church, "The Buffalo Creek Disaster: Extent and Range of Emotional and Behavioral Problems," *Omega* 5:1 (1974): 61–63.

47. Terrence Des Pres, *The Survivor* (New York: Oxford University Press, 1976; Pocket Books, 1977). This is an intense exploration of the survivors of the Holocaust.

48. Bugen, "Human Grief: A Model for Prediction and Intervention."

49. Vernon, *Sociology of Death,* p. 159.

50. Mary Kawena Pukui, E. W. Haertig, and Catherine A. Lee, *Nana I Ke Kumu (Look to the Source),* vol. 1 (Honolulu: Hui Hanai; Queen Lili'uokalani Children's Center, 1972), pp. 135–136, 141.

51. In a similar fashion, mourners' requests directed at the corpse to "take away" quarrels and grudges affecting family members or the community may have relieved guilt feelings.

52. In a study of grief behavior in the black American community, researchers found a discrepancy between expressed norms and observed grief behaviors. Sixty-four percent of the sample studied said that they would control outward expressions of grief, yet researchers note that this expressed intention is not consistent with observed grief behavior, for crying, moaning, wailing, and fainting are all commonly observed manifestations of grief at black American funeral rituals. See Kalish and Reynolds, *Death and Ethnicity: A Psychocultural Study.* Also see Jean Masamba and Richard A. Kalish, "Death and Bereavement: The Role of the Black Church," *Omega* 7 (1976): 23–34

53. Glick et al., *First Year of Bereavement,* p. 303. The authors comment on the need for a balance in the daily concerns of life, on the *bridging* phenomenon that leads the survivor to a future without the deceased, and on the *linking* phenomenon that ties a survivor to the past.

54. John Schneider, *Stress, Loss, and Grief: Understanding Their Origins and Growth Potential* (Baltimore: University Park Press, 1984), pp. 66–76.

CHAPTER 8

1. Such experiences do not invariably lead to personality problems in adulthood, as has sometimes been supposed. Much of the research conducted in the past has focused on disturbed populations, such as patients in psychiatric institutions. As a result, researchers investigating the etiologies, or causes, of present difficulties experienced by patients have tended to emphasize disruptions experienced in childhood. Thus, although it is true that problems experienced by disturbed individuals can sometimes be traced to childhood traumas, the experience of severe loss or trauma in childhood does not necessarily result in personality disturbances. Rather, the difficulty is more likely to be a dysfunctional *coping* with the traumatic experience, not the experience itself. See Richard Lonetto, *Children's Conceptions of Death* (New York: Springer, 1980), p. 184.

2. Committee on Trauma Research, National Research Council, *Injury in America: A Continuing Public Health Problem* (Washington: National Academy Press, 1985), p. 1.

3. For example, children interpreted behaviors such as crying or avoidance as indicating the seriousness of their illness and their nearness to dying. See Myra Bluebond-Langner, *The Private Worlds of Dying Children* (Princeton, N.J.: Princeton University Press, 1978), pp. 7–9.

4. Ibid., p. 10.

5. Ibid., p. 11.

6. Ibid., pp. 12, 135–136. Bluebond-Langner concludes: (1) Children interpret their own behavior and self-images and then act on the basis of those interpretations. (2) They interpret the behavior of others to develop a view of themselves, others, and the objects in their environment. (3) They can alter their behavior to affect the views that others have of them and their own self-views. (4) The meanings they attach to themselves, others, and objects vary with respect to the setting (physical, social, and temporal) in which they find themselves. (5) They can move from one social world to another and act appropriately in each world.

7. These age groupings are generally applicable, though there is overlap between categories and individual differences among children that should be taken into account. See Lonetto, *Children's Conceptions of Death*, pp. 172–173.

8. Studies indicate that terminally ill children experience a greater awareness of death than do their healthier counterparts. Also, they typically have greater awareness of the hospital experience and the accompanying medical procedures. See ibid., pp. 174–175.

9. Thesi Bergmann and Anna Freud, *Children in the Hospital* (New York: International Universities Press, 1965), pp. 27–28.

10. Donna Juenker, "Child's Perception of His Illness," in *Nursing Care of the Child with Long-Term Illness*, 2nd ed., edited by Shirley Steele (New York: Appleton-Century-Crofts, 1977), p. 177.

11. The coping mechanisms of the seriously ill child are discussed in Juenker's excellent article, "Child's Perception of His Illness," pp. 153–197.

12. Judith Stillion and Hannelore Wass, "Children and Death," in *Dying: Facing the Facts*, edited by Hannelore Wass (Washington: Hemisphere Publishing, 1979), pp. 208–235; reprinted in *Death: Current Perspectives*, 3rd ed., edited by Edwin S. Shneidman (Palo Alto, Calif.: Mayfield, 1984), pp. 225–249.

13. Lonetto, *Children's Conceptions of Death*, p. 186. This phenomenon is also dealt with in Sylvia Anthony's classic work, *The Discovery of Death in Childhood and After* (New York: Basic Books, 1972).

14. "The Concrete Jungle," *Science News* 128 (December 14, 1985): 381.

15. Ute Carson, "A Child Loses a Pet," *Death Education* 3 (1980): 399–404.

16. Jane Brody, "When Your Pet Dies," Honolulu *Star-Bulletin & Advertiser*, December 8, 1985.

17. Randolph Picht, "Fido's Final Resting Place," Associated Press story (January 5, 1986).

18. Besides the book *Pet Loss* by Nieburg and Fisher, listed in Figure 8-3, see William J. Kay, ed., *Pet Loss and Human Bereavement* (Ames, Iowa: Iowa State University Press, 1984).

19. Spontaneous drawings can be an excellent method for working with young children to help them explore and express feelings that otherwise might remain hidden, yet disturbing to them. For further information on the use of spontaneous drawings, see Robert C. Burns and S. Harvard Kaufman, *Kinetic Family Drawings: An Introduction to Understanding Children Through Kinetic Drawings* (New York: Brunner/Mazel, 1970), and Burns and Kaufman, *Actions, Styles and Symbols in Kinetic Family Drawings* (New York: Brunner/Mazel, 1972); Helen Ann Desmond, "The Psychological Impact of Childhood Cancer on the Family" (Ph.D. dissertation, California School of Professional Psychology, Los Angeles, 1977); Joseph H. DiLeo, *Young Children and Their Drawings* (New York: Brunner/Mazel, 1970), and DiLeo, *Children's Drawings as Diagnostic Aids* (New York: Brunner/Mazel, 1973); and Gregg M. Furth, "Impromptu Paintings by Terminally Ill, Hospitalized, and Healthy Children: What Can We Learn from Them?" (Ph.D. dissertation, Ohio State University, Columbus, 1973).

20. Erna Furman, *A Child's Parent Dies: Studies in Childhood Bereavement* (New Haven, Conn.: Yale University Press, 1974), pp. 13–14.

21. Religious and philosophical concepts of death may confuse and frighten young children whose emphasis on "concreteness" is not well suited for grasping abstractions. Older children, on the other hand, may gain value from such conceptions, provided these are added to their concrete understanding rather than offered as a replacement for their already-developed death awareness.

22. Quoted in Jo-Eileen Gyulay, *The Dying Child* (New York: McGraw-Hill, 1978), p. 18.

23. Ibid., p. 17.

24. These figures reflect English-language publications and are based on an on-line search of *Books in Print* (Ann Arbor, Mich: R. R. Bowker, 1985).

25. The Walt Disney movie *Bambi,* which portrays a mother's death, recently has been joined by *Harry's Mom,* a story for young children written by Barbara Ann Porte and illustrated by Yossi Abolafia (New York: Greenwillow Books/Morrow, 1985).

26. Lucile Clifton, *Everett Anderson's Good-Bye,* illustrated by Ann Grifalconi (New York: Holt, Rinehart and Winston, 1983).

27. Brochures and information on local chapters of The Compassionate Friends may be obtained by writing to Box 1347, Oakbrook, IL 60521. The Center for Attitudinal Healing is located in Tiburon, California.

28. For more information on the activities of these groups, contact: Brass Ring Society, 7020 South Yale Avenue, Suite 103, Tulsa, OK 74136; Starlight Foundation, 9021 Melrose Avenue, Suite 204, Los Angeles, CA 90069; Sunshine Foundation, 2842 Normandy Drive, Philadelphia, PA 19154.

C H A P T E R 9

1. See John Schneider, *Stress, Loss, and Grief: Understanding Their Origins and Growth Potential* (Baltimore: University Park Press, 1984).

2. Charles W. Brice, "Mourning Throughout the Life Cycle," *American Journal of Psychoanalysis* 42:4 (1982): 320–321.

3. Louis E. Lagrand, "Loss Reactions of College Students: A Descriptive Analysis," *Death Education* 5 (1981): 238.

4. Erik H. Erikson, *The Life Cycle Completed: A Review* (New York: W. W. Norton, 1982), p. 67. Neil Salkind says the final psychosocial stage described by Erikson contains mystical elements and has much in common with the state of self-actualization discussed by Maslow; see Salkind, *Theories of Human Development,* 2nd ed. (New York: Wiley, 1985), p. 117.

5. Lagrand, "Loss Reactions of College Students," pp. 241–242.

6. This example is from Robert Kastenbaum, *Death, Society, and Human Experience,* 3rd ed. (Columbus, Ohio: Charles E. Merrill, 1986), pp. 223ff.

7. The relative absence of death anxiety, or fear of death, among the old should not be interpreted as an acceptance of euthanasia, however. Although death is perceived as normal and acceptable in old age, *choosing* death is less acceptable for the aged than for younger persons. See Russell A. Ward, "Age and Acceptance of Euthanasia," *Journal of Gerontology* 35:3 (May 1980): 428–429.

8. See Harriet Sarnoff Schiff, *The Bereaved Parent* (New York: Crown, 1977), which explores the issues faced by parents in the context of the writer's experience of a son's death.

9. Exhibition note, "Native Peoples," Glenbow Museum, Calgary, Alberta, Canada.

10. Brice, "Mourning Throughout the Life Cycle," p. 322.

11. The authors thank Barbara Sironen for permission to use materials in this section from her forthcoming work on "Pregnancy Loss as Disenfranchised Grief."

12. According to the National Center for Health Statistics, about one of every 400 births results in perinatal death, defined as occurring between the twentieth week of gestation and about twenty-eight days after birth.

13. This is discussed in Susan Borg and Judith Lasker, *When Pregnancy Fails* (Boston: Beacon Press, 1981).

14. Glen W. Davidson, "Death of the Wished-for Child: A Case Study," *Death Education* 1 (1977): 265–275.

15. Kenneth J. Doka, "Disenfranchised Grief," paper presented at the Annual Meeting of the Association for Death Education and Counseling, Atlanta, Spring 1986.

16. See Joy Johnson and S. Marvin Johnson, with James H. Cunningham and Irwin J. Weinfeld, *A Most Important Picture: A Very Tender Manual for Taking Pictures of Stillborn Babies and Infants Who Die* (Omaha: Centering Corp., 1985).

17. Ethical issues involving severely ill infants are discussed in Chapter 10.

18. Alan P. Cleveland, "Sudden Infant Death Syndrome (SIDS): A Burgeoning Medico-Legal Problem," *American Journal of Law and Medicine* 1 (1975): 55–69. See also U. S. Department of Health and Human Services, Sudden Infant Death Syndrome Clearinghouse, *Sudden Infant Death Syndrome Research and Grief Counseling: A Selected Bibliography* (Washington: Government Printing Office, 1981).

19. Some parents are concerned that SIDS may have a genetic basis, thus questions about the conception of subsequent children remain paramount in their minds.

20. Beverly Raphael, *The Anatomy of Bereavement* (New York: Basic Books, 1983), p. 229.

21. Barney G. Glaser and Anselm L. Strauss, *Awareness of Dying* (Chicago: Aldine, 1965).

22. Typically, the dying children who have been studied were not told that their disease would be fatal, yet their anxiety was significantly higher than that of other — even chronically ill — children. Richard Lonetto suggests that the reason for this "lies in the nature of the parent-child interaction," such that, even without being told explicitly, the dying child is aware of the disruptions in his or her family and senses the parents' anxieties. See Richard Lonetto, *Children's Conceptions of Death* (New York: Springer, 1980), p. 177.

23. The study by Myra Bluebond-Langner, it should be noted, was completed in 1976. Thus, a later study might reveal that greater openness toward death and dying in society generally has resulted in a greater proportion of open awareness contexts in the interaction between dying children and their families. Anecdotal evidence from those working with terminally ill children suggests that this may be a valid hunch.

24. Thesi Bergmann and Anna Freud, *Children in the Hospital* (New York: International Universities Press, 1965), pp. 141–151.

25. Lonetto, *Children's Conceptions of Death,* pp. 177–178.

26. Shirley Steele, ed., *Nursing Care of the Child with Long-Term Illness,* 2nd ed. (New York: Appleton-Century-Crofts, 1977), p. 531. Steele cautions against parents performing procedures that cause the child pain. When a parent is asked to help with the IV or a similar procedure, the child may see the parent as someone who is causing or intensifying pain. The parents' role should be to devote attention to providing comfort and support to the child. Steele says, "Parents should be helped to participate in the role of a parent rather than trying to play the role of a nurse."

27. Myra Bluebond-Langner, *The Private Worlds of Dying Children* (Princeton, N.J.: Princeton University Press, 1978).

28. Jerome L. Schulman, *Coping with Tragedy: Successfully Facing the Problem of a Seriously Ill Child* (Chicago: Follett,1976), p. 335. See pages 330–335 in this source for a discussion of coping mechanisms typical of families who cope successfully with a child's serious illness.

29. Raphael, *Anatomy of Bereavement,* p. 280.

30. Marion Osterweis, Fredric Soloman, and Morris Green, eds. *Bereavement: Reactions, Consequences, and Care* (Washington: National Academy Press, 1984), p. 81.

31. For information, write P.O. Box 3696, Oak Brook, IL 60522, or call (312) 323-5010.

32. For information, write National Sudden Infant Death Syndrome Foundation, 310 South Michigan Avenue, Chicago, IL 60604.

33. For information, write 2025 Eye Street, N.W., Suite 1011, Washington, DC 20006, or call (202) 659-5136.

34. Raphael, *Anatomy of Bereavement,* p. 177.

35. Savine Gross Weizman and Phyllis Kamm, *About Mourning: Support and Guidance for the Bereaved* (New York: Human Sciences, 1985), p. 130.

36. Important studies include: Colin Murray Parkes, "The Effects of Bereavement on Physical and Mental Health: A Study of Medical Records of Widows," *British Medical Journal* 1 (1964): 272–279, and "Recent Bereavement as a Cause of Mental Illness," *British Journal of Psychiatry* 110 (1964): 198–204; see also his *Bereavement: Studies of Grief in Adult Life* (International Universities Press, 1972); Ira O. Glick, Robert S. Weiss, and Colin Murray Parkes, *The First Year of Bereavement* (New York: John Wiley, 1974); for a follow-up reassessment, see Colin Murray Parkes and Robert S. Weiss, *Recovery from Bereavement* (New York: Basic Books, 1983); Helena Z. Lopata, *Widowhood in an American City* (Cambridge, Mass.: Schenkman, 1973) and *Women as Widows: Support Systems* (New York: Elsevier, 1979); Paula J. Clayton, "Mortality and Morbidity in the First Year of Widowhood," *Archives of General Psychiatry* 125 (1974): 747–750 and "The Sequelae and Non-Sequelae of Conjugal Bereavement," *American Journal of Psychiatry* 136 (1979): 1530–1543; Herbert H. Hyman, *Of Time and Widowhood: Nationwide Studies of Enduring Effects* (Durham, N.C.: Duke University Press, 1983).

37. Brice, "Mourning Throughout the Life Cycle," pp. 320–321.

38. Justine F. Ball, "Widows' Grief: The Impact of Age and Mode of Death," *Omega* 7 (1976–1977): 307–333.

39. Judith M. Richter, "Crisis of Mate Loss in the Elderly," *Advances in Nursing Science* (July 1984): 45.

40. Judith M. Stillion, *Death and the Sexes: An Examination of Differential Longevity, Attitudes, Behaviors, and Coping Skills* (Washington: Hemisphere, 1985), p. 131.

41. "Marital Status of the Population," in *Statistical Abstract of the United States 1986,* 106th ed. (Washington: Government Printing Office, 1985), p. 36.

42. Stillion, *Death and the Sexes,* p. 126.

43. Ibid., p. 127.

44. Ibid., p. 130.

45. See Phyllis R. Silverman and Adele Cooperband, "On Widowhood: Mutual Help and the Elderly Widow," *Journal of Geriatric Psychiatry* 8: (1975): 9–27; and, by Silverman, "The Widow-to-Widow Program: An Experiment in Preventive Intervention," *Mental Hygiene* 53:3 (1969), in which she describes her initial work in this area at Harvard Medical School's Laboratory of Community Psychiatry. See also Mary Vachon et al., "A Controlled Study of Self-Help Intervention for Widows," *American Journal of Psychiatry* 137:11 (1980): 1380–1384. For information on support programs, write Widowed Persons Service, 1909 K Street, N.W., Washington DC 20049.

46. Osterweis et al., *Bereavement,* p. 85.

47. The aged generally have been held in higher esteem in agricultural than in

industrial societies. Also, in Oriental cultures, such as China and Japan, old age may be accepted more easily because of a cyclical, rather than linear, conception of time. For an account of the aged in modern Japanese society, see Erdman B. Palmore and Daisaku Maeda, *The Honorable Elders Revisited: A Revised Cross-Cultural Analysis of Aging in Japan* (Durham, N.C.: Duke University Press, 1985).

48. Stillion, *Death and the Sexes,* p. 56.

49. Hannelore Wass, "Aging and Death Education for Elderly Persons," *Educational Gerontology: An International Quarterly* 5 (1980): 79, 88.

50. Miriam K. Aronson and Elaine S. Yatzkan, "Coping with Alzheimer's Disease Through Support Groups," *Aging* 347 (1984): 5. The Alzheimer's Disease and Related Disorders Association (ADRDA) is a voluntary organization whose membership includes family members, researchers, and health professionals. For information, write 360 North Michigan Avenue, Chicago, IL 60601.

51. Jon Hendricks and C. Davis Hendricks, *Aging in Mass Society: Myths and Realities* (Cambridge, Mass.: Winthrop, 1977), pp. 284–285.

52. Ibid., p. 282.

CHAPTER 10

1. Margaret Mead, "The Cultural Shaping of the Ethical Situation," in *Who Shall Live? Medicine, Technology, Ethics,* edited by Kenneth Vaux (Philadelphia: Fortress Press, 1970), pp. 3–23.

2. This study is reported by Donald Oken, "What to Tell Cancer Patients: A Study of Medical Attitudes," in *Journal of the American Medical Association* 175 (April 1, 1961): 86–94; reprinted in *Ethical Issues in Death and Dying,* edited by Robert F. Weir (New York: Columbia University Press, 1977), pp. 9–25.

3. The discussion of the Commission's inquiry is drawn from: The President's Commission for the Study of Ethical Problems in Medicine and Biomedical and Behavioral Research, *Making Health Care Decisions: The Ethical and Legal Implications of Informed Consent in the Patient-Practitioner Relationship; vol. 1, Report; and vol. 3, Studies on the Foundations of Informed Consent* (Washington: Government Printing Office, 1982). Unless otherwise noted, quoted material in this section is from these sources.

4. This trend toward greater disclosure can be seen in the fact that a 1961 study by Donald Oken found that 90 percent of physicians preferred not to inform patients of a diagnosis of cancer, whereas a 1977 study by Novak et al. revealed that 97 percent of physicians said they routinely disclosed cancer diagnoses.

5. Joseph Fletcher, "The Patient's Right to Die," in *Euthanasia and the Right to Die: The Case for Voluntary Euthanasia,* edited by A. B. Downing (London: Peter Owen Ltd., 1969), p. 30.

6. Glanville Williams, "Euthanasia Legislation: A Rejoinder to the Non-Religious Objections," in *Euthanasia and the Right to Die,* edited by A. B. Downing, pp. 134–135.

7. Another argument proposed against euthanasia concerns the notion that the time of dying represents an extraordinary, indeed a final, opportunity for enlightenment in the present life. This is a belief held, for example, by some Buddhist sects. This notion may have a biochemical rationale as well, as has been suggested by some recent work on endorphins—natural products of the body that tend to relieve pain while enhancing clarity of thought during the process of dying.

8. The definition of what is essential may encompass what some would consider to be aggressive treatment; for example, the use of antibiotics to combat pneumonia infection in a terminal cancer patient.

9. President's Commission for the Study of Ethical Problems in Medicine and Biomedical and Behavioral Research, *Summing Up: Final Report on Studies of the Ethical and Legal Problems in Medicine and Biomedical and Behavioral Research* (Washington: Government Printing Office, March 1983), p. 31.

10. President's Commission for the Study of Ethical Problems in Medicine and Biomedical and Behavioral Research, *Deciding to Forego Life-Sustaining Treatment: A Report on the Ethical, Medical, and Legal Issues in Treatment Decisions* (Washington: Government Printing Office, March 1983), p. 2.

11. For the legal history of the case, see *In the Matter of Karen Quinlan: The Complete Legal Briefs, Court Proceedings, and Decision in the Superior Court of New Jersey* (1975) and *In the Matter of Karen Quinlan, Volume 2: The Complete Briefs, Oral Arguments, and Opinion in the New Jersey Supreme Court* (1976; Arlington, Va.: University Publications of America).

12. "Florida District Court of Appeals Decides Landmark Case Concerning Life-Sustaining Measures," PR Newswire, April 22, 1986.

13. President's Commission, *Summing Up,* p. 34.

14. Robert McCormick, in *Ethical Issues in Death and Dying,* edited by R. F. Weir, p. 133.

15. This case is cited by James M. Gustafson, "Mongolism, Parental Desires, and the Right to Life," ibid., pp. 145–172.

16. Ibid., p. 163.

17. President's Commission, *Deciding to Forego Life-Sustaining Treatment,* p. 7.

18. This discussion of the "Baby Doe" regulations is based on articles appearing in *Science* from 1983 to 1986.

19. "Postmortem in on Baby Fae," *Science News* 128 (December 28, 1985): 390. Although the infant died three weeks after the transplant, her medical team stated later that the death had resulted from an immune response that was "potentially avoidable" in similar circumstances.

20. For more on the function of "gate keeping," see Renee C. Fox and Judith P. Swazey, *The Courage to Fail: A Social View of Organ Transplants and Dialysis* (Chicago: University of Chicago Press, 1974), p. 33.

21. Douglas N. Walton, *On Defining Death: An Analytic Study of the Concept of Death in Philosophy and Medical Ethics* (Montreal: McGill–Queen's University Press, 1979), pp. 20ff. Also see Eric Cassell, Leon Kass, et al., "Refinements in Criteria for the Determination of Death: An Appraisal," in *Journal of the American Medical Association* 221 (1972): 48–53.

22. Editorial, "Brain Damage and Brain Death," *Lancet* (1974): 342.

23. Clyde M. Nabe, "Presenting Biological Data in a Course on Death and Dying," *Death Education* 5:1 (Spring 1981): 56.

24. In the case of Karen Ann Quinlan, for example, transplantation was not an issue; nevertheless, the decision to withdraw the respirator involved a complex medical and legal debate.

25. Robert M. Veatch, *Death, Dying, and the Biological Revolution: Our Last Quest for Responsibility* (New Haven, Conn.: Yale University Press 1976), p. 32.

26. Nabe, "Presenting Biological Data," p. 53.

27. Veatch, *Death, Dying, and the Biological Revolution,* pp. 21–54. The next several quotations from Veatch are from these pages.

28. In a 1907 study, dying persons were placed on a very sensitive scale to determine whether any weight loss occurs at the moment of death. Researchers noted a loss, averaging from 1 to 2 ounces, leading to speculations about whether the loss indicated the departure of the soul from the body at death. This study was reported by Duncan MacDougall, "Hypothesis Concerning Soul Substance Together with Experimental Evidence of the Existence of Such Substance," *Journal of the American Society for Psychical Research* 1:5 (May 1907): 237–244.

29. Veatch, *Death, Dying and the Biological Revolution,* p. 37.

30. The Harvard criteria call for a second set of tests to be performed on the patient after twenty-four hours have elapsed. They also specifically exclude cases of hypothermia (body temperature below 90° F) as well as situations involving the presence of central nervous system depressants such as barbiturates.

31. Veatch, *Death, Dying and the Biological Revolution,* p. 48. Other clinicians propose the use of alternative or additional criteria, such as measurements of the metabolic products in the blood or cerebral spinal fluid, or the absence of circulation in the brain.

32. Ibid., p. 61.

33. President's Commission for the Study of Ethical Problems in Medicine and Biomedical and Behavioral Research, *Defining Death: A Report on the Medical, Legal and Ethical Issues in the Determination of Death* (Washington: Government Printing Office, July 1981), p. 45.

34. Alexander M. Capron and Leon R. Kass, "A Statutory Definition of the Standards for Determining Human Death: An Appraisal and a Proposal," *University of Pennsylvania Law Review* 121 (1972): 87–118.

35. The Uniform Anatomical Gift Act is discussed in Chapter 11.

36. President's Commission, *Defining Death,* pp. 74–75.

37. Ibid., p. 76.

38. Ibid., pp. 4, 6. The "Harvard criteria" for making a determination of death, published in 1968, have been reliable, the Commission said, in that "no case has yet been found that met these criteria and regained any brain functions despite continuation of respirator support." It pointed out, however, that, although the criteria are intended to define a state of "irreversible coma," or death, the phrase is misleading since the word coma refers to a condition of a living person, whereas "a body without any brain functions is dead and thus *beyond* any coma" (p. 25).

39. Ibid., p. 16.

40. Ibid., p. 7. During the 1970s, about half of all U.S. states had adopted statutes incorporating the cessation of total brain functions as a ground for declaring death.

41. Ibid., p. 18. The Commission noted that the longest such survival exceeded thirty-seven years.

42. Ibid., p. 40.

CHAPTER 11

1. Information about legislation related to the living will in the various states may be obtained from Concern for Dying, 250 West 57 Street, New York, NY 10107; (212) 246–6962.

2. The model Uniform Anatomical Gift Act was approved in 1968 by the National

Conference of Commissions on Uniform State Laws. It provides that: (1) Any person over eighteen may donate all or part of his or her body for education, research, therapeutic, or transplantation purposes. (2) If the person has not made a donation before death, the next of kin can make it unless there was a known objection by the deceased. (3) If the person has made such a gift, it cannot be revoked by his or her relatives. (4) If there is more than one person of the same degree of kinship, the gift from relatives shall not be accepted if there is a known objection by one of them. (5) The gift can be authorized by a card carried by the individual or by written or recorded verbal communication from a relative. (6) The gift can be amended or revoked at any time before the death of the donor. (7) The time of death must be determined by a physician who is not involved in any transplantation.

3. If the necessary funding is approved by Congress, such a network could be in place by the end of the decade.

4. Edwin S. Shneidman, "The Death Certificate," *Deaths of Man* (New York: Quadrangle/The New York Times Book Company, 1973), pp. 121–130.

5. Readers interested in learning more about the duties of the coroner and the medical examiner are directed to Cyril H. Wecht, "The Coroner and Death," in *Concerning Death: A Practical Guide for the Living*, edited by Earl A. Grollman (Boston: Beacon Press, 1974), pp. 177–185.

6. An exception to the requirement that the next of kin's consent be obtained before a voluntary autopsy (that is, not required by law) can be performed would be when the deceased has previously donated his or her body for autopsy under the provisions of the Uniform Anatomical Gift Act.

7. For further discussion of the lawyer's role in serving the terminally ill and the survivors, see the following by Barton E. Bernstein: "Lawyer and Counselor as an Interdisciplinary Team: Interfacing for the Terminally Ill," *Death Education* 1:3 (Fall 1977): 277–291; "Lawyer and Therapist as an Interdisciplinary Team Serving the Terminally Ill," *Death Education* 3:1 (Spring 1979): 11–19.

8. Bernstein presents the three legal stages affecting the terminally ill and their families in "Lawyer and Therapist as an Interdisciplinary Team: Serving the Survivors," *Death Education* 4:2 (Summer 1980): 179–188.

9. Everyone should maintain a record of important family information and pertinent documents. Such records include the vital statistics for each family member; military service records and VA (Veterans Administration) number; marriage, divorce, and adoption papers; names, addresses, and phone numbers of relatives and close friends who should be notified if a death occurs; professional and social organizations that should receive notification; location of wills and other important documents, including insurance policies, property deeds, and tax returns; names and addresses of persons to be contacted upon the death of a family member, including executors, attorneys, bank officials, accountants, funeral or cemetery directors, brokers, and mortgage companies; information about notes receivable and accounts outstanding; information regarding funeral plans and wishes for the disposition of the body.

10. A will should be kept where it can be easily found by the executor and safeguarded against loss or theft. Usually, a will is kept by the person's attorney or trust company (bank). A duplicate may be kept in the home office, but the testator must be sure to destroy all duplicate copies of a will when it is revised.

11. One of the problems with self-help guides to avoiding probate is that the information contained in them may become dated and no longer reflect the most recent

changes in probate and estate tax laws. Although the movement toward taking greater charge of personal financial destiny seems laudable, the risks of relying on limited information should at least be cause for taking a cautious approach.

12. Paul Ashley, *You and Your Will: The Planning and Management of Your Estate* (New York: New American Library, 1977), p. 14.

13. The authors thank Richard G. Polse, attorney-at-law, for valuable assistance in writing this section.

14. Ashley, *You and Your Will,* pp. 76–77.

15. Andrew J. Lyons, "Insurance and Death," in *Concerning Death: A Practical Guide for the Living,* edited by E. A. Grollman, p. 158.

CHAPTER 12

1. From *Letters of E. B. White,* collected and edited by Dorothy Lobrano Guth (New York: Harper & Row, 1976), p. 558. White's comment was in connection with "Death of a Pig," in his *Essays* (Harper & Row, 1977), pp. 17–24. White wrote in his letter, "I tend to write about events or circumstances that raise the level of my perception. The death of this animal moved me, heightened my awareness. . . . As I said in the piece, 'I knew that what could be true of my pig could be true also of the rest of my tidy world.' "

2. Work-related deaths result, basically, either from injuries or from occupational diseases, most of which occur after long-term, low-level exposure to hazardous conditions. For more on this subject, see Daniel M. Berman, *Death on the Job: Occupational Health and Safety Struggles in the United States* (New York: Monthly Review Press, 1978).

3. Ibid., pp. 179–180.

4. Kenneth J. Doka, Eric C. Schwarz, and Catherine Schwarz, "Risky Business: Reactions to Death in Hazardous Sports," paper presented at the Annual Meeting of the Association for Death Education and Counseling, Atlanta, 1986.

5. National Research Council, *Injury in America: A Continuing Public Health Problem* (Washington: National Academy Press, 1985). About 50,000, or more than 90 percent, of these deaths result from automobile accidents, followed by roughly 13,000 from asphyxiation (drowning, suffocation, hanging), 10,000 from chemical poisoning, and 6,000 from burns. Aviation and railroad fatalities each account for approximately 2 to 3 percent of total deaths in transportation accidents.

6. This example is adapted from Robert Kastenbaum and Ruth Aisenberg, *The Psychology of Death: Concise Edition* (New York: Springer, 1976), p. 300. The example is not here as an argument for gun control, for some might argue that lack of a gun increases the risk of violence perpetrated by criminals. Nevertheless, as Lundsgaarde states, "guns . . . do not kill people by themselves. They are simply efficient tools used by people for the killing of people . . . [yet evidence does suggest that] the presence of weapons serves to elicit and escalate aggressive responses." See Henry Lundsgaarde, *Murder in Space City: A Cultural Analysis of Houston Homicide Patterns* (New York: Oxford University Press, 1977), pp. 184–185.

7. Factors influencing accident-proneness are discussed by Kastenbaum and Aisenberg in *Psychology of Death,* pp. 299–323, esp. pp. 301–307.

8. Perhaps as we reach the point where as many women as men engage in activities once considered the exclusive province of men, the group at greatest risk may contain as many women as men.

9. Kastenbaum and Aisenberg, *Psychology of Death,* p. 319.

10. For an excellent account of the personal response of nearby residents to such

disasters, see Robert Leppzer, *Voices from Three Mile Island: The People Speak Out* (Trumansburg, N.Y.: Crossing Press, 1980).

11. Although the number of disasters affecting the U.S. population has increased, this area of death awareness and study has mostly been neglected. Robert Kastenbaum has cited this neglect as an example of "our society's selective attention to death even when it does choose to pay any attention at all"; see *Death, Society, and Human Experience* (St. Louis: C. V. Mosby, 1977), p. 98.

12. "Damage in Mexico: A Double Quake," *Science News* 129 (January 11, 1986): 25; see also Allen A. Boraiko, "Earthquake in Mexico," *National Geographic* 169: 5 (May 1986): 654–675.

13. Kastenbaum, *Death, Society, and Human Experience*, p. 103.

14. U.S. Geological Survey, *Eruptions of Mount St. Helens: Past, Present, and Future* by Robert I. Tilling (Washington: Government Printing Office, n.d.); see also Robert D. Brown, Jr., and William J. Kockelman, "Geology for Decisionmakers: Protecting Life, Property, and Resources," *Public Affairs Report* 26: 1.

15. Kastenbaum, *Death, Society, and Human Experience*, p. 104.

16. *Postvention,* a term coined in the early 1970s by Edwin Shneidman, relates to what can be done in the aftermath of a disaster. This is discussed by Kastenbaum in *Death, Society, and Human Experience*, pp. 105–110. Interested readers can also refer to Vanderlyn R. Pine, editor, *Responding to Disaster* (Milwaukee: Bulfin, 1974), which has chapters on the legal and medical perspectives on disaster, the role of the federal government, the role of funeral directors in providing aid to survivors and caring for the dead, as well as plans for emergency preparedness formulated by the National Funeral Directors Association.

17. Those who come to the aid of the survivors of a disaster may also become "survivors" in the sense that their work of postvention involves an intense encounter with human suffering and tragedy. Consider the experience of a Kansas City doctor who arrived at the scene of the Hyatt Regency Hotel disaster in 1981 to find among the debris bodies chopped in half, decapitated, and maimed. He watched as a critically injured man's leg, trapped under a fallen beam, was amputated with a chain saw. He worked sensitively and professionally as one of the first caregivers to force his way to where the victims were trapped. In the aftermath of the disaster, when things returned more or less to normal, he told officials that he felt the need to spend some time away from reminders of the disaster and take time to cope with his own experience as a survivor. Often, those who provide care and support are themselves given little in the way of support for their own coping needs.

18. Beverly McLeod, "In the Wake of Disaster," *Psychology Today* (October 1984): 54–57.

19. *Science* 230 (13 December 1985): 1257. This office will also collect information concerning patterns in suicide and suicidal behavior.

20. Fame seems to increase this risk. The assassinations of the two Kennedys and of Martin Luther King, Jr., as well as more recent attempts on the lives of political leaders, indicate the additional risk that accompanies political leadership. The murder of John Lennon came as a shock to many, who felt "jolted" when the violence of assassination made an artist and musician a target of the irrational killer.

21. Kastenbaum and Aisenberg, *Psychology of Death*, pp. 283–284.

22. Lundsgaarde, *Murder in Space City.*

23. Lundsgaarde observed that "in parent-child homicides, parents receive a disproportionately lighter sentence for killing their children than do children for killing

their parents." However, the killing of an unfaithful husband or wife by a spouse is less likely to be punished severely than is a parent's killing of a child. Ibid., pp. 90–92.

24. Lundsgaarde says, "What appears so shocking, or understandable as the case may be, about many killings depends upon our personal understandings of and assumptions about the rules that 'should' and 'ought' to govern a particular kind of relationship." Ibid., p. 104.

25. In making these determinations, the criminal justice system — which, in this case, also includes the police investigation — takes into account the intention, motivation, and circumstances surrounding the homicide. Ibid., pp. 3ff.

26. Ibid., p. 124.

27. Ibid., p. 140.

28. Lundsgaarde says, "Intimates form symmetrical social relationships that insulate them within a series of obligations subject to enforcement by social and psychological sanctions. The robber, rapist, killer, or even the self-styled terrorist, is not restrained in his behavior by anything other than criminal sanctions." Ibid., p. 141.

29. Kastenbaum and Aisenberg, *Psychology of Death,* pp. 269ff.

30. Ibid. Italics in original.

31. Glenn M. Vernon, *Sociology of Death: An Analysis of Death-Related Behavior* (New York: Ronald Press, 1970), p. 95.

32. Ibid., p. 95. To gain insight into the experience of death row from the perspective of the condemned men, prison administrators, and death row chaplains, see *Death Row: An Affirmation of Life,* edited by Stephen Levine (San Francisco: Glide Publications, 1972).

33. Kastenbaum and Aisenberg see an inconsistency in society trying to eradicate or prevent murder by itself engaging in killing. They say that capital punishment provides an excuse for taking the easy way out. Also, if this is the best solution that a society can come up with after years of deliberation, then what can be expected of the solitary individual? Citing evidence from psychology and behavioral therapy, which emphasizes the beneficial effects of *positive* reinforcement, Kastenbaum and Aisenberg say "there is little evidence to suggest that imposing massive punishment on one individual will 'improve' the behavior of others"; indeed, it may serve as positive reinforcement of hostile fantasies and murderous tendencies (*Psychology of Death,* pp. 284–285).

34. Ibid., pp. 95–96.

35. Lundsgaarde, *Murder in Space City,* p. 146.

36. Kastenbaum and Aisenberg, *Psychology of Death,* pp. 296–297.

37. Ibid., pp. 281–282.

38. Ibid., pp. 290–294.

39. Arnold Toynbee, "Death in War," in *Death and Dying: Challenge and Change,* edited by Robert Fulton et al. (Reading, Mass.: Addison-Wesley, 1978), p. 367. Kastenbaum and Aisenberg speak of war as "an extension of capital punishment on a grand scale," adding that war "elevates killing into national policy" (*Psychology of Death,* pp. 285–290).

40. Dalton Trumbo, *Johnny Got His Gun* (New York: Bantam Books, 1970), pp. 214, 224. Published in 1939, this book became a National Book Award winner. Set at the time of World War I, Trumbo's novel remains one of the most powerful antiwar statements in literature. In an introductory note to the 1970 edition, Trumbo says that, in modern warfare, "numbers have dehumanized us. Over breakfast coffee we read of 40,000 American dead in Vietnam. Instead of vomiting, we reach for the toast. Our

morning rush through crowded streets is not to cry murder, but to hit that trough before somebody else gobbles our share" (p. iv).

41. Vernon, *Sociology of Death,* p. 46.

42. Toynbee, "Death in War," p. 367. One of the conventions of warfare, Toynbee points out, is to dress the part. The psychological effect of the soldier's uniform is that it "symbolizes the abrogation of the normal taboo on killing fellow human beings: it replaces this taboo by a duty to kill them."

43. Vernon, *Sociology of Death,* p. 47.

44. Joel Baruch, "Combat Death," in *Death: Current Perspectives,* 1st ed., edited by Edwin S. Shneidman (Palo Alto, Calif.: Mayfield Publishing Co., 1976), p. 93.

45. Ibid., p. 92. Baruch explains: "Combat training had never prepared me for anything like this. The death of an enemy was mentioned in aloof terms as if the enemies were stuntmen on a movie set who would get up and walk away after the take. Your own death was never dwelled upon; the training period was set in a world of illusions in which American soldiers seemed invulnerable to combat death."

46. Ibid., p. 94.

47. Personal communication.

48. Ibid. In this veteran's opinion, "those who make a display of telling about their combat experiences, making a point of emphasizing the more gruesome aspects of killing, probably don't remember what it was actually like in the real situation." On the process of readjustment of the combat veteran, see Harvey J. Schwartz, "Fear of the Dead: The Role of Social Ritual in Neutralizing Fantasies from Combat," in *Psychotherapy of the Combat Veteran,* edited by H. J. Schwartz (New York: SP Medical & Scientific Books, 1984), pp. 253–267.

49. Baruch says that most soldiers in combat "are possessed by an overpowering desire for survival and, at the same time, a humane reluctance to kill the enemy. Of course there were dissenters; a substantial minority of them—the rabble-rousers, the hate-mongers, those professional soldiers who actually like to kill—actively relished the idea of staking their lives against those of the enemy in a contest to the death. I know this much: they were a different breed of animal." See Baruch, "Combat Death," p. 98.

50. Robert Jay Lifton and Eric Olson, *Living and Dying* (New York: Bantam Books, 1975), p. 8.

51. Ibid., pp. 123–124.

52. Ibid., p. 8. Such films as *Coming Home, The Deer Hunter,* and *Apocalypse Now* have been credited with helping Americans begin to come to terms with the lessons of the Vietnam war and to move toward healing the trauma experienced by many returned veterans of that war. See John Hellman, *American Myth and the Legacy of Vietnam* (New York: Columbia University Press, 1986), p. 100.

53. Gil Elliot, "Agents of Death," in *Death: Current Perspectives,* edited by E. S. Shneidman, 3rd ed., pp. 422–440.

54. Toynbee, "Death in War," p. 369.

55. Lifton and Olson believe the term *psychic numbing,* which describes the survivors of Hiroshima, applies as well to Vietnam veterans and, indeed, to all Americans who experienced the war via television news reports: "Numbing is the characteristic psychological problem of our age. Jet pilots who cooly drop bombs on people they never see tend not to feel what goes on at the receiving end. Those of us who watch such bombing on TV undergo a different though not unrelated desensitization" (*Living and Dying,* p. 7).

56. Elliot, "Agents of Death," p. 437.

57. Trumbo, *Johnny Got His Gun,* pp. 240–241.

58. Placing the nuclear threat within a historical dimension, Arnold Toynbee states: "Since 1945, the human race has been living under a threat of extinction that had not hung over it since man definitely got the upper hand over all other large beasts of prey on this planet. This happened perhaps about thirty thousand years ago, and, at that date, human beings can hardly have been conscious of the danger of extinction from which they were liberating themselves. Today, on the other hand, they are fully aware of the threat. . . . The invention of the atomic weapon produced an instantaneous change in the nature of war. A five-thousand-year-old wicked institution that had always been cruel and devastating had now become suicidal" ("Death in War," pp. 370–371).

59. John E. Mack, "Psychosocial Effects of the Nuclear Arms Race," in the *Bulletin of the Atomic Scientists* 37:4 (April 1981): 19–20. Some of these young people, Mack says, "have doubts about planning families or are unable to think ahead in any long-term sense. . . . We may be seeing that growing up in a world dominated by the threat of imminent nuclear destruction is having an impact on the structure of personality itself. . . . It seems that these young people are growing up without the ability to form stable ideals. . . . We may find we are raising generations of young people without a basis for making long-term commitments, who are given over, of necessity, to doctrines of impulsiveness and immediacy in their personal relationships or choice of behaviors and activity."

In an article by Edwin S. Shneidman, "Megadeath: Children of the Nuclear Family," in *Death and Dying: Challenge and Change,* edited by R. Fulton et al., pp. 372–376, the effect of the threat of violent, mass death on the lives of those who have come of age since Hiroshima is discussed.

See also Judith M. Stillion, "Examining the Shadow: Gifted Children Respond to the Nuclear Threat," *Death Studies* 10: 1 (1986): 27–41.

60. William C. Adams, et al., "Before and After 'The Day After': A Nationwide Survey of a Movie's Impact," paper presented at the Annual Meeting of the International Communication Association, San Francisco, May 1984.

61. Karyn Charles Rybacki and Donald Jay Rybacki, "Visions of Apocalypse: A Rhetorical Analysis of 'The Day After,' " paper presented at the Annual Meeting of the International Communication Association, San Francisco, May 1984, p. 16.

62. Joanne Silberner, "Hiroshima and Nagasaki: Thirty-Six Years Later, the Struggle Continues," in *Science News* 120:18 (October 31, 1981): 284–287. Silberner notes that "as a direct result of the bomb, 130,000 of Hiroshima's total population of 340,000 were dead by November, and an additional 70,000 died by 1950" (p. 284). Even today, the *hibakusha,* or "explosion-affected persons," continue to suffer the debilitating and fatal consequences of the bomb and its aftermath.

63. Robert Jay Lifton, "Psychological Effects of the Atomic Bomb in Hiroshima: The Theme of Death," in *The Threat of Impending Disaster: Contributions to the Psychology of Stress,* edited by George H. Grosser, Henry Wechsler, and Milton Greenblatt (Cambridge, Mass.: MIT Press, 1964), pp. 152–193.

64. Ibid.

65. Ruth Leger Sivard, *World Military and Social Expenditures — 1980* (Leesburg, Va.: World Priorities), p. 12. Sivard also notes that currently about half a dozen nations possess nuclear explosives, and about as many again are likely to acquire them in the near future (p. 5).

66. U.S. Congress, Office of Technology Assessment, *The Effects of Nuclear War* (Washington: Government Printing Office, 1979), pp. 3–4. This publication provides

an analysis of possible scenarios that could accompany nuclear attack. Another resource for the interested reader is Bernard T. Feld, "The Consequences of Nuclear War," in *Death and Dying: Challenge and Change,* edited by R. Fulton et al., pp. 383–389.

67. Sivard, *World Military and Social Expenditures — 1980,* p. 5.

68. Lester Grinspoon, "Fallout Shelters and the Unacceptability of Disquieting Facts," in *The Threat of Impending Disaster,* edited by G. H. Grosser et al. (Cambridge, Mass.: MIT Press, 1964), pp. 117–130. Simply making people aware of the reality of a threat does not provide an antidote: Grinspoon says, "fear-bearing communications decrease the recipient's capacity for adaptive response" (p. 128).

69. Sivard, *World Military and Social Expenditures — 1980,* p. 12.

70. Howard L. Rosenberg, *Atomic Soldiers: American Victims of Nuclear Experiments* (Boston: Beacon Press, 1980). Also see Thomas H. Saffer and Orville E. Kelly, *Countdown Zero* (New York: G. P. Putnam's Sons, 1982).

71. Lifton and Olson, *Living and Dying,* p. 104. Psychiatrist Jerome Frank has identified three practical steps that can be taken to prevent war: (1) promote increased international communication and cooperation through trade and cultural exchange; (2) break the link between violence and courage by emphasizing new avenues for national pride and achievement; and (3) question the morality of war given the present nuclear situation. See Jerome Frank, "Group Psychology and the Elimination of War," in *Peace Is Possible,* edited by E. H. Hollins (New York: Grossman, 1966).

72. Sivard, *World Military and Social Expenditures — 1980,* p. 5.

73. Dr. Helen M. Caldicott, an advocate of nuclear arms reduction, says: "The world is moving rapidly toward the final medical epidemic, thermonuclear war. Earth can be compared to a terminally ill patient infected with lethal 'macrobes,' nuclear weapons, that are metastasizing rapidly." See "The Final Epidemic," *The Sciences* (March 1982): 16.

74. Quoted in Sivard, *World Military and Social Expenditures — 1980,* p. 11. For an annotated checklist of recent publications on nuclear war and nuclearism in general, see *Publisher's Weekly* (March 26, 1982): 45–51.

75. A revised edition of Hans Selye's classic work, *The Stress of Life* (New York: McGraw-Hill), was published in 1976. In it Selye not only explains the concepts and the physiology of stress, but also offers constructive suggestions for reducing the level of stress in one's life. Also see Hans Selye, "Stress, Cancer, and the Mind," in *Cancer, Stress, and Death,* edited by Jean Tache et al. (New York: Plenum Medical Book Company, 1979), pp. 11–19.

76. See Thomas H. Holmes and Richard H. Rahe, "The Social Readjustment Rating Scale," *Journal of Psychosomatic Research* 11 (1967): 213-218; also see Richard H. Rahe, "Social Stress and Illness Onset," *Journal of Psychosomatic Research* 8 (1964): 35–43.

77. Meyer Friedman and Ray H. Rosenman, *Type A Behavior and Your Heart* (New York: Alfred A. Knopf, 1974). In contrast to Type A, the Type B personality is described as relaxed, easy going, and not especially concerned about deadlines.

78. Malcolm Carruthers, *The Western Way of Death: Stress, Tension, and Heart Attacks* (New York: Pantheon Books, 1974), pp. 24–25.

79. Paul J. Rosch, "Stress and Cancer: A Disease of Maladaptation?," in *Cancer, Stress, and Death,* edited by J. Tache et al., pp. 211–212.

80. The positive uses of stress are discussed in an interview with Hans Selye by Laurence Cherry, "On the Real Benefits of Distress," *Psychology Today* 11:10 (March 1978), 60–70.

81. Jean Tache, "Stress as a Cause of Disease," in *Cancer, Stress, and Death,* p. 8.

82. Ibid., p. 9.

83. Selye, "Stress Without Distress," in *Stress and Survival: The Emotional Realities of Life-Threatening Illness,* edited by Charles A. Garfield (St. Louis, Mo.: C. V. Mosby, 1979), p. 15.

84. See, for example, Herbert Benson, *The Relaxation Response* (New York: Avon Books, 1975).

85. Joseph Eyer, "Hypertension as a Disease of Modern Society," in *Stress and Survival,* edited by C. A. Garfield, p. 56.

86. Eyer notes that some of the social problems that tend to increase the level of stress include community and family disruption, work pressures, population shifts, lack of close social relationships, rapid social and technological change, war and violence, excessive competition in the workplace, and inability to relax or enjoy the fruits of one's labors. Ibid., pp. 63–66.

87. On stress related to general environmental conditions, see Manfred F. R. Kets de Vries, "Ecological Stress: A Deadly Reminder," *The Psychoanalytic Review* 67:3 (Fall 1980): 389–408.

CHAPTER 13

1. "Death Rates" and "Death Rates by Selected Causes and Selected Characteristics," in *Statistical Abstract of the United States 1986,* 106th ed. (Washington: Government Printing Office, 1985), pp. 73–74. For the United States, the overall incidence of suicide is about 12 per 100,000 people.

2. Edwin S. Shneidman, "Suicide," in *Death: Current Perspectives,* 2nd ed., edited by E. S. Shneidman (Palo Alto, Calif.: Mayfield Publishing Co., 1980), p. 432.

3. Ronald Maris, "Sociology," in *A Handbook for the Study of Suicide,* edited by Seymour Perlin (New York: Oxford University Press, 1975), p. 95. Maris adds that "groups with high suicide rates tend to be made up of individuals who are socially isolated from significant others and who, since they do not participate in society, do not benefit from social sanctions or normative restraints" (p. 96).

4. Emile Durkheim, *Suicide: A Study in Sociology* (New York: Free Press, 1951), p. 209.

5. In Durkheim's scheme the mass suicide of members of the People's Temple cult in Jonestown, Guyana, can be considered altruistic suicide. The following sources provide differing perspectives and interpretations about this tragedy: Marshall Kilduff and Ron Javers, *The Suicide Cult: The Inside Story of the People's Temple Sect and the Massacre in Guyana* (New York: Bantam Books, 1978); Jose I. Lasaga, "Death in Jonestown: Techniques of Political Control by a Paranoid Leader," *Suicide and Life-Threatening Behavior* 10:4 (Winter 1980): 210–213; Shiva Naipaul, *Journey to Nowhere: a New World Tragedy* (New York: Simon & Schuster, 1979); James Reston, Jr., *Our Father Who Art in Hell* (New York: Times Books, 1978); Richard H. Seiden, "Reverend Jones on Suicide," *Suicide and Life-Threatening Behavior* 9:2 (Summer 1979): 116–119; Kenneth Wooden, *The Children of Jonestown* (New York: McGraw-Hill, 1978).

6. Charles Brenner, *An Elementary Textbook of Psychoanalysis,* rev. ed. (Garden City, N.Y.: Anchor Press/Doubleday, 1975), pp. 100–101.

7. Shneidman, "Suicide," in *Death: Current Perspectives,* 2nd ed., p. 421.

8. Erwin Stengel, "A Matter of Communication," in *On the Nature of Suicide,* edited by Edwin S. Shneidman (San Francisco: Jossey-Bass, 1969), p. 78.

9. Ibid.

10. Stengel says that if the suicide attempt fails to bring about a change in the conditions that led up to it, the act may be repeated: "It is important therefore in every suicidal attempt to ask what change it has achieved. . . . A purely intrapsychic appraisal is not enough. It ignores the communicative function of the suicidal act. If it is fatal, it is a final message: if it is not fatal, it is part of a dialogue. And you cannot understand a dialogue if you take notice of one participant only." Ibid., p. 79.

11. Edwin S. Shneidman and Norman L. Farberow, "The Logic of Suicide," in *Clues to Suicide,* edited by Shneidman and Farberow (New York: McGraw-Hill, 1957), pp. 31–40.

12. The dying patient's "right" to surcease suicide is the topic of many recent publications as well as much public discussion. The following personal accounts of the dilemmas surrounding surcease suicide provide a useful adjunct to the more philosophical-ethical discussions that are typical of this subject: Jo Roman, *Exit House: Choosing Suicide as an Alternative* (New York: Seaview Books, 1980); Lael T. Wertenbaker, *Death of a Man* (Boston: Beacon Press, 1974).

13. The disproportional rate of suicide among the elderly raises serious questions concerning the adequacy of social resources available to older Americans. The phenomenon of geriatric suicides, along with suggestions of how the number of such suicides might be reduced, is discussed in detail by Marv Miller in his *Suicide After Sixty: The Final Alternative* (New York: Springer, 1979).

14. For readers interested in the role of *seppuku* in Japanese culture, the following resources are recommended: Robert Jay Lifton, Shuichi Kato, and Michael R. Reich, *Six Lives, Six Deaths Portraits from Modern Japan* (New Haven, Conn.: Yale University Press, 1979); Bernard Millot, *Divine Thunder: The Life and Death of the Kamikazes,* translated by Lowell Bair (New York: McCall, 1971); Jack Seward, *Hara-Kiri: Japanese Ritual Suicide* (Rutland, Vt., and Tokyo: Charles E. Tuttle, 1968). In addition, the following historical accounts include descriptions of how *seppuku* was practiced in the context of feudal Japanese culture: Helen Craig McCullough, *The Taiheiki: A Chronicle of Medieval Japan* (Rutland, Vt., and Tokyo: Charles E. Tuttle, 1959, 1979); A. L. Sadler, *The Maker of Modern Japan: The Life of Shogun Tokugawa Ieyasu* (Rutland, Vt., and Tokyo: Charles E. Tuttle, 1937, 1978). Current patterns of suicide in Japan are surveyed in "Japanese Suicide," *The East* 21:5 (October 1985): 46–52.

15. The subject of "romantic" or "literary" suicides, and particularly the suicide of Sylvia Plath, is dealt with by A. Alvarez in his illuminating book *The Savage God: A Study of Suicide* (New York: Random House, 1972). Also enlightening on this subject is Sylvia Plath's early novel, *The Bell Jar* (available in various editions).

16. Sue V. Petzel and Mary Riddle, "Adolescent Suicide: Psychosocial and Cognitive Aspects," *Adolescent Psychiatry: Developmental and Clinical Studies*, vol. 9 (Chicago: University of Chicago Press, 1981), pp. 33–364.

17. Paul C. Holinger and Daniel Offer, "Perspectives on Suicide in Adolescence," *Research in Community and Mental Health* 2 (1981): 148.

18. Donald H. Rubenstein, "Epidemic Suicide Among Micronesian Adolescents," *Social Science and Medicine* 17 (1983): 657–665; and "Suicide in Micronesia," in *Culture, Youth and Suicide in the Pacific: Papers from an East-West Center Conference,* edited by Francis X. Hezel, Donald H. Rubinstein, and Geoffrey M. White (Honolulu: Pacific Islands Study Program, University of Hawaii, 1985), pp. 88–111.

19. Edwin S. Shneidman, *Deaths of Man* (New York: Quadrangle Books, 1973), pp. 81–90.

20. National Center for Health Statistics, *Health, United States, 1984* (Washington: Government Printing Office, 1984), p. 74.

21. William C. Fish and Edith Waldhart-Letzel, "Suicide and Children," *Death Education* 5 (1981): 216.

22. Michael Peck, "Youth Suicide," *Death Education* 6 (1982): 29–32.

23. Peck says, "The data indicate that youth suicide is primarily a phenomenon associated with postpuberty," thus there may be a correlation between the onset of puberty at younger ages and the fact that suicide attempts and completions are also occurring at increasingly younger ages.

24. Introductions to the literature on adolescent suicide include John G. Fuller, *Are the Kids All Right? The Rock Generation and Its Hidden Death Wish* (New York: Times Books, 1981); Peter Giovacchini, *The Urge to Die: Why Young People Commit Suicide* (New York: Macmillan, 1981); Francine Klagsbrun, *Too Young to Die: Youth and Suicide* (New York: Pocket Books, 1977); Joan Polly, *Preventing Teenage Suicide: The Living Alternative Handbook* (New York: Human Sciences Press, 1985); and Brenda Rabkin, *Growing Up Dead* (Nashville: Abingdon, 1978). A useful book for adolescents is Sol Gordon, *When Living Hurts* (New York: Union of American Hebrew Congregations, 1985).

25. L. Bender and P. Schilder, "Suicidal Preoccupations and Attempts in Children," *American Journal of Orthopsychiatry* 7 (1937): 225–234.

26. Richard H. Seiden and Raymond P. Freitas, "Shifting Patterns of Deadly Violence," *Suicide and Life-Threatening Behavior* 10:4 (Winter 1980): 209. Seiden and Freitas believe that "something serious is happening to young people, specifically a double-barrelled epidemic increase of violent death." They add, "It is a pernicious omen which severely challenges our values of the good life and a secure future for our children."

27. Cynthia R. Pfeffer, "Self-Destructive Behavior in Children and Adolescents," *Psychiatric Clinics of North America* 8:2 (June 1985): 215–226.

28. Peck, "Youth Suicide," p. 33–36.

29. Fish and Waldhart-Letzel, "Suicide and Children," p. 216.

30. Peck, "Youth Suicide," pp. 42–46.

31. Josefina Jayme Card, "Lethality of Suicidal Methods and Suicide Risk: Two Distinct Concepts," in *Omega* 5:1 (1974): 37–45.

32. This is probably the most commonly stated estimate. Other estimates, however, place the ratio of suicide attempts to completions at as much as 100:1 by considering the variety of suicide attempts that are reported as "accidents" or as due to "other" causes.

33. For more information on the observed differences between suicide attempters and suicide completers, see Ronald W. Maris, *Pathways to Suicide: A Survey of Self-Destructive Behaviors* (Baltimore: Johns Hopkins University Press, 1981).

34. Edwin S. Shneidman, "Self-Destruction: Suicide Notes and Tragic Lives," in *Death: Current Perspectives,* 2nd ed., p. 467.

35. Estimates range from about 15 percent to 30 percent. For more detailed studies of suicide notes, a useful reference is Edwin S. Shneidman, "A Bibliography of Suicide Notes: 1856–1979," in *Suicide and Life-Threatening Behavior* 9:1 (Spring 1979): 57–59.

36. Edwin S. Shneidman, "Self-Destruction: Suicide Notes and Tragic Lives," in *Death: Current Perspectives,* 2nd ed., p. 471.

37. Ralph Beer, "Holding to the Land: A Rancher's Sorrow," *Harper's* (September 1985), p. 62.

38. One of the earliest listings of "Facts and Fables About Suicide" was prepared at the Los Angeles Suicide Prevention Center in the early 1960s. Further information can be found in Alex D. Pokorny, "Myths About Suicide," in *Death and Dying: Challenge*

and Change, edited by Robert Fulton et al. (Reading, Mass.: Addison-Wesley, 1978), pp. 340–346.

39. This tendency in American society is discussed by Jack D. Douglas in *The Social Meanings of Suicide* (Princeton, N.J.: Princeton University Press, 1967), pp. 324ff.

C H A P T E R *14*

1. As Stephen J. Vicchio points out (in a personal communication), death might be seen as the "meaning" of the present life. In this extreme view, the *reason* for the present life is some other state of existence. This view contains a logical fallacy because it fails to address the question of the meaning of *this* life.

2. Bertrand Russell, *Unpopular Essays* (New York: Simon & Schuster, 1950), p. 141.

3. Chapter 2, "The Problem of Immortality," in Jacques Choron, *Death and Modern Man* (New York: Collier Books, 1964), gives some anecdotal examples of different responses — not all of them favorable — to the prospect of immortality.

4. Mary Kawena Pukui, E. W. Haertig, and Catherine A. Lee, *Nana I Ke Kumu (Look to the Source),* vols. 1 and 2 (Honolulu: Hui Hanai; Queen Lili'uokalani Children's Center, 1972). See also E. S. Craighill Handy and Mary Kawena Pukui, *The Polynesian Family System in Ka-'u, Hawai'i* (Rutland, Vt.: Charles E. Tuttle, 1972).

5. Job 7:9, *The Jerusalem Bible.* Compare this with Job 14:7–12.

6. Daniel 12:2, *The Jerusalem Bible.* There is a parallel development in the use of the Hebrew word *She'ol,* generally defined as the underworld of the dead, a shadowy realm of disembodied souls. *She'ol* is referred to in I Samuel 28:3–25, which gives an account of necromancy. The spirit of the dead prophet Samuel is summoned up from *She'ol* by the witch of En-dor at King Saul's request. Asked by Saul to describe what she sees, the witch of En-dor replies, "I see a ghost [*elohim* = superhuman being] rising up from the earth (*She'ol*)." As the Hebraic concepts were further refined, *She'ol* was divided into two distinct realms: *Gehinom* (hell) and *Pardes* (heaven or paradise). This development is discussed by Lou H. Silberman in "Death in the Hebrew Bible and Apocalyptic Literature," in *Perspectives on Death,* edited by L. O. Mills (Nashville: Abingdon Press, 1969), pp. 13–32.

7. Stephen J. Vicchio, "Against Raising Hope of Raising the Dead: Contra Moody and Kübler-Ross," in *Essence: Issues in the Study of Ageing, Dying and Death* 3:2 1979): 63.

8. Quoted in Lou H. Silberman, "Death in the Hebrew Bible and Apocalyptic Literature," p. 18; from H. Wheeler Robinson, "Hebrew Psychology," in *The People and the Book,* edited by Arthur S. Peake (London: Oxford University Press, 1925), pp. 353–382.

9. See, for example, *The Apology of Socrates,* translated by Benjamin Jowett, *The Harvard Classics,* vol. 2, edited by Charles W. Elliot (New York: P. F. Collier & Son, 1937), pp. 28ff.

10. This position is stated by Vicchio, "Against Raising Hope of Raising the Dead," p. 64. Plato's arguments for the immortality of the soul and the dissolution of the body are presented in the *Phaedo,* translated by Benjamin Jowett, *The Harvard Classics,* vol. 2, edited by Charles W. Elliot, pp. 45–113.

11. *The Meditations of Marcus Aurelius,* translated by George Long, *The Harvard Classics,* vol. 2, edited by Charles W. Elliot, pp. 193–301; see especially section II, 5 and 11, pp. 201–202.

12. Compare Genesis 3:6 and Romans 5:12–15. The Apostle Paul writes: "If it is certain that death reigned over everyone as the consequence of one man's fall, it is even more certain that one man, Jesus Christ, will cause everyone to reign in life who receives the free gift that he does not deserve, of being made righteous" (Romans 5:17, *The Jerusalem Bible*).

13. Ninian Smart, "Death in the Judaeo-Christian Tradition," in Arnold Toynbee et al., *Man's Concern with Death* (New York: McGraw-Hill, 1968), p. 117.

14. Milton McC. Gatch, *Death: Meaning and Mortality in Christian Thought and Contemporary Culture* (New York: Seabury Press, 1969), p. 48.

15. Ibid., p. 78.

16. Vicchio, "Against Raising Hope of Raising the Dead," p. 62. Historian David Stannard's research into the origins and effects of such changing views in early American history reveals the extent to which such conceptual developments can alter people's lives. See, for example, David E. Stannard, *The Puritan Way of Death: A Study in Religion, Culture, and Social Change* (New York: Oxford University Press, 1977); see also David E. Stannard, "Calm Dwellings: The Brief, Sentimental Age of the Rural Cemetery," in *American Heritage* 30:5 (August–September 1979): 42–45; and David E. Stannard, editor, *Death in America* (Philadelphia: University of Pennsylvania Press, 1975). See also Gordon E. Geddes, *Welcome Joy: Death in Puritan New England* (Ann Arbor, Mich.: UMI Research Press, 1981).

17. Renee Haynes has written that persons brought up in the oldest traditional form of Christianity "will have learned to consider two things from which many of their contemporaries have been conditioned to turn away: the fact of mystery and the fact of death." See Renee Haynes, "Some Christian Imagery," in *Life After Death*, edited by Arnold Toynbee et al. (New York: McGraw-Hill, 1976), pp. 132ff.

18. Arnold Toynbee points out that the notion of reembodiment of the dead is still doctrine in most of the world's religions, including Zorastrianism, Judaism, Christianity, Islam, Hinduism, and Buddhism. The first four teach the pattern of immortality that has been outlined in the text; Hinduism and Buddhism teach that reembodiment occurs innumerable times—until the "karma account" is cleared (Buddhism), or for the duration of the current epochal cycle (Hinduism); see Toynbee, "Man's Concern with Life After Death," in *Life After Death*, p. 29. However, the dogmas cited by Toynbee are not adhered to by all the practitioners in these religious traditions.

19. Some of the Eastern teachings concerning reincarnation describe a process whereby certain "tendencies" or "karmic seeds" continue on, to determine the next state of being. In the constant arising and passing away of experience, something is carried over from one state to the next, but this "something" is impersonal and is essentially formless and ineffable.

20. *Bhagavad-Gita* II.27. An alternative rendering of this passage is provided by Swami Nikhilananda: "For to that which is born, death is certain, and to that which is dead, birth is certain. Therefore you should not grieve over the unavoidable." In his commentary, Nikhilananda adds, "It is not proper to grieve for beings, which are mere combinations of cause and effect." See *The Bhagavad-Gita*, translated by Swami Nikhilananda (New York: Ramakrishna-Vivekananda Center, 1952), p. 79.

21. Huston Smith, *The Religions of Man* (New York: New American Library/Mentor, 1958), p. 34.

22. *Bhagavad-Gita* II.22. Swami Nikhilananda's translation states: "Even as a person casts off worn-out clothes and puts on others that are new, so the embodied Self

casts off worn-out bodies and enters into others that are new." In his commentary, Nikhilananda explicates this process: "In the act of giving up the old body or entering into the new body, the real Self does not undergo any change whatsoever. According to Vedānta, Brahman, through Its inscrutable māyā, creates a body, identifies Itself with it, and regards Itself as an individual, or embodied, soul" (*Bhagavad-Gita,* p. 77).

23. J. Bruce Long, "Death as a Necessity and a Gift in Hindu Mythology," in *Religious Encounters with Death,* edited by Frank E. Reynolds and Earl H. Waugh (State College, Pa.: Pennsylvania State University Press, 1977), p. 92; see also pp. 73–96.

24. This theme is explored by David R. Kinsley in "The 'Death that Conquers Death': Dying to the World in Medieval Hinduism," ibid., pp. 97–108. Kinsley's paper expands on the following ideas: "To die to the world while living is to win spiritual rebirth [p. 97] . . . . To die while living is to be unattached to a world of matter that inexorably leads to physical decay and death, to stand aloof and free whether one acts or does not act [p. 99] . . . . To think about death, particularly one's own death, makes one 'alert' . . . to the presence of God [p. 105] . . . To anticipate death, furthermore, is to imaginatively die to the world, to be provoked to discern a world or a way that is not grounded in one's own ego-centered being. And to die to the world is to be reborn within a new possibility, a new frame of reference, a new cosmos, to have transcended the 'old man' . . . . [It] is to be redeemed from the habitual clinging to self that encapsules man in a world of limited possibilities, all of which inevitably involve pain" (pp. 105–106).

25. Dōgen, "The Meaning of Practice-Enlightenment (Shushō-gi)," in Yūhō Yokoi, *Zen Master Dōgen: An Introduction with Selected Writings* (New York/Tokyo: Weatherhill, 1976), p. 58.

26. Philip Kapleau, *Zen: Dawn in the West* (Garden City, N.Y.: Anchor Press/ Doubleday, 1979), p. 296.

27. The Buddha's doctrine of *anatta* (no soul) developed in response to the dualistic teachings common to the Hinduism of his time, which view the self as retaining its separateness throughout eternity. See Smith, *The Religions of Man,* p. 122.

28. Dōgen, "Awakening to the Bodhi-Mind (Hotsu Bodai-shin)," from the Shōbō-Genzō, in *Zen Master Dōgen: An Introduction with Selected Writings,* p. 109.

29. These analogies of transmigration and the quotation are from Kapleau, *Zen: Dawn in the West,* pp. 67–68. Kapleau adds: "Rebirth arises from two causes: the last thought of the previous life as its governing principle and the actions of the previous life as its basis. The stopping of the last thought is known as decease; the appearance of the first thought as rebirth" (p. 68).

30. Dōgen, "The Meaning of Practice-Englightenment (Shushō-gi)," p. 58.

31. From *The Zen Master Hakuin: Selected Writings,* translated by Philip B. Yampolsky (New York: Columbia University Press, 1971), p. 219.

32. W. Y. Evans-Wentz, *The Tibetan Book of the Dead: or, the After-Death Experiences on the Bardo Plane, According to Lama Kazi Dawa-Samdup's English Rendering* (New York: Oxford University Press, 1960), p. xviii.

33. Ibid., p. 29.

34. Evans-Wentz notes that *bardo* literally means "between two" and thus refers to an intermediate or transitional state (p. 28); more particularly, it refers to the "phenomenal existence intervening between birth and death" (p. 2). Chögyam Trungpa suggests that *bardo* refers not only to the interval after death, but also to "suspension within the living situation." He says that the *Bardo Thödol* might well be titled "The Tibetan Book of Birth" or the "Book of Space," since the text refers to the space that

contains birth and death. See Francesca Fremantle and Chögyam Trungpa, editors, *The Tibetan Book of the Dead: The Great Liberation Through Hearing in the Bardo, by Guru Rinpoche According to Karma Lingpa* (Boulder, Colo.: Shambhala, 1975), p. 1.

35. Alternative renderings of this portion of the *Bardo Thödol* text can be found in Evans-Wentz, p. 32, and Fremantle and Trungpa, *The Tibetan Book of the Dead,* p. 41.

36. Fremantle and Trungpa, *The Tibetan Book of the Dead,* p. 1.

37. Kapleau, *Zen: Dawn in the West,* p. 69. The crucial period is the first forty-nine days following death. Services may be held every day for the first seven days, then once a week thereafter for the remainder of the seven-week period. After that, similar rites are extended into the third year, the seventh year, the thirteenth, and so on, up to fifty years.

38. While some of the persons in the following studies experienced what is termed clinical death — a temporary cessation of vital, life-sustaining bodily functions — most of the data are based on accounts from persons "on the brink of death" or "near death." Thus, a more inclusive term, "near-death experiences" or "NDEs," will be used.

The summary of NDEs described here has been drawn from a number of published studies, of which two are particularly worth noting: (1) The Connecticut study, reported by Kenneth Ring, *Life at Death: A Scientific Investigation of the Near-Death Experience* (New York: Coward, McCann, and Geoghegan, 1980), pp. 27–38, consisted of a research sample of 102 respondents. Of the 102 persons, there were a total of 104 near-death experiences, related to the following circumstances: 52 NDEs related to serious illness, 26 NDEs related to serious accident, 24 NDEs related to suicide attempt. (2) A cross-cultural study by Karlis Osis and Erlendur Haraldsson of 877 cases, about evenly divided between persons in the United States and in India. Most were terminally ill, although 163 were patients who recovered from near-death conditions. See Osis and Haraldsson, "Deathbed Observations of Physicians and Nurses: A Cross-Cultural Survey," in *The Signet Handbook of Parapsychology,* edited by Martin Ebon (New York: Signet/NAL, 1978), which deals primarily with the data from 471 cases in which human figures were experienced as part of the NDEs of terminal patients.

39. Ring, *Life at Death,* pp. 157–158. Nearly all the respondents said that their NDE was a "potent antidote to the fear of death" (p. 178).

40. Ibid., pp. 39–66.

41. Ibid., pp. 114ff. In Ring's study, NDEs related to suicide attempts presented a departure from NDEs related to accident or illness. Of the suicide attempters, none experienced phenomena associated with the later stages of the core experience. Ring says they seemed to "fade out" prior to the transcendent elements of the core experience, with the NDE tending to end in a dark, murky void or "twilight zone."

42. Vicchio, "Against Raising Hope of Raising the Dead," pp. 51–67.

43. An excellent introduction to the literature and major points of view about NDEs is available in Stephen J. Vicchio's review article, "Near-Death Experiences: A Critical Review of the Literature and Some Questions for Further Study," in *Essence: Issues in the Study of Ageing, Dying and Death* 5:1 (1981): 77–89. Also see James E. Alcock, "Psychology and Near-Death Experiences," in *The Skeptical Inquirer* 3:3 (Spring 1979): 25–41; Michael B. Sabom, *Recollections of Death: A Medical Investigation* (New York: Harper & Row, 1981); and Stephen J. Vicchio, "Near-Death Experiences: Some Logical Problems and Questions for Further Study," in *Anabiosis: The Journal of the International Association for Near-Death Studies* (1981): 66–87. In considering the data on NDEs, the methods of analysis described in the following sources can provide a basis for distinguishing pseudo-experimental from true research designs and for testing the assumptions of various hypotheses: Ronald N. Giere, *Understanding Scientific Reasoning*

(New York: Holt, Rinehart and Winston, 1979); and Schuyler W. Huck, William H. Cormier, and William G. Bounds, Jr., *Reading Statistics and Research* (New York: Harper & Row, 1974).

44. Information about Hawaiian beliefs concerning afterlife can be found in Handy and Pukui, *The Polynesian Family System in Ka-'u, Hawai'i;* Donald D. Kilolani Mitchell, *Resource Units in Hawaiian Culture* (Honolulu: Kamehameha Schools Press, 1982); and Pukui et al., *Nana I Ke Kumu (Look to the Source),* vols. 1 and 2.

45. See Roy Kletti and Russell Noyes, Jr., "Mental States in Mortal Danger," which includes a translation of Oskar Pfister's 1930 paper commenting on Heim's observations, in *Essence: Issues in the Study of Ageing, Dying and Death* 5:1 (1981): 5−20. The history of research into near-death experiences is also traced in Chapter 7, "Consciousness and the Threshold of Death," in Stanislav Grof and Joan Halifax, *The Human Encounter with Death* (New York: E. P. Dutton, 1978), pp. 131−157.

46. Russell Noyes, Jr., "Near-Death Experiences: Their Interpretation and Significance," in *Between Life and Death,* edited by Robert Kastenbaum (New York: Springer, 1979), pp. 73−78. Also see Russell Noyes, Jr., "Dying and Mystical Consciousness," *Journal of Thanatology* 1 (1971): 25−41; Russell Noyes, Jr., "The Encounter with Life-Threatening Danger: Its Nature and Impact," *Essence: Issues in the Study of Ageing, Dying and Death* 5:1 (1981): 21−32; Russell Noyes, Jr., and Roy Kletti, "Depersonalization in the Face of Life-Threatening Danger: An Interpretation," *Omega* 7 (1976): 103−114; Russell Noyes, Jr., and Roy Kletti, "Panoramic Memory: A Response to the Threat of Death," *Omega* 8 (1977): 181−194.

47. Kenneth Ring, *Heading Toward Omega: In Search of the Meaning of the Near-Death Experience* (New York: William Morrow, 1984). An organization devoted to this study is the International Association for Near-Death Studies at the University of Connecticut.

48. Ian Stevenson, *Cases of the Reincarnation Type,* vol. 1, *Ten Cases in India* (Charlottesville: University Press of Virginia, 1975). Vol. 2 (detailing cases in Southeast Asia) and vol. 3 (cases in Lebanon and Turkey) have also been published. A volume on cases in America is planned.

49. George Gallup, Jr., *Adventures in Immortality* (New York: McGraw-Hill, 1982), pp. 1−3, 183, 197. Females were slightly more affirmative in their responses, with 72 percent answering yes, compared to 61 percent for men, for a combined affirmative response of 67 percent.

50. Ian Currie, *You Cannot Die: The Incredible Findings of a Century of Research on Death* (New York: Methuen, 1978).

51. Joseph Head and S. L. Cranston, editors, *Reincarnation: The Phoenix Fire Mystery* (New York: Julian Press/Crown, 1977).

52. For reports on the work of Osis and Haraldsson, see Karlis Osis and Erlendur Haraldsson, *At the Hour of Death* (New York: Avon Books, 1977), and, by the same authors, "Deathbed Observations of Physicians and Nurses," in *The Signet Handbook of Parapsychology,* edited by M. Ebon.

53. Osis and Haraldsson, *At the Hour of Death,* p. 3. This interpretation of NDEs is also expressed by Raymond A. Moody, Jr., in the reports of his research: *Life After Life,* and its sequel, *Reflections on Life After Life* (various editions). Elisabeth Kübler-Ross also expresses this view in "Death Does Not Exist," *CoEvolution Quarterly* 14 (Summer 1977): 100−107.

54. Osis and Haraldsson, "Deathbed Observations of Physicians and Nurses," pp. 287−288.

55. Vicchio, "Near-Death Experiences: A Critical Review of the Literature and Some Questions for Further Study," p. 80.

56. The presentation of the contrasts between the two models for explaining NDEs expands on a brief analysis given by Osis and Haraldsson in "Deathbed Observations of Physicians and Nurses," pp. 288–289.

57. Ibid.

58. Charles A. Garfield says that such experiences should not be summarily dismissed as hallucinatory. On the contrary, "If the varous Eastern and Western religious traditions and parapsychological disciplines are correct, the period just before physical death is one of maximum receptivity to altered state realities." See Charles A. Garfield, "The Dying Patient's Concern with 'Life After Death,'" in *Between Life and Death*, edited by R. Kastenbaum, pp. 52–53.

59. Robert Kastenbaum, "Happily Ever After," in *Between Life and Death*, p. 17.

60. Ibid., p. 25.

61. Garfield, "Dying Patient's Concern with 'Life After Death,'" pp. 55–57.

62. Ibid., p. 56.

63. The early studies of LSD are reported in the following sources: Stanislav Grof, *LSD Psychotherapy* (Pomona, Calif.: Hunter House, 1980), pp. 252ff; Grof and Halifax, *The Human Encounter with Death*, pp. 16ff; Peter Stafford, *Psychedelics Encyclopedia* (Berkeley, Calif.: And/Or Press, 1977), pp. 23–39.

64. Pain is a composite phenomenon that has a neurophysiological component (the pain sensation) and a psychological component (the pain affect). Grof and Halifax note that "it seems that psychedelic therapy influences the pain experience primarily by modifying the psychological component . . . rather than by obliterating or reducing the neuronal impulses responsible for the painful sensation" (*The Human Encounter with Death*, pp. 120–121).

65. Ibid., p. 127. "As a result of such experiences," Grof and Halifax observe, "the individual ceases to be concerned about his or her own physical demise and begins to see it as a natural phenomenon of the cycling of the life force. This acceptance drastically alters a person's life-style; the individual no longer reacts with panic, fear, pain, and dependency to the changes that are occurring" (p. 18).

66. Stanislav Grof's research with LSD began in the early 1960s at the Psychiatric Research Institute in Prague, Czechoslovakia, where he headed a team investigating the potential of LSD for personality diagnostics and psychotherapy with psychiatric patients. Grof subsequently accepted a post at the Maryland Psychiatric Research Center, where additional studies of LSD-assisted psychotherapy were conducted with dying patients as well as with patients diagnosed with alcoholism. In all these instances, the encounter with mortality through the LSD experience achieved quite dramatic results.

67. Stanislav Grof and Christina Grof, *Beyond Death: The Gates of Consciousness* (New York: Thames and Hudson, 1980), p. 24.

68. Some evidence suggests that LSD may function by interfering with the transfer of oxygen on the enzymatic level. Anoxia, or diminished levels of oxygen in the bodily tissues, is also frequently found with dying patients as well as in conjunction with certain yogic techniques involving breath control. Thus, the chemical changes caused by anoxia in all these instances may somehow activate certain transpersonal matrices in the unconscious, giving rise to the experiences associated with NDEs, certain yogic states, and LSD sessions. For a discussion of this, see Grof and Halifax, *Human Encounter with Death*, pp. 183ff.

69. Stanislav Grof, *Realms of the Human Unconscious: Observations from LSD Research* (New York: E. P. Dutton, 1976), p. 19. Grof says that an analysis of the LSD data "strongly indicates that this substance is an unspecific amplifier of mental processes that brings to the surface various elements from the depth of the unconscious" (p. 6).

70. Ibid., p. 95. Certain transpersonal experiences during LSD sessions involve intuitive insights into "the process of creation of the phenomenal world as we know it and into the Buddhist concept of the wheel of death and rebirth. These can result in a temporary or enduring feeling that the individual has achieved a global, nonrational, and transrational understanding of the basic ontological and cosmological problems that beset existence" (p. 204).

71. Grof, *LSD Psychotherapy*, p. 72.

72. Stanislav Grof and Joan Halifax, "Psychedelics and the Experience of Dying," in *Life After Death,* edited by A. Toynbee et al., pp. 192–193. They add: "Psychedelic drugs have made it possible to study the deep parallels and unusual interrelations among actual near-death and death experiences, maps of the postmortem journey developed by various cultures, psychological events occurring in rites of passage, temple mysteries, and other rituals focusing on death and rebirth, drug-induced states, and other instances of altered states of consciousness." Similar experiences are reported in connection with sensory overload and sensory deprivation, sleep deprivation, fasting, hypnosis, chanting and rhythmic dancing, and various meditative techniques. It would seem from the evidence that "the human unconscious contains matrices for a wide variety of experiences that constitute the basic elements of the spiritual journey of the dying."

73. Grof and Halifax report that this effect seems to occur "whether such an encounter happens in reality, as in dangerous accidents and in those instances that involve survival of actual clinical death, or in a purely subjective fashion, as exemplified by death-rebirth experiences in psychedelic sessions and spontaneous mystical experiences" (*Human Encounter with Death,* p. 190).

74. Grof, *LSD Psychotherapy*, p. 253.

75. Ibid., p. 282.

76. For empirical and theoretical discussions of an expanded model of human consciousness, the following sources are recommended: Seymour Boorstein, editor, *Transpersonal Psychology* (Palo Alto, Calif.: Science and Behavior Books, 1980); Abraham H. Maslow, *The Farther Reaches of Human Nature* (New York: Viking Penguin, 1971); Robert E. Ornstein, editor, *The Nature of Human Consciousness: A Book of Readings* (San Francisco: W. H. Freeman, 1973); Kenneth R. Pelletier and Charles A. Garfield, *Consciousness: East and West* (New York: Harper & Row, 1976); Charles T. Tart, editor, *Transpersonal Psychologies* (New York: Harper & Row, 1975); Roger N. Walsh and Frances Vaughan, editors, *Beyond Ego: Transpersonal Dimensions in Psychology* (Los Angeles: J. P. Tarcher, 1980).

77. Grof, *LSD Psychotherapy*, p. 294.

78. Clyde M. Nabe, " 'Seeing As': Death as Door or Wall," in *Priorities in Death Education and Counseling,* edited by Richard A. Pacholski and Charles A. Corr (Arlington, Va.: Forum for Death Education and Counseling, 1982), pp. 161–169. The metaphorical presentation of death as door or wall has been credited by Nabe and others to Herman Feifel; see *The Meaning of Death,* edited by Herman Feifel (New York: McGraw-Hill, 1959), p. xii.

79. Ibid., p. 169.

80. Ibid.

CHAPTER 15

1. Stephen P. Grant, "Death Education for Police Officers," unpublished paper, March 1985.

2. For most of America's 200-year history, mass death from warfare or disaster has not occurred on American soil. This is not to say that death from such catastrophes as war has not touched the lives of many Americans; but war has often been thought of as something that happens "over there," not "here at home." A notable exception, perhaps, was the Civil War. Still, in many countries, the consequences of warfare have been recent and immediate in national experience.

3. Some researchers forecast that, if present trends continue unabated, by the year 2020 the planet will have become poisoned by environmental pollutants: other predictions are more optimistic. Consequently, many people feel frustrated at conflicting reports of the hazard. This frustration is often compounded by uncertainty about whether government agencies and private industry are telling the whole story.

4. J. Eugene Knott and Richard W. Prull, "Death Education: Accountable to Whom? For What?," *Omega* 7:2(1976): 178.

5. Robert Fulton, "Unanticipated Grief," paper presented at the Annual Meeting of the Forum for Death Education and Counseling, Philadelphia, April 12, 1985.

6. For discussion of this issue, see Sally Gadow, "Caring for the Dying: Advocacy or Paternalism," *Death Education* 3(1980): 387–398.

7. Ron Crocombe, *The South Pacific: An Introduction* (Auckland, New Zealand: Longman Paul Ltd., 1983), p. 73.

8. This lack is due partly to a persistent public attitude that maintains that coping with grief — regardless of circumstances — should not require outside intervention. One result is that some health insurance providers refuse to reimburse their policyholders for therapy or counseling related to bereavement.

9. Damon Knight, "Masks," in *A Pocketful of Stars,* edited by Damon Knight (New York: Doubleday, 1971).

10. Clifford Simak, "Death Scene," in *The Worlds of Clifford Simak* (New York: Simon & Schuster, 1960). Robert A. Heinlein, "Life-Line," in *The Man Who Sold the Moon; Harriman and the Escape from the Earth to the Moon!,* edited by Robert A. Heinlein (New York: Shasta Publications, 1950).

11. Kit Reed, "Golden Acres," in *Social Problems Through Science Fiction,* edited by John W. Miestead et al. (New York: St. Martin's, 1975).

12. Avery Weisman, *On Dying and Denying: A Psychiatric Study of Terminality* (New York: Behavioral Publications, 1972), pp. 39–40.

13. Ibid.

14. This account of Lindbergh's death draws on a description given by Dr. Milton H. Howell, one of Lindbergh's physicians, recorded in Ernest H. Rosenbaum, "The Doctor and the Cancer Patient," in *A Hospice Handbook,* edited by Michael P. Hamilton and Helen F. Reid (Grand Rapids, Mich.: Wm. B. Eerdmans, 1980), pp. 19–43.

Name Index

Abells, Chana Byars, 255
Abelman, Robert, 499
Abolafia, Yossi, 521
Abraham, 441
Abrahamson, Hans, 501
Abramovitch, Henry, 71
Adam, 46, 448
Adams, William C., 532
Adlerstein, Arthur M., 78, 504
Agee, James, 494
Aguilar, Ignacio, 502
Aisenberg, Ruth, 371,
     382–383, 384, 504, 528, 529
Alcock, James E., 540
Alderman, David, 507
Alexander the Great, 416
Alexander, Irving E., 78, 504
Allen, Nancy H., 401
Allo, Clifford D., 363
Altman, Dennis, 509
Alvarez, A., 411, 437, 535
Amoss, Pamela T., 296
Anbar, Michael, 39
Anderson, Sherwood, 245
Annas, George J., 363
Anthony, Sylvia, 78, 107, 504, 520
Antoninus, Marcus Aurelius, 446,
     537
Aquinas, Thomas, 449
Arehart-Treichel, Joan, 497
Ariès, Philippe, 58, 62, 65, 70, 71,
     503, 515
Arlen, Michael, 23, 499
Armstrong, Janice Gray, 39

Arney, William Ray, 136
Aronson, Miriam K., 524
Ashford, Marguerite K., 500
Ashley, Paul P., 344, 355, 359, 363,
     528
Ayers, Bill, 500

Baby Doe, 314–315, 525
Baby Fae, 315–316, 525
Bach, Alice, 255
Badham, Linda, 470
Badham, Paul, 470
Baechler, Jean, 406
Bagdikian, Ben H., 513, 515
Ball, Justine F., 523
Barinbaum, Lea, 518
Baring-Gould, C., 505
Baring-Gould, W. S., 505
Barlach, Ernst, 30
Barr, Robert D., 481
Barton, David, 113, 136
Baruch, Joel, 531
Bashō, 452
Bassui, 456
Bataille, Georges, 503
Battin, Margaret Pabst, 437
Bauer, Marion Dane, 255
Baulch, Evelyn M., 510
Beaton, Janet I., 331
Beauchamp, Tom L., 331
Beauvoir, Simone de, 494
Becker, Ernest, 494
Beer, Ralph, 536
Beethoven, Ludwig van, 32, 264

Belth, Joseph M., 363
Bender, L., 536
Benoliel, Jeanne Quint, 121, 136
Benson, Elizabeth P., 71
Benson, Herbert, 534
Bergen, Bernard J., 136
Bergman, Abraham B., 275
Bergmann, Thesi, 276, 520, 522
Bergner, Lawrence, 511
Berlioz, Hector, 30
Berman, Daniel, M., 528
Bernstein, Barton E., 343–344, 527
Bernstein, Joanne E., 255
Bernstein, Leonard, 500
Bierbrier, Morris, 513
Blauner, Robert, 506
Blegvad, Erik, 257
Bloch, Maurice, 71
Bluebond-Langner, Myra,
     237–238, 259, 275, 277, 519,
     522
Boardman, John, 503
Boase, T. S. R., 503
Bonica, John J., 509
Boorstein, Seymour, 543
Boraiko, Allen A., 529
Borg, Susan, 521
Bosch, Hieronymous, 459
Boswell, James, 462
Bounds, William G., Jr., 541
Bouvia, Elizabeth, 311
Bowers, Margaretta K., 507
Bowlby, John, 259, 504, 517
Bowman, LeRoy, 180–181, 513

Bowman, Pierre, 118
Bowmer, Leon F., 293
Bradbury, Elizabeth, 147, 312, 506
Brahms, Johannes, 32
Brand, Stewart, 132
Brandes, Stanley, 296
Brandon, S. G. F., 470
Brenner, Charles, 534
Brent, Sandor W., 504
Bresler, David E., 512
Brewster, H. H., 516
Brice, Charles W., 521
Brim, Orville G., Jr., 136
Brimigion, Jeanne, 508
Brock, Timothy C., 518
Brodman, Barbara, 502
Brody, Jane, 520
Brown, Michael S., 401
Brown, Norman O., 494
Brown, Peter, 71
Brown, R. J., 516
Brown, Robert D., Jr., 529
Brown, Robert N., 363
Browne, Colette, 296
Browne, Jackson, 32
Bruhns, John, 401
Bryer, Kathleen B., 37, 501
Buchholz, William M., 115–116, 507
Buckingham, Robert W., 510
Buddha, Siddhartha Gautama, 453, 455, 539
Bugen, Larry A., 225, 500, 516
Bunting, Eve, 255
Burciaga, Jose Antonio, 502
Burns, Robert C., 520
Burnside, John, 331
Buscaglia, Leo, 255

Cain, Albert C., 437
Caine, Lynn, 285
Cairns, John, 511
Calder, Bobby J., 513, 514
Caldicott, Helen M., 533
Campbell, Joseph, 501
Cannon, Walter, 396
Caplan, Gerald, 209
Capron, Alexander M., 327, 331, 526
Caputo, Philip, 387, 499
Card, Josefina Jayme, 536
Carey, Mary, 255
Carr, Arthur C., 167, 217, 517, 518
Carrick, Carol, 242, 255
Carrick, Donald, 242, 255
Carroll, David, 167
Carruthers, Malcolm, 533
Carse, James P., 470
Carson, Ute, 520
Cassell, Eric, 507, 525

Cedering, Siv, 476
Chase, Deborah, 136
Chatterton, Thomas, 421
Cherry, Laurence, 533
Choron, Jacques, 437, 470, 501, 503, 537
Church, June S., 518
Clancy, John, 510
Clayton, Paula J., 516, 523
Cleveland, Alan P., 522
Clifton, Lucile, 521
Coburn, John B., 255
Coerr, Eleanor, 255
Cohen, Miriam, 255
Combs, Diana Williams, 503
Combs, James E., 39
Cook, Captain James, 442
Cooper, Jilly, 230
Cooperband, Adele, 523
Corley, Elizabeth, 255
Cormier, William H., 541
Corr, Charles A., 107, 136, 255, 259, 494, 510
Corr, Donna M., 136, 510
Cousins, Norman, 135, 136, 167, 480
Cox, Harold, 515
Crane, Diana, 136
Crane, Hart, 417
Cranston, Sylvia, 470, 541
Crapo, Lawrence M., 289
Crawford, Mary Caroline, 515
Crocombe, Ron, 484, 544
Cummings, E. E., 27
Cummings, Richard O., 511
Cunningham, James H., 522
Curl, James Stevens, 71
Curran, William J., 331
Currie, Ian, 541
Cutter, Fred, 437

Danforth, Loring M., 71
Daniel, 443
Dante Alighieri, 447, 449
Danto, Bruce L., 401
Darby, Elisabeth, 71
Davidson, Glen W., 510, 522
Decker, D., 293
Defoe, Daniel, 376
Degner, Leslie F., 331
Del Vecchio, John, 599
Delbo, Charlotte, 27
Deloria, Vine, Jr., 502
DePaola, Tomie, 255
Des Granges, David, 224
Des Pres, Terrence, 401, 499, 518
Descartes, René, 324
Desmond, Helen Ann, 520
Diamond, Donna, 256
Dielman, Frederick, 119

DiLeo, Joseph H., 520
Dōgen, 453, 455, 456, 539
Doka, Kenneth J., 219–220, 269, 500, 518, 522, 528
Donnelly, Elfie, 255
Donovan, Marilee Ivars, 125, 508, 510
Douglas, Jack D., 537
Douglas, Mary, 401
Downing, A. B., 524
Drings, P., 509
Duc, Quang, 415
Duda, Deborah, 510
Durkheim, Emile, 407–410, 534
Dyck, Arthur J., 331
Dyer, Gwynne, 391

Ebert, Roger, 26, 499
Ebon, Martin, 540
Edelhart, Mike, 511
Edgley, Charles, 187, 514
Eichenberg, Fritz, 29, 499
Eisenberg, Mickey S., 511
Eisenhower, Dwight D., 395
Elias, Norbert, 70, 503
Elliot, Gil, 390, 531
Emerson, Ralph Waldo, 354
Engel, George L., 218, 517
Enkidu, 48, 501
Enright, D. J., 39, 264
Epicurus, 445
Epstein, Gerald, 516
Erikson, Erik H., 75, 84–87, 106, 262, 505, 521
Etlin, Richard A., 71
Evans, Richard I., 505
Evans-Wentz, W. Y., 456, 539
Eve, 46
Eyer, Joseph, 534
Ezekiel, 443

Farberow, Norman L., 412, 437, 535
Farley, Carol J., 255
Farrell, James J., 39, 503
Feifel, Herman, 33, 500, 503, 543
Feld, Bernard T., 532
Fine, Judylaine, 167
Finucane, R. C., 470
Fish, William C., 421, 536
Fisher, Arlene, 256
FitzGerald, Susan, 511
Fletcher, Joseph, 308, 524
Fordyce, Wilbert E., 509
Forman, Eileen C., 74, 506
Fornatale, Peter, 500
Fox, Renee C., 145, 331, 525
Frank, Anne, 27
Frank, Jerome, 533
Frankfort, Henri, 512

Frazer, Sir James G., 44, 501
Fredrick, Jerome F., 218, 517
Freedman, Morris, 214
Freeman, Alan D., 363
Freeman, Howard E., 136
Freeman, S. J. J., 508
Freitas, Raymond P., 536
Fremantle, Francesca, 540
Freud, Anna, 276, 520, 522
Freud, Sigmund, 75, 76, 211–212, 407, 410, 516
Friedman, Meyer, 162, 398–399, 512, 533
Friedman, Rochelle, 268, 296
Fries, James F., 289
Fuller, John G., 536
Fulton, Robert L., 34, 36, 180, 181, 202, 219, 482–483, 497, 500, 513, 518, 544
Furman, Erna, 251, 259, 520
Furman, Robert A., 259
Furth, Gregg M., 520

Gallo, Robert, 123
Gallup, George, Jr., 541
Garfield, Charles A., 132, 167, 465, 542, 543
Garrison, Webb, 59
Gaster, Theodor H., 501
Gatch, Milton McC., 448, 538
Geddes, Gordon E., 538
Geis, Gilbert, 180
George, Joan Neet, 14
Gernsbacher, Larry, 437
Gide, André, 264
Giere, Ronald N., 540
Gilgamesh, 48, 501
Giovacchini, Peter, 536
Girion, Barbara, 256
Glaser, Barney G., 34, 167, 274–275, 507, 522
Glaze, Anita J., 501
Glick, Ira O., 516, 523
Goethe, Johann Wolfgang von, 417
Goldberg, Helene, 182, 513
Goldberg, Ivan K., 518
Goldreich, Gloria, 505
Goldstein, Allan L., 517
Gonda, Thomas Andrew, 136
Goody, Jack, 52, 502
Gordon, Audrey K., 107
Gordon, David, 1–3, 495–496
Gordon, Sol, 536
Gorer, Geoffrey, 34, 212–213, 517
Gottfried, Robert S., 71
Gottlieb, Carla, 499
Goya, Francisco José de, 29
Gradstein, Bonnie, 268, 296
Graeber, Charlotte, 256
Grant, Stephen P., 544

Green, Betty R., 503
Green, Morris, 233, 523
Greenblatt, Milton, 532
Grifalconi, Ann, 254
Grinspoon, Lester, 393, 533
Grof, Christina, 470
Grof, Stanislav, 467–468, 470, 541, 542, 543
Grollman, Earl A., 107, 203, 256
Grosser, George H., 532
Grout, Donald J., 499
Gruber, Howard E., 505
Gullo, Stephen V., 107, 255
Gustafson, James M., 314, 525
Gustaitis, Rasa, 331
Gyulay, Jo-Eileen, 259, 521

Habenstein, Robert W., 195, 203
Haertig, E. W., 211, 501, 515, 519, 537
Hakuin, 456, 539
Halifax, Joan, 467, 541, 542, 543
Hall, Mary, 19–20, 498
Hall, Nicholas R., 517
Hallstrom, Alfred P., 511
Hamilton, Michael P., 509
Handy, E. S. Craighill, 501, 515, 537, 541
Haraldsson, Erlendur, 463, 540, 541
Hardt, Dale Vincent, 517
Harmer, Ruth M., 34, 181
Harrell, Stevan, 296
Harris, Murray J., 470
Harron, Frank, 331
Hatton, Corrine Loing, 437
Hauser, Philip M., 497
Haynes, Renee, 536
Head, Joseph, 541
Headley, Lee A., 437
Hegel, Georg Wilhelm Friedrich, 264
Heim, Albert, 461
Heinlein, Robert A., 486, 544
Hellman, John, 499, 531
Hemingway, Ernest, 417
Hemphill, Charles F., Jr., 363
Hendin, Herbert, 437
Hendricks, C. Davis, 292, 524
Hendricks, Jon, 292, 524
Herodotus, 171
Herzog, Alfred, 517
Hesychius of Jerusalem, 64
Hezel, Francis X., 535
Higgins, William G., 366
Highwater, Jamake, 502
Hilgard, Josephine, 509
Himler, Ronald, 255, 256
Hingson, Ralph, 136
Hippocrates, 300, 305, 308
Hoban, Lillian, 255

Hodges, William, 442
Hoffman, Albert, 467
Hoffman, Frederic J., 27–28, 499
Hogan, Bernice, 256
Holbein, Hans, the Younger, 67
Holck, Frederick H., 470
Holden, Constance, 510
Holinger, Paul C., 535
Holmes, Thomas H., 396–398, 400, 533
Homer, 445
Hoopes, Lyn Littlefield, 256
Housman, Laurence, 26
Howell, Milton H., 493, 544
Huck, Schuyler W., 541
Huffman, John L., 498
Huffman, L. A., 40
Huggett, William Turner, 499
Hultkrantz, Åke, 71
Hunefer, 451
Huntington, Richard, 71
Husain, Syed Arshad, 437
Hutschnecker, Arnold A., 162, 512
Huxley, Aldous, 498
Hyman, Herbert H., 523

Imbus, Sharon H., 507
Irion, Paul, 203
Irish, Donald P., 503

Jackson, Edgar N., 107, 177, 202, 203, 221–222, 233, 517, 518
Jackson, Graham, 229
Jaffe, Dennis T., 512
James, Wiliam, 287, 468
Javers, Ron, 534
Jensen, Maxine Dowd, 343
Jesus, 32, 58, 106, 446, 448, 450, 538
Jewell, Nancy, 256
Job, 443
John, Elton, 32
Johnson, James Weldon, 449
Johnson, Joy, 522
Johnson, S. Marvin, 522
Jones, Jim, 409
Jong, Erica, 487
Jonsen, Albert R., 331
Juenker, Donna, 240, 241, 520
Jury, Dan, 296
Jury, Mark, 296

Kalish, Richard A., 182, 513, 518, 519
Kamm, Phyllis, 212, 214–215, 517, 523
Kanahele, George S., 500
Kane, Barbara, 506
Kaplan, Chaim, 27
Kapleau, Philip, 455, 457, 470, 539

Kass, Leon R., 327, 526
Kast, Eric, 466
Kastenbaum, Robert J., 115, 371, 373–374, 382–383, 384, 413, 465, 498, 504, 521, 528, 529
Katō, Shuichi, 535
Katz, Jay, 331
Kaufman, S. Harvard, 520
Kavanaugh, Robert E., 36, 212, 213–214, 517
Kay, William J., 520
Keats, John, 227
Keleman, Stanley, 206, 516
Kelly, Orville E., 164–165, 167, 512
Kelly, Patricia Fernandez, 502
Kelman, Harvey, 256
Kelsey, Morton T., 470
Kennedy, John F., 23, 81, 95, 173, 221, 498, 518, 529
Kennedy, John F., Jr., 81
Kennedy, Robert, 221, 529
Kerr, M. E., 256
Kets de Vries, Manfred F. R., 534
Khan, Princess Yasmin, 290
Kilduff, Marshall, 534
King, Martin Luther, Jr., 23, 221, 529
King, Noel, Q., 502
Kinsley, David R., 539
Kirsch, Charlotte, 363
Klagsbrun, Francine, 536
Klass, Dennis, 107
Klein, Susan D., 331
Kletti, Roy, 461, 462, 541
Kliman, Gilbert, 505
Knapp, Ronald J., 296
Knight, Damon, 486, 544
Knott, J. Eugene, 544
Kockelman, William J., 529
Köllwitz, Kathe, 30, 31, 273, 426
Koocher, Gerald P., 90–93, 505
Kovic, Ron, 499
Kramer, Stanley, 390
Krebs, Ernst T., 160
Krementz, Jill, 256
Krishna, 452
Kübler-Ross, Elisabeth, 34, 112, 122, 124, 146, 226, 480, 485, 494, 506, 511, 515, 541
Kulstad, Ruth, 509
Kung, Hans, 470
Kurtz, Donna C., 503
Kutscher, Austin H., 167, 401, 518

L'Engle, Madeleine, 256
Lack, Sylvia A., 128, 509
LaGrand, Louis E., 296, 521
Lamers, William M., 195, 202, 203
Lamerton, Richard, 309

Lancaster, Matthew, 256
Langer, Lawrence L., 499
Langone, John, 39
Lasaga, Jose I., 534
Lasker, Judith, 521
Lazarus, Richard S., 401
LeBaron, Samuel, 509
Lee, Catherine A., 211, 501, 515, 519, 537
Lee, Jung Young, 470
LeGoff, Jacques, 71
Lennon, John, 23
Leppzer, Robert, 528
LeShan, Eda, 256
LeShan, Lawrence, 114, 163, 512
Levine, Sol, 136
Levine, Stephen, 120, 167, 223, 470
Leviton, Dan, 74, 500, 506
Lewis, C. S., 233
Lewis, Oscar, 210, 502
Lifton, Robert Jay, 33, 39, 389, 393, 401, 531, 532, 533, 535
Lincoln, Abraham, 179, 222
Lindbergh, Charles A., 492–493, 544
Lindemann, Erich, 210, 516
Lindenmann, Jean, 511
Lingeman, Richard R., 7
Lingle, John H., 518
Linzer, Norman, 437
Liszt, Franz, 30
Lonetto, Richard, 107, 242, 276, 505, 519, 522
Long, J. Bruce, 539
Lopata, Helena Z., 523
Lucie-Smith, Edward, 252
Lundsgaarde, Henry P., 378, 379–380, 382, 528, 529
Lurker, Manfred, 512
Lutkins, S. G., 217, 517
Lyall, W. A. L., 508
Lyons, Andrew J., 528

MacDougall, Duncan, 525
Mack, John E., 532
Macken, Bob, 500
Maddison, D., 516
Maeda, Daisaku, 523
Mahler, Gustav, 32
Mandelbaum, David G., 50–51, 502
Manwell, Juana, 48
Marchant, Guy, 503
Marcus, Morton, 166, 490–491
Margolin, Malcolm, 50, 502
Maris, Ronald W., 406, 408, 534, 536
Marks, Amy Seidel, 513, 514

Marshall, Victor W., 265
Martin, Claire, 511
Martin, Steve, 19
Marx, Jean L., 511
Masamba, Jean, 519
Maslow, Abraham H., 521, 543
Maurer, Adah, 77, 504
Mbiti, John S., 71
McAuliffe, Christa, 22
McCarthy, James B., 83, 504
McCormick, Robert, 525
McCullough, Helen Craig, 535
McGee, Marsha, 498
McKee, Embry, 516
McLendon, Gloria H., 256
McLeod, Beverly, 529
McNeil, Joan N., 259
Mead, Margaret, 300, 524
Meehan, Maude, 271, 288, 435
Menninger, Karl, 411, 437
Metcalf, Peter, 71
Meyer-Baer, Kathi, 503
Miles, Miska, 256
Millay, Edna St. Vincent, 254
Miller, Marv, 535
Millot, Bernard, 535
Mills, L. O., 537
Minton, Frank, 174, 513
Mitchell, Donald D. Kilolani, 541
Mitford, Jessica, 34, 181, 513
Mobley, Jane, 256
Moffat, Mary Jane, 39
Monat, Alan, 401
Monroe, Marilyn, 32
Montagnier, Luc, 509
Moody, Raymond A., Jr., 541
Moody, William J., 363
Mooney, Elizabeth C., 279, 296
Mordden, Ethan, 500
Morgan, Ernest, 203
Moss, Ralph W., 511
Mozart, Wolfgang Amadeus, 30
Munch, Edvard, 30
Munger, Nancy, 256
Munley, Anne, 510

Nabe, Clyde M., 321, 322, 469, 470, 525, 543
Nagy, Maria H., 78, 504
Naipaul, Shiva, 534
Neale, Robert E., 516
Neiberg, Herbert, 256
Nelkin, Dorothy, 401
Netzorg, Gordon W., 363
Neuendort, Kimberly, 499
Nikhilananda, Swami, 538
Nimmo, Dan, 39
Norman, Marsha, 26
Noyes, Russell, Jr., 461, 462, 510, 541

O'Brien, Tim, 499
Offer, Daniel, 535
Oken, Donald, 524
Old Chief Joseph, 50
Olson, Eric, 39, 389, 393, 531, 533
Ong, Vickie, 509
Onzuka-Anderson, Roberta, 296
Ornstein, Robert E., 543
Osis, Karlis, 463, 540, 541
Osterweis, Marian, 233, 523

Pacholski, Richard A., 494, 499
Palgi, Phyllis, 71
Palmerston, 264
Palmore, Erdman B., 523
Parker, Dorothy, 428
Parkes, Colin Murray, 218–219, 233, 516, 523
Parnall, Peter, 256
Parsons, Talcott, 134, 510
Patterson, Paul, 107
Pattison, E. Mansell, 167
Paul, 448, 449, 450, 538
Paz, Octavio, 33, 55–56, 500, 502
Peake, Arthur S., 537
Peale, Charles Wilson, 29
Peavy, Linda, 256
Peck, Michael, 422–423, 536
Pecorado, Philip, 255
Pellegrino, Edmund D., 136
Pelletier, Kenneth R., 543
Peretz, David, 167, 518
Perkes, A. Cordell, 505
Perlin, Seymour, 331, 437
Perry, Johathan, 71
Petzel, Sue V., 536
Pfeffer, Cynthia R., 536
Pfister, Oskar, 461, 541
Phillips, Dennis H., 290
Phipson, Joan, 256
Piaget, Jean, 75, 87–88, 90–91, 505
Picht, Randolph, 520
Pierce, Sandra Girton, 125, 508, 510
Pike, Martha V., 39
Pincus, Lily, 233
Pine, Vanderlyn R., 39, 179, 203, 513, 514, 529
Plath, Sylvia, 417, 535
Plato, 446, 537
Pokorny, Alex D., 536
Polly, Joan, 536
Polse, Richard G., 528
Porte, Barbara Ann, 521
Posada, Antonio Guadalupe, 56, 67
Prattes, Ora, 572
Prull, Richard W., 544
Puckle, Bertram, 180

Pukui, Mary Kawena, 211, 461, 501, 515, 519, 537, 541
Pulaski, Mary Ann Spencer, 505
Pythagoras, 445

Quinlan, Karen Ann, 16, 310, 330, 525

Rabkin, Brenda, 536
Radin, Paul, 71
Raether, Howard C., 513
Rahe, Richard H., 396–398, 400, 533
Ramsey, Robert, 409
Rando, Therese A., 136, 233
Raphael, Beverly, 212, 214, 233, 277, 401, 517, 522
Rasmussen, Linda, 216
Rasmussen, Lorna, 216
Reed, Kit, 486, 544
Rees, W. D., 217, 517
Reich, Michael R., 535
Reid, Helen F., 509
Reiser, Stanley Joel, 39, 137, 331
Rembrandt, 29
Renear, Eileen, 508
Reston, James, Jr., 534
Reynolds, David K., 437, 494, 518, 519
Reynolds, Frank E., 470
Ribar, Mary C., 494
Richards, Marty, 296
Richter, Elizabeth, 256
Richter, Judith M., 523
Riddle, Mary, 535
Riemer, Jack, 471
Riley, James Whitcomb, 18
Rinaldi, Ann, 256
Ring, Kenneth, 458, 460, 462–463, 482, 540
Roback, Howard, 516
Roberts, Leslie, 167
Robinson, Edwin Arlington, 407
Robinson, H. Wheeler, 444, 537
Rogers, William A., 332
Roman, Jo, 535
Romer, John, 512
Roosevelt, Franklin Delano, 229
Rosch, Paul J., 533
Rosen, Helen, 259
Rosen, Hugh, 505
Rosenbaum, Ernest H., 118, 167, 507, 510, 512
Rosenberg, Howard L., 533
Rosenblatt, Roger, 107
Rosenfeld, Alvin H., 499
Rosenman, Ray H., 162, 398–399, 512, 533
Ross, Judith Wilson, 331
Roth, Robert, 499

Rothschild, Annie de, 69
Ruark, John Edward, 136
Rubenstein, Donald H., 535
Rudolph, Marguerita, 107
Ruehlmann, William, 499
Russell, Bertrand, 440, 537
Rybacki, Donald Jay, 532
Rybacki, Karyn Charles, 532

Sabom, Michael B., 540
Sadat, Anwar el-, 206
Sadler, A. L., 535
Saint-Saëns, Camille, 30
Salkind, Neil, 521
Samuel, 537
Santoli, Al, 401
Santora, Joseph C., 500
Sartre, Jean-Paul, 79
Saul, 537
Saunders, Cicely, 126–128
Savage, Candace, 216
Schiff, Harriet Sarnoff, 296, 521
Schilder, Paul, 77, 504, 536
Schildt, Roberta, 505
Schneider, John, 231, 519, 521
Schoenberg, Bernard, 167, 217, 517, 518
Schorsch, Anita, 499
Schowalter, John E., 107, 259
Schramm, Wilbur, 498
Schubert, Franz Peter, 32
Schulman, Jerome L., 277, 297, 522
Schulz, Richard, 507
Schumann, Robert, 32
Schwartz, Harvey J., 389, 531
Schwarz, Catherine, 528
Schwarz, Eric C., 528
Scotch, Norman A., 136
Seattle, Chief, 50
Seiden, Richard H., 534, 536
Seligman, Martin P., 504
Selye, Hans, 217–218, 396, 400, 517, 533
Seward, Jack, 535
Sexton, Anne, 417
Shakespeare, William, 26
Shelley, Percy Bysshe, 227
Shelp, Earl E., 331
Shepard, E. H., 245
Sheskin, Arlene, 518
Shiva, 454
Shneidman, Edwin S., 338, 403, 406, 407, 411, 412, 418, 419, 431, 500, 511, 518, 527, 529, 532, 534, 535, 536
Showalter, C. R., 516
Shumway, Norman, 316
Siegel, Mary-Ellen, 510
Siegler, Mark, 331
Silberman, Lou H., 537

Silberner, Joanne, 532
Silverman, Phyllis R., 523
Simak, Clifford, 486, 544
Simmons, Richard L., 331
Simmons, Roberta G., 331
Simon and Garfunkel, 32
Simonton, O. Carl, 163, 512
Simonton, Stephanie Mathews, 163, 512
Sironen, Barbara, xvi, 521
Sivard, Ruth Leger, 532
Smart, Ninian, 501, 538
Smith, Anne Warren, 257
Smith, Frank, 363
Smith, Huston, 452
Smith, Nicola, 71
Smith, Robert J., 501, 518
Smith, W. Eugene, 472
Sobel, Harry J., 509
Socrates, 440, 446
Sokan, 44
Solomon, Fredric, 233, 523
Sophocles, 26
Speece, Mark W., 80, 504
Spencer, A. J., 512
Stafford, Peter, 542
Stannard, David E., 33, 500, 503, 538
Starr, Paul, 137
Steele, Shirley, 522
Stein, Gertrude, 264
Stein, Marvin, 217
Stein, Sara Bonnett, 257
Steinbeck, John, 350
Steinfels, Peter, 500
Stengel, Erwin, 411, 535
Stevens-Long, Judith, 293
Stevenson, Ian, 463, 541
Stevenson, Robert Louis, 197
Stillion, Judith M., 107, 287, 297, 494, 505–506, 520, 523, 532
Stoddard, Sandol, 510
Strauss, Anselm L., 34, 167, 274–275, 507, 522
Strauss, Johann, 32
Stravinsky, Igor Fyodorovich, 32
Sudnow, David, 117, 207, 507, 514
Suzuki, Shunryu, 456
Swain, Helen L., 90–91, 505
Swazey, Judith P., 136, 331, 525

Tache, Jean, 399, 534
Tart, Charles T., 543
Tatelbaum, Judy, 233
Taylor, James, 32

Temes, Roberta, 233
Terkel, Studs, 195–196
Tetsuo, Yamaori, 501
Thackeray, William Makepeace, 231
Thomas, Lewis, 35
Thomasma, David C., 136
Thucydides, 444
Tilling, Robert I., 529
Tolstoy, Leo, 26, 494
Toye, Randall, 409
Toynbee, Arnold, 385, 389, 471, 530, 531, 532, 538
Trillin, Alice Stewart, 140
Trumbo, Dalton, 385, 390, 530
Trungpa, Chögyam, 457, 539
Turner, Ronny E., 187, 514
Twycross, Robert G., 509

Unamuno, Miguel de, 469, 502
Uris, Leon, 100

Vachon, Mary L. S., 137, 508, 523
Valente, Sharon McBride, 437
Van Der Zee, James, 474
Van Tassel, David D., 297
Vanderbilt, Amy, 18, 498
Vandiver, Trish, 437
Varley, Susan, 257
Vaughan, Frances, 543
Veatch, Robert M., 322–326, 331, 500, 525
Ventafridda, Vittorio, 509
Verdi, Giuseppe, 30
Vermeule, Emily, 471
Vernon, Glenn M., 229, 382, 385, 517, 530
Vicchio, Stephen J., 449–450, 460, 464, 537, 538, 540
Viorst, Judith, 257
Vogel, Isle-Margret, 257
Vojtech, Anna, 256
Volkan, Vamik, 516
Vonèche, J. Jacques, 505
Vonnegut, Kurt, 395
Vovelle, Michael, 503

Wagner, G., 509
Wahl, C. W., 504
Waldhart-Letzel, Edith, 421, 536
Wallace, Samuel E., 518
Wallis, Henry, 421
Walsh, Roger N., 543
Walton, Douglas N., 525
Ward, Russell A., 521
Washington, George, 207

Wass, Hannelore, 107, 255, 287–288, 500, 520, 524
Watterson, Barbara, 512
Watts, Alan, 494
Waugh, Earle H., 470
Waugh, Evelyn, 34, 183
Webb, James, 499
Wechsler, David, 77, 504
Wechsler, Henry, 532
Wecht, Cyril H., 341, 527
Weinfeld, Irwin J., 522
Weir, Robert F., 39
Weisman, Avery D., 167, 489–490, 492, 494, 511, 544
Weiss, Robert S., 233, 516, 523
Weitz, Lawrence, 516
Weizman, Savine Gross, 212, 214–215, 517, 523
Wekstein, Louis, 437
Wertenbaker, Lael T., 535
Wertham, Fredrick, 380, 382
Westall, Robert, 107
Wheeler, Anne, 216
White, E. B., 257, 365, 528
White, Geoffrey M., 535
Wiesel, Elie, 27
Wildavsky, Aaron, 401
Williams, Carey, 470
Williams, Garth, 257
Williams, Glanville, 308, 524
Winslade, William J., 331
Wolf, Anna W. M., 506
Wolfenstein, Martha, 95, 505
Wood, Virginia N., 502
Wooden, Kenneth, 534
Worden, J. William, 212, 215–216, 233, 517

Yahweh, 444
Yampolsky, Philip B., 539
Yatzkan, Elaine S., 524
Yorba, Tomás Antonio, 348–349
Young, Ernle W. D., 331
Young, J. Z., 175, 513
Younger Chief Joseph, 50

Zawacki, Bruce E., 507
Zeligs, Rose, 506
Zimmerman, Jack M., 510
Zimmermann, M., 509
Zindel, Paul, 257
Ziony, Ruth Kramer, 142
Zolotow, Charlotte, 103, 257

Subject Index

Abortion, 219, 267, 269
Accidental death, 45–46
  certification of, 338, 339, 342
  news reports of, 21–23
Accidents, 236, 369–371
  costs of, 369
  death rate from, 12, 236, 528
  industrial, 372, 481
  nuclear, 372, 374
  risk taking and, 367–368
Acholi funeral song, 55
Acquired Immune Deficiency
    Syndrome (AIDS), 123–124,
    133, 485, 509
Acute care. See Hospitals
Adolescence, 85–86
  accidents in, 370
  death rates in, 236
  life-threatening illness in, 239
  nuclear threat in, 390, 532
  suicide in, 418, 420–423
Adulthood
  death of parent in, 286–287
  developmental hypotheses and,
    261, 262
African culture, 46, 52–55, 501,
    502
Afterlife concepts, 41–42, 49–50,
    170, 439–470, 501, 537
  in art, 28, 29
  attitudes toward death and,
    468–470
  mature concept of death and, 76
Age. See also Developmental
  hypotheses

accidents and, 370
grouping by, in African societies,
    52
segregation by, and
    intergenerational contact, 13
Aged persons, 12, 13, 35
  attitude toward death of, 521
  community care of, 294–295
  cross-cultural perspectives on,
    523–524
  developmental hypotheses and,
    262
  future projections about care of,
    487
  health care of, 291–296
  physiological functioning and,
    288–291
  spousal death and, 282
Aging, 265
  stereotypes of, 287
Alcohol abuse, 338, 369, 420
All Souls' Day, 56
Allowing to die, 309. See also
    Euthanasia; Foregoing
    life-sustaining treatment
  in special care nursery, 312–317
Alzheimer's disease, 290–291
Alzheimer's Disease and Related
    Disorders Association
    (ADRDA), 524
Ambivalence, 225, 440
  in suicide, 410–411, 435–436
American Bar Association, 327, 328
American Cancer Society, 133, 142,
    510, 512

American Medical Association
    (AMA), 311, 328
Amish culture, 37
Amyotrophic lateral sclerosis (ALS),
    290
Ancestors, 43–44, 45, 52, 53, 54,
    56, 501, 502
Anniversary reaction, 208
Anoxia, 542
Anxiety, 5, 83, 504–505
  aged persons and, 521
  death education and, 482
  humor and, 18–20
  nuclear threat and, 33, 35
Apparitions, 463. See also Spirits
Appropriate death, 136, 489–490,
    492–493
Art, 28–30, 56, 59, 67, 68, 503
  therapeutic value of, 86, 247, 250,
    520
Artificial heart, 150
Ashes (cremated remains), 515
Assassinations, 23–24, 95, 529
Association for Death Education and
    Counseling, 36
Atherosclerosis, 12, 289
Atomic bomb, 35, 364, 390, 391,
    392, 532. See also Nuclear
    threat
Atomic Energy Commission, 393
Atomic Veterans' Rights
    (organization), 512
Attitudes toward the dead, 42–45,
    178, 211, 440–441, 444,
    502

Attitudes toward death, 5, 16–20, 25, 26, 32, 33, 47, 56, 58–59, 72, 169–170, 264, 365, 419, 473, 500
  afterlife concepts and, 468–470
  aged persons and, 262, 264, 265
  in children, 94–101
  cross-cultural examples of, 48–56
Australian aboriginals, 177
Autopsies, 340, 341, 342, 379, 527
Awareness contexts, 34, 274–276, 522
Aztecs, 55

Bardo Thodol, 457
Bereavement. See also Grief; Mourning
  children and, 241–242
  definition of, 206–207
  funerals and, 174–175
  life change and, 231–233
  social support in, 172, 177, 183, 203, 228, 278
  studies of, 516–517, 523
Bhagavad-Gita, 452, 453, 538, 538–539
Bible, 441, 443
Bibliotherapy, 253–257
Biological death, 114, 319–320, 507. See also Vital signs
Biology of grief. See Grief, physiology of
Biopsy, 152, 155
Black Death. See Plague
Books. See Publications on death
Boston Sunday Globe, 326
Brain death, 325, 330, 526
Brass Ring Society, 259, 521
Brooklyn College, 36
Buddhism, 415, 453, 455–456, 457, 469, 538
  funerals in, 540
Burial, 188, 193
  costs of, 192, 197
  cross-cultural examples of, 6, 64–66, 193–194, 440, 501
  Native American respect for places of, 502
  Neanderthal, 41
  types of, 40, 49, 170, 193–195, 197, 442
Burn-out. See Stress

Cancer, 12, 118, 139, 140–142, 150–151, 153–154, 289, 395, 399, 511. See also Health care institutions; Life-threatening illness
  survival rates of patients with, 510

Cancer Counseling and Research Center, 163
Candlelighters, 278
Capital punishment, 382–383, 530
Care of dying, 36, 70, 109, 111–116, 138, 483, 508
  ethics and, 115
  family's role in, 115, 127, 166–167, 276, 522
Cartoons, 20, 24, 95. See also Humor
Casket Manufacturers Association of America, 515
Caskets, 182, 188
  costs of, 185, 190–192
  sales of, 515
Cause(s) of death, 11–12, 45–46, 300–301
  accidents as, 369
  among adults, 265
  certification of, 338–339
  in children, 236–237
  death certificate and, 338
  suicide as, 403
Cellular death, 321, 322
Cemeteries, 64–66
  costs of burial in, 197, 198
  for pets, 243
Center for Attitudinal Healing, 164, 258, 259, 521
Centers for Disease Control, 369, 376
Central vs. peripheral relationship, 224–225
Centre for Living with Dying, 160, 228
Cerebrovascular disease, 12, 139
Ceremonies, death, 49–51, 52–55, 148, 169–170, 177, 203, 442
  mass media and, 22, 23–24
Certification of death. See Death certificate
Certificate of stillbirth, 270
Challenger accident, 22, 35, 221
  children and, 95
Charnel houses, 65–66
Chemotherapy, 157–158, 163, 239, 511–512
Children. See also Developmental hypotheses
  bereavement and, 80, 81, 87, 95, 100–101, 200–201, 236, 241–242, 519
  books for, 253–254, 255–257, 521
  death rates of, 9, 236–237
  discussing death with, 72, 94–95, 98, 101–106, 250–254, 257, 504, 520
  hospice programs for, 129–130
  life-threatening illness and,

237–241, 271–277, 519, 520, 522
  media influence on, 24–25, 35, 499
  parent death and, 86, 219, 224–225, 234, 245–247
  play activities of, 93–94
  prototothanatic behavior in, 79
  sibling death and, 247–250
  suicide among, 418, 420–423
  support groups for, 258–259
Child's death
  effect of, on survivors, 220, 236, 266, 273, 277–278
  parental mourning of, 31, 202–203, 219, 260, 268–269
Christianity, 46, 469, 501, 538
  afterlife concepts in, 446–450
  in Middle Ages, 29, 58, 63–65, 459
Chronic care. See Care of dying; Nursing homes
Classic vs. ideal caring situations, 113
Clergy
  funerals and, 174, 181–182, 185, 513–514, 514
  perinatal death and, 268
Clinical death, 321
Cocopa, 50–51
Coffin. See also Caskets
  child's drawings on handmade, 200, 201, 202
  "life-preserving," 320
Cognitive development. See Developmental hypotheses
Comatose state, 507
  determination of death and, 320
  ethical issues, 309
Combat death, 221. See also War
Committee on an Aging Society, 296
Committee on Trauma Research, 369, 401
Communication, 166–167
  in disasters, 372–374
  in health care settings, 112–113, 114, 115, 117–118, 120–121, 124
  informed consent and, 305, 506
  seriously ill children and, 522
  styles of, 240, 272–276
  with suicidal person, 431–437
  suicide as act of, 412, 535
  truth telling and, 301–303
Community
  rites of passage in, 6, 7, 33, 171, 203, 221, 228, 440–441, 484
  violence and moral standards of, 377, 379–380

Compassionate Friends, 258, 278, 521
Completion of being, 49, 70
Computers in medicine, 14–16, 150, 337
Concentration camps. *See* Holocaust
Concern for Dying, 526
Consumer Reports, 203
Coping strategies, 5, 116, 146–150, 162–165, 264, 277
in bereavement, 219, 228–231
of children, 240–242, 250–251, 272–276
informed consent and, 306
in life-threatening illness, 511, 512
in risk taking, 367, 368–369
in stress, 400
in terminal illness, 512
Coroner, 338–340, 342
suicide and, 403
Corpses. *See* Disposition of dead
Cosmetic restoration, 180, 181
Counseling, 118, 132–133, 143, 483, 484, 512, 544
in disasters, 374–376
in parental bereavement, 266
Cremation Association of North America, 198
Cremation, 169, 182, 188, 191–192, 193, 198, 438, 515
costs of, 198, 199, 201
statistics, 198
Crib death. *See* Infant death; Sudden Infant Death Syndrome
Cryogenic internment, 197
Cyclical concepts, 49, 451, 523–524. *See also* Rebirth

Dakota, 48
Dance of Death (Danse macabre), 29, 30, 32, 56, 66–68, 503
Day of the Dead, 56, 57, 503
Death benefits, 188, 362–363. *See also* Life insurance
certification of death and, 338
Death certificate, 338, 339
cost of filing, 188
grief listed as cause of death on, 218–219
Death with dignity, 310. *See also* Appropriate death
Death education, 26, 33–36, 473, 479, 481, 482–483
aged persons and, 287–288
Death notices, 69, 112, 172–173, 188, 498
Death rates, 7–9, 10, 35, 141, 497
from accidents, 528
of children and adolescents, 236–237

Death songs, 48, 49
Deathbed promises, 226
Deathbed vigil, 4, 62–64, 111, 503–504
Definition of death, 16, 301, 312, 319, 321–327, 330–331
legislation specifying, 327, 328
Denial, 5, 30, 33, 36, 56–57, 112, 115, 211, 393
Depersonalization, 28
of dying patients, 507
language usage and, 18
in mortal danger, 461
in war, 389
Determination of death, empirical criteria in, 319–327
Developmental crisis, 84
Developmental hypotheses, 73–75, 76–77
adulthood and, 261, 262
aged persons and, 287, 521
cognitive model (Piaget), 87–92
death of parent and, 286
psychoanalytic model, 83–84, 504–505
psychosocial model (Erikson), 84–87, 262
seriously ill children and, 238
spousal death and, 281–282
"Developmental push," 286
Diagnostic related groups (DRGs), 509
Dies irae (Day of Wrath), 30
Disasters, 371–376
grief in, 223
postvention in, 374–376, 529
reports of, in news media, 22–23
survivors of, 373
Disenfranchised grief, 219–221, 269
Disposition of dead, 177, 484. *See also* Burial; Cremation; Funerals
costs of, 185, 193, 197–199, 201
funerals and, 178
laws regulating, 341, 343
Domiciliary care homes. *See* Aged persons, community care of
Down's syndrome, 313, 314, 315
Drawings, 86, 94, 95, 96–97, 246, 520. *See also* Art, therapeutic value of
Durable Power of Attorney for Health Care, 335–336
Dying
in Middle Ages, 62
Native American attitudes toward, 49
in nineteenth-century America, 5–6, 9, 29–30

Dying persons. *See also* Care of dying
caregiver contact with, 508
ethical issues about, 308–312
legal affairs of, 344
LSD therapy with, 466
near-death experiences and, 465–466
social role of, 114, 133–136, 503–504, 506, 507
Dying trajectory, 134–135, 511

Earthquakes, 372
Egyptian culture, 29, 170, 451
El día de los Muertos. See Day of the Dead
Elderly persons. *See* Aged persons
Elisabeth Kübler-Ross Center, 133
Embalming, 179, 182, 189–190, 514
Emergency care, 114, 116–117, 150, 507
Empirical facts of death, 75. *See also* Determination of death
Entombment. *See* Burial, types of
Eros and death, 68
Eschatology
medical, 115–116
in Middle Ages, 503
Estate taxes, 355–358. *See also* Probate; Wills
Ethics, 125, 150, 298, 311. *See also* Foregoing life-sustaining treatment
critically ill newborns and, 270
dying persons and, 308–312
life-extending technology and, 15, 16
neonatal death and, 312–317
nutrition and, 311, 334
treatment options, 309–310
in war, 384–389
Etiquette, 18, 38, 208
Euphemisms, 6–7, 17–18, 180
Euthanasia, 308–309, 413–414, 524. *See also* Allowing to die; Suicide, surcease
aged persons and, 521
living wills and, 334
Executor of estate, 350–353
Exit (British organization), 413
Experimental procedures, 306
Extraordinary measures. *See* Ethics

Fairy tales, 95, 98
Family
extended, 8, 9, 11, 229, 272, 497
funerals and, 172
geographical mobility and, 9–10, 13

Family (*continued*)
　participation in patient care, 111, 512
　violence in, 379–380
Fear of the dead. *See* Attitudes toward the dead
Federal Trade Commission (FTC), 34, 182, 186, 188, 190–193, 199, 201
Fire safety, 370
Firearms, 369, 381, 425–426, 427, 528
Foregoing life-sustaining treatment, 311. *See also* Ethics; Euthanasia
　in emergency care, 507
　living wills and, 333–336
Framingham Heart Disease Epidemiology Study, 399
Freudian theory. *See* Psychoanalytic theory
Funeral directors, 168, 178, 180, 181, 182, 185, 187–188, 202, 514
"Funeral Rule" (FTC), 182, 184, 186, 188, 190, 199, 201, 514, 515
Funerals
　clergy and, 513
　as coping mechanism, 175
　costs of, 182, 184–193, 514
　criticisms of, 34, 171, 180–181
　cross-cultural examples of, 177, 501, 540
　in early societies, 501
　future projections of, 484
　history of, in U. S., 6–7, 171, 177–181
　of LoDagaa, 52–55
　music in, 32
　perinatal death and, 268
　personal choices in, 168
　psychological aspects of, 175, 177, 184–185, 202, 219–221, 517
　public opinion of, 37, 177, 182, 513, 514
　social aspects of, 37, 171, 174–175, 177, 183, 202, 213, 228, 229–230, 232
　statistics, 187
Future projections of death, 483–487

Gallows humor, 20
Gender, 99, 497–498, 528, 541
　related to accidents among young people, 370
　related to spousal death, 283–284
Geographical mobility, 9–10, 13, 228
Gifts, 358

Gilgamesh epic, 48, 501
"Good death." *See* Appropriate death
Grave markers, 65. *See also* Memorialization
Greek culture, 29, 171, 444–446, 450, 489
Grief. *See also* Bereavement; Mourning
　abnormal, 208, 209, 211, 516
　anticipatory, 222
　children and, 241–242
　counseling in, 484, 544
　cross-cultural expressions of, 54, 211, 214, 221, 224, 442, 503, 518, 519
　definition of, 207
　in disasters, 22, 373, 374–376
　disenfranchised, 219–221, 269
　duration of, 177, 208–210, 477, 516
　emotions in, 204, 205, 207, 210–211, 214, 226–227, 229–230, 267, 286–287, 480, 519
　expression of, in hospitals, 506
　factors conditioning, 219–228, 233, 260, 261, 279, 281–284
　high vs. low, 219
　linking objects and, 210, 516, 519
　management of life's affairs in, 216, 519
　physiology of, 177, 208, 210, 212, 213, 217–219, 267, 518
　stage theory and, 210, 212–215, 483, 517
　suicide and, 222–223, 517
　tasks of, 210, 215–217
Guild for Infant Survival, 278

Harvard criteria, 325, 326, 526
Hawaiian culture, 32, 43–44, 45, 203, 211, 229, 441, 460–461, 501
Health care institutions, 13, 108, 111–115, 131. *See also* Care of dying
　aged persons and, 291–292, 293–296
　costs in, 110, 124, 127, 142, 150, 270, 506, 509
Health care triangle, 111
Health and Human Services (HHS), Department of, 314, 315
Heart disease, 12, 139, 140–141, 150, 162, 395, 398–399
Heaven and Hell, 64, 70
Hebraic tradition. *See* Judaic culture
Hellenistic culture, 444–446, 448, 450

Heroic measures, *See* Ethics
Hibakusha, 33, 392, 532
Hinduism, 438, 452–453, 454, 456, 469, 538
Hippocratic Oath, 300, 305, 308
Hiroshima, 33, 35, 385, 389, 390, 391, 532
Holocaust, 27, 102, 223, 385, 386
Home care, 108, 127–128, 294. *See also* Care of dying
Homicide, 12, 376–380, 381
　among children and young adults, 236
　certification of death as, 338, 339, 342
　grief reaction to, 223
Hopi, 51
Hospice care, 37, 124, 125, 126, 503–504, 509, 510
　in hospitals, 129–130
　history of, 126–129
Hospice of New Haven, 128
Hospitals, 109–112, 125, 126
　children in, 238, 239, 520
　grief room in, 506
　hospice care in, 129–130
　organ donation and, 337
　role of dying patient in, 506, 507
　support groups in, 512
Humor, 18–20, 30, 56, 95
Hundred Years' War, 68
Huntington's disease, 290
Hypertension, 289, 395, 400. *See also* Stress

I Ching, 451
Images of death, 63. *See also* Dance of Death
　in art, 28–30
　in mass media, 24–26
　as mirror, 55, 63
　as mysterious stranger, 34
Immortality, 440, 445, 446, 448, 449, 450, 502, 503. *See also* Rebirth
Infant death, 9, 12, 14, 236, 267, 270. *See also* Special care nursery; Sudden Infant Death Syndrome
Infection, 161–162, 511–512
Infectious diseases, 11–12
Informed consent, 117–118, 125, 147, 303–308, 507. *See also* Truth telling
　attitudes toward, 304–306
Inheritance taxes, 358
Interferon, 161
Interleukin-2, 158–159
International Association for Near-Death Studies, 541

International Pet Cemetery Association, 243
Interpersonal relationships. *See* Relationship factors
Intestacy, 354–355. *See also* Probate
Islam, 46

Japan Broadcasting Corporation (NHK), 401
Japanese culture, 44, 198, 199, 477, 523–524
  suicide in, 414
Jivas, 452
Journey of the dead. *See* Afterlife concepts
Judaic culture, 46, 441, 443–444, 448, 450, 501, 537
Judgment, concepts of, 28, 58, 441, 449, 451

Kanikau, 32
Kara (organization), 133
Karma, 452, 453, 455, 538
Kidney machine, 14
Killing. *See* Homicide; War
Knells, death, 30, 59
Korean War, 513

Laetrile, 160–161
Language, 17–18, 175
Last rites. *See* Funerals; Rites of passage
Liber vitae, 58
Life after death. *See* Afterlife concepts
Life cycle. *See* Developmental hypotheses
Life expectancy, 7–9, 293, 301, 497
  theoretical maximum possible, 12, 288, 289
  work satisfaction and, 367
Life insurance, 359–362
Life review, 460–461
Life-style factors. *See* Coping strategies
Life-threatening illness, 117–118, 139, 144–148, 149. *See also* Health care institutions
  children and, 236, 237–241, 271–277
  neonatal death and, 270
  self-concept and, 510
  truth telling and, 302–303
Literature, 26–28, 48, 56, 98, 417, 501
"Little deaths," 205, 235, 515
Living will, 333–336
LoDagaa, 52–55, 175

Los Angeles Suicide Prevention Center, 431
Loss. *See* Bereavement
LSD (lysergic acid diethylamide), 466–468, 542
  dying persons and, 542

Magical thought, 46
  children and, 76, 78, 83, 90–91
Make Today Count, 164–165, 512
Malignancies. *See* Cancer
Malpractice, 113–114, 333, 506
Marital bereavement. *See* Spousal death; Widowhood
Marital deduction, 356–357
Martyrs, cult of, 64, 65
Mass media, 20–26, 206, 498
  influence of, on suicide, 420
  reports of death in, 206, 278, 365, 498–499
Mature concept of death, 75–76, 78, 91–92
Mausoleum. *See* Burial, types of
Medical eschatology, 115–116
Medical examiner, 338–340
Memorialization, 6, 30, 32, 50, 53, 59, 65, 67, 68–70, 176, 209, 263, 444, 478
  art and, 28–30
  costs of, 185, 197–198
  mass media and, 22, 23–24
Memorial societies. *See* Cremation
Mercy killing. *See* Euthanasia
Mexican culture, 55–57, 502
Middle Ages, 29, 57–66
Military service. *See also* War
  euphemisms in, 18
  funeral regalia of, 176
Minnesota Coalition for Terminal Care, 36
Miscarriage, 219, 267, 268–269
Mortality of grief. *See* Grief; physiology of
Mortality rates. *See* Death rates
Morticians. *See* Funeral directors
Mortuaries, 179, 185, 187, 199, 514
Mothers Against Drunk Driving (MADD), 278, 484
Mount Auburn, 69
Mount Pelee, 373, 374
Mount St. Helens, 373–374
Mourning, 32. *See also* Bereavement; Funerals; Grief
  cross-cultural examples of, 177, 207
  definition of, 207
  nineteenth-century American customs in, 38, 178–179, 207, 515

seclusion of bereaved in, 515
Mourning memorials. *See* Memorialization
Mourning restraints, 54
Movies, 25–26, 95, 521, 531
  portrayal of atomic bomb in, 390–391
Mummification, 170
Murder. *See* Homicide
Music, 30, 32, 67, 503
Mythologies, 46

Nagasaki, 33, 390
Naming practices, 44–45, 224, 501
Nandi, 52
National Academy of Sciences, 161
National Cancer Institute, 158–159, 510
National Center for Health Statistics, 521
National Foundation of Funeral Service, 180
National Funeral Directors Association (NFDA), 180, 185
National Hospice Organization, 510
National Library of Medicine, 36
National Organ Transplant Act, 337
National Research Council, 369
National Selected Morticians, 180
National Sudden Infant Death Syndrome Foundation, 523
Native American culture, 40, 48–51, 194, 266, 502
Natural death directive, 333–336
Neanderthals, 41, 440, 501
Near-death experiences, 457–458, 460–466, 469
  LSD and, 468
Necrophilia, 483
Neonatal death. *See* Infant death
Neptune Society, 199
New Jersey Supreme Court, 16, 310
New Testament, 446, 448
Newspapers, 23, 56, 69, 172–173. *See also* Mass media
  death education in, 26
  probate procedures and, 350, 351–352
  reports of suicide in, 404–405
Nirvana, 455
Notification of death, 172–174, 498. *See also* Death notices; Mass media
Nuclear threat, 364, 390–393, 395, 481, 532, 532–533, 533
  near-death experiences and, 462
  psychic distancing from, 393
Nuclear winter, 392
Nursery rhymes, 98, 99

Nurses, 111, 112, 114, 119–121, 477, 508
Nursing homes, 110–111, 125, 126, 284. *See also* Health care institutions
types of, 292, 293

Obituaries, 22, 35, 56, 112, 172–173, 498. *See also* Death notices
Occupational hazards, 366–367, 528
Office of Technology Assessment, 392, 532–533
Ohlones, 49–50
Oncology. *See* Cancer
Organ donation, 336–337
Organ transplantation, 299–300, 317–318, 329, 337, 482, 486
determination of death and, 327
Origin of death mythologies, 45–47
Orphic mystery religions, 445–446

Pain, 127, 509
appropriate death and, 489–490
LSD therapy and, 466, 542
suicide as escape from, 414
Palliative measures. *See* Care of dying; Pain
Panoramic memory, 460, 461
Papago, 48
Parent death
children and, 245–247
effect of, on adult child, 286–287
Parents of Murdered Children (POMC), 278, 484
Patient advocacy, 121–122
Perceived similarity, 230, 518
Perinatal death, 267–270. *See also* Infant death
definition of, 521
Pet cemeteries, 243
Pet death, 80, 91, 242–245, 264, 500
Plague, 29, 68, 139, 376, 485
Platform burial, 40, 442
Pornography of death, 34
Postvention, 529
in disasters, 374–376
Preliterate societies, 41–48, 440–441. *See also* African culture; Hawaiian culture; Native American culture
President's Commission for the Study of Ethical Problems in Medicine, 303–306, 310, 311–312, 314, 328, 330
Probate, 350–354. *See also* Intestacy; Wills

avoiding, 353–354, 527–528
executor's duties in, 350–353
intestate succession and, 354–355
Prolonged grief. *See* Grief, duration of
Protothanatic behavior, 79
Psychic numbing, 531
Psychoanalytic theory, 83–84, 211–212, 410–412
Psychological autopsy, 338, 418
Psychology Today questionnaire, 37, 500
Psychosexual model. *See* Developmental hypotheses, psychoanalytic model
Psychosocial development. *See* Developmental hypotheses, psychosocial model
Public Broadcasting System (PBS), 26
Public Health Services (U. S.), 123–124
Publications on death, 33–34, 36, 479, 500
Puritan culture, 64, 449–450

Quality of life, 70
Questionnaire, *Psychology Today*, 37

Radiation
exposure to, in atomic bomb testing, 512
therapy, 156–157
Rational suicide. *See* Suicide, surcease
Rebirth, 42, 45, 440, 445, 455, 457, 463, 469, 538, 543. *See also* Afterlife concepts
in Hinduism, 452, 453
Relationship factors, 221, 223–225, 279–281
in homicide, 379–380
Respiration, artificial, 321, 323–324, 526
Resurrection, 443, 444, 446, 448, 450, 469
Reversibility, 77, 78, 90–91, 92
Right to die, 310, 334, 482, 535. *See also* Euthanasia; Living will
Rigor mortis, 322
Risk taking, 366–369, 481
disasters and, 372
homicide and, 383–384
subintentioned death and, 418, 419
Rites of passage, 54, 171, 175, 440–441
from war to peace, 389
Roman culture, 29, 64, 65

Romantic view of death, 30, 58, 64, 68, 209
Romeo and Juliet, 68
Rural cemetery movement, 69–70

St. Christopher's Hospice, 126–128
Samsara, 453
Scaffold burial, 40, 442
Sea burial, 194–195
Secular thought, 63, 450, 503
Senufo, 46
Seppuku, 414
Sequential survival curve, 289
Shanti Project, 132–133
She'ol, 537
Shiva, 454
Sibling death, 247–250
Simonton approach, 512. *See also* Visualization
Sioux, 40, 49
Skilled nursing facility. *See* Nursing homes
Social death, 114, 507
Socialization. *See* Children; Developmental hypotheses
Social Readjustment Rating Scale, 396–398
Social support, 264
in bereavement, 37, 174–175, 183, 203, 213, 219–220, 228, 278, 285–286
in life-threatening illness, 132–133, 143, 160, 164–165, 512
Soul, 170, 439, 444, 445, 448, 449, 460, 526
defining death as loss of, 324
South Pacific societies, 484
Spanish culture, 502
Special care nursery, 15, 312–317
Speculum mortis, 63
Spirits, 43, 45, 49, 51, 56, 441, 442, 446, 463
Spontaneous drawings. *See* Art, therapeutic value of; Drawings
Spousal death, 279–286, 516. *See also* Bereavement; Widowhood
Stage theory, 76–77, 78, 87, 146, 512, 517
Starlight Foundation, 259, 521
Stillbirth, 267, 269–270, 516
Stress, 261, 365, 395–400, 417, 534
bereavement and, 217–219
caregivers and, 116–117, 119–123, 508
hospitalized children and, 238, 240

Strokes, 289
Subintentioned death, 338, 418
Sudden Infant Death Syndrome
 (SIDS), 271, 522
Suicide, 12, 402–437
 altruistic, 55, 409, 410, 414–415
 among children and adolescents,
  236, 418, 420–423
 anomic, 408, 410
 certification of death as, 338, 339,
  342, 403
 as cry for help, 423
 definitions of, 406–407
 egoistic, 408–409, 410
 epidemic, 417–418
 grief reaction to, 222–223
 intervention, 426, 430–437
 methods of, 424–428
 in Micronesia, 417–418
 myths about, 431–432
 postvention, 431
 prevention, 340, 430–437
 psychotic, 414
 referred, 415–417
 romantic, 417
 statistics, 403, 420, 425
 subintentioned, 418
 surcease, 413–414, 535
Suicide notes, 404, 429
Suicide prevention centers, 431
Sunshine Foundation, 259, 521
Support groups, 228, 230–231, 484
 for children, 258–259
 parental bereavement and, 278
Supreme Court (U. S.), 315
Surgery, 154–156, 299
Survivor guilt, 210, 214, 249, 266,
 268, 269, 271. See also
 Holocaust
Suttee, 414–415
Symbols of death, 28–30, 56–57,
 169, 170, 174, 175, 178, 207,
 501, 515
Sympathy cards, 18, 213, 243–244,
 498

Taboo of death, 32, 111, 139, 237
Tahitian culture, 442
"Tamed Death," 58
Tao, 451
Tasks of mourning, 210, 215–217
"Teachable moments." See Death
 education
Technology, 8, 13, 14–16, 63, 70,
 108, 479, 485
 ethical issues and, 298, 299–300,
  301, 331
 influence on site of death,
  503–504
 in war, 389–390, 392
Television, 22, 24, 26, 390–391,
 499
 children and, 95, 499
Terminal care. See Care of Dying;
 Hospice care
Thanatology. See Death education
Tibetan Book of the Dead, 324
Tomb art. See Memorialization
Tombs. See Burial; Memorialization
Transmigration, 452, 455. See also
 Rebirth
Transplant procedures. See Organ
 transplantation
Treatment, 150, 153–161
 infection and, 161–162
 informed consent to, 303–308
 seriously ill children and,
  237–238, 239, 240
 for stress, 400
 unorthodox, 158–161
Tristan and Isolde, 68
Trusts, 358–359
Truth telling, 301–303, 524. See
 also Informed consent
Tumors. See Cancer
TV Guide, 24
Type A behavior, 398–399

Undertakers, 178. See also Funeral
 directors
Unfinished business, 225–226

Uniform Anatomical Gift Act, 336,
 526–527
Uniform Determination of Death
 Act, 328
Unknown Serviceman, 176

Veterans, 389, 393, 394, 512
 death benefits for, 362, 363
Vietnam War, 27, 176, 263, 385,
 386–387, 389, 415, 479, 513
 as factor influencing suicide, 420
Violence, 27–28, 376–384
 and suicide, 420–421
Visualization, 163
Vital signs, 319, 321
 defining death as loss of, 323–324

Wakes. See Ceremonies, death;
 Funerals
War, 384–390, 472, 544. See also
 Combat death; Nuclear threat
 burial of dead in, 513
 prevention of, 533
Widowed Persons Service, 523
Widowhood, 175, 209, 222,
 497–498, 516, 518. See also
 Bereavement; Spousal death
 social support in, 285–286
Wills, 343–350, 527. See also
 Intestacy; Probate
 dying persons and, 344–345
 testator's qualifications for making,
  345
Winnebago, 47
Wintu, 49
Woodlawn, 69

X-ray machine, 15

Yokut, 50
Yombe, 53

Zen, 453, 455, 456
Zorastrianism, 194

Credits and Sources

Prologue and Epilogue: Copyright © 1982 by David Gordon. Used by permission.

Page 7: From *Small Town America: A Narrative History, 1620–Present,* by Richard R. Lingeman, G. P. Putnam's Sons, 1980.

Page 14: "Grandmother, When Your Child Died," first published by the California State Poetry Society. Used by permission of Joan Neet George.

Page 19: Reprinted by permission of G. P. Putnam's Sons from *Cruel Shoes* by Steve Martin. Copyright © 1977, 1979 by Steven Martin.

Page 27: "Buffalo Bill's" is reprinted from *Tulips & Chimneys* by E. E. Cummings, by permission of Liveright Publishing Corporation. Copyright 1923, 1925 and renewed 1951, 1953 by E. E. Cummings. Copyright © 1973, 1976 by the Trustees for the E. E. Cummings Trust. Copyright © 1973, 1976 by George James Firmage. From *Complete Poems 1913–1962,* by permission of Grafton Books.

Page 35: Excerpt from "Death in the Open" from *The Lives of a Cell: Notes of a Biology Watcher,* by Lewis Thomas. Originally published in *The New England Journal of Medicine.* Copyright © 1973 by Massachusetts Medical Society. Reprinted by permission of Viking Penguin Inc. and Penguin Books Ltd.

Pp. 38, 69, 178, & 320: Courtesy of Edward C. and Gail R. Johnson.

Page 42: Illustration copyright © 1982 by Eric Mathes. Courtesy of Eric Mathes.

Page 44: From *The Four Seasons: Japanese Haiku Second Series,* translated by Peter Beilenson.

Copyright © 1958 by The Peter Pauper Press.

Page 47: "When Hare Heard of Death," an excerpt from pages 23–24 of *The Road of Life and Death: A Ritual Drama of the American Indians,* by Paul Radin, Bollingen Series V. Copyright © 1945, renewed 1973, by Princeton University Press. Reprinted by permission of Princeton University Press and Doris Woodward Radin.

Page 48: By permission of Smithsonian Institution Press, from *Papago Music* by Frances Densmore. "Papago song" by Juana Manwell. Bureau of American Ethnology Bulletin 90. Smithsonian Institution, Washington, D. C. 1929.

Page 48: Dakota song from *The Primal Mind: Vision and Reality in Indian America,* by Jamake Highwater; Harper & Row, 1981.

Page 49: "Burial Oration" (Wintu Indian) from "Wintu Ethnography," by Cora Du Bois, in *University of California Publications in American Archaeology and Ethnology* 36 (1935). Reprinted by permission of the University of California Press.

Page 55: From *Religions of Africa: A Pilgrimage into Traditional Religions,* by Noel Q. King; Harper & Row, 1970.

Page 59: From *Strange Facts About Death,* by Webb Garrison. Copyright © 1978 by Webb Garrison. Used by permission of the publisher, Abingdon Press.

Page 64: From *Writings from the Philokalia on Prayer of the Heart,* translated by E. Kadloubovsky and G. E. H. Palmer; Faber and Faber, 1951.

559

Page 69: From *CoEvolution Quarterly* 17 (Spring 1978): 135, "Little Prigs & Sages." Used by permission of CoEvolution Quarterly; back issues available at $3.00 postpaid from CQ, P.O. Box 428, Sausalito, CA 94966.

Page 74: "Death Education for Children and Youth," by Dan Leviton and Eileen C. Forman, in *Journal of Clinical Child Psychology* (Summer 1974).

Page 76: From *The Interpretation of Dreams*, by Sigmund Freud, translated and edited by James Strachey; Basic Books, 1953.

Page 79: From *The Words*, by Jean Paul Sartre; George Braziller, 1964.

Page 84: Adapted from *Behavior and Life: An Introduction to Psychology*, by Frank J. Bruno. Copyright © 1980 by John Wiley and Sons, Inc. Reproduced by permission of John Wiley and Sons, Inc.

Pp. 86, 200, & 250: Used with permission of Joe Allen, Brooks Allen, and Janice Laurent.

Page 95: "The Shroud" from *Grimms' Tales for Young and Old*, translated by Ralph Manheim. Reprinted by permission of Doubleday & Company, Inc.

Pp. 98 & 99: From *Journeys Through Bookland*, Volume One, edited by Charles H. Sylvester; published by Bellows-Reeve Company, Publishers, Chicago, 1922.

Page 100: From *Trinity*, by Leon Uris; published by Doubleday & Company, Inc., 1976.

Page 103: From *My Grandson Lew*, by Charlotte Zolotow; published by Harper & Row, 1974.

Page 113: From *Dying and Death: A Clinical Guide for Caregivers*, edited by David Barton. Copyright © 1977 by The Williams and Wilkins Company. Used with permission of The Williams and Wilkins Company and by courtesy of David Barton, M. D.

Pp. 117 & 207: From *Passing On: The Social Organization of Dying*, by David Sudnow; published by Prentice-Hall, Inc., 1967.

Page 118: From the Honolulu *Star-Bulletin*, October 20, 1985.

Page 120: Excerpt from *A Gradual Awakening* by Stephen Levine. Copyright © 1979 by Stephen Levine. Reprinted by permission of Doubleday & Company, Inc.

Page 122: From the book *To Live Until We Say Good-Bye*. Text by Elisabeth Kübler-Ross, Photographs by Mal Warshaw. Copyright © 1978 by Ross Medical Associates, S. C., and Mal Warshaw. Used by permission of the publisher, Prentice-Hall, Inc., Englewood Cliffs, N.J.

Page 125: From *Cancer Care Nursing*, by Marilee Ivars Donovan and Sandra Girton Pierce. Used by permission of Appleton-Century-Crofts.

Pp. 135 & 480: From *Anatomy of an Illness*, by Norman Cousins. Copyright © 1979 by W. W. Norton & Company, Inc. Used by permission of W. W. Norton & Company, Inc. United Kingdom rights by permission of Transworld Publishers Ltd.

Page 140: "Of Dragons and Garden Peas: A Cancer Patient Talks to Doctors," by Alice Stewart Trillin, in *The New England Journal of Medicine*, March 19, 1981.

Page 142: "Scream of Consciousness," by Ruth Kramer Ziony, in *Neworld*, 1977.

Page 145: Excerpt from *Experiment Perilous*, by Renee Fox, published by the University of Pennsylvania Press, 1974.

Pp. 147 & 312: Used by permission of Elizabeth Bradbury.

Page 148: Used by permission of Joan J. Conn.

Page 152: Adapted from *Living with Cancer*, by Ernest H. Rosenbaum; The Mosby Medical Library series, The C. V. Mosby Company, St. Louis, 1982. Used with permission of the C. V. Mosby Company.

Pp. 160 & 228: Used by permission of The Centre for Living with Dying.

Page 164: From *There Is a Rainbow Behind Every Dark Cloud*, compiled by the Center for Attitudinal Healing; published by Celestial Arts, 1978. Used with permission of the Center for Attitudinal Healing.

Pp. 166 & 490: From *Big Winds, Glass Mornings, Shadows Cast by Stars: Poems 1972–80* by Morton Marcus (Jazz Press, 1981, Los Angeles). Copyright © by Morton Marcus. Used by permission of Morton Marcus.

Page 173: Used with permission of the Blanchette family.

Page 174: From "Clergy Views of Funeral Practice, Part One," by Frank Minton, in *National Reporter* 4:4 (April 1981).

Page 177: Used by permission of Edgar N. Jackson.

Page 179: Courtesy of the Athenaeum of Philadelphia.

Page 180: From "Death and Social Values," by Robert Fulton and Gilbert Geis, in *Death and Identity*, edited by Robert Fulton, published by John Wiley and Sons, 1965.

Page 183: From *The Loved One*, by Evelyn Waugh, published by Little, Brown & Co., 1948.

Page 195 (top): From *The History of American Funeral Directing*, by Robert W. Habenstein and William M. Lamers, published by Bulfin Printers, 1962.

Page 195 (bottom): From *Working: People Talk About What They Do All Day and How They Feel About What They Do*, by Studs Terkel. Copyright © 1972, 1974 by Studs Terkel. Reprinted by permission of Pantheon Books, a Division of Random House, Inc., and Wildwood House Ltd., London.

Page 206: From *Living Your Dying,* by Stanley Keleman, published by Random House, Inc., 1974.

Page 210: From *A Death in the Sanchez Family,* by Oscar Lewis; published by Random House, Inc., 1969.

Page 211: From *Nana I Ke Kumu (Look to the Source),* by Mary Kawena Pukui et al.; published by Hui Hanai, 1972. Courtesy of Queen Lili'uokalani Children's Center, Lili'uokalani Trust.

Page 214: From "Notes on Grief in Literature," by Morris Freedman, in *Loss and Grief: Psychological Management in Medical Practice,* edited by Bernard Schoenberg et al.; published by Columbia University Press, 1970.

Page 216: From *A Harvest Yet to Reap: A History of Prairie Women,* by Linda Rasmussen et al.; published by Women's Press, Toronto, Ontario, 1976.

Page 223: Excerpt from *Who Dies?* by Stephen Levine. Reprinted by permission of Doubleday & Company, Inc.

Page 230: From *Class: A View from Middle England,* by Jilly Cooper; Methuen, 1979.

Page 242: From *The Accident* by Carol and Donald Carrick, published by Seabury, 1976.

Page 245: (top): Caption to cartoon by E. H. Shepard; copyright © *Punch.* Reprinted by permission of Rothco Cartoons, Inc. (bottom): From *Winesburg, Ohio,* by Sherwood Anderson, published by Viking Press, 1958.

Page 246: Used with permission of Christine and Donovan Longaker.

Page 252: From *A Tropical Childhood and Other Poems,* by Edward Lucie-Smith; Copyright © Oxford University Press, 1961. Reprinted by permission of Oxford University Press.

Page 254: From *Collected Poems,* Harper & Row. Copyright 1921, 1948 by Edna St. Vincent Millay.

Page 264: From *The Oxford Book of Death,* edited by D. J. Enright, Oxford University Press, 1983.

Page 268: From *Surviving Pregnancy Loss,* by Rochelle Friedman and Bonnie Gradstein; Little, Brown, 1982.

Pp. 271 & 435: Used by permission of Maude Meehan.

Page 275: From "Psychological Aspects of Sudden Unexpected Death in Infants and Children," by Abraham B. Bergman, in *Pediatric Clinics of North America* 21:1 (February 1974).

Page 279: From *Alone: Surviving as a Widow,* by Elizabeth C. Mooney; G. P. Putnam's Sons, 1981.

Page 285: From *Widow,* by Lynn Caine. Copyright © 1974 by Lynn Caine. Used by permission of

William Morrow & Company and Macdonald & Company (Publishers) Ltd.

Page 288: From *Chipping Bone: Collected Poems,* by Maude Meehan; published by Embers Press, 1985. Courtesy of Maude Meehan.

Page 289: From *Vitality and Aging: Implications of the Rectangular Curve,* by James F. Fries and Lawrence M. Crapo. W. H. Freeman and Company. Copyright © 1981. Reprinted by permission.

Page 290: From *Living with Huntington's Disease: A Book for Patients and Families,* by Dennis H. Phillips, University of Wisconsin Press, 1982.

Page 292: From *Aging in Mass Society: Myths and Realities,* by Jon Hendricks and C. Davis Hendricks; Winthrop, 1977.

Page 293: From *Adult Life,* 2nd ed., by Judith Stevens-Long. Mayfield Publishing Company. Copyright © 1984. Reprinted by permission.

Page 304: From *Making Health Care Decisions: A Report on the Ethical and Legal Implications of the Patient-Practitioner Relationship,* Government Printing Office, 1982.

Page 309: From *Care of the Dying,* by Richard Lamerton, Technomic Publishing, 1976.

Page 326: From "Law Versus Medicine," an editorial that appeared November 8, 1981, in *The Boston Globe.* Reprinted courtesy of *The Boston Globe.*

Page 341: From "The Coroner and Death," by Cyril H. Wecht, in *Concerning Death: A Practical Guide for the Living,* edited by Earl A. Grollman, published by Beacon Press, 1974.

Page 343: From *The Warming of Winter,* by Maxine Dowd Jensen, published by Abingdon Press.

Page 344: From *You and Your Will,* by Paul P. Ashley, published by New American Library, 1977.

Page 348: Will of Tomás Antonio Yorba, translated by H. Noya [HM26653], reproduced by permission of The Huntington Library, San Marino, California.

Page 350: From *To A God Unknown,* by John Steinbeck; R. O. Ballou, 1933 .

Page 366: From "Groundfall," by William G. Higgins, in *Sierra* (November – December 1979).

Page 371: Reprinted with permission of Pacific Gas & Electric Company.

Page 375: Reprinted with permission of Chevron U. S. A. Inc.

Pp. 378 & 380: From *Murder in Space City: A Cultural Analysis of Houston Homicide Patterns,* by Henry P. Lundsgaarde. Copyright © 1977 by Oxford University Press, Inc. Reprinted by permission.

Page 387: From *A Rumor of War,* by Philip Caputo. Copyright © 1977 by Philip Caputo. Reprinted by permission of Holt, Rinehart and Winston, Publish-